A History of
ISLINGTON

First published 2005
by Historical Publications Ltd
32 Ellington Street, London N7 8PL
(Tel: 020 7607 1628)

ISBN 0 948667 97 4
British Library Cataloguing-in-Publication Data
A catalogue record for this book is available from the British Library

Other works by Mary Cosh include:
Inveraray and the Dukes of Argyll (with the late Ian G Lindsay) (1973)
Edinburgh: the Golden Age (2003)
The Squares of Islington, Pt I (1990) and Pt II (1993)

Typeset in Palatino by Historical Publications Ltd
Production by Liz Morrell and Paddy Donnelly, 130 St Paul's Road, London N1 2LP
Printed by Edelvives, Zaragoza, Spain

A *History of*
ISLINGTON

by Mary Cosh

HISTORICAL PUBLICATIONS

Contents

Acknowledgments

Thanks are due to many people for help in preparation of this book:

Past and present members of Islington's local history librarians, at the Central and since that department's removal, Finsbury Library.

Members of staff of the British Library and the London Library.

Barney Sloane, formerly of MOLAS, now of English Heritage, and Derek Seeley, of MOLAS, for enlightenment on archaeological discoveries.

Alec Forshaw, Islington Borough Conservation Officer, for kindly reading the draft text and making many useful suggestions.

John Richardson, my publisher, for pointing out many omissions and inconsistencies, for choosing the ilustrations and for compiling the index.

Jim Lagden, of Islington Museum, for support and information notably on the Arsenal Football Club.

Pamela Willis, curator of the Museum of the Order of St John, for support and information over a number of years.

Stella Mason, Philippa Toomey, Marion Harvey, Harley Sherlock, and many other friends and inhabitants of Islington whose interest and encouragement has been of so much value since this project began.

The Illustrations

We are grateful to the following for permitting use of illustrations as follows:

Jean Elrington: *42*

Guildhall Library, London: *76*

London Borough of Islington: *50, 71, 119, 120, 122, 123*

London Metropolitan Archives: *69, 112*

Museum of London: *35, 40, 85*

Victoria County History: *43*

All other illustrations were supplied by the Author or the Publisher

Introduction

No complete history of Islington has been published since Samuel Lewis's of 1842, nor of Clerkenwell since Edward Wood's updated version of William Pinks's history in 1865. Two later Victorian histories dealt with boundaries or other limited aspects. Since the 1960s some half-dozen works have been written, again on particular aspects, or as potted histories based on the earlier works.

This book attempts a chronological history from the earliest times to date, ending with a summary of trends since the end of the Second World War, and mostly on Islington itself. Clerkenwell has regretfully been more summarily dealt with: while its history is undeniably richer than Islington's, to do it justice would require a long work to itself. Here I have attempted to include the most significant and interesting events in Clerkenwell's past, but in general concentrating on the growth and evolution of the old area of Islington.

Some events and influences have unavoidably been overlooked or omitted, doubtless to many readers' chagrin, but prolonged research has now thrown up some very unexpected byways in Islington's history, and these along with the more generally known events and developments are presented here in the hope that they may inform, entertain and in some cases surpise the reader.

Mary Cosh

CHAPTER 1

The Beginnings

During the mild inter-glacial age some quarter of a million years ago, a small band of hunter-gatherers, now termed Palaeolithic men, hunting deer, ox or boar, killed a straight-tusked elephant in the tundra and grassland beyond the swamp north of the Thames. One of the party, no doubt unintentionally, left his flint weapon with the abandoned carcase. In AD 1680 the weapon and the bones were dug up in the fields north of London near what, some century or two later still, was to become King's Cross Road. It was interpreted as being vaguely 'ancient British', and the elephant was then thought to have been imported by the Emperor Claudius in his invasion of AD 43.

That axe's owner would have moved on with his nomadic fellows; but smaller wandering tribes also roamed the land for some miles around, and evidence of their passing has been found in places that aeons later became Pentonville, Mildmay and Stoke Newington, and elsewhere near Sadler's Wells and in the Clerkenwell area.

A mere 10,000 years ago, long after the last ice age, when northern lands were covered by forest and the melted ice had raised sea level and cut off Britain from the rest of Europe, groups of tribes began to clear the woodlands and till the land; but they appear not to have actually settled in these parts. Only many centuries later again, from about 1700 BC onwards, are there signs of scattered habitation, with the River Thames now a trade route and the use of metal widespread; and not until the 7th century BC, when iron was being worked, are there real traces of settlement in the Islington area. A few potsherds found in the Moorfields area suggest occupation at some unknown site. At that time the chief tribe in the south-east of Britain were the Catuvellauni: they were centred round Colchester, and may well have beaten out a track between there and the Thames. It was they whom the Romans encountered in the Claudian invasion, which laid the foundations for London as a trading port and starting-point of roads built to various parts of Britain.

Settlement was mostly along these roads and confined to places near the Thames: the area that was to become north Islington seems not to have been inhabited. The chief road ran east-west along the line of the present Clerkenwell Road/Old Street, near which would have been a few villas and farms; another was an old track, leading north, probably the route of Kingsland Road, which the Romans used, and later still was called Ermine Street. Lesser tracks may have run through what is now Islington. Finds of Roman pottery and coins north of Londinium have mostly been in the Clerkenwell area and the bed of the River Fleet, but one gold and silver hoard of the Constantine period (4th century), discovered in York Way in 1845, might imply a settlement there – or perhaps more likely a hasty flight; while also in the 19th century three gravestones were discovered in the same area, one of a 20th Legion soldier. Indeed the discovery in recent years of a Roman cemetery outside the City seems a clear indication that that area was not intended for settlement, and its presence would be a discouragement in later times.

In AD 61, when the British savagely rose against the Romans, both Colchester and London (which then had an estimated population of about

30,000) were fired and razed to the ground. A cherished theory fervently believed from the 18th to the mid-20th century was that Queen Boudicca's last stand against the Romans had been at Battle Bridge, or what was later called King's Cross, and apparent fortifications in Barnsbury and Highbury were interpreted as Roman military camps related to that campaign. However, the Queen of the Iceni is now thought to have fought near Fenny Stratford, and the supposed Roman earthworks have long been identified as medieval.

The wall with which the Romans encircled the City, between AD 190 and 225, interrupted the flow of the little Walbrook stream, which rose in Moorfields and ran into the Thames to the west. This might have caused the Moorfields area to flood, making that quarter unfit for settlement for many centuries: the Romans may even by this means have deliberately created a marsh as a defensive measure. At all events by the 4th century the Moorfields area was abandoned.

At that time only scattered farmsteads would have existed in the hilly rural area above Londinium, at the edge of the forest that covered most of what is now Middlesex. The slopes north of the City were well watered by springs, rising in the clay and running southwards downhill, through the marshy flats to the Thames.

During the centuries of Roman rule, then, Islington was still not an area where significant events – indeed any at all – are identifiable. Nor do we hear of these parts in the disturbed aftermath of Roman Britain, when Londinium itself dwindled to a mere marketplace of diminished importance. In due course the area north of it was settled by invading Saxons, the mid-Saxons (Middlesex) loosely connected with the kingdom of East Saxons (Essex), while London became a city of the kingdom of Mercia. The mists of anonymity settle through the centuries, as generations of farmers or smallholders continued to cultivate their patch, while Britain was Christianised, invaded and Christianised again. Throughout the time of Danish invasions and Alfred the Great's stand against them, we still hear nothing of this region.

Material evidence of the period remains extremely scanty, even after the excavations of recent years. Not until the end of the first millennium do the clouds lift, with a charter of about 1000 AD revealing, rather surprisingly, the Saxon bishop of London as overlord of two settlements called Gislandune and Tollandune. The names signify that two men called Gisla and Tolla occupied hilltops (duns), where presumably they cleared the forest and tilled the heavy clay, or perhaps kept herds of pigs that fed from the woodland with whose timbers they built their houses. Overlordship of these lands, however, is established as having been granted by the last Saxon kings to the Church – that is, to the new Cathedral of St Paul's; and much of it remained in its hands for more than 500 years.

Excavations near the present Islington Green in 1993 gave a hint of Saxon settlement. We must be content at present, however, with exiguous evidence for knowledge of the period, here so shadowy, though in many other parts of England well documented.

THE NORMANS

With the coming of the Normans the picture changes, at least in terms of visibility, with several important records to dispel some of the darkness.

Although the new King William became owner of most of his acquired realm, granting large tracts to his followers as manors of which they became tenants-in-chief, in Middlesex the situation was different. Here the Abbey of Westminster owned much already, and at the time of the Domesday Survey of 1086 St Paul's possessed most of what is now Islington.

For the first time we get an idea of place. The parish was extensive, forming a rough parallelogram tilted westwards from its southern base, which adjoined what became Finsbury and Moorfields. A major highway sliced it in two longitudinally. This road started from the City, ran northwards through Finsbury, and climbing gradually uphill entered Islington about a third of the way from the western parish limit (the present Angel area). Some quarter of a mile north of this the road forked, the left-hand branch continuing north towards Highgate, the other, at a lower level because of the eastward slope, leading north-east towards Essex.

The two roads, therefore, were known as the Upper and the Lower Street – the latter is now known as Essex Road. A small triangle of land, embraced between the beginnings of the two roads, came to be regarded as 'waste'. This was the eventual Islington Green.

The Upper or main street ran due north for about a mile, turned north-west and then continued almost straight. This highway became known as the Hollow Way, until it crossed the northern parish boundary en route to the Midlands and North. Some halfway along it a second north-bound highway branched off to the right, which traversed the neighbouring Tolendune (Tollington) and left the parish about three-quarters of a mile east of the Hollow Way. This today is the route of Hornsey Road.

Our earliest information on the land contained in this large area is found in the Domesday Survey. By 1086 King William had been twenty years on the throne, though the first half-dozen years of his reign had been occupied in establishing his right (by warfare) to the country; and now in what proved to be the last year or so of his life he was again threatened, in England by the unruly North, and from abroad by the Danes, the French and even the Normans.

The exhaustive analysis of land ownership and worth of England made by the King's representatives, though officially known as the Book of Winchester, was popularly called Domesday because like the Day of Judgement there was no appeal against it. The book's entries for the Islington area are divided between Islington, called Iseldone, and Tollington, called Tolentone.

The name Iseldone or Isledon continued in use until the 17th century. At the time of Domesday the area was, like Tolentone, part of the 'hundred' of Ossulston, an administrative division of the county of Middlesex already in use in Saxon times. The name Tolentone however, is not found again until the 16th century.

In Domesday land ownership was measured in 'hides', which could be 120 acres, but could also be variable depending upon the quality of the soil. Middlesex hides, larger than most, averaged 204½ acres. Parish units were usually 5 hides or a multiple of 5. Ossulston Hundred, containing 220 hides, was second in area only to Elthorne Hundred in the southwest of the county: indeed, it contained a quarter of the county's total hideage and uniquely had 11 five-hide units, almost half its total area.[1]

Much of the county of Middlesex was then undeveloped.[2] Its free population, that is excluding the serfs, was reckoned at only 2,065, though the City probably then held well over 10,000.

The Islington possessions of the Canons of St Paul's consisted of four hides, in two separate estates containing four 'ploughlands' between them. The few lay owners, by contrast, mustered only half a hide each. In the south of the parish there was Derman, son of Algar, identified as 'of London'; and in an unspecified area there was Geoffrey de Mandeville, who also owned large areas in Edmonton and Enfield as well as estates elsewhere in the country. Farther north, Tolentone was held by "Ranulph, brother of Ilgar", granted him by the King,[3] while the Canons, again, owned the four hides of Stanestaple, and a further two in the adjoining parish of Stoke Newington.

At the time of Domesday about half of Islington's total area was under cultivation, namely 12 hides and one virgate (a quarter of a hide). Of this, the Bishop of London had granted five hides and the odd virgate to a tenant-in-chief of whom we now hear for the first time: Hugo de Berners,[4] a Norman whose powerful family was associated with this manor thenceforward for a couple of centuries, and whose name is commemorated in Bernersbury and, later, Barnsbury. His land was enough to support four plough teams, one in his own demesne – the lord of the manor's own personal land. The rest was occupied by villeins and lower-grade peasants.

Villeins, or villagers, made up at least a third of the country's population. In a manner of speaking they were the aristocracy of the peasantry, though like the other peasants they owed service to the lord, usually by ploughing his land without payment, or rendering a proportion of their livestock, in those days usually a pig. In Middlesex, as much as half the population was recorded as being *villani*, a number of them occupying up to a hide of land.

Next below the villeins were *bordarii*, smallholders, averaging only up to an eighth of a hide; and below them again, cottagers (*cotarii*), who held still less land or even none at all. Most paid their rent in kind, or in work. On the de Berners' land one villein held half a hide, six shared three virgates; another half virgate was shared between two bordars, and a mere 2½ acres by three cottars. Bernersbury manor also contained woodlands sufficient to maintain 150 pigs, and Hugo de Berners owned a mill – presumably water-driven – valued at £6 6s 8d.

Elsewhere in the parish, the Canons of St Paul's held enough arable land between them for four teams, also ploughlands and cattle pasture, populated by the families of 7 villeins, 4 bordars and 13 cottars. At Tolentone, Ranulph (see above) had two hides, with 5 villeins, 2 bordars, a cottar and a serf, and cattle pasture and woodland for 60 pigs.

Derman's and de Mandeville's small manors, of only half a hide each, both had land for half a team, but Derman had one villein, while de Mandeville had only one bordar.[5]

The population was then, to say the least, sparse. All these men presumably had families, though Domesday records only the (male) holders, and the number of serfs is rarely recorded at all.

By the 12th century the picture begins to emerge of six large manors and their owners, tenants and sub-tenants.

A MOATED HOUSE

As we have seen, whether from choice or pressure, by 1086 St Paul's had made over almost 40 per cent of the parish to Hugo de Berners. The huge tract of Barnsbury, west of the Hollow Way, extended as far north and west as the parish boundaries, and south and east it sloped downhill to meet the valley of the River Fleet. Two manor houses have been identified for Barnsbury, one in the north approximately where the Odeon, Holloway Road now stands, the other on the site now covered by Mountfort House, on the west of Barnsbury Square. The latter was probably the lord's own and the centre of his demesne land.

Trial excavations in February 2000 of the Barnsbury moat site to the north and west of Mountfort House while revealing no medieval buildings, showed from pottery and tile fragments of the 11th and 12th century, and ox bones with butchery marks, that the site was occupied from soon after the Norman Conquest. It had, however, been regularly cleaned out, and by the 16th or 17th century had begun to silt up until it was entirely 'backfilled' by the 19th. Barnsbury manor house appears as an unusually early example so far excavated in north London: comparison was made with a (late) medieval moated site at Low Hall in Walthamstow.[6]

A 12-foot deep moat at least 20 feet wide, with an embankment on the west side, was still visible until about 1834, in what was known as Reed Moat Field, and the north-west corner was to be seen as late as 1842 when buildings had effaced the rest. Part was even apparently visible at the time of the 1914 Ordnance Survey.

THE KNIGHTS HOSPITALLER

In 1144 a Norman knight, Sir Jordan de Briset, and his wife Muriel de Munteni made a grant of land between Islington and the City to the Order of Knights Hospitaller, or Order of St John of Jerusalem. How Sir Jordan and his wife had acquired the land is not recorded. The purpose of the grant was so that the immensely powerful international Order might build an English Priory. The area chosen, noted for fresh springs and wells, came to be called after the most famous of them, Clerkenwell, the well of the Parish Clerks of the City. A few years later Lady Muriel made a further grant, presumably from her own dowry, to build a convent for Augustinian canonesses adjoining the Priory – the Nunnery of St Mary.

The establishment in the area of the Knights of St John was one of the most significant events in Islington's early history. The Order, founded to aid Crusaders and pilgrims, was based chiefly in the Holy Land, representing the main countries of Christendom. By Jordan de Briset's grant it now secured a footing in England. Before long the Knights extended their property beyond Clerkenwell and included three fields called Commandry Mantells[7], covering 10 acres north of their large Priory church and its monastic precinct. More importantly for Islington, the Order also acquired a large part of the manor of Tollington

– which like Bernersbury covered almost half the parish – formerly including Ranulph's lands. It was also known as Newington Barrow.[8] At several times in the 12th century substantial parts of this land were granted, by Muriel de Munteni and by Bertram de Barrow, to both the Priory of St John and the Nunnery of St Mary. Bertram had inherited the land through Derman, his grandfather. A century later again Bertram's grand-daughter, Alice de Barrow, made a further grant to the Priory (1270–71).[9]

Thus in little more than a century the already powerful Order also became possessed here of a huge country estate, which from its hilly situation became known as Highbury, and at some time before 1348 they built a substantial moated stone mansion as a country retreat for their Prior. As we shall see, this mansion had a short life.

SMALLER MANORS

A small manor was carved out of part of Barnsbury when Ralph de Berners made over property to the Prior and Canons of St Batholomew's, Smithfield. This began modestly with the grant of a small rent in 1176, and continued with a manor granted by a later Ralph, mentioned in 1253. The land formed a triangle enclosed between Hopping Lane (now St Paul's Road), the boundary with Highbury or Newington Barrow, and the Upper and Lower Streets which stemmed from Islington village. It was subsequently named after its new owners: Canons' Burh, or Canonbury.

South and east of Canonbury an even smaller manor held by the London citizen, Derman, formed the parish's southern tip. When Derman's son, another Algar, became the first Prebendary of Islington, probably at the end of the 11th century, Derman presented land to the Church. (A prebend is a member of a cathedral committed to officiating in church services at stated times.) Hence this small estate became known as the Prebend estate, though it contained no manor house, and its lords probably lived in the City. It extended between the high road (the present Upper Street) and the eastern parish boundary, between two southern extensions of Highbury manor, one completely detached, the other almost so.

The six manors of Barnsbury, Canonbury, Tollington, Newington Barrow or Highbury, Prebend, and St John of Jerusalem (most of which was outside Islington proper), between them regulated the whole parish for the next few hundred years. By degrees their lords disposed of parcels of varying size, splitting the lands between different families, and so the history of the area continued in records of marriage dowries and bequests. Information remains scanty until the times of the Tudors apart from dry records of such disposals, which tell us precious little about the characters and personalities concerned.

A MARKET TOWN

The walled City of London's main exits to the north were by Bishopsgate, Cripplegate and Aldersgate, the latter being the departure point of the already ancient highway to the Midlands and North, via Islington. Between the City wall and the Priory of St John, and west of St Bartholomew's church, lay a flat, 'smooth field', its name soon corrupted to Smithfield, and this early proved a conveniently open space to hold a market outside the City's walls.[10] Here, as the chronicler William Fitzstephen described in 1174, peasants brought pigs, cows and oxen for sale; he also mentioned its "celebrated rendezvous of fine horses to be sold" on Fridays. On one side of Smithfield, a group of elm trees was from early times the scene of public executions; on the other, a steep slope led down to the River Fleet and its waterside mills. Fitzstephen also describes the popularity of skating in Moorfields, the marshy area east of Finsbury, when a large pool north of the city walls froze in winter. This was certainly so in the 12th century in Henry II's time – apparently on skates made of bone.[11]

Islington early benefited from proximity to Smithfield's livestock market, and it must also have had a small village market in its own high street, as its width and raised pavements testify to this day. Being so near London, with an accessible water supply from many hillside springs and wells, it soon became a useful spot for cattle drovers from farther afield to lay up their beasts on the way to and from Smithfield. To fatten these animals, areas of local pasture were pressed into service, and more land was fenced to pen the herds overnight. Soon it would have seemed practical to keep permanent dairy herds and make use of these rich pastures for local benefit: and so the tradition of Islington as a dairying centre began – though at just what date is not known.

ST MARY'S CHURCH

The church had been founded before the Norman Conquest, and in 1078 William, Bishop of London, presented its living as part of an endowment to St Leonard's, a nunnery he had founded at Stratford-atte-Bow, east of London. In the next century a curious dispute arose over patronage, lingering on for years between the Dean and Chapter of St Paul's, the landowners, and the Stratford nuns, beginning in 1163 and determined only in 1180 by another bishop, Gilbert.[12] By this the nuns were authorised to continue to hold the living of Iseldon on payment of one mark annually to the Canons of St Paul's, and they further secured the presentation or nomination of the vicars, and also built and endowed the vicarage. So things went on for the next three and a half centuries, until in the time of Henry VIII the nunnery was suppressed along with other convents and monasteries, and the patronage was granted elsewhere.[13]

The first records of the church appear to have been lost, perhaps during the Reformation, and no names of vicars are known before that of Walter Gerkin, who died in 1327, and his still more oddly-named successor, Egidiau de Felsted. Indeed, little is known of any vicar until the late 15th century, and as little of the church building itself. It was probably the first of at least four churches on the site. The small Norman, or probably Saxon building is described as of rough materials, "flints, pebbles, and chalk, strongly cemented together", its dimensions 92 by 54 feet, 28 feet high, with a 74-foot tower and turret; it was furnished at some time with six bells. This rude edifice stood until the late 15th century when it was succeeded by a building in the Perpendicular Gothic style (the date 1483 was at one time found in the steeple).[14]

LOCAL HOUSES

The villagers in Norman and Plantagenet times lived in houses built of timber felled from the extensive woodland, and perhaps of unbaked clay or mud – mud walls are known to have been used in London for building as late as 1212.[15] Of the houses of their feudal superiors we have no record, whether of appearance, size or materials. Prebend manor, as we have seen, uniquely possessed no great house, and its lords may have been wholly absentee. Canonbury is the only house whose site has remained in occupation until modern times, but it changed its appearance completely in the 16th century, when the splendid house built for the Canons, who may have taken over an existing house from de Berners in 1253, but more likely built their own, was substantially altered by Sir John Spencer.

De Berners' own manor house of Bernersbury may have been on the moated site described above, in the southern part of his lands. This is mentioned in 1297 but in 1388 is described as ruinous, and here too no lords of the manor appear actually to have lived, at least before the 16th century.[16] Tolentone's house was sited off the Hornsey Road at what is now Kinloch Street, and was known as the Lower Place: it appears soon to have given way to the Highbury house of the Prior of the Knights Hospitaller, which stood at the brow of the gentle slope up from the boundary with Canonbury manor (now Highbury Grove).

SUB-DIVIDING ESTATES

One example of the subdivision over the years of the large manorial estates, let to sub-tenants in smaller parcels, was in Highbury. An area on the eastern parish boundary named Iveney or Sweveney, later named Spittle Fields, or Eden Grove, lay between Essex Road and what is now Southgate Road, bounded on the north by the present Northchurch Road. In about 1239 Thomas of Stortford, Precentor of St Paul's, granted one mark annually from these lands to the clerks of the cathedral choir, with the proviso that the land would revert to the cathedral should his tenant die without heirs. Only 15 years later Thomas's son William surrendered his right in this tenement to Peter of Newport, Archdeacon of London, who in 1251 in turn granted a 14-acre field south of it to the Priory of St Mary-without-Bishopsgate. The rental was 6s. 8d a year, payable to the clerks. The straw from the field could be used by the nuns for the poor, and its corn could supply them with bread and gruel.

From such minutiae are the manorial records made.

While this parcel maintained its connection with the Church, others came into lay hands. An estate in the north of Bernersbury, called Cutlers or Cotelers, appears to have originated in the land held of Adam de Basing, received from the de Berners family at a couple of removes.[17] Before he died in 1262 Basing, who had acquired a good deal of land in Islington and nearby, including several tenements and a windmill, made over Cotelers to his daughter Avice and her husband William de Hadestok. It then passed to their daughter Joan's son Henry Bedyk, from whom by 1334 Henry the Hayward, of West Smithfield, and Roger Creton, a clerk, held 52 acres of land. These two men granted the house and 50 acres of the estate to St Bartholomew's, with four acres of meadow held from the Priory and another four held of John de Berners. House and land were just within the parish – though often described as Kentish Town – at the north end of the later Maiden Lane or York Way. The fee remained with St Bartholomew's Priory until seized by the Crown at the Dissolution.

For us today the chief point of interest in these tedious transactions is probably that Cutlers may well have been the site of Copenhagen House, haunt of later Londoners as a pleasure-garden until eventually taken over for the Metropolitan Cattle Market. It was replaced by the Cattle Market Tower, which survives today.

The northern hamlet of Tollington continued with that name until the late 17th century, but the name Holloway appears already by 1307 as part of the Great North Road, and by the 15th century copyholders and craftsmen had settled there, and three licensed alehouses are recorded by 1550. The settlement centred round the crossroads – Ring Cross (by Tollington Lane), Lower Holloway by Roffe's Lane (Tollington Way), and Upper Holloway where Hagbush Lane (roughly the north end of Maiden Lane, now York Way) joined the high road.

The main roads through the village continually caused complaint. By 1300 the road known later as Devil's Lane and later still as Hornsey Road became impassable at times, and a new road was made up Highgate Hill. A few years later travellers on the road named from Saxon times 'Hollow Way', 'hollow or sunken road', were being charged a toll by the Bishop of London (1318). Towards the end of the century Islington was granted a 'pavage', with the facility to charge travellers for the upkeep of the road.[18]

The Hollow Way had by then scattered houses on either side. The fields bordering these roads appear not to have been the usual medieval open arable fields; on the other hand, Islington had acquired some common lands that had been manorial 'waste', and these in time formed village greens: the triangular space at the junction of the Upper and Lower Streets,[19] at Newington, and at Kingsland, the parish's eastern tip. Farther south, common fields towards Hoxton and Shoreditch were being used for archery practice, which was especially popular in Finsbury just outside the City walls.

Local industries had begun to start up. The soil here made good brickmaker's clay, and brick kilns were opened on the edge of Clerkenwell by the shores of the Fleet. In the Prebend manor land, not far north of this, part of a field named Hattersfield was dug for clay in the 1340s by a man named Henry Frowyk, in the area later to become Colebrooke Row, and thereafter was known as Tile Kiln Field.[20]

By the 15th century the village boasted a variety of trades: besides the inevitable baker and smith, in 1445 we have a currier, in 1462 a courser and in 1474 a lorimer, all concerned with riding and hawking. A drover and his labourer, mentioned in 1465, are an indication of the cattle trade with Smithfield.[21] This was all part of a trend during the century of an outward shift from the City to surrounding parishes. During this overflow poorer craftsmen, who could not afford the dues to City guilds, moved away, first to outer wards like Bishopsgate, Cripplegate, Fleet Street or Holborn, and then to country parishes like Clerkenwell and Shoreditch.[22]

Dairy farming, for which Islington later became famous, is not yet mentioned, but the equally famous water supply is, and already one of its hilltop spring-heads had been pressed into service, supplying Charterhouse, founded in 1371. The monks received this supply directly from a well-head, later known as the White Conduit from the small white stone house built to protect it.

A water supply for the growing City was always a problem, and by the 16th century several of Islington's hill waters were being channelled downhill. One conduit – possibly that later recorded opposite what is now 14 Highbury Place – was made to carry water to a reservoir at St Giles's Cripplegate, and another near Canonbury House, called 'Cowlese', was by 1433 supplying St Bartholomew's Hospital, and was still operating at least a hundred years later.[23]

During the outward growth in the 15th century, Londoners moving from the City set themselves up in the hamlets along the Hollow Way. Near the junction of what is now Tufnell Park Road was a moated farmhouse, held of Barnsbury manor. One development, this time for the less privileged, was halfway up Highgate Hill, where a well isolated leper hospital, dedicated to St Anthony, was founded in 1473, marked by a wayside cross on the site of which the later Whittington Stone was erected. This stone spuriously prolonged the legend that the destitute Dick Whittington turned back from here, and changed his mind about going home, so as to try again for fortune in London. In fact, Whittington came from a well-to-do family and his home was in the west country and not to the north.

Another leper hospital in an equally distant area had been founded at Kingsland, Islington's extreme edge[24] – a spot equally divided with Hackney, for the hospital itself was just over the parish border. Only half of its attached chapel lay in Islington – the boundary ran through the centre of the building.

New highways and tracks linked these remote parts of the parish and continued in use for centuries, but all were to be obliterated in the 19th century when engineers carved out new straight highways in their place. One such lane is recorded in 1492 from Battle Bridge to Highgate, whose lower part is later referred to as Longhedge Lane and by 1735 as Maiden Lane, now York Way.[25]

I am grateful to Barney Sloane, now of English Heritage and formerly of MOLAS, and Derek Seeley of MOLAS for reading this chapter and providing up-to-date information on local excavations, e.g. around Islington Green.

1   Keith Bailey, "The Hidation of Middlesex", in *LAMAS Transactions*, Vol. 39, 1988, pp. 165-86; see also H G Darby & E M J Campbell, *The Domesday Geography of S.E. England*, OUP, 1962.
2   Bailey, 'Hidation', pp. 175 ff.
3   *The Domesday Book*, ed. Thomas Hinde, Guild Publishing, London, for English Tourist Board, 1985, p. 181.
4   VCH, p. 51.
5   VCH, p. 69.
6   Archaeological Evaluation Report, *17 Barnsbury Terrace, London N1*, MOLAS, March 2000.
7   The name derives from Commandery, the term used for the Order's Priories throughout Europe, and a corruption of Mandeville, the original owners of the land.
8   Hinde, *Domesday Book*, p.181; Bailey, 'Hidation', p. 184.
9   VCH, p. 56.
10   Alec Forshaw, *Smithfield*, London, Heinemann, 1980, pp. 20 etc.
11   F M Stanton, *Norman London, with a Translation of William FitzStephen's Description*, London, Historical Association, 1934.
12   VCH, p. 88.
13   Quoted in John Nelson, *The History of Islington*, London, 1811, p. 278.
14   Nelson, *Islington*, pp. 288–9.
15   Lyndon F Cave, *The Smaller English House*, Robert Hale, 1981, p. 21.
16   VCH, pp. 51, 53.
17   VCH, p. 60.
18   VCH, p. 3.
19   Excavations in 1998 by Pre-Construct Archaeology Ltd at 7–9 Islington Green (north side) during development of the site, revealed traces of 15th-century tenement buildings, including an oven. These were demolished in the 17th century.
20   VCH, p. 73.
21   Ibid.
22   George Unwin, *Gilds and Companies of London*, London, 1908, p. 245.
23   VCH, p. 62.
24   VCH, p. 41.
25   VCH, p. 3.

CHAPTER 2

Pomp, Plague and Revolt

The more memorable events in medieval Islington usually took place at the Priory of St John, at which royalty and members of the nobility had a permanent right to hospitality, as did members of the Order visiting London. The earliest, and one of the grandest recorded royal visits was in 1185, when Roger des Moulins, Grand Master of the Order in the Holy Land, came to London with the Patriarch of Jerusalem during a tour of the Christian kingdoms to drum up support for a Crusade, for which they hoped to enlist King Henry II.

On this visit to the Priory the Patriarch himself consecrated the Order's new church with a circular nave off Fleet Street (part of today's Temple church), built in this form to echo the Church of the Holy Sepulchre in Jerusalem. A few days later the King convened a Council in the Great Hall of the Priory at which he pledged financial support for a Crusade, but would not be persuaded to join in person. Having administered this diplomatic rebuff, he personally escorted his honoured guests to Dover where they embarked for France.

The next King to take advantage of the Priory's free hospitality was King John, during Lent in 1212; together with Prince Alexander, heir to the throne of Scotland (who must have passed through Islington on his way to London) whom the King knighted on Easter Day. The Prince, son of King William the Lion, succeeded his father a few years later as King Alexander II.[1]

THE BLACK DEATH

The worst domestic calamity in medieval times was undoubtedly the Black Death in the reign of Edward III. Beginning in the Middle East, it ravaged all Europe between the end of 1347 and the end of 1349, reaching England in 1348.

At this time when barely 12 per cent of England's population lived in towns, London, with 85 parishes within its walls and its outlying districts such as Southwark, Westminster and Islington, consisted of some 14-18,000 households, a population of at least 60,000. Strangely enough, the plague appeared in England not via the Kentish ports, but from Dorset and the West Country. When it did reach London, possibly as early as November 1348 and certainly by the beginning of the next year, the rich fled, the poor perforce stayed. In outlying areas such as Islington, life seems to have struggled on as normally as possible.[2]

In January King Edward prorogued Parliament because of the 'deadly pestilence'. As deaths increased, graveyards soon proved inadequate. A new burial ground was opened at Smithfield and consecrated by the Bishop, Ralph de Stratford; and another that had a notable future was provided by Walter de Manny, a Flemish gentleman related to Queen Philippa. Early in the year de Manny leased and later bought from St Bartholomew's Hospital a 13-acre field called Spittle Croft, just north of the City and lying between Smithfield and St John's Priory. Here he built a chapel which he dedicated to the Annunciation, and opened the site for burials of City plague victims. This practical action was the precursor to his founding in 1371 a new monastery on part of the site, the Charterhouse.

One contemporary, Robert of Avesbury, reckoned that during two months at the beginning of 1349, the worst period of the plague, as many as 200 corpses were buried here nearly every day. Over the following months, though deaths and burials declined, they amounted in all to 17–18,000 deaths. The 16th-century historian, John Stow, however, put the figure at more than 50,000. He said that this figure appeared on an inscription in the churchyard, and claimed that it was verified in royal charters.[3] William Camden, who saw the same inscription, records on the other hand that it read 40,000.

These new cemeteries were of course supplementary to London's existing graveyards, but although lying outside the City walls, they must have served chiefly for victims living in the City, rather than in surrounding villages like Islington.

The generation following the plague was one of unrest, with a population seriously reduced and demanding higher wages, while the landowners in turn demanded more work from them. The main effect was the gradual end of the feudal system.

There was a further London disaster in the 14th century – the Peasants' Revolt. This was provoked by the imposition of a Poll Tax during the reign of the young Richard II. In the violent disturbances, the Priory of St John in Clerkenwell was attacked, especially as its prior, Sir Robert Hale, was the King's Chancellor and collector of the odious tax.

A motley army of peasants attacked St John's Priory, burning the church and monastic buildings, and beheading the Chancellor and the Lord Mayor at Tower Hill. A mob also stormed the Prior's country residence at

1. A reconstruction of the priory church of St John, Clerkenwell

Highbury, and burnt that as well. The great Clerkenwell church and its priory buildings were rebuilt within a few years, but Highbury's manor house was abandoned and remained an unoccupied ruin.[4]

MANORIAL HAPPENINGS

The ownership of Barnsbury manor, which was in lay hands, passed through a chequered period in the 14th and 15th centuries because of a succession of inheritance by minors who, in each case, were by the law of the land in wardship to the Bishop of London. At one time Edward III himself intervened until one heir, James, was of age. As this young man was shortly impeached and his own son, Richard, was only a boy, the King granted the manor for a period to his own clerks. The manor house – probably the moated house on the site of Barnsbury Square, became ruinous while the land around was farmed.

Richard, though married twice, had no surviving son. His widow Philippa also remarried and held half the manor as dowry, passing it to her new husband for her lifetime. Richard's daughter, Margery, in turn became a ward of the Bishop, who held her share of the manor in trust, while again two thirds of the land was temporarily farmed to the benefit of the King. Margery, who was married at the age of 12, on Philippa's death in 1421 obtained the whole estate, with a confirmation that it was not held of the King.

Complications still did not end. By her first husband, John Ferriby, Margery had no children, but she then married Sir John Bourchier, and as the male de Berners line had failed, her new husband received the title Lord Berners in right of his wife. The manor was settled on their heirs, but as their son died in their lifetime, on Margery's death in 1475 the title passed to their grandson John, aged eight.

This John, the second and last Lord Berners,

was a literary man, translating Froissart's *Chronicles* and producing among other works a life of King Arthur. In 1502 he sold the Barnsbury lands to Sir Reynold Bray, who died only a year later, leaving the estate to his nephew Edmund. But in 1510 Barnsbury and other lands were settled on Bray's niece, also a Margery and presumably Edmund's sister, who married Sir William (later Lord) Sandys. On her death Sandys and their son Thomas sold the manor, then valued at £30 a year, to Robert Fowler, vice-treasurer of Calais.

Thus after 180 years and four generations of minority inheritance, of wardship, third-party management and resettlement, Barnsbury finally ended its connection with the de Berners family.[5]

Islington village at that time extended along the high road from the top of St John Street until past the lane leading to Canonbury. It must have been a string of timber-framed houses and weather-boarded cots. Such houses offered little comfort, even for the rich. It is doubtful if the poor people even slept in beds, but probably they lay side by side on the floor, their animals and yard poultry often sleeping in the house with them.

In the 15th century St Mary's church was rebuilt in the 'late Gothic' style, three-aisled and paved with brick and stone, and with a square tower. The walls were gilded wainscot, the roof panelled, and the altar-piece carved with painting above. It also possessed an image known as 'Our Lady of Islington'.

1   H W Fincham, *The Order of the Hospitallers of St John of Jerusalem*, London, 1924.

2   Philip Ziegler, *The Black Death*, Folio Society, 1977, p. 128.

3   *Ibid.*, pp. 133-4, quoting Stow's *Survey of London*.

4   VCH, p. 57.

5   VCH, pp. 51, 53.

CHAPTER 3

Under the Tudors

In the 16th century our shadowy concept of Islington as a place at last begins to take on more distinct form, and some of its inhabitants acquire flesh and blood. After the unsettled decades of the Wars of the Roses and the battles between Lancastrian and Yorkist kings, establishment of the new regime of upstart Tudors by Henry VII opened a period of greater political stability. There were opportunities for trade and prosperity, and for a new, not to say equally upstart nobility and gentry to establish families, develop estates, and build in newly fashionable styles – until Henry VIII's meddling with the Church and its property caused upheaval in society, the economy and land ownership.

Islington's situation near the City and its natural features made it a favourite spot for wealthy men to build themselves pleasant country houses on its manorial lands, away from the smoke and stench of cramped London-within-walls. East and west of the City there were no hills, and south of the Thames with its single bridge to the City was always outside of main development. But to the north, beyond marshy Finsbury, a mile or so above the City was this airy hilltop supplied with pure water, a major factor at this time when supply depended entirely on rivers, springs and wells. So to the scattered medieval houses of the manors were now added a sprinkling of buildings of greater luxury, by those who acquired portions of their lands.

Henry VIII himself kept a hunting lodge, though apparently with dubious intent, on Islington's eastern fringe at Newington Green. In this timbered, oak-panelled house, its

plaster ceilings embossed with symbolic medallions, his game-bag extended to the young women he was said to keep here as mistresses – though probably not more than one at a time. To this day the road nearby between Ball's Pond Road and Kingsland Road is known as 'King Henry's Walk'.

Most of the characters in the local scene, however, still remain insubstantial shadows, and of one mysterious, perhaps eccentric figure early in that king's reign we know only what we can deduce from his lengthy will, whose details are of some interest.

This gentleman was Richard Cloudesley, who owned a small estate in Barnsbury known variously as Stony Field, Stoney's Crofts, or the Fourteen Acres. It was actually 16 acres two roods, 17 perches, as later surveyed by the parish, on the site of Cloudesley Square and neighbouring streets. When drawing up his will, apparently shortly before his death in January 1517[1], among his executives he named Thomas Docwra, the Welsh Lord Prior of the Order of St John, and Sir Thomas Lovell, an influential elderly statesman who had fought for Henry Tudor at Bosworth in 1485, and was at this time Constable of the Tower of London.[2]

Much of Cloudesley's will consists of charitable bequests to the poor, to the prisoners of Newgate, King's Bench and the Marshalsea, and to the mad inmates of Bedlam, in each case including a load of straw – presumably for them to lie on – and, oddly, another load of straw "laid on me in my grave". He also expressed a wish to be buried near his parents in St Mary's churchyard. The 'Poor Lazars of

Hyegate' and the Friars of Greenwich were also to benefit, with sums for the parish poor-box, and a gown each value 6s. 8d bearing the name 'Maria' in honour of the Virgin Mary, to two poor parishioners of Islington and two of Clerkenwell – provided they were honest and neither sold nor pawned them.

The high altars of both St Mary's Islington and St James's Clerkenwell (then part of St Mary's nunnery) benefited by small sums, 20s in the case of Islington for "tythes and oblations peradventure by me forgotten or withholden, in discharging of my conscience". Further, the churches of St James and of St Pancras, Hornsey, Finchley and Hampstead were all to receive two torches each worth 14 shillings and a gown for two poor men, and Islington church eight torches at 6s each, four to be kept for the Brotherhood of Jesus there, the others to be lit at High Mass so long as they would last.

On the lay side Cloudesley left 40s. for repair of the 'cawseway' between his house and the parish church, and £20 for the "highway between Hyegate-hill and the stony bounds beyond Ring Crosse", with the promise of a further £20 were that not enough.

To pay these charitable and parochial bequests his executors were to devote the rents of the Stony field (a wise proviso, as it proved), and the parishioners were to elect "six honest and discreet men" every year for the responsibility of distributing these profits.

So much for the property. What about the man? In his will he was hoping to safeguard his afterlife by insisting on masses and prayers for his soul. This was a traditional aid to free a soul from purgatory, and release it to heaven, as early as possible. The Brotherhood of Jesus for whose use four torches were to be kept was (says Nelson sternly) "a monkish establishment connected with the church of Islington".[3] Included in the Clerkenwell bequest was 20s. to "the ladies of the same place … to do for me *placebo & dirige*, with a mass of requiem". The priests of the churches named were each to have 20 pence "to pray for me by name openly in their Churches every Sunday, and to pray their parishioners to pray for me and to forgive me, as I forgive them and all the world."

Even in the midst of his instructions for repairing highways Cloudesley suddenly inserts his wish "that there be incontinently after my decease, as hastily as may be, a thousand masses for my soul", every priest to be paid 4d, and 5 marks in pence given to the poor on his burial as "dole for my soul". The Highgate lazars and Greenwich friars must also work for their bequests, the former "to pray for me by name in their bede-role", the latter "to sing a solemn dirge and mass, by note, for me". The princely sum of 6½ guineas went to a priest at "Scala Celi at the Savoy" to sing for him for a whole year after his death, the other obligations were also tied up in detail, and at an annual obit in Islington he generously included his wife's soul and "all Christen souls".

Finally, Cloudesley named grants of lands and tenements made to the Order of St John,[4] to the intent I would be prayed for perpetually", who within a month of his death must appoint "an honest sadde priest" to sing "for my soule, my father and moders soules, and all Christen soules, in the new Chapel called The Hermitage,[5] at Islington's town's end", besides other prayers and masses, again insisting he be named. Even after all this, any money remaining to the executors must be devoted to charity, still "for the wealth of my soul".

Cloudesley, incidentally, appears to have lived not on what was subsequently known as the Cloudesley estate, but by the Angel, as Tomlins puts it, "a little lower down": a lease granted by the Priory of St John on 24 April 1516, not long before his death: demised to "Richard Cloudesley of Iseldon, Gent" their tenement by the Long Causeway, "with the gardens and croft adjacent, late in the tenure of John Mantell, butcher; and also one house called the Shepecote, with a little close adjoining, late in the tenure of the said John Mantell … situate and lie between the King's highway on the east side, and our fields called the Commaunders Mantells on the west and south sides, and the tenement of the aforesaid Richard Cloudesley wherein he now dwells, on the north side thereof".

By this it appears that Cloudesley's actual dwelling with adjoining land must have been alongside the top of St John Street where it ran into Islington's high street. Dame Alice

Owen's School and almshouses, a century later, must have been built approximately opposite.[6]

What did all the safeguarding of Cloudesley's soul signify? Had he, and possibly his parents too, committed some serious and unchristian misdemeanour, so that like many a malefactor invented in M R James's ghost stories, he did not expect to rest quietly in his grave unless heavily protected (by name to avoid any misunderstanding by the powers of evil) by masses and prayers?

Indeed, an 'Antient writer' describing such phenomena as earthquakes, specifically refers to "heavings or tremblements de terre" which occurred "in a certain fielde neare unto ye parish church of Islingtoun ... ye earthe swellinge and turninge uppe euery side towards ye midst of ye sayde fielde", traditionally associated with the burial of "Richard de Cloudesley", his "bodie being restles, on ye score of some sinne by him peraduenture committed".

Perhaps the numerous provisions of his will had been ignored, and clearly an exorcism was required "to quiet his departed spirit". Therefore "certaine exorcisers ... did at dede of night, nothing lothe, using divers diuine exercises at torche light, set at rest ye unrulie spirit of ye sayde Cloudesley, and ye earthe did returne aneare to its pristine shape, neuermore commotion procedeing therefrom to this day, and this I know of a verie certaintie".[7]

The masses presumably continued until the King confiscated ecclesiastical property, for in January 1548 the Commissioners for Dissolving Colleges and Chantries recorded the charitable purpose of Cloudesley's bequest (though they assessed the land at only 12 acres). And for probably this reason the Crown did not seize the land, despite the 'popish' purposes. The rents therefore remained vested in the feoffees until in the early 19th century the then trustees built on the land, cashing in on the housing boom.[8]

SIR THOMAS LOVELL

Richard Cloudesley's friend and executor, Sir Thomas Lovell, evidently also lived for some time in Islington, and was probably the builder of a distinguished house in the Lower Street (Essex Road) known as Ward's Place, although more popularly described, without much foundation, as 'King John's Place'. Nelson scornfully comments how King John was traditionally credited with occupying "almost half the antient buildings in the vicinity of London", much as Queen Elizabeth slept in every old house in the realm.[9] It was between Green Man's Lane and another alley called Paradise Place, and survived until 1800.

Lovell, whose active life comprised many influential Court and State offices, was also a great builder. In 1518 he built the gatehouse of Lincoln's Inn, adorning it with his own arms together with the King's and the Earl of Lincoln's. He also built East Herling Hall in Norfolk, and in 1508 through the death without issue of his wife's brother, Lord Roos of Hamlake, inherited Worcesters, a manor in Enfield, where in 1516 he entertained Henry VIII's sister, the widowed queen Margaret of Scotland. Here it was he died in May 1524, which helps to date Ward's Place in Islington.[10] As a benefactor to the Priory of Holywell, Shoreditch, he was buried there in a chapel he had founded.

Ward's Place passed to the Dudley family, whose arms appeared in one of the windows, and if the owner was once that favoured courtier of Queen Elizabeth's youth, Robert Dudley, whom she created Earl of Leicester, it would credibly explain her reputedly frequent visits to Islington – and also account for a "Squier Minstrel" from the "worshipful tooun of Islington" in Leicester's famous entertainment of the Queen at Kenilworth in 1575.[11]

The rambling, homely exterior of Ward's Place is illustrated in an engraving from a drawing by Stockdale, gabled at one end with a large first-floor window and one still larger of six bays below, a timber carriage entrance with a weather-boarded overhang above. At the south end another small entrance in a triangular bay, with a large oriel window above.

Within its rustic exterior, Ward's Place contained remarkable ornaments: stained-glass windows, carved stonework, fine chimney pieces. One of these was enriched with a plethora of arms: the City, Lovell quartering Muswel, the Priory of St John, the Gardner family, grocers of London, and the Company of Merchant Adventurers. A roundel in an upper window, probably the one with the oriel, displayed a young businessman at his work table, thought to represent 'The Faithful Steward', shown in a room with a tester bed and a cupboard on which stand several vessels including a spouted jug.

One enigmatic small emblem was possibly a rebus: a twisted cord twined round, on one side a spray of roses, on the other a wing, above the abbreviated Latin motto o[mn]ia de sup[ra], 'all things from above', though whether this is associated with the skull holding a tibia in its mouth (as shown in Nelson's illustration), is not clear. According to Nelson the device may have been one of the Merchant Adventurers' Company, and adopted by Sir Thomas. Wings were often a feature on City trading companies' arms, and a rose and wing also appeared above the nave arches of his parish church at Enfield, and on Hadley church tower in Hertfordshire.

In a ground-floor room, shown in a drawing made many years later in 1789, three more roundels survived of a set on the parable of the Prodigal Son. Nelson illustrates one showing the son taking leave of his father, then riding off on his ill-considered adventures. The surrounding legend, in gothic characters, reads: *'prodigus hic patr … sc … que substancia tangit. postulat acceptat sorte* [or forte] *beatus abit'*: 'Here the prodigal [asks his] father if he may take [touch] his inheritance … He goes off happy.' Again the background is shown, in which the money is being counted out for the youth.

In another upper room were roundels of sizeable but much mutilated figures of saints, in places obscured by the later covering of the windows with lath and plaster to reduce the number of lights.[12] One, some 9 inches long, may represent St Mark, seen in armour, cloaked, brandishing a sword and with a nimbus behind his head. In one hand is what seems to be the fluted base of a pillar, and beside him a strangely ram-like lion regards him amiably. All these are symbols of the strong defence of the gospel. In the background are the towers and houses of a town.

These decorations, which may be Dutch or German, seem of 16th-century date. Nelson carelessly tells us only that they come from a "book of drawings" lent him by the late Mr

Matthew Skinner, a keen antiquarian, which he had made before the house was demolished.[13]

Since Sir Thomas Lovell died in 1524, his work on Ward's Place presumably pre-dated his last years. Nearest in date of the other Islington mansions was the rebuilding of Canonbury manor house by Prior William Bolton, Docwra's successor. In the 1520s Bolton elected to build a new house ranged round a courtyard, a layout still discernible today, though like its medieval predecessor the actual appearance of most of the buildings is unknown. The Prior placed his personal stamp in the form of a punning rebus on his name (it appears also in the church of St Bartholomew the Great), a 'bolt' piercing a 'tun' or barrel. One of these is seen over a door in the east range, two more on the fronts of the pretty little garden houses or gazebos which survive at the angles of the demesne walls.

THOMAS CROMWELL

In the 1530s Thomas Cromwell, by then ennobled as Earl of Essex and in high favour with King Henry, had leased manor and demesne from the Prior, who died in 1532, and Cromwell occupied the manor until 1536. But the dodgy days when the King's marital problems assumed religious or political significance soon came upon them, with nobles, courtiers and simple individuals alike having to beware of what they were known to believe, else current favour and prosperity quickly disintegrated into disgrace, imprisonment, even torture and death. When the King determined to confiscate the fat lands of clergy and monasteries, all stability was undermined; then woe betide such parishes as Islington, whose manors still had ecclesiastical overlords.

In his favoured days, Cromwell had also acquired Cutlers, which St Bartholomew's had briefly assigned to Sir Thomas More's son-in-law Giles Heron, and when both gentlemen were attainted Cromwell, who already had Cutlers on lease, secured the whole. But Cromwell's days too were numbered, when he arranged the unlucky marriage with Anne of Cleves, and in 1540 he himself was attainted and Canonbury was confiscated by the Crown.

2. Thomas Cromwell.

development of tidy little estates owned by minor families, rather than huge realms owned elsewhere by increasingly powerful landlords.

Thus it was that from King Henry's time Islington gradually became even more popular with gentry and lesser nobility for new houses, often along the two main village streets. For anyone who had inherited a medieval ancestral home, by the time of Queen Elizabeth and particularly after the end of the threat from Spain, it was the fashion not only to rebuild, but to keep a country house as a retreat from City quarters. So there grew up handsome small mansions along the Upper and Lower Streets, most of which were to survive as increasingly battered tenements for some 300 years, to the admiration of later generations, until ruthlessly swept away by 19th-century improvers. Of these the only one to survive, in its later form, was Canonbury House.

CHANGING ESTATES

Although plenty of records survive of the descent of property and of its disposal after confiscation of the monastic lands, it is hard to feel much interest in a string of names of owners and occupiers of whom nothing else is known. We are often told more about the land itself.

The Priory of St John's large manor of Highbury, or Newington Barrow, was settled by King Henry on his daughter Princess Mary. No attempt had been made to rebuild the Priors' house burned during the Peasants' Revolt of 1381, but its grange had survived, described as 'Castle Hill'. It had a walled yard, garden and pastureland, on the east side of the moated enclosure called Castle Yard. The large 300-acre demesne was mostly woodland – Highbury Wood north of the grange, and north-west again Little St John's Wood – and very little was arable. The woodlands, with timber and saplings, were let, with an order for protection of the young growth, and having settled them on his daughter the King re-leased them. In the 1550s, however, thanks to the keeper's negligence, the woods were deemed 'spoilt' by wandering livestock.[15] The devout Mary, on succeeding to the throne,

In 1541 the King, on getting rid of this rejected wife, granted her an annuity of £20 from the Canonbury income, while most of the lands were granted to another Dudley, John, Lord Lisle, who became Duke of Northumberland. But on the boy King Edward VI's death in 1553 Northumberland lost them again for trying to put Lady Jane Grey, his daughter-in-law, on the throne, and once again Canonbury returned to the Crown. Queen Mary granted manor and reversion of the house and demesne to Thomas, Lord Wentworth, who seems to have undertaken some building there, but sold the property in 1570 to a rich citizen, John Spencer.

Much of the demesne was parcelled out to tenants, who may have built or occupied cottages on the site. In 1565 William Rickthorne, leaseholder of the manor house, held at least part of the land on a 31-year lease; his widow Anne, remarried to Sir Arthur Atye, lived on there after Rickthorne's death in 1582.[14]

The fate of Canonbury was not untypical of estates in Middlesex, whose many dissolved monastic properties were subdivided and leased in smaller parcels to favoured courtiers or merchants on the make. This led to the

restored the land to the Hospitallers, but her sister Elizabeth, once she became Queen, confiscated it again.

A few other estates will suffice for a glimpse of contemporary changes. Iveney, one of the smaller lands which as part of Canonbury belonged to St Paul's, is described in the 14th century as having a house, of which no later mention is made, and right up to the 19th century the land continued as meadow. North of Canonbury, Weryngs, a similar small agricultural property (site of today's St Paul's Terrace and Northampton Park), with the nearby Hides and Hopping Field (along Hopping Lane or St Paul's Road), were let after the Dissolution as 'closes' to two related families, Hayes and Callards, and then, through a Henry Iden, to the Wroth family. In 1587 William Wroth is recorded as possessing 15 messuages and 38 unspecified acres in Islington, Shoreditch and St Giles-without-Cripplegate.[16]

Rents from such lands were intended as income for a lessee's widow or heirs. This happened with 'London Fields' east of Hornsey Road, site of the present Harvist estate – which in the 1560s was let to Henry Iden for income "to bring up Edward and William Wroth". Cowleys, 14 acres mostly meadow with a little woodland, was left by Iden to Callard's descendants.[17] Occasionally actual farms are identified, such as Barton's, of Tollington land in Highbury manor, named in 1557 as one of 12 tenants at Tollington and Stroud. Some of these tenants are defined even from early times as 'Londoners'.

Near Maiden Lane the Cotelers or Cutlers estate – whose lease St Bartholomew's Priory had in 1550 granted with Canonbury land to Giles Heron, Sir Thomas More's son-in-law – seems to have had no houses or inhabitants. In the same area a 20-acre croft was held of the Charterhouse, let at the end of the 16th century to an innkeeper, presumably for grazing. All this again suggests an empty quarter.

In fact, outside the main village, documents reveal only scanty building or habitation in the extensive parish. Battle Bridge was at the extreme south-west fringe near the boundary with St Pancras. North of this was called Vale Royal after the Cheshire abbey to which it had belonged. It was east of Longhedge Lane, now York Way[18] and linked to the Back Road (Liverpool Road) and thence to Ring Cross, a route for cattle to be driven to and from Smithfield, with 'layers' or lairs where they could be herded overnight. Sparse though dwellings were, in the 1550s a miller is recorded here as being punished for sedition, and in 1589 Cliffe, a cobbler, published a book denying the truth of the Church. These trades suggest that they had customers living nearby, perhaps recusants like themselves.

Except at Highbury local woodlands had by now been cleared, and before and after the Dissolution, the thinly populated parish consisted of large tracts of arable or pasture, or different-sized plots of cultivated land with small pockets of inhabitants. Most of the land was copyhold, that is, held from the manor on secure tenure, not to be alienated without payment of a fine to the lord of the manor.

Properties were scattered round other fringes, towards Stoke Newington and Kingsland Green to the east. At the eastern edge, in the 1530s Henry Percy, then Earl of Northumberland, had a house in Newington Green – near King Henry's hunting lodge – where he died in 1537. Was this the timber-framed house on the green's north-east corner, built around a courtyard with the usual wainscoted, gilded and painted interior? Its popular name of Bishop's Place was probably not given until the 18th century.[19]

MARTYRDOMS

Islington's part in the stormy mid-16th century religious history is one of discord and oppression. It became a refuge for harassed nonconformers, Catholic or Protestant according to the times. In 1548, though recorded as having 440 communicants, the parish may well have housed as many recusants and 'fugitives', and its open fields were the secret but not always safe resort of outlawed prayer meetings.

There were tragic encounters. Among the saddest occurred during the last year of Queen Mary's reign, in Advent 1557, when a group of Protestants was betrayed by a 'false hypocrite and dissembling brother', and four of them ended their lives at the stake.

Their leader was a John Rough, a Scotsman,

3. Martyrs being burnt at Smithfield. Old St Paul's may be seen in the distance.

who had been a preacher with the Black Friars at Stirling, and later chaplain to the Earl of Arran; in fact it was Rough who persuaded John Knox to join the ministry. He then travelled abroad, "experienced many vicissitudes in different countries",[20] and ended as a preacher to a small congregation in Islington. They met in secret at the Saracen's Head inn in St John's Lane for prayer and a discourse, under the pretext of hearing the reading of a play.

Among Rough's companions in worship were a tailor named Cuthbert, Hugh, a hosier and a man called Symson. Another tailor who joined them, Roger Sergeant, was in reality a spy, and by his "craftie and traytorous suggestion" betrayed the group to the Vice Chamberlain of the Queen's House. All were arrested. Among the charges against Rough was that under cover of reading the mythical play, he had "read the Communion Book, and … used the accustomed fashion as was in the later days of King Edward VI", by then illegal. Foxe, who relates the disaster in his *Acts*

and Monuments,[21] states baldly that Rough was later burnt at Smithfield (1558), though he recounts nothing of the fate of the rest.

On 15 September that year four persons, who may have been among the "divers others" who had assembled with Rough were burnt "at Islington". They were Ralph Allerton, James and Margery Austoo, and Richard Roth. A contemporary print shows the pyre in a field, with the church tower and its surrounding houses a little beyond and, looming far off, the lofty hills of Hampstead and Highgate. How accurate a picture of the village this may be is doubtful. In the foreground the victims, appearing sustained and encouraged by their faith, are secured by a chain to stakes and surrounded by the large bundles of faggots, to which an attendant is adding others. Sullen village onlookers are kept in hand by pikemen, and a uniformed dignitary, presumably the constable, stands ready to give the order. One can only hope that the victims were quickly overcome by the smoke rather than the flames.[22]

Foxe, however, does give a fuller account in *Acts and Monuments* of some forty "godly and innocent persons" who at much the same period (June 1558) were meeting in the back close of a field "by the town of Islington", to pray and meditate on God's word. They had apparently chosen the place at random, for when a stranger approached, first to observe them over the hedge, and then to join them with the innocent-seeming remark that "they looked like men that meant no hurt", one of them actually asked him who owned the close, and whether they might be allowed to pray.

"Yes", said he, "for that ye seem unto me such persons as intend no harm."

The dissembler then made off – straight to the constable of Islington, Mr King, who within a quarter of an hour appeared on the spot with half a dozen men armed with bow, bill and other weapons. Most of these men he left hidden nearby and approached the group with a single supporter. He carefully observed what books they had, and what they seemed to be up to, before turning back among them with an order to surrender their books. Once they realised who he was, they dared not resist, and the constable's posse came forward and ordered them to stay put.

The group quietly complied. Their captors led them to a nearby brewhouse to await the arrival of a Justice they had summoned. The nearest was not at home, and they were taken before Sir Roger Cholmeley (a resident of Highgate and later to be founder of Highgate School).

The posse seems to have been pretty amateurish, for on their dividing the worshippers into parties of ten or eight under single guards, several found it not hard to escape. Some of the women ran away from the close, others made off during their escort to the brewhouse. The remaining 27 were brought to Sir Roger and the Recorder, who took down their names, called them over singly, and "so many as answered to their names he sent to Newgate". The number had now dwindled to 22. These remaining unfortunates were imprisoned in Newgate for seven weeks before being examined, during which time the keeper, Alexander, was told to inform them that they might be freed provided they would hear a mass. Foxe does not relate whether any of them did, but

records without comment that seven were burned at Smithfield and six at Brentford – 13 in all.[23]

The bitter irony of these executions was that after only a short time, that same November Queen Mary was dead, and with the accession of her sister Elizabeth, a Protestant monarch ascended the throne.

TABLES TURNED

The tables were now turned, and it was *Catholic* recusants who came to lodge in Islington for safety. In 1577 three were reported, and two others were named in 1588. Thomas Worthington, a priest from a French seminary at Douai, was arrested here in 1584; while government spies noted that another priest, Williams, was staying at "Mr Talbot's house", and that Thomas Clarke, a seminarian, stayed some months at the Crown Inn. About 1600, three priests sent to England were expected to lodge in Islington; and so things went on.

While all these were Catholics, at the other extreme Robert Browne, founder of the Protestant Brownist sect, was said to have preached here in the 1570s – apparently in a gravel pit. He certainly seems to have done so several years later, from 1586 to 1589, when he was a schoolmaster in Southwark and preaching around London.

'Woods near Islington' – which sound like the woodlands of Highbury manor – were among meeting places used in the 1590s by Francis Johnson and John Penry, advocates of a 'separatist church'. Johnson and two of his near relatives were arrested with about 50 others.

Arrests in Islington, or condemnations of recusants of whatever religion, did not necessarily mean local inhabitants: they might as likely be from the City, anxious to escape notice and to avoid the heavy legal restrictions. Though only a couple of miles away, Islington was a wholly separate village. In the same way, City craftsmen who had come to London from the country, or from abroad, were moving out because they could not join the closed guilds. The nearer neighbour, Clerkenwell, in particular was a place where clock and watchmakers, jewellers, printers and others could settle and practise their crafts without hindrance. Already by the late 15th century City industries had spread to the surrounding districts, Finsbury, Shoreditch, Bethnal Green and Holborn. First the poorer craftsmen shifted to outer City wards like Bishopsgate and Cripplegate, then beyond the walls altogether. They were joined by craftsmen coming in from the country seeking opportunities, from Hertfordshire or Essex.[24]

A PLACE AWAY FROM THE CITY

Islington, comfortably distant from the walled City and its close-set streets, and from Finsbury's marshes, now included in its two main streets half-timbered and gabled mansions set in gardens, with orchards behind, indisputably rural but a horseback ride from the City's trades and the royal court at Westminster. Perhaps not an easy ride. Roads throughout England were so rough, miry and rutted, and in heavy clay country totally impassable, as many a foreign visitor attested, that Islington would then seem many times the distance from London as today. For the simple litters and crude, uncomfortable coaches, the very approach to the City from Highgate Hill – or worse, up it – must have been an unwelcome enterprise. More would ride than travel by coach, and still more walk than ride. The number of high-road taverns and ale-houses, often small and insignificant, attested not to the drunkenness of the populace, but to the need for refreshment at short intervals along the arduous way. For foot passengers, packmen, carriers, drovers and other travellers, even the well-mounted or carriage borne, 'Halfway House' along the Hollow Way was a blessed respite during a seemingly endless unpaved three miles between the Angel and Highgate village. This inn was substantial enough to issue its own small coinage (tokens) during the coin shortage after the Restoration.

The Angel, first recorded as an inn (but not then named) in 1614, probably originated in late medieval times, at the fairly lonely junction of the Goswell Road and St John Street. Highwaymen were a danger even so near the City, and assembling travellers into a convoy at two or three nearby inns, as described even a century or two later, may well have originated in Tudor times.

London's population was expanding, with the arrival of victims of land enclosures and other 'masterless' men, including criminals and vagabonds, besides strolling players, pedlars and jugglers who had flocked to the capital. These men, regarded as a threat to society, were sometimes not even looking for a job, but were drop-outs for whom London formed a general refuge. Between 1500 and 1650 London's population increased up to eightfold, as both casual labour and charity were available, while opportunities for fraud and theft were limitless. By the end of Elizabeth's reign a criminal underworld was emerging, and much of the population was living on the poverty line.[25]

The fields around London, Islington's among them, were the resort not only of illegal prayer meetings, roving preachers and vagabonds, but of rowdy exercises such as the training of militia, popular local sports – especially archery, notably still in the flat Finsbury area – and of crooks, such as counterfeiters.

Towards the end of the 16th century the High Street was lined with inns. Among Islington's 15 victuallers recorded in 1553, besides those on the west (Clerkenwell) side of the High Street, and three more in Holloway, were the George in 1539, on the west side of the High Street, the Red Lion from 1540 on the east side; later came the Talbot by 1570, the Fleur de Lys about 1588, renamed the Cockatrice by 1618. By 1594 the King's Head opposite St Mary's church was established, and in 1599 the Bear.[26]

On the Lower Street, on the east side and a little north of the Queen's Head inn, was the Crown, the usual rambling and partly gabled structure containing carving and stained glass. This was probably the former residence of some merchant, for one large ground-floor room window included the arms of England, the City and the Mercers' Company, together with combined red and white roses, which suggest a date early in Henry VIII's reign. Like many of its contemporaries the building descended in status over the centuries, had become frequented by strolling players, and was finally demolished about 1795. It was replaced by a form of workhouse for some 200 paupers known as the City Farmhouse.[27]

4. The stage at the Red Bull theatre. From an engraving of 1662.

tune theatre near Cripplegate (in the present Golden Lane), which opened in 1600. It was the income from the Fortune that financed Alleyn's building of Dulwich College and, in Finsbury, the almshouses in Bath Street – which became Pest House Lane. The Red Bull, again a yard theatre, was started off St John Street in 1600 by Aaron Holland, and was used by the Queen's Men. But the real history of early theatre belongs more to the next century.

There were many other forms of recreation. Energetic and even warlike sports had been popular in Finsbury Fields since the Middle Ages, including football, equestrian exercises and fighting with bucklers. The one that proved most significant was archery, especially in the 16th and 17th centuries. The fields were studded with archery marks bearing fancy names and the contests were on occasion watched by the Lord Mayor and Corporation, as described by John Stow in 1598 in his *Survey of London*.

Successive kings, for obvious reasons, reckoned skill in artillery, as it was known, of great importance, honouring the Finsbury Archers and the Clerkenwell Archers by attending their matches. In 1537 they were incorporated by King Henry VIII as the Honourable Artillery Company, whose acknowledged purpose was to defend London in time of war.[28]

THE TUDOR VILLAGE

Unlike in the city, the local water supply appears to have been as prolific as its alcohol; it was still provided chiefly from local springs, to which the open country allowed unimpeded access. In the 1540s and '50s an aqueduct is mentioned, presumably the one from the hilltop White Conduit to the Charterhouse, and springs for a conduit at St Mary's Lothbury were located between Islington and Hoxton. Good farmland and fine cow pastures had already made Islington renowned for another liquid – milk – a product of the grazing land all around the village.

Early maps of the area are uninformative. The so-called Agas map of the 1550s still shows Islington at its extreme top, panoramic as if through a telescope. Almost the only distinguishable building is St Mary's church tower. What is quite clear, however, is that

Theatres as such, though kept outside the City walls, had not come to Islington. On the other hand, an early experiment took place a mere walk across the fields, starting in 1576 with James Burbage's wooden 'Theatre' built in Finsbury fields a little west of Shoreditch High Street, and followed barely a year later by the Curtain in Holywell Lane on the site of the abandoned Holywell Priory. Here from 1597 to 1599 the Chamberlain's Men performed, possibly including Shakespeare. In 1599 both theatres' leases expired, and Burbage's men dismantled the theatre and removed its material to the South Bank, where the Rose Theatre had been built. It was reopened as the Globe.

The end of the century and of the Queen's reign were marked by new theatres, all on Bankside except Alleyn's and Henslowe's For-

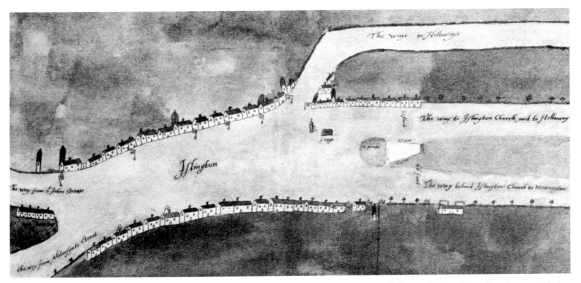

5. Islington High Street in Tudor times. To the left are St John Street and Goswell Road, and going north is what became Liverpool Road. The road divides to the right into Upper Street and Essex Road. It is thought that the signposts indicate inns.

south of this virtually no building existed between the village and the Charterhouse and Old Street. 'The Waye to St Alban' (Goswell Road) is bordered by fields, with apparently a single building opposite the disproportionately mountainous 'Mount Calvary' (Mount Mill, a windmill hill), east of which is what appears to be a brick or tile kiln. On the west St John Street winds northwards, well separated from Goswell Road and equally bare of houses save for a couple approximately level with the single house on Goswell Road, and like that road ending in an undistinguishable cluster of buildings.[29]

Our first real impression of Islington comes from a plan dated about 1590, extending north from the Angel intersection to a point beyond the Green, though unfortunately for our knowledge, short of the church. It shows lines of houses on either side, some on the west extending back rather than along the street; and a tiny sprinkling at the junction of 'The Waye to Holloway' – that is, the Back Road (now Liverpool Road). At this junction the most unexpected detail is the presence of five tall standards along the high street, and two others flanking the Back Road corner: street lamps or signs?

Opposite the Back Road junction is a village pump and 'cage' or lock-up, in mid-street, just short of the Green; then more building on the west side. A single large house on the east side of Lower Street ('the way behind Islington church to Newington') may represent Ward's Place.

At the Back Road junction, by 1601 in a 3½-acre close stood a capital messuage, the Horsehead or Nag's Head (a Nag's Head succeeded it on the spot, with successors almost to this day), owned by Richard Martin and his wife Ellen, along with six houses of craftsmen.[30] Much farther along the Back Road was the six-acre Gosseyfield, on whose site Lonsdale Square was eventually built.

As for St Mary's Church, at some time in the Tudor period it was graced with a peal of six bells and a clock on the west front facing the street. The west front itself was completely obscured by the building of a two-storey porch, which on its upper level contained a parish schoolroom, with storage space below.

Towards the end of Elizabeth's reign was actually a fear that the City and its immediate suburbs were becoming overbuilt with "too many houses". In this expansion the road from the start of St John Street was continuously lined as far as Islington, with its numerous inns, a pond and the parish 'cage'. The more northerly of the inns, with a gateway alongside, was probably the Angel Inn, though not yet mentioned by name.[31] From there building continued on the east as far as the Green; beyond was a noticeable thinning out after the church.

Over the decades the road level had risen from accumulated rubbish or debris, for on entering the church one descended several steps into the nave, then up two more to the altar. The rector's house was on the other side of Upper Street, just south of today's Theberton Street and the house long associated with Sir Walter Raleigh (see page 32). Of unknown date, by 1587 the rectory boasted two gardens – presumably one in front and one behind – an orchard and 45 acres.

No parish registers are extant before 1557, but a curate is known to have been employed from an early date and from the 1540s one was appointed continuously. The vicar's stipend at the time was £30 a year. In the 1560s there were three churchwardens, and in 1577 four overseers of the poor. This kind of appointment constitutes the early form of local government, traditionally supervised by the vestry.

At the Dissolution the rectory and advowson, possessed since Norman times by the nuns of St Leonard's, Stratford-atte-Bow, were taken from them and bestowed as usual on a layman, Sir Ralph Sadler. By various channels, usual enough at that unsettled time, they passed in turn to John Perse, Roger Martyn and John Cheke, and by the 17th century were in the hands of the Stonehouse family.

In 1583 Islington received as vicar a fairly notorious gentleman, the Rev. Meredith Hanmer, of a Flintshire family then settled in Shropshire, who at the age of 23 had served as chaplain of Corpus Christi College, Oxford (1567) and in 1581 became Vicar of St Leonard's, Shoreditch. But he was accused of melting down the brass from graveyard monuments to make counterfeit coin, and was also charged with marrying, with neither banns nor licence, a couple of whom one was apparently already someone else's wife; and as witness in a prosecution for scandal, he is recorded has having "dealt ... leudly towards my Lord [Shrewsbury] in speeches ... This Doctor regardeth not an oath; surely he is a very bad man".[32]

Nonetheless, having taken a doctor's degree

in divinity in 1582, he was considered a good disputant and preacher, a good historian, publishing several works, including attacks on the Jesuit Edmund Campion, and translated the works of the early church historians.

He served as vicar of Islington to 1590, then removed to Ireland, where he became Treasurer of Waterford, and later held other ecclesiastical offices, dying eventually in the plague year there, 1604. One version has him ending ignominiously, even possibly by hanging himself.

CANONBURY HOUSE

The mansions for which Islington became known during the next centuries were increased in the latter part of Elizabeth's reign, starting with a further rebuilding of Canonbury Manor, the one to be seen today. Prior Bolton's work, though recorded as being "builded of new", was more restoration than total re-creation, erecting the range which encloses the curious six-storey brick tower with its flat roof, but otherwise much of his work was to be obscured by later building.

Bolton was not the last Prior. He was succeeded by Robert Fuller, Abbot of Waltham Holy Cross, who held St John's Priory until forced to surrender both it and his Abbey to the King, when Thomas Cromwell acquired Canonbury and Highbury manors.

The best-known period of manor and house begins with the disposal in 1570 by Lord Wentworth, to whom Queen Mary had granted the manor in 1557, to John Spencer, rich Suffolk-born citizen and clothworker. This energetic and patriotic citizen, who always had London's interests at heart, became successively Alderman, Sheriff (1583–4), and in 1595 Lord Mayor. During his mayoralty he made strenuous efforts, in the teeth of opposition, to keep the City supplied with corn in a time of scarcity.[33] He urged the closing of potentially dangerous small postern doors which inhabitants had cut through the City walls; suppressed unruly apprentices who held "several tumultuous meetings" near the Tower, and even had five of them executed. As Lord Mayor, Sir John (knighted 1595) lived at Crosby Place in Bishopsgate, a splendid house which he had recently bought, and here at the beginning of King James's reign he was to entertain the French Ambassador, Marquis de

6. *Canonbury House depicted in 1846.*

tower with its oak newel stair, built unusually on a square and ascending the whole height of the building. The stair turns round a hollow timber centre, in which cupboards and other recesses open (not without a hint of the White Rabbit's domain down which Alice fell, snatching at objects on shelves as she passed). The great enigma is, what was this building for? It had no defensive purpose, but it provided a series of richly panelled rooms, one large and one small on each floor, and led to a flat roof commanding a fine panorama of Middlesex and the City.

Adjoining this group of buildings was a stable range, with an oak folding gate of apparently the same period. The manor house itself ranged round three sides, the west always left open. The south side, which was demolished and rebuilt as houses in the 1770s, we know only through distant exterior views, showing that it included another tower with a central cupola. The grand gabled north wing contains a fine oak staircase, a large ground-floor room rising through two storeys with an elaborate stucco ceiling, and three first-floor rooms also with stucco ceilings.

Sir John Spencer, who married Alice Bromfield, had no son, and his daughter Elizabeth was his heiress. The girl fell in love with the young Lord Compton, of Compton Wynyates in Warwickshire and the new Castle Ashby near Northampton. Having succeeded his father in 1589 at the age of 21, he came to Court, spent a great deal of money, borrowed from "rich Spencer", but succeeded in obtaining only a minor paid court office, as Master of the Leash responsible for the Queen's greyhounds.

Young Elizabeth's father cared less for the title than for the relative lack of money in her lover's family, and opposed the match. The tradition, which there seems no reason to doubt, is that the girl was shut up in Canonbury tower, where her father had just come to live, but Lord Compton disguised himself as a baker's boy, drove up with a cart and by whatever means, got his love out of the tower in a basket. On 18 April 1599 they were married at St Katharine Coleman church.

The upshot was that the furious father disinherited Elizabeth of a fortune computed as anything between £300,000 and £800,000, and

Sully. (The Hall of Crosby Place in comparatively modern times has been re-erected on the Embankment at Chelsea.) But like many a rich merchant, Spencer fancied a country house as well, and Canonbury was the one he purchased, at first renting it out until he came to live there himself in about 1599.

Inside the plain, gabled exterior, considerably less irregular than most of Islington's rambling mansions, were installed a number of fine, elaborate oak chimney-pieces, one of them carved with the Christian and cardinal virtues, and the arms of the City and of Sir John and the Clothworkers' Company (dated 1601). Another in three sections displays robed figures of a man and woman, and Spencer's arms surrounded with "tritons, griffins, serpents, fruit, and other ornaments, finely carved", subdivided by columns with Corinthian capitals, and supported by two figures bearing baskets of fruit on their heads. The main rooms were oak-panelled, the ceilings richly stuccoed.

The most striking though not most beautiful feature of the house is the tall, rather grim

when a son was born to the couple in 1601 their future must have seemed bleak. A perhaps less credible but equally picturesque story is that the Queen was persuaded to intervene, which she did by asking Sir John if he would stand sponsor with her to "the first offspring of a young couple, happy in their love but discarded by their father". The unsuspecting Sir John agreed, even promising to regard the child as his own son, having no heir. One can only picture the fairy-tale ending and resultant reconciliation; at all events the couple moved into Canonbury House, where their next child was born.[34]

The story does not go on so well. Lord Compton was evidently unstable, a gambler and improvident, ending in madness in 1609. Sir John died in 1609/10 and the next stage of Canonbury House belongs to the 17th century in the next chapter.

SIR WALTER RALEIGH

Nearer the centre of Islington, some hundred yards south of the church and on the west side of the main street, was a house associated with Sir Walter Raleigh. A 'Life' published in 1740 states that he was said to have a villa "about a bow's shot on this side the church", and this building survived as the Old Pied Bull inn until 1827.[35] Yet Raleigh's coat of arms was not to be found, as would be customary, in any window or over any chimney-piece. However, Raleigh's early connection with Islington is established by a not very salubrious affair late in 1577, shortly before he made his 'voyage of discovery' with his half-brother; it shows that he already owned a house in Islington, some three years before his voyages established him at Elizabeth's Court.

Walter Raleigh, or Rawley as locally spelt and pronounced in Devon, had as servants two brothers called William and Richard Paunceforth (there were various spellings), who late that year were with a gang which made a riotous and doubtless drunken attack on the defensive outwork Mount Mill, off Goswell Street, then under guard by a party "keeping watch for the Queen at Wenlox Barn".

"Rascals and drunken slaves, come an ye dare, and we will be your deaths!" Thus was recorded the attackers' provocative challenge,

7. *Sir Walter Raleigh.*

as they attempted with drawn swords to storm the little fort. The constable of Wenlock Barn, Anthony Howson, with the watch-party, chased them off, and the two Paunceforths fled with the others, including another Islington "yoman" Giles Harmer, but rounded on the pursuers and seriously wounded Howson, then sought safety in the house of another local, Clement Rigges. Next day, 17 December, Harmer and the two Paunceforths with some other marauders were bound over before the JPs to appear at the next sessions on payment of security, William having to give bail of 100 marks, twice as much as the others. Two days later again, Richard and others were similarly bound for 100 marks, to "answer such matters as may be objected against him".

The two brothers, identified as Raleigh's servants, were presumably doughty young men like their master, who is referred to in the first recognisance as "of Islington" and in the second as "of the Court" (*de Curia*). This sounds as though he had already appeared before the Queen, though he had not yet made his mark, and it was some three years before the dandified young adventurer with his entrenched

8. North view of the house said to be occupied by Sir Walter Raleigh, which later became the Pied Bull.

Devonian burr became a glamorous royal favourite. [36]

As for his house in Islington, with it were 14 acres of land held of Barnsbury manor, extending westwards (along the present Theberton Street, then a footpath), and the 1740 'Life' records that Sir Walter "had purposed to wall in that ground with intention to keep some of his horses therein". Any arms recorded in the house, and some of the decorations, dated from the time of Sir John Miller, a Devon knight living in Islington from 1624. Miller's arms were depicted in the stained glass of a casement window, though surrounding decorations certainly suggest Raleigh: in the parlour was a border of two mermaids crested with a globe, and two seahorses above, supporting a bunch of leaves above the shield, and below, two parrots, one grey, the other green eating fruit. They may well have originally surrounded Raleigh's arms, later replaced by Miller's. Also in the window appeared another parrot and a border of figures and flowers. In the chimney-piece niches were the letters F. H. and Ch, again in a border of cherubs, fruit and foliage. Its main decoration, possibly in compliment to Queen Elizabeth, was a figure of Charity surmounted by two cupids supporting a crown and head, a lion and unicorn couchant below. The ceiling was adorned with the five senses and Latin mottoes, in stucco; in the centre a female figure, her right arm entwined with a serpent biting a hand, in her left a stick pointing to a toad at her feet, the motto, 'Tactus'.

The chimney-piece in the "noble dining room" depicted the Christian virtues. In smaller surrounding ovals, symbolic figures represented the pleasures of taste ('Gustus'), sight, hearing and smell. The five senses also appeared in the stucco ceiling. The parlour also contained some dozen painted panels, of Scriptural scenes.

All of the decoration might have been added in Sir John Miller's time. We shall never know because, like almost every other ancient house in the district, the house became an inn, the Pied Bull, probably early in the 18th century and was destroyed in the early 19th century.

This richly finished house was built sideways on to the street, entered from the lane or footpath leading westwards across the fields. Queen Elizabeth, known to have come several times to Islington, may well have visited Raleigh here.[37]

Of the 16th-century parsonage adjoining Raleigh's house on the south, but set back from the street behind a front garden, we have no description. In the 17th century a new rectory was built on the front garden site.

THE QUEEN'S HEAD

The most famous of other half-timbered mansions was in the Lower Street, the Queen's Head Inn, regarded by those who remembered it in later times as one of London's most perfect domestic buildings. This too was associated with Raleigh, who certainly stayed there even if he did not live in it. It is supposed to have been one of the taverns built after he was granted the patent, in 1588, to license inns and retail wines. It shares with the Pied Bull the tradition of being where Raleigh's servant dowsed him with water on seeing him smoking a pipe.

Its three timber and plaster storeys overhung each other, with bay windows supported on brackets carved as figures. This too over the centuries had to be entered by steps from street level now four feet above. The centre projected several feet to form a large porch – also receding in the lower floors, supported by carved oak caryatids crowned with Ionic scrolls. The chief room or parlour had a chimney-piece with two festooned stone supporters, and above, a carved slab showed Diana and Actaeon, Venus, Bacchus and 'Plenty'. In the centre of the plaster ceiling a medallion probably represented a Roman emperor, crowned with bay, with cherubs on a shield surrounding the letters I M. Round this were dolphins, cherubs, acorns, and a wreathed border of fruit and flowers.

Lord Burleigh was also associated with the house, probably after Raleigh's time. Two carved wooden lions, supporters of the Cecil arms and said to have come from the Queen's

9. The Old Queen's Head in Essex Road. From a drawing by F W L Stockdale.

Head, were long to be seen in a neighbouring yard. A servant of Burleigh's son, Lord Exeter, was buried in the village. Yet another tradition relates that Lord Essex had the house as a summer residence, and that the Queen occasionally visited it. As none of these stories are dated, one must juggle with decades and biographies to make any sense of them.

At one time the house must have been a storey higher, for when the roof was stripped during demolition the workmen found part of a staircase and the floor of another range of rooms. The brick and stone chimneys were vast, the roof lead weighed at least 1½ tons, and the lead gutters were a quarter of an inch thick. In 1829, to great local regret, the house was demolished and its materials sold. Mr Bird, proprietor of the boring building erected on its site, bought and re-erected the parlour chimney-piece (showing Diana and Actaeon), the adjoining oak panelling, and the plaster ceiling.[38] In sifting the sand under the floors, a gold piece of the time of William and Mary was found.

A lane hereabouts, later called Cross Street, linked the Upper and Lower Streets, forming the boundary of a copyhold estate, part of Canonbury manor.

BARNSBURY MANOR

Barnsbury manor, being already in lay hands, had escaped the damages of confiscation. As we have seen, after passing from the de Berners family and being twice sold on, it ended with the Fowlers. Not that ownership was now straightforward. It passed to a cousin of the first Fowler, who sold to (presumably) another relation, Thomas Fowler, merchant of the Staple and water-bailiff of Calais, whose son died in 1560 leaving an infant heir, another Thomas. This Thomas and his son, a third Thomas, were both knighted by James I on his arrival in London in 1603, and the younger knight in 1628 was upgraded by Charles I to baronet. He died in 1656.[39]

The house the Fowlers built, however, was of Elizabethan date. Starting with one on Upper Street beside the rectory, they then vacated it for Cross Street. The Upper Street house was by 1685 replaced by Rufford's Row.[40]

The Fowlers' new house, on the site of to-day's 41 Cross Street, had extensive grounds at the rear, running northwards along the present Halton Road to the boundary of Canonbury manor.[41] It was irregular in shape, built of lath and plaster, its front later modernised and the whole building considerably altered in its later days. The stained glass windows of the oak-panelled rooms included the Fowler arms dated 1588, with those of the Heron family, one of whom had married the first Thomas who settled in Islington. Also dating from the Queen's time (1595) was a stucco ceiling in the first-floor back room, with the arms of England, initials of the Queen and of Thomas and Jane Fowler, with a fleur-de-lys and medallions – similar to the style in Canonbury House.

Historically more interesting than the house was the three-storeyed brick garden lodge, also late 16th century, built at the north end of the demesne, which for reasons often dismissed as frivolous was always known as Queen Elizabeth's Lodge. Though it may have been the porter's lodge, giving access to the house from that end of the grounds, it was more probably a gazebo. On the west side near the top were the Fowler arms with an esquire's helmet in stone – thus dating the building to before Sir Thomas was knighted. A lead platform on the roof afforded a good view to the north of Canonbury's mansion and park, with the woods of Highbury; to the west and south the church and village, and eastwards over the fields to the City.

The theory is that the Queen must have passed through the lodge when visiting Sir Thomas Fowler at the house; or perhaps on her way to Sir John Spencer at Canonbury. She might well have taken a fancy to the little building and proposed to dine or take other refreshment there – or even just have enjoyed the view. Certainly the Queen came often to Islington, as attested by her arms in more than one house.

Whatever personal visits the Queen made to such favoured courtiers, she evidently came from Enfield, on her way to St James's, often enough for it to be found necessary to level hedges and ditches along the way from Islington onwards, to make a clear road for her and her entourage.[42]

1   In present-day terms this may have been 1518 as the new year did not begin until 25 March.

2   Lovell who, after Bosworth, had been created Chancellor of the Exchequer for life, sat as MP for Northampton and was also Speaker of the House of Commons until 1488. He was knighted in 1487 and was made Knight of the Garter in 1503. In 1509 he became High Steward of both Cambridge and Oxford. He died in 1524.

3   The Brotherhood of Jesus was founded in or before 1479 and at least until 1541 kept a priest to say regular masses. (*VCH*, p. 89) The property of such organisations was seized under the Act of 1548 against "superstitious uses" and their income, then £7, was confiscated. From 1551 the parish feoffees were allowed the profits except for 53s. 4d reserved for the Crown. In 1561 new feoffees appointed trusts by which the churchwardens received the profits to distribute as this group of parishioners decided. *VCH*, p.135; Vestry Report to Cloudesley Estate, 1851, p.14, in Islington Libraries. See Nelson, *Islington*, p.301.

4   These include Barrell's, a house with 9 acres, and Sibley's Field, a close which the Lord Prior was to pass to seven named persons (quoted in Nelson, *Islington*, p.304).

5   The Hermitage was on a piece of Brewers' Company land, later known as Hermitage Field, on which Dame Alice Owen's school was built almost a century later.

6   Thomas Edlyne Tomlins, *Yseldon, A Perambulation of Islington*, London, 1858, p. 23n.

7   *Purlet de Mir. Nat.* X.c.4, quoted by Nelson, *Islington*, p. 305n.

8   Nelson, *Islington*, pp. 301–7 and nn.

9   *Ibid*, p. 201, *n.2*.

10   *Ibid*, p. 202, *n.2*.

11   *Ibid*, p. 203.

12   *Ibid*, p. 207.

13   According to Nelson much of the surviving glass was acquired by "the late Samuel Ireland, Esq., of Norfolk Street, Strand".

14   *VCH*, pp. 54, 69.

15   *VCH*, p. 72.

16   *VCH*, p. 59.

17   In 1666 this was defined as a house with eight acres.

18   *VCH*, p. 60.

19   *VCH*, p. 41.

20   Nelson, *Islington*, p. 47n.

21   John Foxe, *Actes and Monuments*, quoted in Nelson, *Islington*, pp. 47-8.

22   John Stow, *The Annales of England* (1585-7).

23   Foxe, *Actes and Monuments*, quoted in Nelson, *Islington*, pp. 48-9.

24   Unwin, *Gilds and Companies*.

25   Christopher Hill, *The World Turned Upside Down*, London, 1972.

26   *VCH*, p. 45.

27   Nelson, *Islington*, pp. 405-6.

28   See, e.g., William J Pinks, *The History of Clerkenwell*, with additions by Edward J Wood, London, 1865, pp. 68-74, 606-7; John Stow, *Survey of London*, (1598 & 1603), Sutton Publishing ed., 1994, p. 129; *VCH*, pp 9, 50.

29   Stephen Powys Marks, *The Map of Mid Sixteenth Century London*, London Topographical Society, 1964.

30   *VCH*, p. 66.

31   *VCH*, p. 13.

32   John Strype, *The Annals of the Reformation*, 1824, Vol. III, pp. 216, 217; William Fleetwood, *Diary*, both quoted in Nelson, *Islington*, p. 282n.

33   Nelson, *Islington*, pp. 225-6.

34   Islington parish registers in LMA.

35   Its 19th-century successor was needlessly renamed 'The Sir Walter Raleigh' in the 1990s.

36   *Middlesex County Records*, Vol. I, pp. 110, 111, in LMA.

37   Samuel Lewis, Jr, *History of the Parish of St Mary, Islington*, London 1842, p. 159.

38   *European Magazine*, March 1808. The room containing these features was burnt out in the 1970s, but the fireplace and its surrounding panelling and part of the ceiling survived.

39   *VCH*, pp. 51-2.

40   Said to have been built by Captain Nicholas Rufford, a churchwarden who died in 1711, aged 72. By 1877 the site had been numbered 289–302 Upper Street. (Eric Willats, *Streets with a Story*, Islington Public Libraries, 1988, p. 206.)

41   Traces of the Tudor garden wall survive off Fowler Road at the boundary of the school playground and the back of Cross Street houses.

42   Pinks, *Clerkenwell*, p. 259.

CHAPTER 4

The Seventeenth Century

THE NEW RIVER[1]

Before Queen Elizabeth's reign ended one of London's major concerns had become the water supply. For some thirty years any new conduits in the City had had to draw from river water from the Thames, of increasingly doubtful purity as the population increased. Early in the next century an ambitious scheme was brought to fruition which was to have a profound effect both on London's and on Islington's own growth and development.

It began with small and abortive efforts. In 1581 an attempt was made to improve the efficiency of river water circulation by a Dutchman, Peter Mauritz, or Morris, who obtained a lease from the City to set up a water wheel and works at the northern arch of London Bridge, from which he could supply local houses through pipes laid under the streets. Its scope was limited, supplying only the south and east parts of the City.

Small, localised schemes, at Broken Wharf for the west and Botolph Wharf for the east of the City were attempted in 1594 and 1600. More ambitiously, at about the same time a former captain in the army, living in Bath, proposed to bring a fresh supply from a distance, channelled from springs in Hertfordshire and Middlesex. This was Edward Colthurst. Most of the supply was intended to cleanse London's many ditches, but about a third would bring water to certain houses in both London and Westminster. The Queen, now in the last years of her life, asked her Lord Treasurer, Lord Buckhurst, to look into the idea, and he secured the City Corporation's approval in 1602 as "a matter very beneficial

and no waie p[re]judiciall to them". Also at the Queen's order, the sheriffs of the two counties pointed out that inhabitants would require compensation for cutting through their land.

At this stage the Queen died. It proved little hindrance, however, as Colthurst then applied to the new King James. On 18 April 1604 he was authorised under Letters Patent to complete his project in seven years, and once it made a profit, was to pay the Crown £20 a year. By the following February Colthurst announced that three miles had already been completed.

Colthurst's efforts spurred others to propose schemes, and a Bill was brought to Parliament in January 1606 "for the bringing in of a fresh Stream of running Water from the River Lee, or Uxbridge, to the North Parts of the City of London". On its second reading the Bill was referred to a Committee including the Recorder of the City, Sir Henry Montagu, and two brothers named Hugh and Robert Myddelton.

With suitable recompense to Colthurst the City was to bring fresh water from the Hertfordshire springs of Amwell, Chadwell and others nearby, by cutting a river no more than 10 feet wide and allow access for workmen and transport. Local landowners and mill-owners were to be compensated.

Negotiations continued for the next two years, including with Colthurst and a drainage engineer named William Ingelbert; after the passing of a second Act in 1607 the latter disappears from view, apparently ending in poverty.

Colthurst announced in 1608 that his

partnership was ready to proceed under the patent he had secured, and requested the City (through the Court of Aldermen) not to hinder his project by pressing their own. He was given two years to execute the work – at no cost to the City.

After some months' silence Colthurst, for the first time naming Islington as the destination of his channel, applied for £2,400 towards the cost, in return for which he would make over two-thirds of the water for the public. Failing this contribution, he would pay for all but keep any profits. The City cannily agreed to the second alternative.

The next move seems unexpected, for in March 1609 it was not Colthurst who was authorised to execute the work, but a Welsh goldsmith, whom we have already met on the committee following the first Bill's second reading.

Hugh Myddelton, born in 1560, was a sixth son, and as such would be expected to make his own way in life. His father, Richard, was Governor of Denbigh Castle, near where Hugh was born. As a youth Hugh prospected for coal to supply the town but soon moved to London where he became a goldsmith, sat in Parliament as MP for Denbigh and was its first alderman. Among his influential customers was the King.

The Myddelton brothers Hugh and Robert, though appointed in 1606 to the committee on the first Bill, were not apparently on the second. It was Hugh, however, who kept the accounts, begun in February 1609 as the First Book of Disbursements on this undertaking, "for the bringinge of watter from the springs of Chadwell and Amwell to the citty of London", from which it appears that during the earlier negotiations he had been Colthurst's partner. The transfer of powers may have been for financial reasons, Hugh Myddelton being relatively rich, whereas Colthurst was not.

Under the new agreement work was to start within two months and finish within four years. Myddelton was granted power of attorney and a formal agreement was drawn up in April 1609. At first Colthurst was responsible for payment of wages, which date from May, and received a weekly allowance of 14 shillings. This payment continued until August 1616, which may signify his death.

10. Sir Hugh Myddelton. An engraving of 1805.

'Mr Wright', who paid for three surveys of the land between Amwell and Islington, must have been Edward Wright, the Norfolk man who had tried to supply water from Botolph's Wharf. He was a renowned mathematician and astronomer, and after initial payments he was paid a regular weekly wage of £2.

The direct distance between Amwell and Islington was only twenty miles, but this grand undertaking, styled 'New River' but effectively a man-made canal, had to follow gradients. The course meandered around the 100-foot contour, adding no less than 18 miles to the total. Where there was a hill, they had to go round; where a valley, they had to carry a channel over it.

Between August and September the number of labourers employed rose from 50 or so to over 130, and their number fluctuated until January 1610 when there were only 17; some difficulties must have been encountered as work ceased except for maintenance, for nearly two years. In the summer four 'walksmen' were paid their first quarterly wages, at this stage for very little work.

The hold-up appears to have been obstruction from land-owners. The first 'loop' round a contour was being negotiated at Wormley. There had never been such an undertaking before and there were plenty of people to object. The City fulfilled its part of the bargain by appealing to the King, via the Privy Council, to remove "all lette and hindraunce" to Myddelton. They ran into opposition in the Commons, who made a strong attempt to repeal both the Acts authorising the now substantial work. The Court of Aldermen appealed, for the work had now progressed ten miles "at the Charges of Mr Hugh Midleton" and cost him £3000.

Numerous hitches over funding, disposal of profits, and local opposition halted progress throughout 1611. The King, doubtless visualising royal gains, bargained for a half-share in the profits, and through the intervention of the Lord Treasurer, Lord Salisbury, across whose lands around Hoddeson the course was already cut, obstructions were removed.

Even passage through royal lands was now made free, and Myddelton was to be reimbursed for half his own expenditure. A minute record of all payments was then kept until 1631.

The formal agreement between Myddelton and the Lord Treasurer (1 November 1611) empowered Myddelton to extract water (a 'quill') from the main City supply pipe to provide free to "the poore people … about Ste Johns Street and Aldersgate Streete which are not able nor fitt to paie for their water". A repeat agreement was signed with the King on 2 May 1612, with the further royal injunction that his people were not to "moleste inquiett trouble or hinder" Myddelton in his task of bringing the springs to the city, "upon paine of his maiesties highe displeasure".

Thus Myddelton and his assignees became deputies for the City. Myddelton divided the undertaking into 36 shares for his partners, the 'Adventurers', according to their contribution, and in future opposition and hindrance were to be strongly dealt with.

Yet work was only resumed by November 1611, when a new figure was brought in, a mathematician named Edward Pond, evidently succeeding Edward Wright (who died in 1615), as 'Arts Man' at £2 6s 8d a week. It was he who now kept track of the river's course, worked on site, with a level, and even kept a tent there made from four ells of canvas. Myddelton too now had a regular allowance until 1620, of 45s 8d a week for himself, "his man & tooe geldeinges".[2]

Thenceforward work proceeded at a good pace. Over the 40 miles from Chadwell spring to what was named New River Head the average fall was about 5 inches a mile, a total of 18 feet. Sluices at several points – at the spring head, at Amwell, Broxbourne and Theobalds – created drops which lessened intervening falls to 2–3 inches. Where the level coincided with the course of a stream a wooden trough was made to carry the river above, or on occasion the stream was carried over the river by a 'flash', notably at Wormley and Enfield Chase. By this means they avoided elaborate aqueducts of the kind the Romans would have built, except at the timber 'Frame' at Bush Hill. Here leaks, which soon presented a problem, were dealt with by a combination of tar, resin, pitch, oakum and tallow. The base was underpinned by 'tileshards', and to caulk the frame a gang of shipwrights was brought in at 2s a day. (At this stage no lead was used.) At certain points wooden arches supported the Frame. Indeed leaks proved a recurring problem, especially on the left (east) bank of the river where over much of the distance the land fell away, and particularly in the more northerly reaches the banks were constantly being raised and strengthened. The river had been barely completed when a great flood at Christmas 1614 caused the river to burst its banks at Brookfield, Cheshunt.

In some places trees barring the way had to be felled. And at certain times weeds choked the river and needed clearing. Then there was the menace of moles, which particularly in the early days were trapped by mole-catchers; gratings had to be made to keep out hogs and geese, and at New River Head itself frogs got into the system and had to be kept off by plugs.

Yet from the north of Cheshunt to New River Head took only 22 months.

A number of Myddelton's fellow-Welshmen were employed, and one Scotsman, Thomas Trenson, who died on the job in December 1609. At times at least 100 labourers were again employed to follow in the wake of the

11. *The New River Head from the north in the earlier part of the 18th century. The figures are in front of the outer pond. Beyond it the brick wall, round pond and water house were all built in 1613.*

excavators, who sometimes had to dig as deep as ten feet. Measuring gauges were first used in December 1609. Carpenters were employed to wharf the banks and build little bridges. Sometimes these were of brick, which cost more. 'Oversight' was by a surveyor and a 'Master Worke man'. Even the King took a part, ordering banks to prevent flooding in Theobalds Park. They even invested in a drum to summon the men.

The river finally wound its way through Islington and the uneven, hilly ground near the Angel. The 'Round Pond' or reservoir was dug and paved, and the famous occasion of opening the sluices and filling the Pond took place on Michaelmas Day, 1613.

This, an occasion of pageantry, was presided over by the Lord Mayor, Sir John Swinnerton. With him were two of the Adventurers: Myddelton's brother, Sir Thomas, who was Lord Mayor elect, and the Recorder Sir Henry Montagu. A different Middleton, Thomas the playwright, had composed a lengthy verse, which was declaimed, paying tribute to Colthurst, "an ancient soldier and an Artisan", William Lewyn the clerk, Edward Pond

the mathematician, and three of the artisans.

The Round Pond formed the reservoir, but its contents were controlled by a curious fairy-tale building known as the 'Water House', which contained the sluices. Sometimes attributed to Inigo Jones, with its quaint, steep-pitched roof it dominated the site, which for two centuries attracted many artists, notably Hollar in Charles II's reign. Unfortunately its interior seems never to have been pictorially recorded.

The House, which rose as high as garrets, contained a counting house, a staircase and a 'Middle room' – perhaps on the middle floor. There was also a gallery, on which one stood to turn the wooden, or sometimes brass stop-cocks. A trapdoor gave admission to the 'cistern house', which was linked by a grating to the Round Pond, and wooden pipes in the cistern's south side acted as distributors to supply the City's streets.

The timber for these pipes, which remained in use until the early 19th century, was elm from Berkshire and other Home Counties, brought by Thames to a wharf where they were bored by special horse machinery at a cost of 7½d a yard to diameters of three, four and six inches. The ends were either sharpened or bored out in order to ram them securely together, the joint strengthened by iron hoops.

To lay the pipes trenches were dug and paved along the streets, often at night, at 3½d– 4½d a yard. The first line was across the fields bordering New River Head to St John Street, Smithfield and Newgate, where it divided to serve Cheapside and Ludgate via the Old Bailey. The second line, from New River Head down Goswell Road, was not made until 1617. The pipes were dragged between a pair of coach-wheels; for laying, they were lifted by chains and tarred ropes and once in place sometimes protected from leaks by packing the surroundings with clay.

All this cost a great deal. At cessation of work in 1610, £707 was spent; at resumption costs rose from £4,424 in 1612 to £6,407 in 1614, when the elm logs were finally bought and laid. Meanwhile, the expected profits did not materialise as London's citizens did not rush to pay the quarterly rental varying between 5 shillings and 6s 8d (the latter being what the poet John Milton's father, then living in Bread Street, paid). According to an Act of the Privy Council in 1618 it had not achieved the expected effect "either in point of proffitt or otherwise". The King was dissatisfied, and it was debated whether either he, or the Adventurers should take control of the works. This resulted in a Charter of Incorporation on 21 June 1619, by which Myddelton was to become Governor, with a deputy and a treasurer of "the Company of the New River brought from Chadwell and Amwell to London", consisting of the 29 Adventurers.

A number of these were Myddelton's relations: Hugh's son, also Hugh, his brother Sir Thomas, nephews William and Richard, and three others. They held their first meeting in Serjeants' Inn in Fleet Street, and subsequently at Myddelton's house. The number of 'tenants' of the water supply rose late in 1618 to 1,000; an increase in supply was sought by drawing water from the nearby River Lea. In 1621 Myddelton took over management of the whole works.

However, at the time of opening the river was not complete, and in 1618 improvements were made at Highbury. These included the creation of the famous 'Boarded River', another 'frame', its purpose to reduce one of the many loops. Until then the river had curved as far as the Holloway Road and Ring Cross to circumvent the valley of the Hackney Brook. It was now carried across in a long, wooden trough raised on banks which took most of 1618 to create; the trough, caulked with pitch and tar, was made by carpenters in August/September 1619. The Boarded River became a notable local feature, until a century and a half later its many leaks obliged Robert Mylne to create an alternative.

After its uneasy start, both financially and administratively, the New River began to pay off. The King received his first dividend or 'Royal Moiety' at Michaelmas 1622 (£433 2s 7d), and on 19 October Hugh Myddelton was created the first engineer baronet. He was further rewarded in 1623 when the City acknowledged "the great and extraordinary benefitt and service" brought by the new water supply – especially as London had by then endured several serious fires. They presented him with a gold chain and jewel, which appear on Sir Hugh's portrait painted by Cornelius Jansen.

After King James's death in 1625 his son, Charles, began to weigh up the greater profits he might receive through granting patents for a rival venture, which might bring water from Hoddesdon. (Where this channel would have ended is another matter.) Although this did not materialise, the King pulled out of the existing arrangement with the New River Company, conveyed the 'Royal Moiety' to Sir Hugh by indenture (1631) and in exchange accepted an annual rent of £500, known as 'the Crown Clog'.

Sir Hugh, now 71 and very ill, within three days made his will and a few weeks later died, on 10 December 1631. At least the years of negotiation and uncertainty had come to a reasonable fruition.

DAME ALICE OWEN AND HER SCHOOL

The New River Head was actually in the parish of Clerkenwell, though so far from the main part of Clerkenwell that it was usually thought of as an Islington feature and did indeed profoundly influence its development.

12. An early Owen's School building. The boy appears to be chasing a pig out of the garden.

Another Clerkenwell establishment, very near the Angel, also affected Islington village. This was Dame Alice Owen's School, founded, at about the same time as the construction of the New River, by a friend of Sir Hugh Myddelton. In origin Dame Alice was Mistress Alice Wilkes, daughter of Thomas Wilkes, a well-to-do tenant-owner of property in the manor of Barnsbury which by 1556 included an eight-acre field, 'the Long Meadow the Greater'. There were a number of local Wilkeses, one of whom, Robert, a brewer, contributed to equipping ships which opposed the Spanish Armada in 1588.[3] The brewing connection was to prove all-important in Dame Alice's life.

Born apparently in 1547, Alice was evidently a privileged young woman, who on walking out in the fields was attended by a maid-servant. The oft-told story of her escapade with cow and arrow is that, on one such expedition, presumably in her teens, she had a fancy to try her hand at milking a cow in one of the lairs south of the Angel where local cattle were kept. As she rose from the stool she had a narrow escape. One of the archers practising in the nearby fields shot off an arrow which, providentially, pierced her tall-crowned hat and not her skull – which it certainly would have done had she moved a fraction earlier. The grateful girl, on recovering from the shock swore that "if she lived to be a lady she would erect something on that spot of ground in commemoration of the great mercy shown by the Almighty in that astonishing deliverance".

The story is recorded in Strype's continuation of Stow's *History of London*, not published until 1720, which relates the episode as when "sporting among other children", she expresses pious thanks that "missing all others", she "did not come to any other harm" than the famous hat piercing. The *Gentleman's Magazine* version in 1791 (vol. lxi pt 1, 217), altogether more flowery, suggests that the marksman was none other than Sir Thomas Owen (sic), the most distinguished of her three husbands, which wound "Cupid revenged with one of his arrows, that made a still deper wound on Sir Thomas". If this far-fetched supposition is true, Owen waited long enough to heal his wound while she married and outlived two other husbands.[4]

Alice Wilkes did not become a 'Lady', but

three respectable marriages entitled her to the married woman's prefix of 'Dame'. Her husbands, in succession, were Henry Robinson, William Elkin, alderman and referred to as Esquire, and finally Thomas Owen, a judge of the Court of Common Pleas. Though she was subsequently sometimes termed 'Lady Owen', there is no evidence that Thomas was ever knighted.[5] She also bore seven children, six sons by the first husband, a daughter by the second, all of whom she married off respectably to gentry or knights, and ended with numerous grandchildren.

In later life, as a widow, the same woman servant reminded her of her girlhood vow, which indeed she had not forgotten, and in 1608 she secured a patent from the King to buy the 11-acre 'Ermitage' Fields, which extended southwards from a passage by the Welsh Harp inn (now the Old Red Lion), bounded by St John Street and Goswell Road to the present Rawstorne Street. Within a few years the end of the New River was to wind diagonally across it.

Nearly a hundred years earlier the Priory of St John of Jerusalem in Clerkenwell had built a chapel there (c.1510), occupied by a hermit or single divine until the Dissolution. Here, at the top end of St John Street, Dame Alice ordered ten almshouses to be built for "poor old widows". Her patent also allowed her other purchases in the 'Charterhouse Closes', north of the present Pentonville Road, which were conveyed by indenture in February 1609 to the Brewers' Company as Trustees, as were Hermitage Fields the same November. Each estate brought in £25 annual income to be used for the almshouses. In 1610 the Dame secured a second patent in order to build a chapel and house for a minister, "who may be able to read to the aforesaid widows... and teach the sons and daughters of the poore", payable from the income of other lands' value up to £30 per annum.

This is the first mention locally of education, and the school was presumably built shortly after, being mentioned in a deed of November 1612, but possibly receiving its first (boy) pupils in 1613. Some 30 boys – 24 from Islington, 6 from Clerkenwell – were thenceforward taught free, according to their benefactor's 'Orders and Rules' issued on 20 September 1613, in which the foundation is described as "lately erected", as "the Free Chapel and School of Alice Owen, of London", though completion of purchase of the necessary lands had not yet taken place.

On 10 June 1613 Dame Alice had drawn up her will in which she increased the £20 intended as the Master's salary by £2 and ordered the purchase of more land of £20 rental value for his future maintenance, ensuring that if it were not completed before her death he should be paid £5 now and £5 until the purchase was final.

She died not long after, on 26 November, and though by then living for years in the City, was buried in St Mary's church, Islington, in the south-east corner, in "a very spacious and costly monument of white and veined marble, enriched with cherubim, fruit and foliage, and with two columns and an entablature of the Corinthian", within an iron railing. On it was her reclining effigy, reading a book, with eleven of her descendants shown as small kneeling figures, and with a lengthy description of her life and achievements (notably the successful disposal of her children's marriages).

This monument unfortunately did not survive the destruction of the church in 1751, when it was declared mostly in too frail a state to remove, and a different monument was placed in the south aisle of the new building in 1754 – in marble, again within iron railings, and retaining part of the original inscription in its letters of gold, ordered by the Brewers' Company. Nine of the original children's figures were also rescued from the old church and removed to the school, to be placed in a niche above its entrance. This survived subsequent moves and is to be seen in the present school.

Even the 18th-century monument deteriorated until, in the late 19th century, Dame Alice was recorded in St Mary's only by a tablet. In 1897, therefore, the school commissioned a statue of their benefactor from the young sculptor George Frampton, who executed it in polychrome, parts being of marble, bronze and alabaster.[6]

The Master, who by the Rules had to be single, and not in any ecclesiastical benefice, was to be selected by Dame Alice and after her death by the Court of Assistants of the Brewers' Company and approved by the Bishop. Among his privileges was to hold chapel, schoolhouse and study above the porch, and garden, rent free; the Governors maintaining the buildings. He was to be paid £5 quarterly, even during illness, as well as two chaldrons of coal a year (which soon proved inadequate), retiring whether from age or infirmity on full salary. As for duties, he was to teach the pupils "the Grammar, fair Writing, Cyphering and casting of accompts" as training for apprenticeship or "some other honest course"; to ensure cleanliness and neatness "in their Bodies and Garments" and nominate two of them to sweep the school every day. As "Custos of the almshouses" he had to ensure that they were supplied with "coal and cloth", read prayers twice daily in the almshouses, keep a register, read out Rules and Orders every quarter, and take any necessary disciplinary measures.

School hours were 6 am. to 6 pm. in summer, 7 am. to 5 pm. in winter. No boys were to pay a fee unless by the governors' consent, and then their care and teaching must not be in preference to the rest. Foundation scholars, elected by the Company at parents' request, had to be certified by their local parish church.

There was to be a regular visitation by the Court of Assistants, and the Master and Wardens were annually, between Easter and Whitsun, to visit Dame Alice's tomb in the church, after which they were allotted 30 shillings "for a dinner, or a refreshing to them".

The buildings extended along St John Street between the Welsh Harp and the Crown & Woolpack (nos 416 and 396). The almshouses, ranged behind a courtyard – which at least by the late 18th century was fronted by a low wall, with steps down to the yard – were of undressed stone with mullioned windows. Each contained only one room with a small garden behind; a pump, also used by the school, stood in the forecourt, and in 1629 two trees were planted there.

The school premises ran back from the road, had a porch, later enlarged to make an entrance hall with benches, and the Master's room above. In a closet to the right were a writing table and cupboard, and over the inner door Dame Alice's device of a pomegranate tree in a lozenge. To the left a door opened into the forecourt, presumably for access to the pump. Not just one arrow but for good measure three were displayed on the apex and the gable corners. When the front was modernised in the nineteenth century, at least in 1828 the shaft of one arrow survived.

The schoolhouse, a single room 50 x 20 feet, was considered large enough to house between 30 and 50 boys; it was wainscoted on both sides and supplied with lockers and hat-pegs. Two large casement windows with brick mullions looked on to the little garden. It was furnished with benches, and a long writing-table. The Master's area at the far end, originally wainscoted with two shelves above, was later enclosed with a desk and cupboard. Other furniture was sparse. As late as 1661 the Master petitioned for a school clock, as they were far from the church and certainly had no watch between them. They were then presented with a striking clock with weights, hung on the right of the front door. There were also many petitions for a bigger coal supply.

At the Master's end a staircase led up to his Spartan quarters of two small rooms, and upstairs again, to a closet in the garret. When the porch was enlarged he was also given the room above it. His own supplies were equally scanty: table, "old wainscot bedstead" with feather bed and quilt and two feather bolsters, two joint-stools, a "carplett" and a mat. They sound like cast-offs, and were renewed in 1672 by a new 'French' bedstead with curtains, a bolster and two pillows, blanket, rug, and a cupboard. In the second, less good room, was more old furniture: a table, backed chair, two old-style stools and, behind a partition, another bed-space. The small porch-room seems to have been practically empty, as were the attic rooms. Below stairs their beer was stored, doubtless a staple fare.

The garden had an arbour as well as shrubs and bushes, also a coalhouse and the privy or 'necessary house'. A vine climbed up the schoolhouse wall. Two gates, surmounted with the Company's arms, led, one to the rear of the almshouses, the other to the adjoining field.

Across St John Street was Goose Farm, whose fields stretched down to the New River Head. On the south side there was soon to be the New River itself, winding across Hermitage Fields, after crossing a vale or hollow east of the inn on the site of the Angel, by the last of its many bridges. The school was, in effect, a country place bordering on the village.

The first Master at the school, William Leake, to whom Dame Alice left a personal bequest of £5, resigned the following year, and indeed the school's early history was not very successful either financially or, apparently, with its masters. Between 1613 and 1628 there were no less than seven, five of whom resigned and one died. After that things improved for a time, Peter Dowell serving from 1628 to 1654 until he died in office, and until 1665 George Lovejoy, who went on to the prestigious King's School at Canterbury. Thereafter came a brisk turnover of five, Lovejoy being followed by two who quickly resigned, and until the end of the century three others who, after serving for a number of years, were dismissed.

The Master's responsibilities were of course fairly wide and demanding and included maintenance and supervision of the almshouses and their inhabitants, as well as the school buildings, apparently without the assistance of an under-master. Some of the almswomen, in fact, were described as less than responsible, pawning their gowns, selling drink and becoming drunk themselves, even entertaining vagrants on the premises. Mr Lovejoy had so little time available for teaching other than the Classics that he had to employ a Writing Master. It was he who obtained the clock, and in general proved efficient enough to warrant the raising of his salary by £4.

Financial problems soon arose when the organisation ran into deficit, most of its annual income of £72 being swallowed up by regular expenditure, leaving only £2 10s. for repairs or emergencies. In 1626 the Brewers' Company felt obliged to take over the regular overdraft, which continued to rise. The Company then suffered a great misfortune, losing its Hall in Addle Street in the Great Fire, along with treasures and equally precious records; it also lost all its breweries on Thames-side. Yet they contrived to carry on Owen's School. Towards the end of the century the property which funded it increased in rental value, with new building, and the Hermitage estate supplied the almshouses with a handsome income which supported the school, whose own property outside London was doing less well. By

the 18th century, however, the school was prospering.[7]

CHARTERHOUSE

Almost exactly contemporary with the completion of the New River and the founding of Dame Alice Owen's charity, was Thomas Sutton's foundation in 1611 of a school and hospital at the Charterhouse. Although it was at Clerkenwell's extreme southern limit, its importance warrants a brief description here. Since its dissolution as a monastery in 1537 the Charterhouse had passed to the Crown – King Henry had used it to store his hunting tents – then to Sir Edward North, and shortly thereafter to John Dudley, Duke of Northumberland. The latter soon lost it when he was executed for his attempt to put Lady Jane Grey on the throne. It then reverted to North, who in 1558 entertained the new Queen Elizabeth there to receive homage before her coronation and progress through the City.

A similar visit and procession was made in 1561, but North, financially ruined by the expense, retreated to the country and in 1565 Charterhouse was sold to the Duke of Norfolk. He in turn was executed (1572) for trying to marry Mary Queen of Scots and place her on the English throne. Next it was let to the Portuguese Ambassador, was lived in from 1593–5 by the Earl of Cumberland and family, and the Queen in her old age gave it in 1601 to the Duke of Norfolk's son, Thomas Howard, Admiral of the Fleet. She stayed there with him in 1603 and James I stayed four days on his arrival in the capital, creating 133 knights and making Howard Lord Chamberlain.

At last in 1611 Thomas Sutton, known as 'the richest commoner in England', bought it for £13,000, only six months before his death, in order to found a school for 44 poor boys and a 'hospital' (almshouses) for 80 poor gentlemen. The first boys joined the school in 1641, under a master and an usher, and the school continued for many years with about 100 boys. [8]

A corollary to the foundation was another service which Thomas Sutton provided for the district in restoring White Conduit at the top of Islington hill, which by royal licence of Henry VI in 1431 had for nearly two centuries

13. The old porch of the Charterhouse, from a drawing by J P Neale, published in 1815.

supplied the Charterhouse with water.

The conduit head survived until 1831, in a white stone building. It stood in the fields on the very boundary of the parishes of Islington and Clerkenwell, with an arch of brick and flint. In 1641 a carved stone was placed on its front in memory of Sutton, with Sutton's arms below (chevron between three annulets, as many crescents of the field), his own initials TS, and FR, on the left, and on the right a monogram of the initials GC and MR. All these may have been benefactors though not, as Pinks suggests, "eminent masters of the Charterhouse".

Though later much robbed and decayed, the building was a famous local feature and gave its name to a pleasure garden until the spread of building overran the entire area.[9]

HICKS'S HALL

Another important innovation in Clerkenwell contemporary with the New River, the Charterhouse and Dame Alice's school, was the establishment of a regular court-house for magistrates. For years they had met in some neighbouring tavern on market days but in 1611 Sir Baptist Hicks established a meeting place at the southern end of St John Street, known as Hicks's Hall, where 14 Justices of the Peace held courts. It became too small for this purpose and the Middlesex Sessions House was built on Clerkenwell Green in 1779–82. The site of the Hall, demolished in 1782, was where St John Street widens just north of Smithfield, and until recent years was somewhat unworthily marked by a men's lavatory. It is today just roadway.

LOCAL HAPPENINGS

While Islington was very much a country retreat from its position as first village on the road north from London, it nevertheless played its part as a place of passage and stopping off, sometimes for royalty. James I,

14. Hicks's Hall, c.1750, in the middle of St John Street, at the Smithfield end.

on his arrival from Scotland in 1603 to take possession of his new kingdom, had been ceremonially met at Stamford Hill by the Lord Mayor and aldermen, and thence escorted "over the fields" to his appropriate reception at the Charterhouse.

Many years later, in 1641, Charles I made a ceremonial entry into London on his return from Scotland with his Queen and his two sons, Charles and James. They and their "splendid cavalcade", however, travelled over the fields from Newton (Stoke Newington) to Hoxton, by Sir George Whitmore's house, Balmes or Baumes, and so to Moorgate. [10]

This recurring reference to crossing 'fields' does not exactly mean forcing their way through hedgerows, but rather the use of field paths and bridleways in order to avoid the rough and ill-paved, or even unpaved, highways as was common practice.

By the early 16th century a 'Long Causeway', between St John Street and Islington church, had been created in aid of pedestrians – who were of course the great majority of travellers. Richard Cloudesley in his will in 1517 had included a bequest "to the repairing and mending of the Causeway" between the church and his house near or below the site of

the Angel.[11] This was presumably why he chose "the new Chapel of the Hermitage at Islington's town's end" for the masses ordered for his soul (to finance which he bequeathed property to the Priory of St John).[12]

A century later Thomas Sutton, when founding the Charterhouse school, according to Stow left 40 marks for mending the highways between Islington and Newington. The 'Long Causeway' was one of not very many attempts to improve the going in certain areas. The stretch from St John Street was still in the 18th century referred to as 'Islington Causeway', or in the vernacular, 'Causey', when on 25 September 1742 a refiner named Swift was stabbed and robbed by "three footpads".[13]

Records reveal some seamier happenings in the Islington area. There were the activities of a card-sharper living variously in Charterhouse, Whitecross Street and eventually merely at 'Islington', who several times got away with it before suffering unpleasant retribution.

He was John Starr or Starre, a ne'er-do-well shoemaker, sometimes described simply as 'yoman' and later as 'a rogue and vagrant'. First detected in 1618 in league with a cordwainer named Leonard Richardson, also of Charterhouse, he cheated a fellow-gambler "by false lay" and lightening his purse by £25, no mean sum. Starr was ordered to appear at the next Gaol Delivery, but seems to have decamped, and is next heard of some months later in Hounslow, at "a common inn", the Maidenhead, with a Hounslow local, defrauding a victim of 44 shillings in a game called 'Thy card and my card' – perhaps a version of Spot the Lady. These two got away.

A year later fate caught up with Starr, now identified as "maintaining himself lazily and craftily" by card playing "to the injury of the King's lieges". His plea of Not Guilty was not accepted by the jury, and he was condemned to the usual barbarous punishment of being "halfe stripped, tyed at a cartes taile with a superscription upon his head shewing his offence", and whipped from gaol to Westminster. Further, he was more appropriately expected to make good what he had won from the aggrieved parties, to put up surety for his future good behaviour, and to appear at the next Session.[14]

ILLUSTRIOUS RESIDENTS

The villages of Islington, Hackney and Hogsdon were places of retreat for the nobility, in houses built largely on the former monastic land. Often these houses were let to others. Lord Compton, although he inherited Canonbury manor from Sir John Spencer, spent only part of his later life here with his family – four of whom were born in Islington. From 1627 to 1635 the Canonbury manor house was let to Thomas Coventry, Lord Keeper, a law-man like his father Sir Thomas the judge. He had been successively Recorder of London, Solicitor-General and Attorney-General, was knighted in 1617, became MP for Droitwich in 1621 and Lord Keeper from 1625. During his tenancy of Canonbury he was created Baron Coventry, and soon afterwards was trying to act as mediator between King Charles and his Parliament.[15] In 1635 James Ferrers, 7th Earl of Derby, writes from Canonbury – where presumably he was a guest – complaining that he cannot get to the court at St James's because of the greatest snow he ever saw in his life.[16]

Highbury manor, with 300 acres of demesne, continued in the hands of the Wroth family after Queen Elizabeth renewed the lease to Sir Thomas in 1562. He had held the farm on lease from Thomas Cromwell since 1541, and on expiration of this further term of 21 years the lease was still further renewed in 1584 and 1594, for 60 years in reversion to Sir John Fortescue, of the Queen's Privy Council. Thence Sir John Spencer obtained the remainder of the lease, which thus also passed to his son-in-law Lord Compton.

Actual ownership, however, was still with the Crown, and in 1611 King James bestowed the manor on his heir, Henry, Prince of Wales, who ordered a survey, from which we know its then condition and the status of its occupants in detail. The report, entitled 'The Plot of the Mannor Newington Barrow, parcel of the possessions of the High and Mighty Prince Henry, Prince of Wales ... taken in July 1611', is signed by the unlikely name 'Rocke Church'.

The estate, totalling 987 acres, was made up of the yard or close known as Highbury Castle, formerly the castle or mansion destroyed during the Peasants' Revolt; the two woods, Highbury and Little St John's, of 43 and 17 acres;[17] and adjoining lands, and had increased in value sixfold since Henry VIII's time.

As major leaseholder, Lord Compton held the demesne of 426 acres, and Sir Nicholas Coote had the modest holding of two meadows amounting to some 32 acres. Eight freeholders of 113 acres included the then Lord Mayor Sir James Pemberton, a goldsmith. On the east side of Tollington Lane the Brewers' Company held two fields amounting to a further 32 acres. Finally the copyholders held 414 acres between them, also including Pemberton and the knights Sir Henry Slingsby and Sir William Ayclif. [18]

Prince Henry died soon after the survey was made, in 1612, and Highbury again reverted to the Crown until granted by the King to his next heir, Prince Charles. The latter granted the manor to Sir Allan Apsley in 1629, who in turn sold on to a Thomas Austen. This was the position – except for the woods, which had not been included in the grant to Apsley – until, during the Commonwealth, a Parliamentary survey was made.

The Fowler and Fisher families appear early in the context of Barnsbury manor, which in 1548 had been in the hands of Thomas Fowler, 'gent'. By virtue of Fowler memorials recorded in the old church we know more of his descendant, Sir Thomas who died in 1625. He had three wives, with issue only by the first, Jane Charlet, daughter and heir of a London tallow chandler. She died in 1601, and their two sons Thomas and Edmund were both knighted in their turn. Sir Thomas's second wife, Mary, was widow of a different Spencer family, that of Sir John Spencer of Althorp, and was mother to the first Earl Spencer. This first Sir Thomas was a Deputy Lieutenant for Middlesex, a "high commissioner for the verge" and commissioner of the peace. It was during his lifetime that the Fowlers moved from their Upper Street house to the better-known mansion in Cross Street.

Of the other noted local houses, Ward's Place in the Lower Street, which had earlier passed to the Dudley family, has also been credited to the Ducies on the grounds of the initials H.D. above the entrance: Sir Robert Ducie, who died in 1634, was succeeded by his youngest son Sir Hugh, who died about 1678. His son, Sir William, who died about 1691, certainly lived in Islington.[19]

PARISH AFFAIRS

From the latter part of the sixteenth century the High Street and Upper Street had been graced with several inns between the junction with Goswell Road and the Green. In the first half of the seventeenth century we find the Horse's or Nag's Head, the Castle, the Bull's Head (renamed the Griffin); and in Highbury Manor the Rose & Crown, the Saracen's Head, the Swan, Cock, Blue Boar, George, Black Horse and Maidenhead.

The famous Angel inn appears not to have been so named until 1638. The first house on this site was shown as an inn in the 16th century and by 1614 it was called Sheepcote and let by the Priory of St John. In 1638 it was enlarged and evidently given its more celebrated name. We do not know of its appearance, nor whether it sported a sign bearing an angel.

By 1601 a number of trades were noted in the southern part of Upper Street, the Hedge Row: collar-maker, vintner, grazier, shoe-maker, tailor, wheelwright and weaver. In 1630 the state was similar, when there were about eleven houses, further including the Nag's Head and Black Horse.

Moving on to the church, details are scanty for the successors to the Rev. Meredith Hanmer: Samuel Proctor, presented in 1590, who shortly moved to Shepperton; William Hunt, and Leonard Cooke. Hunt, appointed in 1639, evidently occupied the rectory in Upper Street.

As for the church officials, by 1612 the churchwardens had risen to three, a number which continued to fluctuate over the years. A parish clerk is mentioned in 1636.

Following Dame Alice Owen's benefactions, several charities and bequests to the poor were founded during the first half of the century: her own to Christ's Hospital of £60, provided

15. The inner courtyard of the Angel inn. An engraving published in 1819.

that the governor give one shilling a week to Islington's poor; another small bequest was made by Richard Martin in 1602; Thomas Hobson in 1614 surrendered the copyhold of the Cock, from whose rents the churchwardens were to pay twelve poor persons 2d each, every Sunday; Nathaniel Loane of St Sepulchre's in 1625 willed £5 4s from the property of Little Old Bailey to Islington's vicar and churchwardens, again for Sunday distribution to twelve poor "of good conversation", 12d in bread and 12d in money. Daniel Parke in 1649 bequeathed from 40 shillings'-worth of rents, mostly for bread on Sundays, but including ten shillings for a Christmas Day sermon.[20] And finally Mrs Amy Hill left £50 to be invested in land yielding 50 shillings a year, of which 30 shillings were to go to the poor on St Thomas's Day, and £1 to be divided between 13s 4d for a sermon, and 3s 4d each for the clerk and sexton.

One wonders how well the poor – probably consisting chiefly of the old and the sick or crippled – managed to scrape through the year on these staple, if not particularly nourishing, benefactions.

Burials of the poor were made largely in the Clerkenwell area, and before the time of the Great Plague burial places included Cripplegate Poor Ground in Whitecross Street, used from 1636 and known as St Giles's Upper churchyard. This was in Bear and Ragged Staff Yard (later renamed Warwick Place). Though several times closed owing to overcrowding, it always contrived to re-open. Behind St James's church in Curtain Road was the Holywell Mount burial ground, created on the site of the old Curtain Theatre. It was used during times of plague.

In Moorfields an acre was set aside "for burial Ease" for London parishes lacking ground, especially St Botolph's, Bishopsgate, which was also used to bury lunatics from Bethlem Hospital. It had been given in 1569 by Sir Thomas Roe, merchant tailor and later Mayor, whose wife was buried there. At her wish he had enclosed her grave-site with a wall. South of St Bartholomew's but still north of the City wall (approximately on the site of the present hospital's west wing), as shown on a plan of 1617, was a large piece of ground known as Christ Church Graveyard. Later

the hospital made use of Bethlem Hospital's ground for burials.

From the beginning of the century plague burials were a recurring necessity. There had been outbreaks in Queen Elizabeth's time, but the reigns of both James I and Charles I, in 1603 and 1625, were heralded by plague epidemics – and Charles II had been on the throne only five years when the Great Plague took hold.

LOCAL AMUSEMENTS

Islington was already in a mild way a place for amusements. It was not a centre for the theatre, although early Elizabethan experiments in theatre building were only a walk across the fields at the Curtain. Like the Fortune, the Red Bull in Clerkenwell carried on illegally under the Commonwealth, but reopened at the Restoration, and seems to have specialised in bombastic, militaristic shows for the masses, and to have gone down and down. Samuel Pepys, a great playgoer (sometimes more for amorous than dramatic entertainment), visited in 1661 but found it a wretched affair, "the clothes very poore and the actors but common fellows". They seemed unable even to draw an audience, for Pepys shared the pit with only about ten others, and reckoned barely a hundred in the whole house. Worst of all, when a boy made a hash of his song, "his master fell about his eares and beat him so that it put the whole house in an uprore".[21] Not surprisingly, within the next couple of years the theatre was pulled down.

There was plenty of other local entertainment, as recorded during the reigns of the first two Stuart kings. In 1628 the poet George Wither writes how

"Hogsdone [Hoxton], Islington, and Tothnam Court,
For cakes and creame had then no small resort"

In 1641 a work named *The Walks of Islington and Hogsdon*, by Thomas Jordan, refers to "a low dramatic piece" played at the Saracen's Head, with visitations of "ladies of fortune and young 'prentices". A tavern named the Hugh Myddelton Head opened in 1614, appropriately opposite the New River Head. Farther afield, in mid-century 'Drunken Barnaby's' *Four Journeys to the North of England* cites Mother

Red Cap's entertainments in the Holloway Road. And the famous White Conduit House, next to the springhead (*see Chapter 3*) was built in 1641.

Outdoor sport, so-called, was duck-hunting in the local ducking ponds, as Ben Jonson tells us in *Every Man in his Humour* ("come a ducking to Islington ponds"), and Sir William D'Avenant includes it in *The Long Vacation in London*:

> "Ho! – Ho! to Islington – enough –
> Fetch Job my son, and our dog Ruffe.
> For there, in pond, through mire and muck,
> We'll cry, hay, duck, there Ruffe – hay duck "

Indeed, one of the ponds pressed into service to become the reservoir at New River Head, "an open idell pool", had long existed as a ducking pond, while another, known as the Wheal Pond, was near White Conduit House.

1   Main sources of the New River include G C Berry, 'Sir Hugh Myddelton and the New River', in *Transactions of the Honourable Society of Cymmrodorion* for 1956 (pub. 1957), pp. 17–46, and *London's Water Supply 1903–1953*; Michael Essex-Lopresti, *Exploring the New River*, 3rd edn, London 1997; B Rudden, *The New River, a Legal History*, Oxford, 1985; R Sisley, *The London Water Supply*, 1899; and Nelson's and Pinks's histories of Islington and Clerkenwell. Robert Ward's admirable *London's New River* was published by Historical Publications late in 2003, when this book was already in proof.

2   Another man now much involved was Howell Joahnes (or Jones?), a ganger employed until his death in 1617 who, once the river was completed and the water-house built, supervised the labourers employed in the streets, and lived at the New River Head. Here he seems to have profited by selling drink and 'victualling', a sideline which after his death it seemed advisable to forbid.

3   The famous politician John Wilkes and his later kinsman Charles Booth Wilkes, assassin of Abraham Lincoln, were evidently descendants of the family.

4   John Stow, *Survey of London, Brought to the Present by John Strype*, 1720 (1893 edn), Vol. I, p. 280; Pinks, *Clerkenwell*, pp. 472ff.

5   At the time and long after, however, it was not uncommon to refer to esquires' or high officials' wives as 'Lady', or occasionally 'Madam', being regarded as obvious "ladies". In Vestry Minutes both Dame Alice's tomb and her bequest are regularly referred to as 'Lady Owen's'.

6   The statue was removed in 1976 to the new school at Potter's Bar.

7   Reginald A Dare, *A History of Owen's School*, Wallington, 1963, chs. III-V.

8   Walter Thornbury, *Old and New London*, London, 1883-5, Vol. II, Chs. XLVII, XLVIII; G E Mitton, *Clerkenwell and St Luke's*, London, 1906, pp. 38f.

9   Pinks, *Clerkenwell*, p. 541.

10 *Ibid*, p. 295.

11 Tomlins, *Yseldon*, p. 23*n*.

12 Pinks, *Clerkenwell*, p. 472.

13 Nelson, *Islington*, p. 15; *Daily Post*, 25 September 1742, quoted in Pinks, *Clerkenwell*, pp. 295, 747.

14 *Middlesex County Records*, Vol. III, pp. 140, 148, 155.

15 *DNB*, Thomas Coventry.

16 This Earl of Derby, a staunch Royalist, in 1649 indignantly refused Cromwell's offer of terms provided he delivered up the Isle of Man. He fought bravely at the Battle of Worcester for Charles II in 1651, but was taken prisoner and executed a few weeks later.

17 These and the figures below disregard the odd roods and perches.

18 Nelson, *Islington*, pp. 131ff. Henry Slingsby, Master of the Mint 1662-85, is mentioned occasionally by Samuel Pepys.

19 *VCH*, p. 14.

20 Like other charities, in Victorian times this was commuted, the rent charge being replaced in about 1881 by £75 invested in stock, with an annual yield of £2.1.4.

21 *The Diary of Samuel Pepys*, ed. Henry B Wheatley, London, 1904, Vol. I, p. 338, 23 March 1661.

CHAPTER 5

War, Plague and Fire

A STORMY PERIOD

There had for some time been rumblings of discontent with the King's arbitrary rule, and London itself was largely anti-monarchy. In the last years before actual warfare, cases were brought against those who spoke ill-advisedly on the King's side. An Islington labourer, John Scullard, in July 1642 in the presence of "the King's lieges", spoke "these wicked and devilish words, 'pox confound the Parliament'", and on the same day in Clerkenwell William Spencer, described as a 'Latin Clerk', complained that the Privy Councillor Henry, Earl Holland, was "raysed from a beggar by the Kinge and that now he did what he could to cutt the King's throate". He also alleged that the parliament had imprisoned Sir Richard Gurney, the Lord Mayor, "for nothing else but because he was an honest man and did the King's service".[1]

Actions against Catholics meanwhile were unremitting, and late in 1640, not long before war broke out, no less than 1430 persons were prosecuted for recusancy, many of them nobility and gentry. They included local people such as, in Clerkenwell, Penelope, Lady Gage and her family, Sir John and Lady Katherine Symons, the Dowager Countess of Portland, and William Ducy, an Islington gentleman, who was however acquitted. The charges were always the same, offenders having been noted by informers as not attending an officially established place of worship for, say, three or six months.

One witness seems to have had a change of heart. Edward Martindall, an Islington victualler, was charged with leaving the court after swearing to give evidence on a Bill of Indictment against "Popish recusants", and had to answer it.

After the execution of Charles I, those who still made their anti-Parliament protest suffered for it. In March 1650 three men, including an Islington butcher, William Norman, were summonsed "for drinking a health to the confusion of Parliament and all those that tooke part with them".[2]

Crime of a less political tinge continued. Islington does not figure greatly for domestic murder during these years, but in February 1653 Thomas Harret was arraigned for killing his wife, and in gruesome fashion was ordered to be "hanged on a gibbet at Islington before his doore 3 houres". Though we do not know where his house was, he was presumably strung up in the street outside it for those hours after his death.[3]

During the Civil War we hear little or nothing of Islington proper, though troops and companies of horse must have passed to and fro on campaigns. The nearest fortification seems to have been Mount Mill, in what is now Seward Street off St John Street, site of windmills north of the walls.

Islington was just outside the fortifications hastily erected north of the City. Interestingly, before the Upper Pond was created at the top of Islington hill, the site was to become an important Civil War fort, built by the Parliamentarians in 1642, which a later map shows was the only one outside the chain of such defensive forts built along the line of the City walls.

The star-shaped earthwork, "a large redoubt

with four half-bulwarks", was known as Fort Royal, not, of course, referring to the Royalists' side but a term for this type of fort then being raised all over England. It would have been surrounded by a palisade of sharpened stakes and fronted by iron pikes to obstruct attackers, while the defenders fired on them from the ramparts. The fort was apparently also intended as a defence against possible 'tumults' by the citizens.

Immediately after the Civil War these forts were destroyed and in the autumn of 1647 that on the site of the reservoir in Claremont Square was levelled – but not entirely. Signs of it appear on later maps, and William Maitland in his *History of London* (1756), describes a path or "covered way" – that is, lined by defensive earthworks – leading from the garden of the pleasure resort, Merlin's Cave, *(see Chapter 7)* as far as the "large Bulwark" at the west side of the Upper Pond. Such remains would also account for the roughness of the open ground seen in some of Hollar's views of the New River Head made in 1665.

When the King laid siege to London during 1642 and 1643, a defensive chain was stretched across St John Street not far from Owen's School, and a breastwork was set up at the Angel. Shops in the area closed, and women and children joined in digging and carrying earth for the fortifications, at the south end of St John Street and near the Upper Pond. Farther north, a small redoubt or individual strong-point was set up near the Pound 'by the Green', while there was also a small fort near Bagnigge Wells.[4]

The Honourable Artillery Company, just south of Bunhill Row, was of course much concerned, providing the parliamentary side with drilled pikemen. Their recruiting ceased, however, from 1644 to 1656, and after restoration of the monarchy the Captaincy-General of the Company was assumed and retained by the Royal Family.

THE PLAGUE

The early years of Charles II's reign will for ever be chiefly remembered for the Great Plague, which eventually spread to much of England, and for London's Great Fire; yet equally importantly, throughout both of these

disasters England was at war with the Dutch.

Plague was certainly no newcomer to London. Deaths are recorded, for example, in 1577, 1578, 1592, and in 1593 were reckoned at over 15,000. The outset of the reigns of both James I and Charles I, in 1603 and 1625, were marked ominously by plague and John Evelyn in his journal refers to lesser outbreaks in 1636, 1642 and 1658. But it was the year 1665 which was to brand itself on the memory.

Islington was little affected – except as a place of refuge from those fleeing the infection. The village already had an unexpectedly high death and burial rate for a place with such a healthy situation, probably because people in bad health moved there in the hope that it would prolong their lives. Also, children might be put out to nurse in Islington who then died there, and people who died in the City were sometimes brought there for burial.

Islington and Clerkenwell tried to guard against infection. One local was charged with striking a constable who questioned his bringing in goods without a certificate of clearance from an infected house in St Giles's, Cripplegate, and another with actually bringing a plague victim from St Martin's Lane into Clerkenwell.[5]

In the City the plague spread extensively from May to November 1665 when it at last began to decrease during colder weather; but by winter it had taken hold in outlying areas such as Chelsea, so that although by the time of the Great Fire it was extinguished in the City, in Deptford, for example it was still rife.

Pepys first notes it on 30 April 1665: "Great fears of the Sickness here in the city, it being said that two or three houses are already shut up." He adds piously, as was being uttered by most citizens, "God preserve us all." Thereafter he notes the steady and alarming rise in plague deaths, its spread in different quarters, and the distressing sights he experienced. His house then was in Seething Lane, a stone's-throw from the Tower. He packed his wife and her maid-servant off to Woolwich for safety, and his own office, the Navy Office, removed out of harm's way to Greenwich, where Pepys frequently stayed overnight.[6]

Of Islington's fortunes during the terrible days of 1665 we have no direct reference. The

Vestry minutes, which start in May 1663, and were for a long time kept only sporadically, were completely abandoned during the outbreak and until after the Fire, and silence reigns on the village's experiences. Our most vivid account is of a famous incident described by Daniel Defoe, whose journalist's compilation appeared only in 1722 as a fictional documentary, though evidently based on sound research. This episode in his *Journal of the Plague Year*, which has the ring of truth, illustrates how the village, separated from the City by open fields, was an obvious refuge, and like other such villages was naturally jealous and fearful for its own safety.

It happened in mid-July, when Islington in the preceding week had had only two plague cases. A London citizen who, like many others, had been incarcerated at home to prevent infection of those outside, attempted to escape. Having broken out of his house in or near Aldersgate Street, he forged northwards towards Islington, where he tried in turn to stay at the Angel Inn and the White Horse, but at both was refused entry. At last he was admitted to the Pied Bull, possibly the one at the corner of the Back Road (Liverpool Road), rather than the house in Upper Street formerly occupied by Sir Walter Raleigh. The only bed free was in the garret, and that for only one night, "some drovers being expected the next day with cattle". He gladly accepted, though his dress suggested he was too fine for so humble a lodging, as he admitted when the servant showed him to it with a candle: "I have seldom lain in such a lodging as this", but agreed to make shift for one night on account of the "dreadful time". Sitting on the bed – possibly the sole furniture in the room – he asked the girl to bring him a pint of warm ale; but for one reason or another, presumably other duties, she forgot.

In the morning he did not appear, and another servant was sent up to call him. He was found "stark dead and almost cold, stretched out across the bed. His clothes were pulled off, his jaw fallen, his eyes open in a most frightful posture, the rug of the bed being grasped hard in one of his hands, so that it was plain he died soon after the maid left him."

This of course raised a tremendous alarm, lest having been free of plague so far, this visitation would start a local epidemic. Indeed (says Defoe), the maid herself who had shown him to the room was first smitten, and others followed. So that during that week (11–18 July) there were 17 deaths, 14 of them of the Plague.[7]

By this time the sickness was so rampant in the City that food supplies were beginning to fail, as country people trying to come in with provisions were stopped well outside the gates. One such place where they were obliged to sell their goods was Bunhill Fields, and beyond that "a great field called Wood's Close, near Islington". Others were Spitalfields, beyond Whitechapel, and St George's Fields. In this way the Lord Mayors, aldermen, magistrates and their households contrived to keep within doors and sent their servants to buy, a method which seemed to prevent further infection.[8]

In the two months from early August to early October London's recorded deaths were 59,870, of which 49,705 were of the plague, the worst weeks being from late August to mid-September.

Islington also appears in Defoe's long and circumstantial story of three men, two of them brothers, who after much argument resolved to flee the City and risk ejection by such villages or towns as they came to. They carried with them a tent made by one of them, a sail-maker, for the purpose. By a tortuous route, they made their way out of London, arriving at Homerton by Hackney, securing certificates of health from the village constables.

"Thus they passed through the long divided town of Hackney (for it lay then in several separated hamlets)", as far as the great north road on the top of Stamford Hill. Near here, on a windy night, for shelter they set up the tent against a barn, a joiner friend acting as scout. He was alarmed by the arrival of a party of 13 people, including women, also on the run and seeking shelter in the barn, "good, sober sort of people". Having mutually established that all were free of plague, Ford, leader of the newcomers, told them that they came mostly from Cripplegate parish, though two or three were from the "hither side" of Clerkenwell, and that they had been some time away from London, keeping together "at the hither end of Islington", where they were allowed to sleep in "an old uninhabited house" with bedding they had brought with them. "But the plague is come up into Islington too", went on Ford (it was early August), "and a house next door to our poor dwelling was infected and shut up, and we are come away in a fright."

The party had then planned to go northwards to Highgate, but were stopped at Holloway, "so they crossed over the fields and hills to the westward, and came out at the Boarded River, and so avoiding the towns, they left Hornsey on the left hand and Newington on the right hand, and came into the great road about Stamford on that side", as the three friends had done from the other direction.

What seems so alien about such an adventure to present-day readers is how very remote these districts seem to be, as if far from a large capital city, so that our travellers were finding it slow progress over by-ways and across fields, through areas today totally urban. The first three travellers, who had a horse, had kept more to the roads, such as they were.

The two parties threw in their lot together, had an adventurous trek as far as Walthamstow, where they were banned by the constables and watchmen, but after much parley were given food, and so continued to Epping and further adventures.

During the last week in July deaths totalled 1,889, of which St Giles Cripplegate had the worst, 554, double St Sepulchre's, the next worst, while Clerkenwell and Shoreditch had respectively 103 and 110. In September the City, its eastern suburbs and Southwark suffered badly, but in Clerkenwell deaths in the week beginning 12 September dropped to 77 and the next week to 76 – Southwark lost 1,636 and 1,390 in the same weeks.

The plague inevitably affected those charged with delivering bodies to plague pits. One died driving a cart with its grisly cargo on the way to Shoreditch, and the horses dragged on unguided until the cart overturned and the bodies were thrown out. Untended horses of another cart, whose driver was either dead or fled, ran too near "the great pit in Finsbury Fields", so that the cart fell in, dragging down the horses – and perhaps the driver too, whose whip was found later among the bodies.

Mount Mill by Seward Street, with its Civil War earthwork fortifications, was among the sites where burials were made "promiscuously" above street level. Later, Defoe records, the site became a "physic garden" and was eventually built over; thousands more were buried in other areas surrounding the City.

During the Great Plague a new burial ground was formed by the Corporation in Bunhill Fields. It had been the dumping-ground for bodies since before 1579 when it had received the skeletons removed from St Paul's charnel-house – hence its name Bone Hill, soon corrupted to Bunhill. In 1665, however, it appears to have been used not for plague victims but for ordinary burials and, as it also seems never to have been consecrated, it was especially used for interments of Non-Conformists as they were not obliged to use the Book of Common Prayer rites. (Among distinguished burials in the 17th and 18th centuries were Cromwell's son-in-law, General Charles Fleetwood, members of the Wesley family, Daniel Defoe, Isaac Watts and in the 19th century William Blake. Bunhill Fields continued in use until prohibited under the Burials Act of 1852.)

The onset of winter cold helped to finish off the epidemic, and by February 1666 Londoners "reckoned the distemper quite ceased". The court returned to Whitehall after Christmas, though many of the nobility and gentry kept away still. In London the more prudent inhabitants disinfected their houses with what remedies were thought efficient, even blowing up gunpowder or burning continuous fires.

FIRE

Only a few months of blessed normality – or rather, the gradual settling down to normality – were followed by the City's next major disaster, the Great Fire, which raged for four days and nights and whose smoke-cloud and flames could be seen from miles away.

This was to affect Islington more permanently. For whereas during the plague, while people died in great numbers or fled, their dwellings survived, the fire destroyed thousands of houses and businesses, and many craftsmen had to settle elsewhere, as conveniently near as possible. In many cases this was Islington.

The fire ceased at Pye Corner, just on the south side of Smithfield where the market's open space prevented its spreading to Clerkenwell. Islington was a short-term refuge. Pepys viewed Londoners camping out on Moorfields on 5 September, "poore wretches carrying their goods there", and having to keep watch over them in what was luckily a spell of fine weather.[9] John Evelyn's is a more comprehensive survey of the event. His peregrinations took him towards Islington and Highgate, "where one might have seene two hundred thousand people of all ranks & degrees, dispersed & laying along by their heapes of what they could save from the Incendium, deploring their losse, & though ready to perish for hunger & destitution, yet not asking one penny for reliefe, which to me appeard a stranger sight, than any I had yet beheld".[10]

In Islington the sole local reference to the Fire recorded by the Vestry occurs in their list of disbursements on 10 October:

"Collected then in o^e of P[ar]ish Church of St Mary Islington ye sume of £17.19.1 for ye releif of poore distressed Citizens of London: whose poverty came by fire."[11]

1   *MCR*, Vol. III, pp. 82, 179. Sir Richard Gurney, Royalist Lord Mayor (1642–3) was from 1642-7 imprisoned in the Tower for authorising the reading of the King's proclamation against Parliament's Militia Ordinance (*DNB*).

2   *Ibid.*, Vol. III, p. 194.

3   *Ibid.*, Vol. III, p. 288.

4   Robert Ward, *London's New River*, London, Historical Publications, Ch. 9, esp. pp. 105-7; Dare, *Owen's School*, pp. 33-4.

5   *MCR*, Vol. III, pp. 375-6, 381-2.

6   Pepys, *Diary*, Vol. IV. pp 379ff, 30 April 1665, *et seq.*

7   Daniel Defoe, *A Journal of the Plague Year*, Folio Society, 1960, pp. 77-9.

8   Defoe, *Plague Year*, pp. 86-7.

9   Pepys, *Diary*, Vol. V. p. 401, 5 September 1666.

10   *The Diary of John Evelyn*, ed. E S de Beer, UOP, 1959, p. 499.

11   Islington Vestry Minutes (VM), Vol. I, end note. This large payment was considerably more than the usual collections, though on 5 November £8.18.8 collected for the poor may also be an outcome of the Fire.

CHAPTER 6

The Later 17th Century

DIGGING FOR BRICKS

In the weeks and months after the fearful time when the sky was reddened for miles around the Great Fire, Clerkenwell was settled by City craftsmen – printers, gold and silver-smiths, jewellers and watchmakers – and artisans. Livelihoods were now at stake. The overflow of course went on as far as Islington, and for the next century London moved out-wards along the road to the north, up Goswell Road towards the New River Head, up St John Street to the Angel and the Great North Road, and farther east, up the old Roman road to Kingsland and Hoxton. Behind these main roads the network of open fields was hardly changed.

The City was rebuilt extensively in brick, and Moorfields and Islington both provided good brickmaking clay. Timber required for roofs, windows and doors was readily imported from the Baltic ports. But in this part of the coun-try there was a shortage of stone.[1]

In 1668 licence was granted to dig brick and tile earth on four acres behind the Swan Inn in the High Street, and on part of an adjoining common field, all belonging to Francis Tredway, who had dug since 1633 in the Preb-end manor area, but had fallen foul of the City archers who used to practise there. Other brickmakers rented land on the Shoreditch parish boundary, paying 6d per 1000 bricks made – 1,700,000 bricks were said to have been produced in the first summer (1673) – and on a 20-acre site by agreement for 10 years from 1691. During the 1680s clay and gravel were also dug on the far west of the parish in Vale Royal (by York Way), and

around Charterhouse Closes, Commandery Mantells and elsewhere.[2]

NEW HOUSES

While the appearance of the City had radically changed, its population had too. With the re-establishment of the Court at Westminster the upper and wealthier classes moved there too, though their fine country houses in and around Islington continued as a good base for some to keep in touch with state events. Yet the rich moved away from the larger houses and a middle class began to settle in what were becoming fashionable rows newly run up by builders. This fashion began in 1684 when Nicholas Barbon, son of the Anabaptist politician Praisegod Barebones, built Essex Street, off the Strand.

But well outside London an earlier example had mysteriously appeared in 1658. This quartet of houses, nos 55–58 Newington Green, of handsome proportions and finish, were in classical mode with round-headed windows and pilasters, yet still retaining Jacobean-style gables. They were securely dated by a plaque on the front, to the last years of the Cromwellian period. Standing as they do alongside a village green a couple of miles from Islington, their origin is a mystery, neither builder nor occupants being known, and their sophisticated appearance in this rural setting, long before other such buildings appeared elsewhere in the London area is like a great question mark.

Of Islington's great houses, the Draper family's house between the churchyard and Lower

Street was sold by Sir Thomas Draper in 1662 to James Cardrow, who from 1666 let it to a tenant who in turn sublet both ends. In 1668 its coach-house and stable, yard and orchard too were separately let and walled off, and the coach-house was actually converted into a double-fronted house. The main building was described as having a great hall, with the usual wainscoted walls and shuttered windows, "some decorated in an earlier manner", and the garden was adorned with fishponds, "a pedestalled sun and moon dial, and ornamental flowerpots".[3]

Stretching from the corner of the Back Road (Liverpool Road) northwards along the Great North Road (Upper Street) was Hedge Row, a town row with ground-floor shops, recorded in 1668. The village now boasted more inns: the Bluebell, the Queen's Arms and Black Boar (mentioned in 1668 and 1674), the Three Cups (1678), the White Horse in Canonbury manor (1691), and another White Horse in Lower Holloway (1700).

The manorial woodland was beginning to be grubbed up. In 1650 Parliament had ordered a new survey of Highbury Manor whose wood then estimated at 43° acres, contained 371 trees, and Little St John's Wood at 35 acres – neither of great size. Part of Highbury Wood had already been felled. (Depredations continued, and by 1710 only 23 acres of coppice survived but no mature trees.)[4]

PARISH AFFAIRS

We now learn something of Islington vicars.

The Rev. William Cave was appointed to St Mary's in August 1662 at the age of only 25, having been educated at St John's College, Cambridge; before coming to Islington he had served at Haseley in Oxfordshire, and at All Hallows in London. He subsequently achieved a DD (1672), preached before the King and the Lord Mayor, became the King's chaplain, and in 1684 Canon of Windsor. He also published several religious works over the years, one of which led to a controversy with the Dutch scholar Jean Leclerc. Evelyn records hearing him preach at Whitehall "to the household" on 25 January 1680, "a learned and pious man"; at his own church "very excellently" on 28 January 1683, and in London on 18 January

1685 when Cave preached before the King. Evelyn also mentions Cave's "several usefull bookes", especially *Primitive Christianity*. His eloquence was felt to be somewhat over the heads of his small Islington congregation.[5]

Cave served at St Mary's for 28 years, until 1691, and in 1713 died and was buried there, leaving four sons and a daughter. A monument was raised to him in the church.[6]

Parish income was derived from both landowners and householders who were rated on land or goods respectively. For example, from 1678 each twenty acres of land was rated at £40 annual rent. Householders were rated £40 for each £1,000-worth of goods or its equivalent.[7]

In the year that Cave was appointed, the Bishop complained to vicar and churchwardens that men of "adverse dispositions" (presumably offensive on political or religious grounds) attended the vestries, and ordered that they be replaced by 24 parishioners of good standing, conforming to ecclesiastical laws.[8] Hence, from the following year official vestry minutes were kept and meetings were supposedly held fortnightly, an orderly state of affairs which instantly lapsed.

Islington's first vestry minutes date from 18 March 1663 when only seven people attended the meeting: the churchwardens, John Davis and William Tiffany, together with Thomas Morris, Ralph Suckley, Phillip Meade, Henry Martin, William Bunion, John Payne and Henry Kettle (himself later a churchwarden). The parish clerk was William Warton. Very occasionally one or two gentry appear – Sir Thomas Fisher, Thomas ?Cower and John Smith Esquires. Certain local notables, including Sir Richard Fisher, seem to have attended meetings only if there were some matter with which they were closely concerned. Other, more assiduous gentry, such as Richard Browne and Jacob Harvey, Esqs, attended meetings for many years.

Class distinctions were affirmed by the normal practice; for gentry by the suffix 'Esq', but the title 'Mr' was always given to distinguish middle-class burghers, merchants and legal men, and was omitted for the labouring classes. Wives were similarly distinguished. The title 'Lady' occasionally occurs, not always with strict accuracy.

The parish officers were appointed annually in April; the two (later three) churchwardens, three sidesmen, four overseers of the poor, and four 'surveyors of the wayes'. The church plate consisting of two flagons, two silver cups with covers, and two plates, was annually entrusted to the churchwardens.[9]

Until well into the next century, the business transacted at vestry meetings was of limited interest to posterity. It included disposal of alms received in collections, or sometimes as donation – such as from the Company of Clothworkers on 16 May 1663. At the first recorded meeting it was ordered that two years' assessment according to the Poor Books be "made and raised for the amending and repairing of the church Vestrey house and Bells and building one or more Gallery or Galleries". This important agreement was undoubtedly the reason for the meeting. On 15 May Kettle, then appointed Head Churchwarden, and the other churchwardens were to examine the bills for the work, "marke the pews in the gallery", and appoint seats there for any who wanted.

Otherwise vestry business continued to deal with the Poor Rate and the appointment of pauper apprentices. Apart from fairly frequent meetings over building the church gallery officials were lax enough, and as already noted, gave up meetings altogether during the Plague in London, until 27 April 1666; though it does appear that Robert Merry, when churchwarden, had made payments and incurred expenses "by reason of the late visitation or great plague" (16 June 1666).

The chief items of interest at this time were that cattle, impounded on the common (off the north end of the Lower Street), were to be "replenished at the costs and charges of this Parrish", and that the order for the "plucking downe" of Mary Rowlett's house, north of Canonbury House, had not been carried out. The Churchwardens were then ordered to demolish it before 20 May, together with "one of the Cottages in the church yarde where Elizabeth ffaucet did lately dye". At the same time the surveyors for the highways were to make a gravel pit on the common and garner what they could find.

Demolition of the cottages was to comply with a statute disallowing the building of cottages with less than four acres of land, a measure to deter the spread of house building in the London area. (Ten years later, the beadle was ordered to report monthly to the vestry on new or divided houses, and on any new inhabitants.)

And in June 1668 in pursuance of a warrant from the JPs, an assessment was proposed on seven months of the Poor's Book in order to raise the large sum of £67 5s for the new workhouse in St James's Clerkenwell, which the Overseers of the Poor were to collect. A warrant was to be issued against any who had not brought in their accounts for the previous year. In view of the vestry's lackadaisical habits, one may wonder whether this was ever executed.

Meanwhile, the Bishop's Court had again intervened, and on 2 August its order was recorded that the parish be fined for not displaying "ye figures of moses & Aaron & ye tenn Commandments" in the church, which were to be put up forthwith, while the post, gate and stiles were to be repaired or renewed. The next March it was complained that affairs were so "out of order", "for lack of frequent Vestreys", that in future they were to meet on the first Thursday of every month.

This they accordingly did – for a few months.

In June 1667 one vestryman, Thomas Norris, had reported on a repair of highways "from Newgate Lane to Ring Crosse" and, provided he produced a copy, it was agreed to reimburse him. At the same meeting the Rev. William Cave, whose physical stamina evidently did not match his intellectual capacity, but who fairly regularly attended the vestry meetings, "justly" complained at having to read the services and preach twice in a day, "by reason of his weaknesse". A subscription was agreed to employ a reader. From 1667 one was accordingly employed, and from 1673 a 'lecturer' was appointed from year to year to preach on Sunday afternoons.

By the 1670s the lecturer's stipend was £30, payable from the Stonefield estate. In 1679 a reader, payable by subscription, was again being sought. Thereafter the vestry selected the lecturer from a choice of candidates, and the stipend was raised from an annual collection. From 1691–6 this lecturer was Thomas Brett, a non-juring divine.

The church received further adornments in 1671 when a new altarpiece was installed, the roof was panelled inside and painted above the chancel, and in 1683 the treble bell of the peal of six was recast.

Some of the minor officers were paid a small salary from at least 1663, when a sexton is named (in 1671 this was a woman), in 1671 a beadle – whose duties included keeping order during church services – and eventually, in 1706, a watchman to assist him. Church-wardens proved a slight problem, the choice of those liable to serve being so small, and the fine for non-performance of the office was raised from three or four pounds to at least ten. Plenty of residents put in a claim for non-service and were declared exempt and, as a precaution, a list was made out in 1676 to avoid anyone's not serving at all, or on the other hand serving twice.

The poor continued to receive bequests from wills. Besides Mrs Amy Hill's donation for a sermon, in 1678 Ephraim Skinner bequeathed five shillings for the minister every Sunday to catechise the poor.[10]

There is little record at this time of Catholic inhabitants, in 1680 two being "suspected". But after the Restoration non-conforming Protestants tended to settle in Islington and neighbouring villages, and thus it was that the many schools were started for which Islington later became well known. Newington Green particularly became a centre for Presbyterians and others, and here in 1672 Samuel Lee, a Dissenting minister ejected from St Botolph's, Bishopsgate, was licensed to teach at his house. Daniel Bull and Mrs Stock also had houses licensed for Presbyterian meetings. Similarly, the Rev. George Fowler, ejected from Bridewell, obtained a licence to teach at his Islington house, and William Barker and George Thwing had licensed meeting places, as did David King at Kingsland Green. After this flourishing period, Presby-terianism declined in the area for at least a century.[11]

NEW SCHOOLS

Perhaps partly because of the reputation of the Owen school, Islington became a favourite centre for small 'academies', conformist as well as non-conformist. Education for the poor was also catered for, with parish children being ordered to school from 1679, twopence a week per head to be allowed for a master and mistress. Twenty years later Dame Sarah Temple left £500 for a rent charge to be paid to the minister and churchwardens for main-taining and educating poor children. (This took three years and a Chancery case to bring to fruition, the money being obtained from her executor, Sir Thomas Draper, in 1702, when 22 acres of land were bought at Potter's Bar.)

Efforts for children's education were of course individual, and far from universal. From 1659/60 a divine in his late thirties, Israel Tonge, held a grammar school class in the gallery of Sir Thomas Fisher's house, and was even said to teach Latin and Greek to girls.[12] In 1669 an ejected clergyman from Dorset maintained boarders at his house in Islington whom he probably educated as well. Newington Green too became especially known for non-conformist academies. Theophilus Gale started one there in 1665, continued after his death in 1678 by his pupil Thomas Rowe. Rowe was in Islington when the famous Isaac Watts was a pupil and re-mained until about 1705. He was among the first to abandon traditional textbooks in favour of 'free philosophy', and was an early exponent of the philosopher John Locke. His pupils included Dr John Evans, Daniel Neal, Henry Grove, John Hughes, poet and drama-tist, Dr Jeremiah Hunt, and Josiah Hort, who became Archbishop of Tuam in Ireland.

Another who moved his academy to Newington Green in the early 1670s was Ralph Button, some of whose pupils themselves became Dissenting ministers; and Sir Joseph Jekyll (1663–1738) who became Master of the Rolls. On Button's death in 1680 most of his students were taken over by Charles Morton, who had formed a Newington Green academy possibly as early as the late 1660s, as London's chief Independent school. By 1682 he had at least 60 boarders in two houses, and added new subjects to the traditional narrow cur-riculum, such as modern languages besides the classics, and "politics as a science". Further, he taught in English rather than in Latin. He too numbered pupils who were to become famous, notably Daniel Defoe and Samuel

Wesley; but in 1685 the vicar of Islington, the Rev. William Cave, reported the school to the authorities and Morton felt it wise to leave England for America. Fellow-teachers managed to carry on the school until 1696.

Like Ralph Button, Thomas Doolittle moved his academy to Islington in 1672, but was in turn forced to leave. In 1680 his students numbered 28, including the boy Edmund Calamy, later to be a historian of non-conformism. The school closed temporarily in 1685 and Doolittle moved.

A school for girl boarders, which may have been non-conformist, from 1689–97 was run by a clothworker, Robert Woodcock, in the Draper family's former house behind Islington church. Another girls' boarding school was kept by Hannah, the wife of John Playford, a musician and publisher, in Upper Street opposite the church, until her death in 1679.

Schoolchildren were expected to attend church; for example in 1664 a Mrs Smith had a pew allotted for herself and scholars – a few among many, for only four years later it was decreed that no more seats were to be so allotted as they were overcrowded. Hence provision had to be made to build galleries if needed, and in 1673 Captain Stacy applied for a gallery for his school.

It will be seen that these schools were very personal foundations, and usually ceased once their founders died or were removed, leaving a child's future education in doubt. This was the norm for many years to come.

CHARITIES

Among major bequests to charity, Mrs Amy Hill's of 13s 4d for a sermon was invested in some ¾-acre of land near the Back Road on which a century later, in 1777, a new workhouse was built. The payment then ceased.

Ephraim Skinner's generous bequest of £700 to Christ's Hospital in 1678 stipulated that the governors were to pay five shillings for 'catechising' the poor and to distribute £5 a year: but the gift would become void should the catechising lapse even for two consecutive Sundays. (It appears to have survived.) In 1685 Dr William Crowne, a London physician, left Islington's poor £50, the interest to be used

to buy bread every Sunday. The will was amplified by his widow, Dame Mary Sadlier, in 1707 by a further gift of £50 for 12d-worth of bread on Sundays. Though the vestry recorded receiving the gift, neither bequest is referred to afterwards. Then in 1694 Robert Hull, an Islington bricklayer, left £3 for the poor to be paid after the death of his wife Jane, and a further £3 which, at her choice, was to go either to Islington or to the Bricklayers' Company.[13]

The problem of the poor was indeed perennial. In Tudor times it was eventually accepted that many were so not by choice but by misfortune or sickness, and various Acts, often ineffectual, were passed to deal with them. Finally a famine in the 1590s, combined with the discharge of often wounded soldiers, flooded the country with beggars, and Acts passed in 1597 and 1601 had set up a more efficient arrangement.

The system was still partly based on the traditional supervision by Justices of the Peace, but from now on parishes annually appointed Overseers of the Poor who levied a Poor Rate, apprenticed pauper children to a trade, and had to supply raw materials to provide work for the able-bodied. Only those considered recalcitrant were penalised, and the workhouse was the last resort. This tough but not wholly unsatisfactory approach survived for more than two centuries, by which time it needed, and got, another thorough overhaul.

Hence charitable bequests by private persons, either from pure philanthropy or believed to be for the good of their own souls (or reputations), were of great significance, supplemented by the weekly church collections set aside for benefit of the poor.

THE BEGINNING OF SADLER'S WELLS

At the end of Charles II's reign springs were discovered which put Islington and north Clerkenwell firmly on the social map for more than a century and a half.

As early as 1575, when Lord Leicester entertained Queen Elizabeth at Kenilworth, a minstrel from Islington was said to have praised "the worshipful village of Islington" as renowned for its "furmenty for porage ...

mylke for theyr flawnes … creame for theyr custards … and of butter for theyr pasties and pye paste", all of high quality and (it was repeatedly pointed out), not thinned down, or mixed with flour or chalk or otherwise tampered with.[14]

Moreover, Islington was on a hill. London was low-lying, smoky and generally befouled, Islington was airy and healthy – and it provided views. Already in 1660 Prospect House[15] on the brow of what was later to become Pentonville Hill, was known for a vista across the fields over the City and its clustering of spires – even in its wretched state after the Fire.

Local specialities were sold at Islington fair, presumably held in the wide Upper Street, and are mentioned among favourite spots in *Poor Robin's Almanac* of 1676:

At Islington
A fair they hold
Where cakes and ale
Are to be sold.
At Highgate and
At Holloway,
The like is kept
Here every day;
At Totnam Court
And Kentish Town,
and all those places
Up and down.

A few years later other delights are recorded. Dairy-farming meant milkmaids, milkmaids were traditionally comely and accommodating, and in 1681 local inns and fields are praised in *The Merry Milkmaid of Islington, or the Rambling Gallants defeated*. Indeed from mediaeval times the walk towards the hill-top through Clerkenwell became lined with places for music and dancing, by degrees adding alcohol in the form of ale, wine and punch, even staging bucolic playlets. A pipe and a mug of ale, especially on Sundays after church or dinner, allowed Londoners to "regale upon a gaudy day with buns and beer at Islington or Mile End", and daily except on Sundays, simpler houses offered breakfasts for fourpence of "fine tea, sugar, bread, butter and milk" – or even coffee for 1½ d.

The spur to the great expansion of 'Merry Islington' lasting until early Victorian times,

was the discovery in 1683 of an abandoned medieval well under Mr Sadler's property.

Thomas Sadler[16], Surveyor of the Highways, who had acquired the land after the Restoration, set up a simple wooden music-house alongside the New River Head. When he ordered a couple of men to dig in his garden for gravel to be used on the roads, a pickaxe struck a hard surface. It was not, as hoped, a chest of buried treasure, but a "Broad Flat Stone", supported by oak posts and surmounting a large, stone-lined well, "arched over and curiously carved". The digger was said to have tried to keep his find from Sadler, who however got to learn of it and had the water analysed.

It proved to be a ferruginous spring, which until the Dissolution had served St John's Priory, its waters dispensed as medicinal by the monks. In the years that followed closure of the Priory it was said to have been covered over and forgotten. Another version holds that it continued in use for public benefit until the Commonwealth, when visiting invalids were warned off as "superstitious".

The discovery of 'Sadler's Wells' – a second was found close by – led to the establishment of a noted place of amusement, and apart from a couple of short closures remains so to this day. Of the many other such places, large and small, that from then on flourished for more than a century, this is the only one to survive.

In 1686 John Evelyn records going "to see Midletons – receptacle of Waters at the New River: & the new Spa wells neere it" (11 June). By the following year it was so well known that "even Islington" was remarked as comparable with Bath and Tunbridge Wells, to which the world now flocked.

A satirical poem in 1691 mocked the place as "The Threepenny Academy"; filled from early morning with beaux, officers bound for the war in Flanders, socially ambitious City tradesmen, whores and country folk, drinking the freely dispensed waters, gambling and listening to (it was claimed) atrociously played opera tunes. Before long there was an obstruction in the flow of the springs, and Sadler had to rely on his concerts.

But this marked a temporary eclipse, while the provincial spas were flourishing. The flow resumed in 1697, by when Sadler had bowed out, or perhaps died, and by 1699 the place was renamed Miles's Music House after a new proprietor. Less palatable entertainments than either music or the water were now in vogue, notably the eating of a live cock, feathers, blood and guts, the lot, by the 'Hibernian Cannibal', washed down with brandy and apparently rewarded with five guineas. So the century ended for Sadler's Wells.[17]

ISLINGTON SPA

At approximately the same time as Sadler's discovery in 1683 came exploitation of another spring just opposite, which for some time was to have a more fashionable history. This later grandly called itself Islington Spa, but earlier, and even more ambitiously, 'New Tunbridge Wells'.

This was in fact a third well discovered by Sadler, which he had earlier sold to a merchant named John Langley and which, under its grandiose new title, soon rivalled his.

The journalist Ned Ward describes both haunts in their early state in his scurrilous verse account, *A Walk to Islington* (1699). Having sampled Sadler's, upstairs among cheesecake eaters, lovers and ale-drinkers to the sound of an organ and fiddlers, and examined a display of paintings of the gods at their amours, he witnessed a display of (he complained) singularly unattractive performers in company with a crowd of unsavoury, rowdy, ill-behaved characters.

New Tunbridge Wells was known by at least 1684, when it was advertised as "the sweet gardens and arbours of pleasure" opposite the New River Head, but in the last decade of the century it was renowned for the chalybeate quality of its waters and their supposed medicinal properties, and its social pleasures were perhaps more modest and less flamboyant than its rival opposite.

These pleasure haunts were of necessity summer resorts, and New Tunbridge Wells opened only from April to August, from 7 in the morning and on two or three days a week. The early visitors were probably the more dedicated to their health, promoted at 3d a glass. Later in the morning more fashionable addicts arrived, along with the usual motley

throng of seamstresses, clerks, shop-men, and the seamier figures of gamesters and cheats. There was, however, a doctor in attendance to give advice if required.

New Tunbridge Wells seems never to have had the elaborate if gimcrack buildings which other resorts offered, but it was famed for lime-walks and arbours, while it boasted a coffee-house and a dance-room, with out-houses which served as gambling rooms. Its greatest days of fame were to come more than a generation later, but even then it was rather a sylvan glade with arbours than a permanent building with the usual Long Room.

Already, other resorts and attractions were near at hand. The Hugh Myddelton Tavern had opened soon after the New River was completed, in 1614. The London Spa was more or less contemporary. On top of Islington Hill was Prospect House looking south over New River Head from what is now Pentonville Road (which was not laid out until 1756). In 1633 it was recorded as "the bowling place in Islington fields[18], and the bowling-green continued for decades. In 1669 it was rated as 'the Prospect' kept by Mr Ireland. By the turn of the century it had become Dobney's, D'Aubigny's, or Bowling Green House, and as Dobney's its fame belongs to the 18th century.

Another local bowling green, at least by 1664, was Busby's Folly, at the corner of what would become Penton Street, named for Christopher Busby, who in 1668 was landlord of the White Lion at Islington; it appears as the meeting-place of a fraternity known as the Society of Bull Feathers Hall. Like Dobney's, it was to change its name and became in succession Penny's Folly and the Belvidere – a name under which it survived as a pub until the 1990s (then renamed Finca Tapas bar) and hence might be claimed to rank with Sadler's Wells as preserving some continuity to modern times.

So indeed might the London Spa, rebuilt as a pub in the 1930s and now a Spanish tapas bar. It nearly matches Sadler's Wells and New Tunbridge Wells in date, starting with identification of yet another chalybeate spring in 1685, when a vintner, John Halhed, advertised its qualities at his Fountain Inn, claiming that the chemist Robert Boyle had visited and praised its medicinal strength. On 14 July that year, ceremonially named the London Spaw in the presence of "an eminent ... more than ordinary ingenious apothecary", namely Boyle, its apparently humble rooms and walks were thrown open. While obviously wishing to attract the great and fashionable, Halhed offered the waters free to the poor. Again, its great days were to come in the next century.

Finally comes an initially more ambitious establishment some way to the west, the Cold Bath, a cold spring discovered in 1697 on the land of Walter Baynes of the Middle Temple, near what is now Mount Pleasant. Being somewhat of an opportunist, he opened it as a commercial bath-house, advertising its cures for 'nervous disorders'. Open from 5 in the morning until 1pm., it cost two shillings to immerse oneself in its icy waters, or half-a-crown if, too crippled to do so unaided, one was lowered in a chair suspended from the ceiling.

The Cold Bath had a gabled house and garden alongside and was surrounded by a high wall which remained long after the area was built up to form a square. At the corners were ogee-capped summer-houses.[19]

1 Stephen Inwood, *A History of London*, Macmillan, 1998, pp. 248, 258.
2 *VCH*, p. 73.
3 *VCH*, p. 14.
4 *VCH*, p. 72.
5 *VCH*, p. 88; Evelyn, *Diary*, pp. 679, 734, 785.
6 The monument was transferred to the 1750s building but lost when the church was bombed in 1941.
7 *VCH*, p. 113.
8 *VM*, Vol. I.
9 The plates or patens, both of about 1636, and the flagons (1637) survive, together with two dishes of 1783.
10 *VCH*, p. 90.
11 *VCH*, p. 101.
12 *VCH*, p. 131; *DNB*, Israel Tonge.
13 *VCH*, p. 136.
14 Lewis, *Islington*, p. 16 & *n*.
15 It later became Dobney's. *(See Chapter 9)*
16 'Mr Sadler' has been credited with the name 'Dick'. The sole reference in contemporary literature and journals is found in the *Gentleman's Magazine*, and he is supposed to have died in about 1699, after which his name disappears and Miles takes over the music house. Clerkenwell parish records show three Sadlers in the death / burial register and one that fits is Edward, 'victualler', who died in 1699 leaving a family. Another Edward, also with a young family, is identified as a Surveyor, and yet another might have been the music-man's brother. We may safely suppose that 'Dick' was either a mistake or an affectionate nickname and that his name was Edward. (Dennis Arundell, *The Story of Sadler's Wells, 1683–1977*, David & Charles, 1978, pp. 2, 6.)
17 Arundell, *Sadler's Wells*, pp. 5-6.
18 Pinks, *Clerkenwell*, p. 710.
19 Warwick Wroth, *The London Pleasure Gardens of the Eighteenth Century*, London, 1896.

CHAPTER 7

Merry Islington

The village of Islington was expanding. After the bloodless Revolution of 1688 which disposed of the Stuart Kings and placed William and Mary, of more distant vintage, on the throne, although wars continued they were, as far as England was concerned, in Europe. At home, settled life was considerably more sober since the death of merry Charles II, but Islington's reputation for merriment increased along with its size. In 1708 it was estimated to have 325 houses; a generation later in 1732 they had nearly trebled to 937.

The number of inns was also increasing: in 1716 there were 56 keepers of alehouses, and by the 1720s about 100 inns and beershops selling spirits – especially gin. Many were in Upper Street, like the King's Head and one in the Lower Road; others were scattered through the parish, three in Frog Lane behind the Lower Road, and more distant, the Rosemary Branch on the far eastern boundary. At Newington Green were the Coach and Horses and three others nearby, one was at Kingsland, three near the northerly Stroud Green, two at Tollington Lane including the Devil's or Duval's House, one at the end of Hornsey Lane, two on Highgate Hill, five in Holloway and Upper Holloway and one at Ring Cross. On Barnsbury's hilltop was the famous White Conduit.

The increase was due as much to rising popularity as a resort as to Islington's proximity for craftsmen and trades after the fire of 1666. With the fashion for Sadler's Wells and the New Tunbridge Wells, and the convenient local presence of other wells and springs which inspired the opening of more

modest establishments, by the mid-18th century there were at least a dozen pleasure resorts.

As early as 1704 there was an outdoor resort off Upper Street known as 'The Last', whose proprietor set out tables in a field behind, where people came to practise archery. By 1730 this place, now well established, had tea gardens, bowling green and a fishpond. Along tree-lined walks were boxes whose seats were cut out of the hedge, and there were two large tearooms and smaller rooms. Its clients were notably not rank and fashion, but citizens and their families who walked up from the City.

In 1728 came the Lord Cobham's Head, named after the Lollard leader of Henry IV's time, Sir John Oldcastle, known as Lord Cobham and the original of Shakespeare's Falstaff. It was near Walter Baynes's Cold Bath, had a canal stocked with carp and tench, and in 1742 was famed for a fine garden with a grove, gravel walks, and supposedly London's finest beer.

In about 1735, Merlin's Cave opened on the hillside south of New River Head, and about 1742, the Mulberry Garden near Cobham's Head. In about 1740, what was much later to become the notorious Highbury Barn started modestly as a small house selling cakes and ale. It developed into a tavern and tea-gardens, when Mr Willoughby laid out a bowling-green – always a favourite feature – and ground for the old game of trap-and-ball. By 1745 when the White Conduit gardens were laid out, north Clerkenwell and south Islington had long been placed securely on the social map, for King George II's daughters, the Prin-

16. *Merlin's Cave, Spa Fields 1840. This public house stood to the west of New River Head from about 1730.*

cesses Amelia and Caroline, had 'discovered' New Tunbridge Wells.

It was, rather, a re-discovery. Earlier the Spa had fallen out of fashion, and in 1714 was described as deserted:

The ancient drooping trees unprun'd
   appear'd;
No ladies to be seen; no fiddles heard.
                (The Field Spy)

But a couple of decades later, in May 1733, the sister princesses set a fashion, their carriages regularly leading a morning procession that rolled up the hill to the gardens, sometimes welcomed by a salute of 21 guns. For a time they made it all the rage; one morning 1600 people were said to have attended. In a print of that year by George Bickham the modish throng is seen leaning against the balustrade surrounding the well as the server hands up glasses of the disagreeable liquid, while other visitors stroll among the young trees against the background of low single-storey, gabled-roof rooms. Verses were set to an accompanying air *(Charms of Dishabille):*

Behold ye Walks, a chequer'd Shade,
In ye gay Pride of Green array'd. . .
Red Ribbons group'd with Aprons blew; Scrapes,
Curtzies, Nods, Winks, Smiles & frowns, Lords,
Milkmaids, 'Dutchesses and Clowns,
In their all various Dishabille.

Informality was indeed the rule, which the Princesses possibly considered one of the chief attractions.

A physician famous for his pills, calling himself Dr Misaubin though Cambridge had refused him a degree, was in attendance, along with the inevitable thieves and sharpers – Lord Cobham was robbed of his gold repeater watch – and an exhibitionist known as the Tunbridge Knight displayed himself wearing a yellow cockade and carrying a hawk. The notoriety lasted for a season or two, but then royalty, and fashion, moved on, while the more motley attendance remained.[1]

New Tunbridge Wells (soon more usually known as Islington Spa) possibly enjoyed its modish spell because at Sadler's Wells the waters seem to have dropped out of use. Nor were its gardens so important, for from 1698

17. Islington Spa in 1737

at Sadler's Wells music began to be the draw. Henceforward as Miles's Music House it was the home of rustic concerts, against the backdrop of the New River, "the pleasant streams of Middleton", and herds on "herbage green and bleating flocks". Unlike New Tunbridge Wells, it also offered evening entertainment.

Miles continued as host until his death in 1724, and his partner Francis Forcer's son, also Francis, described as educated and gentlemanly, continued until his own death in 1743, introducing such additional entertainments as rope-dancing and acrobatics. The programmes were innocuous and uplifting enough; it was the clientele who could let the place down. At the time of Queen Anne's death in 1714 it was still more popular than the spa opposite, until the latter's royal attention.

The area was rough, however, not least from the minor criminals it attracted. As a safeguard against the local footpads linkboys would wait outside with their torches, and from about 1733 horse patrols were available to escort visitors back to the City and Westminster. It was even considered worthwhile to advertise moonlight nights.

The musical programme at Sadler's Wells, according to the actor Charles Macklin reminiscing some years later, consisted of "horn-pipes and ballad-singing, with a kind of pantomimic ballet, and some lofty tumbling" – all in daylight, while the audience "smoked and drank porter and rum and water as much as we could pay for". Entrance was 3d, while for 6d the more modish few could sit at the side.

The younger Forcer, when he found himself rivalled by New Tunbridge Wells in 1735, tried to secure a licence to charge for entertainment as well as drink, to revive the varieties of a previous generation. Though unsuccessful, he was allowed to advertise programmes at 5 pm. and sometimes at 1 pm., including occasional pantomimes. When the Licensing Act was introduced in 1737, limiting dramatic performances to the Royal Patent Theatres (Drury Lane and Covent Garden), unless resorts included music as well, Forcer duly "new modelled" his music-house to provide more attractive accommodation.

This 'new-modelled' house is the one to be seen as the backdrop to Hogarth's famous painting *Evening* in 1738. The hen-pecked husband, a nearby cow's horns cunningly appearing behind his cuckolded head, lugs the baby, with a put-upon dog and two spoilt brats, while his plump, bad-tempered wife sails towards the Sir Hugh Myddelton's Head.

18. Cricket at White Conduit Field in 1784.

The New River, or perhaps the Round Pond, washes the front of the picture, along with one of the famous hollow timber pipes.

An advertisement of 1740 lists the performers and their 'diversions', mostly dancing, followed by a pantomime and rope-dancing by "Mademoiselle Frederick Kerman, lately arriv'd". Prices were increasing: half-a-crown for a box, ls 6d for the gallery.[2]

NEW BUILDING

Although the fields still stretched behind, by 1732 Upper Street contained several rows of houses, mostly named after the men who had them built: Oddy's Buildings, Chad's Row, Yeates Row and Pierpont Buildings and Rents on the east side, where John Pierpont had ac-

quired land in 1718. Between was a sprinkling of detached houses, for example the new, late-17th-century vicarage near Raleigh's former house, which became the Pied Bull Inn. In Cross Street, Fowler House had been let from 1673, and by 1690 14 new houses were built nearby. Other upper-class houses had declined in status, and the new rows named from their builders were distinctly bourgeois. Nicholas Rufford, for example, from the 1670s onwards a vestryman, sidesman of the church, and churchwarden, in 1688 founded Rufford's Row on the site of the former large house on the corner of Upper Street and Cross Street. He had already in 1685 created Rufford's Buildings on the east side of the High Street, next the inn later known as the Blue Coat Boy.[3]

So by the 1730s the main roads were mostly long built up, notably the west side of the High Street, and Upper Street as far as the present Highbury Corner. Here John Wells, a brickmaker, was probably the builder of Wells or Wells's Row, letting houses there in 1722 and owning brick kilns to the west. Part of the High Street's east side was still fairly open, though the Lower Street (Essex Road) was mostly built as far as Greenman's Lane, while lanes were being built to the south-east, but farm land continued round Pierpont Row. The triangle of land between the two main roads and Cross Street had many houses. Facing the Green was Old Paradise Row, and south of it almshouses and others, with a narrow passage leading through to the fields.[4]

The fields themselves were of great importance, owned as they were by dairy farmers and used as lairs for cattle on their way to and from Smithfield. The dairy industry suffered a serious if temporary outbreak of cattle distemper (rinderpest) in 1714, killing many animals. During more than two months 667 cattle were lost or destroyed, and only 550 survived. Farmers' fortunes thus varied considerably: John Radcliffe, who had 200 head, lost only 12, whereas Mr Rufford out of 72 lost all but 10, and Samuel Pullin lost 38 out of 87.[5]

Some of the open land was already planted with nursery gardens and orchards. During much of Charles II's reign Catherine Comondall, who leased Draper's house near the churchyard, had made a living by selling produce from the fruit trees and herb garden; while in 1692 one-and-a-half acres on the south side of nearby Church Lane were leased by Andrew Butter, who lived there in a house built for him by the landlord and also grew fruit trees and plants. In the early 18th century besides nurseries there were even botanic-gardens, some owned by keen amateurs such as Dr Pitcairn, and in 1727 a gardener was renting grounds of a large house, with a green-house – perhaps again Draper's.[6]

Some roads were cut through to avoid Upper Street, particularly the Back (Liverpool) Road to Ring Cross, which already by the late 16th century served for driving the herds to Smithfield. One such early lane, Longhedge or Longwich Lane (York Way), known by the 16th

century, ran from Battle Bridge and by 1735 was known as Maid or Maiden Lane (though Rocque in his map of 1746 calls it Black Lane, possibly for Black Dog Lane after a tavern near the top of Highgate Hill). It also had other names, notably Hagbush Lane.

In the 1670s and 1680s the parish had been under constant pressure to repair the road from Holloway to Highgate and Tallington Lane, under an indictment from the JPs based at Hicks's Hall in St John Street. With the establishment of the turnpike trust, the parish surveyors of the highways were responsible for raising a sum from the parish in lieu of the traditional 'statute work'. But the roads remained rough, still with little maintenance. The turnpike trust, set up in 1716, by a decade later controlled $6\frac{1}{2}$ miles of the parish's main roads, as far as Holloway and Highgate Hill, and Ball's Pond Road; later it worked in conjunction with Hampstead and Highgate Trust and Marylebone Trust.

A surviving mediaeval, not to say feudal practice, in the form of annual 'statute work' owed by the parish for highway maintenance, was from 1718 commuted to a tax payable to the Turnpike Trustees, and every year the Vestry ordered its Surveyors to compound with the Trustees for this sum. It was long limited to a ceiling of £100, but gradually expressed as a figure regarded as mutually acceptable.[7]

As for industries, apart from dairying the chief was still brick-making. By the 1730s, besides John Wells's kilns between Highbury Corner and the Back Road, there was Hattersfield by River Lane near the New River, also known as Tilekiln field.

PARISH AFFAIRS

The Vestry's meetings were still sporadic, mostly very parochial in content. For example, small almshouses east of the Green were possibly the six built by the Vestry in 1710, near the watch-house, which seems to have been built in 1680. The parishioners, invited to make a choice between paying a rate for the watch, or acting as watch themselves, thriftily chose the latter. In the autumn of 1706 the first six men were appointed to act as nightly watch for the six months until Lady Day (25 March).

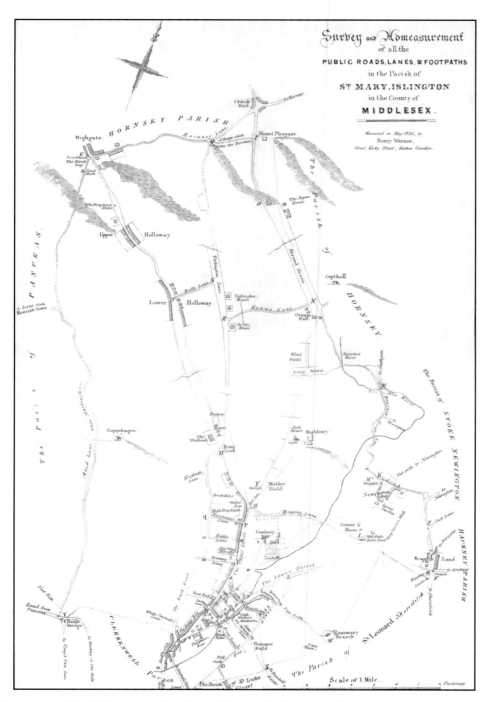

19. Islington parish in 1735 surveyed by Henry Warner. It shows very little development beyond the High Street and Green. The Back Road is today's Liverpool Road, going north to the workhouse on Holloway Road. At Highbury, Jack Straw's Castle is on the site of the old residence of the Prior of St John Clerkenwell, burnt down during the Peasants' Revolt. The New River comes in from the north-east.

The parish was also responsible for the work-house, and in 1726 a house for the purpose was taken at the safe distance of Stroud Green; but the site was inconvenient, and two years later they were discussing an improvement, finally building or renting a house near Ring Cross jointly with Hornsey. An apothecary was also employed. The problem, however, continued to be perennial.

The other main parish service was the up-keep of a fire brigade, and in 1716 a shed for two fire engines was rebuilt north of the church porch, where it still remained after the new church was built in mid-century.

CHURCH MATTERS

The old Vicarage House was subsequently let when the new one, known as Parsonage House, was built in its grounds and held on long lease.

As for the church, two of its bells were recast in 1706; in 1708 a clock and sundial were added to the tower, and from 1710 a charity school was established in the upper storey of the porch. The tiled roof, square steepled tower and Gothic arcades were seriously decaying and in need of frequent repair. Parishioners were dissatisfied, and in 1711 the Vestry applied unsuccessfully to rebuild under the London Churches Act – which ambitiously proposed 50 new churches for the capital though in the event only a handful were built. Complaints of St Mary's inadequacy were soon increasingly frequent.

Islington continued to have a significant role in London's religious history, as much in non-conformity as in the established church. At the Restoration, when the advowson reverted to private ownership, it was members of the Stonehouse family who presented the living to Cave in 1662 *(see Chapter 6)* and eventually in 1738 to the Rev. George Stonehouse, a family member.

The Rev. William Cave, who had resigned the living in 1691, lived until 1713 despite his apparently frail health, and was buried in Islington. Pluralism continued. His successor, the Rev. Robert Gery, was for two years rector of Allhallows the Great, and in 1701 was installed as a Prebendary of Lincoln. He appears to have made no great impression in Islington parish, though occasionally attending vestry meetings in his early days as vicar. He died in 1707 and was also buried in Islington.

His successor, the Rev. Cornelius Yeate, was Archdeacon of Wiltshire and died in 1720: "a gentleman of great probity and learning", said his obituary notice in the *Daily Post* on 14 April, in the unrevealingly laudatory platitude expected of such announcements, "generally esteemed for his exemplary life" and practice of virtue. Yeate, who also attended vestry meetings, was generally referred to as 'the Archdeacon'.

The Rev. George Kerie, vicar from 1720–33, though briefly dismissed by Nelson in his *History* (who misnames him Carey), left a more positive memory. During a wet season in 1725, when the unfortunate haymakers lost heavily, he made house-to-house calls in the parish to collect "a handsome sum" to be distributed to them at the church. It is also sadly recorded that in August 1721 his only son was drowned in the New River.

The Vestry minutes suggest a more active intervention in parish affairs by this vicar, and Mr Kerie attended meetings rather more frequently than his predecessors, who had generally limited their appearances to occasions for appointing a lecturer or some other personal concern. On 22 March 1722 Kerie was doubtless responsible for an order to the churchwardens to buy the Vestry Clerk "a decent & proper gown to attend divine service in", and for fees, once settled, to be "entred fair into this Vestry Book and be Confirmed" – both orders surely emanating from the new vicar/new broom. Soon after this Jacob Harvey, one of the parish gentry, Philip Oddy and others were ordered to make an abstract of the parish's title deeds, gifts and donations for examination by the Vestry. (This had to be ordered again in 1744.)

In June 1723 Kerie was present at discussion of a "dispute ab^t the present Churchwarden" (apparently concerning finances), and naturally at a meeting in October 1724 for choosing a new lecturer after the death of William Hendry. On this occasion George Waite, the minister elected, received almost twice as many votes as the other two candidates, supported by many of the regulars like Oddy, Samuel Pullin, the Sebbons (father and son) and the more socially distinguished Jacob Harvey and Sir Thomas Halton. The vicar also attended meetings about the worsening condition of the church.

Parish affairs had evidently deteriorated into confusion at the beginning of 1727. A committee of 12, appointed on Boxing Day just past, headed by Kerie and this time meeting at "the Crane in the Lower Street", reported inefficiencies which led to vital basic tidying up – yet another committee being appointed to examine the parish "Books Papers Deeds Writings & Evidences". These were now to be kept permanently in the Vestry Room in a chest with three locks – and keys held by the vicar, churchwarden and Vestry Clerk.

Further, the list of fees for marriages, christenings and burials, settled in 1717 and again in 1722, was to be re-entered, and a fair copy sent to "the proper Court at Doctors Commons", the body of practitioners of canon and civil law. Another committee headed by the vicar was also appointed, doubtless to continue these reforms.

Storms ranged from parochial to ethical. Often much meeting time was devoted to allocation of pews, a perennial subject of contention or jealousy. Great significance was attached to the importance, or otherwise, of where one sat, with the presumption that the galleries seating charity children, and scholars with their schoolmasters or mistresses, were lower in the scale. A new parishioner might be allotted a gallery seat until a better became available. Seats in the old church were defined as in the north, middle (presumably the most sought-after) and south aisles, or by nearness to either Lady Owen's monument, the pulpit, reading desk, or place where the communion rites were kept. Certain pews under the gallery were specifically assigned to the cattle drovers who were such a regular presence in the parish, others were kept for parishioners' household servants.

If an extension, by taking in part of a neighbour's pew, were authorised at a sitter's request, the necessary carpentry was at the sitter's expense. On some occasions there are strong hints of bad feeling when would-be occupants are specifically excluded. In April 1727, after the Vestry approved a number of allocations (including allowing Jacob Harvey a whole pew,

altered at his own cost), the sexton was ordered not to admit anyone to an inhabitant's vacant pew until after conclusion of the Second Lesson, "as he will answer the same at his peril". Even then he had to give preference to locals above strangers. At one point in 1736 a rule was made that an existing occupant had to approve a newcomer. Some parishioners showed a distinctly un-Christian possessiveness over their seats.

Soon afterwards there was a scandal about a bastard child, fathered by one Adam Burgoin on Martha Nicholson, who was actually his own granddaughter-in-law. The parish had to prosecute the father via the churchwarden at the ecclesiastical court.

Not that the vestry was meeting more frequently or regularly. There would be an annual flutter on Boxing Day and on Easter Tuesday for election or nomination of Surveyors, Churchwardens and Overseers, and for some years for setting pensions granted to the poor. Then a long gap usually ensued until the autumn, and on several occasions meetings ordered were not recorded at all (or perhaps did not even take place).

Islington's spas and pleasure gardens have been described at length in the classic works, Warwick Wroth, *The London Pleasure Gardens of the Eighteenth Century*, London, 1896, and Septimus Sunderland, *Old London's Spas, Baths and Wells*, London, 1915. (See also Chapter 9).

1   Wroth, *Pleasure Gardens*, pp. 17-18.
2   Arundell, *Sadler's Wells*, pp. 8ff.
3   Nelson, *Islington*, pp. 121-2, *VCH*, p. 15. Other regular serving Vestrymen who gave their names to short rows and courts were Philip Oddy and James Terrett.
4   *VCH*, p. 15.
5   *VCH*, p. 70; *Islington Medical Officer of Health Annual Report, 1865*, p. 10.
6   *VCH*, pp. 71-72.
7   *VCH*, p. 5; VM, Vol. II, *ad loc*. Most of what follows in this chapter is derived from the Vestry Minutes

CHAPTER 8

Spiritual Vicissitudes [1]

PULPIT DISTURBANCES [2]

These were stirring times in the Church, in which Islington was to play a prominent part, though not surfacing in the vestry records until April 1739. The Rev. Richard Streat who served the parish from 1733 resigned in 1738, and his successor, the young Rev. George Stonehouse, aged only 24, proved to have distinctly Methodist leanings. He quickly ran into trouble by introducing the Wesley brothers and other unlicensed preachers to the strictly conforming St Mary's pulpit, exciting serious local opposition.

Stonehouse was descended from a Royalist family of clerics and his inclination towards nonconforming preachers is perhaps surprising. Like John Wesley, he had connections with the Moravian church of central Europe, whose devotees under Count Zinzendorf had been persecuted and were now in exile. They made many friends and converts in England, and others in Scotland. Indeed Stonehouse's actions savoured more of tolerance than did those of his leading parishioners. 'Methodism' was a derogatory nickname which stuck, and the preaching of the brothers John and Charles Wesley and George Whitefield, even before they established their Foundry chapel near Bunhill Fields, a mere mile or so away, were deeply suspect among the devout orthodox.

John Wesley, recently returned from Savannah, Georgia, made a missionary tour throughout England and was back in London in the spring of 1738. On 20 April he records the first of many visits to Stonehouse in Islington, with James Hutton, son of a clergyman with whose family he usually stayed in Great College Street. On the first of these visits his brother Charles notes that "they dined and talked of the mystics. At four they had tea, and conversation." They then went on to another supporter, "sang, and, apparently, covenanted together, singing and reading prayers." This was a frequent pattern of their visits to Wesley's mother, their numerous siblings, disciples, or other ministers.

John Wesley was always on the go, whether abroad, travelling in England, or in London. His day was divided between missionary visits, communal prayers and singing, religious 'converse', and preaching, interspersed with hospitality by his various hosts. He visited Stonehouse on 24 April and on 10 May, when he records in his own journal that the young vicar was convinced of "the truth as it is in Jesus". Yet, he continues ominously, "From this time till Saturday the 13th, I was sorrowful and very heavy, being neither able to read, nor meditate, nor sing, nor pray, nor do any thing..."

In September Wesley preached twice in one day in Clerkenwell at "St John's Chappel", as he called it, and a couple of days later it was Charles who "read prayers in Islington Church, and preached with great boldness. There was a vast audience, better disposed than usual". But Charles adds revealingly, "None went out, as they had threatened, and frequently done heretofore; especially the well-dressed hearers", whenever he mentioned Hell, or "urged that rude question, 'Do you deserve to be damned?'"

This is the first reference to the unruly disturbances that the Methodist gospel mission

20. *John Wesley, from a painting by William Hamilton, 1788.*

21. *George Whitefield.*

excited at St Mary's. John Wesley, by contrast, did not remark on such outbreaks in his daily notebook but continues on the usual neutral lines, as on 4 October: "3 Islington, prayers; 4 at Mr Stonehouse's, singing, conversed, prayer, tea, conversed; 5.45, walked, conversed. . ."; and two days later, after a visit by both brothers to Hoxton, John "walked and read as far as Mr Stonehouse's, where, after burying a corpse, he broke his fast, dining at five o'clock".

He seems to have been working on Stonehouse's conscience to adopt Methodist beliefs, shortly afterwards writing to a fellow-preacher, "Mr Stonehouse hath at length determined to know nothing but Jesus Christ and Him crucified; and to preach unto all remission of sins through faith in His blood."

So it went on for about a year, during which John and Charles, though never formally appointed ministers at Islington, visited either to pray and 'converse', or occasionally preach and act as curates. Islington and Stonehouse occur frequently in their journals. For example on Christmas Day Charles preached there in the morning "and gave the cup", while Stonehouse preached in the afternoon. That December George Whitefield returned to

England from his prolonged mission in Georgia, and John, who for some days had been preaching in Oxford, hastened back to see him. Whitefield now joined their Islington visits, though he was in the West country when Wesley himself for the first time was subject to trouble here: on Sunday, 25 February 1739, preaching in the afternoon, "Many here were, as usual, deeply offended. But the counsel of the Lord, it shall stand." To Whitefield he wrote, "the church was almost as hot as some of the society rooms used to be … The fields after service were white with people praying God." The word 'hot', referring to their spiritual state, is contrasted with the phenomenally cold winter weather outside.

In the spring of 1739 Wesley went to Bristol on a continued mission – there as elsewhere greatly magnifying the numbers in his congregation (the following June, for example, he claimed 7,000 at Moorfields, and at Kennington Common the same afternoon, a modest 15,000).

Meanwhile, however, Stonehouse and the three missioners between them had provoked Islington Vestry into action. It was Whitefield who finally roused the rumblings of disapproval into outbreak – or, to change the metaphor, fanned the fatal spark of Stonehouse's activities.

Whitefield records in his *Journey to Savannah* how that April he assisted in giving communion in Islington, when a large crowd listened to his discourse. But next day the churchwardens intervened and refused to allow him to enter the pulpit, and like many of his dissenting brethren he was obliged to preach to the crowd in the churchyard, mounted on a tombstone.

This caused a great stir. At a time when the local administration was largely concerned with the poor state of the highways and mismanagement at the workhouse, the vestrymen became involved with the directions of the Church's 52nd Canon. A committee was appointed from the parish heavy artillery to wait on the vicar on "special parish affairs". This consisted of his predecessor, Rev. Richard Streat, his Lecturer, the Rev. Thomas Scott, four JPs of the local gentry – Jacob Harvey, John Elliott, William Booth and Thomas Pargiter (a relative newcomer, only recently accommodated with his family in a pew) – and regular stalwarts, Samuel Pullin, Richard Bull and others.

Stonehouse was greatly blamed by conservatively minded parishioners for the "disturbances" he had caused by admitting these unlicensed preachers, and in August they took the case to a higher authority. The sum of his transgressions put to the Bishop, the Rt Rev. Edmund Gibson, was that, despite the Vestry's "peaceable & Gentle" attempts to modify Stonehouse's actions, his defiance in "Irregular Illegal and Arbitrary proceedings . . . willfully persists . . . to the great disorder and Confusion" of public worship and offence of devout worshippers, and was actually discouraging church attendance. These illegal assemblies were taking place not only at the church but in Stonehouse's own vicarage, where he and other preachers (notably the Wesley brothers) expounded heretical doctrine. Further, Stonehouse had begun to refuse Communion to certain members of the congregation; the deputation named in particular, Thomas Emlin, a vestryman in this respect, though we are not told the reason for his refusal.

These acts transgressed against canons of the established church, such as no. 71 forbidding unauthorised preaching, no. 28 forbidding refusal of the sacrament, and so forth. And by encouraging strangers from outside the parish to take Communion at St Mary's Stonehouse was in violation of two further canons.

What seems to have been almost the last straw was that Stonehouse had lately been married, without banns, licence or even parental consent, to a girl described as "an Infant", that is to say under age. It took place at Highgate Chapel and the bride was Mary, daughter of Sir John Crisp, baronet. Stonehouse finally overstepped the mark by proposing to engage as his curate another dissident, who was in fact John Wesley's nephew, John Wesley (sometimes spelt Westley) Hall.

Information on the contretemps was taken to the Bishop, initially by Captain Robert Cumming, supported by the Churchwarden Samuel Dennis, the vestrymen James Terrett, William Deakin and the oddly named Thomas Science. They took with them the "representation" of Stonehouse's misdeeds, signed by parishioners, but were at first deferred and called to attend the Bishop on another day. On 3 September a slightly different deputation waited on his Lordship, and the Bishop, on learning the facts, felt obliged to take up the matter with Stonehouse who, not surprisingly incensed, summoned the Churchwarden Dennis and threatened prosecution "in a very Severe manner", if Hall's preaching were interfered with.

None of this campaigning appears in John Wesley's journal. (And curiously no mention of Wesley appears in the Vestry minutes.) His notes continued so apparently oblivious to the Islington furore, and especially to the actions of its local governors, that it is as if both were describing totally different events. It was while Wesley was in Bristol that the outburst over Whitefield occurred, and he briefly returned to London in mid-June 1739, taking communion and preaching in Islington. He also visited his mother who had been living in the country with the Wesley Halls and had come with them to London, before he returned for some weeks to the West. Back again in London, on 3 September he dined with Stonehouse – the very day when the second deputation waited on Bishop Gibson.

The churchwardens, notwithstanding Stonehouse's reaction, resolved on drastic measures, and on Vestry authority arranged that any of them or their sidesmen should be on guard beside the pulpit to make sure that neither Hall nor any other unqualified preacher entered it, promising official protection should the case be taken to law. The vicar responded by refusing the sacrament to several more parishioners, and their appointed committee then sought legal advice.

Still ignoring these broils, Wesley calmly noted on 14 September, "I expounded again at Islington; but, the house being too small for the company, I stood in the garden; and showed them how vainly they trusted in baptism for salvation, unless they were holy of heart."

Stonehouse applied to the Bishop for a licence to employ Hall. Predictably, the Churchwardens, with Thomas Science and Edmund Cooper (one of those refused the sacrament) in November waited on the Bishop again, begging him to license neither Hall, "being a Common field preacher and a holder of Assemblies in private Houses in an Unlawfull Manner", nor any other so "disagreeable" to the locals, to preach in their church.

This is the last reference by the Vestry to the whole affair, and minutes thereafter return to the prosaic matters of the state of the roads and the appointment of officers.

For some time Wesley, now established at the Foundry in Tabernacle Street, continued his frequent visits to Stonehouse whenever in London. He also preached at the new St Luke's Church, referring to it as "our parish church", and commenting that the service "was such a sight as, I believe, several hundred communicants, from whose very faces one might judge that they indeed sought Him that was crucified".

In June 1740 Stonehouse capitulated by resigning, selling the vicarage on 1 July. Yet he seems to have stayed on – perhaps in the other vicarage house – at least until September, when Wesley visited him for the last time on the morning of 24 September, spent an hour with him, and seemed to be suffering from disillusionment over his acolyte. "Oh what 'persuasiveness of speech' is here! Surely, all the deceivableness of unrighteousness. Who

can escape, except God be with him?"

Stonehouse was said to have removed to Woodstock, but it was in the Bristol area that he died in 1793, "in inglorious 'stillness'", comments Wesley's biographer. But Wesley did visit him again, at East Brent in Somerset in 1781, when he observes disapprovingly, if enigmatically, "Perhaps if I had his immense fortune I might be as great an oddity as he."

Interestingly Nelson too, in his *History*, does not mention the religious strife, limiting his account of Stonehouse's career to a brief, bland note and relegating the broils to a short footnote. He may well have frowned on the incursion of Methodism and chosen to ignore or at least underplay it.

Stonehouse's successor was another well-born clergyman, the Rev. Sir Gilbert Williams, a baronet from Breconshire who, although his subsequent actions suggest autocratic arrogance, at least did not offend the orthodox over doctrine or conformity. The unfortunate Lecturer, Thomas Scott, died on 18 July 1740, it was claimed from the strain over Stonehouse's activities.

Scott's successor was elected on 2 September 1740 from among no less than 12 candidates, and the Rev. John Ditton was chosen by a large majority. (Four of the unsuccessful candidates received well under 10 votes each.) Thus ended the unseemly scenes and disturbances in pulpit, churchyard and vicarage.

A DILAPIDATED CHURCH

There were other serious church concerns to preoccupy the Vestry and (at least through their purses) the congregation. These were the dangers caused by the increasingly alarming state of the 15th-century building itself. The church, besides being equipped with oak pews and wainscoted walls, had a gallery and altarpiece, made in Charles II's reign; its east window contained remains of old stained glass, and it was adorned with a number of monuments. Though problems had been recorded as early as 1675, the fabric steadily deteriorated, until a major event in the middle of the 18th century was its total rebuilding. Its condition had long caused concern in spite of work carried out, and again on 26 July 1685 it was reported as "verry much out of repair". Lead guttering had to be replaced more than once (in 1682 it was stolen), the bells were recast in 1706, and further additions were made such as the two-storeyed porch, partly for the charity school, partly for a Vestry room. The gallery, another addition on the north side, had been built by Sir Richard Fisher in 1685 at his own expense, to provide a family pew, and was entered through a door knocked out through the existing wall. In fact, the church had been greatly tinkered with, and as already reported in 1682 its centre had begun to sink.

In 1711, like several London parishes the Vestry applied to rebuild under the Act for 50 New Churches. Even though it was "very Ruinous & in great Need of being rebuilt" and a dozen skilled surveyors had reported on its condition, they were turned down.

After they petitioned in 1718 under the same Act, again without success, a period of more tinkering followed: roof tiles, repairs to aisles and even pews, Communion rails and adjoining pavement. The only part of the church in which maintenance appears to have been successful was the tower clock, kept in order by a succession of experts.

Needless to say, it was often the vestrymen who secured the jobs, thanks to their professions. In 1726 the steeple timbers had rotted and were renewed with "good yellow fir" by vestryman Robert Chandler. Special parish rates paid for the work, usually 2d in the pound, and (for example) it was Chandler who repaired pews and aisles besides the steeple.

Clerkenwell, by contrast, in 1733 benefited from the New Churches Act by acquiring St Luke's Church in Old Street, designed by John James and Nicholas Hawksmoor, whose originality was manifest in its magnificent fluted obelisk 'spire'.[3]

At St Mary's, after a lull of a few years, there was concern over the pulpit, in this case for the care of souls rather than the safety or comfort of bodies, for Stonehouse wanted pulpit and sounding board raised to improve acoustics, no doubt to enable his unlicensed preachers to be better heard (October 1738). But no matter who preached from it, the position was found unsuitable. Three vestrymen, including Robert Catherall (Surveyor in 1734 and a Churchwarden in 1736), who examined

it in May 1739 pronounced "the Prop in the North Isle" to be "useless". This suggested that they feared the whole building might be about to tumble about their ears.

Further, in November 1740 a heavy storm damaged the roof, and a new 4d rate had to be imposed to pay for its repair. Legal costs against the vicar for unorthodoxy were bad enough without his incurring heavy parish expense for moving the pulpit as well. Late in 1740, Stonehouse having now departed, it was agreed that the aisles, now sunk below street level, should be raised, so that a new pulpit could be built in the middle of the church to allow a preacher's voice to carry more effectively (9 Nov. 1740). Only in July 1741 was a bricklayer, John Corneck, employed to level the aisles, and in August 1743 repairs were made to the Vestry Room and south side of the church.

The next trouble, which arose during Sir Gilbert Williams's rectorship was an undignified disagreement actually referred to the law. There had been a fixed conviction among parishioners that "from time immemorial" upkeep of the chancel had been the vicar's responsibility. Unfortunately Williams, who appears as rather intransigent, and seldom bothered to attend vestry meetings unless directly concerned, affirmed in no uncertain terms that it was no responsibility of his. The parish then sought legal advice from Dr George Hay at Doctors' Commons on whether they might bring a suit to enforce Williams' taking on the restoration; but before responsibility was resolved, the physical future of the whole building had come under threat.

In October 1750 three reputable surveyors were employed to inspect the church from top to bottom. They were Benjamin Timbrell, James Steere and George Ufford, of whom certainly the first two, men at least in their fifties, were well established carpenters (who at that time often doubled as architects). Timbrell indeed was one of London's leading Master Carpenters and like many contemporaries was sought after as a speculative builder in Mayfair and elsewhere, for example on the Berkeley and Grosvenor estates. He also bought and rebuilt three houses in St James's Square on the site of Chandos House, and sometimes designed for himself, such as nos

1-3 Crown Office Row in the Inner Temple.[4] He was among the contractors for Grosvenor Chapel in South Audley Street. In this very year, 1750, he was about demolishing and rebuilding a house for himself in Fulham.

While Timbrell was perhaps the more fashionably distinguished, James Steere or Steer, carpenter and joiner, would be, in 1758, Warden of the Carpenters' Company and, had he lived another year would probably have become Master. From 1736 he had been Surveyor to St Thomas's Hospital, and indeed much of his work was in surveying. He also had Islington connections, was architect of the Welsh Charity School on Clerkenwell Green in 1738 (this now houses the Marx Memorial Library), and soon after designed the east wing of Guy's Hospital, in conventional Palladian style.[5] Only a few years before his employment to examine St Mary's Church he had designed an obelisk which he hoped would be erected in Smithfield to commemorate "the Cruel Triumph of Popery", as a warning should a Catholic sovereign ever reign again in England – all of which suggests that he may have lived in this part of London.[6]

The report of 18 October 1750 on the examination of St Mary's Church by these "able and experienced" surveyors, was damning. They stated that "the walls in general are Extremely out of an Upright and very ruinous, and that the timbers to the Roof are Decayed and Extremely bad, Likewise the Paving … and that the Pavement … is very much under the Surface of the Road and Church yard". The whole church, they concluded, was so ruinous as to be incapable of repair, had to be demolished and totally rebuilt.

Churchwardens and Vestry were in a quandary. They might well win a legal case against the vicar for restoring the chancel, but to what purpose if the whole building had to go? And if the church were rebuilt, whose responsibility would be its chancel?

Legal advice from Dr George Hay showed that "the Vicar's Chancel" did actually belong to him, and that like his predecessors he was entitled to the profits from burials there or from its pews. Sir Gilbert had indeed received fees for chancel burials (presumably in the vaults beneath), and for pews which he had

let, specifically, for burials of William Smith and Richard Tuckwell in 1747, and pews for two ladies for which he received a guinea a year. The survey by the "able and Experienced Workmen" revealed that at least £34.13s was needed for repairs which, when the parish applied to Sir Gilbert he "Refuses or Neglects". In the meantime, it was agreed that previous repairs undertaken by Churchwardens, without Vestry orders or even consideration by any vicar, had been "ignorant and trifling". Dr Hay agreed that the Vicar having taken the profits, had also to take the responsibility. "The Commendum & Onus should go together." The parish seemed to have a strong case. On the other hand, under the circumstances was it worth pursuing? And had any vicar ever actually paid for repairs?

The parishioners agreed to suspend legal action in view of the urgency of rebuilding. But they had achieved a notable moral victory: the Rev. Sir Gilbert caved in. He conceded the parish's case in quite gracious terms, asking as a favour and not as of right, that supposing the church were *not* rebuilt, during his lifetime the parishioners should undertake the repairs. This the Vestry agreed.

In effect, both sides had won, for it was merely an establishment of principle, since there was no doubt that the decaying church had to come down.

REBUILDING THE CHURCH

The Vestry applied to Parliament for an Act to demolish and rebuild.[7] Once this was authorised, trustees were named to raise £7,000 capital, both by loans in the form of life annuities, and with the usual assessment or parish rate, in this case a shilling.

Exterior views of the old church had been engraved several times, especially in the 1730s by Bernard Lens, drawing-master in the families of George I and George II, and the third Bernard in generations of a family of artists of Dutch origin. This building was now demolished by Samuel Steemson, a local carpenter and builder, who allowed the parish £110 for the materials, which he was to clear away.

In July 1751 the church closed for services. Islington's church was demolished in only a month and according to contract. The most arduous part of the destruction was its tower, which proved so strongly built that it was realised too late that it could have stood for another couple of centuries; but the locals insisted on destruction. Gunpowder was tried on the stronger parts, but used so sparingly for safety's sake that it had no effect. The tower was finally disposed of by shoring it up with timber while a large fire was built to undermine the foundations, so that it came crashing to the ground. So speedy was the demolition that the new church's foundation stone was laid as early as 28 August 1751, by James Colebrooke, Islington's most considerable landlord, with the usual engraved copper plate commemorating the event.

For the next three years St Mary's services were held in a rented building known as the Tabernacle near the Fox on Islington Green, fitted up for worship at a cost of £100. As for the new building, its cost, unusually, proved less than expected, as some of those who purchased annuities conveniently died after receiving only a year's interest.[8]

The architect for the new church, or surveyor as he was usually described, was Launcelot Dowbiggin (c.1689–1759), "citizen and joiner of London", one of a family of surveyors and joiners who appear to have come originally from Lancashire. He became Master of the Joiners' Company in 1756, but had earlier got into trouble for supposedly working against the employment of George Dance to design the Mansion House, though in the end he personally undertook joinery for the building. In 1746 he had contracted for the tower of St Mary's Rotherhithe, of which it is not clear whether he or Benjamin Glanvill was architect. His son Samuel followed in his footsteps as joiner and surveyor.[9]

Dowbiggin's design has been described as rustic, its chief feature the tower surmounted by a balustrade with corner urns and an openwork, domed temple-structure crowned by a stone steeple. The rest of the building was simply plain brick with stone dressings and round-headed windows. It was finished in less than three years, and opened for worship on Sunday, 26 May 1754.

The new building's other chief ornament was on its pedimented west front, a semicircular domed portico supported on Tuscan columns, entered by a flight of five semi-

22. *The rebuilt St Mary's, c.1820*

circular steps. The interior, with nave and aisles containing 91 pews, ended in a Venetian east window with paired Ionic columns. The roof spanned the whole building, so that the only interior supports were the Tuscan pillars carrying the galleries, which held 62 pews. The coffered ceiling was divided in the centre by four semicircles, their circumferences adorned with stucco flowers. A marble font, central mahogany pulpit and reading-desk, and mahogany altar compartmented by Doric columns, completed the fittings. A modest mahogany-cased organ at the West end (replaced much later by Byfield and Greer) was installed only in 1772.

The length of the new church was 108 feet, its width 60, the tower 87 feet high to the balustrade, and 164 to the top of the spire's ball and vane.

The six bells from the old tower were rehung in the new (recast in 1774), with a subscription to cast two smaller bells to complete the octave. (The tenor bell, weighing 16 cwt, was again re-cast in 1808 "to improve the tone".) Each bore a verse inscription.

John Nelson, nearly 60 years later Islington's first historian, offers restrained approval of the new building, rather damning with faint praise: "though perhaps not formed according to strict architectural rule … allowed to be a light and handsome edifice", with "throughout an elegant plainness".[10]

It was by Nelson's time too small, the parish having already in the previous decades launched into its dizzying population increase. Indeed the church's size proved a problem within a decade, for in 1764 new pews had to be built at the back on both north and south sides. And worse, within some thirty years it was found to have been shoddily built.

For his work Dowbiggin was paid 100 guineas (£105), with a further 18 guineas "for extra trouble". The contract for the building was £6,319, plus £50 for its brass chandelier, £73 for the clock and £13. 14s 11d for its four dials, one on each face of the tower. Other expenses were £490 (later) for the organ, some £210 for the bells and frames, £93.10s for the churchyard walls and sundries, and £55.17s 1d for unspecified extras. The grand total was £7,340.[11]

The 30-hour clock was the work of Thomas Wilkins who offered to construct it "in an Iron frame, the Wheels Brass, the Pinions Tempered, Great Wheels Eighteen Inches Diameter with three Dials, one minuted, the other two plain Hours, to strike on a Bell Eighteen Hundred wt for Fifty five pounds". This was exclusive of the mason work, painting, gilding the hands, carpentry and scaffolding. The Vestry settled for the fee with extra for striking the hour on the great bell and the quarters on two bells. A Mr Sanders Oliver cut the dial plates to his own design, which a painter, John Maxey, painted black with "the figures in proper lines for Hours and Minutes on one plate and for Hours only on the other two to be gilded in a Strong proper and Exact Workman Like Manner", for 17 guineas including the gilding.[12]

In the new church were installed monuments removed from the old, including, besides part of Dame Alice Owen's, one to the Rev. William Cave of 1713, and to his son-in-law the Rev. Robert Gerie, who had predeceased him in 1707. There was also a tablet to the architect Dowbiggin, which Nelson does not think worth mentioning. He does however give an exhaustive list of indoor and churchyard memorials, few of which, curiously, record the faithful members of the Vestry who served Islington for many years.

One vital adjunct to the church which Steemson, having removed it from the old building, would not part with, was the King's Arms, obligatory by law to be displayed in every church, and for nearly three years he refused to give them up. Not until April 1757 did the Vestry insist on his surrendering them, as it was agreed that, properly cleaned and fixed against the tower at the west end, it would be "an Ornament", besides conforming to the law. The Vestry Clerk accordingly delivered to Steemson a copy of their opinion, and the arms were appropriately installed.

The church was barely completed before the matter of the chancel was raised again, amplifying the clause in the Act confirming the Vicar's rights in perpetuity. The parish had built church and chancel, argued the Vestry, so could the Churchwardens seat anyone there, or only the Vicar? And if he had a right to nine chancel pews, should he not seat Mrs Paul and her young ladies' boarding school, to whom he had let the vicarage, just as they had sat in the chancel of the old church? On the first Sunday of the opening the young ladies were allowed to sit in the West end galleries, which were empty, but Mrs Paul's name was not entered on the vitally important seating plan, nor was she given a key, and the Vestry Clerk told her she was the Vicar's tenant and ought to be in the chancel.

Dr Hay of Doctors' Commons, again applied to for a ruling, declared that this 'Occasional Permission' granted her no right and she had therefore to take her pupils to the chancel.

Further, the Vestry complained that placing the pulpit in the middle aisle was inconvenient, obscuring the altar and leaving little room to pass on either side, whereas in the old church it had been north of the chancel. Dr Hay pointed out that it could not be moved without a licence, and should the vicar also object to the inconvenience they had to seek a Faculty. They seem to have abandoned the idea. Still further, the delicate matter of pew seating had to be undertaken from scratch. The inevitable committee was formed, of Churchwardens and trustees. Plans were drawn, places allocated, and for some time to come an intensive game of musical chairs was played between seats.

They now had what seemed a fine new church, one of the parish's major achievements of the century, and for the next generation one of the Vestry's greatest anxieties was largely settled.

Whether or not a small organ was originally installed at the West end of the church, in April 1770 the question of installing a good one came under discussion, agreed to be "not only a very great Ornament ... but also of great use". The churchwardens were instructed to apply to Doctors' Commons for a Faculty, and then to the Trustees for the Rebuilding to buy an instrument with the money allotted it from rates and duties. In the ensuing months, while the Vestry was heavily preoccupied with the matter of watching and lighting the parish, the Trustees undertook this task and in April 1772, at the time of the annual parish appointments, a poll was held to elect an organist.

Miss Jane Crook, possibly the daughter of the vestryman James Crook, applied for the post. She had a rival in Mr Bartholomew Davis, but in the poll captured 212 votes and Davis only 12, and she was therefore appointed on an annual basis, the post being renewed every Easter Tuesday along with the other parish officers – except that, as a lady, Miss Crook received no official salary, but was supported by voluntary contributions. She continued organist for many years.

The church received other, more portable adornments in 1785 when several Vestrymen, either in concert or in competition, presented furnishings: from Henry Wright "a Crimson velvet Cushion and Covering trim'd with Gold Fringe & Laces for the Pulpit", from Joseph Manwaring jr Esq., similar fittings for the Communion Table, and from Charles Brown, also for the Communion Table, a damask cloth and two napkins – at the time when many newcomers were moving in and seeking pew sittings. There were indeed so many gifts and legacies that it became necessary to acquire a new 'Benefaction Table'.

However, there had already been dissatisfaction because the church, when little over 20 years old, had been outgrown by its parishioners. Although in November 1777 a motion was negatived that it could not contain the inhabitants, the following January it was decided that the objections had to be met, and new galleries were proposed on both north and south sides. Samuel Dowbiggin, Launcelot's son, produced drawings and an estimate for £610, and the matter was referred to the Trustees for Rebuilding, who had never been disbanded. The Trustees, however, pointed out that under the Act for rebuilding the church they were given no authority for such alteration, and the churchwardens had to apply for a Faculty, that is a permit from the consistory of the church, without which alterations to the fabric or even to permanent furnishings and monuments might not be made. The problem was, for the time being, shelved.

When the churchyard also proved too small, in the spring of 1782 the adjoining ground held by the nurserymen, the Watson brothers, became available for sale and the Trustees were asked to treat with the owner, George Iveson Tapps, Esq., with a view to purchase. This too hung fire for some time.

The steeple clock also frequently required attention. In 1786 John Brice – perhaps the brother of Robert, recently appointed Sexton on the death of his father, Robert senior – was offered a rise to eight guineas from the former seven for the care of two church clocks. In May 1788 a Mr Thwaites was discharged for refusing to wind up the clock for £5. John Brice reappeared, offering to fit "Wires and new Lines", and to maintain both clocks for an annual eight guineas. He thus joined the army of officials annually reappointed every Easter Tuesday. However, by October 1789 the clock required urgent repair and William Dorrel, a clockmaker in Bridgwater Square near the Barbican, dismantled and repaired it for six guineas. This seemed to serve until 1793, when the churchwardens employed William Vale, who again found it much out of repair and was commissioned to maintain it "in a proper & Workmanlike manner" for a maximum of £8 per annum.

All this suggests a certain amount of tinkering with problems, reflecting to a minor degree the much more serious discovery in 1786 that Launcelot Dowbiggin's architectural standards, or Samuel Steemson's quality of building, had been inadequate or suffered neglect since the church was completed. The churchwardens called in no less an adviser than Robert Mylne, the distinguished architect descended from the family of Scottish Master Masons, who at the age of 34 had been appointed surveyor to the New River Company. He was of notoriously hot temper and as an architect was of high principles, just the expert to discover flaws in the church structure which had escaped the Vestry members.

Mylne spent a month inspecting the church from top to bottom, and his report, dated 9 July 1786, was discerning and thorough. Nor was it the first time he had examined the fabric during the 32 years since its completion. He pointed out that cracks had been drawn to his attention about 24 years earlier, when the church would have been only eight years old. There was now considerable settlement – as had happened to the medieval church – especially in the heaviest part of its tower, lobby and spire, which had caused fractures in the brick and stonework surrounding doors, windows and other openings. He doubted, however, whether these cracks would prove dangerous, observing that settlement, and the "effects of various pressures" could happen to all buildings, but here they had been neglected too long. He recommended that they have "the Works cut open, stopt, and filled in, with the best of materials", to prevent weather damage and also to remove "every unseemly appearance".

Repairs were also needed in the body of the church, roof, cornices and parapets. While the spire itself seemed secure, he recommended lightning conductors ('Electrical Rods'), pointing out that "the church stands on the most elevated ground in a circuit of many miles" – a fact not at all obvious today.[13] The 42-foot flagstaff erected at a corner of the tower in 1776 he condemned as no asset as its instability in wind caused it to loosen stone joints near it. This the Vestry agreed to remove and to place it more safely on the roof at the East end.

The chief danger was in the square tower between lobby ceiling and base of the spire, which Mylne remarked disapprovingly "does not seem to have been attended to, in its original construction" by making what he regarded as essential ties from corner to corner. The rehanging of the bells 18 years after the church was built had, like the flagstaff, added to its weakness. Indeed, were all the bells to be rung together "in full play" the violent motion could seriously endanger the church. He proposed 2-inch-square iron ties fixed at three different levels which, "screwed up tight on the outside", could draw the walls together at the point of the cracks.

Minor repairs included replacing decayed fir timber with oak, work on the bell frames and clock dials, some re-slating, and improvement to the dangerous approach to the tower (unfortunately not described), not to mention cleaning and whitening the interior.

Mylne added a significant rider on the effect of the great increase in Islington's population in the past decades, so that there was now insufficient room for living or dead. He assumed (wrongly as it was to prove) that the churchyard could not be extended, and that more land at a distance had to be bought.

As for the shortage of seating, he suggested bringing the gallery fronts forward while reducing their bulk and narrowing the passages behind. By doing away with the 'cross passages' room could be made for another row of seats. Further, by raising the floor the corners of the landing at the top of the stairs could be brought into use. The Charity Boys' seats could be pushed back to "the useless space over the Vestry", which was "enclosed for no purpose".

By the end of August the Vestry had agreed to nearly all Mylne's recommendations, except a suggestion to dig out the ground below the chancel floor, which was not vaulted like the rest and was used for occasional burials – and would in time, to put it mildly, prove "very inconvenient" to the pews above. Excluding the digging under the chancel, which would have cost another £100, the total estimate was £535, its heaviest items the iron ties for the tower (£150), and altering the galleries (£100). The Vestry, having approved the findings, imposed a 6d in the pound rate (shortly raised to 9d) to pay for the work. The contract was given to Benjamin Williams (March 1787). During the repairs the church was closed for five months.

When the work started Nathaniel Clarkson, a 30-year-old local artist, offered to present a painting to replace the East window, the subject being the Annunciation, with "emblems of the law and the Gospel" in chiaroscuro on either side. His offer was gratefully accepted with a formal vote of thanks, a courtesy which only then, towards the end of the century, became regular practice.

Curiously, the vestry minutes are completely silent over the most spectacular aspect of the church repairs, which was an extraordinary device used to protect the spire during works. This was the creation of a basket maker named Thomas Birch, and was a kind of woven scaffold of wicker-work, made of willow, hazel and other limber branches, wrapped round the whole of the temple-structure, dome and spire in tapering stages and encircled by an external flight of steps. The builders carried on the work inside this basket-like attachment. It cost nearly £800, but Thomas Birch was paid a mere £20 for his ingenuity.

According to the *European Magazine* (LII, 338), quoted by Nelson in his *History* (312, n.l), Sir William Staines, a former Alderman, had invented this form of scaffolding, first used on the repairs to St Bride's spire when conventional scaffolding poles were blown down. Birch then used the contrivance on the steeple at St Albans, and it was "brought to the greatest perfection by him at Islington".[14]

While Birch's fee was modest, his personal takings were apparently generous, since the curious contraption was advertised in the newspapers, bringing not only locals to see it but visitors from other parts of London and from neighbouring villages.

VICARS

The Rev. Sir Gilbert Williams, unlike his predecessor, continued as vicar of Islington until his death in 1767. He was followed briefly by the Rev. Richard Smith who died and was buried in Islington in 1772, and then by the much more distinguished Rev. George Strahan.

Strahan, born in 1744, was, like George Stonehouse, a young man when he came to Islington, and like Stonehouse, he had famous connections, but unlike him enjoyed celebrity rather than notoriety. Through his father William, a successful Scottish printer who had settled in London and printed Dr Johnson's *Dictionary*, he knew not only Johnson but Benjamin Franklin as well. Strahan was educated at University College, Oxford, taking his MA the year before his appointment to St Mary's, Islington in 1772. Continuing in the pluralist tradition of his predecessors, he also became rector of two Essex villages, Prebendary of Rochester (1818), and rector of Kingsdown (1820). His philanthropy is underlined by his association with Benjamin Franklin, whose benefactions he evidently shared. (*See Chapter 12.*)

Like his father, Strahan was a friend of Dr Johnson, who used to visit him at his Islington vicarage. The great man was actually staying at Strahan's house for a few days during his last illness in 1784. Boswell in his *Life of Johnson* records returning from Edinburgh in May, when Johnson was temporarily recovered from dropsy, "I but just saw him for a coach was waiting to carry him to Islington, to the house of his friend the Reverend Mr Strahan, where he went sometimes for the benefit of good air, which ... he now acknowledges was conducive to health."

After Johnson's death Boswell notes that Strahan "had been always one of his great favourites", and in that last illness "had ...the satisfaction of contributing to soothe and comfort him. That gentleman's house at Islington ... afforded occasionally and easily an agreeable change of place and fresh air; and he attended also upon Johnson in town in the discharge of the sacred offices of his profession."

Being with Johnson at the end, Strahan reassured Boswell "that after being in much agitation, Johnson became quite composed, and continued so till his death". He was a witness to Johnson's will on 8 December 1784. In a codicil, among numerous small bequests of books, and in contrast to the others who mostly got one book each, was left a much larger collection: "Hill's Greek Testament, Beza's Greek Testament by Stephens, all my Latin Bibles, and my Greek Bible by Wechelius".[15]

The young rector was also in part Johnson's literary executor, publishing his *Prayers and Meditations* in 1785 from material which Johnson had personally given him.

The Reverend George Strahan served as vicar in Islington for more than 50 years and died at the age of 80 in 1824.

DISSENTERS [16]

In great contrast to what was to happen in the 19th century, in the 18th a mere handful of Dissenting chapels or meeting-houses came into being in Islington and Clerkenwell.

London's first Methodist preaching-house was Wesley's 'Foundery', a ruined gun-foundry which his supporters repaired and opened in 1739. It was replaced by a purpose-built chapel only in 1777–8, the one which, though much altered, survives in the City Road to this day. Wesley's own house along-side the present chapel was the first of several to be built in 1779; others built slightly later were demolished. The Foundery chapel was enlarged in the middle and later 19th century, gutted by fire and eventually rebuilt in 1899, containing some of the original seats.

George Whitefield's Tabernacle of 1752–3, in what was then appropriately named Tabernacle Row (now Leonard Street), also replaced an earlier, wooden building. Though described by one critic as "a mass of architectural deformity", it was a model for his later chapel in Tottenham Court Road. It was rebuilt in 1868 and closed in 1958.[17]

While the Wesley brothers and Whitefield were based in Clerkenwell, other Dissenters were settling in Islington in the 1740s, though the great migration of Dissenters and their ministers was happening meanwhile in nearby Stoke Newington. Islington's earliest purpose-built chapel was 'The Meeting', at the corner of Lower Street and Green Man's Lane. It was the work of the Independents, predecessors of the Congregationalists, in 1744, replacing a house which they had been able to license for meetings the previous year. This, and the Methodists' establishments in Clerkenwell, long existed in isolation. Initially The Meeting was very simple: plain brick with a pantiled roof and a side wing containing a small vestry room. Pulpit and desk were placed on the long (east) side, and it had no galleries until 1768. The Meeting was enlarged and improved in the early 1820s.[18]

A generation passed between the first Wesley/Whitefield chapels and the next Methodist establishment when, in 1779, the Countess of Huntingdon took over the grandiose Pantheon after it had failed as a pleasure-dome. Her Spa Fields chapel was in use until 1886, when Exmouth Street was curtailed for the building of Rosebery Avenue, and then rebuilt as the Church of the Holy Redeemer, while the Huntingdon connection moved to a new chapel in Lloyd Square.

Islington's three other chapels of this period were of different denominations. St James's Pentonville, built on Henry Penton's land, was conceived in 1777 as an Anglican chapel-of-ease for Clerkenwell. Although Penton succeeded in having a clause inserted in the Paving Act which encouraged such a building to serve his new estate of Pentonville, disagreement over the vicar's stipend delayed progress for ten years. It was built only in 1787–8 by Aaron Hirst, one of the proprietors, and though conforming to Anglican rites, not being on the Establishment it ranked as a Non-conformist chapel. Eventually disgruntled locals succeeded in ending this anomaly by persuading the Church Commissioners to buy out the proprietors and acquire the building as an Anglican church. It was consecrated in July 1791, and then did indeed serve as chapel-of-ease for St James's Clerkenwell.

In Islington parish itself there were two chapels other than the Lower Street meeting-house. The first was the inspiration of a blacksmith, John Ives, a devotee of the preacher Jeremiah Garrett. The two of them set up a chapel in Church Street (now Gaskin Street) off Upper Street. The building, begun in 1788, plain and almost barn-like, took five years to complete. It was said to be partly built of stone quarried from the old Clerkenwell church, just demolished and rebuilt. In 1793 it was leased by George Welch of Colebrooke Row, who then let it to a relative of the Countess of Huntingdon, Thomas Wills, who had been a minister in her church. In 1800 it was taken over by the Rev. Evan Jones and was the forerunner of the chapel built in Upper Street in 1814–15 (subse-

23. The original Islington Chapel.

quently rebuilt in 1867).[19]

Lastly came a small venture which was to launch a long and distinguished history. About 1793 a celebrated preacher, the Rev. Hugh Worthington, living in Highbury Place and then minister of Salters' Hall in the City, opened a small meeting house in rural Highbury Grove. This closed after only three years, and in 1799 the building was taken over by local evangelicals and reopened as the 'Union Church', so named as being an ecumenical group. The venture thrived so well that the building soon became too small, and in 1806 they built Union Chapel in the new Compton Terrace. The Highbury Grove building was converted to become a house (no.18 Highbury Grove). From such small beginnings great developments followed. [20]

1   Except where otherwise stated, this chapter section is based on the Vestry Minutes, Vol. II; on George Whitefield's *Journal of a Voyage from London to Savannah, 1737*; and *The Journal of the Rev. John Wesley, A.M.*, ed. Nehemiah Curnock, London, 1909 edn, Vol. I, pp. 453-60 and Vol. II, pp. 77-390, *passim*. See also Frank Baker, *John Wesley and the Church of England*, London, Epworth Press, 1970, pp. 18ff.

2   This section is based on the Vestry Minutes, Vols. II and III.

3   Badly damaged in the Second World War, it was restored in 2002 and is now used by the London Symphony Orchestra.

4   Destroyed during the Second World War.

5   Also destroyed during the Second World War.

6   Howard Colvin, *A Biographical Dictionary of British Architects, 1600-1840*, London, John Murray, 3rd edn, 1995, p. 980 (Timbrell), 920 (Steer).

7   Nelson, *Islington*, p. 289.

8   Nelson, *Islington*, p. 291 and VM, Vol. III.

9   Colvin, *British Architects*, p. 321.

10   Nelson, *Islington*, pp. 309-10.

11   Nelson, *Islington*, p. 312.

12   VM, Vol. III, 3 August 1753. Much of the rest of this Section is based on Vol. III of the Vestry Minutes.

13   The danger of being struck by lightning was thus the greater, as had happened to St Bride's Church in the City in 1764. Mylne's own diaries, mere notebook entries as an aide-memoire, reveal that he attended a "Board" in Islington on their new fire engine on 27 June 1786 and on 29 August "Waited on the vestry of Islington Parish when the works to be done were finally settled and explanation given". Of his final report, on 16 September when he was also concerned with the embankment of the New River at Bush Hill (replacing the old Boarded River), he records: "Wrote out for Islington Church, particulars of electric rods, and corrected Mr Reynold's draft for the other work." (Robert Mylne, MS Diaries).

14   Nelson, *Islington*, p. 286.

15   James Boswell, *The Life of Samuel Johnson*, Folio Society, 1968, Vol. II, pp. 502, 596-7, 591.

16   For much of this Section I am indebted to Philip Temple's invaluable *Islington Chapels*, Royal Commission on the Historical Monuments of England, 1992.

17   It is now the Central Foundation School for Boys. See Temple, *Islington Chapels*, p. 43.

18   The Chapel closed in 1864 when the congregation moved to River Place, and the Green Man pub (no. 144A Essex Road) was built on its site. *Islington Chapels*, p. 121.

19   The rebuilt Islington Chapel in Upper Street of 1887 closed in 1979 and became a recording studio. The Gaskin Street chapel became a school, then a memorial hall, then served baser uses as a skating rink and a factory and was demolished in the 1970s. (*Islington Chapels*, pp. 72-73, 122) (*See Chapter 27*).

20   Temple, *Islington Chapels*, pp. 82-3.

CHAPTER 9

Still Merrier

Apart from the important change in Islington's aspect brought by rebuilding the medieval church, the chief interest in the parish in the later 18th century was undoubtedly its social life centring on its now numerous pleasure gardens.

In the decade after the new church was completed, Sadler's Wells itself set a new phase when it was rebuilt as a theatre in 1765. By the mid-18th century the pleasure garden/tea-house craze was in full swing on the fringes of London generally and round Islington particularly. Samuel Lewis in his *History* describes the favourite outing on a Sunday after church and dinner, to "regale .... with buns and beer at Islington". Sometimes, too, one would breakfast out. He also relates how, going north from Clerkenwell, one could pass in a single walk (if in rather an odd order) Walter Baynes's Cold Bath, the Lord Cobham's Head, the Sir John Oldcastle, both near the corner of Coppice or less genteelly Codpiece Row; then past the Ducking Pond on New River land. Continuing towards Islington were the London Spa, the New Wells, Mulberry Garden, Shakespeare Head and Jubilee Gardens, then the fashionable New Tunbridge Wells or Islington Spa, and near it Sir Hugh Myddelton's Head, Farthing Pie House (named quite literally), and Sadler's Wells. To one's left were Merlin's Cave, Bagnigge Wells, the English Grotto, and farther uphill, White Conduit House. Though strictly in Clerkenwell, these were mostly on the border with Islington proper.

The radical tailor-reformer Francis Place, who was born in 1771, relates rather disap-provingly in his autobiography how his father – a *bon viveur* and lecher who (Place suggests) ought to have been saving their money – used often on a Sunday afternoon to join those who "drink tea smoke and indulge themselves in liquor". His father's favourite resort was the rural Bagnigge Wells in King's Cross Road, where he often took the whole family, though sometimes much farther afield to Hornsey Wood, Winchmore Hill, Clapham Common or even Wimbledon: "The smaller children were dragged along in a child's chaise. A bottle of wine was always put into the seat of the chaise … sometimes provisions for the day … These journeys were to me excessively fatiguing" (everyone had to share in dragging the chaise). Yet he admits he did enjoy them.

Later, as an apprentice in the 1780s, Place himself frequented resorts such as White Conduit House, one of the many which he recalls (in the 1840s) "in a state utterly indescribable now for the public sight". Yet ten years later again, married and with two children, on fine Sundays he and his family often walked to White Conduit House and beyond through the fields to Copenhagen House, both very crowded on a Sunday. "We carried the children nearly the whole of the way and returned as we went never spending a single halfpenny."[1]

By the 1770s there were so many resorts in and round London that Elizabeth, 1st Duchess of Northumberland, in 1773 felt it necessary to list all places of pleasure, including theatres, in her diary (first mentioning the licensed theatres Drury Lane and Covent Garden). She leads off with the Islington area: "Sadler's

Wells, Bagnigge, Battle Bridge; Dog & Duck, Islington" before continuing with other famous haunts: "Vaux Hall, Cupers Gardens, Grotto, Ranelagh". Next she lists Marylebone Gardens, Astley's, Almack's (surely a grand odd one out here), then back to "Pantheon, Mobs, Do. in Spaw Fields". She even listed available lectures, exhibitions, including one on stained glass, "Mrs Wrights Figures, Wildman's Bees, besides Wild Beasts in every Street in Town, The Royal Academy Exhibition ..." And so on.[2]

Pierre Chantreau, a Frenchman visiting England in 1788 and 1789, bestowed elegant praise on the pleasure resorts. *"Le nombre en est prodigieux dans les environs ...Dessinés, plantés, distribués avec autant de gout que d'intelligence, quelques uns retracent, en petit, le Ranelagh ou le Vauxhall."* Furthermore, *"Le propreté, la promptitude avec lesquelles on est servi et qui n'appartiennent qu'aux Anglois, la société toujours numbreuse quel'on y trouve, rendent ces endroits recommandables et précieux pour l'étranger."* Although he does admit that one would not expect to see *"les gens de bon ton"*, and that *"ladies"* – that is real ones – would only visit incognito. Chantreau too includes White Conduit House and Bagnigge Wells in a list of five *"les plus fréquentés"* scattered across London.[3] So the standard both of resorts and clientele was varied enough.

An unidentified cutting of 1789 in Place's collection estimates that on Sundays, of the many who visited such gardens were "sober, 50,000; in high glee, 90,000; drunkish, 30,000; dead drunk, 5,000; – total 200, 000." (sic)

Closest together were the north Clerkenwell group, extending southwards towards the City and north towards and even past the Angel. This area of fields had been from time past studded with "open idle pools", some used as ducking ponds, and some now forming adornment to the gardens. The whole New River estate remained fields until after the turn of the 19th century. From the humble cake house at the foot of the lane towards the City (which later became Amwell Street), to Merlin's Cave, the English Grotto, New Wells and others, small resorts were often cheek by jowl with larger, more ambitious establishments.

DOBNEY'S, BUSBY'S & THE THREE HATS [4]

A favourite among entertainments of earlier origin, on the brow of Islington Hill (Pentonville Hill as it became), was Dobney's, the former 'Prospect House' – for obvious reasons, with its fine view across to the City. Until Pentonville was built in the 1770s, carriage access was for decades only by Islington High Street through the gate of the White Lion, and thence down the hill.

In 1718 its greens were advertised "for the accommodation of all gentlemen bowlers"; and when later it was run by a Frenchman named D'Aubigny, his name was anglicised as Dobney's Bowling Green House. After his widow, who died aged about 90 in 1760, a Mr Johnson took it over as Johnson's Prospect House. He evidently had ambitious ideas and in 1767 engaged a famous equestrian performer named Price. According to one version Price had been a show-rider at the Three Hats north of the Angel, and was said to have performed at some time before the King. A poster of about 1767 shows vignettes of his exploits, standing on horseback, hanging over the saddle, and riding two or perhaps three horses at once. These entertainments started at 6 o'clock in the season, and from performances here and elsewhere Price was said to have made a fortune of some £14,000. In 1769 there were varieties such as Philip Jonas, a juggler, and an exhibition of a 60-foot-long skeleton of a whale.

After a brief spell in 1770 as a boarding-school run by the Rev. John Davis, entertainment resumed under the name Jubilee Gardens (recalling David Garrick's Shakespeare Jubilee in 1769) and newly equipped with boxes and a gallery. Here in 1772 the remarkable Daniel Wildman, a bee-keeper who ran a 'Bee and Honey Warehouse' at 326 Holborn, supplying bees to the nobility and gentry, turned his skill to public account in a hybrid show, 'Bees on Horseback'. Standing astride, his face covered by a mask of bees and, it was claimed, holding the bridle in his mouth, he fired a gun to alert certain bees to 'march' across a table, while the rest swarmed in the air, then both sets returned to his face. For this daunting sight one paid a shilling, or two shillings for a seat.

During the 1770s the fame of the place declined, its gardens were neglected and untrimmed, though the adjoining house north of the bowling-green had a couple of tea-rooms, and was let out as apartments. It was said to be a popular Sunday goal for fatigued "'prentice beaux and belles", leaving the dust of London for tea, syllabubs or ale at Dobney's (as it was often still known).

More changes followed. A tradition was established in 1780 of holding debates and lectures in the house, by then called the Shakespeare Tavern and Jubilee Gardens; but only a year later the whole place was auctioned – house, kitchens and bakehouse and two dining-room outbuildings, each holding up to 200, not to mention the large gardens, bowling green, and trap-ball ground.

By this time Pentonville, a suburb in the country, had been created, and the establishment no longer prospered. In about 1790 Winchester Place (part of Pentonville Road) was built, encroaching on house and ground, though a part remained as gardens until finally built over in 1810.

A nearby resort, similarly dating from the 17th century in a series of guises was Busby's Folly. Christopher Busby was landlord of the White Lion in Islington High Street in 1668 and at his Folly (at the corner of today's Penton Street and Pentonville Road) a curious fraternity met, the Society of Bull Feathers Hall. Here too was a bowling-green. From 1731 it was known as Penny's Folly, and from 1769 became popular under a German, Zucker, for a composite upstairs show of 'the Learned Little Horse', which answered set questions presumably by a neigh or a stamp of the hoof. Zucker's wife played the musical glasses, and the "admired and unparalleled Mr Jonas" exhibited unspecified "matchless and curious deceptions" – doubtless the same magician who performed at Dobney's. To attract audiences, before the show started at 6.30 the Little Horse was advertised as "looking out of the windows up two pair of stairs".

There were also gardens, but the show place was the large room with 14 windows where performances took place. A versifier in 1762 claimed that Zucker had already made his name elsewhere before taking over Penny's Folly, and that Greenwich Park, White Conduit House and Chelsea all paled before his "amazing" show.

24. The Three Hats.

The house, like Dobney's with its splendid view, was pulled down by 1780, possibly because Zucker died, and the appropriately named Belvidere Tavern was built in its place with a famous history of its own.[5]

The Three Hats was just in Islington, an inn by the High Street and next to where the Pied Bull at the corner of Liverpool Road now stands (itself now renamed All Bar One). It was a fairly latecomer, where from 1758 in a field behind the inn, the exploits of another pioneer equestrian performer, Thomas Johnson, might be seen, displaying his skills standing, progressing from one horse to two, then three. An experiment of standing on his head while riding had to be abandoned, apparently because it "distressed" the audience. He later joined Price at Dobney's, but seems also to have continued at the Three Hats, where it is recorded that in the summer of 1766 he performed before the Duke of York (not to mention 504 others).

His successor in 1767 was Sampson, in a 5 o'clock performance with "a proper band of music". He was soon joined by his wife, "to prove that the fair sex are by no means inferior to the male, either in courage or agility", as he invited the gentry to witness. At least by the following year the place was well enough known to be quoted in Isaac Bickerstaffe's comedy, *The Hypocrite*, where Mawworm confesses to being a reformed tearaway whose expeditions included regular visits to the Three Hats. Not perhaps an advertisement for respectability.

In 1770 Sampson's act was accompanied by a 4-o'clock match of Double Stick, a "renowned manly diversion" between teams of young West Countrymen, "those who bear away the most heads" to win two guineas. This time Sampson and a German assistant performed before the match. In 1771, however, he was persuaded by Price of Dobney's to sell his horses to a rider named Coningham who performed for two seasons.

In his *History* Nelson gives a circumstantial and perhaps partly apocryphal account of the relationship between Sampson and Price, describing it as a bitter rivalry. One of them, presumably Sampson, took on a "female of dashing appearance and some personal attractions" whom he sent to watch Price's act, by implication as a lure, because the two supposedly fell in love or, as Nelson delicately puts it, formed "an intimate connexion", adding still more delicately that as a result Price found himself "unable to perform feats of horsemanship" and had to give up, leaving the other without a rival. This may well be a fabrication, though Nelson's assertion that the two riders preceded Astley and Hughes as the first equestrian performers in England is probably true.[6]

An advertisement describes Coningham's programme in detail: first a gallop round the field three times standing and without reins; next, dismounting while riding to fire a pistol, then leaping back and forth over the horse some 40 times; then he would "fly" over three horses at speed and (the account becomes muddled with enthusiasm here), leaping over one, then two horses as *they* leapt over a bar, and playing the flute while standing free on two horses. He was joined by the Sampsons, husband and wife, who were evidently still not quite horseless, and a "Mr Brown, &c",

thus making the show "the completest in the kingdom". This 5 o'clock performance cost two shillings for front seats, one for back. Almost as an afterthought it was boasted that Coningham would "fly through a hogshead of fire upon two horses' backs, without touching them".

The wonders continued. Sampson returned in 1772 both as performer and riding master when the 'Hats' became a riding school (advertised along with Astley's and Hughes'). But perhaps the horses were losing their individual attraction, for at Whitsun 1772 as a contrast "a young gentleman" was advertised as picking up 100 eggs, placed a yard apart, within an hour and a quarter, and putting them in a basket, replacing any which he broke, all for a 10 guineas wager. The day after, a group of "smart girls" was to run six times round the riding school for a prize of a holland shift.

This seems to have signalled the end of the horses, and the Three Hats continued as a teagarden until, like everywhere else in the area, it was overrun by houses. In 1779 the constables arrested and took to Clerkenwell Bridewell "upwards of twenty fellows who were dancing with their ladies", apparently to press them into the army.

WATERING PLACES

In the 1740s we hear little of the famous Islington Spa, but after 1750 for some twenty years plenty of visitors lodging there or nearby seem to have taken the waters. "A very pretty Romantick place", wrote a young lady visitor to her family in 1753, though the water, which resembled those of Bath, "makes one vastly cold and Hungry". Luckily the public breakfasts continued, followed by afternoon dancing between 11 and 3, for which one paid 1s 6d. Unlike some places it maintained a reputation of respectability by excluding doubtful characters. The dancing blended oddly with the recommendations to visitors suffering from gout, rheumatism or other stiffness of the joints, and 'nerves'.

An analysis of the water in 1733 by Dr Russel had declared it to contain iron which could cause giddiness unless drunk with ordinary spring water – as indeed Lady Mary Wortley

Montagu had found.

In 1770 John Holland took over and introduced a morning band recital. Though also popular as a 'genteel' tea-garden the Islington Spa was apparently so only in the bourgeois sense, and its status dwindled, becoming local and citified. In any case in 1777 Holland became bankrupt and next year John Howard, who took over, added a bowling-green on the St John Street side. Following or perhaps initiating the example of culture set by Dobney's, he introduced a series of Lent lectures on astronomy, illustrated with an orrery. Howard maintained the music in the morning and sometimes (with tea) in the afternoon, until the end of the century after which the fashion for such resorts began to wane.

This decline in popularity also affected the Pantheon, one of the cluster of entertainments round Spa Fields on the edge of the Northampton estate. Here were the famous London Spa, the New Wells and the English Grotto; and here too, adjoining an inn, was one of the local 'ducking ponds' (south of what was to become Exmouth Street) – perhaps even the one Samuel Pepys visited as a boy with his father.

The Pantheon, which did not open until 1770, was thus late in the canon, if spectacular enough in appearance to have promised success. It was a rotunda, centred on a vast stove and circled by two galleries – in fact in layout not unlike the famous Ranelagh Gardens in Chelsea. It was built and its garden laid out by a tavern-keeper named William Craven at a cost of £6,000.

The Pantheon was near enough to the City to attract tradesmen, their journeymen and apprentices, as well as maidservants, especially on their only free day, Sunday. Like the White Conduit House and Bagnigge Wells it boasted an organ, but the local Justices soon forbade its performance on the Sabbath. The usual refreshments were served. In spite of limiting the sale of drinks after ten at night, it seems to have acquired a fairly unsavoury reputation, with 'ladies' accosting visiting men (so a journalist claimed) with the harmless sounding request for "a dish of tea". At the rear was a four-acre garden, with the usual walks, seats, shrubberies and fruit-trees, a summer-house, pond and a paltry

pretence at a 'canal'. But accounts by visitors are usually tinged with scorn, and after a mere four years, in spite of high attendance, Craven was declared bankrupt.

Apart from its remarkable appearance, the Spa Fields Pantheon's chief claim to notice is its later history. In 1779 it was taken over by the devout Selina, Countess of Huntingdon, friend of the Methodists. She renamed it the Spa Fields Chapel and converted the adjoining tavern as her house.

PLEASURE GROUNDS

Among the leading pleasure gardens, and at this time the most northerly of this group, was the White Conduit, on the top of Islington Hill with views towards Highgate and Hampstead. It too had a 17th-century origin as a wayside alehouse, traditionally built by men who used to drink by the hilltop spring which had supplied the Charterhouse. The conduit itself was in the field opposite the alehouse, as early drawings show.

Nearly a century later it was still a humble, low building, but some time in the 1730s or so it was rebuilt and given the 'Long Room' which so many resorts demanded. Its garden was laid out from about 1745 with arbours and a fishpond. In 1754, probably until his death in 1766, the owner was Robert Bartholomew, who added a 'Long Walk' and screened visitors from "people in the fields" by building a wall seven feet high. Refreshments were tea, coffee, pure milk direct from the cow, and unspecified "liquors", supplemented apparently by little more than hot loaves, but these were famous, and were cried in the streets until the demise of the place about 1825.

Cricket was played in an adjoining field (see ill. 18), bats and balls provided, and continued as long as the area was still free of building (until the 1820s). In about 1784 it boasted a "club of gentlemen", whom a print shows playing with the then contemporary equipment. When the land was eventually built up, the club moved to Marylebone to become Lord's and the Marylebone Cricket Club.

The Long Room had an organ and advertised its "most copious prospects", but like most of

25. The White Conduit House, published in 1819.

the local resorts the White Conduit House was never fashionable, claiming a respectability of the sort which evoked patronising comments from journalists for its popularity as a City Sunday outing, especially at about 5 o'clock.

> Now the heart
> Of 'prentice, resident in ample street,
> Or alley, kennel-wash'd, Cheapside, Cornhill ...
> His meal meridian o'er
> With switch in hand, he to White Conduit House
> Hies merry-hearted.

A description of the crowds follows, including families with children and dogs adorning "fair Islington's plains", "prig with prig" and "the gaudy beau, And sloven mix", the workaday drudge, hairdresser, wig-maker, cattle keeper who strut with "gold-bound hat And silken stocking". And a final scornful compliment:

> The red-arm'd belle
> Here shows her tasty gown, proud to be thought
> The butterfly of fashion.[7]

This was where the impecunious young Oliver Goldsmith, in his late 20s in about 1768, though already famed for his *Citizen of the World* and *The Vicar of Wakefield*, was one Sunday embarrassed on meeting and treating the family of a rich tradesman to whom he was in some way indebted, only to find an empty purse when it came to paying the waiter. (There the anecdote tantalisingly ends.)[8]

Later White Conduit House was frequented by the chief Cashier of the Bank of England, Abraham Newland, who commuted between the City and his fine new house in Highbury Place; and later still by George Cruikshank, who scared visitors by satirising them in his sketches.

By 1774 the gardens were admired for their walks, central pond and avenue and its alcoved hedges adorned with "genteel boxes" for tea-drinkers. Like the boxes at Vauxhall they were fronted with so-called Flemish paintings, while another painting formed a *trompe l'oeil* at the end of the grounds.

By the 1790s the owner was Christopher Bartholomew, presumably Robert's son (born about 1741), who, before selling on in March

91

1795, further improved the gardens. At the height of his prosperity he owned both White Conduit House and the Angel Inn, and was said to be worth £50,000. On one occasion he celebrated winning a lottery by giving a public breakfast in the gardens. But the lottery was eventually his downfall: he lost his fortune, and died poor in lodgings in March 1809. His former haunt, the White Conduit, survived him for another generation.

THE LONDON SPA & BAGNIGGE WELLS

Of the many pleasure gardens on the borders of Clerkenwell and Islington which burgeoned from simple beginnings, among the most famous were Bagnigge Wells and the London Spa. The latter, on the corner of what became Rosoman and Exmouth Streets, seems to have faded into obscurity after John Halhed's grandiose launch in 1685 – surely no coincidence that several chalybeate or 'medicinal' springs were discovered in that area at much the same time. It was probably frequented by the poor and humble, and in 1714 was certainly going through a time of neglect; but in 1720 it was in favour again, with popular arbours of jasmine and shady trees, ninepins and skittles and now frequented by "numerous blended companies". Opening like most places in the spring, on May-Day it was the haunt of milkmaids and their lovers, dancing to a fiddler. An illustration of the time shows dancing in a ring beside the gabled, weather-boarded, lattice-windowed inn, a tempting avenue stretching in alluring distance towards the horizon of hills (or more likely ambiguous clouds).

For Londoners pure spring water was probably almost as much a draw as ale, though the Spaw's home-brew was popular, for which as *Poor Robin's Almanack* describes in 1733:

Sweethearts with their sweethearts go
To Islington or London Spaw.

In Spa Fields a fair was held for the many Welsh living in these parts, for which in 1754 George Dodswell, then landlord, advertised "the usual" roast pork and "the oft-famed flavoured Spaw ale". And as in several hostelries, tokens were issued in lieu of coins.

The London Spa's subsequent fame seems to have been as an inn, as it remained until recently, though rebuilt in the 19th century and again 100 years later. Now a tapas bar, its historic name has regrettably been changed to 'Don Pedro'.

More ambitious and even more celebrated, Bagnigge Wells was in the vale of the Fleet at Bagnigge Wash, actually just over the border in St Pancras parish. (Its odd name perhaps stems, like other Bag- names, from a Saxon named Bacga, or from some word meaning a small animal, like a badger). It was an old house, but as a pleasure garden a late foundation. The house was associated with Nell Gwynne who was supposed to have had it as a sheltered summer place. It was also associated with a nearby old inn named the Pindar of Wakefield, enshrined on the Bagnigge gateway by a stone reading

S T
THIS IS BAGNIGGE
HOUSE NEARE
THE PINDAR A
WAKEFIELDE
1680

(The stone survives today on the wall of 62–63 King's Cross Road.)

Not until 1757 were the properties of its well water discovered, when the then tenant Mr Hughes, a keen gardener, being unfavourably impressed by the condition of the plants which he watered from his garden wells, asked a doctor John Bevis for an analysis. Bevis diagnosed in one the inevitable chalybeate content and the other as having cathartic properties, valued for reasons other than gardening. By the spring of 1759 Hughes had cashed in on the discovery and opened the gardens to the public, the next year publishing a pamphlet on its virtues. One of the 40-foot-deep wells was behind the house, which adjoined the road, the other 40 yards north. Water from both was channelled to a double pump over which was built a small pillared, domed 'temple'. The chalybeate water sometimes induced giddiness, as the young Miss had found at Islington Spa, while the cathartic or purgative water was brackish and bitter. Mercifully, three half-pints were reckoned

26. Entertainments at Bagnigge Wells in 1772.

enough. To drink it one paid 3d, or half a guinea for a season ticket. Later, when tea-gardens were the attraction the fee was raised to 6d.

The dimensions of the obligatory Long Room were 78 x 28 feet; it was converted from the panelled and low-ceilinged banqueting hall of the old house. Over one chimney-piece was a sculptural survival, a garter of the Order of St George, over another a circular niche with the bust of a woman in Roman dress, supposed to be Nell Gwynne, bordered with festoons of fruit and flowers. Less happily, among the added features was a distorting mirror at one end, and at the other an organ played in the afternoons by one Charley Griffith. There was also, in the grounds, a water organ. After 1772 neither instrument was allowed to be played on the Sabbath.

Bagnigge Wells remained popular for about 40 years, until almost the end of the 18th century. The disgusting waters were taken in the mornings by perhaps a couple of hundred people and, more palatably, breakfast was served. Tea was taken in the afternoons in the Long Room, and negus, a hot beverage of claret or port and water, sweetened and with lemon juice and nutmeg, was a popular drink.

Here too the versifiers quickly went to work:

> Ye gouty old souls, and rheumaticks crawl on,
> Here taste these blest springs, and your tortures
>   are gone...
> Obey the glad summons, to Bagnigge repair,
> Drink deep of its streams, and forget all your care.[9]

A later verse defines the social context:

> Bon Ton's the space 'twixt Saturday and Monday,
> And riding in a one-horse chair on Sunday;
> 'Tis drinking tea on summer afternoons,
> At Bagnigge Wells with chayney and gilt spoons.[10]

Yet Bagnigge Wells was perhaps less 'respectable' than some of the others and was patronised by pickpockets and highwaymen living it up. The most famous was Sixteen

String Jack – namely John Rann, a favourite with the ladies and admired by Dr Johnson. Acquitted on some charge by Sir John Fielding in 1774, who besought him to reform, Rann appeared the very next Sunday at the Wells in scarlet coat, tambour waistcoat, white silk stockings and laced hat, sporting the bunch of eight ribbons on either knee which had won him his nickname. But the visitors took such offence at his presence that he was thrown out of a Long Room window. Four months later he was hanged at Tyburn for robbing Princess Amelia's chaplain, Dr William Bell.

In the gardens behind the house and the Long Room, besides the domed temple for the pumps and the water organ there were walks, box and holly hedges, trees, flowerbeds, ponds with goldfish and silver fish and one with a statue of Cupid riding a swan, its beak forming a fountain. Between the east and larger west gardens ran the Fleet River, crossed by three bridges and lined with natural foliage of willows, shrubs and meadow plants, with seats for smokers and drinkers not allowed elsewhere. Hidden among the trees were two rustic lead statues. There were arbours all round trailing honeysuckle and briar, a rustic cottage, and a grotto built like a two-storey castle, lined with shells, fossils and scraps of glass. Finally there were a bowling-green and skittle alley. By 1791 a bun-house had been built near the mansion. Altogether a delightful retreat whose loss we must mourn.

At that time the Wells were run by John Davis, Hughes's successor, until his death in 1793. It was still visited by apprentices and small tradesmen and their wives, though there were also young Templars and junior officers. Still the verses flowed like the fountains and the Fleet.

"Come prithee make it up Miss, and be as lovers be", sings a 'prentice trying to tempt his love after a tiff:

> We'll go to Bagnigge Wells, Miss, and there we'll
>   have some tea,
> It's there you'll see the lady-birds, perched on the
>   stinging nettles,
> The crystal water-fountain, and the copper shining
>   kettles …

Not to mention the gold and silver fish which, he repeats alluringly, "wags their little tails".

So far the decline was not very great, but after the century ended there was to be a distinct change in tone.

CANONBURY TAVERN

In contrast with Clerkenwell, Islington proper had few resorts to show. Even the White Conduit House was strictly just in Clerkenwell. Its chief boasts were Canonbury Tavern, Copenhagen House and later, Highbury Barn.

The least pretentious was probably Canonbury House tea garden, adjoining the park of Canonbury manor house. The Tower was let as lodgings at least by 1740 (when Ephraim Chambers the encyclopaedist died there) and accommodated such young Inns of Court members as Oliver Goldsmith from 1762–4, and much later American visitors, notably Washington Irving. But in the 1750s, before anyone had thought of surrounding the ancient house with desirable villas, Benjamin Collins[11] built an inconsiderable alehouse to the east, which later, under James Lane, once 'a common soldier', acquired outbuildings which included the mansion's former stables. It now became a secluded tea-garden, also known as Canonbury House, run by a Mr Sutton after Lane died in 1783, and by Sutton's widow on his death soon afterwards. She again greatly enlarged the place and organised more corporate, parochial and club dinners (says Lewis) than almost any other London tavern.

Renamed Canonbury Tavern, or Canonbury House Tavern, it also had a bowling-green and improved gardens covering four acres, still within the precincts of the estate, with fields beyond. Indeed it was praised in the *Sunday Ramble* in 1797 as "a place of decent retreat for tea and sober treatment". It was surely frequented by those summer lodgers at the tower. So quiet was it that it hardly figures in records. In early Victorian times it was rebuilt as a tavern on the north side of Canonbury Place.

COPENHAGEN HOUSE

By far the most westerly of Islington's resorts was Copenhagen House, in the fields north of Maiden Lane. Perched on its hilltop (the eventual site of the cattle market in Market Road) it was visible for miles. It formed part of a country walk down to the vale and up again towards Hampstead.

It was a 17th-century house, held by some to have been built by a Dane accompanying the King of Denmark who visited James I in 1606, but stylistically more likely built about 1660. Certainly it had Danish associations, supposedly occupied as a refuge from the Plague by the Danish Ambassador in 1665,[12] and is shown on a map in the 1695 edition of Camden's *Britannia*.

Early in the 18th century it seems to have been an inn, and before 1740 was an assembly place for what became the noted Highbury Society. This group of dissenters originated with the repeal of the Schism Bill, passed on the very day of Queen Anne's death in 1714. It

was a Tory bill aimed at preventing Dissenters from keeping academies and imposing other restrictions, and was repealed by the Whig Government under George I. Protestant nonconformists in the Islington area formed a society to celebrate its demise. They used to assemble on holidays at Moorfields and on the long walk to Copenhagen House amused themselves by bowling an ivory ball at different targets along the way.[13]

Copenhagen House came to notoriety in 1780 when its landlady, Mrs Harrington, was brutally robbed at the time of the Gordon Riots. A band of rioters passed the house on their way to attack Lord Mansfield's house at Kenwood; although they did not then attack Copenhagen House, Mrs Harrington and her maid sent off an alarm to Justice Hyde, who despatched a party of soldiers as garrison until the danger ceased. From their high situation above London the household witnessed as many as nine fires blazing in the capital.

William Hone gives a graphic account of the

27. Copenhagen House, drawn by T H Shepherd in 1853.

burglary by a gang of vandals. Three of them attacked the landlady in her bed with cutlass, crowbar and pistol, a fourth standing guard. They ransacked the drawers for money and threatened to murder the little daughter for crying. Then in an act of mindless destruction they ran off the barrels in the cellar and smashed the bottles, and even destroyed a round of beef – except of course for what they could eat and drink themselves. Returning to torment Mrs Harrington for more money and finding £50 hidden under her mattress, they were so enraged that they nearly cut her throat before making off with the money.

Rewards were offered, and a Clerkenwell watchmaker named Clarkson was arrested, who under promise of mercy ratted on his tradesmen companions. All were executed while he was pardoned. He was later hanged as a receiver of a stolen box of plate from Fetter Lane.

Luckily for Mrs Harrington, the notoriety the house enjoyed as a result of the affair soon compensated her, and her landlord Mr Leader remitted a year's rent of £30. He also exploited the occasion by demolishing an old timber building on the west side to build an upper Long Room for tea, with a lower room for drinkers and smokers.[14]

Copenhagen was also famed for the game of fives, which locally originated here in Mrs Harrington's time, and was described to William Hone by a Shropshire girl employee (later to be Mrs Tomes, landlady of the Adam and Eve, Islington), who first introduced it. She had become friendly with a Highgate butcher compatriot who used to visit the house, and in talking of their home sports they decided to play their own game of fives here. The girl personally not only "laid down the stone in the ground", but even made the special ball, and playing it together they aroused the interest of visitors. "It got talked of", she related, and was soon established as part of the house's fame. John Cavanagh, an Irish house-painter and a champion player, praised in a memoir by Hazlitt as best in the world, used to hold matches here for a dinner or a wager, appropriately playing against the kitchen chimney wall, which resounded so much that the cooks inside would stop and say, "Those are the Irishman's balls."[15]

In the 1790s the landlord was Robert Orchard, who in this time of political division over the French Revolution was a supporter of the London Corresponding Society which held meetings in the adjoining fields. In October 1795 they held a large gathering with several speakers, for whom platforms were set up. There was much talk and much acclamation, but perhaps little effect: an "Address to the Nation", a "Remonstrance to the King", who had ignored their previous address, and a few resolutions on "the state of affairs". Then they dispersed.[16]

Following Orchard was the more unsavoury Tooth, by contrast a backer of rough sports, especially dog-fights, whose disreputable owners assembled with up to 60 dogs, taking over the fives-court on a Sunday for matches watched over flowing pints. This and bull-baiting (the bulls were kept in the next field) carried on until stopped by the magistrates in the next century.

William Hone, invaluable recorder of minutiae, recalls that as a boy he used to wander here in the fields in summer "to frolic in the new-mown hay" and enjoy the hedgerows and birdsong, though he hardly ventured near the house with its outdoor drinking-benches because of the "boisterous company within". As Hone was born in 1780, this would probably be in the rowdy days of Mr Tooth.

In 1825, when already builders were encroaching northwards, Hone describes the house as still "alone in the fields, between Maiden Lane, the old road to Highgate on the west, and the very ancient north road, or bridle-way, called Hagbush lane, on the east". He notes that it is not listed in the 1624 rental of the manor of St John.[17]

HIGHBURY BARN

Highbury Barn originated from the manorial barn of the Priors of St John, which before 1740 had given way to a small cake-and-ale house of the same name. The Court Baron of Highbury or Newington Barrow manor long continued to be held here. Like many such places it was popular for its fine view of London and adjoining country. And like Bagnigge Wells it was frequented by Oliver

28. Highbury Barn, published in 1819.

Goldsmith and friends, as a country jaunt from their Temple quarters. Here they would find colleagues and fellow-scribblers, and could dine at one o'clock on two courses and a pastry for 10d each (including tip). At 6 they would go on to White Conduit House for tea, then sup at the Globe or Grecian to end the day's holiday.

In about 1740 the Highbury Society transferred their meeting-place here from Copenhagen House, thus acquiring their name.

In the 1770s the manor of Highbury was taken over from Sir George Colebrooke by John Dawes, a City stockbroker, who also lived at Canonbury House, and in both places it was Dawes who initiated development. From 1778 he began to enclose ground surrounding a landmark called Jack Straw's Castle for a park, and at a cost of nearly £10,000 in 1781 built the fine Highbury House where he lived until his death in 1788. It was then sold to Alexander Aubert, FRS. Highbury Barn tavern was opposite the house, and the tea-house with the usual bowling-green and trap-ball ground was sold with it. Known also as Willoughby's tea-rooms from its then landlord, it was further expanded by taking in Highbury Barn or Grange, including a large barn equipped to serve as a 'Great Room'.

Willoughby thus brought in new custom,

and after his death in December 1785 his son carried on until at least 1792, further expanding the garden and amusements and installing his own brewery.

This was an opportunity to cater for a local Assembly for the well-to-do locals now living in Highbury Place and Highbury Terrace, begun in 1774 by a London builder, John Spiller. The monthly meetings were held in winter and spring, besides vast dinners held for clubs and societies, particularly in later years.

Highbury was then barely a hamlet, and the few old buildings and the new Highbury House, standing at the crest of a slight rise, enjoyed the rural views for which many parts of Islington were famed. The famous days of Highbury Barn, however, belong to the 19th century.

Such other resorts as Islington boasted were humble and limited in scope. Nearest to Highbury Barn was the Devil's House, named from Duval's Lane (an alternative name for Tallington Lane) which derived from the famous highwayman Claude Duval. The house, weather-boarded and moated, was on the site of the former Tolentone manor-house. A landlord in 1767 who tried to change the name to the more seductive 'Summer House' opened the moat stocked with tench and carp to anglers, and also provided popular hot loaves and fresh milk as well as tea. It functioned as an inn until at least 1811, and the house survived at least until 1849.[18]

In the south, in Frog Lane (now Popham Road), was the Barley Mow, again a tavern in the 1790s which included a tea-house, later to be the haunt of the painter George Morland. Finally, the Rosemary Branch, a modest place of entertainment at the extreme eastern fringe of the parish. Though existing in the late 18th century, its story belongs rather to the 19th.

SADLER'S WELLS
Sadler's Wells is the only one of these establishments to have survived, though in a very different form, to this day. The younger Forcer (*see Chapter 7*) died in 1743, and by at least 1746 the proprietor was Thomas Rosoman, who commuted the admission price for gallery and pit for the cost of a pint of wine, while boxes paid half-a-crown, so that audiences were

smoking and drinking throughout performances. In 1753 Rosoman secured a licence as an accredited theatre.

The entertainment continued varied: harlequins, acrobats, rope-dancers. A wire dancer, Michael Maddox, from 1752 to 1757, conjured with a long straw while he perched on the wire. In 1755 he was joined by Miss Wilkinson, who also played on the musical glasses. Then in 1763 came Giuseppe Grimaldi, known as 'Iron Legs', as ballet-master and leading dancer who continued for many years. He is better known for his son, Joey, who was born in 1779 and made his debut, as a monkey, at the age of two.

The first great days of Sadler's Wells began in 1765, when Rosoman pulled down the wooden music-house and replaced it with a real theatre, which was to last for more than a century. He installed a proper stage, scenery, and seats with ledges on their backs to hold bottles and glasses. He charged three shillings for a box including a pint of wine and heavier stuff such as port and punch. Pit and gallery were respectively 18d and a shilling, plus 6d for wine.[19]

A stream of celebrated performers now graced the theatre, still including harlequins, wire and rope dancers like Spinacuti with his monkey who imitated Blondin on the tight-rope, waving flags, pushing a barrow, hanging from his heels and more. There were comedians like the famous Tom King from Drury Lane, and Rosoman ventured into staging small 'burlettas' or 'musical dialogues', and pantomimes. The reign of the Charles Dibdins, father and son, authors of plays and songs, began in 1772, and continued with Charles the younger and Thomas King as proprietors and managers.

An impressive collection of playbills and advertisements has survived, of which the following is just one example:

"The AMUSEMENTS of this place will
 continue this and every Day: Consisting of
LADDER DANCING, by Mons. Richer.
SINGING, by Mr LOWE, Mr Kear, Mrs
 Burnett, and Miss Dowson,
DANCING, by Mr Atkins, Mr Le Mercier, Mr
 Byrne, Mrs Stephens, Miss Collett, Miss
 Valois, &

TUMBLING, by Mr Rayner, Mr Huntley, Mr
 Richer, and Mr Garman.
Variety of pleasing Performances by Mess.
 Sigels.
And ROPE DANCING by Mr Ferzi, and
 others.
To which will be added, an Entertainment of
 Music and Dancing (never yet performed)
 called HARLEQUIN NEPTUNE.
The Music composed by Mr DIBDIN.
 and the Decorations, & c. entirely new.
The Amusements will open with a new Musical
 Piece called the SEASONS; and in the
 course of the Evening will be performed
 another, called the RAREE-SHEW MAN."

Already in 1773 the first alterations to the subsequently much rebuilt theatre took place by raising the roof and transforming the interior. It began to be added to the fashionable summer theatres, its audiences now including royalty, the Duke and Duchess of York and Duke and Duchess of Gloucester. From 1780 a string of celebrities performed, including the noted singer John Braham (né Abrahams), singers, tumblers, dog-trainers – and the famous tragedian Edmund Kean.

Joey Grimaldi's career as clown lasted from 1781 for nearly 50 years until he could scarcely move. The illegitimate child of a dancer, Rebecca Brooker, he was only two on his first appearance (according to himself he appeared first at Drury Lane). His severe and exacting father, who died in 1788 when Joey was barely ten, certainly exploited him. Joey's infant role as monkey was to accompany his father in an act during which he was swung round at speed by a chain round his waist. One evening in 1782 the chain broke and Joey flew from stage to pit, luckily into the arms of a startled old gentleman.

His pay at Sadler's Wells was poor, at Drury Lane better. He regularly had to walk, or run, between the two theatres, for Sadler's Wells morning rehearsals at 10, to appear at Drury Lane at 11, home for dinner at 2, back to Sadler's Wells for the 6 o'clock show and finally, Drury Lane until 11, with barely time to change his costume, which he might do 20 times a night. Once he and a fellow-actor ran the whole way in eight minutes, timed by their stop-watches. Luckily for him the Drury

29. Sadler's Wells and the New River c.1813

Lane salary trebled and at Sadler's Wells rose from three shillings to £4.

When barely sixteen Grimaldi fell in love with Maria Hughes, daughter of the partner-proprietor Thomas Hughes, but they had to wait to marry until 1797, when the couple moved to 37 Penton Street, "the Regent's Park of the City Road".[20]

It was undoubtedly Joey Grimaldi who formed the basis of Sadler's Wells fame. He also left an indelible mark on the appearance, costume and name of the English clown.

STRENUOUS SPORT

Other forms of amusement included watching the sufferings of would-be athletes, some of them described later by Lord William Pitt Lennox. The earliest he quotes is in 1765, when Mr Mullins, a watch-case maker from Shoreditch, at the age of nearly 50 "walked without shoes and stockings from Shoreditch Church to St George's Church, in the Borough, and back again, for a wager of 6 guineas". He allowed 40 minutes for the feat (taking into account the poor state of the roads), and achieved it in $46\frac{1}{2}$. Five years later a costermonger named James Parrott ran the length of Old Street, from the Charterhouse wall to Shoreditch Church wall, a measured mile, in four minutes, the best odds being that it would take $4\frac{1}{2}$. This was nearly two centuries before Roger Bannister established the then record in 1954.

In the 1770s there were several other such wagers, including walking from Hicks's Hall to York and back, 200 miles each way, one of them in five days. Foster Powell, an attorney's clerk at New Inn and in his thirties, undertook several wagers, having gained a taste for them after a business trip to York which he decided to do on foot and took a little over 6 days. Slightly built and 5' 8" tall, but with stout legs and thighs, he continued this hobby until his late 50s.

In 1775 John Green, in a wager of 10 guineas to walk 7 miles in an hour, eat a cold fowl and drink a bottle of wine, was beaten by a butcher named Hancock in a contest on the City Road.

A great year for such feats was 1791, when a young man who walked 22 miles starting along the Essex Road, took 5 minutes less than his allotted time of 4 hours 5 minutes. A month later a man in his 60s – considered a great age – for 50 guineas ran from Shoreditch church to the 8-milestone past Edmonton, beating the hour's allotment by 10 minutes. Just to vary this pastime, a journeyman baker, Anthony Thorpe, ran a mile round the Artillery Ground, tied in a sack, in $11\frac{1}{2}$ minutes. Not to be outdone, Mr Shadbolt, a publican at Ware known as Goliath, ran 21 miles to Shoreditch while pushing a cart in the 10 hours allowed, showing little sign of fatigue.

Shoreditch was often the starting-point or goal, probably because the road north, the old Roman road, ran straight. Two men ran from Shoreditch to Enfield, 10 miles, the winner taking 61 minutes, and a champion known as the Warrington Walker walked 11 miles round the Artillery Ground in 5 minutes under 2 hours, the wagered time, vaulting every 3 miles, and 4 times at the end (1750). And in 1764 Mr and Mrs Willis, a Moorfields glass grinder and his wife who between them weighed 32 stone, starting from home at 3 in the morning ran to Windsor Castle Gate and returned, apparently in a cart, in less than 9 hours, having wagered for 10.

There were horse wagers too, like Cooper Thornhill of the famous Bell at Stilton, who in 1745 bet he could ride three times between Stilton and Shoreditch in fifteen hours. He was allowed an unlimited number of horses. Each trip took well under four hours, and the total of 213 miles took him 11 hours, 33 minutes and 52 seconds, nearly $3\frac{1}{2}$ hours below the limit. Finally, in 1793 Mr Skipway, of Hoxton, "trotted his pony Jack, 10 hands high, 10 miles in 41 minutes and a half on the Kingsland road", having bet it would take him less than an hour – and later the same day on the same road for 10 guineas he beat Mr Badkins's bay galloway in a 10-mile trot.[21]

1   *The Autobiography of Francis Place*, ed. Mary Thale, Cambridge UP, 1972, pp. 28, 29n, 81 n.3, 158.

2   *The Diaries of a Duchess*, ed. James Greig, London, 1926, pp. 206-7.

3   Pierre Chantreau, *Voyage dans les trois Royaumes d'Angleterre, d'Ecosse et d'Irlande*, Paris, 1792, Vol. II, pp. 132-4.

4   For these resorts see Wroth, *Pleasure Gardens*, and Sunderland, *Old London's Spas*.

5   It was eventually renamed as a Tapas bar, part of the 1990s mania for suppressing tradition in favour of gimmicky names.

6   Nelson, *Islington*, pp. 93-4n.

7   From W.W. (Woty) in *The London Chronicle*, 1760, Vol. VII, p. 531.

8   Nelson, *Islington*, p. 42n.

9   From *The London Magazine*, June 1759.

10 George Colman, prologue to David Garrick's *Bon Ton*, 1775.

11 Nelson (*Islington*, p. 252), says he was Church-warden in 1754, but that was *Joseph* Collins, a Vestryman, so either Nelson muddled the two, or perhaps they were related.

12 William Hone, *The Every-Day Book, and Table Book*, London, 1826, Vol. I, pp. 857f; Tomlins, *Yseldon*, pp. 204-5n.

13 The society survived until 1833.

14 Hone, *Every-Day Book*, Vol. I, pp. 862-3.

15 Hone, *Loc. cit.*, quoting William Hazlitt in *The Examiner*, 17 February 1819.

16 Nelson, *Islington*, p. 74n.

17 Hone, *Every-Day Book*, Vol. I, p. 860.

18 It stood near the junction of Hornsey Road and Seven Sisters Road. At the south-east border of Highbury Woods, in about 1716 a house known as Cream Hall was built by a family called Guidott, which became a popular place of resort. (*VCH*, p. 64).

19 Arundell, *Sadler's Wells*, pp. 23f. Rosoman built a house for himself, which survives at no. 24 Islington Green.

20 Later 24 Penton Street, at one time thought to be the only identified surviving house of Grimaldi in London. For his career, see *Memoirs of Joseph Grimaldi*, edited by Boz, London, 1838.

21 Lord William Pitt Lennox, *Fashions Then and Now*, London, 1878, Vol. II, pp. 165-78, 214-221.

CHAPTER 10

Governing the Parish

VESTRYMEN

Before the late 19th-century reform of local government and the creation of councils in place of vestries, we rely much on vestry minutes to tell us about our then governors, and have to put together information from often scanty evidence.

Amateurish and lackadaisical parish management had in the 1720s shown at least a temporary change for the better, whether by the influence of the still young Rev. George Kerie, already incumbent for some years, or more likely, the bureaucratic attitude of a new Vestry Clerk. His records, in a fine clerkly hand, are not only considerably neater, but are drawn up in methodical, if boringly repetitive wording. Vestry meetings, now prefaced by a note that they had been announced in church, are given explanatory headings. Minutes of the last meeting are regularly read, and committees *ad infinitum* are appointed: for auditing the Churchwardens' accounts, for investigations into problems, for Workhouse management, and (for a time) to determine pensions of the poor, who are summoned to learn their allowances.

Meetings began to be more fully attended, though not more frequent. Indeed less so, perhaps because, with sub-committees attending to specific tasks, whose records have not survived, much parish work was done outside vestry meetings. Hence tantalising gaps over what happened in cases referred for enquiry.

Appointing parish officers was an annual ritual. On Easter Tuesday Churchwardens were elected by the vestrymen and subsequently sworn in. A list of nominees for Overseers of the Poor was submitted to the JPs at the County Sessions House in Clerkenwell (Hicks's Hall), of whom three were picked. Surveyors of the Highways were similarly nominated in a list ratified by the JPs, which for many years was dealt with on Boxing Day, but from 1767, in accordance with a new Act of Parliament the date was changed to on or nearest to 22 September.

In the earlier years there were a number of baronets who served as vestrymen, but after the death of Sir Richard Fisher, in an apparent slight class-shift these disappear, although there were always several Esquires. The rest were in a respectable trade or craft, or were referred to merely as 'Gentleman' – that is, not in a trade or profession for their livelihood.

What is hard to picture is the appearance and costume of these characters. No portraits are known; one must imagine sober-suited, respectable burgher figures, with the Vicar in cassock, Beadle and Vestry Clerk in black gown. Nor, until about mid-century, do we know where or in what style of house any of them lived. Occasionally the names Ring Cross, Newington or Kingsland – all distinguished as outlying – appear, otherwise we must assume they lived somewhere in the clustered village between the Angel and Canonbury Lane. Seldom is there any indication of what vestrymen did for a living. For a few years a trade is shown for those nominated as Overseer of the Poor although more are identified as 'Gentleman'. Occasionally one becomes upgraded to 'Esquire', such as Joseph

Manwaring in 1778, and Samuel Pullin in 1793, no doubt having acquired or inherited a small estate. Of the occasional trades or occupations mentioned, we have, for example, Richard Beesum of Lower Street, as carpenter and John Haime of Lower Side as collar maker (1779), Daniel Sebbon of Upper Street as farmer (1780) – then these identifications cease.

A number are well-known local names which recur regularly over more than one generation. Some were prosperous land owners or farmers while some have been embalmed in history by the names of rows of houses they financed or had built: Philip Oddy in Oddy's Row – a long-serving vestryman, who died in 1786 at the age of 93; Walter Sebbon in Sebbon's Buildings at the north end of Upper Street. Samuel Pullin, another of Islington's noted dairy farmers, financed the building of Pullin's Row (now 84–8 Islington High Street), and also served as Overseer of the Poor in 1784–5.

A vestryman might be called on to maintain the church clock, though not actually identified as a clockmaker, such as Thomas Wilkins from 1754–7 (his bill was not paid until 1760, after his death), or John Brice in the 1780s.

One inhabitant, Giles Jacob, a compiler of legal works, was pilloried by Pope in *The Dunciad* in 1733. He, in return, attacked Pope in angry satirical 'letters' written to Lady Mary Wortley Montagu, in a work called *The Mirrour*. As this lady, he maintained, had charitably accepted a copy of his work, he gave her his address in case she wanted to reply – an unlikely supposition. He lived at "Mes Jones's in Rufford's Buildings beyond the Church in Islington" (now nos 2–78 High Street), thus distinguishing his address from Rufford's Row, now nos 289–302 Upper Street.[1]

One parish benefactor whose work unfortunately perished long ago was Nathaniel Clarkson (1724–97). By profession a coach-painter, he also painted portraits which he exhibited in the 1760s, and historical works. According to Nelson his house was on the "North-west corner of Church Street" (now Gaskin Street) and Upper Street. Its wainscoted walls he adorned with chiaroscuro paintings "representing *Design, Sculpture, Architecture* etc.", which survived until Nelson's day, though were evidently gone when Cromwell wrote *Walks in Islington* in 1835. Cromwell also mentions Clarkson's "initials in the fanlight over the door", and a painting of Henry VII.[2]

Clarkson, who was a member of the Court of Assistants in Merchant Taylors' Hall, served as an Islington vestryman from the 1760s. Though occasionally recorded as nominated for office, he always seems to have been excused on one ground or another. For example, in 1767 as constable for Canonbury; in 1768 as Overseer together with the Islington Benjamin Franklin *(see Chapter 12)*; and in 1769 (by then described as 'Gentleman') as Surveyor of the Highways. In 1787, on the strength of his offer of the painting for the church, he was recorded as a church benefactor.[3]

Another who served as a vestryman was William Wickings (c.1757–1841), later Surveyor to the County of Middlesex, during which time he was architect of St Mary Magdalene church in Holloway Road. Like many architects of the time he was more usually described as 'Surveyor'. In 1793 Wickings presented the Vestry with an attractive view of the church seen from the south-west, in an "Elegant Carved and Gilt frame".[4]

We are able to piece together scanty information about these gentlemen from evidence of their vestry services: as Overseers of the Poor, parish Surveyors, or (grandest of the offices) Churchwardens. Or they might be nominated for Constable or Headborough – a dual office by then largely ceremonial – for one of five 'Liberties' or parish areas: Upper and Lower Barnsbury, Canonbury, Prebend (the St Peter's area) and Newington Barrow or Highbury.

Most of the named persons we encounter, however, are unfortunately just names in a record with no dimensions or known personalities. For hardly any have we a description of appearance, character or history. Vestry minutes do not record their deaths, unless their office, or pew, has to be re-filled and they are then mentioned as 'deceased'. Mostly they quietly disappear without trace.

BOUNDARIES AND ROADS

The duties of the Surveyors of Highways were sadly neglected, and the deplorable condition of the roads continued, causing frequent and deserved complaint. Though the Surveyors were regularly called upon from the late 17th century to repair the main roads to the north, and roads bounding the parish – notably Tallington or Tollington Lane – or to Newington and other parishes, their all too frequent failure is revealed by the several indictments issued by JPs or the courts.

Attention to parish boundaries was, however, meticulous because of parish liability for a border site. There was a famous, perhaps not apocryphal, 16th-century precedent over ownership of the Angel area, when Islington supposedly refused to bury a pauper found dead in a nearby ditch as "not in their parish", so that Finsbury, the manorial area comprising Clerkenwell and St Luke's, had to bury him. However, Islington thereafter referred to the Angel as its own.[5]

Thomas Tomlins, in *Yseldon, A Perambulation of Islington*, paid tribute to the historic 'perambulations' of the parish with a detailed rehearsal of the exact spots and lines of directions between definable locations. His work, published in 1858, records at the beginning the exact survey made in 1735 by Henry Warner of Great Kirby Street in Hatton Garden, which was accompanied by the first detailed map of the parish with lengths of streets in miles, furlongs and poles. For example,

BE Causeway and Footpath, from the south end of the Back Road at B, along the Upper Road through both Holloways, to the Black Dog at Highgate (3M, 2F, 3P);

or

W Footpath, from Frog Lane to Rosemary Branch (2F, 32P).

X Footpath, from Frog Hall through the Provence (i.e. Prebend) Field to the posts on the east side of X (1F, 36P).[6]

In 1730 Islington, called on to join with Hornsey to lay gravel in Hornsey Lane, indignantly replied that responsibility had always been Hornsey's, never theirs.

During the 18th century the Churchwardens sometimes reported removal or damage of a boundary stone, and the officers, or even a committee, had to inspect the site, if necessary together with the neighbouring parish's representatives. This happened, for instance, in 1755, when the campaign for building the vitally important 'New Road' from Paddington was in full swing. Yet Islington seems to have ignored this and was wholly concerned instead with the removal by Mr John Jennings of a boundary stone "in the Lane near the Boarded River House". Having seen this replaced, the Churchwardens and other officers were stirred by the incident to make the rounds and ensure all stones were in place.[7]

The time-honoured ritual of beating the bounds, supposedly annually, but later supposedly every three years or even more sporadically, was at least in early days literally interpreted – the landmarks were often emphasised by beating tattoo-like on the backs of some luckless boy or boys, so it might well be a rowdy occasion. In 1711 we learn of "Madam Amy Wright" (as more grandly disposed ladies sometimes styled themselves) complaining of the rude behaviour of boys who insulted her at her garden wall near Kingsland.

It was no mere ceremony, however, because of frequent disagreements over which parish was liable to maintain a highway. Islington, often in trouble with the Turnpike Trustees for neglect, was also in dispute, sometimes friendly, sometimes not, over exactly where the boundaries were.

In 1792 the vicar, Rev. George Strahan, with the Sexton, Vestry Clerk and a couple of vestrymen, met the St Leonard's Churchwardens on Islington's eastern fringe at the Rosemary Branch, to fix their mutual boundary. They found that a stone with '$\underset{\text{M.I.}}{S}$' engraved on it, nearly opposite the tavern had been moved ten feet to the west. From there they employed the usual device of an imaginary oblique line between it and a similar stone to the west, this time of St Leonard's, at "the corner of Mr Rhodes's field opposite to the Barley Mow". To fix the boundary north east of the Rosemary Branch they agreed to have a stone block sunk flush with the ground, and along a road leading to Mr Scott's brickfields bordering the Lower Road another stone "specifying that the Boundary of this Parish extends 26 feet S from the front of said Stone". To complete the markings, three more stones were to be erected as guides.[8]

Another expedition made in March 1793 to the Newington Green area by the Surveyors of four parishes, Islington, Hackney, Hornsey and Newington, was to establish the joint limits by measuring distances with their poles between Newington and Kingsland Greens. Starting from the west, from Hornsey boundary east to Newington boundary was found to be 55¼ poles jointly in Hornsey and Islington: this they declared to be divided between the two, 27¾ poles from Hornsey boundary eastward to be Hornsey's, 27½ poles to the first Newington boundary to be Islington's. Next, from Newington boundary eastwards to the south western boundary at Cock and Castle Lane, was jointly Islington and Newington, similarly divided as 32¾ poles each to the two parishes. At the latter boundary a brick arch was to be made across the road from the pond, jointly maintained by both parishes. Decision on the rest of the lane, ending at the north side of Newington Green, belonging partly to Hornsey, partly to Islington, was deferred.

Finally the 16 poles from the north side of Newington Green from Coach and Horses Lane near the 'Meeting', to the corner of Green Lanes turnpike road, was jointly owned by Newington and Islington, and was divided equally, 8 poles to each.

These settlements appear to have been amicable. The worst misfortune, the Indictment of 1793 which placed the whole onus of repair of Maiden Lane on Islington, ended a long and vexed legal battle coming to a head in 1794 *(see Chapter 13)*.

In 1734 a new Bill for repairing the highways included the roads from Islington to Highgate and Hampstead, and St John Street to Kingsland. But in the parishioners' view more important were the half-mile or so from Ball's Pond Road to Newington Green, much used by travellers and "heavy carriages" and, surprisingly, Cross Street, a mere 250 yards, so named as being the link between Upper and Lower Streets. These streets were constantly torn up and damaged by ballast carts used for road repairs, and the Vestry begged that

they be included in the Bill. It was hoped that the Trustees could allot some of the heavy tolls collected on the main roads to repair these two others.

After some dispute it was resolved that while turnpike money should be reserved for major turnpike roads, the new Bill, limiting other improvements to specified roads, would act against local interests. A committee headed by Thomas Science, that active vestryman, was formed to attend the Commons debates. Parliament refused their petition.

VESTRY TROUBLE
The Vestry was never out of the wood. In January 1735 the Surveyors were fined £5 each at a Special Session (held at the Red Lion Coffee House in Clerkenwell), for failing to submit a list of defaulters on statute work on the highways, obligatory since medieval times. The Surveyors argued that they had not been issued with a warrant for the purpose until too late, and the Vestry felt obliged to reimburse them. However, the Vestry applied to the Commons to bring in a Bill amending the local turnpike Acts. The Trustees agreed to spend £10 of the £100 statute payment on repairing the "Cross Street Road". Soon afterwards a proposal was raised at a General Sessions of the Peace where it was agreed, after considerable argument (September/October 1735), that the disputes be ended by the Surveyors 'compounding', in lieu of statute work, for £100 annually.

As long ago as October 1681 a petition from the parish officers and inhabitants had been made to the General Quarter Sessions, that Islington had never had a Watch-house for the Constables for night watches, nor a whipping post, nor a 'cage' for "Night Walkers and other loose idle and suspicious persons". This lack, it was claimed, hindered the Constables in their duties, so that vagrants often escaped. Though watch-houses were subsequently built, they were still claimed to be unfit and "useless", and many complaints were made to the JPs. In May 1763 the JPs took a hand, ordering a committee to report at Hicks's Hall on "proper Places for the Securing of Night Prisoners". The Vestry promised "proper regard" to any Sessions Order, and in June determined that existing lockups should be at once rebuilt "in a substantiall manner" financed by an assessment on the inhabitants. Charles Palmer, Esq., acting as go-between, headed a committee to effect this, while another committee would inspect them and organise repairs.

Estimates made for carpentry by John Hall, for a bricklayer, James Burton and a smith, Richard Williams, totalling £24 6s 2d, were submitted to the JPs for orders.

At the same time the fire engines were found to need repair, quickly attended to by Mr Richard Ragg, engine-maker, for 15 guineas "by making a New Cistern, a Brass Flanch, two Suction Pipes" each 7 feet long, and a 40-foot leather pipe with brass screws. This took a mere three weeks.

In September the subject of lighting again came under consideration. It seemed as if a new broom was sweeping Islington clean. But then for more than three years silence ensued on the subject of the Watch-house.

By the end of 1766 when apparently nothing had been done, the Watch-house was again declared "ruinous" and repair admitted to be out of the question. The Churchwardens, with a committee including Hamilton Crosse Esq., Walter Sebbon, Samuel Pullin and others, discussed the expense of rebuilding. Another vestryman, William Sharwood,[9] produced plans and an estimate for £71 1s 10½d, which the Vestry agreed. The same site was used, with an offer to repair and set up the stocks in a suitable place without further charge. Most of the expense was met from the next year's Poor Rate, fixed for 1s 10d in the pound in September 1767.

Responding rather lackadaisically to the Order of Session of May 1763, the Vestry reported that they had ordered Watch-house, Cage and Stocks and asked for instructions for the inhabitants to undertake watch and ward. They did make progress in ordering Sharwood to make the stocks, and William Watson, the Colebrooke Row gardener, was asked to level the ground round the Watch-house which was evidently liable to flooding.

Soon after this the dishonesty of Mr and Mrs Lane at the Workhouse was revealed, with their dismissal. (*See Chapter 14.*)

After a short period of quiescence, in May 1769 it was found that the two fire engines

(which from 1768 were to be regularly tested four times a year, were again reported "decayed" and "useless". This time the Vestry resolved to buy new ones "of the fourth size", with leather pipes, sockets and other equipment.

The committee reported in August 1769 that they were to buy two more leather pipes and 18 buckets, all equipment to be marked with the parish name. The following April, still under-equipped, the committee was ordered to dispose of the two old engines and use the money towards a new one "of the first size".

The engine-keeper, John Ashley, at the post-Easter appointments and nominations, resigned in 1769 and thenceforward John Green, the Beadle and Bellman, was appointed to act in addition as Engine Keeper, at a mere £2 a year.

LIGHTING UP THE DARK

Services we now take for granted were then in their infancy. Street lighting seems to have been unknown until well into the 18th century, and any provision had been left to individual parishes. Householders might fix lamps outside their doors, similarly public buildings might display some illumination, but in general darkness was one of the reasons why foot-travellers were so vulnerable at night, and why horse patrols were offered to escort visitors back to central London.

Not until 1761 were laws on lighting passed, and late that October the usual committee was appointed (meeting at the Mitre inn opposite the church) to raise the subject with the JPs. On Boxing Day the head Church-warden, William Thomas, reported that Thomas Nash had agreed "to Trim, Light and Clean and Keep in repair" at least 60 lamps, at 3s 4d a month each (a generous payment), financed by a 4d-in-the-pound rate. The following year another committee was appointed to contract with "a proper person", and from then on the lamps were lighted by decree from Michaelmas (25 September) until Lady Day (25 March). The rate was raised to 5d. Not all parishioners conformed. The next April Mrs Mary Lenore in Pierpont Row[10] was "distrained" by JPs' warrant for refusing either to pay the duty or display a lamp in front of her house, "according to the Act".

From 1764 the vestryman Matthias Hollis

30. The parish lock-up on Islington Green, a short-term incarceration until prisoners could be transferred to the County authorities.

was appointed collector of the rate, for a fee of £3, raised to £4 in 1767, and in 1769 the parish rate was increased to 6d. The period for lighted lamps was solemnly reiterated every year until 1770, when it was merely resolved that lamps were to be lighted in winter.

Except where otherwise stated, information in this chapter comes from the Vestry Minutes, Vols. II-IV.

1   *The Complete Letters of Lady Mary Wortley Montagu*, ed. Robert Halsband, Oxford, 1965, Vol. II.

2   Nelson, *Islington*, pp. 310, 315; Thomas Cromwell, *Walks Through Islington*, London, 1835, p. 262n.

3   Nelson, *Islington*, pp. 315; VM, Vols. III, IV.

4   Colvin, *Dictionary of Architects*, p. 1,048; VM, Vol. IV.

5   Pinks, *Clerkenwell*, p. 548, quoting *The Gentleman's Magazine* of October 1823.

6   Tomlins, *Perambulation*, p. 13. The letters are those marked on his map. Two MS drafts in a grangerised copy of Tomlins's book, held in Islington Local History Library, recording his difficulties in researching and publishing the work, note that those who helped and encouraged him with material included William Upcott and George Daniel. (*See Chapter 19.*)

7   VM, Vol. III, 26 October and 26 December 1755.

8   VM, Vol. III.; and see Tomlins, *Perambulation*, pp. 177-80. His account, always very detailed, discusses every deviation of every boundary road and its possible reasons.

9   William Sharwood died in September 1771 as Churchwarden, shortly after completing extensions to his Watch-house.

10   Now rebuilt as part of Camden Passage antiques market.

CHAPTER 11

Academies and Schools

A PLETHORA OF ACADEMIES

Islington's popularity for genteel schools, dating at least from the middle of Charles II's reign, was in the 18th century well established and many a youth educated at one of these academies, as the small boarding schools liked to style themselves, went on to relative fame. Young ladies were also educated here, though little is revealed about exactly what they learned.

Dame Alice Owen's school was long undoubtedly chief in the parish. Perhaps because of its fame, and because villages near the City were desirable places to educate one's children away from 'the Smoke', Islington continued to be a draw, demonstrated in the allocation of pews in St Mary's Church.[1]

Already in 1673 Captain Stacy was granted a pew in the South gallery, and all other school-keepers still without pews were requested to attend a vestry meeting in order to be allocated one. Early in 1681 Mr Thomas Torry (or Terry) and his "Scollers" took over a pew formerly used by Mrs Playford and her boarders. The implication was that she had died, as it was a condition that the pew be restored to her husband should he wish to let his house as a school. A couple of years later Mr Torry was confirmed in the pew at a half-yearly 10 shillings pew rent. Torry / Terry seems to have died in July 1695, when his pew was allotted to Mr William Vickers and "Scollars", presumably his successor.

Meanwhile in 1686 the Vestry ordered that all parish, that is to say pauper, children or orphans were to be sent to school – without stating where. This was perhaps at first at

Owen's, for the children were given gallery pews in 1724, but a school was made for them only in 1734 – the room above the Engine House where the fire engines were kept adjoining the old church. Two years later a special gallery pew was reserved for menservants, oddly enough alongside the charity girls' pew, while the next two pews beside the charity boys was for maidservants.

Also in 1734 we first learn of one of Islington's most celebrated early private schools, when Thomas Science, a clockmaker, was allotted a pew with his son, while his wife Mrs Goodlife Science – sound Puritan name – and her school boarders remained in the gallery. On Mrs Science's death John Shields married her daughter and continued the school for boys "with great reputation", and again we hear of their being seated in the gallery.

This school continued under various successors for many decades, always retaining a high reputation, in an ancient house in Upper Street. It was later numbered 107 (between the present Theberton Street and the King's Head pub, described by Nelson as opposite Rufford's Row (itself later numbered 289–302 Upper Street). The timber and plaster house dated from Queen Elizabeth's time or soon after, with stucco ceilings "in crocket work, with medallions", says Nelson, similar to Sir Thomas Fowler's Cross Street house. It contained a chimney-piece showing Adam and Eve with the Tree of Knowledge in the Garden of Eden, which might or might not be a suitable exemplar for the "seminary of youth". It remained for many years.[2]

Nelson, writing in 1811, dates the school

from "about 60 years ago", namely about 1750. The pew seating shows it to be a few years earlier than that. John Shields ran it, while also serving as a vestryman, until his death in 1786. His pupils included the founder of the Royal Humane Society, William Hawes, whose father kept the Thatched House in the Lower Street, and the Islington historian John Nichols. Another pupil of wider fame was a historian of Russia, the Rev. William Tooke, FRS (1744–1820), who became a chaplain at the English church at Kronstadt and later at St Petersburg. Among his published works was *A History of Russia from Rurik to Catherine II* (1800).[3] After John Shields' death the school was run by John Price, and after Price's death in 1793 by Edward Flower.

The Science/Shields/Flower establishment was the most successful of many local private schools. We hear in 1705 of Mr Debora's "scollers", in 1715 of Mrs Sneape giving up her school, possibly on retiring, when her pew was given to Philip Oddy, in 1714 of a pew for Mr Francis Duboias (a mis-spelling of Dubois?), and Mr Gordon and scholars in 1734.

Judging from pew allocations, most schools consisted of not more than a dozen pupils, such as could be accommodated in a single house by doubling up sleeping accommodation. Over the century the tradition of sending boys and 'young ladies' to be educated in Islington increased. In mid-century, for example, we find Mrs Dannold and her young ladies in 1741; Mrs Elizabeth Paul and hers in 1754, mentioned again in 1761; David Davies [4] with three pews in the gallery in 1755, with leave for three rows behind for his boarders from Owen's school, Mrs Jane Courant's scholars in 1763. The children, whether privileged boarders or charity boys and girls, were customarily relegated to the galleries along with the servants, but as the decades went by their days in the pews were numbered as Islington's population increased.

A 1790s Directory names nine schools in Islington in 1787–9, mostly in Upper Street and its 'Rows', such as Hornsey Row (Mr Duff) and Rosoman's Buildings. Mr, or rather Monsieur Charron in the Lower Street kept a boarding school for young ladies and presumably specialised in French. By the 1790s, when Charron was still in business, the total of schools had risen to 14. Two were academies kept by clergymen, the Rev. John Rule, whose establishment was at the north end of Colebrooke Row, and the Rev. A. Croles, in Queen's Head Lane. The latter numbered among his pupils Thomas Uwins (1782-1857), who became a not unsuccessful painter in the 1820s.

One teacher not named in the Directory, perhaps because of her total lack of success in the profession, was Mary Wollstonecraft, who in 1783 transferred from Islington to Newington Green but had no better luck there, and closed her pupil-less establishment in 1785.

In 1777 overcrowding had made it necessary to enquire into the seating of schools in the church. It was found that to build new galleries the churchwardens had to apply for a Faculty (*See Chapter 6*). The best that could be managed was to squeeze in a couple of new pews at the back of the church.

A bleak announcement was made in the Vestry on 22 September 1787, that "The number of Boarding Schools in the parish having increased and still increasing", in future no boarding school keeper would be allowed church accommodation for pupils.

Could they have known it, Islington was on the threshold of a huge increase in population which would transform the parish, its appearance, services and economy. For the present, at Easter 1793, notice was taken that "on account of the Great Encrease of houses & Inhabitants", it would be expedient to elect an additional Beadle.

At this time however, as Britain was on the brink of a war with France, there were other problems to deal with.

OWEN'S SCHOOL

Owen's school had undergone a troubled period. William Smith, an MA, a sound classical scholar and conscientious headmaster who had run the school from 1666, maintained the building in good condition and was awarded a gratuity "for his diligence". However, he was admonished in about 1676 for laxity in keeping the register and neglecting the obligatory daily prayers. He also frequented City taverns where he fell in with Catholic dissidents. Here he met Titus Oates, a former pupil of his at the Merchant Taylors' School where Smith had taught before going to Owen's. Oates was now a suspect character with a criminal record and Smith, rather easily led, was incautiously persuaded at Oates's instigation to write some Latin verses partly concerning the Virgin Mary.[5] He was arrested, cross-questioned by the Bishop and, though the House of Lords dismissed the evidence as hearsay, he lost his licence to preach in 1678 and consequently his job.

Smith also fell foul of the vicar of St James's Clerkenwell, Dr Slater, who replaced him as Master of Owen's by a clergyman's son named John Clutterbuck. He, however, proved so inept that in 1692 he too was dismissed. The next Master, Willam Vickars, was also removed for dealings with a 'disreputable' woman.

Meanwhile Smith who, fortunately for him, had been provided with a testimonial by the Governors that "he was an industrious and careful person in his place, and a very loyal subject to his sacred Majesty and Government", later refused a lure from Oates who was then fabricating the 'Popish Plot'.[4]

Though scandals over Smith and his successors as Owen's headmasters died down, the Governors themselves were in trouble when in 1708 Barker, one of the Islington Surveyors, complained to the Brewers' Company that besides "other great abuses" the almshouse pensioners were insufficiently paid. He was allowed to examine the Company's books, then backed up his complaint with the support of the vicar, Dr Cornelius Yeate, and several vestrymen. After unsatisfactory meetings and consultations the case was referred to the Court of Chancery. The Company was charged with misusing profits from Dame Owen's charity to build cottages which proved a financial liability, instead of spending them on the school and almshouses. Worse, in terms of Islington, they had kept too few almswomen, had stinted them on pensions, clothing and food supplies, and had neglected the Master's salary, the scholars' examinations and even their education.

By a skilled defence the Company evaded many of the charges, but their minute books revealed the truth of others. After several years of litigation and delay, judgement was pronounced by the Lord Keeper of the Great Seal in October 1718, quashing the claims of mismanagement and denying the Vestry's attempt to remove the charity's management from the Company. Their escape was perhaps undeserved, and the Lord Keeper reproved them for allowing the cost of the annual Visitation Dinner, for which Dame Alice had allowed 30 shillings, to escalate. It now significantly sank back by 40 per cent, to its original limit. Thereafter the Vestry kept a close eye on the charity.

The Governors now saw to it that school and almshouses were newly whitewashed, and timber and railings repaired – not to mention the clock and bell. The next series of Masters proved unexceptionable until Thomas Dennett, appointed in 1717, ended ignominiously in 1731 by deserting and abandoning the school until its plight was reported to the Governors and a temporary stand-in appointed.

Henry Clarke endured vagrants using the school porch as a squat, in spite of being ordered off by the watch. Meanwhile Dame Alice's tomb was decaying, and after only a few years Clarke resigned through ill-health (1738).

Another peaceful period followed, until the Vestry renewed complaints over the condition of the property, and vacancies among almswomen and scholars. However, Vestry insistence that increased revenue was to be spent on repairs and improvements was complied with, and the pensions were raised from £6 8s 6d a year to £8.

A new Master, Richard Shilton, was often absent on unspecified business, in spite of reprimands, and in 1746 was accused of mismanagement. His severity with the boys was criticised, and the school was found to be "decaying". Shilton escaped further action by conveniently dying (July 1750). This paved the way for noticeable improvement.

The next two Masters were luckily a success. David Davies, who served until 1791, was strict, business-like and decisive. One of his practical improvements was to persuade the Governors to connect the school with New River water, hitherto dismissed as too expensive. He also improved almswomen's allowances, and when the parish church was rebuilt in 1754, he renewed Dame Alice's tomb. Though rather independent and aggressive for the Company's taste, he was too efficient to be ignored, and his successor Alexander Balfour in 1791 took over a flourishing concern.[6]

1   Pew allocation is recorded in the Vestry Minutes, which also record other information on pews and attempts to increase seating accommodation.

2   Nelson, *Islington*, pp. 113-4.

3   *DNB*. Tooke's son, also William, FRS, became President of the Society of Arts and was prominent in the foundation of London University in 1823 and St Katherine's Docks in 1825.

4   The name is spelt Davis in the Vestry Minutes.

5   Oates was trying to persuade Smith to turn King's Evidence with the promise of being reinstated in his post. Smith recorded a true version of the case, eventually published in 1685. (Dare, *Owen's School*, pp. 36-8.)

6   Dare, *Owen's School*, pp. 39-46.

CHAPTER 12

Some Personalities

THE TWO FRANKLINS

The appearance in 1761 of the name Benjamin Franklin as an Islington vestryman, again from 1767–9, and in 1768–9 as an Overseer of the Poor, seemed to show that the famous American patriot and statesmen lived for a time in Islington. This is a false trail, yet there may be a connection.

The Pennsylvanian Benjamin Franklin had been in turn printer, newspaper publisher, experimental scientist (in 1752 a pioneer in electricity), postmaster, negotiator, inventor (for example of the 'Franklin stove'), and public servant. In 1761, aged 55, he was on the second of three prolonged visits to Britain, this time representing his home state in a dispute over the Penn family's lands. His third and last visit was from 1764–75, after which he left for France and finally returned to America the next year, when war with England was imminent.

Franklin was a friend of Islington's vicar, the Rev. George Strahan, having earlier in his life shared with George's father, William, the trade of printing. He later corresponded with William Strahan, who at one time informs him with other family news that George, his second son, is at Oxford. The latter, when vicar at St Mary's Islington after 1772, was evidently his friend.

Benjamin Franklin certainly had some knowledge of Islington, as shown in an anonymous paper he contributed to the *Public Advertiser* (1 January 1770) as part of a vain campaign to persuade the British Government to repeal legislation imposing taxation on the American colonies. He interestingly quotes Isling-

31. The 'Pennsylvanian' Benjamin Franklin, after a painting by M Chamberlin.

ton to illustrate the injustice of taxation without representation: Supposing (he suggests) the Government decreed that Middlesex had a right to tax Islington parish, while refusing to admit "Deputies from that Parish to the County-Meeting". He goes on, "Could it be reasonably expected that the Inhabitants of the parish of Islington should contentedly submit to such gross Partiality?" Why should he pick out Islington as an example unless he knew something of the place?[1]

A sad and topical correspondence, probably during this last visit to England in the 1770s, illustrates Franklin's philanthropy and his friendship with George Strahan. His papers include letters from Thomas Taunton, an impoverished pensioner of some unnamed City Company. These pitiful, well-nigh illiterate letters bemoan the old man's unhappy lot, living in penury with his daughter on a mere 15 shillings a quarter, crippled by the stone and desperate with pain. They are also full of gratitude to Franklin and Strahan as his only friends. The undated letters, probably written at some time between 1772 and 1775, show Taunton as lodging successively "at mr. Turners At no-5 In the Vinard walk near the Smallpox Ospatell Clarkenwell", at "mr. Houes neare the Cocke at holay [presumably Holloway] Ieslington", and progressively moving farther out, "at mr. Slaters neare the Lair at Hogsdon". But they also reveal the acute distress of the many poor, old and sick who depended on some minute Company pension. At one time Taunton is too ill to go to the "Hall" to collect the money, and the Treasurer kindly sends it to him. Illness confined him indoors the whole winter, unable even to get to church a mile away, at best a journey for him of an hour and a half; though on his way home he used to visit an acquaintance for dinner, so that Sunday was usually his red-letter day. But when "a sodon shake" perhaps loosened the stone, he gruesomely suffered five days of haemorrhage through the penis, in much pain and the surgeon ("mr Repells at Higgat") was at great trouble to stop the bleeding, which left him very weak.

One day he fruitlessly made the long journey to Lambeth Palace to seek the late Bishop's old cook, hoping she might get his daughter a job for "Experence in the Chiken bisnes". This would indeed have been a great service to them both, but alas, the old cook had left. In his last despairing plea Taunton relates how only the daughter and a few acquaintants keep him afloat, while he is "bad with the gout, Stoan, and asma, and woer out being upords of 78 years old".

Undoubtedly both Franklin and the Rev. Mr Strahan will have answered the poor old man's pleas with gifts of money or perhaps in kind, but we know no more of how he fared, or when he died.[2]

The "Ospatell" Taunton attended would have been the London Smallpox and Inoculation Hospital, founded in Windmill Street for free inoculation in 1746. Under Dr Thomas Archer from 1747 it became a centre for teaching and research in inoculation, and was visited by leading physicians from Europe. In 1752, needing larger accommodation, it moved to Cold Bath Fields, with an increased capacity for 130 patients, yet still with long waiting lists. Late in 1758 Dr Archer gave Benjamin Franklin figures on the success of inoculation, showing that of patients who suffered smallpox "in the common way", one in four died, but of those inoculated, only one in 261.[3]

The 'Islington Benjamin Franklin' first appeared as vestryman in 1761, in the year the American returned to Philadelphia from his second British visit, and also in 1767–9 which coincides with his third visit. But any attempt to identify the celebrated American statesman with an Islington vestryman falls down on several counts. There is no such evidence in Franklin's letters (which in personal terms are sadly unrevealing), and besides, while the Islington Franklin's signatures appear in the Vestry Book, the American always signs his letters "B.F." Finally, whenever he stayed in London it was at the same lodgings in Craven Street, and in spite of his evident knowledge of Islington he plainly did not live there.

However, in view of Franklin's friendship with the Strahan family, it seems not impossible that the Islington Benjamin was the son of a mutual friend or relation, a Londoner who knew the American from an earlier visit and named his son after him.

ALEXANDER CRUDEN

Among eccentrics living in Islington in the mid- to late century were two at the opposite extremes of respectability. Alexander Cruden, chiefly remembered for his work *Cruden's Concordance*, was born in Aberdeen in 1699 and educated at Marischal College, where he took an MA, intending to enter the ministry.

32. Alexander Cruden, pictured with his Concordance to the Bible.

Moving to London at the age of 18 he worked as a private tutor, and though apparently of a gentle disposition he was already displaying such oddities of behaviour that he was suspected of insanity. This was explained as the result of a disappointed love affair, and for a time he was privately confined.

Cruden worked variously as a press corrector and a bookseller, kept a shop in the Royal Exchange, and in the 1730s embarked on research for his famous *Concordance of the Scriptures*, which he completed thanks to enormous assiduity, without a contract or even financial backing. Though he dedicated the published work in November 1737 to George II's Queen Caroline, any possible expectation of reward from her was frustrated by her death in the same month.

Depressed and with few prospects, he closed his shop, but for some weeks was again confined in the barbarities of a private asylum, this time in Bethnal Green, which he recorded in detail (chain, handcuffs, strait waistcoat). He brought an unsuccessful action against the warden. This too he recorded and published, though it was long enough before improve-

ments were made to such establishments.

Cruden continued as an accurate and reputable proof-corrector, and undertook several jobs for booksellers; but the sad cycle of confinement for lunacy, subsequent publication and court action, was repeated in the 1750s. Contributing to his reputation for eccentricity he styled himself 'Alexander the Corrector', meaning in this case reformer of morals, such as restoring Sabbath observance, with personal exhortations to the youth of Oxford and Cambridge. His mania extended to applying – needless to say without success – for a knighthood, and to daubing walls with graffiti attacking the politician John Wilkes. More acceptably, he would actually intervene in mobs and "tumultuous assemblies", and thanks to his respectable appearance and gentle demeanour sometimes even succeeded in breaking them up and dispersing the crowds.

Meanwhile he was working on a second edition of the *Concordance*, published in 1761 and presented in person, again with a dedication, to the new King George III. Cruden was also correcting a paper known as the *Public Advertiser*, published by the future Parliamentary reporter Henry Woodfall.

Cruden's philanthropy was notably displayed in saving a sailor named Potter from being hanged for forging a will. He visited Potter in Newgate Prison, exhorted and converted him to religion, and by earnest application to the Secretary of State, Lord Halifax, secured a reprieve. With this encouragement he continued his Newgate visits in the hope of reforming and converting other prisoners, a labour hardly to be equalled until the work of the admirable Mrs Fry.

For much of this time Cruden was living in Islington at what is now 49 Camden Passage. In 1769 he returned to Aberdeen, spending about a year in continuance of his efforts to reform his fellow-men, especially the young. He then returned to his Islington lodging, but on 1 November 1770 was found dead one morning by his landlady, on his knees in prayer, possibly having had an asthmatic attack.

Cruden had never married. He was said to have paid court to the daughter of Sir Thomas Abney, a JP, in 1755, but she refused him. His life was indeed passed in good works – in his careful publications and compilations, strong Calvinistic opinions, and active help to young persons. He used to attend services at Calvinist meeting-places, including Dr Conder's at the Pavement, Moorfields.[4]

A MISER

No less individual, but at the opposite end of worthiness, was the Baron Ephraim Lopez Pereira D'Aguilar, in fact a near neighbour of Cruden with a house at 21 Camden Street (now Camden Walk). He also owned a small farm on the west bank of the New River. A Portuguese Jew born in Vienna in 1740, he owned much land in and around London, and made two profitable marriages by the first of which he had two daughters. His second marriage in 1767 was to a rich widow, with whom he lived in some luxury in the City in Broad Street Buildings, keeping numerous servants, carriages and horses.

Affairs went downhill during the American war, when D'Aguilar lost a profitable estate, his marriage appears to have failed, and he himself (says Nelson) "became rude, slovenly, and careless", affected poverty and lived as a recluse. He was prosecuted for cruelty to his wife, but escaped by pleading poverty. He retreated to a house off Aldersgate Street where he slept at night, but passed the day-time at his so-called farm by the New River. He was said to lure destitute females to his household by taking them on as servants but ultimately keeping them (as Nelson piously puts it) as "ministers to his debaucheries". He also kept their resulting offspring, even several families at a time.

His sumptuous furniture from Broad Street Buildings was now kept in a couple of houses at Bethnal Green, and at other country houses he owned at Twickenham and Sydenham. All the premises were kept locked and unoccupied, save for the meanest maintenance. At Sydenham he kept some starving cattle. This was also the state of his New River farm, "a perfect dunghill" known derisively by disgusted locals as 'Starvation Farm', where the emaciated animals, which he seems to have occasionally fed himself with the most meagre rations, died slowly of starvation, their skeletal frames visible by the river bank. Some

33. Baron D'Aguilar, an engraving of 1802 in the 'Wonderful Magazine'.

were reduced to cannibalism before expiring. Numerous tales were told of the Baron's meanness and the extremities to which his livestock was reduced.

Himself filthy and meanly clad, D'Aguilar was sometimes pelted with refuse by indignant locals. His daughters, who fortunately had married, he mostly shunned, yet in his last illness the younger tried in vain to attend him but was driven off with curses. He allowed neither a doctor to visit nor even a fire in his room, dying (intestate) at Shaftesbury Place in 1802, aged 62, of inflammation of the bowels.

The Baron's untouched riches (despite his losses) were inherited by the daughters, along with his rabble of a household, impoverished women and their children. An auction of his Islington property lasted for two days and realised £128 for his emaciated cattle, £7 for his once fine coach, now falling to pieces and bought by a villager simply for its springs. The Shaftesbury Place house (off Aldersgate Street) contained a valuable library, and he supposedly had £30,000-worth of diamonds and jewels, 7 cwt of plate, and some equally valuable merchandise, cochineal and indigo, which he had long hoarded in hopes of making a high profit. The whole was said to have realised over £200,000.[5]

SAMUEL ROGERS

Islington, until modern times, has few famous literary and artistic connections. Among its literary luminaries in the Newington Green area, which was indeed a haven for dissenting writers and ministers, at this time were Daniel Defoe – at least in his schooldays – Mrs Barbauld, and the poet, Samuel Rogers.

For the early life of Samuel Rogers we must take into account his background, especially the influence of the Rev. Richard Price, who was in a way his boyhood mentor.

Going back more than a generation, Daniel Radford, son of a Chester linen draper and grandson of an evicted Non-conformist minister, the Rev. Philip Henry, had on his father's untimely death been brought up by another minister, the Rev. Matthew Field, author of a Bible commentary. Radford came to London and set up in a partnership in Cheapside, and in 1731 married Mary, daughter of Samuel Harris, an East India merchant, who lived in a large red-brick house (once Sir Richard Halton's) on the rural Newington Green. They settled on the west side of the Green in the house "nearest London".

Radford had taken into partnership Thomas Rogers, a glass manufacturer from Stourbridge. Rogers's son, also Thomas, who came to work for them, married Daniel's daughter, Mary, in 1760 at Islington parish church. The newly married pair first lived at no. 52 the Green, where their son, Samuel, was born in 1763. Soon afterwards Thomas joined a firm of Cornhill bankers known as Welsh and Rogers. The large Radford house passed to him and his family in 1767 and the family was now both well-established and well-to-do. Thomas, who went to the City in his own carriage, is described by a relative as wearing a

34. Samuel Rogers.

light-coloured dress coat with huge cuffs, a three-cornered hat, and his powdered hair in a queue. The family owned an umbrella, then a great rarity, kept in the hall to be held over ladies' heads by a footman as they stepped in or out of their carriage.

The Rogers family also acquired no.35 Newington Green to incorporate into their main house, which was refronted: this family house Samuel Rogers was eventually to sell in 1797.

Samuel's early life gives some insight into not only the wealthy families living on the Green, but also the remarkable, gifted Dr Richard Price (1723–91), who had been private chaplain to Mr George Streatfeild at the house once lived in by Defoe in Stoke Newington. In 1758, after Streatfeild's death, Price was appointed minister to the Unitarian Chapel on the Green, and became a great favourite with the Rogers family, especially in due course with the boys. He regularly turned up at their house in the evenings, straight from his study in his dressing-gown, and they were all influenced by his conversation and his Bible readings and commentary.

35. The Peerless Pool in 1811. It was near today's Old Street roundabout.

Price, a man of great talents, was evidently a fairly quixotic personality. Among scientific works he published, one had an important influence on the development of life assurance. He owned both a telescope and a microscope, and would demonstrate scientific experiments at his house. He was especially good with children.

Once he challenged two men in public office, a Commissary and a Commissioner of Customs, to a hopping race across "the first field between the meeting house and Stoke Newington". He won. Another challenge he lost: to leap right over the Rogers's lawn – when he became entangled in a honeysuckle and "away went the honeysuckle and the doc-

tor together". He took a regular afternoon swim in the Peerless Pool at Shoreditch, and according to the Rogers boys, had once actually leapt across the New River – quite an achievement at twelve feet.

Not surprisingly he was absent-minded and might well go down to his study to take supper forgetting he had supped already. In greatcoat and spatterdashes he rode an old, half-blind horse (which he quite often fell off, once into a "basket of beans" at Covent Garden), and was hailed affectionately by carmen and orange-sellers with the cry, "Make way for Dr Price!" His popularity was due to his standing up for people's rights.

He helped Mary Wollstonecraft to open her

school on Newington Green (see p. 118), though it proved not so much a failure as a non-starter. Miss Wollstonecraft's pew at his chapel was on the East side, next to the Rogers family in the south-east corner farthest from the pulpit. Mrs Barbauld, whose husband Rochemont Barbauld was later minister, was next again. Samuel Rogers became a trustee of the chapel, and many years later in 1844 signed a petition in support of the Dissenters' Chapel Bill, by which 'orthodox Dissenters' would be able to turn out Unitarians from their places of worship.

At that time Newington Green started a weekly supper club, meeting in turn at Dr Price's, the Rogers's and the latters' tutor, Mr Burgh, who kept a school at the south east corner of the Green.

Samuel Rogers records in his *Reminiscences* that their father asked him and his brothers what career they wanted, and to his annoyance Samuel said "to be a preacher" – "for it was then the height of my ambition to figure in a pulpit". Doubtless his admiration for Dr Price had a lot to do with it. Though Samuel did not become a dissenting preacher, his father did abandon the Church of England and joined Dr Price's congregation.

As children the boys played hide-and-seek in a hayloft on the Green and spent their pence at a nearby toyshop. When Samuel was nine the children were taken by their nurse to Sadler's Wells, a trip which greatly impressed them. When he was 13 his parents gave a great children's ball. But about that time their mother died, and their house was then run by Mary Mitchell and a distant cousin, Mrs Mary Worthington. Later Miss Mitchell moved on to Samuel's brother Henry's at Highbury, until her death in 1812.

Samuel recalls how he and his brothers, in their schoolboys' cocked hats, "ran about the fields, chasing butterflies". His first school was Mr Burgh's, and when this moved to Colebrooke Row Samuel went with it.

Though much influenced by Dr Price's precepts, he did not go into the ministry, but entered his father's bank, where he worked until his father's death. However, he remained a supporter of the Unitarians, accepting neither a fixed creed nor orthodox doctrine – including the Trinity.

One day in 1791 while walking back from the bank in the City, he was greatly impressed by the sight of a respectably dressed crowd in mourning, entering two-by-two into what proved to be John Wesley's house. Following them in curiosity, upstairs he found himself in a drawing-room where, laid out on a table, was the waxen-faced corpse of a short man in clerical robes, gown, cassock and bands, Bible and handkerchief in his hands, his face framed by grey hair. It was John Wesley himself of whom devoted followers were taking a solemn leave.

When Samuel's father died in the spring of 1793, he left the bulk of his money to Samuel as his eldest son, who was able gradually to transfer the banking business to his younger brother Henry and thenceforward became a traveller and gentleman of leisure.

He had already begun to contribute to the *Gentleman's Magazine*, and in 1791 published *Pleasures of Memory*. In 1797 he left Newington Green and moved to St James's, where as a poet and man of means his friends were other men of letters. Yet even many years later he liked to return to his well-loved one-time chapel, and visit his old friend Mrs Barbauld and others, whom he greatly entertained by anecdotes of his now eventful life among the celebrated.

Samuel Rogers might be said to be famous for knowing everybody, and for being able to entertain them, in all senses. Yet he became increasingly waspish, once making the excuse that he had a weak voice, "and if I did not say ill-natured things, no-one would hear what I said".[6]

The American poet and essayist Ralph Waldo Emerson describes a breakfast at Samuel's house, the latter then an old man famous for his company and his works of art. He sums up succinctly: "I suppose, no distinguished person has been in England during the last 50 years, who has not been at this house ... like some modern pantheon." Rogers displayed (he says) "cold quiet indiscriminate politeness", which sounds as though he was not seriously interested in his guests. However, he kept them well amused with anecdotes on Scott, Wordsworth, Lord Byron, the Duke of Wellington, Mme de Staël, Talleyrand, Fox, Burke. He also showed them autographs and letters, including of Milton, Washington, Benjamin Franklin, Dr Johnson, even Mozart, to name but a few. He even had some original pages of *Waverley*. This was of course at his Westminster house, but the occasion, and the precious collection of paintings and sculpture, were characteristic.[7]

In 1824 Washington Irving called on Rogers, apparently this time at Newington Green, for in walking with him to his brother's at Paddington he says they passed White Conduit House. Rogers was in his element, every now and then "stopping to speak with various persons … the Duke this, Sir Harry that", and speculating on "the character and concerns of people whom we met", while recounting anecdotes about Lord Byron, whom he had met at Pisa. Their call was a family visit, to dine also with Rogers's sister and "several nephews".[8] Such typical encounters illustrate the rich quality of Rogers's life, whether entertaining notabilities at his house, or out in the streets, he knew everybody who was worth knowing.

Described when he was 81 as "a slight, aged figure, with a peculiarly and rather cankered-looking visage",[9] Rogers lived until 1855 when he was 92 years of age, and in 1850 on the death of Wordsworth, he was offered the position of Poet Laureate. He refused.

MARY WOLLSTONECRAFT

Mary Wollstonecraft's sojourn in Newington Green was both brief and fraught. Born in Spitalfields in 1759, she lived with her family in Hoxton, Hackney and elsewhere. In 1784 with two of her sisters and her friend Fanny Blood, she moved to Islington (address unspecified) and advertised in vain to teach young lady pupils. Hearing of a large old empty house on Newington Green they moved there and tried again, with slightly better success. In the teeth of competition with the many existing schools the fairly basic education they offered attracted just a few day pupils.

Probably Mary's happiest experience here was meeting the radical Rev. Richard Price whose principles greatly influenced her. Yet, though regularly attending his chapel she was never converted to his Dissenting beliefs.

Thanks to Price's wide acquaintanceship

which included such thinkers and philosophers as Benjamin Franklin and Joseph Priestley, Mary was enabled through a local schoolmaster to visit Samual Johnson, then near the end of his life at his friends' home in Highbury.

After barely two years at the Green, in 1786 Mary returned from a visit to France to see her dying friend, Fanny, only to find the school closed for lack of pupils. With mounting debts the sisters left for teaching jobs. Mary, not surprisingly anxious and depressed, took on a governess's post with an aristocratic family in Ireland.

Yet during her time at Newington Green Mary Wollstonecraft contrived to write, at great speed, her first published work, *Thoughts on the Education of Daughters*.[10]

1   *The Papers of Benjamin Franklin*, ed. Leonard W Labaree, Yale UP, Vol. 17, 1973, p. 19.

2   *Ib.*, Vol. 9, 1966, pp. 256, 267-9.

3   *Ib.*, Vol. 8, 1965, pp. 285 & *n*, Genevieve Miller, *Adoption of Inoculation for Smallpox in England and France*, Philadelphia, 1947, pp. 146-56.

4   Nelson, *Islington*, pp. 392-400; *DNB*, ad Keay.

5   Nelson, *Islington*, pp. 386-92.

6   *Recollections of Samuel Rogers*, London, 1859; A J Shirren, *Samuel Rogers: The Poet from Newington Green*, Stoke Newington Public Libraries, 1963; *Reminiscences and Table Talk of Samuel Rogers*, ed. G H Powell, London, 1903.

In November 2004 a portrait of Dr Price by Benjamin West was among works put up for auction at Christie's by the insurance firm Equitable Life, who had owned it since 1864. Its sale was opposed by the minister of the Newington Green Unitarian church, the Rev. Cal Courtney, who had hoped that it might be acquired by the National Gallery or Tate Gallery to be kept in Britain. However, the portrait, which depicts Dr Price holding a letter from Benjamin Franklin, attracted no immediate bids at the auction, but was sold in absentia for £32,000 to the National Museum of Wales at Aberystwyth. (*Islington Tribune*, 26 November 2004)

7   *The Letters of Ralph Waldo Emerson*, ed. Ralph L Rusk, New York, 1939, Vol. III, p. 425.

8   *Journal of Washington Irving (1823-1824)*, ed. Stanley T Williams, Cambridge, Harvard UP, 1931, p. 198.

9   David Masson, *Memories of London in the Forties*, Edinburgh & London, 1908, p. 108.

10 Claire Tomalin, *Life and Death of Mary Wollstonecraft*, Penguin Books, 1992.

CHAPTER 13

Highways, Buildings and Boundaries

THE NEW ROAD

A highway which was to have a profound effect on the village of Islington, but which its Vestry seems to have completely ignored for many years after its completion, was known as 'the New Road'.

Until this was formed, Londoners wanting to cross the capital from west to east, or even to the north, had no alternative but to travel via Piccadilly and the Strand, or by the Oxford Road leading to Holborn, over 'the stones', as the capital's paved streets were known. These streets were notoriously congested, and on top of the usual traffic there was the hazard of cattle being driven to Smithfield from practically anywhere. Contemporary drawings and engravings almost always show a flock of sheep or herd of cattle among the fashionable urban throng. It was largely this which dictated the campaign to make the New Road.

A group of influential gentlemen therefore proposed the building of a road from the Edgware Road at Paddington through Marylebone, crossing Tottenham Court Road, and continuing via Battle Bridge to Islington, and this was put to the Trustees of the Islington Turnpike in 1755. It could only be achieved with the consent of the land-owners, notably the Dukes of Grafton and Bedford whose estates stretched across the north of London. Though the road was planned to skirt their boundaries there was fierce opposition from the Duke of Bedford. The Duke of Grafton, owner of the land farther west, was in favour.

Also strongly in favour were those involved in the Smithfield cattle trade and the "Graziers, Salesmen, Butchers, Drovers and Dealers in Cattle" submitted one of many sup-portive petitions to Parliament. The heavy traffic through London (they pointed out) was a physical danger to their cattle, some of which were regularly either maimed or driven to panic flight, killing or injuring passers-by or damaging traders' goods. Besides avoiding such accidents and dangers, the Bill's main objects, after a survey of the fields was completed, were "free and easy communication" between Essex and Middlesex without passing through London, preservation of the paving, and lessening street congestion. Moreover, such a road would be a national defensive measure. In times of public danger, military forces could "easily and expeditiously" use this "circumvallation" of London to reach their destination.

The Act was passed in May 1756, and the Trustees of the two relevant Turnpikes met to consider a last survey and arrange purchase of the necessary land. This involved removal of trees and other obstructions, and hence compensation to the respective land-owners. Oddly enough one stipulation was that the road should be unpaved, as the chief traffic was expected to be cattle. However, experience soon showed that carts engaged in building the road turned the surface into mud in winter, and when the road opened in 1757 ballast had to be used to level it. Within a few years it was fully paved.

By the terms of the Act the New Road was a minimum of 40 foot in width, and no building was allowed within 50 feet on either side. Covering these rural fields from Paddington to Islington, well north of the ducal estates and of 'the stones', the New Road was London's first by-pass.[1]

MORE TOLL ROADS

In most respects Islington's concerns remained distinctly parochial, largely dictated by its now visible growth. Its older mansions had been subdivided and adapted to baser uses, while from the 1760s the village was being built up with new high-roads and terraces. In 1761, the first year of King George III's reign, a gentleman named Charles Dingley[2] initiated building of a road to link Islington's southern limit at the Angel with the Dog-House Bar, a toll-gate near the end of Old Street where the City's hounds were kept (their huntsmen too lived nearby). He obtained an Act

> "for making, widening, and repairing, a Road from the North-east Side of the Goswell-street Road near Islington ... and near to the Road called the *New Road* over the Fields and Grounds to Old-street Road, opposite to the Dog-house Bar, and ... from the *Dog-House Bar* to the end of Chiswell-street by the Artillery ground".[3]

This vital communication was completed and opened on 29 June, 1761. The City Road, as it would be called, created a more direct connection with the west part of the City than the winding St John Street and Goswell Road, which led only to parts outside the walls. It performed a useful service by linking with the New Road, thus creating a spacious through-route to the City and a major junction at the Angel.

Shortly afterwards a turnpike gate was erected just beyond the Angel at the entrance to Islington village at the end of White Lion Street. (It was moved in about 1800 nearer to Liverpool Road, but proving a cause of accidents because of a sharp turn, in 1808 it was moved again to a final position midway between the two sites.) The gate was in the usual form with two small buildings, in this case octagonal, with pyramid roofs and central chimneys, one on either side, and a set of three fine standard lamps. There was also a weighing-engine to check the freights of carriages and goods passing through. The whole cost the Highway Trustees about £700.

The Act of 1766 for the City's paving, lighting and street cleansing, also fixed the sites for Islington's other toll-gates, including the City Road, Ball's Pond Road, and Holloway.

In all, Islington now contained 6 miles, 4 furlongs and 7 poles of turnpike roads, directed by the Hampstead and Highgate Trust.[4] Dingley, who died in 1769, was eventually commemorated for his pains by having streets off the City Road re-named after him[5] – though not until long after his death .

The City Road, cutting off nearly a mile from London's existing north exit, ran in a straight line past the Fountain, near Peerless Pool (just by the present day Old Street roundabout), then past the Shepherd and Shepherdess, to the Angel. Nearing Islington it ran between fields and cattle pastures, along an existing track which was straightened and paved in the course of only four months. With lamps alongside and footpaths on either side, it was considered the City's finest exit road.

A street which has retained many of its original houses and whose upkeep was always of importance to the Vestry because it linked Upper and Lower Streets – hence its name – was Cross Street. The earliest houses are on the north side (1720s), while on the south side the long terrace at its foot on the high pavement, facing what was then Fowler House, was built in the 1760s by men who worked on Robert Adam's Adelphi, as several doorcases show. Another short terrace nearer Upper Street dates from 1785.

The 1766 Act also dealt with street lighting, imposing a new duty on the Vestry which, as usual, appointed an *ad hoc* committee to deal with it. The Vestry had in fact been considering the matter since 1761, making annual contracts with local suppliers.[6]

NEW DEVELOPMENTS

The City Road probably contributed to the growing practice of City dwellers building or acquiring houses beyond the built-up area of London. On the higher ground of north Clerkenwell and south Islington, they often had pleasant rural views towards the villages of Highgate and Hampstead.

Not far away, between the New River and Islington Green, a group of houses and later a row was gradually formed from 1768, by degrees becoming the north end of Colebrooke Row. This was on land owned from 1761 by Sir George Colebrooke (who had inherited

Highbury Wood from his father James. Adjoining this were six acres of nursery ground acquired from Colebrooke by two brothers named Watson – one of whom, Willliam, attended intermittently as Vestryman from 1767.)[7] More of the Row was built in 1772–4, but Sir George became bankrupt and the land, together with Highbury Wood, was sold.[8]

Opposite this little group, on the west side of the New River, was the infamous Starvation Farm (see Chapter 12), abutting which was a cottage later to be the home of Charles Lamb. Built about 1760, this house was substantially altered a century later, and has now only a superficial likeness to the original.

Nearer the Green remained farm-land, owned until 1800 by the Pullin family. Northwards was the land known as Hattersfield or Tile Kiln Field, on part of which Bird's Buildings – a new kiln was established by Thomas Bird – went up in 1769. This group surrounded the spot where the New River emerged from the culvert running diagonally under the Lower (Essex) Road. The river then flowed along in between the houses of Colebrooke Row and the later Duncan Terrace.

Two houses (nos 56 and 57 Colebrooke Row), were possibly built in or after 1717 as part of the brewhouse and kilns of Walter Burton, a vestryman, and in 1718–19 a Surveyor of the Highways. No. 57 seems to have been the Castle Inn. The next two (58 and 59) were freestanding, then combined into one as a school by the Rev. Mr Rule, but again occupied separately in about 1795. Two houses built by the carpenter and builder, Samuel Steemson, in about 1745 and 1755, on part of Tile Kiln Field which he leased, are now 54 and 55 Colebrooke Row.

At the south end of the Row was Woodfall's Cottage, set back in a garden and dating from mid-century though surprisingly not shown on contemporary maps. Here from 1772 to 1776 lived the future Parliamentary reporter William Woodfall.

In the last decade of the 18th century the west side of the New River began to be developed, though Colebrooke Cottage (Lamb's house) had stood in isolation for a generation before. 'New Terrace' (later confusingly named Colebrooke Terrace, and now 55–58 Duncan Terrace) was built by James Taylor, a young surveyor, on Clay Pit Field. This was part of the land sold earlier by Colebrooke to raise money. Building continued southwards towards the City Road, and by 1794 Taylor also built Charlton Crescent (since renumbered as part of Charlton Place) and Charlton Place at right angles, leading back to Upper Street.

There were a number of nursery grounds before house-building swallowed them up. In 1756 William Redmond advertised growing "a fine auricula" which he named 'Triumph'. Dr William Pitcairn (1711–91), who lived in Upper Street opposite Cross Street, created a botanical garden covering more than 4 acres behind his house, which was continued after his death. Its existence explains why at this point no street connects Upper Street directly with Barnsbury. Pitcairn, born at Dysart in Scotland, studied at Leyden University, was granted an Oxford doctorate in 1749, admitted to the Royal College of Physicians and in 1750 was elected a Fellow. From 1775 to 1785 he was its President.

DEVELOPMENTS IN HIGHBURY

At the turn of the 1770s little could residents of the garden-fringed Colebrooke Row have imagined that they, and Islington, were on the brink of the huge expansion of which the development of their own small area was only the prelude.

Already in 1767, about the time when the north end of Colebrooke Row was being built, the 8th Earl of Northampton had leased the then empty Canonbury House, with its outbuildings and grounds, to a city stockbroker John Dawes, for 61 years. Dawes introduced the pattern of demolishing the old in favour of the new, knocking down the south range of the manor-house and replacing it with a short terrace of five houses to form Canonbury Place. These he leased to the Earl and occupied one himself.

Although until after the turn of the century little else in the building line took place in Canonbury, Dawes soon turned his attention to acquiring manorial lands in Highbury, on the site of the moated Prior's house, at the top of what is now Highbury Hill. (Eton House flats are now on the site.) In 1781 Dawes built

36. Highbury House in the 1790s.

37. Highbury Place, early 19th century. The view is from today's Highbury Corner.

Highbury House for himself.[9] By 1774 he had already leased part of this land to a builder, John Spiller, who set about lining the fields with a handsome terrace in modish style. Between 1774 and 1779 Spiller had built Highbury Place in three consecutive rows, some with coach-houses and other outbuildings, ascending the slight slope to the top where he kept the end house for himself. The architect was his son, James, who had studied under James Wyatt.[10]

These houses were on 67-year leases, and in 1776 Spiller was protected from competition by a guarantee from Dawes that the fields opposite on the west side should not be built on. In 1779, when Spiller built Highbury Terrace on the other side of the fields, it was well above the existing row, and here these elegant terraces which seem as if they might have escaped from Bath – given the more commonplace brick instead of fine stone – remained in isolation for decades (and even preserve the local illusion to this day).

TROUBLE ON THE ROADS

Still in hot water over highway upkeep, in the 1770s the Vestry was reported by the Surveyor, William Hyde, Esq., for neglecting the repair of 'Tollington als Devils Lane', as well as Heame and Hopping Lanes. Although this proved contentious enough it was child's play compared with the long-running disagreement with St Pancras over responsibility for Maiden Lane (now York Way). The dispute was not settled for nearly 20 years, and then only to Islington's great disadvantage.

The case was repeatedly heard at King's Bench. Mr John Weston and other land-owners in the Lane charged the parish with continued failure to repair. Judgement invariably went against Islington. For some years the Vestry got by with compromise, guaranteeing to spend £60 a year on upkeep, until in 1782 two new Surveyors, Henry Wright and John Jackson, declared that even "to make it barely passable" would need the huge sum of £1,287. The JPs threatened closure, but the Surveyors "waited on the occupiers" and persuaded them to sign an affidavit that the Lane was of no public use. A return to King's Bench ended in deferred judgement, but to

avoid a large fine, which would require raising a new rate, a meeting was arranged at the Queen's Head, Holborn between the Surveyor and Mr Weston and others on the prosecution side. By offering payments for eight years and covering costs, the Vestry hoped it was now cleared of further obligation (April 1784).

The Vestry had enough trouble some time after this concerning the road from Newington Green to Bowes Park in Edmonton, when Islington was threatened with a charge in lieu of 30 days' work (1789). A committee, including Henry Wright and Nathaniel Clarkson, pointed out that none of the road was in their parish, and in 1793 this claim was finally settled.

By that time, to Vestry chagrin, after nine years of quiescence the Maiden Lane case had surfaced again. Islington was found guilty of non-repair on the grounds that it "appeared beyond doubt" that at least part of the road was within their limits (May 1793). As the sum now needed had risen to £3,000, it was allowed that because of "the magnitude of the object" to Islington, further discussion was reasonable.[11]

Islington certainly had strong points in its favour. It was in a situation similar to several other parishes, as Maiden Lane was the boundary with St Pancras, as shown in the map of 1735, and there were even boundary stones. It was a narrow lane linking Islington with St Pancras parish, including its church. As for any concern on Islington's side, the Vestry pointed out the road's "inutility", for it did not link with its other highways. Mr John Weston (who by this time had died) had actually erected a notice-board "when he was at variance with the parish", identifying the parish boundary as 20 feet from his property and in the middle of the road. This notice-board proved to be the king-pin of the case – but not in the way expected.

In October 1793 when the jury inspected the site, taking other features into account they determined that Islington was justified in seeking relief from liability to repair. During a further deferment of the case, a committee headed by the Rev. George Strahan and including Henry Wright, Edmund Clutterbuck and William Wickings, obtained useful advice from Mr George Wood of Middle Temple and consulted the Surveyors over the cost of necessary repairs. Even erecting a toll-gate would raise only a small proportion of the cost, and it seemed as if their only course might be application to Parliament. In February 1794 the committee reported that George Wood had considered their evidence perfectly admissible and that the Sessions had been unfair to refuse a hearing. Armed with an apparently watertight case, they referred back to King's Bench for a ruling that St Pancras parish was liable both for repairs and to maintain a moiety for upkeep. In support they quoted historical records from Lambeth Palace, St Paul's Chapter House and the Steward of Cantelowes Manor in St Pancras.

Yet to their dismay the Chief Justice did not even call some of the vital evidence, and while admitting that by English law a road between two parishes was *prima facie* the responsibility of both, and in natural justice other features seemed to be conclusive for Islington, by his reasoning the famous notice-board put up by Mr Weston was conclusive *against* Islington. With so unfair a judgement Islington's Surveyors and the committee were left with the unwelcome realisation that they "could only lament the Opinion given by his Lordship".

Their only recourse seemed to be to seek authority to collect a toll. But the road was only a lane, ill-paved and little used, and receipts from tolls would be very low. It was therefore accepted that it should be made into a good carriage road and hence be taken over by the Turnpike Trust. On hearing the tale of woe, the Trustees agreed that at their expense it should be made a good turnpike road which they would maintain, provided the parish paid for the application to Parliament (6 Nov. 1794). York Way remains the boundary with St Pancras (Camden) to this day.

THE POPULATION GROWS

The official figure for Islington's population was not ascertained until the Census of 1801, when it was given as 10,212. After this it rose, or rocketed, through most of the 19th century.

But in the 1770s with the building of new streets the effect of a rising population could already be seen. When in 1777 the Vestry was arguing about how St Mary's Church, still little

more than 20 years old, could contain all the parish inhabitants, the pressure on seating was increasingly visible. New pews had to be fitted into the aisles and in April 1778 no less than 44 new seatings were confirmed in a church hitherto needing no more than about 10 at a time. Even a year later there were 24, clearly newcomers, for only their surnames, not Christian names, were known and with addresses given for the first time. Some were in new streets such as Bird's Buildings, Camden Street and Highbury Place.

Before the first Census, population estimates were usually based on the number of houses, and Nelson's figures for the 18th century are calculated for 1708 as 325 houses, for 1754, 937, and by 1788, 1,060. The first two figures he took from published sources, Edward Hatton's *New View of London* (1708) and Seymour's *Survey of Londo*n (1754), the third from a manuscript note of 1793 by the Vestry Clerk, John Biggerstaff.

In 1793, when the number of inhabitants was calculated for the first time, Biggerstaff estimated that there were 1,200 houses, which seemed to imply 6,600 persons.

So far the biggest increase in houses had been in the first half of the century, then a steady increase for some years, then another sudden rise. The 1801 figures of 1,745 houses and 10,212 inhabitants, reflected the combined effect of the Napoleonic Wars and the huge influx of people from country to town because of the century's great industrial advances. The picture was changing very rapidly.

Nelson justifiably doubts the accuracy of the earlier figures and points out that Islington had a changing temporary population from its many lodgers, especially during the summer. The large increase in St Mary's Church pew sittings, however, may be more associated with a rise in permanent dwellers.

By 1787 the Churchwardens had to devote so much time to pew allocations that they had to present the particulars at separate meetings: for example in September there were an unprecedented 114 newcomers, again inhabiting new streets and terraces such as Britannia Row, Highbury Barn, Bray's Buildings and Lamb Lane. In March 1788 there were 64, which took three meetings to settle.

Yet the seating problems continued. As we

have seen, with the number of private schools also increasing, the Vestry had to discontinue the time-honoured custom of admitting the proprietors and their pupils. In March 1787 Mr David Davies of "the Brewers School" – that is, Owen's – had to be told that their children could not be given pew space, and in September it was uncompromisingly announced that "the number of Boarding Schools in this parish having increased and still increasing", it was no longer possible to provide seats for *any* boarding-school keeper.[12]

HOUSING THE DEAD

In 1786 Robert Mylne, Chief Surveyor at the New River Head, when consulted on repairs to the church, had advised the Vestry to bear in mind the great increase in parish population in the 30 years since the church was built. With room neither for living nor dead, he suggested buying land for an enlarged churchyard at a distance, for "bound as it is by the Highway on one side, and by houses and valuable property on the three other sides of it", they could not hope to acquire adjacent property. In this instance, fortunately for the Vestry he was to be proved wrong.

On the death of a parishioner, John Briggs, his small estate between the east boundary of the churchyard and Lower Street, was put on the market. In May 1790 the parish agreed to offer for it. The usual committee, this time 13 vestrymen headed by the vicar, the Rev. George Strahan, agreed a price of £2,000, and as with financing the building of the church, the capital was raised by offering annuities, the costs minimised by selling a house and outbuildings on the site for £800.

Settlement took some time. As the property was within the manor of Canonbury, there was the matter of enfranchising the land. Eighteen months passed before the committee dealt with it, and after a couple of applications to Lord Northampton's Steward, Mr Boodle, it was learned that the Earl was in such poor health that his estate was being managed by Trustees – and one of these was in Switzerland for his health. Another seven months passed before the Trustees finally dealt with the matter and at last the Vestry

was free to apply to Parliament for official enfranchisement.

By 1793 the land was theirs. In November it was agreed to use the 'green' removed when levelling the land for burials, in order to fill a pond which had adorned John Briggs's grounds, and the new burial site was consecrated in late December. Future burials in the old churchyard (except where families already had a site) were henceforward forbidden.

1   *Survey of London*, Vol. XXIV, *King's Cross Neighbourhood*, LCC, 1952, pp. 114-15.

2   According to Nelson (*Islington*, p. 19n.) Dingley acquired some fame for attempting (unsuccessfully) to introduce a sawmill into industry at Limehouse.

3   Nelson, *Islington*, pp. 19-20.

4   *Ibid*,, pp. 20-21.

5   Dingley Place, dating from 1832, was originally named George's Row and Dingley Road of 1876 started as Harcourt Place.

6   Information on lighting, officials and highways is found in VM, Vol. III. No. 53 Cross Street, end of the 1785 terrace, was stripped to its wall surfaces in the 1990s to reveal original wallpapers, and otherwise 'excavated' by its then tenant, Martin King, who rescued many historic features and items, notably a pair of cotton leggings with a note that their owner, George Shaw, went to Jamaica in March 1795.

7   Nelson, *Islington*, p. 384.

8   Adjoining these are the original Colebrooke Row, nos 34-36 and 41-53, built in 1768 and 1772-4. Nos 32 and 33 were destroyed in the 1950s.

9   Nelson dates Highbury House as 1778, the *VCH* as 1781.

10   *VCH*, p. 38.

11   The Maiden Lane dispute is recorded in VM, Vols. III & IV.

12   Nelson, *Islington*, pp. 11, 408; VM Vol. IV.

CHAPTER 14

The Workhouse, 1723 – 1777

The poor were regarded as an incubus, with which each parish dealt independently; hence the local poor rate. Moreover, there was a long-entrenched attitude that, except for the old and ill, poverty was in some sense a crime, or at the least one's own fault.

An Act passed in 1723 aimed to reduce the number of outdoor or 'casual' paupers, by driving the able-bodied unemployed indoors to a workhouse. (Until 1782 the 'Workhouse Test' was rigorously applied. But the 'work' concept was a counsel of perfection: in only a few scattered instances was any real effort made at a literal interpretation as 'a house of industry'.

Compliance with any Act was usually slow, not least in Islington. Only in 1726 did the Vestry begin discussions with Hornsey parish, which had established a workhouse in Stroud Green. In September Philip Oddy was authorised to discuss it with Mr Serjeant Cheshire, and it was agreed that Islington and Hornsey Overseers of the Poor unite, at least for a year. Within two years the Islington Overseers decided that Stroud Green was inconveniently far, and the long search began for independent premises, rented or purpose-built. As no house appeared suitable, in October 1728 they decided to build, preferably in the 'Back Road', today's Liverpool Road.

This proved to be the start of half a century of muddle, mismanagement, inadequate personnel and unsatisfactory premises. Indeed, the only regular features were dishonesty, and the death-toll.

To find a site, the inevitable committee was appointed. Some sites were ruled out for high price and complexities of title. Others were off the Back Road, accessible but isolated, including the Hundredth Acre, a parish-owned "little field or Close" occupied by Richard Flower, "near the lane turning from thence into the Town by Justice Harvey's new built Wall". While they were negotiating to issue £40 annuities to finance a deal, based on the (also parish-owned) Cloudesley or Stone Field estate, now leased to Samuel Pullin, Justice Harvey objected to the proposed building's being too near his house. The search dragged on.

Two more land-owners, Sir John Austen and Sir William Halton, applied to for use of "a Peice of waste", "with all convenient speed", evidently refused despite the urgency. Eventually, by February 1729 the Vestry had decided to rent rather than build[1] and in April found a suitable house at Ring Cross, at the junction of the Back Road and Holloway Road. It was the site of a medieval cross, and the Workhouse was about a furlong north of that junction. A list of vestrymen was drawn up to act as lessees or trustees: the Vicar, the Rev. Mr Kerie, the Churchwardens and Overseers, two JPs, Richard Browne and Jacob Harvey, and eight vestrymen including Samuel Pullin and Thomas Science. These Trustees were to engage a Master, Mistress and workhouse officers, supervise admissions, and suggest rules for good management. A lease for the 'House & Appurtenances' was executed on 12 June, and once the Workhouse was operating the committee was discharged.

The pensioned poor were summoned before the Vestry annually after Easter for review.

In 1729, for example, of 44 pensions approved as continuing, 39 applicants were allowed four, six or eight shillings. Three were reduced to a shilling, and only two granted as much as ten. Four women did not appear and presumably their pensions lapsed. In 1730, only five adult pensions were continued, one at only four shillings, the others ranging from 10 to 16 shillings. Six children were allowed six or eight shillings, and Widow Dobson was ordered to the Workhouse. Isobel Gresham, being very poor and promising to leave the parish at once, received a single payment of half-a-crown for her children. One may wonder where they went.

The Vestry also took note of how children who appeared before them were dressed, and approved that they were "newly cloathed" by the Overseers, who were authorised to dispense clothing as they saw fit.

From then on, while pensions were continued for 'outside' poor, most were consigned to the Workhouse, where although officially intended for employment as well as keep, little attention seems to have been paid to work.

The Workhouse's organisation, or lack of it, seemed tailor-made for misrule.

The Master's salary was £16 a year paid quarterly, with a month's notice on either side, though the Vestry might pay a month's salary in lieu. The Master on his side must apply in writing to an Overseer for approval by the Vestry.

The first Master, Mr Robert Samuel, continued in the post after his first year and was joined by Mrs Anne Bannister as Mistress, at £8. As Mrs Bannister was pregnant (by whom is not stated: she was possibly a widow carrying a posthumous child), two guineas were allowed for her lying-in. The appointment was not a success, nor were most of those which followed. Mrs Bannister perhaps felt that a new baby increased her need for money, or perhaps was just naturally dishonest. Only six months later goods were found to be missing at the House, which enquiry showed that she had pawned or stolen. After an Overseers' inspection, Master and Mistress were both discharged, and Mrs Bannister was prosecuted for theft.

Mr and Mrs William Edwards were engaged in their stead, ordered to keep proper accounts and were paid £24 a year between them. Sarah Stone at £4 was appointed the Mistress's assistant.

Robert Samuel and Anne Bannister proved to be prototypes of a string of crooks and misfits who followed, and indeed setting up the Workhouse was only the start of trouble. A stream of problems, to do with management, catering, site and governors' behaviour, added up to a continuing disaster story. In 1733 an inspection committee was set up, which included William Booth, Esq. and leading vestrymen Philip Oddy, Samuel Pullin, Thomas Science and James Terrett.

From 1732 an annual rota was drawn up to supply the workhouse with medicines and medical services by four apothecaries, starting like the other parish officers on Easter Tuesday. First was John Poyner, a vestryman, with a regular fee of £36. The three who followed Poyner were, supposedly, Mrs Penelope Morris, Moses Durell and Charles Fowler; but the scheme seems not at first to have been regularly enforced. Three years later the Vestry was still discussing the fee for medicine supply (hopefully reduced to £20), and if no apothecaries accepted the offer, the Churchwardens were ordered to advertise.

John Poyner applied again, but because of the distance from the "town" the offer was raised to £30 though apparently not as a permanent arrangement. Supplies seem to have been sporadic and privately made by unauthorised agreements with Overseers. After Easter 1740 a regular system was started, again first with Poyner and for £36, as it remained for many years. Supplies and payments were to be through the Vestry, by order, and all attendances had to be by contract, for the outside poor as well as those inside the Workhouse. No apothecary might supply medicines except by signing a contract in the Vestry Room at Easter. Thenceforward this was always observed.

Poyner contracted frequently during the next years, alternating with William Windows, Thomas Shirley and others. For some reason the fee in 1759 was reduced to £26 – possibly Poyner was sick or dying, unable to fulfil the duties, for he disappears from the record and for a time his successors continued at only £26 – including his wife or widow,

Mrs Anne Poyner, in 1763. In 1766 the figure was again £36 for Thomas Shirley (in 1767 Mrs Poyner similarly benefited), where it stayed. In 1773 the name John Poyner reappears, probably the son.

Pensions continued under annual review. In May 1734, one Edward Rush was allowed seven shillings a month, "he being Sick and having a Wife and four small Children"; Katherine Thompson with breast cancer "in a very bad condition" was given a rise to six shillings. Two boys were removed from their foster nurse's care to the Workhouse, a bleak prospect, and in another case requiring proof of residence, a weekly shilling was granted until the husband could prove settlement in the parish before a JP.

The House was still mismanaged, and in 1737, in an attempt at reform, weekly inspections were ordered by the Churchwardens. Again officers were found to have private agreements for the supply of provisions, no doubt with interested tradesmen (themselves perhaps vestrymen). Unauthorised admission to the Workhouse was also forbidden.

As usual officialdom worked slowly or not at all. Two years later (May 1739) the committee of management had again to be reminded to meet weekly, and tenders for provisions were again invited. In 1740 a malt mill was ordered. The number of inmates, assessed every spring, at this time averaged about 40, many of them children. One or two were occasionally discharged: children were sent out to apprenticeships, and one "lunatick" woman inmate was sent to Bedlam.

Problems surfaced again in 1741. The Master had to retire through "infirmities", and the house was declared inconvenient; but after six weeks the Overseers had found neither new house nor new Master. Advertising the joint post in August 1742 at £20 (or £12 and £8 if not a married couple) brought applications from three couples and a widow, and James Corneck and his wife were chosen.[2]

Unsatisfactory Masters were the norm, and the Vestry seemed to have a genius for choosing them. In any case the job seemed to be regarded as a sinecure for the old and ailing, and several died after only a short time in office. The Cornecks were another failure. In April 1743 they were summoned to a vestry meeting to answer complaints, but were nevertheless continued in office if only temporarily. When they did attend they made, significantly, several contracts for provisions.

Settlements for supplies from butchers and grocers were made half-yearly. These included officially "good" cheese and butter from Mr William Thomas, beef and mutton in "pieces", by Benjamin Sweetman, an Overseer, for "Beef the thick flank Leg Mutton piece Clod & Sticken and Legs Mutton about three Stone, wth Neck Mutton Occasionally for sick persons", "Good" small beer at 8 shillings the barrel from Mr Harvey and milk by "Winchester Quart" from Edward Crane at 15d – or Walter Sebbon offered for the same should he object. Vestrymen seem to have cashed in on the contracts, and the repetition of "good" is suggestive. We never hear what happened to the food on arrival at the Workhouse and much probably ended up with the Master and Mistress. The record's wishful thinking does not match the traditional ugly picture of Workhouse life. Nor did it improve. The Cornecks were found wanting during several inspections by the Overseers and their supporting committee. "Great Abuses are Committed there", very likely in part from misappropriation of the grand-sounding supplies. Early in February 1744 the Cornecks were discharged, and Andrew Francis became a temporary governor.

The Poor at their annual examination were able to enlighten the Vestry. The Cornecks were shown to be guilty of "partialities and Neglects", and a formidable body of Churchwardens, Overseers and interested parishioners were again ordered to visit and "admonish" the couple to be "Careful to behave better" (14 March 1744).

Late in May Henry Hughes was appointed Master, apparently to satisfaction, for apart from the annual Apothecary's contract there is silence for a couple of years until Hughes died, and in his place Andrew Hoatson was appointed (August 1746).

Then in 1748 the question of more convenient premises arose again. A Mrs Adams offered a house in Lower Street (Essex Road) on a 20-year lease at £16 "clear of taxes", but the Vestry unanimously rejected it, and the old building continued to deteriorate. By November 1748 Hoatson too had fallen sick and died. His widow Jane was allowed £2.10 a year, and Jane Corneck, in view of her age, was granted a pension of £3 a year.

The next Master and Mistress, William and Sarah Stimson, proved no longer-lasting. This time it was the wife who died, in the summer of 1750. Mrs Corneck was one of four applicants petitioning for her place – unsuccessfully, though her pension was increased to £5. The post went to Elizabeth Upton.

At the same time sad little domestic dramas were enacted when John Bannister, possibly a son of the discredited Mrs Anne, went bankrupt, and the Overseers were ordered to "lay down" a maximum of four guineas for his furniture and remove it to the Workhouse, leaving some for use of his wife and two children. But before long an Overseer, Richard Mason, reported that after paying the four guineas for Bannister's goods, he had had to leave it all for the wife who needed furniture to keep her family by taking in lodgers.

Next came a maintenance case. The father of a crippled 7-year-old boy who had been some time in the Workhouse died: his very name, 'Mr Thomas Islington', suggests that he himself had perhaps started life as a parish foundling. A friend who had sold the dead father's effects was to hand over the money to the Overseers for the boy's maintenance (August 1751).

Death still relentlessly stalked the workhouse Masters. By September 1752 William Stimson too was dead, and a new master was engaged, William Bodell, out of three who applied (including Stephen Rasbury, a vestryman). After two years as if on cue he too died. Was there perhaps something toxic in the very air of the Workhouse? The Vestry (who were at the time still arguing over responsibility for the chancel) then appointed John White out of only two candidates. In less than two years (May 1756) the Overseers were complaining that in spite of reproof White, too, "daily" neglected his duty. Summoned to a vestry meeting, he boldly affirmed that for him to be more attentive was not "convenient", and from Midsummer he was accordingly dismissed. After a brief lull, or perhaps a muddling through, in January 1757 Samuel

Burton was employed.

By the next Christmas the old Workhouse was found "so much decay'd that it is now unfit for the reception of the poor", and the overseers gave notice that they would quit the building on Lady Day (March 25th, old New Year's Day). The usual committee was appointed to seek an appropriate house, and met, as quite frequently, at the King's Head opposite the church.

On 8 January 1758 Jacob Harvey reported that the committee had found only two possible buildings, the White Hart Inn and the house formerly Dr Poole's, both in such poor condition that they needed inspection by "proper persons" to assess repairs and costs. The Vestry did not approve of the inn, and asked the committee to get an estimate for Dr Poole's, but also to seek another alternative. Dr Poole's was the old Ward's Place, which had been used as a smallpox hospital since 1740.[3] After a week John Boustred, as Upper Churchwarden, reported that Walter Sebbon, representing Mrs Elisabeth Grimstead, was offering Dr Poole's at £20 a year, but with an estimated £73 10s for repairs and £10 for glazing. The Vestry discharged the committee.

Churchwardens and overseers now negotiated for some months, for "a House near the Meeting in the lower Street" – that is the same one – at £13 rent clear of taxes and repairs. They made an agreement early in July, yet more than another six months passed before the Vestry even met again, and then only for the annual Surveyors' nomination and pew allocation.

Muddle at the old Workhouse continued, and in February 1759 the usual complaint of "great Neglects and Mismanagements" was aired against Master and Mistress. A month later, after a desperate notice in the *Daily Advertiser*, the Vestry considered five applications, three of which were referred for a committee decision. Only two applicants turned up, and John Shot Clark and his wife were chosen.

The vestry minutes are silent on the outcome of the building negotiations, but Nelson's *History* confirms that the former Ward's Place/Dr Poole's became the Workhouse for a time. The Clarks moved in on 31 March, and Clark made the constructive, if belated proposal to employ the poor in "spinning Linnen and Woollen or picking Oackum, or other Employment for the Family Business", according to ability and subject to parish committee inspection. This would certainly keep people occupied, though with the lurking danger of exploitation.

Even this apparently positive move did not work. At the very beginning of 1760 the Churchwarden, George Brown, complained that on New Year's Day the Clarks "behaved in a very scandalous and abusive manner to him". The Vestry decided on summary dismissal, with £5 in lieu of a quarter's notice. For lack of a successor, a few days later they gave Clark a short extension, and not until May was a new couple engaged, Thomas and Rebecca Lane, to start early in June. Still the casualty rate was high. In May 1763 Mrs Lane died, so a new Mistress was required. Christian Emerton, a widow, was appointed at the usual £8.[4]

After the usual two years trouble surfaced again. By April 1765 Thomas Lane was dead. His brother John the Beadle was reprimanded for neglect of duty, but excused himself because of gout and other illness. This, interestingly, was considered adequate qualification for succeeding his dead brother as Master, and not surprisingly he "willingly" agreed. (John Green, his successor as Beadle and Bellman, served for a number of years, in this case evidently to satisfaction.)

Again not surprisingly, John Lane did not shine as Master, and less than four months later the Workhouse committee reported "abuses" by both Lane and Mrs Emerton. Summoned for reprimand by the Vestry on 6 August, the vestrymen were naïvely satisfied by their promise to take more care.

At this stage of the saga of muddle Thomas Cogan, a leading Vestryman (who after some years' service becomes promoted from 'Mr' to 'Esq.', perhaps on acquiring landed property) moved for a committee to consider better regulation. Put to a vote, this was surprisingly negatived. This may have been for bureaucratic reasons, for after more debate it was decided to appoint a committee to "enquire" into abuses and determine on better regulations – a modification in the method of approach. The members were as usual the

Churchwardens, Overseers, and 13 vestrymen including Cogan, fellow-Esquires Hamilton Crosse, Samuel Bolton and Charles Palmer, and the ubiquitous Walter Sebbon and Samuel Pullin.

After asking for more time, this committee eventually reported through the Vestry Clerk on Boxing Day 1765. Without specifying the "abuses", they urged that in the parish interest the poor be employed, showing that Clark's suggestion of five years earlier had still not been taken up. The committee had consulted Thomas Perrin, Master of the St Sepulchre's Workhouse, on a "Machine" costing no more than £31 9s. for spinning hemp and flax, on which Perrin proposed to have the inmates instructed. The plan was adopted, and the officials were ordered to keep the machine in constant use. Most of the same committee were called on to be a committee of management – Churchwardens, Overseers, 20 vestrymen and any interested local inhabitants.

Under one of several new Parliamentary Acts, from July 1767 "Gentlemen Inhabitants" were to be appointed Guardians of poor parish children. The Vestry appointed Hammond Crosse, Thomas Cogan, Roger Altham (a proctor), with the vestrymen Charles Brown and Thomas Dale.

As for the Workhouse, at the Easter appointments John Lane was cautiously continued as Master, and since the Mistress, Mrs Emerton, had now died, out of three applicants the Vestry voted for Mrs Elisa Leppington.

Priority was now the rickety premises themselves. In July 1767 more poor people had applied for admission than the house could hold, and anyway it was in such poor condition as to be "improper to be repaired" or extended. A committee of 13 appointed to seek either a site or a better building and agree on cost, consisted of the usual officials with Hamilton Crosse and Cogan, and included Charles and George Brown, possibly brothers.

But in the winter new scandal erupted. A Workhouse committee examining the House Book of expenses, which by Overseers' order had been managed since October by the Beadle John Green and his wife, found on 8 December so great a saving on the bread bill that they suspected "great Mismanagement" by the Master and Mistress, and the Vestry took the sensible if rather overdue step of asking the suffering inmates for their views.

Questioned separately, eleven women declared that under the Beadle's direction the bread allowance had been exactly the same as when John Lane and Mrs Leppington had controlled it. The "saving" now on pounds of bread meant that presumably much had formerly gone to the Master's table.

Lane and Mrs Leppington in their turn were accordingly dismissed, Lane with a weekly pension of seven shillings, until new Overseers were appointed after Easter. Mrs Leppington was allowed three shillings a week during pleasure, payable by the Overseers, and Lane was threatened that unless he leave before Lady Day his pension would not be paid.

The vacancies were announced in church, sealed applications delivered in writing to the Churchwarden. At a ballot on 4 February (1768) when only those who had paid the Poor Rate to date were eligible to vote, of three candidates Thomas Roberts and his wife Magdalen were elected by a rousing majority. At the renewal of offices on Easter Tuesday following (when Constables and Headboroughs for four of the Liberties were nominated), the Robertses were appointed Master and Mistress.

In September the Poor Rate was fixed at 1s. 6d in the pound, from whose receipts were payable George Brown's bill for the Workhouse meat supply and Amery & Company's for its beer. The Robertses, for a change, fulfilled their supervisory duties to satisfaction, so that the following Easter as a reward "for their care" the £20 stipend was actually increased by a £5 gratuity.

At Easter 1768 among nominations for Overseers of the Poor had been the Islington

38. The new workhouse, near the corner of today's Barnsbury Street and Liverpool Road. From a print published in 1819.

Benjamin Franklin (*see Chapter 12*) and Nathaniel Clarkson, painter of the picture for the church (*see Chapter 8*). Franklin, Thomas Oldershaw, a long-standing vestryman, and Benjamin Gee were appointed, and in August or September the following year, when their term had expired, Franklin and Oldershaw reported Poor Rate arrears by eight inhabitants, including two women. They were asked to pursue the debts.

Others were now taking a hand in Workhouse affairs. In September 1770 John Flower, a Cripplegate dealer or merchant in Beach (Beech) Lane, offered to clothe and maintain the poor at a certain price (not recorded). The Workhouse committee concluded it was "not for the advantage of the Parish" – in other words, either Flower was profiteering, or they were too mean to accept.

Soon after the almost statutory two years in the service, both the Robertses were dead, and the ballot for their successors produced 67 votes for John Bowtell and his wife over two competitors. They took over at Christmas from the Beadle John Green and his wife, who had again acted as temporary caretakers.

The Bowtells' appointment was at last both satisfactory and prolonged, serving for several years and earning a gratuity of £8 above their £20 – in spite of a perhaps admonitory notice in 1774 that their appointment was "during pleasure" (of Churchwardens and Overseers).

There had to be trouble, of course, this time again in 1772 over the buildings. It had been hoped that the addition of two rooms on the yard side would suffice, and William Sharwood produced plans for the end of August. Walter Sebbon, still representing Mrs Grimstead, agreed on a repairing lease at £13 clear rent, for a range of between 7 and 11 years, and the alterations were presumably made, though by September Sharwood too was dead.

The House still proving "very Inconvenient and improper", the number of inmates having shot up to about 120, the Vestry agreed on a new building. This time the appointed committee was headed by the Vicar, the philanthropic Rev. George Strahan, and decided on "the 100 Acres" property in the Back Road, bequeathed a long ago by Mrs Amy Hill. For good measure they made instructional visits to other parish Workhouses, and finally adopted an earlier plan submitted by Richard Jupp, a Clerkenwell-born carpenter/architect, with changes to the staircase and some small additions.[5]

This necessitated an Act of Parliament, applied for in the name of the Vicar, the Churchwardens, Overseers and 14 others, including the painter Nathaniel Clarkson, Sebbon and several gentry: Thomas Cogan, Richard Strong and John Dawes of Canonbury House. The Act allowed for borrowing up to £1,000 based on annuities of the lives of persons aged 50 and over, at a maximum 8% interest. A 20d in the pound rate was also fixed.

The Act received the Royal Assent in 1777 and the new Workhouse was built in what became Barnsbury Street, near to Liverpool Road, and here it remained for the next century.

Regulation of Islington Workhouse is covered in VM, Vols. II-IV.

1   VM, Vol. II, 2 October and 3 December 1728, 26 February 1729.

2   Corneck's brother or perhaps son John, a bricklayer, had worked on church repairs and in 1739 was also a Vestryman.

3   According to Nelson it was used for inoculations as an 'outhouse' to the hospital on the site of King's Cross Station, was later a soap factory and then let out in tenements, which would account for its dilapidated state. (*Islington*, p. 205.) In 1744 an Independent meeting-house was built alongside, its back wall probably the garden wall of Ward's Place.

4   Richard Emerton, presumably Christian's husband, named as Beadle in 1762, had died by the following March. His son Edward, was passed over for the post in favour of John Lane, probably brother of the Workhouse Master, Thomas Lane.

5   Richard Jupp (1728-99) was a son and namesake of the Master of the Carpenters' Company, whom he eventually succeeded, and may have studied in Italy or France. He was appointed architect of Guy's Hospital (1759) on John Steere's death. He designed Dyers' Hall in Dowgate Hill (1768-70) and Pain's Hill (1774). From 1768 until his death he was Surveyor to the East India Company and may have designed their East India House (later rebuilt). (Colvin, *British Architects*, pp. 566-7.)

Chapter 15

Fin de Siècle: Revolution in the Air

War Preparations

The 18th century ended with the winds of radicalism, reform and revolution blowing hard. London, like other towns, attracted those displaced from the countryside by developments in agriculture and, although its own industrial background developed very differently from the north of England, the capital was affected by the influx of artisans, unskilled labour and the downright poor, all seeking jobs and homes. And now there was the war. From 1789 many an apprehensive glance was cast at France and when in 1793 Britain finally declared a war which, apart from the brief respite in 1802-3, was to last more than two decades, there was constant fear of a Napoleonic invasion.

In 1796 Islington, like other London parishes, was ordered to raise a quota of men for the army and navy. Modest enough: the figure of ten included Stoke Newington and Glass House Yard liberty, Islington finding eight and the others one apiece. Offering a bounty was agreed as the most likely way to attract the men.

The Treasurer of the Marine Society, Samuel Thornton, circulated a letter to Islington and other parishes soliciting subscriptions to fund such grants to "Sea men and Land men" for the King's service. On 5 May the Churchwarden, John Jackson, reported that eight men, who had agreed to serve in the Navy for a 20-guinea-bounty plus two guineas'-worth of clothing, had been approved by the Recruiting Officer, and were now on board their ships. One wonders what rude awakening greeted them there.

The man who cuts the most colourful figure in Islington in the war-time crisis is Alexander Aubert (1730-1805), a Swiss gentleman who, although born and at first educated in London, was sent to Switzerland at an early age, and having prospered there returned to London in 1752 to join his father's business. Already in 1753 he was director, and later Governor, of the London Assurance Company, and during the French Revolution

39. Alexander Aubert.

40. A view from the top of St Mary's church towards the City of London c.1789, drawn by C H Matthews 1841

chaired a society to suppress sedition. But his chief taste was for science and astronomy, becoming an FRS in 1772, FSA in 1784, and in 1793 a Member of the Imperial Academy of Sciences of St Petersburg.[1] Also skilled in mechanics, Aubert was invited to chair the trustees for the completion of Ramsgate harbour, which in conjunction with his friend John Smeaton, he achieved with some skill.

Having in 1786 built a private observatory near Deptford at Loampit Hill, in 1788 Aubert bought Highbury House, with other adjoining property, some time after the death of its builder John Dawes, and lived here until his death in 1805. In the grounds, whose paddocks,

shrubberies and hothouses he greatly improved, and filled in a moat at the front of the house, Aubert built a tower on which he installed the clock from St Peter le Poer church in Broad Street. More importantly, he added to the house a well-equipped three-storey observatory of his own design, with a solid block of stone to support the instruments. These were products of the best makers, notably a reflecting telescope by James Short bought from the collection of Topham Beauclerk, who had died in 1780.[2]

According to Nelson's *History*, Alexander Aubert was a local favourite, thanks to his "good humour, hospitality, affability, and po-

Anderdon but it was Aubert who was chosen as their commandant, with the rank of Lt-Colonel. Their uniform, on which its eager bearers seem to have spent much time and consideration, was (as Nelson relates) "a blue jacket with white facings, scarlet cuffs, collar and epaulets, and trimmed with silver lace; white kerseymere pantaloons and short gaiters, helmets, and cross belts". The Government supplied arms and accoûtrements, and thus clad and armed, many a local gentleman must have appeared as seductive as did Mr George Wickham of the Hertfordshire militia.

Several of the vestrymen's gentry signed up, and at the next Vestry meetings their enthusiasm showed in their being listed with their acquired rank. On 1 May 1798 Aubert appeared not as 'Esq.' but as 'Lt. Col.', at a meeting intended to debate their contributing "to the public defence". It was adjourned, however, presumably to allow a larger number to attend. On 5 May besides the vicar, the Churchwardens, an Overseer and John Hole – one of the gentry who seems habitually to have taken the chair except when the Vicar was present – there were 24 others, four of whom are given their rank: Major Wheelwright, Lt Thwaites, Lt Harries and Captain Gibson.

A stirring resolution was unanimously made: "That at a time when we are threatened with Invasion from a foreign Enemy it is the duty of all good Citizens to put aside every party difference and to unite in one common exertion". That is, to protect people and property. It was further resolved that the inhabitants be recommended to join the new Volunteers and, as the cavalry corps was now raising, to subscribe to its expenses, John Hole acting as Treasurer.

The Volunteers' declaration and resolutions were ordered to be printed for circulation to the inhabitants. They had been in touch with the Lord Lieutenant, and learned that the Government had accepted their offer of service. A vote of thanks was offered not only for the Vicar's usual "impartial chairmanship", but also to the local farmers who, via the Lord Lieutenant, had offered the services of their waggons, carts and horses.

Yet parish life went on as usual, and Aubert (at the next meeting reverting to simple 'Esq.')

liteness upon every occasion". Among his many distinguished friends were William Pitt the Younger, and Henry Dundas, the Scottish Secretary of State (later Lord Melville), and he was esteemed for his abilities by the King himself.

In Islington Aubert naturally served as a member of the Vestry, and also naturally it was he who had the initiative in 1797 to propose and launch a local corps of military Volunteers. This comprised one company each of cavalry and infantry, funded by voluntary contributions, in numbers soon rising to more than 300 gentlemen from the surrounding area. They served under a captain, J P

and John Hole were both included in the list of Guardians of Poor Children.

As in the event the dreaded invasion by Napoleon did not happen, we lack information on the Loyal Islington Volunteers' activities, though they must have enjoyed their drilling and manoeuvres as greatly as did – for example – the similar corps in Edinburgh in which the young Walter Scott and many contemporaries served.

After four years, Nelson tells us, a dispute between Aubert and some of his officers led to resignations, and numbers began to fall. At the beginning of the new century the Volunteers were disbanded, but the still loyal members presented Aubert with a magnificent silver cup, skilfully decorated and inscribed with a congratulatory address:

This Cup
was presented by the late Corps of
Loyal Islington Volunteers
to Alexander Aubert, Esq.
their Lieut.-Col. Commandant, in testimony
of their respect and esteem
for him, in approbation of his firm and
spirited behaviour in support of the
honour and independence
of the corps, previous to its general
resignation,
and in grateful acknowledgement
of his judicious and liberal conduct
upon all occasions
as their Commander.

The inscription also records that they were "embodied" on 4 March 1797, and when they "unanimously resigned" on 20 January, 1801, the two companies consisted of 314 members.[3]

The corps also compiled for Aubert an appreciative address on his activity, generosity and liberality, emblazoned on vellum, and signed by the Corps Secretary, John Biggerstaff the younger, who with his father had long served as joint Vestry Clerk.

Next year the short peace of Amiens was signed, but with its collapse in 1803 a new military body was raised, the Volunteer Corps of Infantry commanded by Mr Wheelwright, of Highbury, and instructed as Adjutant by Mr Dickson, formerly in the army. Their uniform was slightly less flamboyant – scarlet and black jacket, pantaloons of light blue or grey, and short gaiters.

Aubert was said to be associated with this corps only in an honorary capacity (being then in his seventies), but on the granting of its colours he invited, significantly, "nearly all the respectable inhabitants of Islington" to a dinner and ball in the 74-acre gardens of Highbury House. By October 1806 as the Volunteers' funds were found to be insufficient to continue, they were dissolved, and their hardly glorious but at least picturesque existence came to an end. Colonel Aubert predeceased them by just a year, on a visit to a friend in Wales to see a glass factory near St Asaph, where he became overheated and took a chill of which he died. His body was brought back to Islington and was buried in a vault below the church.[4]

1   *DNB*, Alexander Aubert.
2   Topham Beauclerk (1739-80), friend of Dr Johnson, was grandson of the 1st Duke of St Albans, hence directly descended from Charles II and Nell Gwynne.
3   Nelson, *Islington*, p. 146. The cup is now at the Victoria and Albert Museum.
4   Nelson, *Islington* pp. 141-8.

CHAPTER 16

A Growing Village

NEW HOUSES AND SOME WHO LIVED IN THEM

Islington's expansion as a desirable place for the middle classes to live, starting in the late 18th century, had been initiated by Henry Penton's venture in creating Pentonville, north of the New River Company's lands. Sadly, almost nothing of the original suburb-in-the-country survives, except for a few scattered houses at the top of the hill. Even Aaron Hurst's church, a chapel of ease for St James's Clerkenwell, was unreasonably demolished in the 1980s, though its façade has since been successfully represented in a replica. The justly named Belvidere Tavern at the corner of Penton Street was rebuilt and in the 1990s renamed as a Spanish tapas bar. Even Pentonville's grid system has only partly survived. When it was laid out there was nothing to impede it and no adjustments were needed to fit existing streets for there were none.

Among Pentonville's early residents was a noted Scottish clockmaker, Alexander Cumming, who started his career at Inveraray in mid-century under the patronage of the 3rd Duke of Argyll, and moved to London where he was commissioned to make an astronomical clock for King George III. With workshops in the Strand, he settled with his brother, John, in the new Pentonville. In 1804 Cumming wrote to an old friend describing the pleasures of life in the area, including its own "Assembly", namely White Conduit House on the brow of the hill, fronted by a street then called "the parade" (now Penton Street), though as yet still few houses.[1]

Other town-style ventures in a country setting, Highbury Place and Terrace which soon followed, remained for many years with no nearby development. And Canonbury, apart from John Dawes's experimental venture adjoining the Tower and Manor House, contained only a few houses, none yet identifiable by street name.

In 1803 the 9th Earl of Northampton signed an agreement with "Henry Leroux", an entrepreneur in Stoke Newington, presumably of Huguenot forebears and perhaps to be identified with the architect-speculator Jacob Leroux.[2] This was for a large plot of land bounded on the north by Hopping Lane and on the west by the north end of Upper Street. Leroux started a fine row of houses on Upper Street named Compton Terrace, after the Northampton family, flanking a new chapel to which the Independents in Highbury were to move. A lease in 1805 refers to "an intended square", that is Canonbury Square.

Leroux did not get far, for by 1809, with only a handful of houses built, he was bankrupt and Canonbury's development was delayed until after the Napoleonic wars had ended.

The other development round the turn of the century was on either side of the New River on former Colebrooke land where in the 1790s a "New Terrace" had appeared, later confusingly named Colebrooke Terrace and later still to become nos 50–58 Duncan Terrace. These were the work of James Taylor, a young builder/surveyor whose office was at the top of City Road. At the end of the century another short row of handsome houses (nos 1–10 Duncan Terrace) went up at the City Road end, to be followed in about 1820 by four more. An ornamental feature to these houses was the New River, on its last reach towards New River Head, flowing in front of their doors.[3] Cross Street, always an important highway, linking Upper and Lower Streets, with Fowler House and its grounds at the foot, had already been developed. To this day it remains largely a late-18th-century street, especially on the south side with its linked series of houses, the lowest range on a high pavement, and built by craftsmen who had worked at Somerset House.

This was approximately the extent of building until the end of the war generated the outburst of development that was to transform Islington from a village and create its now characteristic appearance of terraces and squares. By the time this building boom ended with the financial crash of 1825, some of the prettiest streets such as the Cloudesley and Stonefield estates had been begun or at least planned. Stonefield, for centuries in parish hands and let to tenants by the parish office, was then with the influential dairy farmer and Vestryman, Samuel Rhodes. An offer to build a military barracks on the site in 1805 fortunately did not materialise. A proposal to take it on was made in 1809 by the Corporation of London, by then already under pressure to remove the nuisance of Smithfield to a more rural spot. However Islington's dairy farms could not survive much longer as greater profits could be made from building.[4] An Act of 1811 enabled the Trustees to grant land building leases, persuading the Vestry that such profits could finance the building of a much-needed Chapel of Ease for St Mary's, for which a private Act was then put to parliament.

This project too did not materialise as planned, for the expense of William Wickings's design for St Mary Magdalene in the Holloway Road outraged the Vestry.[5] The Stonefield or Cloudesley plan hung fire for a few years though a short terrace in the Back Road (71–79 Liverpool Road) was built just outside the limits of the estate in 1814, while within the estate drainage was laid down. Only in 1818 was the first terrace begun actually within its bounds. Soon afterwards, in 1821, the parish began building on its own Glebe land,

creating Elizabeth Terrace (now Cloudesley Terrace).

Building in London since the Great Fire had theoretically been controlled by Building Acts, though only that of 1774 was very effective. A chief preoccupation was, of course, fire prevention, for example by setting back the window sashes within reveals, instead of flush with the walls. Other rules governed thickness of walls, and types of building material, hence the use of brick rather than timber. There was also an attempt to prevent houses encroaching dangerously on street space. Though professional surveyors were employed in parishes to enforce the Act – such as those annually appointed by Islington vestry – much depended on their quality.

Yet there was no regulation on the width of new streets, height of houses, nor on their ventilation and lighting, and no control over building of basement rooms, or of keeping streets as throughways – hence the number of dank alleys and cul-de-sacs, especially in Clerkenwell, built to cram in as many small houses as possible. By 1840, thousands of Londoners were living in slum conditions. Houses built on the large estates were under the control of their land-owners, who generally preferred to let on building leases rather than sell. But in their estates in Islington and Clerkenwell the Earls of Northampton had not adequately supervised the terms of leases, especially not preventing building on back gardens, so that cheap housing soon covered formerly open ground and overcrowding became serious.

As long ago as the late 16th century London's increased housing had caused alarm, and regulations forbade building within a mile of the City. Hence the expansion of such nearby villages as Islington and St Pancras, separated from London by fields. In the second half of the next century Clerkenwell had more than doubled its number of houses, and in each of the 19th century's first two decades it rose by another quarter, until in 1821 there were calculated to be 4995 houses with 202 more uninhabited and 185 still building. By 1831 the stock again increased by more than 1,000, and (for example) the whole of Spa Fields was already built over.[6]

Two important changes, one bringing temporary benefit, the other causing great hardship, resulted from recent Acts of Parliament. One was the Cholera Act of 1832, enabling houses to be entered for cleansing and fumigation, and the setting up of emergency hospitals, but these lapsed once the epidemic died down. The other was the tough Poor Law Act of 1834 which, at a time when unemployment was regarded almost as a moral crime, ended outdoor relief and forced able-bodied poor into spartan workhouses. More of the poor sought refuge in London, where many could not find jobs, and crowded into districts like Clerkenwell where sweated labour might be available. Here they filled its increasing number of courts and alleys, slums as soon as they were built. Not until the 1840s was there any attempt to address the problem.

Besides the influx of displaced country workers seeking jobs, Clerkenwell and Islington's proximity drew clerks and artisans from the City, whereas the better off, higher in income and the social scale, sought more distant new suburbs such as Paddington or Pimlico.

Clerkenwell and St Luke's, between them suffering the worst conditions, were beginning to affect their neighbour Islington, partly the fault of slovenly Vestry government – for example in continuing to allow open drains in the streets which caused infection, particularly during the cholera epidemic of 1831–2.

In 1839, in affluent St George's Hanover Square and rural Hackney, female mortality was as low as one in 57, but in Islington one in 50, and in both Clerkenwell and St Luke's, one in 38. During the epidemic more than 20% of trades-people and more than 22% of the labouring classes died, yet of the gentry, a mere 6½% and in a second cholera outbreak in 1848 the situation was hardly better. The sole improvement, ineffective because permissive like most such legislation in these decades, was to empower entry to fumigate buildings, funded by the Poor Rates.

In 1801 Finsbury/Clerkenwell, at 55,212, was five times more densely populated than the village of Islington at 10,212, and in 1821 had risen to 86,223. By 1861 Islington had outstripped it – 155,291 compared with 129,073, after which for several reasons Finsbury's population began to decline. At first it

dropped by 5,999 in a decade, then by 10,000, while Islington until the 1920s still increased. Even in 1851, when in density Clerkenwell had risen to 170 persons per acre and St Luke's to 245, Islington had still reached only 30.[7]

As for the class structure, in 1831 when Islington's population was 37,316 and the number of houses calculated as 6,830, by far the highest proportion of inhabitants were classed as in the retail trade and crafts (33,666), and as many as 3,254 servants were women – but only 314 men.

SURVEYING THE BOUNDARIES

The remarkable increase in building in Islington made necessary, in 1802 and 1803, exhaustive boundary surveys. They were carried out along with parish officials from neighbouring Hackney and Clerkenwell. In 1801 it was announced that there had been no perambulation for 8 years, and to ascertain the boundaries it had become necessary to hold them more frequently. In 1805 the situation again required a new perambulation.

In May 1805 William Wickings, who the previous year had completed a 3-year stint as Churchwarden, offered to provide within two years an "Exact Survey Admeasurement and fair drawing of all the Houses Buildings and Lands" in the parish, with a "Field Book of references" and a plan, including all buildings and improvements made before Midsummer 1806 at a scale of 3 chains (66 yards) to the inch with an engraved reduced-scale plan.

After some argument the Vestry approved the proposal, referring it to a committee of the Vicar, Churchwardens and Overseers with half a dozen Vestrymen. Only three weeks later they accepted an offer from Richard Dent, of Camden Place, Camden Town, for a larger plan on these lines, showing every house, outhouse, garden and enclosure, with owners and occupiers recorded in a book, for £350. This invaluable document was at first refused in favour of a cheaper, smaller-scale alternative; however, once they had enquired into the surveyor's capabilities, Dent's more detailed plan was approved.[8]

The settlement of boundaries between the top end of Goswell and City Roads in 1803 had included a stone to be fixed on a house

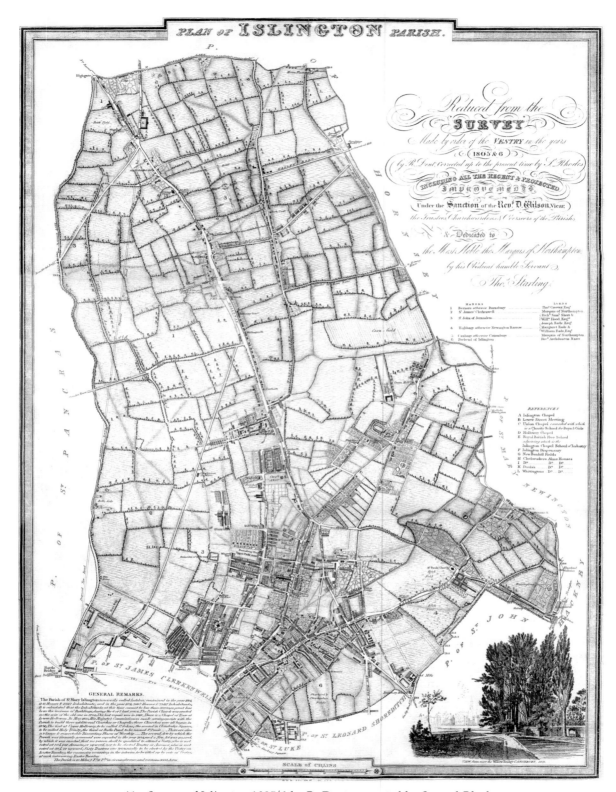

41. *Survey of Islington 1805/6 by R. Dent, corrected by Samuel Rhodes.*

(Samuel Cox's) east of the Blue Coat Boy inn by the Angel, inscribed with the exact spot of the boundary. Mr Robert Dalby, who had built several houses for 'respectable families' in the field adjoining Goswell Street, attended the Vestry (12 April) to request permission to move a footpath which would interfere with the house he intended building for himself, and produced a plan showing where he wished to enclose an alternative path across the New River.

This caused a slight flurry. The Vestry Clerk was instructed to purchase copies of the various Acts concerning the New River Company, and the Vicar and Churchwardens went to view the site. On their recommendation permission for the path was refused (30 June 1803). Dalby built his house, however, and although altered some half-century later, it stands today as the top, double-fronted house facing uphill at the junction of Goswell Road and the City Road.

BUILDING ON THE HEIGHTS

Islington, still very much a large village despite its late 18th-century growth, was so far beyond London limits as to be classed among outer suburbs such as Hackney, Stepney or Kilburn. Local descriptions of the heights north of Pentonville and the White Conduit were less about the village than about what could be seen from it: "the most pleasing prospects imaginable", observed the lawyer Edward Pugh[9], a real panorama of the City, Marylebone, Paddington, northwards to Hampstead and Highgate, and round to Kentish Town, Hornsey and Muswell Hill. The point was, all this could then be *seen*. At the village's north end, half a mile north of St Mary's Church Canonbury House was "on an eminence"; a little higher was Highbury Place, "a noble row of houses"; and higher still Highbury Terrace, "commanding a beautiful prospect". In the 1820s the prospects began to be hidden.

Already in 1826 William Hone, bemoaning the loss of the "extensive prospect" from White Conduit House, once "the pleasantest spot near to the north of London", and recalling the "beautiful pastures and hedge-rows which are now built on, or converted into brick clamps", foretells all too accurately how "In a few short years, London will distend its enormous bulk to the heights that overlook its proud city; and like the locusts of old, devour every green field, and nothing will be left to me to admire, of all that I admired."[10]

South of the Angel in Clerkenwell the Earl of Northampton had begun to develop his estate with Northampton Square, adjoining the site of the old manor-house off St John Street; while the New River Company was covering its fields between the Earl's lands and Pentonville, starting with a terrace off the top of Pentonville Hill (1821) which by 1827 would form part of a new square, Claremont.

The houses were variants of the conventional terrace form, many of them in the New River style, setting a pattern of square-headed first-floor windows in a sunken semi-circular brick surround. Many had ironwork balconies or window-guards, some had stuccoed ground floors simulating rustication, front doors were usually framed by pilasters and crowned by fanlights of varying design.

A more unusual style was observed in the hillside estate of the Gloucestershire landowner the Rev. Lloyd Baker, in rows of often paired pedimented villas, or terraces whose houses were grouped in pairs to give an illusion of being semi-detached, quaintly original, begun only in 1825 though planned in 1818.[11]

All such estates contained at least one square, lessening the number of houses the developers could fit into the available space but, thanks to the square's central gardens, maintaining some variety in what soon became that term of vilification: "the March of Bricks and Mortar". This spoliation George Cruikshank was to record in 1829 in his punning cartoon *London Going out of Town*, as seen from his window in Amwell Street. This former field-path skirted New River Company land, to connect the brow of Pentonville Hill with the lanes bordering the north fringe of Clerkenwell. Cruikshank showed the ignominious retreat of London's surrounding fields, invaded by anthropomorphic houses and builders' tools, while rows of kilns like artillery spew out a rainbow-shaped stream of bricks.

42. Double villas in Lloyd Baker Street. Watercolour by Jean Elrington, 1997.

NEW ESTATES

In Islington itself the chief developments were in the Cloudesley estate, Barnsbury and the Milner-Gibson estate in the 1820s and 1830s, and Lord Northampton's Canonbury, resumed by 1819 in Compton Terrace, and Canonbury Square by 1821.

There were architectural curiosities here too, particularly in Barnsbury, and more particularly in its squares. Barnsbury Square itself was a happenstance, a number of disparate buildings grouped round a garden; Lonsdale Square of the 1830s, by Richard Cromwell Carpenter – usually a church architect and devoted to the Gothic – was an indulgence in Tudor Gothic with picturesque gables and Elizabethan-style windows, and must be unique among squares. The relatively late Milner Square (1840s), by the experimental Roumieu and Gough, lofty and vertical despite its heavy entablature and unbroken skyline, has a monumental, almost overpowering effect.

Canonbury Square too showed its complex history by lack of uniformity in both layout and style: with a large villa on the north side, south of that its earliest terrace differing slightly from the rest, and none of the sides joined to each other.[12]

The old manorial lands were built over by owners keen to profit from building villas and terraces on their land, on the Prebend estate as well as in Barnsbury and Canonbury. The already partly-existing Colebrooke Row and Duncan Terrace were filled in piecemeal, and in the 1840s a more modest district was created nearby with its own church, St Peter's, in the area of the new Canal.

The curious spur of land near the parish's south-eastern angle, from near Ball's Pond Road to Newington Green, owned since 1673 by the Mildmay family, had descended in the late 18th century to an heiress, Jane Mildmay. Her husband, Sir Henry Paulet St John, who died in 1808, had added Mildmay to his own name and took the family's coat of arms. After the building slump his widow joined the band of developing land-owners, obtaining an Act giving licence to build in 1827. The area, predominantly farmland, surrounded the scat-

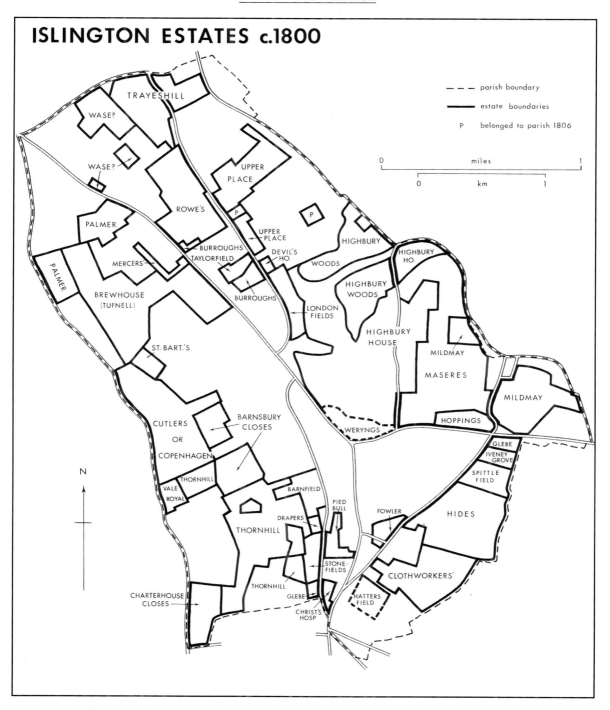

43. *Islington estates c.1800. (Reproduced from the* Victoria County History of Middlesex, *vol. VIII)*

44. *In the 18th century, and for half the 19th century, most main roads were in the control of Turnpike Trusts who were entitled to charge a fee for use of the road. Above is the turnpike in St John Street. Below (45) is the Islington turnpike near the junction of High Street and Liverpool Road, looking north.*

tering of good-sized houses with gardens round the Green. On the south, at either end of Ball's Pond were the large Barr & Brookes (later Brookes & Co.) and Bassington's nurseries, the latter bounded in part by Kingsland Green. Despite the Act, like the later Thornhill estate this area was slow to develop. Similarly the nearby Clothworkers' estate did not take advantage of the renewed building activities until the 1840s.

The outlying Newington Green area also remained mostly rural until mid-century, its few houses surrounding the Green and the rest farmland. On the south, from the end of Ball's Pond Road to Kingsland Green, stretched a string of terraces as usual individually named, such as Strahan Place and Brunswick Place. The latter was bordered at the back by trees and ended in Bassington's Nursery.

At the south-west corner of the Green the poet Samuel Rogers lived in a large villa until his removal in 1797 *(see Chapter 12)*. A friend and neighbour was the famous Mrs Barbauld, blue-stocking and educationist. The old Unitarian chapel, built in 1708, remained as a centre of religious gatherings, and the area retained its tradition of being home to Dis-

senting clergy and their academies.

As the building rash spread Barnsbury was further enlarged in the 1840s, notably with the building of the Thornhill estate, owned by a family which held land chiefly in Huntingdonshire and Cambridgeshire, from whence came a number of street names. This development was continued down to the Caledonian Road, referred to when planned as 'the Parliamentary road'.

ALMSHOUSES

One form of housing catering for small numbers, which proliferated in Islington and Clerkenwell and nearby areas such as Hoxton, was the almshouse. A great many had flourished here since the 17th century and even earlier, a number of them sited only a little outside the City, housing retired members of City companies or their widows.

Lady Holles's almshouses in Curtain Road were founded as early as 1539; also among the earliest were City Green Yard in Whitecross Street, founded by Sir Thomas Gresham for eight poor persons; the Girdlers'

46. Anna Barbauld. From an engraving by Henry Meyer.

47. Dame Alice Owen's almshouses in St John Street, c.1830.

Company in Bath Street, by George Palyn for six poor members of the Company in 1609; and the Haberdashers' in Pitfield Street, in 1692 by Robert Aske with a bequest of £31,905 for 20 poor men of the Company and 20 boys, to be maintained, clothed and educated. Besides Lady Owen's (1609), other 17th-century foundations were John Walter's in Cross Street (1651), John Heath's in Frog Lane (1648) for 10 freemen of the Clothworkers' Company, and Lady Lumley's in 1672 for six persons in the City Road.

Many more were founded in the 18th century, notably Mrs Davis's in Queen's Head Lane, endowed in 1793 for eight widows. The Dutch almshouses in Crown Street, Finsbury, were endowed by Dutch merchants at different times and housed 20 persons aged 60 and over, with 14 tenements for indigent Dutch in Austin Friars. A foundation for French Protestants in Bath Street, founded in 1718, at one time housed as many as 230 Huguenot refugees; and Mrs Alice Hinton's in Plough Alley, Barbican, was founded in 1732 for 12 widows of Cripplegate. The Dyers' Almshouses, built in 1755 in the City Road for 16 poor members of that Company, were removed to Ball's Pond Road in the early 19th century.

The almshouses founded by Richard Whittington in the City in 1421, did not move to their prominent position by the Archway Road until 1822.

Almshouses, small by their nature, accommodated only up to a dozen or so inmates, sometimes as few as six, usually widows. But for those lucky enough to have been married to a member of a City livery company it meant a roof overhead for no weekly rent, a supply of coals and basic food. Less fortunate widows had to depend on parish charity.

A survey made in 1854 showed that then no less than 23 of these establishments survived in this area, including Whittington's and Owen's. Seven of them were in Hoxton and Kingsland, 11 in Finsbury and Clerkenwell and only five in Islington, which included Cutlers' in Ball's Pond Road, Mrs Davis's in Queen's Head Lane, Heath's in Frog Lane, near what was to be built as Tibberton Square, and Whittington's. Three of these had been founded in the 16th century, seven in the 17th and six in the 18th.[13]

THE MARCH OF TERRACES

The type of small-to-medium-sized house that spread like a rash over Islington, Pentonville and the rest of Clerkenwell, with their dull, cramped little sitting rooms, was well illustrated by George Cruikshank outside and in, and by Dickens's early illustrator 'Phiz'. They were the homes of minor professionals such as piano-teachers (for the daughters of genteel families), clerks in City offices, medium tradesmen, petty legal employees, dressmakers, well-to-do craftsmen. Contemporary writers describe them and their homes with a certain impatient scorn. *Ainsworth's Magazine*, for example, edited by the novelist and journalist Harrison Ainsworth, is full of disdain for the desecration of one-time open fields to create them, and the ravaged surroundings, then too soon for any gardens or trees to have grown.

Thomas Carlyle, then living in Edinburgh, poor but by now rising in fame, during his first visit to London in 1824 stayed initially with his friend the Rev. Edward Irving at 4 Myddelton Terrace (later to become part of Amwell Street). He was in London partly to join the travels of his employers the Bullers to whose sons he was tutor, partly to see his work *Wilhelm Meister* through the press.

He records how he "regularly lost my way for the first 3 or 4 days", overwhelmed by London's "great desart of Brick" stretching seven or eight miles either way, "clusters of streets and houses hanging round it with scarcely any interruption ... streets not broad [very unlike Edinburgh, which however he hated] or very crooked, and not always *very* narrow, jammed together in ... complex and perverse fashions". But he was impressed by the "roomy squares with trees and grass plots intermingled, which gives an air of freshness". Some of these squares must surely have been in Islington and nearby, for he goes on, "The unbuilt spaces are full of brick kilns; there are some villages in the neighbourhood, where the sulphrous smell of them is very offensive." These would be kilns in the Fleet valley below Pentonville, only minutes away from Irving's house.[14]

After a spell away, Carlyle was back in Pentonville, where he took two-roomed lodgings which, for someone who in Edinburgh was always changing his lodgings through one shortcoming or another, he describes with unexpected satisfaction. He was at 23 Southampton Street (now Calshot Street), one of Pentonville's newer streets – the suburb had begun at the hilltop and crept downwards – a few doors from where the clown Joey Grimaldi later lived at no. 33. It was "a fine, clean quiet spot" owned by "a middle-aged cleanly, substantial, most discreet looking person", with "a tidy girl for a servant" and an asthmatic single old lady lodging on the ground floor.

This household may be taken as typical of many such houses in many such Islington streets, and Carlyle's description is as apt as any:

"I occupy the whole 2nd floor, with my bedroom and parlour, and above me, there is nothing but 2 empty rooms ... The room which is of moderately large dimensions with 2 windows looks out upon a little empty space, neatly paved with clean tiles, a green wooden railing, then the flagstones, then a new smart street communicating at the distance of a few score of yards with the New Road, one of the greatest thoroughfares

48. *Thomas Carlyle.*

49. *Upper Street, junction with Cross Street*

50. Holloway Road c.1840. To the right is the site of the later Northern Polytechnic.
Watercolour by C H Matthews.

in London. The bedroom looks out upon green plots (one of which belongs to the house), then a field cut with walks, and beyond this a neat building which I believe is some public charity,[15] and beside it among other houses the chapel of St James' Clerkenwell. Both rooms are about the neatest I ever inhabited; papered and cleaned like bandboxes, and quieter than I supposed any were in this monstrous place ... After half past 10, there is scarce a murmur to be heard till towards 7 in the morning, and throughout all the day there is nothing that even approaches to noise."[16]

A couple of days later he writes to Jane Welsh of "this quiet airy street, in my own trim and comfortable apartments". We may note his comment on "green plots" rather than gardens – at this stage the new street's occupants had hardly had time to cultivate gardens.

Only a few days later Carlyle oddly dates a letter from 18 Salisbury Place – an evident slip of memory, for he describes his lodgings in almost the same terms, including the old lady and the garden. He is now bounded on the top storey by "an occasional ancient gentleman" and "an asthmatic lady on the ground

floor". It is still "the best I have lived in; clean as a new guinea, even elegant", with its back view of the "green plots", and all for 16 shillings a week including dinner, "cheap for this most expensive of cities", yet to him "excessively expensive".[17] But he did suffer from the watch continually calling the time, "a wretched mortal with a voice like the howling of wolves ... that it is 'Paast ney-een'".

Carlyle dismisses Edward Irving's Myddelton Terrace house as "like most London houses ... hampered and unsubstantial" – and London itself "as a town ... not worth looking at above a week". However much he hated living in Edinburgh, he evidently found it as a city superior to London.

Later, established with his wife Jane Welsh near Mecklenburg Square, his strictures on London living could apply equally well to nearby Islington:

"You are ill-lodged, in brick houses, thin as shells, with the floors all twisted, and every article indicating its showiness and its weakness. You are ill-fed, unless you can live upon beef; your milk is of the bluest, your water of the muddiest; [he was now outside the New River supply] your eggs rotten, your potatoes watry [sic] and exactly about 10 times the price they are in Annandale, namely one penny per pound!" Yet, he graciously concedes, "there is a great charm in being here".[18]

Carlyle's general description of London daily life could also apply to Islington:

"the people are situated here like plants in a hot house ... the carman with his huge slouch hat hanging half way down his back, consumes his breakfast of bread and tallow or hog's lard, sometimes as he swags along the streets, always in a hurried and precarious fashion, and supplies the deficit by continual pipes and pots of beer. The fashionable lady rises at 3 in the afternoon, and begins to live toward midnight ... You are packed into paltry shells of brick-houses (calculated to endure for 40 years, and then fall); every door that slams to in the street, is audible in your most secret chamber; the necessities of life are hawked about thro' multitudes of hands, and reach you, frequently adulterated, always at rather more than *twice* their cost elsewhere ... you are assailed by vast shoals of quacks, and showmen, and street-sweepers, and pickpockets, and mendicants of every degree and shape. . .

"Yet the people are in general a frank, jolly *well-living*, kindly people."[19]

This was high praise, for Carlyle at this stage of his life tended to dislike more people than he liked, and often cooled considerably towards those he did like.

1   Mary Cosh, 'Clockmaker Extraordinary. The Career of Alexander Cumming', in *Country Life*, 12 June 1969.

2   Canonbury Square and Compton Terrace were begun by Henry Leroux, of whom we know little except the bankruptcy which prevented his completion of the job, but he was likely to have been the son of Jacob Leroux, architect and builder. Jacob, articled in 1753, exhibited at the Royal Academy, practised in Great Russell Street and as a JP was on the committee for building the Coldbath Fields prison (1784, built 1788-94: *See Chapter 34*). He also designed an elegant 'Polygon' in Somers Town which was left unfinished. Charles Dibdin in his *Musical Tour* (1788) accuses Jacob as the "architect, brickmaker, and trading-justice ... with a dastardly speciousness", who made a fraudulent agreement by which Dibdin lost £250, for "the skeleton of a building" near St Pancras "which was blown down by the first high wind after the licence was refused". Jacob's work in the area near Islington (and the unusual surname) suggests the connection with Henry Leroux. (Colvin, *British Architects*, p. 611, Jacob Leroux.)

3   Mary Cosh, *The Squares of Islington*, Part II, Islington Archaeology & History Society, 1993, pp. 57ff.

4   VM, Vol. V, 7 February and 4 April 1809.

5   VM, Vol V, *ad loc.*

6   Pinks, *Clerkenwell*, pp. 13-14.

7   *VCH*, p. 13. Density in East London was 290 and in central London, St James's for instance, 215.

8   VM, Vol. IV, 24 May 1805.

9   Edward Pugh [=David Hughson], *Walks Through London*, 1817, p. 378.

10   Hone, *Every-Day Book*, Vol. I, p. 1,204.

11   Mary Cosh, *The Squares of Islington*, Part I, Islington Archaeology & History Society, 1990 pp. 3, 26.

12   Cosh, *Squares*, Part II, pp. 41, 43.

13   J Weale, *The Pictorial History of London*, London, 1854, p. 216.

14   *The Collected Letters of Thomas and Jane Welsh Carlyle*, N. Carolina, 1970ff.; Carlyle to his brother Alexander, 25 June 1824, Vol. III, p. 93.

15   This was probably the home for 'fallen women' in Pentonville Road.

16   *Carlyle Letters*, Carlyle to his mother, from 23 Southampton Street, 12 November 1824, Vol. III, pp. 194–5.

17   *Ibid*, Carlyle to his brother John, 21 November 1824, Vol. III, pp. 206-7; 30 November 1824, Vol. III, p. 209.

18   *Ibid.*, Carlyle to his mother, 22 January 1832, Vol. VI, p. 95.

19   *Ibid.*, Carlyle to his brother Alexander, 14 December 1824, Vol. III, pp. 219.

CHAPTER 17

Ups and Downs in Entertainment

SADLER'S WELLS

The prolonged war did not mean the end of fun for those at home, particularly in a place like Islington. At the turn of the 19th century it was at the peak of popularity, and Sadler's Wells Theatre especially was firmly established. Grimaldi had been a regular attraction since his debut in 1781 at the age of three and in 1801 the actor Edmund Kean first appeared, as a boy, an instant success.

From the late 18th century there had been several changes of management. In the 1780s Tom Arnold and the actor Richard Wroughton bought out King and Serjeant for £12,000, and as manager Wroughton aimed at greater 'respectability'. So the Wells now ranked with such minor theatres as Astley's Amphitheatre and the Royal Circus at the Surrey Theatre in St George's Fields, while the patented 'Winter' theatres, invoking "noxious laws" tried in vain to suppress their competitors.

Sadler's Wells, as the oldest of the non-patent establishments, in 1788 led a counter-attack with a Bill to legalise their performances, and other minor theatres followed suit, but the Wells bid misfired. The Lord Chancellor, Lord Thurlow, dismissed their claim, asking "Is it because they are the oldest offenders ... No – all, or none!"[1] Soon afterwards Wroughton issued shares to friends and associates, such as Arnold's son, Mrs Siddons's husband, and Richard Hughes, manager of several provincial theatres, who now became manager. Seat prices were raised, except for the gallery which remained at a shilling.

From 1800 the theatre was under the patronage of the Duke of Clarence, and remained so until he became King in 1830. In 1802 Wroughton moved to Drury Lane, new shareholders joined, including the brothers Thomas and Charles Dibdin the younger, and Charles took over as manager.

After several years' gap the sale of wines resumed in 1803, but a dreadful catastrophe brought this to an end. On 15 October 1807 a quarrel started between a couple of the audience, and there were cries of "Fight!" which people in the gallery misheard as "Fire!" In their panic all rushed to the stairs, knocking each other over, several people were crushed and 18 were killed, many more injured. Surgeons from St Bartholomew's were hurriedly sent for, and the management later held two benefit nights to help the victims' families.

The theatre's earlier fame as a spa was re-established when in 1800 the well was accidentally re-discovered, down a flight of steps, ringed by stone "in the space between the stage-door and the New River."[2] Then in 1804 a different use for water was found. It was decided to produce aquatic spectacles by bringing in water from the New River Head to a tank created under the stage. Its irregular dimensions must have been dictated by the geology: 90 feet long, 5 deep, and in some places 24 (some said up to 36) feet wide. Pipes and engines were installed to allow for sprays and jets, and when in use the stage floor was wound up and the tank revealed.

The first water feature was staged on Easter Monday, 1804 as an 'incidental', based on a *Naumachia*, the Roman spectacle of a naval battle. This was such a success, not least because no other theatre could compete with it, that

51. Sadler's Wells Theatre in 1830

such displays became included among the evening's varied programme, and the Wells became known as 'the Aquatic Theatre', an attraction which continued nearly 20 years.

Among the earliest water scenes staged was the Siege of Gibraltar, with ships modelled on gun-boats, and floating batteries representing the Spanish fleet, which sailed up to assault the Rock, while the land artillery hurled bombs and rockets at the besiegers, who retaliated with their brass cannon. "Some were sunk", writes the historian Brayley, "others were set on fire, and blown up and, to conclude the mimic display, Sir Roger Curtis was represented saving, as in reality, the Spanish sailors from a watery grave." To crown it all,

an above-stage tank let loose cascades and cataracts, lit by fireworks and "Bengal lights", an explosive mixture including potassium nitrate and sulphur which gave out a blue-white light. The Duke of Clarence, who with other nobility and gentry visited these displays several times, claimed it was better than the Press Gangs at recruiting for the Navy. Small wonder that so spectacular a kind of performance long remained popular.[3]

Charles Dibdin wrote several pieces for the aquatic shows, usually melodramas in which heroes rescued maidens from drowning, or villains threatened to hurl them from crags to the waters below. Or even children who fell in, to be rescued by a dog.

151

52. Charles Dibdin

In 1805 the 21-year-old Henry Temple – who was to become the Prime Minister Lord Palmerston – was "highly entertained" by a piece based on Johnson's tour of the Hebrides. "In the last act they actually drown two people on the stage in Fingal's Cave; they let in a great quantity of water from the New River, and a boat with two men in it is made fairly to sink. In the first part a lady jumps out of a boat and swims to shore: really whatever faults our dramas possess they are accurate and lively presentations." The play was Dibdin's "grand Caledonian Melo-Dramatic Romance", *An Bratach or, The Water Spectre*.[4]

Only a few days later a young American, Benjamin Silliman, attended the theatre with a friend. They walked to it across a grassy field where young men were "playing at ball" including a game "resembling cricket", admiring the handsome, well made and healthy appearance of young "genteel" Englishmen in elegant, un-foppish dress (less showy than the Americans). He describes the Fingal's Cave scene in great detail as the last act of a long melodrama and climax to a very varied evening, including "low buffoonery" in the

opening clowning – probably Grimaldi, though he does not say. "The clown pulling off his boot let out a yell of pain, and pulled out his foot gripped in the teeth of a large rat, while he ran around the stage in apparent consternation". This was "received with great applause". There was also "a great deal of dancing" by girls in loose pantaloons, seemingly meant as a semi-oriental costume, of which Silliman says rather stiffly, "I shall say nothing more than that they danced with much spirit and elegance". Next a popular song, based on the recent capture of a West Indian fortress by a boat's crew from a British ship of war, was received with enthusiasm.

Though Silliman observed that in general actresses seemed so coarse-featured, fat and ugly that he wondered how they could ever go on the stage, this particular performance "was to me a perfectly novel and an entertaining exhibition".[5]

Water spectacles alternated with the usual variety programme, which included Grimaldi's harlequinades, and pantomimes, drama, burlettas and equestrian acts. The effect was, like early cinema shows, a series of 'shorts', and a single evening might consist of displays by tumblers and trampoline artists, a dramatic dance piece, a short musical sketch, Sieur Scaliogni's Dancing Dogs, a dancing bear which beat a drum at command, a pair of tight-rope dancers, including the celebrated La Belle Espagnole fresh from a Paris triumph, still leaving time for a comic sketch and an 'Oriental' conjurer. All for two shillings in the pit (afterwards raised to three).

Unfortunately in 1823 the New River water was cut off, the tank destroyed, and the stage was lowered by several feet to be available for orthodox drama. For instead of endless series of divertissements, straight plays were now becoming popular, and like other theatres, Sadler's Wells began to stage full-length plays or farces. Many of these were written by Charles Dibdin.

The Dibdin brothers were illegitimate sons of Charles the elder, the famous dramatist and song-writer, by Harriet Pitt or Davenant; he was author of many dramas, comedies and sketches, and a composer for Covent Garden and other theatres. The two sons, though less famous were also successful and prolific, both became actor-managers at Sadler's Wells and wrote a number of its pieces.[6]

Grimaldi, of course, was a byword for comedy and clowning. Many are the descriptions and illustrations of his act. Lord William Pitt Lennox in his early *Recollections* describes a visit in about 1810, when the clown was in his early 30s and Lennox a boy of about 11.[6] He was taken with a friend to the Wells by the flamboyant Margravine of Ansbach – an English lady by the way – whose appearance was a spectacle in itself. He describes the harlequinade, a series of ingenious pantomime changes, a pump turning into a cow, a shop turned into a view of the Mint, Tilbury Fort turned into a warship, a wicker basket with wheels made of huge cheeses suddenly turned into "a fashionable drag".

Grimaldi would appear "in a driving-coat made out of blankets, large tin plates for buttons, a bunch of carrots and greens as a bouquet [Grimaldi often fooled about with anthropomorphic vegetables], and a low-crowned hat", and mounted the box like a member of the Four-in-Hand Club. His singing produced as much excitement as his acting and clowning.

"The juveniles", declares Lord William, "were in a state of perfect rapture from the drawing up of the curtain until its fall."[7]

Grimaldi's family in 1794, some years after his father's death, had moved to Penton Place, a newish 6-roomed house with a garden. He fell in love when barely 16 with Maria, the daughter of the then Sadler's Wells proprietor, Thomas Hughes, but because of his relatively humble position they had to wait for three years before even becoming engaged. In 1797 the family moved again to 37 Penton Street, "the Regent's Park of the City Road, in those days", comments Dickens. In 1798 Joey first appeared billed as 'Mr', in *The Monster of the Cave, or Harlequin and the Fairy*, which so exhausted him that he was unable to attend the next day's review or 'call' of the new play.

Grimaldi and Maria married in May 1799, but their happiness was brief, for in October 1800 Maria died in pregnancy, leaving him inconsolable. At Christmas, however, he returned to appearing at Drury Lane, having moved to Baynes Row by Warner Street, and later to Braynes' Row (now no. 8 Exmouth

53. *Joey Grimaldi.*

Market). Drury Lane closed from June to September, and when the leading Sadler's Wells clown, the French acrobat and juggler John Baptist Dubois, left in 1802, Grimaldi took over. He introduced changes in costume and technique, and according to Dibdin "founded a New School for Clowns" – in fact, the style which he was to make traditional. He was soon remarried, to Mary Bristow, a Drury Lane actress, and in November 1802 they had a son.

In these early years of the century Grimaldi had a few disasters, including his own brother John who reappeared after 14 years at sea. They had an affectionate reunion, but John promptly vanished again with a large sum of money. On the professional side, however, Grimaldi was doing well under Charles Dibdin with the many pantomimes Charles and Thomas wrote for him, including his greatest success *Mother Goose*. For his alternative theatre he transferred to Covent Garden, had a season in Dublin, then on return lost his money to a dishonest landlord.

Sadler's Wells in these war years was very popular with sailors and their girls. There is a story that one evening a deaf-and-dumb sailor with his shipmates, sitting in the front row of the gallery, was so transported with glee at Grimaldi's antics that his faculties were apparently miraculously restored. From conversing in deaf-and-dumb language, he turned to his neighbour and cried, "What a damned funny fellow! … Speak! Ay, that I can, and hear too!".

Grimaldi continued with clowning and pantomime (then an all-season entertainment), performing simultaneously at Covent Garden and at the Wells. After his show at the Wells he would leap into a carriage still in his clown's dress, which he had no need to change, and career off to Covent Garden. One night when no carriage turned up, he raised some curiosity running through Clerkenwell in the rain. When he passed the lighted shops, someone shouted "Here's Joe Grimaldi!" and a cheering mob pursued him through Holborn. There he found a coach but the crowd still followed, cheering even more when he stuck his head out of the window with "one of his famous and well-known laughs". He turned up at Covent Garden with "the dirtiest bodyguard that was ever beheld".

In 1814, resuming at the Wells with *The Slave Pirate*, Grimaldi had his best ever benefit night, earning £263 10s. His own son Joe first appeared as Man Friday in *Robinson Crusoe* – history repeating itself 33 years after Grimaldi's own debut (a nice story, if not wholly confirmed).

When his former father-in-law Thomas Hughes died in December that year, Grimaldi had to carry on clowning, attending the funeral between rehearsal and show, though on the first night of *Harlequin Whittington*, he could scarcely struggle through the part.

One of his greatest feats was to perform three times on the same night at different theatres, which one of the managers insisted could be done by keeping a swift chaise-and-four constantly in waiting. Curiously enough, though it caused a lot of anxiety, he felt no more exhausted than after a single performance, even though sustained with only a glass of ale and a biscuit.

In 1811 after never a day's illness Grimaldi was taken ill with shortness of breath and was off for a month, and afterwards was never fully in health again.

Over his career of 38 years he missed only one Sadler's Wells season –1817. That year he fell out with Dibdin who, when the clown's articles expired, agreed to raise his salary only from pounds to guineas, but countered by reducing his benefit events from two to one. The upshot was that Dibdin replaced Grimaldi for the season with another clown, Paulo, son of the rope-dancer Paulo Redigi.

This caused a great outcry. Grimaldi, returning from a visit to Egham, found the streets covered with placards reading "No Paulo!" "Joey for ever!" (and one or two even "No Grimaldi!"). Dibdin tried to make an announcement that the change was Grimaldi's idea. Grimaldi attended to make his own announcement but there was no need, the audience had stayed away, less than a quarter of the seats were filled. Next day the newspapers remarked on the shabby action, and Grimaldi was offered jobs in theatres all over the country. Sadler's Wells had the worst season it had ever known and there were rumours of a takeover. Grimaldi made more money than the Wells had ever paid him, and after rather angry negotiations he returned – as part proprietor, with a summer release for touring (1818).

But this arrangement was not a success. The theatre made a loss after he left on a northern tour, and with the cost of shares and other demands, he began to regret not sticking to acting, for he seemed as poor as ever.

Things went on no better. Before the 1819 opening Dibdin resigned as acting stage manager, and Grimaldi had to sacrifice his summer tours and take over. However, his new pantomime *The Fates, or Harlequin's Holy Day*, made a profit. That spring, too, he first sang what was to be his most famous song, *Hot Codlins*.

Grimaldi now began to suffer seriously from the "painful infirmities" – probably arthritis – which dogged him ever after, and his refusal to give up shortened his life.

They still lacked a stage manager, and in 1820

he tried renting the theatre to another company, Howard Payne, which unfortunately ended in a loss. Grimaldi meanwhile made a tour to Dublin, which proved to be his last season there. In the winter his son had his first regular season at the Wells.

Letting the theatre ended in misunderstandings and "coolness". By 1822 Grimaldi, with his health in gradual decline, took no part at Sadler's Wells and could undertake no tours. But against doctors' advice he could not resist a profitable offer from the Coburg Theatre (later the Old Vic) – during which he was sometimes too ill to appear. After a reviving trip to the Cheltenham waters he embarked on what was to be his last Covent Garden season, a lavish staging of *Harlequin and the Ogress*, or *The Sleeping Beauty*, which ran until the following Easter (1823). The new melodrama, *The Vision of the Sun*, which followed, proved almost too much for Grimaldi, stiff, weak, debilitated and suffering "cramps and spasms". As he staggered offstage attendants had to support him, even carry him to his dressing-room.

His stage career was over. He wept. It was 3 May 1823, and his son Joey took over his part. Grimaldi was never to resume his act, though he long vainly hoped things might improve. A last attempt at Covent Garden ended in a return to the Cheltenham waters, but he was now crippled.

Unfortunately his son turned out undependable, reckless and drunken, sometimes violent, at one time even found insane. Grimaldi did not see him for several years, except on stage at the Wells – or his son shunned him in the street. The proprietors of the Wells commissioned Thomas Dibdin as actor-manager, with the now unemployed Grimaldi as 'resident assistant' at £4 a week and a lavish, extended season for a full year (1825), too ambitious for their finances. Grimaldi cut his own salary to £2, and they introduced pony-racing in the adjoining paddock, which helped. In 1828 Grimaldi was persuaded to try a last benefit at both theatres, and on 17 March held his farewell show at the Wells.

To a crammed house, a variety bill and masquerade were followed by Grimaldi's farewell address and fireworks. After struggling with a "trifling part" he told the audience that,

though he felt like "a very aged man" he was only 48 years old, and had been on the stage until the last years of his life. He gave the audience his grateful thanks, was overcome with emotion and had to be led off, breaking down in the green room in painful weeping "impossible to alleviate".

In material terms the evening brought him £230, with another £85 later in gifts, but he was too overcome to carry out the Covent Garden engagement and it had to be dropped. The chagrined Grimaldi instead made his last ever appearance on a benefit night at Drury Lane on 27 June 1828 at which he was able to perform sitting – yet again could scarcely continue to the end among the audience's cheers. Helped off-stage by the manager and his son, after swallowing a glass of madeira he was able to take leave of friends, made a farewell bow on the theatre steps, and his carriage was followed by hundreds.

This last benefit earned Grimaldi a total of £850, yet he was still scared of being poor. From the Drury Lane Theatrical Fund he obtained a pension of £100 a year. With finance now secure, he was again plagued by his son's reappearance "in a state of insanity", destitute from drink and only occasionally getting a job.

Late in 1832 Joey junior got a benefit at the Wells, so successful that he then achieved a part at the Coburg; but after celebrating his 30th birthday with his parents, he left, and was seen no more.

The Grimaldis moved in 1829 from 8 Exmouth Street to 23 Garnault Place (demolished in the 1970s for student accommodation), then after trying Woolwich in the hope it would be good for their health, they finally returned to Pentonville in 1835. News of their son's sudden collapse and death so shocked Grimaldi that he too, galvanised into rushing to tell his wife, collapsed again. Two years later his wife died, and the gregarious Grimaldi, left on his own moved to a furnished house at 33 Southampton Street (later renamed as 22 Calshot Street, and unfortunately demolished in the late 1970s). It was a "neat little dwelling", next door to a former servant of his brother-in-law Richard Hughes.

Here he dictated his memoirs, and in the evenings was carried, hoisted on a friend's back, to a nearby tavern – perhaps the Clown, near the top of modern Rosebery Avenue. This life continued for a couple of years, while he completed the memoirs on his 57th birthday on 18 December 1836. Less than six months later, he was found dead by his housekeeper, on the morning of 31 May 1837; and so he never saw his memoirs published. He was buried in the churchyard of St James's Pentonville, in a grave next to Charles Dibdin.[8]

By 1820 Sadler's Wells had been in four hands, including Hughes and Grimaldi. The ground landlord, incidentally, was the Gloucestershire landowner, the Rev. Lloyd Baker, who was also owner not only of the land on which the Lloyd Baker estate was about to be built, but also of New Tunbridge Wells.

The theatre's interior, entirely done over in 1803, and again in 1825, held about 2,200 (400 in boxes, 1,000 pit, 800 galleries). Brayley in 1826 minutely describes the layout, including the Royal or principal box, on which the Royal arms were displayed for the not infrequent visits of royalty. The boxes were lined with richly decorated flock paper, with gilt mouldings on the fronts, and the ceiling was painted like the sky as if seen through an opening surrounded with garlanded flying cupids. The saloon or foyer was "very tastefully decorated with painted compartments of latticework and flowers, relieved by an open sky". As a renewed luxury, wine was again sold, thanks to a reduction of duty on port which made it available at 3s. 6d a quart.[9]

With Grimaldi's ill-health and retirement, Sadler's Wells staged less circus-type material, rope-dancing and balancing acts, and aquatic spectacles ceased in 1823. Dramatic entertainments increased: burlettas, ballets and pantomimes. Pony-racing was billed as "a Novel Entertainment, on a scale never before Exhibited at ...any other Place of Public Amusement in London". In a small enclosure behind the theatre, opening at 4pm., the races started at 6, claimed as "Newmarket in Miniature", with grand titles such as 'King's Plate'.

Even in the 1830s Sadler's Wells retained a whiff of rurality. The poplar-fringed New River still lapped at its doors until the trees were felled in 1848, and for some people it was still a favourite haunt, "old-fashioned, unpretending ... the very ruggedness of its

uncouth architecture" lending charm. It was to remain a minor seasonal theatre, a summer jaunt to the suburbs.

The ill repute of actors and particularly actresses was no myth. Some were so poorly educated that they could barely repeat their lines correctly, let alone convincingly, and despite a few handsome exceptions the women were complained of as fat and coarse-featured. While the Duke of Clarence was patron, advertisements were extravagant and exclamation-mark-ridden, perhaps to mask an actual loss of fashionability.

Plays and melodramas became topical, including scenes such as 'the New London Bridge', 'the Old Queen's Head at Islington' (demolished in 1829), the King's Head, even the Tottenham Court Road, by the scene-painter Greenwood (1830). But there was a fall in its popularity until the theatre reopened in 1832 under new management with the building again improved and the company enlarged. An approving press report claimed that "the fastidious" need have no scruples over "the gentility of the locality", for a recent audience included the Earl of Glengarry and party, Lord and Lady Fitzroy Somerset, Lord Alvanley and party, and so forth. They were probably slumming. Next year the management changed again when a prolific local playwright, George Almar, living at 43 Wilmington Square, presented topical Islington and Finsbury dramas with titles like *Peerless Pool and The Knights of St John* – billed as "a new Grand military and Chivalric Spectacle" (though it seems to have survived only one season). There was also an unsuccessful attempt to renew the water spectacles.

Almar, born at Mistley in Essex to a merchant who lost his money at the end of the Napoleonic wars, had decided to try his fortunes in India. Almost on the eve of departure he visited the Coburg Theatre – and transferred his ambition to the stage. After trying several theatres, in 1834 at the age of 32 he settled for Sadler's Wells.

A typical production was the comic pantomime, *The Red Cow, or the Archers of Islington and the Hog of Highbury*, which followed the adventures of a couple of apprentices, a comic Finsbury draper fond of archery and "himself a bit of a beau", the landlord of the Robin

Hood Tavern at Hogsden or Hoxton, frequented by archers, and for good measure "a Demoniac", the Wild Hog of Hogsley Hole. The scenery, equally topical, included an "Extensive view of Islington and Finsbury Fields as they appeared in the 15th century", bounded by Clerkenwell Nunnery, Aldersgate, the City walls, and so on. The audience might love this sort of local show, but it was an unlikely draw for the condescending aristocracy, and in 1836 and again in 1837, the management changed once more.

The staging of single evening shows for charitable institutions, such as the Somers Town Benevolent Harmonic Union, suggests a desperate effort to keep going. In 1838 they installed "additional warm air stoves", and continued to bill new productions in such terms as "an entirely New and Original Local Drama (written expressly for this Theatre)". This was a puff for *St John's Priory, or Islington in the Olden Time* (1837), part of the popular vogue for romanticised versions of medieval England, a spin-off from Sir Walter Scott's historical novels. The other usual fare was now comic pantomimes, French-style romances, and 'medieval' tales. There was even a highly up-to-date 'laughable' interlude on The Omnibus – London's new public transport.

The Wells staggered on for some years, in a period when most national theatres were similarly degenerate, if not closing altogether. From 1841 the theatre advertised itself as the "Theatre Royal Sadler's Wells and the New Royal Amphitheatre of Arts", said to be under the patronage of the young Queen Victoria. Thomas Greenwood, son of the one-time scene painter, became lessee in 1842.[10]

At almost the same time a new management under Mrs Warner and Samuel Phelps came on the scene in a noble effort to turn the tables and make Sadler's Wells "what a theatre ought to be". Their reign was to last a triumphant 18 years.

THE END OF THE PLEASURE GARDENS

The irony of the decline and fall of the pleasure gardens lies in the glaring contrast between these acres of groves, shrubberies, bowers and other rustic delights and 20th-century Islington, with by far the smallest acreage of park and open space in London.[11]

Although the Islington Spa continued into the 19th century, its day had long passed and it descended into a mere tea-garden. Worse, the water supply dwindled, and when in 1826 a new proprietor tried to revive it as a spa, it was too late – the building rash had begun and it interfered with the flow of water. In 1840, a row called Spa Cottages was built over most of the site, though the proprietor's house survived at 6 Lloyd's Row. After 1842 a Dr Molloy lived there, treating patients with six-penny doses of the water, or a guinea a year. In 1860 the spring dried up altogether. The slip of gardens opened in 1895 – alongside Rosebery Avenue opposite Sadler's Wells – marks the site, and as late as 1914 at 6 Lloyd's Row a small room resembling a grotto survived above the blocked well, while on the front of the house the inscription 'Islington Spa, or New Tunbridge Wells', was visible.

Like any long-established form of amusement, the fashion for spas and pleasure gardens declined and gave way to others. Bagnigge Wells became by degrees a lower-class resort; people still drank the waters for 3d and were amused by threepenny concerts, games of bowls and the usual refreshments, but in more plebeian style. The gardens closed in 1844, though the spring survived at Spring Place (later renamed St Helena Place) until 1858, and a pub in King's Cross Road still bore the name of the Wells.

Francis Place in his autobiography recalled, at the turn of the century "the concourse of men women and children on Sunday evenings at Bagnigge Wells – White Conduit House – the Boot and Bowling Green – Copenhagen House & Hornsey Wood House. At the two former I well remember the difficulty in finding seats & waiters to bring the tea cups & hot water – extra gates were opened on Sundays & often Struggling to get in like the theatre", and spending what seemed a large sum, two, three or even more shillings per party, even on weekdays "when the organ and singing attracted". By the time he was writing, though such places were not yet held to be "immoral or improper", no respectable person would dream of attending one.[12]

The moral fall came rather later. In 1884 the journalist James Greenwood wrote that by about 1860 those pleasure gardens still "flourishing wholesomely" had sunk in repute to "little better than a haunt of vice and profligacy, patronised chiefly by fast young shopmen in the habit of taking liberties with the money-till, with dissipated apprentices and factory lads, and their equally precocious and unscrupulous young female companions." "Dens of iniquity", indeed, to be found in every suburb, clinging to the now fictitious name of tea-gardens ("all fudge"), where beer and stout were the mildest drink, whisky-and-water more fashionable and spirits the commonest. The chief amusement was now a dancing platform, considered rather 'fast', and 'refreshment boxes', whose discreetly lit depths acted as a concealment. Greenwood, a moral writer, observes how increasing scandals ended in warnings from the police and eventual closures.[13]

But in the late 1830s the 'Vite Cundik' or the Eagle were frequented by Cockney holiday-makers, for genteel flirtations in their "snug arbors". Or the long walk to Hornsey Wood, or a picnic on the banks of the river Lea, were still a rural temptation.

Some like Edmund Yates later looked back with nostalgia, remembering how even in the late 1830s he, his jolly grandfather, a one-time actor, and his dog, on summer evenings would walk from his cottage in Kentish Town across the fields to Copenhagen House, "or further afield to the Hornsey Sluice-house", near where Finsbury Park was eventually created.[14]

A facetious contemporary sketch of the same date, however, on Cockney misadventures in country pursuits, describes a venture to the White Conduit. The youngish Mr Wiggins, courting the youngish widow at her chandler's shop, eventually asks if she "vos never at the Vite Condie, or the Eagle" on a Sunday, and when she admits she would need a "prutector", he escorts her. "Seated in one of the snug arbours of that suburban establishment", she pours the tea while he butters a hot roll, with clumsy badinage; he calls for "two glasses of brandy and water, stiff, and three cigars", lays hand on heart and claims he needs a wife. Sadly, the romance fizzles out, he is tiddly on the walk back, next learns from her shop-boy that she is a fraudulent debtor, and so on.[15]

White Conduit House had started the century prosperously. Its landlord Bartholomew, who also owned the Angel and property in Highgate and Holloway, and made much capital out of hay-crops, ran into bad luck when his lottery wins became losses. A new lucky win restored his fortune, but he squandered it on gambling, was reduced to poverty and died aged 68 in a garret almost starving.

Though a Cockney retreat, the White Conduit had fashionable habitués, including Lord William Lennox and other 'West End exclusives' and St James's clubmen. Lennox and friends hired a first-floor room with a bay window to see a balloon ascent, but on the day, the crowd outside waited with increasing impatience for more than an hour until a notice was put up that the astronaut had pocketed his fee and absconded.

When one of the party, Sir George Wombwell, a Peninsular veteran, sticks his curly head out of the window some of the crowd declare he is "a Roossian" and that it was supposed to be "a foreigneering gent that was to go up". As tempers mount a youth shies an apple at his head, a shower of missiles breaks the window and the Peninsular hero and the rest retreat, until Lord William (so he claims) pacifies the mob and they are allowed to leave, with cheers and hand-shakes.[16]

The end of Copenhagen House came in 1855 when the City Corporation, having at last grasped the impossibility of continuing Smithfield Market on its existing site, purchased house, grounds and 75 acres of adjoining land, to set up the Caledonian Cattle Market. The house was then demolished and on its site was built the tall market clock-tower. The innkeeper of the Lamb, one of the four pubs built at the corners of the land, in 1863 leased the cricket-ground for a few years to the Marylebone Cricket Club – in the tradition of the old House.

The tea-garden known for at least 80 years as the Shepherd and Shepherdess, just off what was later built as the City Road, had in the 1820s been renamed the Eagle, the name used by Dickens in *Sketches by Boz*. Among its specialities were allegorical paintings on the walls, chairs which had been used at George IV's coronation, an organ and an 'automatic piano' – some kind of early pianola or barrel organ. At the beginning of Queen Victoria's reign it was again renamed, as the Coronation Pleasure Gardens, and a larger organ was installed in the redecorated saloon, the gardens given fountains and lit by lanterns in the evenings. Entertainments varied from opera to tightrope walkers in the Grecian Theatre.

So it continued until its transformation by Ben Conquest, father of the more famous George, as The Grecian.

The Grecian at the Eagle was pre-eminent among 'saloon theatres', which were actually music-halls until the law made them become licensed theatres. The proprietor Thomas Rouse (writes John Hollingshead, reminiscing many years later), sat in his private box nightly with an air of "stern authority", holding "a huge walking-stick like a drum major's staff". He showed both taste and discernment, for example following the style of the famous Madame Vestris at the Olympic by upgrading his programmes for middle- and lower-middle-class audiences, with mainly opera and ballet, a high-class programme costing 6d in the City Road. In 1834, for example, his company included a dozen artistes, now forgotten though then popular, a ballad-singer, a comedian, a singer and composer, a dancer, a pantomimist, and others who went on to play at West End theatres.

Frederic Robson, a "meteoric actor", was held to be the most remarkable of the century, and though he had a fine career at the Olympic, most of his best farce parts started from 1839 at the Grecian.

Operas played here included *La Sonnambula*, fresh from the Opéra Comique in Paris, *The Barber, The Elixir of Love, Daughter of the Regiment, Don Pasquale, Bohemian Girl, Freischutz* ... in productions simple enough but performed by a capable company sometimes of star quality. This was particularly so between 1834 and 1845.

A scornful ballad on the contrast between the Grecian and the old Shepherd and Shepherdess on almost the same spot was written in 1883 by G. R. Sims, jeering at this place "where the costers prevail".

What a change from the days when they christened
  the spot!

Then of course it was charming and green ...
Now I gaze with disgust on the ill-favoured boys,
And the bold little hussies who gawk,
While I sigh for that era of pastoral joys
When here might a shepherdess walk.

Twenty years earlier Ewing Ritchie, though conceding the cockney origin – "from time immemorial" – for apprentices and clerks, claimed it was not "fast" but a family place, with Conquest's theatre actually showing full-blown tragedies besides farces, and with the dance-floor as well. Many of its faithful habitués were, strangely enough, 'juvenile swells' up from the country, whose parents innocently supposed them safe; living in Islington or Hoxton remote from the temptations of the Metropolis. In fact they found the Eagle handy to visit, accompanied by 'unfortunates', namely prostitutes with "painted faces, brazen looks, and gorgeous silks", while they smoked cigars, drank pale ale, and aped the slang and vices of the more sophisticated. The relatively innocent youths were balanced by fat old women with baskets of 'prog' and squat old tradesmen with pipes, and bagmen homing from the City.

The juxtaposition of green apprentices and rough City workers Ritchie found reprehensible, in this haunt "not far from a lunatic asylum, and contiguous to a workhouse", with the lack of female company for these youths other than women of the town. He adds a moral reflection on the deficiencies of society which left no choice for thousands of low-paid young men from the provinces.[17]

Mr Balfour, a witness in a Parliamentary report on Public Houses, claimed that for women, the Eagle was "the most detrimental place", with its enticing gardens adorned with statues and large theatre with regular performances, patronised by "common streetwalkers". In the boxes and alcoves adjoining the gardens, they lured young lads to be "plied with drink". On Sunday evening there would be no play, but, said Balfour reprovingly, "I have seen gentlemen come out drunk". He described the attractive features, Chinese room, ballroom, concert room, all crowded with drinkers with many women servants and prostitutes. Conquest, who must have read this report, took no action, intending to retire as rich as had his predecessor.

The audiences were happy. The fat ladies admired its beauty, the pictures, 'miraculous' gas jets, trickling fountains and grottoes, while they drank bottled beer and enjoyed "questionable sausage rolls".

And there were spectacles to be admired. An acrobat supposedly made a balloon flight in which, in place of the usual 'car' carrying the aeronaut, he attached a horse, and astride this steed floated above the streets letting off fireworks.[18]

On the credit side, with seats ranging from 6d to two shillings, thoughtfully provided with ledges for one's glass of beer or spirits, and penny buns, sandwiches or even a hot supper brought by a servant to the gate, and smoking permitted everywhere, it had obvious attractions. This 'people's opera house' transformed the City Road (says Hollingshead) into "a little unsophisticated German town, with its beer-garden, palm-garden, and cheap and good music". A nice comparison.

There were also variety shows, but music was the chief attraction, and although the Salvation Army later took over the building, the Grecian was a true parent of 1890s' music-hall.[19]

NO MORE FIELDS

The rural setting had long vanished under bricks and mortar.

"One of the longest but most pleasant ways I have walked is from Paddington to Islington, where you can see on the left a fine view of the nearby hills, with the village of Hampstead on one of them, and on the right an ever-unfolding prospect of the streets of London. It is dangerous to walk alone here – especially in the afternoon and evening – for only last week a man was robbed and murdered on this road."

That was in 1782, the impression of a German visitor named Carl Philip Moritz.[20] In half a century the view altered completely. Thomas Cromwell, describing Islington in 1835, was witness to changes that had already been in evidence for a decade.

"Few are the suburban districts ... which have been more fertile in changes ... than that of Islington. The distant and unpretending village of a former age, besides having become almost an integral part of London through the immense increase of intermediate buildings, now comprises within itself a mass of population, respectability, and wealth ... while, at the same time, the major part of the large parish of Islington continues to partake of the rural character ... whether as regards the delightful undulations of its surface, or the extent of the views it commands from a variety of elevated situations."[21]

So by the 1830s Islington was a suburb, though still a leafy one. Indeed, elderly gentlemen in the 1850s reminisced nostalgically over the rural beauties still enjoyed in the 1820s, even if chiefly in the form of surviving pleasure-gardens, by mid-century only a cherished memory. The rash of bricks and mortar spreading like a dirty phrase over the whole of the New River estate, Barnsbury and Canonbury, swallowed up the once green fields.

Less than another decade later Dickens could compare it with the growth of Washington, D.C. "Take the worst parts of the City Road and Pentonville, or the straggling outskirts of Paris ... preserving all their oddities, but especially the small shops and dwellings, occupied in Pentonville (but not in Washington) by furniture-brokers, keepers of poor eating-houses, and fanciers of birds ..." Washington, he suggested, was a compound of these, plus a bit of St John's Wood, with wider streets and rebuilt in wood, and with elements of the brickfields which had invaded Islington and neighbouring areas before giving way to the houses of which they became components – as illustrated by George Cruikshank's famous 1829 cartoon, *March of the Bricks and Mortar*, based on his own Amwell Street experience.[22]

One place which still retained a simple rural charm was the far-flung Hornsey Wood, sole survivor of the mediaeval manorial forest. "The most tea-drinking place north of the Metropolis", writes John Fisher Murray in 1845, it was approached by any of several pretty roads, via Islington, Highbury or the Sluice

House by the banks of the New River, or from Highgate or Hampstead.

At the Sluice House "cockney anglers", cooped up in a tiny room, paid a shilling to angle (in vain) for sticklebacks or roach. Then up the gentle hill to the tavern against the wood, "a little scrubby patch of some dozen acres", kept as a wilderness and an attractive change from the manicured arbours and cramped gardens of the customary resort. Hornsey Wood had "a little meadow, a little lake, with little boats on it", and natural surroundings – rural views as far as Epping Forest, and nearer at hand the vale of the river Lea. It provided the usual facilities, ballroom, orchestra, bowling-green, but Murray waxes most lyrical about the rural aspect, itself soon to be swallowed up like all the rest by housing.[23]

The general story of these pleasure-resorts, repeated throughout Islington and London, is of decline, first in popularity, then in shabbiness, then in respectability until public opinion, become prudish, ends them in either quiet closure or law-breaking and police intervention. So it was with them all. Highbury Barn was about the last to survive, after undergoing many changes, but that belongs to a later generation.

There is a large bound collection on Sadler's Wells in the British Library, Th. Crs. 49, Vol. 8 [= 1790–1815] and a Sadler's Wells Collection of press cuttings in the Local History department of Finsbury Library, London.

1   Edward Wedlake Brayley, *History and Descriptive Accounts of the Theatres of London*, London, 1826.
2   Lewis, *Islington*, p. 438.
3   Arundell, *Sadler's Wells*, pp. 73ff.; Brayley, *London Theatres*.
4   *The Letters of Viscount Palmerston to Laurence and Elizabeth Sulivan, 1804-63*, Camden 4th Ser., Vol. 23, Royal History Society, 1979, p. 42.
5   Benjamin Silliman, *A Journal of Travels in England, Holland and Scotland … in the Years 1805 and 1806*, 3rd edn (enlarged), New Haven, 1820, pp. 16-18, 105.
6   *The Reminiscences of Thomas Dibdin*, New York, 1970; *DNB* Charles Dibdin (1768–1833), Thomas Dibdin (1771–1841).
7   Lord William Pitt Lennox, *My Recollections from 1806 to 1873*, London, 1874, Vol. I, pp. 167-8; Boz (Dickens), *Grimaldi, passim*; Arundell, *Sadler's Wells*, pp. 79ff. Lord William Pitt Lennox was the son of the 4th Duke of Richmond, a spectator at the field of Waterloo, served in the army, later an MP and author of some indifferent novels.
8   Boz (Dickens), *Grimaldi, passim*; Arundell, *Sadler's Wells*, pp. 79ff.; Brayley, *London Theatres*.
9   Brayley, *London Theatres*, pp. 56ff.
10 Arundell, *Sadler's Wells*, Chapter 10.
11 In the year 2000 the percentage of open space in Islington, despite increases in the 1990s, was a mere 5.3.
12 Francis Place, *Autobiography*, p. 28n. 2. For the pleasure gardens see Wroth, *Pleasure Gardens*, Sunderland, *Old London Spas*. See also Chapter 7.
13 J Greenwood, *Dining with Duke Humphrey*, London [1884].
14 Edmund Yates, *His Recollections and Experiences*, London, 1884, Vol. I, p. 38.
15 Robert Seymour, *Humerous Sketches*, London, 1838 (1866 edn illustrated by Alfred Crowquill).
16 Lord William Pitt Lennox, *50 Years of Biographical Reminiscences*, 1863, Vol. II, pp. 13-18.
17 G R Sims, 'A Street Song' in *Ballads and Poems*, London, 1883; Ewing Ritchie, *The Night Side of London*, London, 1861.
18 A N Bennett, *London and Londoners in the 1850s and 1860s*, London, 1924.
19 John Hollingshead, *My Lifetime*, London, 1895, Vol. I, pp. 25-28.
20 Carl Philip Moritz, *Journeys of a German in England in 1782*, p. 59.
21 Thomas Cromwell, *Walks Through Islington*, Preface.
22 Charles Dickens, *American Notes*, London, 1842, Chapter VIII.
23 John Fisher Murray, *The World of London*, London, 1845, Vol. II, pp. 83f.

CHAPTER 18

An Outbreak of Religion

While in the 18th century the number of Dissenting sects had greatly risen, the Established Church suffered a fall in vigour, and by the early 19th century when England was said to have nearly 11,000 livings, almost half had no regular incumbent, even a curate (1813). This caused the Establishment great anxiety, for as the country's population rose in the decade 1811-21 by nearly ¼ million, and by still more as time went on, parishes expanding in population had no adequate provision of churches, a gap which the Non-Conformists were not slow to fill.

Islington's parish church of St Mary's was already beleaguered by the end of the 18th century, a state which intensified as the new century progressed. In 1803 a chapel-of-ease seemed a likely solution. In the new suburb of Pentonville west of the Angel, a second church was already serving Clerkenwell, Aaron Hurst's St James's on the hill (1788, though for some years not admitted to the ecclesiastical establishment). While the problem was recognised in St Mary's parish, for some time the Vestry tinkered with it by its desperate attempts to provide more seating through in-

54. St James, Pentonville, built in 1788.

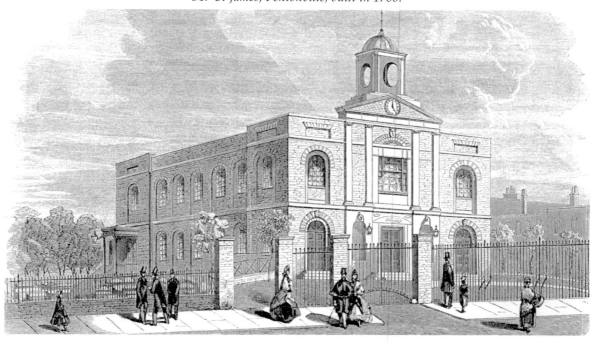

55. St Mary Magdalene on Holloway Road, with a churchyard extending to Liverpool Road.

ternal adjustments.

There was then official silence until in 1811 William Wickings, a vestryman who was also an architect, was asked to build a church in the Holloway Road, where there was space for both fabric and churchyard. In view of the parish's continuing search for more burial ground since the 1780s, the latter was of some importance. The builder was named Griffiths, and the cost, £20,000, proved unexpectedly large – indefensibly, even scandalously. A committee of investigation found that much of it was wasted thanks to an absence of a specific contract, "the Architect having left them in the dark as to certain works", and often applying for more funds.[1]

Wickings, who from 1805-14 was Surveyor for Middlesex, and twice President of the Surveyors' Club (1807 and 1820) might be put in the category "as an architect he was a good surveyor". At all events little praise has been accorded to his St Mary Magdalene's (1812). "Undistinguished classical" is Colvin's verdict. It was appropriately large: "a tall, gaunt six-bay box" (Pevsner), in detail mostly Tuscan for porch and gallery columns. As in its mother church, a painting was installed above the reredos, here *Noli Me Tangere*, again painted locally by a vestryman, John Tibbetts, who in 1814 served as Churchwarden.

On the credit side, with the church came a

new parochial school, built at the rear alongside what became Liverpool Road.

In 1818 the serious shortage of churches throughout England led to the setting up of a national church building fund, administered by a Commission, limiting individual expenditure to £20,000. The allocation for London was 33, for most of which the new 'Grecian' style was chosen, less for looks than for relative cheapness: the more expensive churches were built in the newly fashionable Gothic.

'Commissioners' Churches', as they were called, suffered from this limitation of funds, and the campaign lagged. In 1824 a further £½ million was granted, and local contributions were sought. Islington, one of three parishes receiving the most grants – eight each – was among the new outer suburbs to benefit.

In the 1830s it was calculated that of London's now 1½ million inhabitants, still one third were receiving no religious instruction, and Bishop Blomfield aimed his sights higher, forming a Metropolitan Churches Fund (1836) to build and endow more London churches.

DANIEL WILSON

The problems of St Mary's parish are well illustrated during the eight-year incumbency of the Rev. Daniel Wilson snr, struggling with the continuing church shortage.

His predecessor, the Rev. George Strahan, who lived to be 80, was described as "a fine specimen of the old school of divines … courteous in manners – a good scholar – an excellent preacher – regular in the discharge of official duties". He was generally loved and admired by his whole congregation.[2]

Under him in 1818 St Mary's Church underwent further repairs and alterations, including a new roof. Thomas Cromwell, writing in 1835, considered this a change for the worse, the new ceiling "inferior in construction and design", while the interior was darkened by "filling the lobby with pews" for the new parishioners, preventing access to galleries and nave from the side doors. All this cost £2000 in contrast to the works in 1787 which had cost less than £800. (The church was further "repaired and beautified" in 1830.)

Dr Strahan's afternoon Lecturer, Dr George Gaskin, who resigned in 1822, was in the pluralist tradition, being also Rector of Stoke

56. Rev. Daniel Wilson snr.

which he endured a further prolonged convalescence.

Wilson's new parish, which still had many rural elements despite its spectacular population increase (from 10,000 to 30,000), was described as having "strong local attachment, combined with good sense, friendly feeling, religious principle", but "marred by occasional outbursts of party spirit easily provoked, and with difficulty, allayed". The Rev. Daniel before long instigated great changes. For the past couple of decades in the closing years of his predecessor the venerable Strahan, "Islington slept. Under his successor it awoke" – to repeated controversy.[5]

Although his style did not suit everybody, Wilson was already famous before he came to Islington. Henry Edward Fox (who later succeeded as 4th Baron Holland), a young gentleman of decided opinions, on hearing him in 1822 at Bloomsbury Chapel pronounced his sermon "bombast repetition", giving "about 50 descriptions of the New Zion", each time "exactly with the same thoughts but differently expressed", "and this, with a few theatrical attitudes and variations of voice learned of Kean [the famous tragedian], was the amount of his whole sermon. Upon the whole it was trash ..."[6]

The quality of sermons was of great importance to contemporaries, and apart from the traditional duty of attendance it was indeed largely why people went to church. On arrival at Islington Wilson again did not universally please, and though at this stage he was fairly restrained he was "abrupt, fearless, decided, active, uncompromising" – in fact an Evangelical preacher, and many feared this "new doctrine". One angry parishioner declared he and his family would not enter the church again, but Wilson found out where he lived, at once called on his family and (says his biographer) "all was set right in a moment", for "few could resist him when he wished to please". As prejudices lessened, more joined his congregation, until St Mary's had standing room only. The less devout complained that "There's no such thing as getting a comfortable game at cards now, as in Dr Strahan's time". One old High Churchman, who also threatened to leave the parish, was won over, finding after all "that religion is heart-work".

Newington and St Benet, Gracechurch, and left St Mary's on being granted a prebend's stall at Ely.[3]

When Strahan died in 1824, the advowson was in the hands of Mr William Wilson, of Worton in Oxfordshire. He presented the living to his nephew and son-in-law Daniel. Son of a prosperous Spitalfields silk merchant, Daniel Wilson had been educated at the Rev. John Eyre's school in Hackney. Though he was apprenticed to his silk manufacturer uncle, he was determined to enter the Church. Overcoming his father's resistance this serious, dedicated young man took a degree at St Edmund Hall at a time when Oxford was little concerned with either religion or scholarship, became a tutor there and later its Vice-Principal, and married his cousin Ann Wilson. From 1809 to 1824 he was vicar to a small select congregation at St John's Chapel in Bedford Row.

Wilson's transfer to Islington followed a long and serious illness which had caused him to move in 1820 for health reasons to "what might be called a country house at Barnsbury, Islington" (writes his biographer).[4] On 2 July 1824, his 26th birthday, he was inducted, and preached his first sermon for 8 months – after

Wilson, though he lived to be 80, was far from robust: weakness continued for the rest of his life, and in the pulpit he had to sit on a stool, on whose cross-bars he would mount when excited, towering over the congregation in a manner admittedly not graceful but "impressive and earnest".

At this time the two Sunday services were conducted by the Vicar in the morning and his Lecturer in the afternoon, but early in 1825 Wilson asked the Vestry to consider an evening service. At a meeting attended by 200 and lasting nearly four hours, the prolonged discussion was not so much on the number of services as on payment or otherwise for pews. At last it was unanimously decided that pews should be free, and (by a large majority) that the Churchwardens, on behalf of the parish, should pay the expenses. On 27 February an exhausted Wilson – who as he recorded in his journal had spent the meeting "standing, speaking, talking, and calling to order" – first opened St Mary's for an evening service.

Wilson is recorded from the beginning as holding Morning Prayer twice a week, with the Eucharist on saints' days and early Eucharist on Sundays,[7] which Evangelical arrangement was held to have proved beneficial to the Church in England generally, inspiring philanthropic attitudes such as supporting the freedom of slaves.

NEW ANGLICAN CHURCHES

Under the 'Commissioners' Act' Islington was reckoned to need three new churches, in spite of the anxiety caused by the expensive St Mary Magdalene's, for which the debt was still unpaid. To lessen parishioners' distrust the new Vicar issued a circular letter pointing out that the parish, already numbering 30,000 souls and, with land let for more building, expecting a further rise to 50,000, still possessed only these two Anglican churches which held only 2,500 between them – just one-twelfth of the population. A minimum of three more would be necessary, and would cost £30,000 or more. Wilson urged local support to the tune of 3d in the pound rate to raise £12,000, the rest to be funded by the Commissioners. Perhaps, he said persuasively, 3s. 4d per family? – a small sacrifice for adequate church accommodation? In a diplomatically worded appeal, he hoped this would generate no "heat and contention".

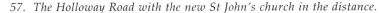

57. The Holloway Road with the new St John's church in the distance.

58. St Paul's, Ball's Pond Road, 1905.

The plea proved "irresistible". A full discussion was held in the Vestry, and Wilson circulated another letter "as a pledge of gratitude and praise to God", were they successful, pleading for the appointment of "men of decided evangelical piety", promoters of the 39 Articles.[8]

"Who could tell into whose hands these churches might one day fall?" asked sceptics in the whirl of consultation, opposition, discussions with the Commissioners and parishioners, and prayers and exhortations from the pulpit. Bishops, even archbishops, were drawn in, and finally three churches were agreed, to contain a total congregation of 5000.

Building started with St John's in Upper Holloway, with 1,782 sittings, on a site given by the Corporation for Relief of the Widows and Orphans of Clergymen. Its foundation stone was laid in 1826 in the presence of many leading clerics, notably the Archbishop of Canterbury, with a long procession from St Mary's bearing banners and masonic emblems, and followed by dinner at the

Canonbury Tavern. It was consecrated by the Bishop of London, Dr Howley, on 2 July 1828. The architect was the young Charles Barry, in his early 30s, son of a well-to-do Westminster stationer and largely learning his architectural skills while articled to a firm of Lambeth surveyors.

A few months later the Bishop consecrated Barry's St Paul's, Ball's Pond Road, similar in design and accommodation, but with the tower liturgically at the reverse end. At £10,947 it cost slightly less, thanks to Lord Northampton's offering the site at a nominal price. Largest of the three, though with no tower, was Holy Trinity in Cloudesley Square, also begun in 1826 on parish land (the Stonefield estate), costing £11,535 and providing 2000 seats. Here Barry's model was the chapel of King's College, Cambridge; and it was consecrated in March 1829. The vicar presented each new church on the day of consecration with a set of Communion plate worth 100 guineas. The three churches' completion proved for Wilson an unforgettable

59. Trinity church in Cloudesley Square, drawn by Thomas H. Shepherd.

achievement.

At the same time nine Sunday Schools were launched in the parish's poorest areas, under voluntary teachers who set up lending libraries, and before long these increased to 15, which the Vicar duly visited in turn.

In 1825/6 progress was halted by the financial crisis throughout Britain – not helped by a period of severe weather. In an unprecedented move, Wilson raised £100 from parish contributions to aid the poor, forming the nucleus of a Benevolent Fund.

There was unseemly dissension when the afternoon Lectureship once more came up for nomination. The Lecturer, the Rev. Mr Denham, elected by the parishioners and financed by voluntary contributions of about £100 a year, was about to resign and the late Dr Strahan's curate was expected to apply. Wilson announced that he personally would conduct the afternoon service – a precedent dating from the time of old Dr Cave, for whom a Reader and later a clergyman was provided when he was too frail to conduct both serv-

ices. This was forgotten, however, and at a stormy meeting parishioners voted that they themselves would appoint a Lecturer. While the sober and respectable held back, the demagogues stepped in. In July 1826, after angry arguments and attempted adjournment, and uproar against a background of furious meetings and placards of protest, it was grudgingly accepted that the Vicar held the right.

1827 opened in an atmosphere of enthusiasm: 400 were turned away one March Sunday from an over-full church, and there were now strong links with other churches. Wilson met the notorious Edward Irving *(see pp 170-1)* at a breakfast, whom perhaps unexpectedly "I liked enormously".

As Wilson really believed his own life was drawing to a close: he resisted advice to build a library on his Barnsbury Park house, "tired of houses and building, and I see the end of life so near". In fact his most famous days were still to come. When the Bishop of London attended a confirmation service in March 1827, expecting perhaps "three times the usual number", actually 700 attended. Next, Wilson initiated setting up a Proprietary School for "upper classes" to provide a good education at moderate fees, an undertaking which went through many misunderstandings, offences and reconciliations. When at last concluded in October 1830, the new school in Barnsbury Street was opened, again by the Bishop.

Personal sadness for Wilson had now intervened, for his already ailing wife fell terminally ill during a visit to Clifton and, sinking rapidly, died in May 1827. They had been married 24 years.

Next year brought another controversy over an error in election of parish trustees under the local Act. A group called for "Opposition to the Vicar", and party spirit was revived. Wilson mostly kept in the background, while his supporters tried to nominate trustees for the next two years. At another stormy meeting the Churchwarden, Mr Woodward, was assailed by "motions, amendments and points of order" before (in the small hours) a settlement was reached.

In 1830 more Anglican district churches were authorised for the poor areas of the parish, including its western fringe. First came All Saints beside the Chalk Road, as Caledonian Road was then usually known, on a site near Curtis's Wharf on the canal, purchased from the landowner George Thornhill, MP. Its timid Gothic style by W. Tress was not very inspired: as Goodhart-Rendel described it, "a mean box with a sort of show E-front; quite awful, but perhaps cheap".

A damning judgement, but certainly accurate about the low cost, £4,412, three-quarters of it raised by subscribers in "the largest and poorest population of any district in the parish" (it was close to the area of noxious industries round Maiden Lane). Thus did the new *Islington Times* newspaper point out in May 1857, when already the church needed urgent repairs. All Saints had one environmental virtue, that it provided a vista-closer across the Chalk Road at the foot of Wynford Road, south of the Regent's Canal. (By the late 1970s the vista had been lost by infilling and the church was demolished in a period of sweeping destruction of redundant Anglican churches. It has not been replaced by anything remarkable.)

Two other 1830s foundations were after Wilson's rectorship had ended, and were the work of Henry William Inwood, designer of many churches including the Neo-Greek St Pancras, and of his pupil E N Clifton. St James's in Chillingworth Road, where the Liverpool Road joins the Holloway Road, has had an unenviable fate. It too had a Grecian-style front, with four Ionic Erechtheum-style pilasters, a pediment and what Pevsner calls a "hungry SW tower", almost unbelievably narrow when viewed (as most often) from the south. However, again the style was chosen as much for cheapness as aesthetics, also serving a poor and unprovided quarter.

The land was offered by Miss Sebbon, a relative of the long-serving vestryman Walter Sebbon. It was hoped, and proved, that it would bring uplift to the district. However, perhaps because it was built for less than £4000, within a year expensive but necessary alterations cost more than half as much again, including the provision of porches and an organ, above which 80 charity children could be seated. This church, after serious bomb damage in World War II, was temporarily used as a church hall for St Mary Magdalene, and later as an offshoot of the Almeida Theatre, until it was acquired for studios and workshops in the early 90s. Then, monstrous additions including two giant columns, two additional storeys and rear extensions resulted in a gross caricature.

Of the three the happiest fate has been that of St Stephen's in Canonbury Road, also by Inwood and Clifton together with Inwood's brother Edward. Here Inwood tried the Neo-Gothic style then becoming fashionable. Completed in 1839, and unusually orientated (because of its site south of the street) with altar at the West end and entrance from the East, its chief features centred on the entrance front. Unpretentious as it was, still it boasted a spire. A critic in the *Gentleman's Magazine* (July 1838), on seeing the design at the Royal Academy could hardly contain his scorn: "An exceedingly bald elevation, showing a square naked wall for its principal front ... We here witness three architects conjoined in building a brick wall: a century ago one was deemed sufficient to design and execute a cathedral."

Despite the architectural strictures St Stephen's flourished, establishing a missionary tradition and a rapidly increasing congregation, while three of its early vicars served for 67 years between them. In the Second World War, like St Matthew's in Essex Road ("the ivy church") by A. D. Gough in 1850, St Stephen's in October 1940 was burnt out by incendiary bombs. After the war St Matthew's was demolished, and the two districts merged under St Stephen's, which had at least retained its external walls. The church, its interior restored in a very different style, continues to be a lively parish centre.

In 1834 the young Charles Barry designed St Peter's, another Gothic church, for the unpretentious new area south of Colebrooke Row to which it gave its name. Completed by 1835 and costing only £3,407, in 1842 it was given a slender spire by Roumieu and Gough, with flying buttresses and other adornments.[9]

Meanwhile in Clerkenwell, in 1826–28 William Chadwell Mylne, Surveyor to the New River Company, had built the large St Mark's in Myddelton Square, centre of the Company's new residential estate, in fashionable Gothic with an impressive tower. Some of its stone was re-used from the demolished Colen Campbell Wanstead House.

These churches, built by the beginning of Queen Victoria's reign, proved to be early forerunners of a spate of religious building.

THE CHURCH MISSIONARY SOCIETY

After his wife's death Daniel Wilson immersed himself in work. He attempted, unsuccessfully, to launch a Mutual Assurance Society, tried to change Smithfield's market day to avoid interference with Sunday services, and with better luck established a local association for the Church Missionary Society.

He capitulated over enlarging his house at 9 Barnsbury Park (having given up the idea of finding a suitable vicarage) by adding to it a large library entered by a winding stair, 35 feet long and capable of holding 12,000 volumes. Visitors would find the vicar at his work-table by the fireplace, "immersed in papers". Here he held his annual church meetings, conducted family prayers, or entertained friends to breakfast. Here, too, he inaugurated the Islington Clerical Meeting, a gathering of clergy which became annual and was continued by his son, expanded and eventually moved (1920) to Westminster. For a short while his mother and sister shared the otherwise lonely house while his sons were at college and daughter at school, until his mother too died in 1829.

Also in Wilson's time the Church Missionary Society was founded, launching a college for training missionaries in Barnsbury Park in 1820. In 1824 it moved to a new college building in Upper Street, provided with a library and lecture room, thus establishing Islington as a "missionary parish". At right-angles to the main road, it was designed by William Brooks, who also designed Finsbury Unitarian Chapel and the London Institution at Finsbury Circus. The land was bought by the Church Missionary Society for £2,180, and the brick building, "plain but handsome", held 40 students. It stood in a garden, reached by a flight of stairs from the hall, with secluded paths for contemplation.

Its site is now taken by Sutton Dwellings (1915), which stretch back to the street called College Cross, the only clue to the existence of the College.

There was also a non-denominational college at Highbury. This had opened at Mile End in 1783 as a Congregational training college. For a number of years it was at Hoxton, and in 1826 it removed to Highbury, to a new building on six acres, where it too catered for about 40 students. In 1848, however, it moved again and the building was sold the following year to the Church of England Missionary and Training Institution, which made additions for school buildings. The College building was sold in 1913, together with its six acres, and was taken by the Woolwich Arsenal Football Club, which had moved from south of the Thames.

Wilson's time in Islington was nearing its end. Having long been concerned with the church in Calcutta, he invited Dr Turner, its Bishop, to preach at the new Church Missionary Association in Islington. On Turner's death in 1831 Wilson was called to succeed him, and after much heart-searching he accepted. In April 1832 he resigned the living and was consecrated Bishop at Lambeth.

60. The Church Missionary Society College, pictured in 1827. It is now replaced by Sutton Dwellings between Upper Street and College Cross.

After a farewell public breakfast at Canonbury, Wilson senior took leave at Court, kissed the King's hand, preached his last parish sermon to a crowded congregation in an address lasting an hour and 40 minutes, and sailed for India on 18 June. The bells were rung in his honour, a large crowd assembled round his house to say farewell, and relatives accompanied him and his daughter to Portsmouth.

Wilson did not return to Islington until 1845, on Church business for India. Although taken ill with jungle fever, he attended the Church Missionary College; saw London's new buildings – especially the new Houses of Parliament designed by Barry – preached a last sermon, and in August 1846 again sailed for Calcutta, where he died in 1858. In his will he did not forget his old parish, leaving £1,000 for the poor, and £2,000 for a new Church Building Fund, for the shortage of churches was now as serious as ever.[10]

The advowson being with his family, Wilson's son, also Daniel, succeeded him as vicar and was inducted to St Mary's in May 1832 – where he was to serve until 1886.

NON-CONFORMIST INROADS

Meanwhile in non-Established churches there had been great expansion. Perhaps the most notorious – and locally most ill-fated – was built for the Rev. Edward Irving off Duncan Terrace, beside the New River.

Irving (1792–1834), a friend in youth of Thomas Carlyle, was an MA of Edinburgh University who after a spell at teaching became assistant minister to the celebrated Dr Thomas Chalmers in Glasgow. Having made a reputation for rousing sermons, he moved to London in 1822 as minister at Hatton Garden Chapel, where crowds of the aristocracy, the rich and famous flocked to hear him preach, though several wrote off his florid sensationalism as bombast. Irving was elegant, dark and startlingly handsome save for a squint which many felt gave him a sinister appearance.

Irving lived in Myddelton Terrace, recently built beside the New River's upper reservoir, in what shortly became part of Claremont Square (Carlyle visited him here more than once). He was renowned not only for preaching for well over an hour, but for tyrannising worshippers: for example at prayer meetings at his house his flock might try at their peril to escape before he permitted them. In

time he became still more extreme, "speaking in tongues", all of which ended with his expulsion from the Presbyterian church for heretical practices.[11]

Near the end of his career, Irving's devoted followers built him a church in Duncan Street, for like the Methodists of almost a century earlier he had been reduced to preaching in Islington's fields. Before he died, supporters styled themselves the "Holy Catholic Apostolic Church", and after his death in Glasgow in 1834 they continued to flourish, in 1854 founding the Catholic Apostolic Church in Gordon Square.[12]

Probably the most famous Non-Conformist chapel of the 19th century (though its chief fame was to come after its rebuilding in 1876-7) was what came to be called Union Chapel, removed to Compton Terrace in 1806. This chapel was to provide some of Islington's most distinguished ministers of the 19th century, starting with the Rev. Thomas Lewis who served from 1804 (when it was still meeting in a house in Highbury Grove) until 1852.

The other chapels built before Queen Victoria

61. The Rev. Edward Irving.

62. The rebuilt Union Chapel in Compton Terrace, early 19th century.

came to the throne were Claremont Chapel in Pentonville Road in 1818–19 (much of it now home to the Crafts Council), Angel Baptist Chapel in Chadwell Street (1824, and at the time of writing its future uncertain), Maberly Chapel in Ball's Pond Road (1825), the Scottish Presbyterian Chapel in Colebrooke Row (1834), and the Northampton Tabernacle (now the Roman Catholic SS Peter and Paul) in Amwell Street (1835). The Catholic St John the Evangelist in Duncan Terrace, and Vernon Baptist Chapel in Vernon Street followed in 1842–3 and 1843–4, the former a result of the Catholic Relief Act of 1829 liberating Catholics from long-standing restrictions.

*   *   *   *   *

In the 1840s the obligation to attend church was considered binding. An American clergyman visiting Britain in 1844 commented that on Sunday morning churches were well filled, and no shops except those of a few Jews were open, and some confectioners' and cigar shops "half open". Butchers' stalls in markets in poor areas opened until church-time, while drink shops opened after church came out, for the benefit of families who liked beer with their dinner. As for Sunday morning traffic, it was mostly omnibuses carrying people to and from church. The afternoons many people devoted to fun, and large crowds walked long distances to tea-gardens or to take boat trips. Indeed, Sunday was for many years the only day of leisure.[13]

1. Cromwell, *Walks Through Islington*, pp. 131-6; VM Vols. IV (January 1811) and V; Colvin, *British Architects*, p. 1,048; Bridget Cherry & Nikolaus Pevsner, *The Buildings of England, London 4: North*, Penguin Books, 1998, p. 657. The builder, Griffiths, was probably John William Griffith of Clerkenwell (*c.* 1790–1855), a surveyor like Wickings, though at this time very young. He later designed the parochial schools in Liverpool Road, west of the Chapel of Ease churchyard (1815f.) He was father to William Pettit Griffith, architect in Clerkenwell (b. 1816). (*VCH* p. 236) On the other hand the builder might have been Thomas Griffiths, trade or profession unspecified, who was Churchwarden from 1811–14 (VM).

2. Rev. Josiah Bateman, *The Life of the Rev. Daniel Wilson, DD*, London, 1860, p. 232.

3. Cromwell, *Walks Through Islington*, p. 84.

4. Bateman, *Life of Wilson*, p. 230.

5. *Ibid.*, p.232.

6. *The Journal of Henry Edward Fox, 1818-1830*, ed. Lord Ilchester, London, 1923, p. 99.

7. Canon Sidney Ollard, *Short History of the Oxford Movement*, London, [1915], p. 195. See also a summary of Wilson's life in *The North Londoner*, 17 April 1869, p. 163.

8. Bateman, *Life of Wilson*, pp. 240f.

9. *Ibid.* pp. 247f. For the churches, see Cherry & Pevsner, *London 4: North, ad loc.*; Nikolaus Pevsner, *London, Except the Cities of London and Westminster*, Penguin Books, 1951, p. 226 (quoting Goodhart-Rendel on All Saints); Mary Cosh, *A History of Saint Stephen's Church, Canonbury*, p.p. by St Stephen's Church, 1989.

10. Bateman, *Life of Wilson*, pp. 232–258.

11. Mrs Oliphant, *The Life of Edward Irving*, London, 1862, Vol. II, Chapters 4-7.

12. The Gordon Square church later became the London University Church, now converted into flats. The small classical church behind Duncan Terrace (by Stevenson and Ramage in 1834), was almost completely rebuilt in 1854 by G Truefitt. It closed in 1962 and was burnt down in 1967. (Temple, *Islington Chapels*, p. 120).

13. Rev. Henry Colman, *European Life and Manners*, Boston & London, 1849, Vol. I, p. 213.

CHAPTER 19

More Characters

CHARLES LAMB

We have several accounts of Charles Lamb when he was living in Islington, in the 1790s at no. 45 and later 36 Chapel Street (now Chapel Market), and from late 1822 to 1827 when he lived at Colebrooke Cottage beside the New River (as it flowed between Colebrooke Row and Duncan Terrace – the grassed strip now marks its former course).

Charles Lamb, born in 1775 in the Inner Temple, where his father was a law clerk, had known the slightly older Coleridge as a school-boy at Christ's Hospital. They met again when Coleridge came down from Cambridge in 1794. During Lamb's lifetime his friends also included William Hazlitt, the Wordsworths, John Keats, Thomas De Quincey, Leigh Hunt, Robert Southey and many others in the literary field – most of whom visited him at Colebrooke Cottage and his later homes. But he himself was bound to daily drudgery with the East India Company, from the age of 17 until he retired aged 50 in 1825.

He early took to writing, and contributed to several periodicals including the *London Magazine*, in which his *Essays of Elia*, later published in book form, established his fame between 1820 and 1823.

There was a streak of insanity in the family on Lamb's mother's side, and he himself suffered a derangement when he was 20. His younger sister Mary, whom he looked after with care and affection, in 1796 in a fit of madness killed their mother. It was at their Chapel Street lodgings that this tragedy took place.

Brother and sister were devoted, and she collaborated with him in 1807 on their *Tales*

63. Charles Lamb.

from Shakespeare. At times when she was mentally deranged, he had to escort her across the fields to Balmes House, a well-known private asylum in Hackney.

Colebrooke Cottage, where the pair moved in December 1822, was the first house that Lamb, who was by now 47, had ever owned, and he was naturally eager to share his delight with his friends. To Bernard Barton he wrote his well-known description of house

173

and garden (2 September 1823):

> "I have a cottage at Colebrooke-row, Islington; – a cottage, for it is detached, a white house with six good rooms in it; the New River (rather elderly by this time) runs (if a moderate walking-pace can be so termed) close to the foot of the house; and behind is a spacious garden, with vines (I assure you), pears, strawberries, parsnips, leeks, carrots, cabbages, to delight the heart of old Alcinous. You enter without passage into a cheerful dining-room, all studded over and rough with old books; and above is a lightsome drawing-room, three windows, full of choice prints. I feel like a great lord, never having had a house before."

Long afterwards the house was substantially altered, and Lamb's description no longer fits: the hall-less entrance and the three-window drawing room are gone. Today there are only two such windows, and the garden was long ago swallowed up by John Webb's lemonade factory. The New River has since been stopped off at Stoke Newington, but its course is marked by the gardens along Duncan Terrace.

Lamb also wrote to Robert Southey, with whom he had recently ended a misunderstanding after Southey's criticism of him in the *Quarterly Review*, inviting him to visit his new abode: "A detached whitish house, close to the New River, end of Colebrooke Terrace, left hand from Sadler's Wells".[1]

The most celebrated event that took place during Lamb's occupancy is probably the one caricatured by Cruikshank in his cartoon *Drowning*, though that takes place at night, depicting a decrepit watchman feebly waving his lantern while the yelling reveller sinks from sight. The unrailed New River along Colebrooke Row was often criticised as a danger to pedestrians, and a notorious ducking was suffered by Lamb's elderly writer friend, George Dyer, as he describes with some poetic licence in his Elian essay 'Amicus Redivivus". 'In fact Lamb was out at the time, but describes seeing Dyer leaving the cottage after a Sunday morning visit, and "instead of turning down the right hand path by which he

had entered – with staff in hand, and at noon day, deliberately march right forwards into the midst of the stream and totally disappear". Lamb pretends that he hurls himself forward, seeing "the silvery apparition of a good white head emerging", and Dyer's upright staff, wielded unlike Excalibur by an unseen hand, and drags him on his shoulders to the bank. Here he is besieged by a babel of well-meaning passers-by who now "in philanthropic shoals" bombard him with advice, "the application, or non-application of salt, &c" while Dyer seems on the point of expiry.

One bright spark has the wit to suggest a doctor, whom Lamb describes as expert in such emergencies: gravely middle-aged, one-eyed, clad in "sad brown" now darkened to nearly black by (Lamb supposes) his "frequency of nightly divings". The doctor, who lodged at or frequented the Sir Hugh Myddelton's Head, supposedly daily revived the nearly drowned. Dyer, a non-drinker, is persuaded to drink a tumbler of cognac and revives.

Barry Cornwall, as the barrister/writer Brian Waller Procter was professionally known, who happened by that same morning, gives what was more likely the true account. Approaching the house he sees the "track of war ... like that left by a large Newfoundland dog", and on ringing the bell learns from the maid that Lamb was not at home, Mr Dyer had fallen in the water and "My Missus is in such a fright". Upstairs he found Dyer swathed in blankets, his stubby grey hair standing on end like needles, and garrulous from a stiff brandy-and-water, while Miss Lamb ransacked his wet trouser pockets for his keys and money. While she twittered, Dyer chattered: "It certainly was *very* extraordinary, I really thought it was the path. I walked on and on, and suddenly I was in. But I soon found out where I was."

"I should think so", drily observed Barry Cornwall, and left him to the care of the one-eyed "itinerant doctor" from the nearby pub, who was cannily improving its sales by prescribing plenty of cognac.[2]

Another barrister, Henry Crabb Robinson, a one-time correspondent of *The Times* and the sort of man who called on and entertained Everybody, was exactly Lamb's age. The two used to take country walks to Enfield, Hampstead, or call on Mrs Barbauld at Stoke Newington. Lamb was less interested in scenery than in the walk itself, and "his great delight", notes Robinson in 1814, "even in preference to a country walk, is a stroll in London".

Robinson mentions calling at the Lambs' after swimming in the Peerless Pool off the City Road, and on one such evening in 1815 "at Islington during a long shower", "wetted to the skin", he was "consoled by finding Wordsworth at the Lambs'". (The Lambs must then have been at either Russell Street, Covent Garden, or Chapel Street.) In 1824, when Robinson and Lamb visited Mrs Barbauld after dining together, Lamb was unusually "disputatious with her and not in his best way. He reasons from feelings ... she from abstractions and verbal definitions. Such people can't agree."

Also in 1824, over tea at Lamb's house Robinson met the Rev. Edward Irving and Thomas Carlyle. Contrary to usual impressions, the handsome Irving struck Robinson as very ugly, "more like an Italian assassin than a Gospel preacher" – probably because of that squint. "There is so little sympathy between Lamb and Irving", observes Robinson, "that I do not think they can or ought to be intimate."

Several writers describe Lamb's appearance. The American traveller Nathaniel Willis, meeting brother and sister at a breakfast at the Temple, described the essayist as "a gentleman in black small-clothes and gaiters, short and very slight in his person, his head set upon his shoulders with a thoughtful, forward bent, his hair just sprinkled with grey, aquiline nose, and a very indescribable mouth" – which he puzzled to interpret as indicative of humour, feeling, good nature "or a kind of whimsical peevishness".

Mary Lamb he described as small, bent, rather deaf, and evidently not in good health. He charitably supposed that earlier in life her features had been handsome, and she still had a "bright grey eye ... full of intelligence and fire".[3]

George Daniel, the 'collector', met Lamb in his lodgings at Russell Street, in 1817 and noted his "noble head" with only "a few grey curls amid crisp ones of dark brown", and fancied those expressive, thoughtful features had

an almost "Hebrew cast". Daniel, pleased with the Colebrooke Cottage move, helped Lamb to arrange his folios of Beaumont and Fletcher, Ben Jonson and so on in the pleasant dining room, and in the drawing-room to hang portraits of poets in the best light, the Hogarths in their ebony frames, and to arrange Chelsea shepherds and shepherdesses on the chimney-piece. In the pretty garden behind, where birds thronged on lawn, housetop and windowsills, Lamb grew vegetables and fruit for his dinner table and flowers for his hearth. Roses were his favourites, and he would seldom go out without a buttonhole.

Extraordinarily proud of this first house-ownership, he lived abstemiously and for the first time kept early hours, took long summer walks in the fields and picked wild flowers. He recalled an "early and transient courtship here in rural 'Merrie Islington', but bemoaned the current encroachment of "horrid bricks and mortar".

That same autumn of 1823 Daniel dined there with Robert Bloomfield, another poet, and they wandered on Lamb's favourite outing, to Newington and Queen Elizabeth's Walk. Lamb also loved to sit at the top of Canonbury Tower, studying the stars until the cold drove him down again. Its then tenant, "Goodman Syme", a fellow-antiquary, entertained him in the oak-panelled room where Goldsmith had written *The Traveller* in 1764, fortified by drinking buttermilk; while Lamb would look lovingly at Syme's small painting of Shakespeare in a carved gilt frame. (A Highbury banker later gave the portrait to Daniel.) He endlessly prowled up and down the Tower's winding stair, "peeping into its sly corners and cupboards, as if he expected to discover there some hitherto hidden clue to its mysterious origins".

Lamb also frequented Islington's ancient inns, especially the oak parlour at the Old Queen's Head in Lower Street, then still surviving. There he met the dreadful Theodore Hook, infamous practical joker, who accompanied him back to his cottage where "lightsome and lissome" Lamb in vain suggested a turn round the garden. Burly Hook, "pursy and puffy", with a nose like a red-hot poker, and who hobbled (says Daniel) like a fat goose, declined.

At the Sir Hugh Myddelton's Head Lamb was sure to run into "some playgoing old crony", and would drop in at Sadler's Wells to watch Grimaldi. He loved London spectacles like the Lord Mayor's Show, and still more Bartholomew Fair, nor could he ever pass a Punch and Judy show without stopping to watch it to the end.[4]

One who, unlike other writers, was always deeply antagonistic to Lamb, never sparing in viciously unflattering shafts, was Thomas Carlyle. Long after the Lambs had left Colebrooke Cottage he described the ageing writer as "a miserable, drink-besotted, spindle-shanked skeleton of a body", crackbrained and "sinking into drink, poor creature", only grudgingly admitting him to have humour, "a genuine, but an essentially small and *Cockney* thing... not genius, but *diluted insanity*". In a *Notebook* diatribe he again writes off Lamb as almost insane, rubbing it in: "pitiful, ricketty, gasping, staggering, stammering Fool ... witty by denying truisms, and abjuring good manners... Besides he is now a confirmed shameless drunkard, *asks* vehemently for gin-and-water in strangers' houses; tipples till he is utterly mad ..." By that time Carlyle, now acclaimed as a writer, was more disposed than formerly to be charitable about celebrities he met. Why he was so vicious about Lamb is not clear, but the invective did not lessen.[5]

Lamb's literary friends recorded pleasant evening gatherings. Despite Carlyle's strictures Lamb was described as abstemious, but Carlyle, who seemed to despise him only less than he did the poet Thomas Campbell, even in earlier days suspected him of taking drugs: he "walks as if he were quarter drunk with ale and half with laudanum".[6] Waspish to the end, Carlyle finally visited in November 1833, when Lamb had not long to live, "whom by God's blessing I shall not soon see again. The man is clearly verruckt [crazy]"; "clamours for 'gin-and-water' with a rude barbarism ... [and] more and more obstreperous". Carlyle was not above repeating himself.[7]

At Colebrooke Row Lamb's nervous tensions faded and his health improved. In fact, there he was in his element – comfortable in his own house, retired from work drudgery, and entertaining old friends. In mixed company he was not at his best, but among friends his liveliness, scholarship and wit had full play. In spring and summer Daniel, now a near neighbour, walked with him to Hornsey and farther, "through healthy villages over-looking glorious landscapes and picturesque cottages surrounded by garden ground"; dining at Finchley at the Bald-Faced Stag – all charming rural spots which in another generation or two would be swallowed up in suburbs. Then in the spring of 1827 Mary's health made it necessary for them to leave this idyllic setting and move to Enfield, but this was not a success, nor later was living at Edmonton ("the very dreariest and dullest of all his domiciles"), where Lamb died in 1834.

George Daniel, who had not heard of Lamb's death, called one day to find closed shutters and heard the tolling-bell. At first he feared it might be for Mary. But on crossing to the churchyard, to his horror he found himself at Charles Lamb's open grave, and endured the most sudden and saddest shock of his life.[8]

MORE FAMOUS CHARACTERS

Samuel Rogers and Charles Lamb are the chief of Islington's resident literary characters. Turning the pages of contemporary memoirs and letters one is unlikely to find writers and painters who lived there or even went there, except for the many visiting Charles Lamb. In the 19th century artists tended to live in Marylebone, Kensington or Chelsea, authors in Bloomsbury, Kensington or elsewhere in west London, or in Hampstead and Highgate. There were indeed famous literary visitors: Oliver Goldsmith, who was a summer visitor to Canonbury Tower and wrote *The Traveller* there. A later lodger was Washington Irving, while Thomas Carlyle, as we have seen *(Chapter 16)* lodged in Pentonville in 1824.

Much is made of the fact that Thomas Paine started on *The Rights of Man* in 1790 in an Islington pub – whether the Angel or the Old Red Lion has never been fully established – as a riposte to Burke's *Reflections on the French Revolution*. Paine was not an Islingtonian but a Norfolk man and he completed Part II of the book elsewhere.

With some historic characters the connection with Islington was in their childhood and

64. Oliver Goldsmith.

65. Washington Irving.

probably schooldays. Edward Lear (1812–1888), traveller, water-colourist and arch-creator of Nonsense, was born and spent his first ten years at Bowman's Lodge, Holloway, a house which, like so many others, later became a ladies' seminary and on which site in the 1850s Bowman's Place and in the 1860s Bowman's Mews were built.

There is a claim that Benjamin Disraeli was born in Upper Street. His father, Isaac D'Israeli, born in 1766 of a Levantine Jewish family which removed to England from Italy in the mid-18th century, was author of a number of works such as *Curiosities of Literature* which he wrote in six volumes from 1791, and *Calamities of Authors* (1812–13). For a time Isaac and his family lived in Canonbury, "behind the tower". According to Dr John Jeaffreson, a respected local doctor who lived at no 10 Trinity Row (now nos 207–220 Upper Street), the D'Israeli family moved to no 9 where they lived for about a year or 18 months. This period may possibly have coincided with the birth of Benjamin in December 1804. Benjamin was certainly at school in Islington for a time, perhaps at Miss Roper's 'Academy' in

Colebrooke Row. Trinity Row was absorbed into the famous local drapery store, Rackstraw's, in the 1860s.

A much later inhabitant of Upper Street was the artist and dainty children's book illustrator, Kate Greenaway. Born in 1846, through her drawings she set a fashion for a quasi-Regency children's dress style. Her father, John Greenaway, an engraver and illustrator on the *Illustrated London News*, had moved to Islington from Hoxton. His wife, Elizabeth, kept a millinery and fancy-goods shop at no 123 (now 147) Upper Street from 1852–78. Kate, too, was at school locally, at Mrs Fiveash's at 12 Richmond Terrace (now 52 Richmond Avenue) and attended art classes at Canonbury Tower. She had a studio in College Place, off Liverpool Road.

Charles Dickens certainly knew Islington well, describing aspects of it in his novels, and Harrison Ainsworth, though he seems not to have lived there, lampoons its shoddy, intrusive suburban terraces often enough in his writing. Islington's chief artists were George Cruikshank, Thomas Hosmer Shepherd and later Walter Sickert. On the other hand, Islington seemed to attract collectors, antiquaries and literary journalists.

JOHN NICHOLS

Born a generation before Charles Lamb, and probably the most notable of his Islington contemporaries, one of the antiquarians and printer/publishers who then distinguished the parish was John Nichols, editor from 1792 to his death of the *Gentleman's Magazine* – which was published at St John's Gate. Nichols's father Edward had also lived most of his life in Islington and in 1769 and 1770 served as Churchwarden.[9] John, born in 1745 opposite St Mary's Church, was educated along with several others who were also to become famous, at the popular school run by John Shields, successor to Mrs Science. On the death of an uncle who, had he lived, would have furthered a naval career, John was instead apprenticed when not quite 13 to the noted printer William Bowyer, whose partner he in time became. Like the schoolmaster Shield before him, Bowyer encouraged the young Nichols's literary leanings. In 1774 Nichols published essays on the origin of printing, which brought him learned friends. In 1778 he joined the *Gentleman's Magazine*, and meanwhile published a stream of literary and art anecdotes – including Hogarth's (1781) – and correspondence, sometimes in many volumes: Richard Steele's in 1788-91, works of Swift, an edition of Shakespeare's plays.

A keen antiquarian, who became an FSA of London, Edinburgh and Perth, Nichols between 1780 and 1800 produced *Bibliotheca Topographica Britannica*, a ten-volume collection of works which might otherwise have perished without trace. He also compiled accounts of the Progresses of Queen Elizabeth and James I, the former of which was used by Sir Walter Scott in writing *Kenilworth*. Nichols collaborated with Richard Gough, a fellow-antiquary who became a close friend. In spite of his many biographical miscellanies, including those of his business partner Bowyer, he was perhaps happiest with topographical antiquities, starting with the history of Leicestershire, probably his most important work (1795–1815). In 1788 he published *The History and Antiquities of Canonbury*, while contemplat-

ing a similar work on Islington itself, unfortunately never written.[10]

A portrait shows a middle-aged Nichols with an expression full of bonhomie, and he was honoured and respected for his good-tempered, benevolent nature. His first wife, Anne Cradock, whom he married about 1767, died in 1776 at the age of 36, a year-old son dying only a couple of months afterwards. Later he married Martha Green, of Hinckley, Leicestershire, who also died young, aged 32 in 1786. A son, John Bowyer Nichols, like his father became an FSA. [11]

In 1804 John Nichols became Master of the Stationers' Company, an honour greatly prized as "the summit of his ambition". He continued to live in Islington at 14 Highbury Place, though his office was off Fleet Street in Red Lion Passage, where in 1807 he had a fall which broke his thigh. Even worse, two years later a fire destroyed both printing office and warehouse and, worst of all, their contents. Comforted by friends and by his work, Nichols was sustained by further research and publications, and lived to be over 80, dying on 26 November 1826 on his way to bed. His funeral was attended by many distinguished friends and acquaintances. He was buried near his parents and his dead children, in the churchyard opposite the house where he was born. His important collection of papers was given to the Bodleian Library.[12]

WILLIAM WOODFALL

A year younger than John Nichols was the Parliamentary reporter William Woodfall (1746–1803). He and his elder brother Henry Sampson Woodfall started their careers as apprentices, the elder to their printer father, the younger to a bookseller. Henry was to become printer of *The Letters of Junius*. William was a printer of his father's *Public Advertiser* and later of other newspapers. He also became an actor and dramatic critic in the provinces, and on returning to London lived from 1772–1776 in a pretty cottage set back behind Colebrooke Row.[13]

Woodfall now turned to journalism, editing the *London Packet* (1772–4) and working on the *Morning Chronicle* (1774–89). He acted as proof corrector for Alexander Cruden (*see Chapter*

66. William Woodfall.

lection to become a collector and antiquary.

Humphry, tactfully known as his godfather, had him apprenticed about 1797 to a bookseller in Pall Mall, where he rapidly developed his collecting, so successfully that when the London Institution in Finsbury was founded he was appointed Sub-Librarian (1806). This post, which he held for 28 years, enabled him through his connections with publishers to indulge his passion. He assembled the papers of such historic characters as Henry Hyde, Earl of Clarendon, and the antiquary Ralph Thoresby of Leeds, both eventually published. His paternal inheritance of pictures in oil and crayon, drawings, engravings, and correspondence with artists and other leading personalities, crystallised the tastes by which Upcott eventually became 'Prince of Collectors', "father of one amongst our maddest fashions of the time."[15] In his collection of contemporary autographs he in time amassed 32,000 letters and 3,000 portraits, besides many other manuscripts.

Among Upcott's major discoveries were John Evelyn's diary in 1818, and Thomas Chatterton's poem *Amphitryon*, which turned up in unlikely circumstances at a City cheesemonger's. Another historic document he secured was the 'confession' of John Felton, assassin of Charles I's Duke of Buckingham – which after Upcott's death was blown away at his own front door when a boy was collecting his papers for the auctioneers.

Upcott appears not to have married; though an Elizabeth Upcott, described as wife of William Upcott, Esq. and dying at Cullompton in Devon in March 1847, aged 66, would indeed have been his contemporary. However, there was a rumour that his resignation from the London Institution in 1834 was punningly attributed to his having "extra-illustrated" the resident housekeeper "in a family way". This evoked an acquaintance's comment, "Like father, like son". It was then that Upcott retired to the little Upper Street house (opposite Cross Street, depicted on the jacket of this book) which became known as 'Autograph Cottage', described unflatteringly as simply "a bare brown wall towards the south, with a space of poor garden ground, and a high railing between". Inside, writes Joseph Mayer, it was "quaintly old fashioned and ... a veritable

12). It was however after he left Islington that his fame as a Parliamentary reporter was established, being the first to publish a verbatim account of Commons speeches the morning after the debates. Here a remarkable memory served him well, said to be so retentive that, without notes, which were then not allowed to be taken in the Commons, he could absorb whole speeches and report them supposedly accurately. (Although of course we have no means of knowing just how exact his record was.) Woodfall's attempt to publish a Parliamentary *Diary* lost out to *Hansard* but he continued as a respected drama critic. He died in 1803 at the age of 57.[14]

WILLIAM UPCOTT

Of a later generation William Upcott (1779–1845), who ended his days in Islington, was the illegitimate son of the painter Ozias Humphry. The artist had been a friend of George Romney and William Blake, studied in Italy and later painted in India, but in his fifties lost his sight. Among his bequests to his son William were engravings and letters which doubtless encouraged the boy's predi-

museum", crammed with letters, manuscripts and prints by the ten thousand. The walls were hung with paintings not merely by Ozias Humphry but by Thomas Gainsborough, and every possible receptacle was stuffed with books, autographs, cuttings and portraits. In 1833 Upcott lost a large collection of gold and silver coins in a burglary, but admirers raised a collection or a grant from the Institution to reimburse him.

Described as a kindly man full of "cheerful and agreeable conversation", Upcott, like William Woodfall, was blessed with a phenomenal memory which "furnished an inexhaustible fund of anecdote". In his autobiographical notes, compiled in 1816 for a Norwich banker friend, Mr Dawson Turner, he described how his life-time's hobby "galloped me into half the sale-rooms as well as among the printsellers, booksellers, coin dealers … till I have been … almost penniless with the pursuit". He writes in December 1834 to his friend Robert Nasmyth in Edinburgh of the bedlam that reigned in "the confusion of every room – every chair – nay every floor – of my Cottage. Only a single Table is allowed for Meals, and the rest are literally spread over with scraps of various kinds which I am endeavouring to arrange previously to the pasting and binding up into volumes."

The following March he wrote to Nasmyth's wife of a violent storm which had caused huge local damage: "Houses have been blown down in this neighbourhood – others unroofed from the falling of stacks of Chimneys, which I witnessed – and the Tiles have quitted their resting places, in various directions. I do not know when I have heard the Wind more rumbustical than during the past three weeks." As he lay terrified in bed "the Windows and doors were rattling with all their might, to put me in a terrible fright for the safety of my own *batch of Chimnies*, which have stood many a blast …in days long past." While the weather was still unsettled, "wet one day, a gleam of Sunshine the next", he was hoping for a repeat Edinburgh visit in the spring. In 1836 he circulated a description of his autograph collection.

Robert Pearse Gillies, a minor Scottish writer who was in London in 1835 or 1836, describes calling on Mr Upcott in his "frugal retirement at Islington" to solicit a report for some literary work. Upcott himself opened the door "with a sheaf of papers in his hand", and when Gillies tentatively offered his card "he replied very courteously that my name alone was a sufficient introduction". Leading the way to his study he informed Gillies that he had that very moment opened a large box of Lord Buchan's papers which he had bought from the executors. Gillies said he had known Lord Buchan well, though he had not been in touch for at least 12 years, and was invited to look at the first document, "a sort of literary testament" about the disposal of the papers. By extraordinary coincidence, studying the document he read that he himself was the very person Buchan would wish to be his literary executor.

"Mr Upcott dropped the paper in his utter amazement. That the individual thus named … should suddenly appear in the house of a stranger at the very instant … was an accident so unexampled that it might well be classed with the supernatural."[16]

Much of Upcott's 'retirement' must have consisted in acquiring such files of family papers, going through them with a toothcomb, and endeavouring to reduce them to order among his other thousands of manuscripts.

William Upcott died in September 1845 from an illness incurred during a long railway journey (second class) – which he had actually made to investigate rail travel's uncomfortable conditions. He took to his bed, "listening to the rumble of Islington omnibuses which pass every three minutes" and, more pleasurably, St Mary's quarter-hour chimes, "my favourite church clock". A fortnight later he was dead.

The vast Upcott collection, emptied from his cottage and auctioned by Sotheby's at Evans's Rooms in Covent Garden, attracted great crowds. In the 11-day sale, books that he had picked up for shillings were sold for guineas. The sale realised over £4,000 – an irony for a man who had lived so modestly. An engraving of his portrait was circulated to his many friends. Upper Street and Islington were the poorer for his death and the disposal of his life's collection. Fortunately for posterity, much of it ended up at the British Museum.

GEORGE DANIEL

A younger contemporary of William Upcott was Lamb's friend the writer and book collector George Daniel, born in 1789, who lived at 18 Canonbury Square. Said to have had a career in business, he nevertheless passed much of his time in literary pursuits, composing satirical and even religious poetry, some of it published in 1814 in *The Modern Dunciad*. He wrote a couple of Drury Lane farces, and more weightily, edited two works on drama, John Cumberland's *British Theatre* (1823–31), and Davison's *Actable Drama*.

Much of Daniel's verse is doggerel, sometimes amusing. In one of his works, the verbose *Democritus in London* (1852), the foreword dated from his house in Canonbury, Daniel describes in loving detail the Old Queen's Head, demolished more than 20 years earlier. He mentions the tradition that here Sir Walter Raleigh was dowsed by his servant when smoking a pipe. Elsewhere in the book a footnote castigates the grandiose terms popular in "the present age of affectation", such as "purveyor" instead of tradesman, "mart" and "depot" for his shop and warehouse, and a chef becoming an "artiste", a publican a "licensed victualler", while society "progresses" and conspirators "agitate" – even the scruffy Battle Bridge area, "region of dogcarts, dusthills, and demireps!" has become "King's Cross".[17]

Daniel's main achievement was as a collector of published works, particularly of Elizabethan books, ballads, and works on the theatre, and original portraits or prints of stage celebrities. Much of his collection was unique, and throughout his life he ferreted out rare works, actually owning four Shakespeare First Folios and many of the Quartos. He collected 17th-century books, 'Jests', songs, missals and autograph letters, including those of Dr Johnson, David Garrick, Jonathan Swift, Alexander Pope, which after his death were sold as a lot for £62. Many of his treasures he picked up for mere shillings at bookstalls.[18]

William Hazlitt's grandson, William Carew Hazlitt, used to encounter Daniel sometimes at Sotheby's auction rooms, and particularly remembered him for the kid gloves he wore. Once when an 'ordinary lot' was knocked down to a Mr Daniel, who was sitting beside him, he asked if he was the famous collector. "No, sir", was the answer, "if I were to buy all that Mr Daniel does, I should have an Alexandrian library."

"The" Daniel was vain of his treasures, and always reckoned his possessions as better than others. Hazlitt meeting him once in Long Acre tells him he has secured a fine copy of the Water Poet, John Taylor. "O yes, sir, I saw it", says Daniel carelessly, "but not quite so fine as mine!"

Charles Lamb, when he visited Daniel, liked to look at his books – but was apparently not allowed to handle them. "I would not have allowed that", Daniel told Hazlitt, "Why, Mr Lamb would turn over the leaves of a volume with a wet finger – and I always kept a particular copy of old ballads for him."[19]

While Daniel was buying prices were low, whereas by the time of the sale after his death values had enormously increased, and books he had bought for 4d sold for £300. Sotheby's sale of his property in 1864 was catalogued as "the most valuable, interesting and highly important Library … together with his collection of original drawings and engraved portraits of distinguished Actors and Actresses, beautiful water-colour drawings of the first quality, Barrett, Cattermole, Cooper, Cox, Dewint, Harding, Prout, Pine, Stanfield, Stothard, Wilkie, and other eminent artists, miscellaneous objects of Art, Interest & Curiosity, Beautiful Pottery and Porcelain of Chelsea Manufacture, and other fine examples of art and vertu".

The sale took ten days, preceded by two viewing days. One day was devoted to 'Garrickiana' and contemporary authors like Gay and Goldsmith, another to Johnson and included *Letters of Junius*. The fourth day was exclusively on Islington, including Nichols's *Antiquities of Canonbury*, with prints, playbills, cuttings on the parish, and views of White Conduit House and Bagnigge Wells. (These in contrast with the four-figure takings for the others, went for a mere £77.) The biggest total was on a day which included the Shakespearean collection and Scottish works, some by Sir Walter Scott (nearly £6,000 the lot); another day had Upcott's Library Catalogue, two more were of prints and views, and finally came a day of 'objects', among them Garrick's cane and buckles, vases, tradesmen's tokens, snuffboxes, and water-colours.

Henry Huth, fellow-bibliophile and benefactor to the British Museum Library,[20] walked in just as the dealer, Joseph Lilley, was triumphantly holding up a famous collection of ballads from the Tollemaches of Helmingham Hall. None of the proceeds went to Daniel's own family. One of his children came in on the viewing day preceding the sale, as his father had never shown them his collection. Yet to others he tended to show off his triumphs, always claiming their superiority. He was, says Hazlitt, "a virtuoso rather than a connoisseur. He studied the commercial barometer, and knew the right things to buy."[21]

WILLIAM HONE

Whereas William Upcott and George Daniel salvaged invaluable records of the past, William Hone and George Cruikshank were among those who have our gratitude for their recording what was then present but would soon disappear or be destroyed – Hone in his writing and Cruikshank in illustrations.

London, and England, owe a great deal to William Hone, radical bookseller, editor and publisher, for describing that fast-vanishing world. Though constantly at work his life was mostly a struggle. Despite his weekly issues of *The Everyday Book* (1826–7) – which he dedicated to Charles Lamb – *The Table Book* (1827–8) and *The Year Book* (begun 1830), all of which sold in large numbers, the profit was so small compared with the outlay and his labours that he and his family were often very poor.

Born in Holborn in 1780, itself then not far from the country, Hone began his working life, like many boys at the time, at thirteen, as a lawyer's clerk. A voracious reader, he was largely self-educated. He married young, and soon went into a bookseller/publisher partnership in Fleet Street.

As an atheist and pro-reformist radical, during the French Revolution and the repression at home he got into trouble by publishing scurrilous pamphlets, anti-Government, anti-Regent, and in 1817 was put on trial on three counts of anti-ministry propaganda. Although he defended himself so ably that he was acquitted, the struggle left him exhausted.

He moved to Ludgate Hill, where he continued his public protests with satires, seditious pamphlets and caricatures, and was vilified from the pulpit and by the Government as a blasphemer. Nevertheless, his pamphlets sold by the thousand. He was for years a close friend of George Cruikshank, who produced many illustrations for his works, and though the two later quarrelled, before Hone's death in a cottage in Tottenham they were reconciled. Hone was also one of those who had the friendship and admiration of Charles Lamb, in whose house he could stay when Lamb was away, and was a friend of Francis Place the Utilitarian, reforming tailor.

Hone's *Everyday Book* was the first of his publications of an original kind, a miscellany of information and anecdote on curiosities, traditions, survivals, folklore, often recording what would otherwise have been forgotten, and many dealing with Islington. Friends and acquaintances fed him with jottings and stories. Cruikshank was, at the start, his illustrator, and from January 1825 Hone himself tirelessly produced weekly instalments at 3d, eventually collecting them to be published in book form. He was particularly interested in rural events, and in the country near London (all he ever had time to visit), and culled much material from his library of ancient books. But with the cost of production, fees and travel expenses, his labours did not bring him money; instead others profited from them and in one case stole from him. By degrees he had to sell most of his treasured library.

In one of several periods of melancholy and depression Hone removed himself from his family to work in a room at the back of Pentonville, where he could see the fields round Islington, but bad weather made him return to the City, where he found only debts and writs. A trusted assistant's fraud landed him in the King's Bench Prison, where he lived 'within the Rules' in a nearby house, and his family had to take refuge with friends. Here he produced *The Table Book*, but finally had to sell the rights in his works, and retreated with his family to the former house of Samuel Rogers's friend Dr Richard Price, the reforming minister, near Newington Green. By late 1829 they had to return to London, where friends set them up in a humble coffee-house/

hotel in Gracechurch Street, which he ran with his family until it wore them out. At the same time he was working on *The Year Book*, a monthly, now not as proprietor but as a paid writer, while the publisher grew rich on this and on Hone's former works.

Although Hone lived in the Islington area for only brief spells, he knew it well from visits and study. To him we owe accounts of Sadler's Wells, Canonbury, Raleigh's house (by then the Pied Bull), the New River, as they were in the 1820s – while bemoaning the changes already taking place – and what he had learned of their past.

In 1834 the one-time atheist became converted to the Congregational church, a comfort to him though he remained antipathetic as ever to the Established Church. With declining health he and his family retired with his remaining books to a small house and garden in Tottenham, where he spent his last years, reconciled with Cruikshank before his death and visited by the rising young Charles Dickens. It was Dickens who in an appeal for subscriptions for Hone's family, summed up this wayward, principled, ever-struggling fighter for justice and for the aspects of England that he loved, in one simple, understated sentence: "He was not a common man."[22]

CRUIKSHANK

Born in 1792, the artist and cartoonist George Cruikshank lived through more than three-quarters of the 19th century. His Scottish grandfather had been 'out' as a Jacobite in the Forty-Five rising, and his father Isaac, born in Edinburgh, an established artist and political caricaturist, moved to London in the 1780s and married a Perthshire lady of rather higher social class than his own, who had been educated by the Countess of Orkney. George, their second son, was born in London and though undervalued in his lifetime, was to make the 1820s and later decades the great age of British book illustration. At first he had wanted to be an actor rather than an artist, and spent some time on the stage, but already from 1810 he had been producing satirical political sketches as well as children's book illustrations, and met William Hone, whose works he also illustrated.

Like his father and his fellow-caricaturist James Gillray, Cruikshank was inclined to the bottle and led a somewhat raffish life. Between 1824 and 1849 he lived in three different houses in what is now Amwell Street, starting in the then Myddelton Terrace, now part of Claremont Square. Here he produced all the work on his pictures except for the 'biting in' of the etchings, for which he kept an assistant. To help him he promoted his kitchen boy, appropriately named Joseph Sleap, for he had a habit of dozing off, as Dickens found when he visited – and used him as a model for the Fat Boy in *Pickwick Papers*.

Among Cruikshank's prolific output were illustrations for Grimm's folk-tales and novels of Harrison Ainsworth including *The Tower of London* and *Jack Sheppard*, and *Ainsworth's Magazine* and *Bentley's Miscellany*. Later he produced *The Bottle* (1847) and *The Drunkard's Children* (1848) as part of the campaign to promote teetotalism. He himself had to give up drink in order to weather the financial storm when his Finsbury bank failed during the 1846 railway crash. He had great problems pulling through, while soon after, in May 1849, his wife died of phthisis when only 42.

Cruikshank illustrated for both Charles Dickens and William Thackeray. Among his most famous cartoons is *London Going Out of Town* (1829), depicting the encroachment on the countryside as seen from his own back window.

Although he became famous for his works – his *Comic Almanack* folded in 1853 after years of popularity – he fell out of fashion in later years and his style and subjects were considered dated. He retained his skill and was hardworking to the end, but became increasingly poor, his income largely maintained through the efforts of friends.

After his death in 1878 the journalist George Sala wrote in the *Gentleman's Magazine* of calling on him as a young man in Clerkenwell in 1843, in fear and trembling with some of his own sketches, but found himself received very kindly by Cruikshank, "in a shawl-patterned dressing-gown", with his little spaniel who had appeared in Hone's *Table Book* "basking on the hearth-rug". Cruikshank spent two hours with the young aspirant, gave him useful advice and encouragement, and when Sala left trembling this time with gratitude and joy, suddenly called him back on the doorstep for a parting maxim, "It's a very precarious profession" – with the final warning that he must work harder than a coal-heaver.[23]

Islington maintained its high quota of printer/booksellers and journalists into the 19th century and Victorian times, no doubt enhanced by Clerkenwell's historic association with the printing industry – and Grub Street was not far away. In the Victorian age Sala, the brothers Frederick and James Greenwood, William Harvey ('Aleph') and George Sims are only the best known of those who wrote copiously about the area, which provided them with good and sensational copy.

A CURIOUS BAPTISM

Sensational indeed was a curious adult baptism which took place in 1821 at St Mary's Church. It was of a portly lady named Olive or Olivia Serres, born in 1772 and thus a few months short of 50, who claimed to be a daughter of the late Henry, Duke of Cumberland by his first marriage. She had formerly been reputedly the daughter of a Warwick house-painter named Robert Wilmot, and was early married off to the royal marine painter Thomas Serres, but they later separated. Only in about 1817 did she discover who was her real father and took up her case with the Prince Regent and the Government. She produced (Islington's historian Lewis says) "several absurd and contradictory documents", in particular a supposed will of the King in which she was left £150,000.

Her latter-day baptism was recorded facetiously by a newspaper, *The Traveller*, on 12 September 1821. On the previous Thursday, 6 September, at about 11 am. what appeared to be a nobleman's carriage drew up at the curate's house (presumably the Rev. Dr George Gaskin's) and then drove on to the churchyard, causing some attention when the occupants got out. "A portly well-dressed dame, apparently about fifty, [was] handed from the coach by a dashing young fellow of not more than half her age, and to whom it was concluded the lady was now about to bestow her fair hand at the altar."

Bystanders were wrong, for after some time – the party having not thought to send for the parish clerk – it proved to be for a baptism. Inquisitive locals next day found in the parish register the record: "Olive, only daughter of the late Henry Frederick, duke of Cumberland, by his first duchess, baptised Sept. 6, 1821; born April 3, 1772."[24]

The secret marriage of King George III's brother Henry, Duke of Cumberland, had been only one of the numerous scandals associated with the Royal Family, when in 1770 there was a rumour of his marrying Olive Wilmot, said to be the daughter of a clergyman. If this marriage was legal, it was not accepted, and within a year the Duke again married, Mrs Horton, illegally or bigamously, though the birth of Olive (Serres) in 1772 suggests he must still have been cohabiting with Olive Wilmot.

Her claim of legitimacy was not recognised, however, and although there were a number of payments and pensions allowed by the Crown for unofficial offspring of its scions, rendering the claimant respectable by a church baptism did not avail her. Why Islington church was chosen for the ceremony is not known, and the lady died poor and unrecognised within the Rules of the King's Bench on 21 November 1834.

The assiduous diarist Thomas Creevey records how at a 'City Feast' in November 1820 he was fascinated at the sight of (as he calls her) "the Princess Olivia of Cumberland", whose royal birth he did not doubt for a moment. "She is the very image of our Royal family. Her person is upon the model of the princess Elizabeth [George III's third daughter, who married the Landgrave of Hesse-Homburg], only three times her size." He was especially transfixed by her "brilliant rose-coloured satin gown" and "fancy shawls" draping her shoulders *à la* Lady Hamilton, and she was dripping with diamonds and "feathers that would have done credit to a hearse". The procession to the hall for dinner was delayed for ten minutes when the 'Princess Olivia' insisted, as a member of the Royal Family, on sitting at the Lord Mayor's right hand, but the Mayor strongly resisted, and the lady was finally banished to another table.

Her petition to the House of Commons was

supported by many who were taken in by the extraordinary royal resemblance, but unfortunately she could not produce any credible evidence for her claim.[25]

The matter had repercussions, as in 1866, long after the supposed daughter's death, a Mrs Ryves was claiming to be the Duke's grand-daughter and petitioned for recognition (unsuccessfully) to the Court of Probate and Divorce.[26]

1   Charles Lamb to Bernard Barton, *The Letters of Charles Lamb*, ed. E V Lucas, London, 1935, Vol. 2, p 394. *The Life and Correspondence of the Late Robert Southey*, ed. by his son, the Rev. Charles Cuthbert Southey, London, 1849-50, Vol. V, p. 153.

2   Charles Lamb 'Amicus Redivivus', in *Last Essays of Elia*, London, 1833; Barry Cornwall, *Literary Recollections*, London, 1936, pp. 132-3.

3   *The Correspondence of Henry Crabb Robinson with the Wordsworth Circle (1808–1866)*, ed. Edith J Morley, Oxford, 1927.

4   George Daniel, *Love's Labour's Not Lost*, London, 1863, pp. 1-31.

5   *Carlyle Correspondence*, Carlyle to Jane, 29 August 1831, Vol. V, p. 375; *Two Notebooks of Thomas Carlyle*, ed. Charles Eliot Norton, New York, Grolier Club, 1898, (2 November 1831), pp. 217-8.

6   *Carlyle Correspondence*, Carlyle to Thomas Murray, 24 August 1824, Vol. III, p. 132.

7   *Carlyle Correspondence*, Carlyle to his brother John, 13 November 1831, Vol. VI, pp. 50-51.

8   George Daniel, *Loc. cit.*

9   The Islington historian Samuel Lewis identifies John Nichols as the 'Old Inhabitant', donor in 1806 of £10 to the parochial schools where his father Edward was educated. (Lewis, *Islington*, p. 383 & n.)

10   Lewis, *Islington*, p. 177n.

11   A daughter, Mary, born 1784, married John Morgan and lived in Highbury Place, her husband dying in 1832. A daughter by his first wife married the Rev. John Pridden, FSA, Rector of St George's, Botolph Lane. (Lewis, *Islington*, pp. 180, 239)

12   *Ibid.*, pp. 176-80.

13   Because of its situation, when the houses were later numbered Woodfall's Cottage became no. 32A, and does not even appear on Baker's map of 1805. The cottage, with nos 31-33, was unfortunately demolished in the early 1950s and replaced unworthily in 1959 by Hermitage House

14   Lewis, *Islington*, p. 351; *DNB*, Woodfall.

15   Joseph Mayer, *Memoirs of Thomas Dodd*.

16   Robert Pearse Gillies, *Memoirs of a Literary Veteran*, London, 1851, Vol. III, p. 240.

17   George Daniel, *Democritus in London*, London, 1852, p. 136.

18   In 1876 the antiquarian Joseph Mayer (1803–86), writing in *Temple Bar*, described seeing in a Cheshire country house, a bound volume of some 1,000 "letters, receipts, agreements, hoary play bills, and ancient critiques" once at the Upper Street cottage, and described as the cream of Upcott's collection. Mayer, himself a collector of Greek coins and Egyptian antiquities, acquired at least part of the collections of Upcott and Thomas Dodd. (*DNB*).

19   William Carew Hazlitt, *The Hazlitts*, London, 1912, pp. 323-30.

20   Henry Huth's father, Frederick Huth, started life as a clerk in a merchant's firm in Hamburg, came to England in 1812 and set up a successful business in the City as F. Huth & Co. At one time he lived in Finsbury where two sons were born and later moved to Clapton. Henry Huth lived from 1851-78. (*DNB*).

21   W C Hazlitt, *The Hazlitts*, pp. 378-9.

22   John Wardroper, *The World of William Hone*, London, Shelfmark Books, 1997, pp. 1-18.

23   George August Sala, in *The Gentleman's Magazine*, February 1878.

24   *The Traveller*, 12 September 1821; Lewis, *Islington*, p. 252.

25   Maurice Marple, *Wicked Uncles in Love*, London, 1972, pp.xiii-xiv.

26   *Creevey*, ed. John Gore, London, 1948, p. 202 & n.; See also *Annual Register*, Vols xiii, p. 331 and xliii, p. 150.

CHAPTER 20

A Revolution in Transport

NEW ROUTES

In an expanding city roads, waterways and what travels over them become of vital importance. Islington's highways, inadequate in coverage, ill-constructed and ill-maintained, now became paramount as the increasing population needed forms of transport.

The New River, created for drinking water, of course carried no traffic, but canals did, and London now belatedly received its own in the Regent's Canal. But before that the main-road highway from the North, which entered London at Highgate, achieved a daring improvement that triumphantly survived a serious initial setback. This was begun as a tunnel through the notoriously steep bank at the top of Highgate Hill, authorised by Act of Parliament in 1809 and started by Robert Vazie. It would have been England's first main-road underpass, but on 14 April 1812 between 4 and 5 am, a disaster occurred when the whole thing – 130 feet so far – collapsed. Not enough bricks, and poor-quality cement.

Disastrous though this was, it created the basis of a ready-made cutting through the earth, which John Nash was called on to turn into an Archway carrying Hornsey Lane – now severed by the collapse of the tunnel. The bridge he designed to carry the Lane was built in the style of an aqueduct, with three smaller arches above the main road-arch. This was completed in 1813 and what was later called the Archway Road provided an easier alternative to Highgate Hill.[1]

At much the same time Nash was engaged in building a canal through Islington. London was late in the great canal race, the boom hav-

67. Highgate Archway, designed by John Nash, pictured in 1814.

ing been decades before. Its nearest canal was the Grand Union built in 1793, connecting the East Midlands via the Oxford Canal with the Thames at Brentford. In 1801 an extension of the Grand Union was begun to the small village of Paddington. As the new East India and St Katharine's Docks needed better communication with west London, after a false start a further extension was started, north of the New Road and clear of London's ducal properties. After a great deal of landlord and

68. The Regent's Canal, entrance to Islington Tunnel.

vested-interest opposition, an 8½-mile route was agreed, an amended Act passed in July 1812 – just after the Highgate tunnel collapse – and Nash, who knew nothing about canal building (nor did his assistant James Morgan), undertook this controversial operation. It needed a long experiment.

Their chief problem was creating 12 locks, three of which occurred between Camden and City Road Basin, to deal with the fall in land level between Camden Town and Limehouse. They dealt with this by making double locks, partly to conserve the scanty water supply, partly to lighten the time of passage. The lie of the land also necessitated two tunnels, a short one through Maida Hill by the new Regent's Park (another of Nash's creations), and a long one of 986 yards under the top of Islington's hill. The whole canal also required 40 bridges and seven basins. It was completed in eight years.

There were many hold-ups, financial and legal rather than engineering: Thomas Homer, who had thought of the idea in the first place, made off with the subscribers' funds in 1815;

however, he was arrested and transported. William Agar, an intransigent lawyer and land-owner with a mansion off St Pancras Way, kept up continual litigation, and only in 1816 was the dispute with the Regent's Canal Company resolved, to heavy criticism of the Company in Parliament and elsewhere. For labour, eventually engagement of 20,000 unemployed paupers as 'navigators' was authorised and a Government loan obtained. The complicated stretch from Hampstead Lock, and the long Islington tunnel, took from 1813 to 1816 to complete. The canal entered Islington under a bridge at Maiden Lane (York Way). Here a basin known as Battlebridge or Horsfall Basin was created. The canal next passed under what would become the line of the Caledonian Road and then, in order to pass through the hilltop, the famous Islington tunnel was created to Morgan's design. It was too narrow to allow for a tow-path, so that when a barge entered it, the horse would be uncoupled and led over-ground across the High Street to rejoin the barge where the tunnel emerged, after passing under the New River, at Colebrooke Row. The boatmen, lying across the barge roof, had to 'leg' it through, pushing their feet against the tunnel walls.

The last bridge, Frog Lane lock and City Road Basin were completed in 1819–20, and on 1 August 1820 the canal opened triumphantly to the sound of bands playing national airs in the tunnel. Nash, Morgan and celebrities travelled in the City State Barge, and a salute was fired at the City Road Basin.

The finished canal linked the Thames with the Midlands trade, and City Road Basin superseded Paddington Basin for distribution of goods in London.[2] It was more important as a departure point for local deliveries. This especially included building materials for the housing boom, and, by 1835, London's coal. Horsfall Basin, completed in 1825 and privately owned, was conveniently near warehouses and depots.

But in fact the canal company had – almost literally – missed the boat. The great age for canals ended as the railway age took over, and the Regent's Canal came in too late to succeed. When the London & Birmingham Railway was opened in 1837, Midlands traffic moved to rail, though the canal continued to carry timber, and coal for the gas works. In other respects its trade dwindled, and in mid-century there was actually a threat to convert the canal into a railway.

NEW ROADS

At much the same time important new roads were being built as through-ways, to facilitate both the crossing of London and its exits. The chief roads had always been radial from the centre. Congestion in the centre was due partly to its twisting streets, partly the continual passage of flocks and herds to and from Smithfield, so that London was almost nowhere free of them.

Among the first of the new highways to be built was the New North Road in 1812, whose function was shown by its name: to continue the road from the North, from near Highbury Corner to Shoreditch. A private Act was obtained by a company of shareholders (52 Geo.III) "for making a public Carriage-road from the present Turnpike-road near the south

end of Highbury-place, Islington, to Haberdashers'-walk, in the parish of St Leonard, Shoreditch".

Between north Islington and east London this saved $\frac{3}{4}$ mile, yet for some 30 years it was little used. But it had the usual effect of a new road of giving a spur to building in new streets constructed towards Hoxton. At Canonbury the New River was bridged at a point known as the Horseshoe – and here from about 1823 more houses were built.

Other important roads were made farther north. Junction Road, laid out in 1811, also described its function: a link between the upper part of Kentish Town and the north end of the Holloway Road. It remained free of houses until the 1850s. Camden Road, connecting Holloway with the new suburb of Camden Town, was authorised in 1825, laid out in 1826 and eventually in 1831–3 linked with the still later Seven Sisters Road to end at Tottenham. The latter road was named after seven ancient elms near the Tottenham boundary at Page Green, said by some to have been planted by seven sisters about to be separated, by others to be the site of the burning of martyrs. By 1840 the trees were claimed to be 500 years old, though when felled in 1852 their estimated age was 300. Seven more elms were then planted to replace them, which by the end of the 19th century had also disappeared.[3]

Caledonian Road was begun in 1826 on the west of the parish, to connect Battle Bridge and Holloway, skirting Pentonville hill and the Angel. Again a company was formed, raising £60,000 capital in £50 shares. Running east of Maiden Lane (York Way), it lay within the parish boundary, traversing the Thornhill estate. As on digging out the ground a chalk substratum was found suitable as a foundation, it was first known as the Chalk Road, but when the route was still being surveyed in 1823 an orphan asylum was built in the fields for children of expatriate Scots, hence named the Caledonian Asylum. This eventually gave its name to the new highway. As on other highways, the terraces by degrees built along it were given individual names, Sutherland, Caledonian, Lansdown and so on, until subsumed in the overall name in the 1850s.

The chief feature of these new highways was

69. 'Near the Caledonian Asylum, Caledonian Road', 1838.

that, not being 'organic', like old lanes which wound between fields and boundaries, they ran straight from source to goal, cutting through the land after negotiation with the owners. They also linked parts of London long isolated from each other for lack of direct communication. Finally, cutting through undeveloped land, they facilitated building so that eventually they became ribbons of development across London, and backbones to new subsidiary streets.

GETTING ABOUT

'Transport' at that time was mostly on foot – the romanticism of coach travel is exaggerated. Only the comfortably off owned even a horse. Professional men and well-to-do merchants and tradesmen set up a carriage (an expensive indulgence); the less well off, who in any case had no space to house a carriage, usually hired a horse when required from a livery stable, such as owned by John I'Ons in Islington off Upper Street, next to Canonbury Lane, or another stable in Essex Road. The great mass of people walked every day, miles if necessary, though on the whole one worked near where one lived.

For the poor, travel between towns was by carrier, unless they could afford the stage coach. Charles Dickens, in *Sketches by Boz*, paints a very unglamorous picture (1835), such as might describe the Angel, starting with the booking-office: "a mouldy-looking room" peopled by shabby, despondent characters, the coaches subject to the tyranny of fellow-passengers, not to mention "waiters, landlords, coachmen, guards, boots, chambermaids", the stout coachman himself bursting out of his "rough blue greatcoat"; while early rising for a 6 am. coach, and the bustling flurry of departure, were a mere prelude to the discomfort of the journey itself, cramped, rocking and often chilly.

There was also a strict hierarchy of the road. Flora Tristan describes in her *London Journal* in 1840 how carriages with a coat of arms took precedence, followed in order of status by "middle-class carriages with 4 horses", then those with only two, while these prevailed over "cabriolets and tilburys, hired landaus over coaches, coaches over omnibuses, omnibuses over cabs, and so on ... down to the trap, and even it has the right of way over the cart".[4]

The Angel being on the highway to the

north, Islington's High Street and Upper Street might well see top-class carriages as well as the regular stream of stage-coaches. But the lowlier types would be more usual. The only public transport in town was the short-distance coach. These lumbering vehicles, like ordinary stage-coaches covered the London area, carrying some half-dozen inside and two or three on top, but could be boarded only at a booking-office (most likely a pub). Within London they stopped only at the termini, though outside 'the stones' or paved streets area they could be hailed anywhere. By 1825 there were plenty of these coaches, more than 400 plying for instance between the City and Paddington, Clapton or Hackney, with a daily service to distant suburbs.

These short-stagers had 12 major routes from the City. One ran 11 coaches to Islington, some made more journeys; but fares, based on the cost of fodder, were high. The service was heavily regulated because hackney carriages had the monopoly.

Hackney carriages dated from the 17th century, supposedly named from an office which issued licences there to coaches for hire. More probably, the name's origin is from the French 'hacke-nee', a nag. They held a monopoly until 1832 and became a byword for abuses. By the 19th century there were some 1100 of them.

The earliest cabs for hire were old hackney coaches, cast off by their owners when shabby, just as their horses were old hacks no longer good for anything else, and the drivers were drunken and scruffy. The horses, treated with unspeakable brutality, were kept going by all kinds of cruelties until they became no good even for that trade, and were finally sent to the knacker's yard.[5]

In 1829 came an important innovation, the horse omnibus. Starting in a small way, within a few years it revolutionised transport. This too was an idea borrowed from Paris, where a service had begun in 1819, said to be run by a Monsieur Omnès, who made a Latin pun on his name with the slogan "Omnes Omnibus", "all for everyone". On 4 July 1829 George Shillibeer (1797–1866), who had encountered these vehicles in Paris, was so far-seeing as to launch a similar service in London. Shillibeer's omnibuses, following the New Road, ran from Paddington to the Angel

and thence down the City Road to the Bank, and thus avoided 'the stones'. The full fare was a shilling, from Islington it was 6d either way. Two vehicles provided five services a day, at 9 o'clock, 12, 3, 6 and 8 from Paddington Green, returning at 10 o'clock, 1, 4, 7 and 9 p m The carriage held 20 inside passengers in two rows lengthwise, and ran, rather eccentrically, with three horses abreast.

George Shillibeer, who had urged setting up such a service for at least a year, was at pains to emphasise its quality as well as value, such as that the "three beautiful bays abreast" were "after the French fashion". He also at first dressed his two young conductors, sons of a naval officer, as midshipmen. They were shortly replaced by men in "velvet livery", and (unlike the traditional rude coachmen) were advertised for their courtesy.

The Shillibeer buses were also the first to run a regular service, with vehicles keeping to a timetable, moving on whether full or not. They were also slightly cheaper and held a few more passengers than the crammed short-stage coaches. However, this new service catered only for the more well-to-do, and Shillibeer, though by next year running six buses, had no capital, and had to reduce his three horses to two. Rivals soon entered the field in other districts, like Hammersmith, and by 1831 Shillibeer's route was served by 90 vehicles, only a dozen of them his. This rivalry caused unseemly struggles. "A more desperate and reckless set of fellows than those connected with the London omnibuses, never existed in a civilised country," was the verdict of the journalist James Grant in 1842.

There were hazards: conductors sometimes actually manhandled passengers to force them to board their bus, and rival drivers would race each other, keeping dangerously close. Yet, according to Grant, there were not many accidents, despite the drivers' fondness for a gallop. [6]

The usual length of an omnibus was 12 feet, its width four feet. Charging the same fare for all journeys made long trips good value. There were no tickets until in 1857 ten-per-cent discount vouchers were issued for £5-worth of tickets, which on the first day sold 10,000.

In 1832 short-stage carriages within London were also allowed to stop anywhere for passengers, and in competition Shillibeer sent some buses via Oxford Street, but in 1834 he gave up, and ran services elsewhere. (His later career was sadly unsuccessful, going bankrupt, fleeing to France to dodge his debts, and later imprisoned in the Fleet. He ended as a funeral director, and died in 1866.)

Steam was now all the rage, and Islington figured in road experiments with the new power. Walter Hancock (1799–1852) patented several steam vehicles, mostly trying them out along the New Road. They had names such as Era, Erin, Enterprise, Autopsy (meaning 'see for yourself'), and Automaton. The Autopsy, propelled by an endless chain from the engine shaft which turned the rear axle, was tried out for some weeks by Hancock on the City / Pentonville route, then with another vehicle, the 'Infant', from the City to Paddington. By the end of 1833 London had more than a dozen steam vehicles. The faster Era and the Autopsy, easily steered and running on coke and water, competed with horse buses on the same route, but often broke down. Hancock

also tried the Autopsy along the Liverpool Road, and by 1836 his fleet had become a regular service on the Paddington-Islington route. He complained that horse-bus drivers tried to scare his drivers off the road by scattering stones, but it seems more likely that the large wheels of steam vehicles themselves broke up the surface. In 1836 the Automaton, steered by a wheel, ran from the City Road to Epping, averaging up to $11\frac{1}{2}$ miles per hour, with seats facing the driver.

Shortage of capital and his company's apparent inefficiency hampered Hancock in developing the clumsy contraption, actually the first powered vehicle designed specifically as public transport. The machinery was at the back, the driver sitting on a front platform, from which passengers entered. It did not appeal. He went on experimenting until 1840, competing with other firms, but that year the Turnpike Act imposed such heavy tolls that, coupled with the preferred service of horse buses, steam road vehicles ended their short career. [7]

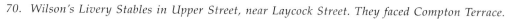

70. Wilson's Livery Stables in Upper Street, near Laycock Street. They faced Compton Terrace.

Bus Economics

After the removal of certain restrictions in 1832 other firms rivalled Shillibeer. E & J Wilson ran a service called 'Favorite' – etymology French, not American – from north London including Holloway, to the City and Central London and was soon the largest company. In 1856 the newly formed *Companie Générale des Omnibus de Londres* took over several companies, including Wilson's 48 buses operating from the Highbury area and soon, renaming themselves the London General Omnibus Company (LGOC), standardised their enlarged fleet. Among their new stables was Highbury Yard, the largest in London, opposite Union Chapel on the site of Laycock's Farm, a 20-acre space entered from Upper Street and extending to Liverpool Road. Its stables each held 40 horses – ten for each omnibus, and in a large shed the vehicles were parked and cleaned overnight. [8]

A stranger arriving in London found it necessary to learn the distinctive colours of the omnibus services, such as the Favorite, which was green. Styles of vehicles evolved. In the 1840s the Favorite was installed with a second row of four seats behind the driver, and another firm, Adams & Co., had a 'clerestory roof' with two back-to-back rows the length of the bus. Use of the roofs – after all, in stage coaches passengers had always sat 'outside' – soon became established, but for many years no lady could possibly ascend the stairs or sit above exposing her legs (though 'modesty boards' were installed).

If they were wise, passengers boarded a crowded bus, for if empty, its driver might dawdle to pick up more, and complaints (even parliamentary action) seemed to lead only to more abusive language. By 1842, however, there was an attempt by a private partnership to take over certain vehicles, employ men for their civility, and distinguish themselves by the colour of livery and hats.

By then London had about 600 hackney coaches, charging a minimum of a shilling a mile, subsequently charged by the half-mile, and licensed to carry four, though some former noblemen's carriages could take up to six. The driver, often happy to squeeze in more, did not hesitate to overcharge obvious strangers. The capital now also had between 600 and 700 omnibuses, each bus except in bad weather averaging 120 passengers daily, when the takings might be £3. It was not very profitable, as a vehicle cost up to £150, not counting the heavy expense of the horses, wages, duty, and wear and tear.

By the late 1850s, with 1,300 conductors, 5,870 horses, often greys, were calculated to be drawing buses. Horses were indeed the highest cost of the service, averaging nearly half of the outlay, £2 19 6½ d a day. Wages were another 9s 9d, and the rest went on maintenance, licence, tolls and administration. The profit was reckoned at 6s 1d. Maintenance was of great importance, horses costing so much to keep, and fodder expensive in a wet summer. They might cover up to 15 miles a day in three hours' work-time, and setting down in mews stables along the route saved extra journeys when off duty. Conductors and drivers, on the other hand, were on duty all the time, sometimes 16 hours a day.

1   Simon Morris & Towyn Mason, *Gateway to the City*, Hornsey Historical Society, 2000; See also Joan Schwitzer, 'Highgate Tunnel: or, The Secret Arch, 1812', in *Hornsey Historical Society Bulletin*, No. 32, 1991.

2   *VCH*, p. 6.

3   In 1955 seven Lombardy poplars were planted by yet another sisterhood.

4   Flora Tristan, *Journal*, p. 151.

5   See, e.g. G A Sala, *Gaslight and Daylight*, London, 1859, p. 57. In 1831 the Hackney Carriage Act regulated conditions for carriages for hire in London up to a radius of five miles from the GPO. As the Act ended the monopoly, there were soon several rivals. The Act's many loopholes led to an amending Act in 1853.

6   *VCH*, p. 5; John R Day, *The Story of the London Bus*, London Transport, 1973; James Grant, *Lights and Shadows of London Life*, London, 1842, Vol. I, pp. 243ff.

7   G A Sekon, *Locomotion in Victorian London*, London, 1938; Day, *The London Bus*; T C Butcher & Michael Robbins, *A History of London Transport*, London, 1963, Vol. I.

8   Day, *The London Bus*; J E Ritchie, *Here and There in London*, London, 1859, p. 190. Omnibuses were also built in the yard.

CHAPTER 21

Water Supply and Public Health

HOLLOWAY'S WATER COMPANY

Towns cannot live without a water supply, even if only wells and springs; nor can houses exist without some form of sanitation, even if only privies and cesspools. Although by the early 19th century the New River Company was only one of nine water companies supplying London, Islington was better provided with water than many districts. Between 1805 and 1811 the existing Southwark, Lambeth and Chelsea water companies were joined by five others: Vauxhall, West Middlesex, East London, Kent and Grand Junction. Few of them supplied pure water.

The author of *The Picture of London* in 1802 praised the "most wonderful" system which supplied London houses with lead pipes to "almost every room" (some exaggeration here) "with unfailing precision and regularity" via mains under the chief streets, from which half-inch pipes served the houses. The advantage of a central supply at high level, such as Islington had, was that second-floor rooms or even higher could benefit, and the New River Head pumps raised the supply higher still.

Unlike New River water brought direct from Hertfordshire, water supplied by other companies came straight from the Thames, three at Hampton, and two more at Molesey. However, all underground sewers discharged into the Thames, and pollution was increased with the pressure of population, not to mention the effluent from rivers like the Fleet and Westbourne. "The common water is abominable", wrote Robert Southey, also in 1802, in the guise of a visiting Spaniard "Don Manuel Alvarez Espriella". "It is either from a vapid

canal in which all the rabble of the outskirts wash themselves in summer, or from the Thames, which receives all the filth of the city."[1]

The *Picture of London* author in a rider urged the New River Company to exact "severe penalties" on "the many thoughtless and wanton persons" who bathe and throw filth into the river, at Islington and other places. It was to be many years before this danger was generally appreciated. Between 1831 and 1866 there were four serious outbreaks of cholera, and not until the second (1848) were significant lessons learnt.

In the late 18th century the Round Pond, the New River's central reservoir, had been supplemented by two others, the High Pond (round which Claremont Square was built 1821-7), supplying Pentonville and later the New River estate; and another in today's Dartmouth Park Hill towards Highgate, built on the same plan. The Upper Holloway area, then sparsely populated, had no supply, as the Company thought it a poor investment.

In 1809, therefore, an enterprising local land-owner named George Pocock began to raise water for Holloway from artesian wells. He had in 1800 acquired from Lord Northampton 40 acres of land west of Holloway Road, which became known as Pocock's Fields. (Pocock was, until recently, commemorated in a pub name opposite Caledonian Road underground station.) Here from about 1806 he built small streets such as Cornwall Place and George's Place (now George's Road). In 1809, at the south end of Cornwall Place he sank a 172-foot well and built a steam engine at the top, with machinery to supply water to the whole neighbourhood. Under a private Act he formed a joint stock company, the Upper Holloway and Islington Waterworks and raised 200 £50 shares, 60 of them for himself "for supplying with water Upper and Lower Holloway, Highbury, Canonbury, Upper Islington, and their respective vicinities", with power to raise a further £10,000.

By 1810 Pocock had sunk a second artesian well, costing £2,000, said to yield pure, sparkling water straight from the chalk – a great boon – and moreover, supplied by a local entrepreneur. But as soon as the New River Company got to hear of it they hastened to lay their own water-pipes to Holloway, and with competition from so powerful a rival Pocock's shares lost their value, and his company was ruined.[2]

As a result of this dog-in-the-manger, far from altruistic action the New River Company now supplied all Islington with water.

SANITATION

A supply for drinking and washing was one thing; waste disposal quite another. London's local rivers and streams like the Fleet or the small Hackney Brook, which for centuries carried off sewage and surface water, no longer sufficed, nor did the universal cesspools adequately contain household waste. 'Filth', as it was termed, collected in rooms and cellars and in the yards of humble dwellings and hovels, creating "stench, effluvia and poisonous gases", and whatever drains there were became totally inadequate. No water closets were installed in houses before 1811. By the late 1840s thousands of houses still had neither water nor waste pipes, indeed no drainage at all. In 1850 it was estimated that some 80,000 London houses, a quarter of the whole, had no piped water, and even if they did, much came straight from the polluted Thames. London's death rate rose higher than for the whole of Britain. In the capital's expansion after its long stagnation during the French wars, Islington's inhabitants had risen in round figures from some 10,000 in 1801 to 22,000 by 1821, and by 1831 to 37,000.

To complicate matters London was not an entity but a series of unrelated parishes, and the City remained immune from legislation.

Funded public services were not just non-existent but anathema: *laissez-faire* was all. Responsibility rested on the individual, and if the individual was a landowner, MP, JP or other magistrate his general object was to maintain the status quo. As for public health, whereas the 17th century had been one of plague and the 18th of typhoid, the 19th showed every sign of becoming the century of cholera.

CHOLERA

A cholera outbreak began in 1831 in the eastern river areas. Though Medical Superintendents were appointed to set up temporary hospitals, action was permissive, and remained so for decades, and next year when the epidemic ended these hospitals closed. Even records were sporadic, and the quoted numbers of deaths were only estimates. In any case, until Pasteur's discovery in the 1870s of bacteria as the spreaders of disease, infection was believed to be caused by 'foul air' or 'effluvia'.

Until 1847 London's sewers were under the direction of eight Commissioners, for the City, Westminster, Holborn, Finsbury and so on, but as they were independent of each other, in laying drains they had no regard to neighbouring districts: at every parish boundary shapes and sizes of drains changed, from large to small, from straight or circular to egg-shaped, and being of different dimensions, leaks were common. In some cases, notably round the River Fleet, the river itself served as sewer, fed not only by local springs – Sadler's and Bagnigge Wells, Chad's Well and the Clerks' Well – but by any other source of water whatever. Even the piped water supply was not constant, but limited to a few hours a day and none at weekends, while many households were served only from standpipes in the street.

Urgent though this situation was, reformation was tardy, partial and often ignored. The reforming Local Government Act of 1835 did not apply to London. In 1838 in 20 metropolitan parishes or unions 77,000 paupers were recorded, of whom 14,000, nearly one-fifth, caught a current fever and nearly 1300 died. In 1840 a Select Committee, set up to enquire into the health of towns, reported many correctable defects, but no action followed.

One witness to that Committee, Dr Francis Mosely, quoted Islington as "so far out [of London] that there are generally very great sources of sickness from similar causes, a number of courts running out of High Street [the notorious Angel rookery] in perhaps as unwholesome a state as any in the central part of London". The Chairman agreed that "there is a great neglect of sewerage, and draining, and cleaning, there", believed to be the source of fever. However, from its relatively high position there was no lack of air, and with the parish surroundings still open ground Islington was actually no unhealthier than many other districts. In 1849 it did not rank badly in the general analysis of sickness and death.

In the years 1838–42 cholera deaths per 10,000 were in Islington 200, in Clerkenwell 242 and and in St Luke's 276 (Mayfair 179, London 252), but population density in these areas showed considerable differences: Islington still only 28 per acre, Clerkenwell 202, St Luke's 242 (Mayfair 57 and London 29). Of cholera deaths per 10,000 in the 1847–8 epidemic Islington had 22, Clerkenwell 19, St Luke's 34 while Mayfair had only eight; but London's average overall was 62.[3]

In nearly two decades since the 1831 epidemic little had changed unless for the worse, and the death rate rose along with the population. Into the bargain, late in 1847 there were epidemics of typhus and influenza.

This and the second cholera outbreak stirred the Government to tardy action. A Royal Commission concluded that a competent central authority was required, and in 1848 a Metropolitan Commission of Sewers was set up. Except for the City which still kept its independence, under this London was allotted seven area Commissions with wide powers – the first Parliamentary recognition that the capital should be treated as an entity.

1   [J Feltham], *The Picture of London*, 1802; [Robert Southey], Manuel Alvarez Espriella, *Letters from England*, ed. Jack Simmons, London, 1951, p. 90.

2   Lewis, *Islington*, p. 370; *VCH*, pp. 82–3. The two wells were reported as still existing in 1856, screened from view by small buildings in St George's Road. By then nobody had a legal title to them and the first issue of the *Islington Gazette*, 20 September 1856, urged the parish to acquire them in order to set up baths and wash-houses.

3   Henry Jephson, *The Sanitary Evolution of London*, London, 1907; The Rev. Thomas Beames, *The Rookeries of London*, 2nd edn (revised), London, 1852, p. 150.

CHAPTER 22

Houses in a New Suburb

A TRAVELLER'S TALE

The story of housing in the 19th century is one of glaring contrasts: relative elegance giving way over the years to florid comfort, contrasting with shoddy building and squalid living.

Our best insights into social habits and conditions usually come from outsiders – 'foreigners'. Locals are too familiar with their daily lives to comment, though journalists, like Thackeray or Harrison Ainsworth, treat us to illuminating, usually ironic, accounts of the life of the common man. So, after Carlyle telling us in the 1820s about his spick and span Pentonville lodgings, twenty years later another outsider still describes his Islington circumstances with approval. The Rev. Henry Colman, a Unitarian minister from Boston, Massachusetts, and an agricultural expert, spent three years in Europe (1843–6) studying agricultural conditions in the Old World. When in London after first staying in a central district where lodgings were both noisy and expensive, he was glad in July 1845 to have "escaped the distracting bustle and din of London, for quiet lodgings at Islington".

Irritatingly, he never tells us where, apart from being 4 miles from Charing Cross. It may well have been Barnsbury, or Canonbury. Like Carlyle, though, Colman describes his new habitat with satisfaction, "in a quiet clean street, and every thing seems agreeable". London lodgings for anything between 18 and 30 shillings a week were not always of required standard, "But here, with small, though neat accommodations, I am to pay only 10 shillings, without any extras whatever. It can hardly be called out of London, though it is quite removed from its bustle and interruptions." Four months later he is still satisfied. "I like my lodgings at Islington very much, and now think I shall not go into town. They are very clean. The servant is neat and attentive; my landlady, a little young woman of about 25, very pleasant and anxious for my welfare", and despite the "very long walk at night" if he goes into town, at home he can be uninterrupted, especially at night. He had at first enjoyed a very social life, and often dined out or went to the theatre. By 1846, however, living more quietly as work called, his Islington lodgings, distant from the centre, proved both excuse and safeguard.

"I continue to like my boarding place", he writes in February, "or I should go into town; but my little landlady is as kind as possible, and omits nothing that she can for my comfort." Though he admits that dining at home alone is "absolutely miserable", leaving time to feel homesick, breakfast-time was more cheerful, even if the menu sometimes sounds unusual. "With the newspaper in one hand, and my cup of tea in the other, I do not feel the want of society", on a summer Sunday, rising at 6.30 with birds "in crowds whistling under my window among the trees, which make almost a forest behind the house". After answering his letters and writing up his report he breakfasts at 9, "on my plain boiled rice and tea".

That day he dines with a friend's family (six beautiful children, ruddy and happy) in Barnsbury Villas. They enjoy an afternoon drive in a gig to Edmonton and Southgate, "fine roads, cultivated fields, splendid private dwellings, magnificent parks, umbrageous forests", and the "New River, green hedges, fields with hay-ricks, cattle and sheep, farms and fragrant air …", features soon to disappear from any trip to London's northern outskirts.[1]

Colman remarks in February 1846 how London is expanding so much as to astonish even those accustomed to it,[2] but he finds the new building of "most extraordinary beauty and taste", its suburbs "a series of cottages, which, to my view, exhibit the perfection of rural architecture. We, I think, have a good deal to learn in that matter": for example, American churches he thinks "an utter disgrace".

MORE HOUSES

London's rapid expansion was by now greatly changing in style. House features were becoming heavier and more Baroque, such as window surrounds, and details more elaborate as the severe post-Georgian fell into unpopularity.

The streets and squares of Barnsbury spread in the 1840s and 1850s, Highbury for the first time began to take shape, and more streets were added in Canonbury. The map of 1841 published with Lewis's *History* still shows little change, its most remarkable feature probably a semi-circular layout of streets projected but never built east of the present Hornsey Road. The area was instead to become a waste of railway land and industry, except for Queensland Road, later a tough area visited by police only in threes, and subsequently demolished to be subsumed among the surrounding industrial area.

Until the new railways began to draw capital-dwellers out of London, growth was contained by infilling of its many open spaces, and by a break-up of the small estates whose owners were keen to profit from building. In north Clerkenwell this applied to the New River Company and Lloyd Baker estates, in Islington to Canonbury, and Barnsbury with the Cloudesley, Milner-Gibson and slightly later Thornhill estates; there was similar expansion in Highgate and Hampstead. Railways even brought an opportunity for build-

71. Thornhill Crescent in the 1920s.

ing in more distant villages, rapidly turning them into suburbs.[3]

Expansion in the 1840s and 1850s included, notably, the deferred development of Barnsbury's Thornhill estate, projected by George Thornhill in the '30s, but slow off the mark. It developed with Hemingford Road and the footings of the cross roads leading down to it, and Thornhill Square and its environs, including Matilda and Everilda Streets. It acquired St Andrew's Church, also St Thomas's Church of 1860 by A W Billing alongside Hemingford Road, which survived until the 1950s. Its site is now part of a rare Islington park.

In Barnsbury front gardens were unusual, but in Canonbury the Alwyne group of streets in the late 1840s, and Canonbury Park North and South about 1860, were created as semi-detached villas, with gardens both front and back. This area too had its new square, at first named Canonbury Park Square but in 1863 to spare confusion renamed Alwyne Square.

North of this Holloway remained as two distinct hamlets, Upper and Lower, Holloway Road still running through fields and built up ribbon style. In fact behind the road the northern half of the parish was still rural.

In the south and east of the parish the Clothworkers' Company developed their property from 1846–58 with Arlington and Union Squares, Wilton Square and the roads bordering the canal and New North Road, at first slowly, then with gathering speed. The area is agreeably noteworthy for its unusually wide streets for reasons never quite clear, but bordering low-rise houses.

Alongside the New River, St Peter's area, starting with the former River Lane, was built in relatively humble style in the '40s and '50s. The usual series of terraces included the pretty Noel Road (1841), a desirable terrace with back gardens running down to the canal – but again no front gardens. Highbury's development was by a brickmaker, Henry Rydon, who in 1850 obtained the land from Francis Maseres to create a private gated road, Highbury New Park, its villas in gardens uniquely high-class in the area. It was served at first by a temporary iron church (an increasingly popular device in those days of

rapid growth until a permanent church could be supplied). In this case it was to be St Augustine's (1870), by W G Habershon and E P L Brock, with the advowson held by the Rydon family. Already in the 1850s villas and semi's were being built at the extremities of Islington and Highbury, for example in the new area of Tufnell Park, one of several which adopted the grandiose title where no park was to be seen. There were even political overtones, for with the social and economic unrest shown in Chartism and anti-Corn Law agitation, new building societies began to lay out plots just large enough to qualify owners for a vote, in the hope of increasing the number of possible Liberal voters.[4]

DESCENT INTO SLUMS

While building spread its tentacles to convert Islington from village to suburb, the poor suffered on many counts. Through removal of well-to-do families to still rural areas where they benefited from easy transport, their abandoned houses were taken over for multiple occupation, when they became slums. The influx of families seeking jobs was housed in new rows of jerry-built hovels run up by speculative builders, slums before they were even occupied. From the 1840s philanthropists and journalists alike publicised the dire situation, tackled, if at all, in ineffective ways. Mostly the bad housing was concentrated in Clerkenwell, which with the rest of Finsbury and St Luke's was among London's worst problem areas; but Islington, though rather better off because slightly more distant from inner London and on a hill-top, had its share.

One major problem area was the extreme west of the parish, adjoining the unsavoury quarter ironically known as 'Belle Isle' between the Caledonian Road and York Way. This was traditionally the home of nuisance industries, where from the late 1840s cheap houses were run up to serve their workers. Even so, there were some streets in the neighbourhood originally 'respectable' but fallen on evil days. "Hundreds of modern houses", wrote George Godwin in 1864, "built in decent suburban neighbourhoods as if for one family only, are made to contain several." As an example he quotes Bemerton Street (now re-

198

built and with different problems), a stone's-throw from Caledonian Road, a row of four-storey houses including basement, unexceptionable on the outside, but "dangerously crowded within". One eight-roomed house was occupied from top to bottom. In the basement front lived an old couple, in the back, two lodgers. "In the parlours, there are a man and his wife and eight children. On the first floor, a man and his wife and infant; two girls, sixteen and eighteen years of age, and occasionally their mother, – all in the front room; and in the small back room, two women, a girl, and two young children. On the second floor, a father, mother, two grown-up sons, an infant, and a brood of rabbits. Two women and two boys in the back room make the whole population of the house thirty-four." Next door housed 33. No bathroom is of course mentioned, but Godwin adds that "ventilation is not attended to; the drains get out of order, the 'traps' are destroyed, and the atmosphere is poison." (A trap was a device to prevent the escape of sewer gas from the drains.)[5] In another Islington house, situation unspecified, two persons had died of diphtheria. It had two water-closets but no regular water-supply, "through a disarrangement of the cistern", which overflowed on to the dustbin and on to "vegetable refuse" cluttering an outhouse, and a choked drain caused sewage to seep back into the yard. Most nearby houses were let out as lodgings. In one, the couple's child, sharing their one room, died of diphtheria in less than two days. Two costermonger families occupied the basement, "damp and unwholesome" where "fish and other offensive matter" was kept overnight, besides "dogs, cats, children, and dirt". The upper floors were equally over-occupied, as much by rabbits as by families, apparently a commonplace. An uncovered dustbin, and an inadequate water-closet at the foot of the stair, made for an "offensive atmosphere". Godwin claimed, in fact, that the house contained more than 200 people[6] – hard to credit, unless it was laid out with rows of beds like a house of refuge.

Another area of noxious courts forming a veritable rookery was, surprisingly, around the Angel. The names of some of these, Rose and Crown Court, Black Horse Yard, Swan Yard, indicated that they grew round former inn yards.[7] This warren of decadence and filth off the east side of the High Street, described in 1853 in terms of outrage, was entered through "sewerlike" passages, like entering a noisome vault. One entrance was flanked for years by the ruins of a burnt-out house, which nobody took the responsibility of clearing away.

The writer describes at each court entrance the "half-a-dozen men and women, in the most filthy and tattered garments, idling about, indulging in obscene jests, or swearing and fighting". Passers-by were offended by "sounds which we could not put down on paper without polluting it". Unwashed, barefooted children in filthy rags exhibited total wretchedness, language "tainted with moral leprosy", signs of having sunk "into all kinds of vice".

Within the courts "men with ferociously leering eyes, unshaven chins, uncombed hair, and dirty in their whole body, in clothes tattered and torn [were] seated on bottomless chairs, and smoking short clay pipes, cursing, swearing, or teaching the dogs they have stolen to fight each other". As for women and girls, "youthful charms and health are speedily disappearing before the ravages of filth, want, and immorality ... in the most scandalous state of brutalization. . ." And so on, in an almost endless recital of degeneration.

The shoddy buildings themselves were coated with filth, unpaved and "a mass of mud, offal, and decaying matter". Windows which had long ago lost any glass were stuffed with "besmeared bunches of paper, torn petticoats, or squashed hats" – a combination of bad ventilation, worse drains and inadequate water supply. Most of this degradation was attributed to the unscrupulous landlords, who had allowed such disgusting tenements to be run up by speculative builders. The answer was seen to be nothing short of total destruction of the filthy courts and alleys and removal to "airy and comfortable but simple dwellings, well supplied with water".[8] In Clerkenwell the situation was equally serious for a different reason – loopholes in the building leases on Lord Northampton's estate. Evidence on this disgraceful area given to the Royal Commission on the Housing of the Working Classes revealed a situation which had gone on for many years. Housing here was stigmatised as among London's "most deplorable slums", with "overcrowding, inadequate sanitation, insufficient ventilation, and generally poor repair". After two years it was still found unsatisfactory. Of 475 houses inspected, seven major defects were reported. These included the lack of water supply to the mis-named WC, which was a feature in 294 houses; 52 had defective designs and 32 defective cisterns. Other disgraces concerned dustbins (106 with none, or only "defective"), gullies, sinks and drains, and paving of yards. Here too, many former family houses had deteriorated into dirty, dilapidated tenements.

The Northampton estate building leases mostly dated from 1815 and 1818, which while containing the usual covenants had failed to prevent further building or infilling on the site, and in 1831 cheap tenements were run up unchecked in back courts. Nor were the maintenance orders observed, and landlords were able to convert the older houses to tenements. Lord Compton, giving evidence for his father the Marquess, admitted that the covenants ought to have been enforced, and Henry Trelawney Boodle, agent for the estates, also admitted blame for being too trusting with middle-men, and failing to enforce supervision. [9]

IMPROVEMENTS

Progress towards a desired ideal of "airy and comfortable … dwellings, well supplied with water" was a long time coming, with many false starts and wrong decisions. Not until the 1840s was there any attempt to improve the quality of housing, and then the first tenements were aimed solely at the 'industrious poor' – the responsible working man and his family.

In 1841 the Metropolitan Association for Improving the Dwellings of the Industrious Classes (note that 'industrious' – not 'industrial') was founded by the Rector of Spitalfields. The chairman was Sir Ralph Howard, and one promoter was the distinguished Dr Southwood Smith. In 1845 the Association received a Royal Charter. A Royal Commission on the 'Improvement of the Metropolis', and Edwin Chadwick on the 'Sanitary Condition of the Labouring Poor', made reports in 1842, aided by the establishment of the registration of births and deaths, as part of the duties of the Guardians of the Poor. The Royal Commission's remit covered the effect of improvements and amenities in London, and it concluded among other matters that benefits would result from freeing bridges from tolls, and creating new streets – chiefly by gouging through slummy old lanes and courts.

In 1844 a Labourers' Friend Society, founded as long ago as 1827, launched the Society for Improving the Condition of the Labouring Classes, which had royal patronage and was presided over by Lord Ashley (later Earl of Shaftesbury), a great philanthropist, and again supported by Southwood Smith. This was the first model dwellings society, proposing both planned housing and allotments to reduce pauperism – the former with some success, the latter not. At the Great Exhibition in 1851 a group of model cottages was displayed with Prince Albert's blessing. (They were later removed to Kennington Park, where they still are.) But the Society had already in 1849 created Thanksgiving Building in Gray's Inn Road, mainly for single women and financed by collections made since the second cholera epidemic of 1848.

There were other attempts at new model housing for the 'industrious artisan' at Bagnigge Wells Road below Pentonville. The first such experiment was on poor 'made-up' ground, hence limited to two storeys, a double row of facing tenements housing 23 families and 30 widows. Completed in 1846, they were grim and too closely built. But however tentative, this was a start to introducing cleanly and hence healthier living. In 1847 another tenement for 110 families was built opposite the Fever Hospital near Battle Bridge. This was large indeed, providing separate facilities for water supply, kitchens and lavatories, yet with rents between 3s 6d and 5 shillings it was intentionally too dear for the poorest.

The significance of all this was that the target for help was indeed the labouring poor, that is, not the destitute, unemployed, or unskilled. The object of philanthropy was the respectable workman who was in a job.

However, destruction of slums was not accompanied by their replacement with any-thing better – the poorest of the poor were merely evicted, needing to find somewhere else to exist in still more crowded hovels.

In 1848 when London was swept by its second cholera epidemic, dire though this was, thanks to its relative cleanliness the Bagnigge Wells tenements suffered less than might have been expected.

The epidemic stirred the Government to pass its first Public Health Act, again a tentative move because it was permissive, a timid result of Chadwick's report. It provided for the setting up of local Boards of Health, under a General Board. The Act was largely ignored; however, one positive result came in 1851 with the passing of the Common Lodging Houses Act, which provided homeless men with decent accommodation in dormitories, with common kitchens and washrooms. This was reinforced by the Labouring Classes Lodging Houses Act, with the similar object of increasing the housing supply, exemplified by the model cottages shown at Prince Albert's instigation at the Great Exhibition.

The general view at this stage was that poor sanitary conditions led to poor housing, not vice versa, so that the housing problem became primarily one of sanitation.[10]

According to the credo of the times, the industrious poor should be aided, cleanliness inculcated and disease thus eradicated, and the poorest must be removed from their degrading conditions. Nobody had yet seriously worked out where they should go. Improvements were introduced in areas neighbouring Islington, such as Angela Burdett-Coutts's founding of Columbia Square in Bethnal Green (1859–62), and the Society for Improving the Condition of the Labouring Classes' Thanksgiving Building in Gray's Inn Road. A Nuisances Removal Act in 1855 aimed at reducing overcrowding, but was limited to registration, not removal, of crowded insanitary houses. The Angel Rookeries were exposed in 1853; yet in the next decade it was as if housing activity was on hold – except for the middle classes, who were busy building and buying villas and semis in place of the earlier Georgian rows – until the 1860s brought a fresh surge of activity. Meanwhile sanitation and re-formed local government (the two were connected) took over as the main objective of the times.

1   Colman, *European Life and Manners*, Vol. I, p. 338, Vol. II, pp. 16–17, 52, 73ff.

2   *Ibid.*, Vol. II, p 67.

3   M Harrison, *London Growing*, London, 1965; Donald J Olsen, *The Growth of Victorian London*, London, 1976.

4   Francis Shepherd, *London 1808–1870: The Infernal Wen*, London, 1971; Donald J Olsen, *Town Planning in London*, London, 1964.

5   G Godwin, *Another Blow for Life*, London, 1864, pp. 36-7, 39-40.

6   *Ibid.*, pp. 39-40.

7   *VCH*, p. 17.

8   *Islington Athenaeum*, 9 July 1853 [in Islington Local History Library]. In 1875 these courts were declared "unfit" and (or example) Black House Yard was rebuilt in 1883 by the Improved Industrial Dwelling Co. Ltd. and named Torrens Buildings after the author of the 'Torrens Act' – themselves demolished in 1972.

9   Parliamentary Papers C. 4717 xvi, T Holdings, p. 339; 1887 (260) xiii, quoted in Olsen, *Town Planning in London*, pp. 102ff.

10   Fred Berry, *Housing: The Great British Failure*, London, 1974; Octavia Hill, 'Cottage Property in London', from *Fortnightly Review*, November 1866 (published in *Homes of the London Poor*, London, 1875).

CHAPTER 23

Forms of Education

REBUILDING OWEN'S SCHOOL

Dame Alice Owen's endowed charity school was the nearest Islington possessed to a grammar school. Private academies abounded in the 19th century, but parents unable to pay their fees were reliant on the parish for the education of their children. For example, the primary school opened in 1710 above St Mary's church porch for 24 charity boys and girls was maintained by the minister and parishioners. In 1738 a school for Welsh charity children was built in Clerkenwell Green, but was removed in 1752 to Gray's Inn Road. *(See Chapter 36.)* So things went on until the early 19th century.

A girls' school of industry was founded in 1801 by Islington Chapel, a girls' school in 1807 by Union Chapel and a boys' in 1814. By 1833 there were several infants' and the so-called National Schools run by the churches. By 1810 St Mary's church porch school had moved to Rufford's Row on the corner of Upper Street and Cross Street, with 46 boys and 34 girls, boys dressed in grey, girls in blue, where it remained until about 1860. Similarly, in 1815 a church school opened at the rear of the new Chapel of Ease, on half an acre of land presented by Samuel Rhodes and financed by subscription. Built by the Rhodes estate surveyor John William Griffith, it catered for 400 children.

There were also, notably in the Stoke Newington, Hackney and Newington Green area, day and boarding schools run by ejected Nonconformist clergy, which provided a sound education.

Owen's School, after its difficulties of the past, had been from 1791 under Alexander Balfour, at first seeming a worthy successor to David Davies. However, he began to neglect Foundation pupils in favour of fee-payers, in the manner of many schools which, with the rising population, were taking on more than their quota of pupils. Balfour was also criticised for unfair punishments – beating boys about the head with a book, locking them in the coal-shed, pulling their ears and perhaps more humiliating if less painful, making them clean knives and black shoes.

The historic limit for Owen's pupil numbers was still 30, and the Governors refused Balfour's request for an annexe to hold 20 more, with the chance of expanding the limited classics curriculum to include science, history and modern languages. Eventually he was allowed the £200 extension, and a new room for private pupils. Balfour, who claimed that he funded about a third of the cost himself, at one point acquired as many as 55 new pupils, including boarders.

In 1814 the Governors were keen to introduce Andrew Bell's 'Madras system' of supplementing the masters by training senior boys as 'Monitors' to teach the younger ones. Balfour objected, in spite of their offer to send his own son (who was his assistant) to learn the new method.

Under a new Act of 1818 relating to charities and education of the poor, the reluctant Governors were obliged to investigate the school's past achievements. This revealed that Balfour had without authorisation allowed Baptists to hold Sunday services in the schoolroom, even attending with his family –

72. The rebuilt Owen's School, c.1905.

a contravention of Established church regulations for which he was severely reprimanded. His son, the assistant master, later had a breakdown and entered an asylum, which so affected Balfour that he had to take leave of absence, but sadly did not recover. Although he handed over to a deputy, he resisted pressure to resign, continuing in office until his death in 1826. His successor too fell ill after a few years, dying in 1833 while the school was temporarily closed.

More private schools were springing up in this increasingly sought-after district, where land values were increasing in proportion. The provision under Dame Alice's bequest was no longer realistic, and it was obvious that the school urgently needed to be enlarged. The chief obstacle was the legal complexity of making changes in Owen's Trust. While the Hermitage Estate financing the almshouses had rocketed in value, the Orsett Field financing the school merely doubled in value to £45. A plan in 1819 to combine incomes, allowing

two-fifths to the school, took some years to materialise, though in 1826 the Governors set about a building plan. The architect William Pocock designed a new school as centre-piece to a row of rebuilt almshouses, entered from St John Street but facing the New River.[1]

Not until 1830, however, did the Court of Chancery rule on the finance, when the Master of the Rolls approved (at great length) that the proposed two-fifths of total rental be applied to the school. The Brewers' Company draft proposals were foiled by a complaint to the court by a Mr William Bromley of improper management, which delayed rebuilding until 1838. Another inspection and fresh report then led to a change of plan.

Owen Street had now been built, bisecting the estate and connecting St John Street and Goswell Road. The Crown and Woolpack inn was on the north side of the new road. The Court suggested siting the enlarged school on the triangle of land thus created separately from the almshouses, alongside the new road, to house 120 boys and with a six-roomed Master's house. Pocock worked on the revised plan believing that it would not exceed £2,000 but to the Governors' alarm all tenders proved well above, one of them not far from £3,000. This brought about Pocock's disgrace, and in October 1830 he was dismissed.

The lowest of several tenders, offered by William Cubitt, got the contract. At last by August 1839 the new school was begun and was ready for inspection the following January. An appropriate inscription commemorated the Company's achievement, in the name of the Master, Edmund Calvert, and Wardens.

Cubitt's were allowed the materials from the old school and almshouse buildings, and apart from fragments almost nothing survived. Two of the original arrows (see Chapter 4) were discovered within the wall above which they had been placed, and were kept by the Master – but though they survived until at least 1926, they have since disappeared.

The gabled new school, described glowingly in Lewis's History was if anything more Jacobean in appearance than the old: red brick with stone facings, central gable in the Dutch style, and an oriel window. Pupils entered at the sides. The large central arch led to a groined hall, a cloakroom and the substantial schoolroom, 45 by 20 feet with two square-headed, five-light windows on either side. At the top end the Master's seat, framed by oak panels, was set below a tablet inscribed with the School Rules in gold. Part of Lady Owen's monument with her heraldic arms above, removed from the old church on its demolition, was re-erected here with nine of the original 11 figures of her children. Lewis's detailed description includes an illustration of the Master's house and a copy by Charles Cripps of Lady Owen's original portrait in Brewers' Hall. The architect, George Tattersall (1817–1849), still only 23, was Surveyor to the Brewers' Company and son of the fashionable horse auctioneer.[2]

More classrooms were added in 1846 and 1860. The number of pupils rose quickly from 42 to 84, in 1852 to 111 and by 1858 to its maximum of 120. The age of admission was between 7 and 11; education and books were free to the age of 14. Entry was contingent on parents' 'petitions', with the Vicar and Churchwardens' approval, presented twice yearly by the Court of Assistance.

A record in 1852 shows six classes averaging 17 boys, the smallest learning arithmetic, spelling, reading (New Testament and Catechism). Only the Second class of 38 boys was larger. The Sixth (top) class was taught more advanced arithmetic, reading (of history), grammar and, more sophisticatedly, 'the Globes' – a modernised syllabus dispensing with Latin and introducing some history and geography.

In this period of great advance, the school had its longest-serving Master – 45 years. He was John Hoare, trained at the National Society's Central School in Westminster, and was appointed to Owen's in 1833 at the age of 32. Hoare's military appearance matched his disciplinary approach. He it was who oversaw the move to the new premises, and over the years his annual salary rose from a mere £81 to (in 1864) an impressive £250, with a matching increase in his yearly gratuity. He also appointed extra staff, some of them 'visiting': such as a Drawing Master, one of whom was Cubitt & Co.'s Surveyor Charles Allen (1852–6). There was a French master (1855–8) who also taught part-time at another Brewers' School, and was followed by the long-serving Monsieur Masse (1858–89). Later came Hoare's own son William Sheppard, who in time became Second Master. From 1865 there was also an assistant master for the younger boys. Most of these changes and expansions took place after the mid century, and Hoare himself remained in charge until 1879.

PRIVATE SCHOOLS

By 1833 Islington boasted two proprietary schools, 51 private day schools and 38 boarding schools, whose pupils presumably lived outside the parish, or were perhaps paid for by guardians – as were the unfortunate children described in Nicholas Nickleby.[3] Charity and National schools catered for a total of 578 boys and 447 girls, plus 642 infants, free or for a few pence a week; and the boarding schools 798 boys and 421 girls. Small private schools were the norm for children of town families with any means, of which suburbs like Islington had a large supply. The middle class, at whatever rung of the ladder, who could not afford one of England's major schools for their sons, or had no entrée to either a grammar school or one like the Charterhouse run by philanthropic institutions, sent their children to such a medium-rank suburban private school. A number of these 'academies' were also for young ladies. It was a badge of gentility, of a sort. At the top of the social scale, Of the public schools attended by upper and middle-class boys, London had four, two of them at different times in Clerkenwell: the Charterhouse followed by the Merchant Taylors. Their syllabus, limited to the classics, had scarcely changed in centuries, and such schools were regarded by some as 'nurseries of vice'. Grammar schools too had a limited curriculum, but Owen's School, having upgraded itself to grammar school status, offered a better range of subjects.

Below this were the 'proprietary' secondary schools financed by shareholding proprietors, professional or business men. Islington had one in Duncan Terrace and one in Barnsbury. Proprietors might nominate one boy (possibly their own son) per share held, and more if they paid a fee. If the boy were not their son, consent of the directors had to be obtained. The schools, run in conjunction with King's College, Cambridge, were not intended for local tradesmen.

The first of these, founded in 1830 at the corner of Barnsbury Street and Milner Place, soon had 80 boys rising throughout the decade to 170. The headmaster was an Anglican clergyman, and the curriculum, besides the inevitable classics, included mathematics, modern languages, even Hebrew. Boys were prepared for the universities, for commerce and for government examinations. Similarly the school at the corner of Duncan Street and Duncan Terrace ran for a number of years from 1839.

From the 1840s there were also a number of commercial schools, one at 32 New North Road, preparing boys for commerce and the professions; another, East Islington Commercial School, next to the new cattle market in the Essex Road (see Chapter 24), took fee-paying boys whose parents could not afford a proprietary school. In 1852 the School of Science and Art, in connection with the South Kensington

73. The Proprietary School at the corner of Barnsbury Street and Milner Place.

Science and Art Department, opened in Windsor Street, also off the Essex Road, for sons of tradesmen and artisans. Besides the sciences, subjects included Physiology, Mathematics, English and book-keeping, to Civil Service standard.

All these catered for the increasing numbers of middle-class boys. One preparing pupils for the public schools and universities was the Barnsbury Park Collegiate School, which ran for over 30 years from about 1849 as a day and boarding school for 'gentlemen's sons', teaching modern languages, science, and subjects with a mercantile bias.

At this level girls were not wholly neglected. The Queen's College Institute for Ladies in Brecknock Road, set in two acres on the edge of Tufnell Park, prepared girls for whatever examinations were open to them. By 1851 it had 64 boarders aged up to 19, with 14 governesses, including an Italian singing teacher, and French and German language teachers. Another small school with pretensions, calling itself Histon House College, also in Barnsbury Park and with a garden and even a croquet lawn, prepared day girls and boarders for Oxford and Cambridge examinations, though in 1851 it ran to only 12 boarders.[4]

Then there were the private 'academies'. A Directory published in 1828 shows London ringed with them, and while many parishes or outlying villages such as Richmond, Twickenham, Lewisham or Acton boasted only one, some parishes were traditionally popular. In Chelsea there were 20, in Kensington 11, in Hammersmith 9. Chiswick, where some dozen years earlier Thackeray had placed Miss Pinkerton's academy, in fact had only two for boys and one for girls. In this Directory Islington was credited with as many as 61 and in adjoining villages Hoxton had 5, Stoke Newington 6, Hackney 11, Dalston and Homerton 6, Kingsland 3 and Clapton one.

Girls, who were not admitted to grammar schools, were better provided for by these schools than boys, with 17 schools in Hammersmith, 27 in Kensington, 11 each in Chelsea, Peckham and Kentish Town, 10 in Walworth, 9 each in Hampstead and Hoxton.

Islington, along with Pentonville, Clerkenwell and Holloway (the Directory class-consciously describes most of these places as 'near London') has 26 for boys, 35 for girls. The size of schools is not usually quoted, and given that Islington contained few large houses except in Colebrooke Row, Duncan Terrace and Highbury Place, one cannot suppose an establishment as spacious as Miss Pinkerton's. Pupils were doubtless housed in dormitories with as many beds as the small rooms could hold. The proprietor/proprietress probably lived on the ground floor, and could feed only as many as their dining-room would accommodate. Of girls' academies 14 were quoted as 'Pentonville' – which often meant Colebrooke Row or one of the squares – others in the City Road area, two in Barnsbury Park, three elsewhere in Barnsbury, only one in Canonbury (Miss Oates's finishing school at 7 Canonbury Place, "very select"). Another finishing establishment for a limited number was in Mildmay Row off Newington Green. Indeed, several termed themselves finishing schools, some taking a few pupils, others "not limited", and most quoted moderate terms. Only three such schools gave numbers: Mrs Hogsflesh's finishing establishment for 16 young ladies (at 20 guineas a year), Miss Kirshaw at 42 Claremont Square, into which she crammed 20 girls, understandably at moderate terms, and Mrs Nesbitt on Islington Green, also for 20 girls.

Young gentlemen were similarly catered for in 'Pentonville' (six) and Barnsbury (four). One, 'Thornhill Academy', was in Southampton Street, Pentonville – the street where Grimaldi died and earlier Thomas Carlyle lodged. Mr J R Everett, of Grove House in Cross Street, offered 20 boarders a classical and finishing education for 26–30 guineas. Some were called a 'Preparatory Seminary' – presumably for one of the public schools.

Of the few who gave more particulars, the Rev. R Brazier, at Prospect House, 4 Maberley Terrace in the Ball's Pond Road, offered a limited number of young gentlemen a liberal education in a "pleasant and salubrious" location about two miles from London, with "every indulgence, consistent with their improvement", and "pledges himself to pay every possible attention to their morals, health, and comfort".

Only three of these boys' schools appear to have been run by clergymen, and two were kept by ladies. The Rev. W Briggs at 20 Claremont Square, an Oxford MA, took just four pupils to prepare for public school, university entrance or holy orders, at a mammoth 100 guineas a year, teaching Latin, Greek and French, and "including every expense except washing, stationery, &c." He would also attend boys and girls at their own home, for the quite high rate of five shillings an hour.

At the Colebrooke House Academy in Colebrooke Row the Rev. R Simson, an Edinburgh graduate, had two assistant masters and combined "the sedulous study of the Classics, with a course of Mathematics", aimed to "cultivate the intellectual powers, refine the taste, form and consolidate habits of observation and reflection, and store the mind with a general knowledge of the various branches of English Literature". He advertised the situation as "one of the most pleasant and healthy in or about London", all for 30–35 guineas a year. The contrast in charges with those of the Rev. Mr Briggs is noticeable.

Nearby, Mr Joseph Box at 117 Britannia Street, off the City Road, provided a select academy to qualify young gentlemen for such careers as "Foreign or Domestic Trade, the various Public Offices, Maritime Pursuits".

Like the Rev. Mr Brazier, six grandly styled 'professors' offered their services for arithmetic or writing as visiting masters at the schools, or privately in families. Of more exotic subjects, London itself was only thinly provided with experts on astronomy and "use of the globes" (only four), or the classics (seven), and Islington boasted none of these. But it could offer two dancing masters, or professors as they almost always termed themselves, out of London's total of 46: most were French. Of 193 drawing and painting teachers most lived in Soho, Bloomsbury or Marylebone, though Islington had 11, including two women. Again four were in Pentonville; 11 were styled professors of landscape or architectural drawing (Pentonville 5), out of London's 94; and two men and four women taught drawing and flower painting. There were also several music teachers, four ladies and a gentleman teaching piano, organ, or other 'finger' instruments, three men teaching strings or harp – but strangely, none specified singing.

There were even two instructors in fencing, gymnastics, 'Callisthenic Exercises', and 'Drill Serjeants' Riding Schools', one of whom was, not unexpectedly, John I'Ons who kept the livery stables and riding school off Upper Street, and Mr Peters of 13 Cloudesley Square taught gymnastics. Of two mathematics masters, Mr Quelch of Tabernacle Row off City Road offered "Algebra, Book-keeping, practical Measuration, and Land Surveying, with the Use of the Instructors". But there was not a single teacher of elocution, reading and grammar, geography, or any foreign language.

There is a strange discrepancy between this, the *London Masters' Directory*, and Pigot's, also published in 1828–9, which quotes 40 'Gentlemen's academies', only two of which appear in the former, although all but 10 of the list are apparently day schools. The girls' list does overlap, and again Pigot's numbers far more than boys, totalling 60, of whom 11 are also in the *Masters' Directory* (and of those, three have different addresses, in spite of the two works being contemporary).

Whatever the true total, it was strikingly large, surpassing the numbers listed for other parts of London by a wide margin. The reasons were probably multiple: Islington was conveniently near the City, was in a healthy hilltop situation, and was known for leisure activities.

TEACHING THE POOR

For the many children below the middle, professional and trading classes education in the 19th century was nationally, to put it bluntly, a mess. There was no system, and at the time of Queen Victoria's coronation it was reckoned that over 30% of men and nearly 50% of women could not sign their names in the marriage register. As late as 1840 the visiting Frenchwoman Flora Tristan (who indeed found little good to say about England generally) declaimed, "In England there is no 'free' education of any kind; he who has no money must forget cultivating his mind or increasing his knowledge. Access to libraries, museums, churches and scientific collections is practically impossible for the working class."[5]

The basic problem for education of the working class was how to deal with religion. All attempts to establish a satisfactory national educational framework for the poorer classes foundered on how, or whether, to teach religion, and Bill after Bill, starting with Samuel Whitbread's in 1807 and Lord Brougham's in 1820, was defeated by the Lords or entrenched MPs fearing the effect on the Church of England if alternatives to the Church schools were explored. Meanwhile both Establishment and Dissenters formed their own organisations. The Church of England in 1811 founded the National Society for promoting the education of the Poor in the principles of the Established Church – and thus misleadingly named their schools 'national'. In 1814 the non-denominational British and Foreign School Society was founded. Between them these formed distinctive religious educational organisations, and continued at loggerheads. The state kept out of it.

Apart from the religious question, official reluctance to educate the working class was partly a fear, in these post-revolutionary times, of an articulate proletariat which might spell political – radical – trouble. Besides stirring up labour unrest, their education would be expensive and with no commercial value. Higher education was seen largely as vocational training for the clergy and the professions, or as a harmless way of occupying leisured youth.

There were parochial and charity schools, of which Clerkenwell's, opened in 1828 in

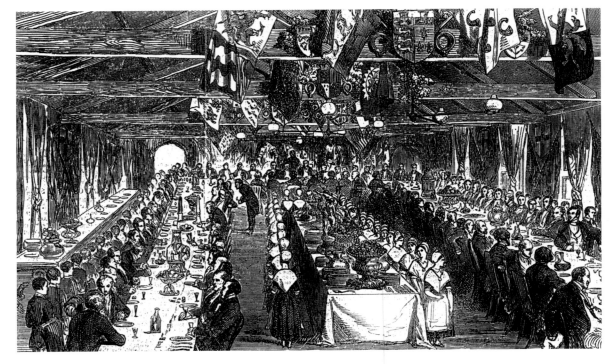

74. A dinner to mark the 150th anniversary of the Clerkenwell Parochial Schools, held in 1850.

Amwell Street, was an example. The new parochial school attached to St Mary's Chapel of Ease, in the Liverpool Road, was run on the Madras method. This reduced the overall cost, but until 1846 provided no kind of teacher training.

In 1833 the National Society and the non-denominational British Society were each granted £20,000 to build schools in large towns, supplemented by voluntary contributions. Though by now numbers at school had doubled, there was a great shortage of both schools and teachers, for which in 1838 Parliament recommended a grant.

Again the religious question intervened. The effort to introduce non-denominational teaching was defeated by the Church's demand for control, and the belief that state backing would contravene religious liberty.

Below the 'respectable' working class were the very poor, about whom, except for the few charity schools, nobody bothered until philanthropists took a hand and encouraged the Ragged School movement for those at the bot-

tom of the pile. First, the London City Mission in 1835 offered basic teaching to destitute and homeless children in the poorest areas, and by 1840 were providing for some 570 children. Then in 1844, 40 pious gentlemen met in (it was said) a Bloomsbury cowshed to form the Ragged School Union, aiming like the Mission to provide education for the poor, and until the Education Act of 1870 at last authorised national education, Ragged Schools employed up to 450 paid teachers, aided by thousands of volunteers, to teach 25,000 children, and their parents on Sundays.

The object was rehabilitation as much as basic education, to reclaim children from the squalor and lack of spiritual value in their lives. Islington and particularly Clerkenwell started a number of Ragged Schools, among the most famous being in Lamb and Flag Court off Clerkenwell Green, and in nearby Field Lane.

Lamb and Flag School, the largest in London, was founded by Mr Humphreys, a City Missionary in (says Vanderkiste) "a small, confined, and unhealthy room" among the courts round Saffron Hill, an area described by *The Times* in 1846 as of "excessive depravity". Missionaries visiting the area in 1841 had commented in shock that they had never seen "such awful scenes or heard such shocking language", or encountered literally hundreds of filthy, half-naked children. The argument for taking on their education was not least that such waifs could never gain entry even to a charity school. When the campaign to come to their aid began, appeals brought in funds, clothing, Bibles and spelling books – and two trained teachers.

Before long the movement was supported by the Queen and Prince Albert, and its progress was demonstrated in its annual reports. The children's patent lack of any knowledge of religion led to the humble schoolroom's opening for Sunday evening services, hoping also to tempt parents from the pub. Very soon the philanthropic Earl of Shaftesbury lent his active support and chaired the meetings, as did members of the clergy.

In 1852 the Lamb and Flag's wretched room was enlarged, partly to let in some air, and also to bring in more pupils – like the youths who idled or scrapped around the courts. The scope was extended to a statutory penny bank to encourage saving, to provide Christmas treats, and to promote cleanliness. One active supporter was the noted Rev. Robert Maguire, vicar of St James's, Clerkenwell, who later became its President.

Lamb and Flag was only the best known of the Ragged Schools. Also in Clerkenwell were schools in Red Lion Street (now Britton Street), and Field Lane or West Street, Saffron Hill. The rising number testified to the district's dense overcrowding in its notorious courts. Saffron Hill was described in 1843 as "proverbially the dirtiest in London; very possibly the dirtiest in the world". In the almost equally squalid St Luke's a school opened in Honduras Street by Golden Lane, and in Pentonville, one in Payne Street (a street demolished after the 2nd World War).

Islington itself soon set up Ragged Schools: in Elder Walk off Lower Street, in Sermon Lane (now subsumed in Tolpuddle Street), a proverbially mean street; in Bryan Street, White Conduit Fields, and farther north, in Brand Street (now Rollit Street, off Hornsey Road).

Sermon Lane, to take one example, by 1852 had admitted 399 children, slightly more boys than girls, and by then had 159 pupils in equal numbers, averaging more than 110 a day. Few could read when they started, but a persevering mistress brought them up to Bible reading standard. An 'industrial class' for some 50 girls, led by several ladies, was eventually taken over by a professional teacher with the ladies' assistance. The ladies also made home visits to the families. Clothes were distributed, and more than 50 children obtained jobs. New rooms were built opposite the school, and opposite where Penton Primary School was to be opened in 1891. A bazaar and donations helped pay for the ground and building costs. At a new evening school there, 26 out of 85 boys could now read, though daily attendances were nothing like so many. But though behaviour had improved, because of a shortage of teachers "their progress is not so great as might be expected".

Charles Dickens, as is well known, like Miss Angela Burdett-Coutts took a great interest in Ragged Schools. In 1848, not long after they were first established, he suggested that the boys ought to have some means of washing before starting school, in the form of a large trough of running water, soap and towels, with an attendant to ensure they were orderly. He also argued that teaching ought to concentrate on "the broad truths", which could be imparted by the volunteers and gentlemen helpers, rather than stuff the children with well-meant but incomprehensible theological concepts. He had great admiration for the zeal of the teachers, but questioned the usefulness of (as he had heard one lady attempting) "injudicious catechising" in questions about the Lamb of God.

In *Household Words* in 1852 Dickens recalled his first visit ten years earlier to a wilderness of abject poverty and obscene squalor: "mounds of earth, old bricks, and oyster-shells – the arched foundations of unbuilt houses ... the odds and ends of fever-stricken courts and alleys", an area of "profound ignorance and perfect barbarism", where well-wishers were gloomily convinced that inhabitants *would not come* to be improved".

Despite that pessimistic outlook the Saffron Hill School had opened, with every possible disadvantage: "no means ... no suitable rooms ... no power or protection from being recognised by any authority", and confined to "a low-roomed den, in a sickening atmosphere, in the midst of rain and dirt and pestilence". The children, scowling and suspicious, old for their years, quickly perceived the lack of experience in their dedicated but naive volunteer teachers, "made blasphemous answers to scripture questions, sang, fought, danced, robbed each other". They broke in, blew out the lights, scattered the books in the gutters.

After two years of zeal and persistence, Dickens found the place, like other Ragged Schools, "quiet and orderly, full, lighted with gas, well whitewashed, numerously attended and thoroughly established".

The managers also aimed to help the many homeless by renting one of the miserable nearby houses, and with a dozen or so cheap beds provided a dormitory as dispiriting as the schoolroom, dark, stifling and ruinous, with tiny rooms. So unsuitable, in fact, that its very efficacy was questionable. But this too was now improved, and better still, a school of industry was started, where besides teaching the basic Three R's it had attentive groups of shoemakers and tailors, making and mending for themselves and for others.

The dormitory was reserved for those attending the school, and shirkers were not allowed in. The 'meals', a small portion of bread, hardly tempted the idle. The room was now clean, cheap and efficient, windowed on all sides and equipped with a stove, with a glazed cubicle for the 'presiding officer'. Dickens described in detail its facilities and well-run programme. In would come the night-sleepers, "thieves, cadgers, trampers, vagrants, common outcasts of all sorts", but unlike in a casual ward their behaviour, and reception, was of kindness.

He concluded that with however small an annual grant, the Ragged Schools "would relieve the prisons, diminish county rates, clear loads of guilt and shame out of the streets, recruit the army and navy". In fact, he declared hopefully, training would turn them into useful citizens, and they might even be reclaimed to religion.[6]

In 1856 a Royal Commission under the Duke of Newcastle enquired into schools, and in 1860 its Vice-President, Robert Lowe, basing a 'Revised Code' on their report, introduced the highly unpopular 'Payment by Results', which fixed grants solely by attendance and examination marks. This unsatisfactory system lasted for many years.

No matter what the odds, or shortcomings in experience of volunteers and sponsors, the Ragged Schools did continue to achieve notable progress until well after the Education Act of 1870 brought schools to all.

SELF-IMPROVEMENT

A totally contrasting form of public education and socialising was characterised by the literary and scientific institutions which grew up towards the middle of the 19th century. Part of a worthy crusade for self-improvement, in view of the limitations of education, they were a middle-class counterpart to the Mechanics' Institutes which also characterised the age. Working men's groups were being formed by the 1820s, and in 1823 the co-editors of the

75. The Islington Literary & Scientific Institution in Almeida Street, when in use by the Salvation Army.

76. Interior of the Institution.

Mechanics' Magazine, J.C. Robertson and Thomas Hodgskin, met with a group in a Clerkenwell coffee-house for reading, discussion and music. They began to campaign for educational institutes in London for 'mechanics', as working men were often termed. With the help of the philanthropist Francis Place and a group of fund-raising radicals, in 1824 the London Mechanics' Institution opened in Chancery Lane under Dr George Birkbeck – forerunner of Birkbeck College. Some 60 of these institutes were launched in London by the 1840s, out of a total of about 700 nationwide and they included the Literary and Scientific Institutes which had a more middle-class tinge.

The Islington venture in this field started in 1832, when (as Samuel Lewis phrases it) "a few gentlemen fond of scientific and literary pursuits, and desirous of extending the advantages of which they themselves were consequently sensible", decided to broaden their activities to a wider field. After initial discussions they advertised their aims in a circular letter and in November outlined the plan at a public meeting at the Canonbury Tavern. Here a literary society was unanimously agreed on, a committee elected, and at subsequent meetings the structure and officers were fixed. Starting in 1834 with 261 members, by the time Lewis was writing (1841) membership had risen to 561. In these years a number of such societies were founded, including one at Highgate (which flourishes to this day), and the Islington group. After meetings held at Thomas Edgeworth's Academy the Institute moved into its own newly-built premises in 1837.

This Greek-style building in what was then

named Wellington Street, now Almeida Street, was designed by the architects Roumieu and Gough, who soon afterwards built Milner Square a short distance away. The foundation stone was laid on 10 April 1837, the builders were the local firm of William Spencer Dove of Trinidad Place, and the building was completed in March 1838 and opened in November, funded by £10 shares.

Though altered in 1842, the building substantially contained a lecture theatre, a library and reading room, a museum, a laboratory and apparatus room, classrooms, offices and a committee room. The semi-circular theatre, seating 500, was at the rear behind the temple-front, and the library contained over 5000 volumes. The 'philosophical apparatus' was presented by the President, Charles Woodward, FRS. In the museum were "specimens of natural history and objects of art, apparatus for philosophical experiments". There were monthly meetings or lectures at which politics and religion were scrupulously excluded, at one of which, in January 1840, a Mr Pettigrew unrolled an Egyptian mummy brought from Thebes to demonstrate the methods of embalming. From the mummy-case inscriptions it appeared to be that of a priest's daughter, but disappointingly few interesting possessions were found on it.

The improving entertainments provided by the Institute included the occasional string quartet, which appears to have proved lucrative. There were gradations of membership, life membership for £25, £10 shareholders subscribing a guinea and a half annually, entitling them to all the privileges, a vote at general meetings and introduction of family members at a guinea a head, and ordinary members at two guineas who were also entitled to introduce "one lady, a resident member of their families", for a further guinea.

The elegant building with its projecting giant portico and pillars, and flanking entrance porches, fronted on to the reading-room. A stone staircase led to the committee room and the museum which was above the reading-room. In the basement were the housekeeper's quarters.

The first Librarian was Joseph Simpson, who, in 1855 after eight years, resigned to take "a favourable business opportunity" and was succeeded by W E Jenkins, formerly of the similar institute in Marylebone. A report on that year's proceedings may serve as an example of the Institute's eclectic activities, which included "a Microscopical Soirée", and lectures on Byron, Electro Chemistry, Peter the Great, Beau Brummell, "the Coloured Residents in London", Florence, the Earth, the Moon, Manufacture of paper, the Character of George IV, Shells, and Boccaccio. Classes were also held in elocution, Philosophy and French.

The Institute was considered of sufficient significance to merit an entry in Knight's *Cyclopaedia*, one of the many tomes published to coincide with the Great Exhibition of 1851. The society flourished at its respectable middle-class level for about 40 years. By the time the 1870 Education Act took effect, however, the need for such institutions was declining, and the centre became of less importance locally. In 1875 the building was rented to the Wellington Club, and the hall and premises let for meetings of different associations. In 1890 the Salvation Army acquired it and converted it in 1904 as one of their Citadels.[7] Today, the revamped building houses the Almeida Theatre.

LOCAL NEWSPAPERS

In 1828 an *Islington Gazette* was launched, and ran for all of three issues before, like so many other ventures, dying of inanition. Ambitiously sub-titled "Monthly Miscellany of Local Intelligence, combined with Literary and General Information, and Amusement", it was a magazine in format and content rather than a newspaper, and its third issue, for instance, opened with the last of three articles on the scope of Dame Alice Owen's bequest.

This *Islington Gazette* was published by C. Hancock, of "Eliza Place, near Sadler's Wells", and was circulated among four named sources, including Hilton's Reading Room in Penton Street – another sign of the times – besides through "different newsvendors in Islington, Holloway, and Pentonville".

A few years later a longer-lasting paper was launched. In its first issue the new *Penny Magazine* advertised, in a single week in November 1836, Sheridan Knowles lecturing on the drama, and elsewhere W T Brande (Esq.) at the London Institution in Finsbury Circus on

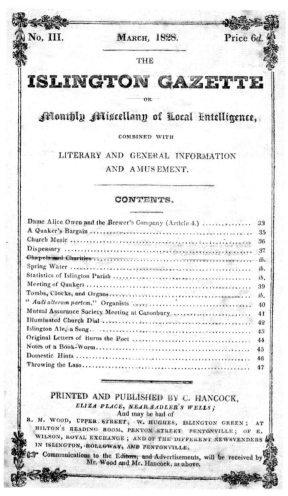

77. The third edition of the Islington Gazette, *a 'monthly miscellany of local intelligence', March 1828.*

chemistry, Mr Chalklen on "The Sublime in Objects and in Writing", whatever that meant, at the Palmer House Academy in Holloway Road, and in Hackney at the Eastern Literary and Scientific Institute, T R Jones Esq. on Insects. The new magazine was printed in Palmer Terrace near Ring Cross (now 145–185 Holloway Road) at the Holloway Press. Indeed, several societies existed with a cultural purpose, devoted to organising lectures with an educational flavour for the respectable middle class.

The attitude of the time might be summed up in an advertisement on the back cover of the third *Islington Gazette*, by Mr Harton of 4 George's Place, Holloway, with ten years' practice behind him and "an extensive knowledge of Ancient and Modern Languages". He expressed his desire of "extending his Connexion amongst the respectable Inhabitants of Islington, Highbury, and Holloway, guaranteeing to introduce his Pupils, by a lenient and amusing method ... to a critical knowledge of those Sciences which are indispensable to the formation of a man of business or a scholar".[8]

Educational references are found in VM, Vols. IV-VI.

1   Dare, *Owen's School*, p. 46. This site was, in fact, where the Girls' School was to be built in 1886.
2   Lewis, *Islington*, pp. 421-3; Dare, *Owen's School*, pp. 47-55. Tattersall set up offices in Pall Mall, designed Tattersall's stables at Willesden, and soon after Owen's was completed published a treatise with illustrations of stables, kennels and other racing buildings. (Colvin, *British Architects*, p. 958.)
3   Although Dickens certainly did not have Islington in mind when the scandalous Yorkshire schools were exposed as convenient dumps for unwanted boys, the agent for William Shaw, master of the Greta Bridge school on which Dotheboys Hall was based, actually lived at 10 Frederick Place, off Goswell Street. For the range of schools in Islington, see *VCH*, p. 118.
4   Information on the private schools is found in *The Boarding School and London Masters Directory*, 1828, and Pigot & Co.'s, *London and Provincial Directory*, 1828-9.
5   Flora Tristan, *London Journal*, p. 185.
6   *VCH*, pp. 119ff; see e.g. Charles Dickens in *Household Words*, 13 March 1852, p. 577 ('A Sleep to Startle Us'); R W Vanderkiste, *Six Years' Mission ... Among the Dens of London*, 1854.
7   Lewis, *Islington*, pp. 42ff. The Institute building later went down in the world and from 1952 was used as a small factory, Beck's Carnival Novelties. The murder of the proprietor brought this to a rather unfortunate end and in spite of interested applications such as from the Orange Music Centre (1972), it languished until in 1981 the whole building was transformed for the Almeida Theatre and gained a new and flourishing lease of life. In 2002/3 it was substantially restored.
8   *Islington Gazette*, Nos 1 & 3, 1828; *Penny Magazine*, No 1, 5 November 1836.

Chapter 24

Markets and Shops

Smithfield Problems

Islington's proximity to the City had brought it into the orbit of Smithfield Cattle Market, in circumstances and in prosperity. Smithfield, between Clerkenwell and the City, had enjoyed a Royal Charter since 1327, and like London's other leading markets, Covent Garden and Spitalfields, it was wholesale – dealing not with consumers but with the trade. Livestock was driven there from all regions, and Islington at the end of the Great North Road had for centuries been the convenient spot to hold animals overnight in cattle lairs, before their last lap to the market. On that last mile of St John Street there was, of course, a proliferation of taverns on either side.

With passing centuries Smithfield, while retaining picturesque characteristics, became the cause of great abuses. Cattle and sheep coming from the west were driven straight through central London, notably Oxford Street, adding to the already heavy traffic congestion, and conditions in the market itself showed it to be ill sited, ill constructed, ill ventilated, and lacking sanitary regulations. Every weekend thousands of terrified animals were driven in by shouting drivers with their dogs, goading the luckless beasts towards the "labyrinth of pens", lashing bullocks to the railings by their heads until they nearly choked, half-strangling frightened calves as they penned them up. Sundays were spent in sorting them out ready for the Monday market.[1]

Among the many contemporary descriptions, Thomas Carlyle's is as vivid as any.

Passing through when the day's trade was mostly over he viewed it from the steps of a doorway:

> "An irregular space of perhaps 30 acres in extent, encircled with old dingy brick-built houses, and intersected with wooden pens for the cattle. What a scene! Innumerable herds of fat oxen, tied in long rows, or passing at a trot to their several shambles; and thousands of graziers, drovers, butchers, cattle brokers with their quilted frocks and long goads pushing on the hapless beasts; hurrying to and fro in confused parties, shouting, jostling, cursing, in the midst of rain and *shairn* [dung] and braying discord such as the imagination cannot figure..."[2]

This was in 1824, when dissatisfaction over central London's being overrun by the constant driving of flocks and herds through crowded thoroughfares, and the noise, dirt and confusion of Smithfield grated on people's consciences.

Yet the situation remained unchanged and unimproved for years. A long diatribe in the *Lady's Newspaper* in 1849 described Smithfield as "an anomaly in civilisation" excused only by its long existence. Facilities "of the worst description ... gave rise to cruelties and unheard-of barbarities to the cattle exposed for sale, and great danger and inconvenience to the public on market days". Its "filthy slaughterhouses and the consumption of diseased meat" endangered health, it was "a resort for thieves and persons of the worst character", and its Sunday preparations were a profanation. To cap it all were "the brutal insolence of savage drovers", and the danger of being trampled or gored by panicking animals.[3]

Yet in 1852 another writer seemed entertained by the market's unique quality, its "cunning costermongers and ruddy-faced countrymen", their costume and dialect from all over the kingdom, and its many eating-houses serving immensely fat joints and rich puddings, customers eating a pound of meat at a time and downing a pot of porter at one gulp. The picturesque aspect was perhaps promoted since the Great Exhibition in 1851 had added to London's tourist attractions.[4] This writer, Thomas Miller, admitted the less attractive side, its deafening cacophony of shouting drovers, barking dogs, bleating sheep, bellowing bullocks, squealing pigs, and the thundering of carts on cobbled pavements. Almost worse was the regular dishonesty as bullying, swindling salesmen shamelessly cried up broken-down beasts.

By 1852, a campaign to close the market had been going on for nearly half a century. In 1810 the City's Court of Common Council had approved a proposal to remove it to the open fields between Sadler's Wells and Islington, a suggestion that died without trace. In 1818 the Court and Aldermen presented a similar Bill to Parliament, but met a storm of opposition from property owners and butchers. (As things turned out, such a move would have been pointless, as the new market would soon have been swamped by building.)

In 1828, a Committee of the House had heard damning evidence of the market's increasing inefficiency, now reduced in size to 3° acres and therefore even more overcrowded, its very entrance blocked by butchers' carts. A major recommendation which excited heated argument was to introduce proper French-style abattoirs, regulating slaughter and allowing the animals rest before their end. Another proposal was to move the market to a distance such as Hackney or Kilburn, where "abundant pastures" would be available for fodder, or alternatively to Southall.

The building of ten slaughter-houses was also proposed, four of them north of the Thames, including one "about Haberdashers' Alms Houses, at the Great North Road". This too was ignored.[5] The City's vested interests still prevented closure, but as a slight palliative the market was enlarged, carts were (officially) banned, and stricter rules were imposed if not enforced.

The anti-Smithfield campaign was now active, and the Committee of the House plainly favoured the market's removal if for health reasons alone, the objectors being "a few interested publicans and butchers who have slaughter-houses adjacent". The City Corporation petitioned Parliament almost annually to end the cruelty and nuisance, by enlargement or better, by removal. Visiting foreigners were astonished at the sight of animals driven through London streets, simply because they had done so since mediaeval times when Smithfield was well outside the City. London's enormous increase in size during the past half-century, not least in the City Road and Islington area, had created an impossible situation.

Lewis Pocock, of the Islington farming family, a brewer and City Liveryman, who lived at Kilburn Priory, in March 1829 submitted that Islington could offer a good 10-acre walled site, only a couple of miles from the present market but well outside London streets, and well served by roads. Enlarging Smithfield even by an acre would cost £120,000, against the comparatively modest costs of a new site with land available for abattoirs. Butchers could easily ride there, it would have no outside distractions, and carriage roads would suffer no market-day hindrance.

Pocock's suggested site was west of "the excellent establishment of Mr Laycock", with provision of a house for the Clerk of the Market and the Market Keepers, money-takers' offices, and efficient arrangements for identifying and registering the animals, their arrival, owners and other particulars. Such details suggest that Smithfield lacked even these elementary records and precautions. There would be no Sunday movement. The animals would rest overnight (4d a night per 'beast', 2d per sheep), to prevent the cruel and "feverish haste" with which London drovers notoriously handled and slaughtered their animals. Precautions included a protective outer fence, avoidance of crowding and cruel handling by tying animals head-to-wall to prevent scaring by passers-by, pens graduated in size, and buyers' viewing-places.

Pocock estimated costs at £23,000, including £7,000 for the site, and detailed costs of wall, roofing, Clerk's house and offices, railings, water-pipes and tanks, and wages for the Clerk, under-clerks, market keepers, cattle workers, four watchmen and 20 labourers. This compared favourably with Smithfield's City charges of £5,255, salesmen's fees amounting to about £11,300 for two nights for over 150,000 beasts and nearly as many sheep, and about £7,500 drivers' charges, totalling £24,218. He calculated a profit for the proposed new market of more than £19,000.[6]

Suggestions and arguments were now rolling in, many published as broadsides, critical of present conditions and pressing for removal. In 1833, a petition by about 90,000 people for Sunday closure of markets and unregulated places like gin-shops, resulted in a Select Committee, chaired by Sir Andrew Agnew. They put forward a Bill for the Better Observation of the Sabbath (March); but while prohibiting gin-shop opening under threat of heavy penalty, it also introduced unpractical regulations, forbidding even a Sunday meal in a pub unless one had stayed overnight. It also debarred Sunday hiring of vehicles, except for church or sick visiting – ignoring the thousands who could travel in their own carriages. However, by moving markets from Monday to Tuesday, the evils of Sunday work and traffic would be lessened.[7]

MR PERKINS' MARKET

At last a concrete offer was put forward for an Islington site, by a landowner from Bletchingley in Surrey. He was Mr John Perkins, who bought 15 acres of Thomas Scott's brickfield on the Lower Road (Essex Road), where for a sum over £100,000 he proposed to build a market with adequate drainage and water-supply.

There was instant opposition from the Corporation and City publicans, not to mention the salesmen, who feared that a new well-organised market would tempt corn-dealers to come in as well. By the time Perkins' preparations to build had begun, the powers were ranged against him. Just before Christmas

78. *The entrance to Mr Perkins' cattle market.*

1833 the Master Butchers held a protest meeting at Butchers' Hall in Little Britain, on the grounds that since Smithfield had been improved, the market in Islington was needless, and that there was better access to Smithfield since the building of New North Road, avoiding driving cattle through Holborn. They claimed also that abattoirs were "unfavourable" to humane treatment.

By then Perkins' new market's handsome entrance portico was built – a kind of echo of Ridley's floorcloth manufactory along the road, with a pediment and tall entrance arch flanked by smaller pedestrian entrances. Cattle sheds and lairs were also complete, and they were already gravelling the centre for sheep pens and the covered Market Exchange. Pinnock's new *Guide to Knowledge*, providing a very inaccurate engraving, urged the authorities to support it as a boon for economy and humanity. During the next months resolutions were taken to resist the Bill for Islington Market by the Corporation and other bodies. Mr William Giblett, an aptly named Bond Street butcher, as chairman argued against introducing the French abattoir system on the rather specious grounds of the "very serious amount of damage and alarm created by the fast driving of carriages" (or butchers' delivery vans) – and more understandably, that they would lose £5 million a year. Mr Deputy Hicks condemned the plan as "a *plot*" of muddle-headed anti-butchers to end slaughtering in London under the guise of preventing cruelty, whereas it was they who, a year earlier, had scotched a Bill against cruelty. The petition to Parliament to end slaughtering in the City and forbid driving cattle through the streets would, he said, force butchers to the expense of sending cattle miles away, with the danger of meat going off. Among other emotional arguments, Mr Hicks praised London butchers for "their industry, their integrity, and he would fearlessly add, their humanity and general good conduct", their reputation "not easily to be shaken ... by cant and hypocrisy". These starry characters now faced ruin.

Perkins' Islington establishment was seen as the thin end of the wedge, for the Government was now talking of four such new markets. A petition to the Lord Mayor and Court of Common Council insisted that Smithfield was indispensable, a single market was best, and far from closing, it should be enlarged. Perkins persisted. The Islington Market Bill had its first reading on 14 March 1834 and was referred to Committee on 24 April, where the Parliamentary Agent Charles Pearson argued fiercely against it, in a polemic extending to 38 pages in the report.

Maintaining that the Islington market would need a lengthy sewer to the Thames, he tried to prove that it was lower in elevation than Smithfield and could never be well drained. He also disclaimed the good road access, as some roads were not yet even applied for, especially on the de Beauvoir estate on the Hackney side and on Thomas Scott's land. However, the Bill passed.

Late in 1835, when the market was largely built, Samuel Rhodes brought a case against Perkins for compensation for loss of his property required to make the roads. He had called in an architect, Joseph Parkinson, familiar with local property, who claimed it was good building land, mostly undeveloped, and he estimated a high value as some 80 houses (4th-rate) could have been built there. He quoted as an example Mr Brookes, who had converted his market gardens to building land,

but as the 'carcases' of houses were now left unfinished, high compensation was being demanded.

Perkins' counsel, Mr Thesiger, replied that Rhodes had already been offered £1,200, more than the land was worth, and dismissed the arguments about the roads as specious, and the action as a ploy to secure compensation. He reminded the claimant that Perkins was paying the Corporation a large annual sum, and if the same were now awarded to Rhodes but the market failed, his compensation plea would have been based on an inflated premise.

Yet, in summing up, the Under-Sheriff Mr Burchell deemed that the claimant was entitled to full payment for his lost land, though he urged the jury not to propose "vindictive damages" as the action was taken under Act of Parliament, for the public good. The jury returned for Rhodes, who was awarded £1,307.

In the teeth of such odds, the market in Essex Road opened on 10 April 1836, to a cacophony of protests from vested interests. It was 15 acres in extent and enclosed by a 10-foot wall, it was near the Ball's Pond turnpike and thus accessible to major roads. Cattle sheds for 800 animals in pens and stalls provided accommodation for feeding and watering until market day. Sewers had been laid, a wind-pump and cisterns installed, there was an inn with stabling for the drovers, and the central circle intended for a salesmen's and graziers' Exchange was served by good roads, under construction, as were the contentious French-style abattoirs. The arched entrance containing offices was set back 60 feet from Essex Road, where a short row of houses with shop fronts was built "in the embellished style now common in the new streets of the metropolis". These were the present numbers 324–340, whose Tudoresque gables somewhat resembled Lonsdale Square. The Corporation, enlisting support from certain journals in its vindictive campaign, accused Perkins of "charlatanry and delusion . . . palmed on the public", and "trickery and misrepresentation" in getting the Bill passed, on the pretext of wanting to break the City's monopoly while trying to close Smithfield altogether.[8] Every possible petty objection was wheeled out. They even argued that Smithfield was not really in central London but "not a mile from the Peacock in Islington, which is not I fancy called London". Perkins' effort to build abattoirs was derided because "no Englishman was offended by the sight of fine cattle driven through the streets". St John Street and Clerkenwell might as well complain of noise at night as Mayfair of carriages after a ball.

Insults in the name of outraged philanthropy were hurled at Perkins and his achievement, with the pretence that never in 20 years had the writer heard of ill-usage at Smithfield, nor of a farthing lost through neglect.

Sadly, the rest of the story is soon told. Sales figures were not encouraging. In the first few weeks, for example, while Smithfield sold 2,346 'beasts' and 15,010 sheep and lambs, Islington sold only 346 and 2,300, a poor showing of which the hostile press made great publicity. Supporters did their best. Perkins advertised his venture by poster, listing the many counties backing him, mainly in the Midlands and East Anglia, and claiming aristocratic land-owners such as Coke of Holkham, the Duke of Norfolk, and Lords Lynedoch and Ludlow, who declared themselves convinced of the good promised by the reformed-style market.

Had it not been for the entrenched opposition, Perkins' market would have had everything going for it – clean air, space, accessibility both from the main roads from north and east and from the City, and new buildings. Samuel Lewis, who in his *History of Islington* lists its accommodation as 7,500 cattle and calves, 40,000 sheep and 1,000 pigs, ignores all the well-rehearsed arguments against Smithfield and timidly claims that such an attempt to rival it "in a comparatively inconvenient situation, could not be otherwise than vain", and quotes the pathetic figures for its first 8-months' sales, of all animals Smithfield 1,140,697, Islington 87,845.[9]

The Corporation and Smithfield's vested interests effectively saw Perkins off (just as they saw off later a new fish market in Limehouse to rival the inaccessible Billingsgate), and after struggling against adverse publicity and derisory sales, within a year his market closed (1837), remaining in use only for cattle lairs.

For the next few years the market was derelict, as if awaiting reopening, and indeed ten years later it seemed just possible that it might. The anti-Smithfield campaign revived, and thoughts turned towards Islington Market. Early in 1847 William Hewitt, of *Hewitt's Journal*, urged the public to walk over one Sunday to take a look at the 10 acres of abattoirs, 15 of animal space, sheds and pens for thousands of animals, awaiting the "dawn of common sense in London". The author recalled seeing this "vast scheme interrupted by as vast a disappointment" and never fully completed. Waxing lyrical over the unrealised opportunity, the perfect alternative to Smithfield, which had lost its promoter Perkins £100,000, he urged its resuscitation.[10]

By degrees public interest was roused. Nearly two years later agitation from the new Sanitary Reform movement led its new proprietors in January 1849 to repair the now decaying buildings and open the site to visitors. Several thousand were said to come if only out of curiosity. It was still being used in a very small way, boarding cattle by the day or week, with a few sales. Its capacity was again advertised, and the public were reminded that the site was larger than Russell Square or Lincoln's Inn Fields. An added attraction was the East and West India Dock Railway (later to become the North London Railway) a mere quarter of a mile away.[11]

But Mr Perkins in the meantime had died, and his two sisters not unnaturally had no interest in reviving the venture. In 1850 the Islington Cattle Market Company were negotiating for a public slaughterhouse, and in 1851 the late Mr Perkins' brother-in-law, the MP Mr Trotter, offered the site for sale to the Court of Common Council. In 1852 it was auctioned, but as building and residential land rather than as a market. On the space were built the long and rather monotonous streets, Northchurch, Englefield and Ockendon Roads, and but for the surviving gabled houses in the Essex Road, now fronted by shops, one would never know that this contentious market had ever existed.

By then even the Corporation, the landowners and the butchers admitted that Smithfield, as a live cattle market, was doomed.

LOCAL SHOPS

The Post Office Trade Directory of 1841 lists for London 430 corn dealers, 2,408 bakers, 1,634 butchers (meat was a relative luxury), 2,676 grocers and tea-dealers, 1,696 merchants – that is to say wholesale dealers – and 4,416 publicans. During the first half of the century, shops were still small single-fronted affairs, and the life of the shop assistant was probably a good deal harder than that of the house servant.

In the food trade, poultry was disposed of from Leadenhall Street, fish from Billingsgate, dairy produce from Newgate Market, and vegetables from Covent Garden, while at Smithfield two million cattle and sheep were sold annually. Dairy products, fruit and vegetables were also usually sold in the markets and often in the street.

Tradesmen at that time had to have certain skills. Grocers especially had to blend their own teas, mix spices and cure their own bacon. Sugar, sold in conical sugar-loaves, had to be cut and ground, coffee to be roasted. All goods on sale were separately weighed and packeted in the shop.

A branch of trade which today means little or nothing was that of the oil and colourman, who dealt not so much in artist's materials as in those essential household adjuncts, oil for lamps, cooking oils, and house paints. Candle-makers too were vital providers, from the wax candles of the rich to the tallow of the poor, and the useful taper. And of other essentials for daily living, cutlery came from Sheffield while clocks and watches were made in Clerkenwell. Sugar refining was done in Whitechapel, often by Germans, while many dairymen came from Devon or Wales. Welsh people were especially employed in north Clerkenwell. Cheesemen came from Yorkshire or Hampshire, bacon dealers from Wiltshire. As for beer, though country ales were popular, brewing was a favourite London trade. In the clothing trade, besides tailors, bootmakers, hatters, hosiers and mercers, all were skilled specialists. Drapery and haberdashery goods were often the province of travelling pedlars and chapmen. Clothing materials were also localised: cotton came from Manchester, linen from Leeds and Northern Ireland, silk from Derby, Manchester or Macclesfield and other northern sources – though Spitalfields still housed a few strug-

79. Shops in the High Street, 1850. On the left is White Lion Street: the site there is now occupied by Prêt à Manger. To the right is the turnpike and the beginning of Liverpool Road.

gling handloom operators, for example in the umbrella and parasol trade. Wool came from Yorkshire, lace was from Nottingham, gloves were from Worcester (or Derby, if silk), and hats and 'beavers' from London itself – for example Mr Wontner's factory.[12] The silk plush to make hats was found in Spitalfields, but also imported from Lyons. Small dress accessories came from Birmingham. And the essential needles to put all together came from Redditch.

The shops selling these wares were, as we have seen, modest in size, though from Regency times increased sophistication began to appear, especially among linen drapers who wanted to be fashionable. Desire for a good address led to taking over and rebuilding a shop-front on a modish site, "a good outside", says Pierce Egan in *Real Life in London* (1821), "being considered the first and indispensable requisite", regardless of expense. A shop owner would often sink all his capital in the process and on stocking the interior (on credit), hoping to lure customers by the dazzling frontage or his "puff" advertisements. One elegant shopping place was Ludgate Hill, the prime attraction being its glass windows – so much so that one countryman supposedly thought a certain shop must be a looking-glass factory. In their modest way Islington's High Street and Upper Street were also a fashionable if local centre.

In about 1835 the young Charles Dickens wrote of the changing style of shopping in *Sketches by Boz.* He observes how in the late 1820s linen-drapers and haberdashers indulged in an 'epidemic' of display, chiefly "an inordinate love of plate-glass, and a passion for gas-lights and gilding". As it spread, "quiet dusty old shops . . . were pulled down; spacious premises with stuccoed fronts and gold letters were erected instead; floors were covered with Turkey carpets, roofs supported by massive pillars; doors knocked into windows . . . one shopman into a dozen." The fashion shortly spread to chemists, then to public houses.

A prime cause of this revolution was the expanding cotton industry, pouring out Manchester goods in the form of sheetings, shirtings, linens and velvets, and promoted by the hard sell – salesmanship becoming a vital feature of shopping. Apprentices became counter-hands, though still lodged at the shop. They were, too, almost entirely young men, the shop-girl's emergence coming much later on. During the inordinately long shop hours – 'early closing' was a much later concept – the luckless shop-man or boy was expected to be ever on his feet and attentive. The idea of a Saturday half-day was tardy in coming: shopkeepers and moralists feared that leisure time would only induce drinking. In fact it was to spur the popularity of sports – and bicycling. For a long period about half of shops opened on Sunday mornings as well. Wages, between about £25 and £40 a year, usually included board, with young shop assistants quite commonly sleeping in the attics above the shop and storerooms, or in the larger shops in dormitories.

The awful Mrs Caudle, eternally treating her mild husband to 'curtain lectures' during the watches of the night, defends their conditions. "What are shops for, if they're not always to attend upon their customers?... Humanity, indeed, for a pack of tall, strapping young fellows . . . And what do they have to do? Why nothing, but to stand behind a counter, and talk civilly . . . and as a matter of principle – I'll always go to the shop that keeps open latest."[13] This was in the 1840s, and a common attitude for many years after.

One of Islington's earliest recorded shops that survived until the later 20th century was Beale's in the Holloway Road, founded by members of an old-established Hertfordshire family from the Royston area: farmers, millers, innkeepers. They first opened a bakery in Oxford Street in 1769, and another in Wigmore Street before a nephew, Edward, moved to Islington in 1829 and started up at 45 Popham Street. *His* nephew, William, having learned the job from his uncle, moved to a shop in Holloway Road in 1866. In 1869 having acquired adjoining properties, on the site of 372–4 Holloway Road and 2–10 Tollington Road, he built a shop in grand Gothic Revival style, in red brick with stone and mosaic decoration, designed by the architect F. Wallen.

This was the usual style of a success story in retailing: an enterprising, ambitious tradesman having started in a small way, as did Edward Beale – and much later the Jones Brothers – made a success of a small shop and acquired the one next door, then one next to that, and so on. Later they or their descendants in the late 19th or early 20th century combined their string of properties in a total rebuild as grander architect-designed premises, at the same time expanding to take in a wider range of specialised goods.

Similarly in 1867 William Jones came to London as a draper's apprentice. Later, with his brother John, he opened a small shop in Holloway Road, enlarged it several times as they became successful, eventually owning numbers 348–66 Holloway Road, which they rebuilt.

On the whole shops were meanwhile still small, independent one-man affairs. It was drapers who first introduced mass-produced goods and became the go-ahead side of trade. Novel examples were sales of 'seconds' or defective goods, issuing handbills advertising a reduction for the sake of quick returns, and among the less smart shops, price tickets (not considered genteel). Indeed, prices were not really fixed until the 1850s, and price tickets were hardly seen until the age of the department store. [14]

A fictitious account of certain shops in a facetious work by Albert Smith gives a thumbnail account of their appearance in the 1840s. One is curiously termed "a doctor's shop" – just like a chemist's and druggist's but for its framed Apothecaries' Company diploma displayed in the window. It is supposedly in the St John Street area, "a blue-bottle shop, as we used to call them, with penny pitch-plasters in the window . . . and the red bull's-eye lamp over the door formed a principal object in the thoroughfare".

The window has an elaborate display of "elegant arabesques of teeth upon black velvet tablets . . . mysterious instruments and chemical apparatus, of curiously incomprehensible shapes . . . packets of soda-powders, whose blue and white envelopes give an animated appearance to the window, heightened by the dusky red of the ready-made pitch-plasters, and the doubtful white of the plaster-of-Paris horse, which occupied the centre pane . . . announcements in gold letters upon gloss slips, similar to those we see at pastry-cooks, except that they notified 'bleeding', and 'patent medicines' instead of ices and ginger beer".

A doctor living in the next street casts doubt on this shop's respectability, claiming that it "also sold lucifers, Windsor soap, jujubes, and tooth-brushes". [15]

Some shops benefited from others' failures. Early in the 1850s Edward Wason Freeman, a dealer in Leghorn hats, advertised from 11 Clerk's Place (off Islington High Street) that "prior to the breaking up of large establishments" he had bought up stock from different manufacturers and could now offer "an enormous amount of Goods, consisting of Plain and Fancy Straws, Tuscan, &c.; which I am determined to sell at a shade of profit". He attributed his success to a depression in Continental trade, doubtless the result of the 1848 revolutions which swept Europe, leading to quantities of goods being brought to England and sold at a loss. Claiming to be "one of the largest Buyers and Importers of Leghorn Hats, Swiss Trimmings, Tuscan Plaits, &c.", he had secured the first offer, and now preened himself on the elegance and sophistication of his goods and their sale "under the Superintendence of an eminent *Marchande des modes*". [16] Such superiority sounds unlike the rackety main Islington street of to-day.

At the lowest level something that passed for a shop is described by Andrew Mullins, a poor boy who made good, brought up probably in Clerkenwell early in the century, living with his parents and two siblings in one top-floor room in a house containing a dozen families. In the lower part a porter's wife ran "a miscellaneous store, called a green-grocer's", which also ran to a side of bacon, a barrel of small beer, red herrings, a black can of new milk', and also "Warren's blacking and Flanders' bricks". In the window were displayed "lolly pops, Buonaparte's ribs, and bulls'-eyes". One pane of the window exhibited Andrew's father's cobbler's signboard. [17]

In the 1840s a French touch was considered a lure. Gillingwater's, at 140 Upper Street at the corner of Barnsbury Street, specialised in dressing-cases, gentlemen's wigs and other ornaments, and offered haircutting rooms "attended by Parisian and British Artists" and "received the Fashions from Paris every Week". The 'artists' also dressed ladies for Court appearances and would wait on them "at any distance". [18] Meanwhile England was not yet wholly industrialised, the power-machine had not yet taken over from the hand-worker, and specialist flower-makers and featherdressers still worked in Clerkenwell. The new railways and steamships had so far not made a great effect on foreign markets.

THE ISLINGTON BAZAAR

From the turn of the half-century a new kind of shopping appeared, signifying increased middle-class prosperity: Islington's fashionable High Street/Upper Street was adorned with a free-standing block opened as the Islington Bazaar. The very name conjured up a picture of the exotic East and oriental imports. The entrepreneur was Mr William Timewell of Essex Road, and although it incurred criticism and like many enterprises its launch was delayed, the opening in July 1851 with a grand concert was hailed as a splendid venture supported by "the wealthy and respectable inhabitants of the favourite and very extensive district of Islington".

Like many a village or market town main street, High Street and Upper Street were originally a broad market-place in which, as building pressure mounted, the open space was encroached on by free-standing blocks with narrow passages behind. Islington Bazaar was to be one of these. "We fear this will prove a bad speculation", observed *The Ratepayer* in November 1850, "and are sorry that the piece of ground . . . has not been appropriated to a better purpose." But it was a sign of the times.

It was indeed a new departure, a block 175 feet long with four entrances leading to a central 'promenade', designed to accommodate 15 shops on either side, with a gallery above for stalls – and lit by gas. It occupied part of the wide section in the High Street. The grand concert opening, surely one of the first ever given in Islington, included not only singers (two of them *foreign* – a real sign of fashion) but instrumentalists claimed as celebrities: one, Leon Reynier, the First Violin, from the Paris Conservatoire, another was Frederick Chatterton, harpist to the exiled Queen of the French. This ensured the Bazaar's right to be a "favourite place of resort, where business and amusement may be combined". Recitals on alternate evenings followed, and the room

doubled as a lecture-theatre, open to visitors. Even the 10-minute omnibus service to the West End (price 4d) was advertised as a draw.

The press generally were supportive of the venture, yet it was perhaps not the unqualified commercial success it claimed to be, for in ensuing years it was let to different firms. Indeed, as it had been an expensive venture to launch, popularity was essential, "with a view to afford that accommodation to the Respectable inhabitants of Islington, Highbury, Holloway and their vicinities which has been so long needed . . ."[19]

Tenancy seems to have changed fairly often. A year after opening sales were being advertised for Burton and Graham's "new Auction Rooms" at the Bazaar, of "Tunisian, French and Swiss Collections from the Great Exhibition". There were said to be more than 17,000 items, as well as dress fabrics "fresh from the Workshops of 13 Eminent British Merchant Manufacturers", all brought from the City, for a six-day sale running from 10 in the morning to 8 at night. Exotic items advertised included "Indian prayer carpets", porcelain, gold embroidered shawls, caskets inlaid with jewels, painted gauze shawls and silvery tissues from India, and many more luxuries such as oriental carpets. All was optimistically offered to "Ladies of the highest Rank, as well as to the demands of millions".

The following October the Rooms were let to the British and Foreign Commercial Association, converted to a warehouse and sale-room for other luxury textile goods "for the express object of providing the Nobility, Gentry, and the Million" at wholesale prices, at least 30 per cent below normal retail – apparently a novel idea in salesmanship, borrowed from Paris. Another new idea was the promise that "warehousemen" would not (as was then customary) badger customers by bullying salesmanship, but would avoid "abuses which are sanctioned by employers in shops, in furtherance of their nefarious pursuits". This time the goods came from other British markets – muslins and damasks from Manchester, woollens from Leeds, shawls from Paisley and other Scottish centres.

The next occupants, advertising in 1854, were Margetson and Haywood, merchants in bedding, cabinet furniture, carpets and general upholsterers. Thomas Tomlins in 1858 refers to the Bazaar as "the large building opposite Pullin's Place and Rufford's Buildings . . . now occupied as an Upholsterer's Show Room".[20]

FASHIONABLE STREETS

In the later 19th century not only Upper Street but the Holloway Road attracted carriage trade. And with public transport at five-minute intervals costing only 4d a ride, Islington was well placed for shopping. So fashionable was it that in setting up his shop in 1863, William Whiteley hesitated between Upper Street and Westbourne Grove – but apparently opted for the latter because it was then *less* fashionable, so that he would there meet with less competition.

In the northern part of Upper Street were Rackstraw's and T R Roberts, two enterprising firms who were expanding both premises and scope. One way and another Islington became a place to buy underwear. In 1881 *Sylvia's Home Journal* recommended Islington

as "classic ground" for buying a trousseau and especially for lingerie – for example, E Avis & Co. specialised in handmade, and in 'Spatula' corsets. R Allin, at 73 Upper Street (and also at 464 Kingsland Road) provided hand-made underwear and styled themselves "The Universal Outfitter" with a variety of choice.[21] In the 1880s, indeed, any enterprising, rising trader with some capital could set up shop with a reasonable hope of success.[22]

The multiple store arrived only in the 1890s, by which time Beale's in the Holloway Road were delivering to 2,000 families a day, and kept 14 horses and vans for delivery, and 15 horses and vans for catering. They had banqueting rooms at the Athenaeum in Camden Road (a building that previously housed a Literary & Scientific Institution), and Assembly Rooms in Holloway Road. Jones Brothers, meanwhile, continuing to be enlarged, had warehouses, workshops, rooms for their assistants above the shop, and stabling for 50 horses.

There was also great expansion in the grocery line. Thomas Lipton, a friend of Edward,

80. Rackstraw's in Upper Street. The site is now occupied by Budgen's supermarket.

Prince of Wales and of William Whiteley, ran 70 shops, of which at least one was in Islington, and other grocers followed. Sainsbury's started in 1869, and in 1882 John James Sainsbury opened his first Islington shop at 48 Chapel Street, managed by his son John Benjamin. This proved so great a success that one Friday it reached record sales of £400. It had open windows, and was one of the shops that kept a stall outside. Cheese was sold from the left-hand window, bacon from the right, and on the stall eggs – which at that time cost a shilling a dozen – and 'Ostend rabbits' and pickled pork. In 1887 only three doors away, at number 51, the firm established its first shop specialising in game, and in 1889 another provisions branch followed. Even so there was room for expansion, and in 1894 Sainsbury took over George Jackson the 'butterman's' at number 44, and converted it into a dairy. This was not a success and closed in 1916, but the game branch increased in sales and in 1898 moved to 43 Islington High Street nearby. Trade at these individual shops continued until conversion to supermarket style in the 1960s.[23]

The small size of the average shop limited it to single types of goods, such as tobacco, sweets, or toys. Larger shops installed the popular 'cash railway' by which payment and bill, placed in a kind of cup on an overhead line, were despatched by a lever. Shop interiors, contrasting with their garish exteriors often plastered with advertisements, were not glamorous. In poorer streets only cheaper goods of inferior quality were sold in humble settings.

Shopping remained local until early in the 20th century when the department store and the lure of the West End took over. At much the same time the obsequious personal service from the assistant and even from the proprietor gave way to the more impersonal.[24] In the late 19th century the more prosperous suburbs were so well supplied that for fashion shopping the West End was still not essential. Not only Whiteley's in Bayswater, but Islington, Hackney, Clapham and Brixton could offer stylish service: "quite independent of the City and of the West End", writes Besant in 1909.[25] There was of course a hierarchy, as Booth points out in 1903: so that by the 1870s "Walworth is as much above Bermondsey New Road as Lewisham or Holloway would consider themselves above Walworth".[26]

1	John Wight, *Sunday in London*, London, 1833, pp. 68ff.
2	Carlyle, *Correspondence*, Carlyle to his brother Alexander, 14 December 1824, Vol. III, pp. 218-9.
3	*The Lady's Newspaper*, 20 January 1849.
4	Thomas Miller, *Picturesque Sketches of London*, London, 1852, p. 174.
5	*The Mirror*, 2 February 1828.
6	Guildhall Broadsides 27/7, Guildhall Library, London.
7	Wight, *Sunday in London*.
8	*Northampton Herald*, 7 May 1836.
9	Lewis, *Islington*, pp. 308-9.
10	*Hewitt's Journal*, 6 February 1847.
11	*Weekly Dispatch*, 4 January 1849.
12	For Wontner's factory, see Chapter 25.
13	Douglas Jerrold, *Mrs Caudle's Curtain Lectures*, London, 1846; 1902 edn, pp. 121-4.
14	Beale's Limited, *Two Hundred Years 1769–1969*, p.p. pamphlet, 1969; for Jones Bros' rebuilding, *Warehousemen's & Drapers' Trade Journal*, 14 May 1892; *The Builder*, 22 October 1892, p. 325; Alison Adbergham, *Shops and Shopping*, London, 1964, revised edn 1981, and *Shopping in Style*, London, 1979; L C B Seaman, *Life in Victorian London*, London, 1973.
15	Albert Smith, *The Adventures of Mr Ledbury, and his Friend Jack Johnson*, London, 1886 (1st edn 1840s).
16	*Islington, Hornsey, Highgate & Kentish Town Family Newspaper*, No. 1, 5 May 1855.
17	Robert Seymour, *Humorous Sketches*, London, 1838, Vol. II.
18	Advertisement in Islington Local History Library, Shops Collection.
19	*Lady's Newspaper*, 19 July 1851; illustrated handbill, 1852 and other, mostly undated and unidentified, cuttings in Islington Libraries, Local History collection. See also *VCH*, p. 15. The building was demolished in the 1960s and left as an open space and Angel bus stops.
20	Tomlins, *Yseldon*, p. 91*n*.
21	Adbergham, *Shopping in Style*, p. 140.
22	Adbergham, *Shops and Shopping*, p. 151.
23	Sainsbury's Journal, [?1989]; 'Two Hundred Years 1769–1969', Beale's Ltd, 1969.
24	Alastair Service, *London 1900*, London, 1979.
25	Walter Besant, *London in the 19th Century*, London, 1909, p. 30.
26	Charles Booth, *Life and Labour of the People in London*, Second Series, Industry, 1903, Vol. III pp. 68-9.

CHAPTER 25

Working Lives

AGRICULTURE

Before Islington was built over, agriculture, and especially dairy-farming was its most important occupation. And while some crops were evidently grown, as London expanded in Tudor times grazing was important enough to convert arable land back to pasture, which butchers rented for fattening cattle. In 1714 a serious outbreak of Rinderpest or cattle fever occurred in the parish. It was carried by a virus which caused acute inflammation of the mucous membrane and intestines. In this outbreak 667 cows were destroyed, including most of those of the local farmer Rufford (62 out of 72), and nearly half of Samuel Pullin's (38 out of 87).[1]

Early in the 19th century large farms began to take over from the small dairymen, and Richard Laycock and Samuel Rhodes, already important farmers and local vestrymen, became even more prominent. Samuel Pullin, another vestryman, farming land near the Angel off the High Street, had maintained up to 100 cows; his name was perpetuated in Pullin's Row, a terrace in the High Street. By about 1810 his farm was taken over by Samuel Rhodes, owner of even more cattle, also making thousands of loads of hay, which was kept stacked nearby.[2] Rhodes bought 3 acres of Hattersfield in 1810 from Gerard Noel, all land which in the next couple of decades was built over. He also owned land off Liverpool Road, of which in 1815 he gave half an acre for schools for the new St Mary Magdalene;[3] further, he had invested in land in Stoke Newington (1821), which later family members, after using it for brickfields, then devel-

oped for housing.[4] The Rhodes family also held a great deal of farming land in St Pancras – one of their descendants was the colonialist, Cecil Rhodes, who founded Rhodesia.

Richard Laycock was active in farming for 40 years until his death in 1834. His land stretched north and west of Upper Street, cut through by a lane to Liverpool Road, nowadays called Laycock Street. His hay was stacked near Hornsey Road, and he owned more land at Enfield. Laycock's farm was even larger than that of Samuel Rhodes, with up to 700 cows and more than 100 carthorses to draw the grain and root-crops used for feed. On his Islington land, besides the inevitable stables and cowhouses were all kinds of barns, storehouses, blacksmiths' and wheelwrights' shops, not to mention sawpits and

81. Trade card for Laycock's Dairy Farm in 1847. It was sited across today's Laycock Street between Liverpool Road and Upper Street.

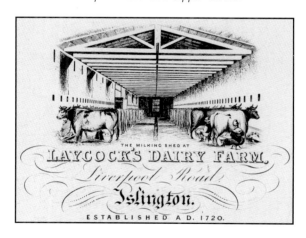

carpenters' shops. He lived on Upper Street in Sebbon's Buildings, fronting his land, and owned much of the adjoining property.[5]

Laycock kept many of the lairs where cattle were herded overnight before being driven down to Smithfield. His lairs were covered, hence more profitable than many others along Liverpool Road.

During Rhodes's and Laycock's lifetimes, local farming was encroached on by building, and they themselves turned farmland into brickfields and ultimately to houses. By the 1840s, cowkeeping survived, but on a much smaller scale. Laycock's successor in 1841 still owned 16 acres of ground, half a dozen cow-sheds each housing over 60 cows, and 5,000 sheep. And well into the 1850s there were more than 50 cow-keepers who owned a few

cattle, scattered through Islington (and even Clerkenwell), but mostly in the more distant, less built-up parts of Holloway and Upper Holloway – even still in Barnsbury. Two of these keepers had 293 and 119 cows each, but the rest far fewer, and living conditions for cattle, by then decidedly cramped and unhealthy, contributed to epidemics and health hazards of the still growing population. Licensing for keeping cattle was not brought in until 1862.[6]

BRICKS AND TILES
In parts of Islington the soil was good for brickmaker's clay. As we have seen (see Chapter 1), in the 14th century clay was being dug in the Prebend manor area east of the High

82. Randall's tile kilns near Battle Bridge.

Street, and recorded again (or still) in the 1590s and in Charles I's time. In 1668, digging was licensed for brick and tile earth in a field behind the Swan inn in the High Street[7] and in 1769 by Thomas Bird behind Bird's Buildings, followed by more such licences, and to a lesser extent was starting up in places such as Vale Royal on the west of the parish.

Then in the 18th century kilns were set up in the Prebend area, in Hattersfield or Tile Kiln Field (1727 and 1735), where Walter Burton had a brewhouse, and near Highbury Corner and Liverpool Road by a brickmaker, John Wells (presumably builder of Wells Row at the north end of Upper Street).[8] And Thomas Scott, who had bought a dairy farm between Frog Lane and Essex Road, bought more land in 1791 between there and the Rosemary Branch, where he started brickfields and began building.[9]

By the 19th century the west side of the parish was equally productive. Adam's tile kilns were the source of chimney pots and garden pots (1810), and in 1828 they were joined by a rival when Randalls moved to Maiden Lane from Bagnigge Wells. By the following year Adam's site included eight acres for tile-making and brick-burning, with large and small kilns, sheds, and workmen's cottages.

NOXIOUS INDUSTRIES

The Maiden Lane area, downhill from the more salubrious heights and close to the River Fleet, became a natural site for less desirable industries, and increasingly important when the new canal provided valuable water transport, and Horsfall's Basin was created. The small settlement of humble cottages became thoroughly industrialised and far from healthy. By 1829 it was wholly a place of noxious industries, known ironically as Belle Isle.

Here were a horse slaughter-house, factories for making grease and for cartwheels, varnish, chimneypots, and a 'feather dressing' factory owned by a Soho firm, Broad, Heal & Co. Another factory in a former pottery boiled bones for making knife handles. A Mr Scheldt's factory made 'patent' yellow paint, a former brewery in 1811 became a vinegar works, while E P Smith, Vaux and Bell's, mustard makers active in 1811, had closed already

by 1829. All these factories were near Battle Bridge, today's King's Cross. A little farther north, Belle Isle had Warner's coach and cart grease works, Margett's (Parker's by 1829) chemical works, the large varnish factory of Wallis and Sons of Long Acre, and another horse slaughterer. Near Battle Bridge, in Albion Yard off Balfe Street, a white lead factory existed from 1832 and between Albion Yard and Maiden Lane was the Pontifex Brass Foundry in Edward Street (now Railway Street). The St Pancras Ironworks was established in 1856.

By the 1850s[10] many poor-quality houses for the workers had been built. There was a local population of nearly 200, and new inhabitants suffered from unpleasant if not toxic fumes and generally disagreeable surroundings. When in 1848 the sanitary inspectors called, they found a repulsive area with open drains, redolent with the smell of pigs kept by many locals alongside their hovels.

Incongruously enough, from the early 1840s a model colony was established nearby according to the principles of the philanthropic industrialist and co-operative promoter Robert Owen. This was in three or four streets between Belle Isle and the Caledonian Road. It was set up by Pierre Henri Joseph Baume[11], Marseille-born socialist, who had served until 1825 as private secretary to King Ferdinand of Naples, then came to England, made money, and used it in idealistic ventures as here at Belle Isle and later on the Isle of Man. Baume let out plots on which he helped with building cottages for a community for whom he set up a school and mission. Appropriately called the Experimental Gardens, and also Frenchman's Colony, or Island (odd recurrence of a name for a very un-island-like site), it was an idealistic small-scale contrast to the neighbouring hell-hole of Belle Isle. Like many such ventures of this period, it did not outlast the initial enthusiasm, and in less than a dozen years seems to have petered out, though in 1851 48 families of craftsmen and labourers were still living there.

By about 1853, though new terraces were beginning to rise in the district, noxious industries continued as a notorious scandal for more than 20 years.

LIGHT INDUSTRIES

Islington's most famous industries at this time, apart from building and brickfields, were its floor-cloth factory and the Rosemary Branch white lead mills. Rubber and associated industries were also established. As early as 1801, at the south end of Hornsey Road, Elizabeth Duke & Co. took out a patent for waterproofing clothes, chiefly army uniforms, and for treating canvas, especially for sails. This prospered during the Napoleonic Wars, but business then fell off, and the works later passed to a Mr Jones, becoming a dye-house, In about 1833 they were demolished and replaced by Ingram Place on the site (in 1877 renumbered as 1–39 Hornsey Road).[12]

According to Lewis's *History*, another rubber works was established in about 1830 by Cornish & Sievier of Holloway, as the Indian Rubber factory, known as the Holloway Mill. This made such items as elastic webs for belts and braces. The works were at the end of the grounds of a 17th-century house owned by one of its co-founders, Robert William Sievier, at the corner of Red Cap Lane (now Elthorne Road), opposite the Mother Redcap inn. Sievier (1794–1865), a stipple-engraver and sculptor, was also a versatile inventor of manufacturing processes, and experimented in electric telegraphy. He doubled the size of his house (which became known as the Old Manor House), and adorned its front with one of his sculptured reliefs.[13]

The firm was incorporated in 1837 as the London Caoutchouc Company – by one of the first Acts to which the young Queen Victoria gave Royal Assent – using steam machinery and employing about 100 workers. For over 20 years Sievier exhibited at the Royal Academy and became an FRS in 1841. His works included portrait busts of the Prince Consort and the king of Prussia, and a statue of Dr Edward Jenner in Gloucester Cathedral.[14]

Also in Hornsey Road, near the corner with Hanley Road, was a lampblack and printer's ink factory. This was set up in 1828 by Thomas Davison, a printer from Whitefriars, Fleet Street, and the product was of high quality; but the process was vulnerable and by 1833 the building, complained of locally, had already been three times burned down. It was again rebuilt with better safety precautions

and its horse-driven machinery was replaced by steam power; the process was served by a 200-foot deep well.[15] The factory was sold in 1853 to Shackell & Edwards, when it continued a nuisance, especially the ink-making.[16]

The famous floor-cloth manufactory, whose Palladian building in Essex Road is now the Borough's Social Service department, was so imposing that contemporary local historians both recorded and illustrated it. Built in 1812, by 1829 it was owned by Samuel Ridley, who ran it in his capacity as "upholsterer workman and floorcloth manufacturer". After passing to his son, and eventually through partnerships, it became Probyn's beer bottling factory in 1893. The grandeur of the building was in Ridley's time marred by strings of advertising lettering covering façade and side walls, and by the fact that its pediment, engaged columns, balustrade punctuated by stone balls, and round-headed ground-floor windows, were not balanced by a single upper-floor window.[17]

This was not the only local floor-cloth manufactory. Another, equally imposing though less handsome, was established across the border in St Pancras by Mann and Surgons at the junction of Camden Road and York Way. It too had classical aspirations, though a clutter of outbuildings rather destroyed the effect.[18]

The white lead factory was at the extreme south-east limit of the parish, behind the Rosemary Branch. Here from 1783 had been a tea-garden, later a pub, famed for its acre of pond on which summer boating and winter skating were popular until it dried up with the spread of house building. In 1788, soon after the Rosemary Branch opened, a lead-grinding works powered by a windmill was built by the Rotherham ironmasters Walker & Co. which had connections with Walkers, Maltby & Co., a London white-lead firm in Upper Thames Street. A second windmill was built in 1792, unusual in having five sails, and for many years the pair formed a striking background to the Essex Road, seen in the distance beyond Ridley's floorcloth factory.

Cromwell refers to the "mystery" of the manufacturing process, described as the action of strong acid on "common lead", when the resulting vapour corroding the metal "reduces it to a white calx, which is afterwards

83. Samuel Ridley's floor-cloth factory in Essex Road.

ground to a proper consistence for use".[19]

By 1833 the sails had been dismantled and like most others, the factory ran on steam, in this case a machine of 20 hp. The firm was under the name of T & C Maltby, employing about 50 people. Two-thirds were women, whose health was considered "less injuriously affected by the unwholesome processes" than "the robuster sex". How this conclusion was reached is not explained. Works were still in existence in 1865.

There was also a variety of small workshops in the parish. One overflow from Clerkenwell was the small watch-spring works and Bull & Smith's cut-glass factory, in Britannia Row off Essex Road. There were also 'rectifying spirits' for gin-distilling, soap making, and variants of the printing and paper-making trade such as the pasteboard maker Thomas Creswick's horse mills in 1816, near the south end of Liverpool Road.

FASHIONABLE HATS

An industry whose founders and their descendants were to make an impact on both Islington and the City was the Wontners' hat factory. Early in the 19th century Thomas Wontner & Co. established a business off the Essex Road in Green Man's Lane, a street named after an old pub. Here up to 50 men were employed sorting skins, especially seal and beaver, for the making of fashionable gentlemen's hats. In 1808 Thomas Wontner built himself a villa north of the lane, which – though the house itself has unfortunately disappeared – was to be the beginning of Tibberton Square, starting with a row of houses he himself built on part of his garden. It was named after his wife's Worcestershire village.

Wontner (1747–1831), a Herefordshire youth, had come to London with his wife and brother, to be apprenticed to the hat trade. He prospered and with his watchmaker brother John moved from their Minories factories to

Islington. Thomas became Master of the Worshipful Company of Felt Makers. His descendants continued to live in the house and are today distinguished figures in the City.[20]

BEER AND SODA WATER

Two sorts of liquor were produced locally. Chief was the distilling and brewing centred in Clerkenwell, but in 1840 Messrs Ufford and Oldershaw, both leading vestrymen (Oldershaw was the son of a former Vestry Clerk), ran the Highbury Brewery off the Holloway Road. By 1840 a well-shaft in the grounds, 104 feet deep, could produce almost 1000 gallons of water an hour. In 1887 the water-level had fallen to 150 feet, and another well was sunk.[21]

On the soft drinks side was John Webb's celebrated soda water factory, opened in 1831 at the end of his garden. It was at the back of Charles Lamb's former cottage in Duncan Terrace, to which Webb had moved, and where he lived until 1844. Advertised as Soda Water maker to the Queen, his factory, powered by steam, was a favourite visit for people eager for information on manufacturing. It later extended as far as Islington Green.[22]

1   *VCH*, p. 70.
2   *VCH*, p. 71.
3   *VCH*, p. 126.
4   *VCH*, pp. 147, 191.
5   *VCH*, p. 71.
6   *Ib*.
7   *VCH*, p. 73.
8   From 1722. *VCH*, p. 15.
9   *VCH*, p. 21.
10 *VCH*, pp. 74, 30.
11 Lewis, *Islington*, p. 70. *VCH*, pp. 30–31. *DNB*, Baume (1797–1875): his name here was anglicised.
12 Cromwell, *Walks Through Islington*, p. 342.
13 Lewis, *Islington*, p. 279; *VCH*, p. 33.
14 *DNB*, Sievier.
15 Cromwell, *Walks Through Islington*, pp. 339–40.
16 Lewis, *Islington*, p. 280; *VCH*, p. 74.
17 In the days of Probyn's bottling factory, the writing was replaced by the more decorative addition to the front of a pair of giant beer bottles. On the factory's conversion in 1972 the picturesque bottles were removed, a matter of some regret.
18 Cromwell, *Walks Through Islington*, pp. 149, 196.
19 *Ib.*, p. 109.
20 Information on Wontner's hat factory was kindly supplied by the late Sit Hugh Wontner and Mr Giles Wontner. See Nelson, *Islington*, p. 186; *Tibberton Square 1839–1979*, Islington Borough Council 1979 (pamphlet); Cosh, *Squares*, Vol. II, p. 146.
21 In 1914 the brewery closed and was taken over by the Brewery Tap, a nearby tavern built in 1815 by the owner of Highbury Barn Tavern, William Willoughby. On the site is now the Flounder and Firkin (54 Holloway Road). (Eric Willats, *Streets with a Story*, Islington Local History Trust, 1988, p. 117.
22 The factory was moved to Lambeth in 1924.

CHAPTER 26

A New Spate of Anglican Churches

By 1840, with Islington's population risen to about 55,000, the Anglican church could cater for just half of the parish inhabitants. By the end of the Crimean War in 1856, when population had more than doubled to about 115,000 church accommodation was merely a quarter of that theoretically needed.

As we have seen *(Chapter 12)* there had been a big expansion of Anglican church building in the first third of the 19th century, largely promoted by the efforts of the Rev. Daniel Wilson Snr, but this soon proved inadequate. The problems were persistent, in an age when religion among the educated and professional classes was fast becoming paramount, and from the 1850s the race between the Established Church and the Non-conformists to fill the gap was to cause a great boom in church building. With the priorities of the time, lack of accommodation for 30,000 souls was seen as a spiritual rather than corporeal problem: few gave as much attention to how many were badly housed, or not housed at all. The primary importance was to serve them through the house of God.

There were also other battles to fight. In 1838 there was great activity by an Association for Promoting a Due Observance of the Lord's Day in Islington. Through a circular issued to 'Masters and Heads of Families', it urged Sunday closing on shopkeepers, who indeed while fearing the loss of custom were said to "almost hail with joy the prospect of a weekly day of rest". The circular therefore exhorted local residents to keep the Sabbath in mind, and to refrain from buying on Sundays, or if employers, to pay wages early on Saturdays so that staff could do their shopping on Saturday night. There was also a meeting that December, with the Vicar in the chair, on a memorial to the Treasury opposing any change in Sunday Post Office business – namely, the proposed Sunday posting of country letters via London's Post Office was contrary to divine law.

In 1854 the religious journalist Ewing Ritchie calculated that the Church of England in London had about 409,000 worshippers, while leading non-conformist churches totalled just over half as many: Congregationalists 100,000, Methodists 60,000, Baptists 54,000.[1]

The 1851 Census of Religious Worship, revealing Islington's shortage of churches, was published only in 1854 during the Crimean War, not an auspicious time to expand, but from 1856 peace offered an opportunity to seek funds. In June 1856 the Rev. Daniel Wilson the younger, through the Islington Church Home Mission, sent to the Church Missionary Society a provisional committee to publicise its campaign. By circulating 7,000 copies of its plan, they amassed more than £5,000 in contributions.[2]

In December at the Parochial Schools in Liverpool Road, with Archibald Tait, Bishop of London in the chair, the Islington Church Extension Society was inaugurated. Wilson, like his father before him, urged a vigorous campaign. On a modest reckoning of 590 persons per 1,000 as capable of attending church, the parish was calculated to need 66,700 seats. Existing Anglican churches provided only 36,150. So, the shortfall was already almost 50 per cent, and population was increasing twice as fast as what the Church could supply.[3]

Twenty years earlier, with a 42,000 population and 9,500 seats, thanks to the then Bishop Blomfield the Metropolitan Churches Fund had voted the three new churches £1,000 each. Disappointed that now not even £10,000 had been raised, Wilson set an example by doubling his own contribution to £100 a year, and proposed that 20 gentlemen repeat their single offers of £50 for several years.

While there was encouraging support in rich areas, poor areas could not contribute. A study of 10 local areas disclosed interesting contrasts. In Arlington Square district, where "a new town has recently grown up" with some 17,000 inhabitants, St Philip's church had been built, but for lack of funds it could not be consecrated by the Bishop, let alone opened, and services were held in a carpenter's shop.

There were two temporary churches, St Luke's, a sub-district of St James's Chillingworth Road, built of wood, and St Barnabas, Hornsey Road, made of iron. While new permanent sites were being made available, in St Bartholomew's, a sub-district of St Stephen's Canonbury Road, in St Michael's (St Andrew's district) and St Clement's near Arundel Square (St James's), services were held in local schoolrooms. So they were at St Silas, off Copenhagen Street, and St Michael's, Caledonian Road, both schools built by Randall of the tile kilns. All Saints district off the Caledonian Road, with only 1,100 seats available for a population of 17,000, needed two churches. The densely populated Angel district and the lead-works area near the Rosemary Branch, at the parish's south-east tip, had no churches at all. These were only the most urgent cases. Foreseeing still further population expansion, churches would also be needed in Highbury New Park, Hornsey Rise (sites were promised in both), in Tufnell Park and Seven Sisters Road.

As for funding, the new Society's committee believed that the sum would soon be raised were each of the 20,000 present worshippers to save even a penny or two a week. But they had to keep their feet on the ground. Though they might build churches, Bishop Tait warned, would the poor enter them? The middle classes went to church, the masses didn't, or wouldn't, so enthusiastic ministers were urgently needed.

The Bishop was therefore surprised to learn from Daniel Wilson that Islington was not only synonymous with world mission – thanks to his father Wilson senior, now Bishop of Calcutta – but it had also a "great home mission". For example, besides the temporary wooden and iron churches, and the schoolroom meetings, services were being held in such makeshift quarters as a cattle shed, a roofed walled garden, and even at the Favorite omnibus yard. So, Wilson argued, potential congregations already existed.

As prominent Church members came forward with donations and support, comparisons with Europe were made: Islington's population was exceeded in France only by Paris and three other cities, and by only one in each of Hungary, Denmark, Poland and the Low Countries. Even in Russia there were only two cities more populous.

Further, with no religious provision for at least 30,000 Islington inhabitants, the 'stone and lime' campaign must not obscure attention to the soul. The backbone of the 'great cause' was the middle classes, while 'free seats' did not ensure strict attention. Children, for instance, usually stowed away in a gallery corner, were left unattended – and unattending.

The Rev. Daniel, repeating in some detail his cogent argument on the crisis, of population rise outstripping the church's spiritual provision, pointed out where money was failing to appear, contrasting well-to-do Highbury, population now up to 2,000, which had built "without much difficulty, an ornamental church" (Christ Church), and populous Arlington Square with 6,000, nearly all of "the industrial classes", where the church built months ago was prevented from consecration by its debt of £1,700.

His proposed Church Extension Society with a six-year target of 10 churches each seating 1,000, would still raise capacity only from 21,000 to 31,000, barely half of the shortfall. [4]

A great outburst of church building followed in the 1850s and 1860s – the Kentish rag period – when at least 17 Anglican churches were built or planned, in stone, and about the same number of non-Establishment churches, Baptist, Methodist, Congregationalist and many others, usually in brick.

84. Christ Church in Highbury.

In 1867 Timbs noted in *Curiosities of London* that of this number built during the last 40 years or so, five were the work of Dove Brothers, the Barnsbury builders. These were St Stephen's Canonbury (1839), St Andrew's, Thornhill Square (1852–4), St Philip's, Arlington Square (1855), St Thomas's, Hemingford Road, architect A. Billing (1859) and St Clement's, near Arundel Square, by George Gilbert Scott (1864–5). In both building and attendance the Established Church was now keeping abreast of the rest. The growth continued in the 1870s, to which belongs the once famous Smithfield Martyrs' Memorial Church in St John Street, begun 1869 and consecrated 1871. This originated with a desire to commemorate the Smithfield Martyrs of the 16th century, as close as possible to the place where they had suffered. It also relieved the church of St James's Clerkenwell of its burden of population, serving the newly growing district of about 8,000 mostly working-class inhabitants, many of them very poor.

For the Martyrs' church a design by E B Lamb was rejected as ugly, and Blackburne's was adopted, with a West tower made of stock brick with Bath stone dressing, and doorways of Ancaster stone. Internally, an aisled nave led to an apsidal chancel with flanking chapels, and columns were of red Mansfield stone, in French early-Gothic style. The West front was adorned with a frieze of 17 statues of English Protestant martyrs, bas-reliefs of martyrdoms, and medallions including of William Tyndale, John Wycliffe, and so on. Scrolls on the walls recorded the martyrs from the House of Lancaster to the last in Tudor times. The church was variously reckoned to hold 900 or 1,000. Lord Shaftesbury laid the foundation stone.

In 1895 the rather top-heavy turreted tower with its high belfry stage proved to be unsafe and was repaired; further repairs were necessary in the new century, and in 1940 the church suffered severe bomb damage. In spite of emergency work it was found necessary to demolish it in 1956. The church has been poorly followed by an undistinguished block of Council flats. [5]

Smithfield Martyrs' church was among those preceded by a temporary iron building. Another was St Augustine's in Highbury New Park (architects Habershon and Brock) – large but "crude" according to Pevsner – begun in 1870 to hold 1,400. Meanwhile Dr Gordon Calthrop officiated nearby for five years in an iron church which itself could hold 900. When it was built the district, also new, was "a region of broad roads and handsome villas ... almost countryfied", as Ewing Ritchie put it. Its inhabitants, "only rich people and people apparently well-to-do", all attended Calthrop's iron church. In this part of Islington there were no poor, so church collections were disposed of between neighbouring churches. The congregation included students from the nearby Church of England missionary college, who also taught in local Sunday schools. Calthrop, a Cambridge man compared by some to the famous preacher Dr Spurgeon, was a good platform and outdoor speaker. Indeed, Ritchie claimed, "the North of London is favoured as regards clergymen".

A humbler church starting off with a temporary structure was St Thomas's, Hemingford Road, of 1859–60 by Arthur Billing in Decorated style. It was a poor district and at that time a new one, numbering 3,000 persons. Here the Rev. George Augustus Todd worked for some months in 1855 with neither church nor school, at times preaching out-of-doors in Pulteney Street (itself later demolished to form Barnard Park). That winter they found a room, then a larger room, then formed a Sunday school for 25 "neglected children of the neighbourhood" until able to build a schoolroom. Numbers increased, until the permanent church was completed by Dove Brothers in 1860. Critics condemned St Thomas's for being cheap (they were very short of funds, and it cost less than £5,000), and that it did not run to a tower, merely a bellcote. It was damaged during the 2nd World War and later demolished, its congregation merging with St Andrew's, Thornhill Square. St Thomas's site is now part of Barnard Park.

St Andrew's was an altogether grander affair. Its architects were Newman (with whom Billing was to go into partnership) and Johnson; its site was presented by the estate's owner, George Thornhill. The church, which cost £6,000 and could hold more than 1,500, was consecrated in January 1854.[6] It was cruciform, in what contemporaries termed 'Middle Pointed' style, in Kentish rag and Bath stone, with tower and spire at the West end of the south aisle. The pulpit was of Caen stone.

These are just a few of the backgrounds to the building of Islington's Victorian churches.

To summarise: churches of the 1850s were: St Matthew's, Essex Road, starting in 1836 as a temporary Episcopal chapel and built 1850–51 (demolished); St Mark's, Tollington Park (1854) and St Jude, Mildmay Grove (1855), both by A D Gough with later alterations; St Philip's, Arlington Square (1858) (demolished); St Luke's, Penn and Hillmarton Roads (1859–60).

In the 1860s were: St Mary's, Hornsey Rise (1860–1) by A D Gough; St Clement's, Arundel Square (1864–5) by Sir George Gilbert Scott); St Bartholomew's, Shepperton Road (1865); St George's, Carleton Road by George Truefitt, and St Saviour's, Aberdeen Park by William White – the church commemorated by John Betjeman – both started 1865; St David's, Westbourne Road (1866–9) by E L Blackburne, St Matthias, Caledonian Road (1868).

In the 1870s: St Augustine, Highbury New Park (temporary 1864) (1869–70); St Paul's, Kingsdown Road (1870); St Anne's, Poole Park (1871); St James the Apostle, Prebend Street (1873–5), St John the Baptist, Cleveland Road (1873); St Peter, Dartmouth Park Hill (1879–80).

In the 1880s and 90s: St John's, Highbury Park (iron 1875) (1882); Emmanuel, Hornsey Road (1884); All Saints, Dalmeny Road (1884–5); St Saviour's, Hanley Road, (1887–8); St Thomas's, St Thomas's Road (1888–9); St Andrew's, Whitehall Park (1894–5).

By 1914 there were 41 Anglican churches in Islington, mostly with attached missions. In 1989, after mergers and demolitions, there were 18.

1   J Ewing Ritchie, *The London Pulpit*, London, 1854; Circular, "Masters and Heads of Families", 1838, issued by the Association for Promoting a Due Observance of the Lord's Day in Islington. (Islington Local History Library)

2   1851 Census of Religious Worship (published 1854).

3   Reports of Proceedings at the Inaugural Meeting of the Islington Church Extension Society, London, 1857.

4   *Ibid.*

5   Pevsner, *London Except the Cities*, p. 114, dismisses the church in two lines as "quite uncommonly ugly". Contemporary descriptions in *The Builder*, 25 February 1871 and *ILN*, 1 July 1871.

6   Cherry & Pevsner, *London 4: North*, p. 654. In 1978 St Andrew's Church was subdivided, not altogether felicitously, to accommodate a meeting space and children's play-groups alongside the congregation area. The fine pulpit was unfortunately removed.

CHAPTER 27

Religion in Many Forms

UNION CHAPEL

Islington's most famous non-Established Victorian church was undoubtedly Union Chapel, removed from Highbury to Compton Terrace and first acquiring its name in 1806 as an Independent foundation. In 1847 it joined the Congregational Union. The church was greatly enlarged under the Rev. Thomas Lewis, in 1836 extending its influence by setting up a school behind for 400 poor children.

Its greatest days followed during the Rev. Henry Allon's ministry, from 1852 to 1892 – Lewis and Allon between them matching the long Anglican ministry of the Daniel Wilsons, father and son, at St Mary's. One of Allon's achievements was to build up Union Chapel's musical fame from a very low standard, adding to the tune-book, introducing a chant, not used until then in non-conformist churches, and in 1859 forming a choir.

Despite old-guard opposition to change, Allon greatly increased his congregation, as the local population rise included many well-to-do Dissenters. In 1859–61, when membership had more than doubled, the church had become "inconveniently crowded", and the building was enlarged to hold another 250 people. At the same time the brilliant Dr Ebenezer Prout was appointed organist. In 1864 Allon achieved the Congregationalists' highest honour, becoming Chairman of the Union, and in 1866 he became an editor of the *British Quarterly Review*. In 1871 Yale University granted him an honorary DD.

Union Chapel's popularity continued to grow to such an extent that by 1876 it was completely rebuilt. After a spell in the customary iron church (in Highbury New Park, taken over from St Augustine's), and alternating with services in Myddelton Hall off Upper Street, the new building by James Cubitt opened in December 1877 to a fortnight of celebration. This huge edifice, the building we know today, is almost unique among non-conformist churches in having adapted the Gothic style to its requirements. Further, its plan was based on Santa Fosca, Torcello, its octagonal interior designed with uninterrupted sight-lines, while a new organ by the famous 'Father' Henry Willis was installed. The solid tower, a new local landmark, was completed only in 1889. One much prized acquisition, donated by Americans in 1883, was a piece of Plymouth Rock, from the landing-place of the Plymouth Fathers of 1620. It was installed above the door to the rear offices.

This was the crowning achievement of Allon's ministry. Having wanted to resign in 1891 he was unanimously persuaded to complete 40 years' service, but unexpectedly died in office just short of that at Easter 1892. Huge crowds turned up at his funeral.

Although Henry Allon's successor, the Rev. W H Harwood, introduced useful changes, as the local population at last began to decline, so did the church's popularity, until its very existence was threatened.[1] In the late 1980s Union Chapel was re-established both as a successful place of worship and, thanks to its fine acoustics, for musical performances and recordings. However, at the time of writing (2005), it is proposed to abandon the use of the church for musical events, and this is causing much dispute among the church members.

HARECOURT CHAPEL

In 1870 Ewing Ritchie remarked on the usually small size of Baptist chapels, and complained of their (to him) "narrow and illiterate" ministers; whereas the Congregationalists had in 1849 founded a chapel building society to aid the building of 87 chapels and were increasing by the year. Yet in 1855 a writer in *The Builder* had noted that with its population now 110,000, Islington parish could still accommodate only 30,000 worshippers, and religious bodies were felt to have done too little to provide. The Congregationalists, he argued, had of late years added only one church .[2]

In that year Harecourt Chapel was built for £3,500 to a design of W G and E Habershon, by the Coleman Street builders Rowland and Evans, then working on the Clothworkers' Estate. It was the work of the London Congregational Chapel Building Society, and replaced the Hare Court Chapel in Aldersgate. Its mission was to proselytise in poor districts by opening schools and meeting rooms, whose members acted as teachers, evangelists and visitors. Harecourt Chapel formed five such centres, and ran schools, ragged schools, nurseries, homes and mothers' meetings.[3]

Also known as Canonbury Chapel, the building was octagonal, in brick, and was considered "very neat", in form a Greek cross with transverse arches, open timbered roof and Gothic lantern turret, and transeptal seats orientated to the centre. The ground floor held 630, the galleries 500. On its completion each workman was presented with a Bible – and a gratuity – which their high workmanship seemed to justify.

The chapel, at the corner of today's Harecourt Road (renamed from Alma Road) and St Paul's Road, was burned out in 1982 and demolished in 1989. A new church stands on the site, also octagonal, by Hodson Rivers.

METHODISM[4]

Clerkenwell in 1778 was the home of John Wesley's original Methodist chapel, and in 1934 Islington was the site of London's last Methodist Central Hall. In Wesley's own day, as we have seen, St Mary's parish church was

85. Spa Fields chapel, by G Breun in October 1826.

the scene of disturbed, and disturbing, services. During his last years Wesley maintained a personal link with the parish, often visiting his friend John Horton, drysalter, at 25 Highbury Place, to write and meditate. In 1791 Horton was an executor of Wesley's will.

The Spa Fields or Northampton Chapel, opened by the Countess of Huntingdon in Wesley's lifetime at the former Pantheon, was demolished in 1886, and rebuilt in 1888 as the high Anglican Church of the Holy Redeemer.

In 1788 meetings were started in a chapel of the Calvinistic Methodists on nursery ground in Church Street (now Gaskin Street), by a blacksmith, John Ives who had been inspired by a preacher. When completed in 1793 the chapel was leased to a relative of the Countess of Huntingdon. It was a plain, barn-like structure with a simple gable-end, supposedly partly using stone from St James's Church, Clerkenwell, then being rebuilt. In 1801 an independent congregation took over and built an addition for a school of industry for girls. In 1814–15 the then minister, the Rev. Evan Jones, had a new chapel built (the New Islington Chapel) which could hold 1,390 people, at the corner of Church Street and Upper Street. The Rev. Mr Jones also opened a "commercial" graveyard in the adjoining nursery garden, known as the "New Bunhill Fields Cemetery" (1814).

The chapels had a varied history. The newer, Upper Street building was demolished for road-widening and was replaced by a fashionably designed chapel in Queen-Anne-style red brick, by Bonella and Paul, in 1887–8. (Closed in 1979, it is now a recording studio.) The unpretentious Gaskin Street building, meanwhile, once superseded, became a British School, then a parochial school for St Mary's church (1814–61), a memorial hall, a skating rink, a factory and was demolished in the 1970s. The graveyard had been closed in 1853 under the London Burials Act, but in 1996 excavations began in the area behind the site of Collins' Music Hall (Anderson's Yard) prior to building new apartments, extending as far as Gaskin Street, and the burial ground was uncovered. (Popular belief in "plague burials" in or near Islington Green appear to be unfounded.)[5]

The Gaskin Street Calvinist Methodists

86. Islington chapel at the corner of Upper Street and Gaskin Street, demolished for street widening.

moved to Providence Place, tucked away behind Upper Street, where in about 1820 Islington Tabernacle and Islington Green Chapel were built, the latter taken over by the Baptists in 1853 until they moved to Highbury Place in 1888. The chapel, which still exists, was converted to industrial use. The Tabernacle lay behind, used by Calvinists of the Countess of Huntingdon's Connexion until the 1860s, after which for a time it was a United Methodist Free church.

In the 1820s Methodist meetings were also held in a private house in White Lion Street, and after it burned down, a brick chapel with columned stone portico was built in 1826 in Liverpool Road. Financed and regulated by 12 trustees, it held about 950, with a Sunday school behind for nearly 400 children. Richard Barford, a member, bought and presented the freehold to the trustees, building houses behind which became Barford Street. In the open surroundings, then still used as cattle lairs, the minister used to preach to the drovers bringing their cattle to Smithfield.

This chapel burned down in 1848, and was rebuilt next year to hold 1,129 people. At the same time the London Fever Hospital was built a little way up the road, replacing the old hospital on the site of King's Cross station, so that from 1862 the chapel stood between the hospital and the Agricultural Hall built on the site of the lairs.[6]

There was some reshuffling between the different non-conformist congregations. For example, about 1838 a neat little Wesleyan chapel and Sunday school was built in George's Road, at the top end of Liverpool Road, at the east end of what was then known as George's Place. In 1857 its congregation moved to the new Drayton Park, while the Society of Friends took over George's Place until in 1883 they too moved on to a new meeting house in Mercers Road.

The Highbury Hill (Drayton Park) chapel was planned at the house of its chief subscriber, Francis Lycett, at 2 Highbury Grove. Designed by Charles Law, with the luxury of central heating, it was paid for by subscription and voluntary contributions. It was launched in September 1857 with members from Liverpool Road and George's Road. The school, begun in 1859, was to become one of the most important Wesleyan schools, and the two buildings stood alone in the road until the late 1880s when the suburb of Highbury was developed.

By 1875 the church had increased to over a thousand members. Becoming head of a new circuit with Mildmay Park church, it planned more chapels such as those in Caledonian Road, Green Lanes in Stoke Newington (1874), and Finsbury Park. Sunday services were crowded, with carriages lining up outside the church. A mission was started in the nearby notorious Queensland Road.

Local members such as Francis Lycett raised funds to build chapels elsewhere in the new Islington suburbs besides Drayton Park: Mildmay Park (1862), Archway Road (1864), Caledonian Road (1866), Finsbury Park (1871) and Holly Park (1876). Lycett, a partner with the glovers Dent & Allcroft, was knighted in 1867. He later moved to 18 Highbury Grove

and died in 1880.

In 1875 the Highbury Circuit, now eight societies, was divided into three, but its success began to wane as new members tended to be from poorer families, leading the churches into debt until well into the 20th century, when in 1924 Highbury chapel joined the London mission.[7]

Clerkenwell, Finsbury, Shoreditch and Hoxton became great centres for Methodist chapels. New places of worship built in Clerkenwell included the Leysian Mission, started in Whitecross Street in 1886, removing in 1903 to a large new building in City Road, which still survives near the Old Street roundabout. The Wilderness Row church moved to St John's Square in 1849 (burnt down in 1941, rebuilt 1949, finally closed in 1957). The curious little triangle called Wilton Square by the Regent's Canal was the site of a small Welsh Calvinist Methodist chapel built in 1853 to hold 400, and rebuilt in 1884 with a schoolroom.[8] In Britannia Fields, also by the canal, where by the 1850s new streets were being run up as the Packington estate, another chapel was built for the secessionist Methodist New Connexion in 1854. Since 1834 this had met in the leader's own house, then in Wenlock Hall and again in private houses, until the Gothic chapel was built for them near Britannia Bridge. Its first minister the Rev. William Booth, who was to found the Salvation Army, resigned from the Packington Street chapel in 1865 to form the Christian Mission in Whitechapel, which became the Salvation Army in 1878. Booth, later world famous as General Booth, kept up his connection with the chapel and sometimes held services there. (It closed in 1964.)

On the west of the parish, in Caledonian Road, in 1841 the foundation was laid of a large galleried chapel with a capacity of 860, at the corner of today's Carnegie Street close to the canal. It included a school with hall and classrooms, and a basement kitchen. At first the Wesleyan Methodist Association Chapel, in 1857 it became a united Methodist Free Church, and in 1907, the King's Cross Mission.[9]

At Clayton Street (now Tilloch Street), Caledonian Road, was one of the five chapels from which the Packington Street Methodist New Connexion Circuit was formed in 1856. There was also Twyford mission hall, behind 28 and 30 Twyford Street (1860s), later removed to 62–64 Gifford Street; and in the 1880s the Centenary Mission Hall was established at 177 Copenhagen Street. (All three were later demolished for building Council flats.)

In 1866 the Wesleyans built a Gothic chapel with a spire at the corner of Caledonian and Hillmarton Roads, for a society which had met since 1863 in York Place off Barnsbury Park. It held 1,000, as usual had a schoolroom, and grew rapidly until the early 20th century, but had to close in 1916. After a spell as a Liberal Catholic Church, it was demolished.

One survivor in Caledonian Road, built in 1870 at the corner of Market Road with the usual gallery and schoolroom, was a permanent meeting place for a society of Primitive Methodists which had met successively in Market Street, Richmond Road (St George's Hall) and Hemingford Road (Hemingford Hall). As a religious centre for the Metropolitan Cattle Market, and for the Primitive Methodists, known as the 'Connexional Chapel'", it held conferences and became head of a Circuit.[10]

THE BAPTISTS

Compared to the Congregationalists and the Methodists, Baptists in Islington got off to a slow start. Originating in the early 17th century, they promulgated adult baptism. They also generated a stricter sect, the Particular Baptists, who would baptise only their own members. Baptists did not appear in Islington until about 1830, and remained comparatively few in number – in 1851 less than 800, but by the end of the 19th century they had increased to nearly 6,000. Then as the 20th century progressed, like other denominations they declined in numbers, many moving out to more distant suburbs.

Their history in Islington was complicated by the amount of interchange between the chapels themselves, many of them either built or later taken over by different denominations. As an example of the complexities, in about 1832 the Rev. Robert Stodhard, a minister of the Countess of Huntingdon's Connexion, built Providence Chapel off Islington Green, then let the chapel itself and ran a school just

behind it, which in 1838 he also let as a chapel, the Islington Tabernacle. In 1853 the Tabernacle was taken over by Strict Baptists, who later moved into the main chapel building – which had meanwhile been used by, in turn, Calvinistic Methodists, Baptists and Wesleyan Methodists. Then in 1888 the Strict Baptists moved from Providence Chapel to a new building to which they gave the same name in Highbury Place. The 1830s chapel by the Green was then used by the general Baptists until about 1931.[11]

Similarly the handsome little chapel in Chadwell Street, pedimented, stuccoed and with a columned portico, was built for Calvinistic Methodists on a site leased in 1821 from the New River Company by Thomas Elliott, Esq. of Claremont Terrace. When two years passed with no building progress, pressed by the Company he completed the building in 1824 – including, contrary to contract, a house behind and other houses on either side. The chapel was also confusingly known as Providence Chapel. The Methodists remained here only until 1827, and on their moving out (probably to Rawstorne Street) the building was temporarily occupied by a congregation of Scottish Presbyterians who had moved out disgruntled from Regent Square. Then they too moved to a new church in Colebrooke Row, and the Chadwell Street building was occupied by different congregations in turn, and as a school, until the Strict Baptists took it over in 1855. They renamed it Mount Zion Chapel, and built a baptistery under the floor. In 1897 they added a Sunday school in White Lion Street, and in the 1920s Thomas Elliott's house at the rear was demolished to make way for a school.

Another early building, in Wilderness Row, (a thoroughfare later integrated into the newly-cut Clerkenwell Road) had started with the Methodists in 1769, when John Wesley preached there. Welsh Calvinists took it on in 1785, enlarged it in 1806 and in 1823 the Wesleyans used it until they too moved into their new St John Square chapel in 1849. Next came the Strict Baptists, who probably rebuilt it, renaming it Zion Chapel, until 1878.

Vernon Chapel was built in 1843–4 on New River Company land by the Rev. Owen Clarke, Secretary of the British and Foreign Temperance Society, who leased land on either side so that it formed the north side of Vernon Square. This brick chapel, gabled and with pinnacled buttresses, contained a school in the basement. After Clarke died in 1859 his congregation was evicted for defecting on the rent, and a minister and congregation from Spencer Place chapel moved in. The building was later enlarged and galleries were added by an architect member of the congregation, John Goodchild. In the 1930s it developed structural problems, and after landmine damage in the Second World War needed considerable restoration.

John Barnett, a member of the Providence Place chapel off Islington Green, designed in Gothic style a Baptist chapel near the foot of Cross Street, in 1852, on the site of the demolished mansion Fisher House. In 1856 a Sunday school building was added at the rear with an elaborate open truss roof (to-day used as a studio). The chapel was bombed early in the 2nd World War, the Sunday school hall then serving as chapel until it was rebuilt in 1957. The post-war buildings also include a new manse, a community room and two attractive enclosed gardens.

One of the more unusual settings was the desolate Belle Isle area, where in 1864 a mission from the Camden Road Baptist church set up a Sunday school above a cowshed. In 1878 they moved to Brewery Road nearby, but the building like a number of others was destroyed by bombing in 1940.

Like many other non-conformist churches, most Baptist places of worship were built or occupied in the 1850s and 1860s, such as the Salem Chapel in Wilton Square, on land leased from the Clothworkers' Company (1843), the Camden Road Church in 1853–4, and the Upper Holloway Chapel on the corner of Tollington Way in 1866. This was more than once enlarged and remodelled, but was eventually demolished in 1989 to build a new chapel.

As Philip Temple points out in his invaluable work, this proliferation of chapels in the middle Victorian period, generated partly by the huge population expansion and partly by the spread of religious enthusiasm, eventually "became a fashion rather than a necessity". He notes: "Chapels were often built in a burst of confidence without adequate regard

for practical considerations, much too large for their congregations, too expensive to maintain, or … in styles which soon went out of date. Some were downright shoddy." (pp.11–12) They could later be, as recent generations have found, a positive embarrassment. The mania at that time for building in the traditional Anglican form, namely Gothic, led to fancy fronts giving on to barn-like structures behind. Like so many churches, in order to accommodate as large a congregation as possible, they usually contained galleries. An example among the grander Baptist churches was that designed by C G Searle in 1853-4 in Camden Road. Of fashionable Kentish rag, it was in Perpendicular style, with flanking octagonal towers, whose spires were removed after 2nd World War damage. It too went out of use, and in 1989–90 was converted to become a hostel and day centre.

NUMEROUS SECTS

In 1851 Islington was reckoned among the ten Middlesex parishes with the most non-conformists. In 1860 it numbered 15 sects, by 1870, 20. By the end of the century 29 sects were known to have held services, of which in 1903 twenty survived. In view of the composition of the parish's population, Evangelicals were the most popular, for which Islington became well known, and their missions were the most successful.

Throughout the 20th century the numbers declined fairly sharply, and indeed by mid-century many chapels (and Church of England foundations) had either gone out of use and been converted to secular purposes, or been demolished.

So many non-Established places of worship were built in 19th-century Islington that they warranted in 1992 a book of their own (Islington Chapels, by Philip Temple). Of 75 still standing in the 1990s only eight, including two Roman Catholic churches (the Northampton Tabernacle SS Peter and Paul, and St John the Evangelist, of 1835 and 1842–3 respectively), date from the early 19th century. Twenty-six were from the 1850s–80s, mostly Methodist and Baptist, with three other Roman Catholic including the famous St Joseph's or "Holy Joe's" on Highgate Hill. Fifty-two built in the second half of the century have been demolished, again chiefly Methodist or Baptist, with some Congregationalist, not counting various forms of church hall. Twenty-one from earlier decades have also gone. Yet in the latter part of the 19th century almost every street seemed to boast a church or chapel.

Calculating the number of non-Anglican churches and chapels built in Islington is like counting the Rollright Stones in Oxfordshire. Of the 75 listed in 1992, including those converted or used as Mission Halls, perhaps surprisingly 21 were 20th century. Conversions and rebuilding made numbers ambiguous, but the majority were built in or after the 1850s. Of the 50-odd demolished, about 18 were of pre-1840 date and most of the rest built between then and the 1880s. Altogether a formidable number, testifying to the explosion of piety in mid-to-late century and its subsequent falling-off.[12] Most were Wesleyan, Congregational, Baptist, and Welsh tabernacles. Four were Roman Catholic, built after abolition of restrictions – one, indeed, St Mellitus, is a conversion, built as Congregational in 1870–1 by C G Searle and acquired by the Catholic church in 1959, for which its Classical architecture seems particularly felicitous.

ROMAN CATHOLICS

In the 1820s the Established Church had been worried about encroachment by Protestant Dissenters. In the 1840s it was in fear of resurgent Catholicism, freed by the passing of the Catholic Relief Act of 1829. Although by 1839 there were still only ten Catholic churches and chapels in London, including St Mary's in Moorfields, the perceived danger led in 1846 to the formation of the group called the Islington Protestant Institution. By then the number of Catholic places of worship in Britain had increased from about 30 in 1792 to 622. These included St John the Evangelist in Duncan Terrace, opened in 1843. In addition 12 colleges and 42 convents and monasteries had been founded and 818 missionary priests were active.

In the first Annual Report of Islington's Institution, in November 1847, the "danger" of the consequences of Catholic Emancipation was discussed at length.

The Institution resulted from a decision that

it was "high time" for Islington Protestants "to awake out of sleep". A committee framed an address to parishioners, rules were discussed at a public meeting, and local committees were formed. Lectures were given by James Lord at, among others, the two St Mary's churches, St Paul's and Highbury Vale, and visiting clergy gave quarterly addresses at the Parochial Schoolroom on the state of Popery throughout the world. Addresses were also published to the 'Operative Classes' and electors (who were urged to vote only for Protestants). A petition was even addressed to Parliament, objecting to a Bill legalising Jesuits. The Rev. Daniel Wilson of St Mary's Church was needless to say a leading activist.

In 1850 the Catholic Province of Westminster was established by Pope Pius IX, comprising Westminster diocese and 12 others, and the Archbishop, the Rev. Edward Henry Manning, was consecrated in 1865. By 1870 London had 50 Catholic churches, by 1879 123, served by 241 priests.

In Islington by the 1870s, besides St John the Evangelist there were St Peter's in Clerkenwell, St Joseph's, Bunhill Row, the Sacred Heart of Jesus in Eden Grove, Holloway, and the Blessed Sacrament in Copenhagen Street. Elsewhere in north London there were St John the Baptist in Hackney, the Augustinians' Church, Hoxton, and Our Lady and St Joseph, Kingsland. Many of these new churches were "of a size and beauty which 30 years ago would have been deemed a folly even to hope for". Further, a single Catholic church was considered as equivalent to several Protestant churches – because of the frequent services, not to mention catechisms, regular daily masses, and work of their benevolent societies. Priests attended hospitals, Newgate Prison and the Debtors' Prison in Whitecross Street. They seemed especially successful in 'low neighbourhoods', and ran charities, an orphanage, even a Catholic Shoe-Black Brigade.[13]

Islington's St John the Evangelist, of brick with two asymmetrical towers, was sandwiched between the houses of Duncan Terrace, and so had no space for aisles or transepts, and the clerestory windows were necessarily built high. It was apsidal, its chapels and confessionals contained in arcades, and had a marble altar and pulpit. It was designed by

87. The Roman Catholic St John the Evangelist in Duncan Terrace.

J J Scoles. On the fringe of a poor district, the church became a centre for Irish worshippers. A famous rector, the Tractarian Canon Frank Oakley, known as a great friend of these Irish, who called him 'Father O'Kelly', had served at Lichfield Cathedral and All Saints, Margaret Street before his conversion in 1845. He served at St John's until his death in 1880.

Fr Oakley, presumably as class-conscious as his contemporaries, commented in *The Tablet* (18 May 1850) on the "repugnance" of "a person of refined and sensitive feelings" at "the proximity of our squalid poor", recommending that the church have a central aisle to separate free and appropriated seats. In this way peer and poor might be equally near the altar and God, though kept apart from each other. Yet Fr Oakley, along with two young converts from Oxford about to become Jesuits, preached a mission in Islington's stinking courts around the Angel, gathering his congregation by ringing a cow-bell in the High Street. This led to questions in the House of Commons.[14] In 1852

Fr William Young followed Oakley's example by holding masses and confessions in the courts and tenements.[15]

For 27 years until 1907 St John's was served by Fr Oakley's successor, Canon Leopold Pyke.

Islington's other chief 19th-century Catholic church was the Sacred Heart of Jesus at Eden Grove, Holloway, of 1872, one of many founded by Canon Cornelius Keens. It was similar to Christ Church in York Way, but smaller, also in brick with stone dressings, a lofty nave, high Gothic chancel arch and stone for the capitals, windows, side chapels and arches. There was a high East window, and a stone High Altar, rebuilt in the 1880s.

The present church of Our Lady of Czestochowa and St Casimir in Devonia Road, taken over as a Polish Catholic church in 1930, was originally New Church College, the national seminary of the Swedenborgians in England. Begun in 1852 by Edward Welch and added to from 1865 by Finch and Paraire, its simple Kentish rag frontage conceals an astonishingly high interior, with a traceried reredos in Caen stone, and a south wing, formerly a schoolroom but now a side chapel. A set of modern stained glass windows by Adam Bunsch depict Poland's wartime struggle for independence.[16]

There was also a small 'temporary chapel' of St Joan of Arc in Kelross Road, Highbury.[17]

Though officially legalised, Catholics were still held in suspicion by many, including the missionary writer R W Vanderkiste. He recorded how he was verbally assaulted for being a Protestant by a violent and bigoted Irishman, and how in St Giles's parish a fellow-missionary had been thrown downstairs. He also described "two of the most desperate characters with whom I ever met", namely two gigantic sisters of the "Roman Catholic superstition", one of whom shortly died of drink, and in such religion as they had, "clung to some of the deadly errors of Catholicism". To Vanderkiste and many of his fellow-apostles anything Catholic savoured of bigotry, superstition and delusion. Most inhabitants of that part of Clerkenwell, if not Irish, were fighter-refugees from Poland, Hungary and Italy. They lived in a barrack-like loft until, as often happened, they emigrated to America. One unfortunate young former lieutenant, when dying, was assiduously visited by Vanderkiste who, pointing out that no priest had visited, preached to him of divine truth. "Fragments of Romish superstition, however, hung about him to the last", while "I *of course* catechised him continually". So to the bitter end these unbending minds confronted each other in piety.[18]

THE JEWS

Jews, excluded from England by King Edward I, had no legal status in England until the time of Charles II, when they began to come in from Amsterdam and settled in the Houndsditch area. They were allowed to build their first English synagogue beyond the City boundary, and took a field in Mile End area for burials. Towards the mid-18th century rich Sephardic descendants, more or less accepted, moved westwards, their early East End homes being taken over by the poorer, less privileged

Ashkenazite Jews from Germany, though later a more prosperous group emerged.

The synagogue at Bevis Marks in the City long observed the rigid rule against their setting up elsewhere in London, and not until the 1860s was a move made into Islington. In 1865 Solomon Andrade was permitted by the Sephardic Congregation to open a minyan or synagogue which he built in an Essex Road garden. The Ashkenazim meanwhile had started a minyan in 1861 in Upper Street, and after several moves, in 1868 built an imposing Italianate North London Synagogue in Lofting Road, Barnsbury.

The 1880s saw further growth, with the Sephardic Jews allowed to establish a larger synagogue in 1883 at Mildmay Park, holding regular services until the late 1920s. The Ashkenazim opened a second synagogue for Canonbury in Poet's Road (also known as the Dalston Synagogue). Two decades followed with inhabitants moving westwards from the

88. The synagogue in Lofting Road. The site is now taken by flats.

East End. In certain parts of Islington the greeting 'Good Shabbas' was commonly heard, and Highbury New Park was popularly known as 'Highbury Jew Park'.

After this period the changes brought by two wars caused wholesale moves and evacuation. The North London Synagogue in Lofting Road was demolished in 1960 and replaced by flats, and in 1967 the Dalston Synagogue in Poet's Road ceased to function.[19]

From about 1840 there had arisen a schism between a Reform group and the Jewish Elders, who in 1842 excommunicated them. The Reformers consecrated their own place of worship, which was legally recognised later under the Dissenters' Chapels Act, and their excommunication was 'purged' in 1849. It was this reform group who became the West London Synagogue, representing some 40 congregations, which in the late 1840s opened their own cemetery in Islington close to the North London Railway, in Kingsbury Road off the Ball's Pond Road. It is one of a small group of Jewish burial grounds in London, and as the earliest of the Reformed Synagogue might be said to be historically a parallel to Bunhill Fields. Of 13 Jewish burial grounds existing in London in 1995, seven dated from before 1850 and indeed two in Mile End were founded in 1657 and 1733 respectively. All were totally exclusive to the Jewish community, following their own burial systems and surrounded by high brick walls.

At Kingsbury Road the distinction was kept between the low horizontal slabs of Sephardic burials, and the more 'conventional' headstones of the Ashkenazim. The inscriptions provide valuable genealogical information, including of families' origins. The burials were of prosperous Victorian middle-class members of the reformed or breakaway synagogues, besides many representatives of noble and distinguished families. Among those buried there was the Rev. Professor David Woolf Marks, founder of the London Reform Community, who died in 1909. Others included the mathematician Professor James Sylvester, the first practising Jew to attend Cambridge University (1814–97); the first Jewish baronet, Isaac Lyon Goldsmid, FRS (1777–1859); the first Jewish QC, Sir Francis Goldsmid (1808–78); and the founder of the *Daily Telegraph*,

Joseph Levy (1812–88).

An attempt in 1995 to take over the land for building and disinter the burials was, not surprisingly, defeated by strong opposition.[20]

THE SANDEMANIANS [21]

There is a wealth of contemporary literature on the variety of London's Victorian religious life, much of it written by clergy, some of whom might even be classed as 'clerical journalists'. Already in 1839 James Grant had written *The Metropolitan Pulpit*, describing a number of ministers, many of them in Clerkenwell – not least the notorious Edward Irving. It included Dr Waugh at Spa Fields chapel, and the Reverends Thomas Mortimer at St Mark's, Myddelton Square, John Blackburn at Claremont Chapel and John Dorman in Rawstorne Street. Islington itself figured with the less remarkable Rev. John Hambleton at St Mary's Chapel of Ease in Holloway Road.

Other writers who in the 1870s produced interestingly comprehensive works were J Ewing Ritchie with *The Religious Life of London* (1870) and the Rev. Maurice Davies with *Unorthodox London* (1876). Dozens of other works were published on specialised aspects, Catholicism, the Oxford Movement, individual churches and preachers (for example, Moody and Sankey), and missions, charities and atheists. Most are enlightening, often indeed entertaining.

Among the unusual churches visited by both the Rev. Maurice Davies and Ewing Ritchie was the Sandemanian or Glasite chapel in Barnsbury Grove, a small turning off Offord Road. It had acquired a temporary lustre when Professor Michael Faraday was an elder and preacher in 1840–44, and again 1860–64; in fact it was said to be haunted by his ghost. Since then it had become (says Ritchie in 1870) modest in aims and supporters, "a very plain and humble folk".

The Glasites were founded in Scotland in 1728 by a deposed Presbyterian minister, John Glass, assisted by his son-in-law, Robert Sandeman. Their creed was "simple belief", in a church subject to no covenant. In London, starting in the Barbican in 1760, they moved in 1862 to Pocock's Fields in Barnsbury, building a small brick meeting house for 400 people at the corner of the "Roman Road" (now Roman Way). Unlike many sects they did not include a school or Sunday school. They ran their church by Elders, who sat together in superimposed desks rather than using a pulpit.

The Sandemanians, who allowed no form of betting or card games, based their creed on a belief that by his death Christ would save mankind (as stated on Glass's tombstone) "without thought or deed on the part of man" – which one might think a cheering rather than a gloomy doctrine. However their service, which ran from 11 to 1.30 p.m., bored Ewing Ritchie excessively, and appeared "illiterate" in both preaching and prayers. Yet he was surprised at how many people attended, and how "respectable" they seemed. Deploring the lack of "oratorical ability" of elders and deacons, he declared he endured "the worst sermon I ever heard in my life".

The Rev. Maurice Davies in 1876 was no more enthusiastic. Knowing little of the sect except their dictum of "faith without works", and their holding a "love-feast", he had heard stories of a "kiss of peace". Unimpressed by both the modest building and the dismal, protracted prayers and psalms, he was surprised at the congregation's apparent calibre, in spite of the endless scripture readings. At a moment when one might expect the service to finish, there was a further half-hour of sermonising, in which congregation and preacher joined in shedding tears.

Davies could not help noting the pretty young women beside whom he might have sat for a kiss of peace, but after the intensely depressing sermon he found he might not even stop to chat, but as a stranger was expected to leave.

A disagreement within the ranks caused some members in the 1860s to move to a chapel in Highbury Crescent. In general Sandemanian numbers then declined, until in 1899 the Barnsbury chapel closed. In 1904 the building was converted into North London's first telephone exchange and Faraday was commemorated in the name of the adjacent small street.

THE SWEDENBORGIANS

The Rev. Maurice mentioned above also visited the Swedenborgians, who preferred to be known as the New Jerusalem church: Emanuel Swedenborg was regarded as only the medium through whom their truths were revealed, and the sect was actually formed many years after his death in 1772.

Swedenborg, an engineer, with some medical knowledge and a gift for hypnotism lived much in London. He 'saw the light' in 1745 and began to converse with angels, to some extent like the Irvingites, though Swedenborgian ritual was closer to the Church of England, a number of whose clergy were said to support their doctrines. One was the Rev. Augustus Clissold, of Stoke Newington.

Davies, who attended a Swedenborgian service in Devonshire Street (now Devonia Road), apparently in the 1860s, was impressed by the choral parts, chanted by the choir and congregation as a refrain after the minister read portions from the Apocalypse describing the New Jerusalem "coming down out of heaven". He later visited their chapel at Argyle Square, King's Cross, surprised to find it a handsome building resembling an Anglican church, communion table in the chancel, flanked by reading desk and pulpit, and two elderly clergy vested like Anglicans. A large open Bible symbolised that their teaching was from the Word of God.

The music was of high quality, and the sermon, not unorthodox, would (he felt) have passed as 'Broad Church' except for some curious Swedenborgian phraseology: 'Jehovah' universally for 'the Lord', plurals like 'hells', 'falses', 'evils', and such forms as 'conjugial' and 'esse' (for 'essence'). He noted the large congregation's "intellectual" appearance, and concluded that they added to their "slightly rationalistic views of the Trinity and Atonement a highly allegorizing method of scriptural interpretation", not unlike Spiritualism.

A REFORMED MAN

Davies's search for unorthodox Christianity also drew him to hear Bendigo, a reformed prize fighter, at the Cabmen's Mission Hall at 'King's Cross Circus', which he found via a basement door to a Sunday school. It was thinly attended. A few children and some men and women teachers were among the small congregation, who while waiting for the service to begin sang a hymn to the tune of *Home Sweet Home*. One little man sang the 'real' words which, Davies remarks, contained "as many aspirated syllables as possible", all omitted by the singers.

At 11 they repaired to the hall above, "a neat building with a double gallery", its pulpit and benches in stained wood. After a further quarter hour "three awakened cabmen behind me" exclaim "Here's Ben!". In goes a big man to the tiny vestry, whence shortly emerge the Rev. Mr Dupee "in violently clerical costume", and Ben "in lay attire on his right hand … while a timid tenor in the gallery sang 'I will arise' to a harmonium accompaniment".

A hymn, then a prayer by Dupee with "frequent and loud ejaculations" from the company, a prayer that Brother Bendigo may be spared to fight as valiantly for Christ as he has "his country's battles", and "in a stentorian voice, and amid much interjectional applause, that Infidelity, Ritualism, and Popery might be put away … and that Her Majesty might be converted! There were also special suffrages for lunatics, cabmen, and prisoners!"

After more hymns and a Bible lesson "rather misread", a brother of the minister preaches in a strong Nottingham dialect, "a capital old fellow, and told first-rate stories of adventures he had had when selling Bibles at fairs", and of being arrested by a policeman for the same offence and going off with him singing *Pretty Polly Hopkins*. This he now repeats, marching up and down, while the congregation join in, stamping their feet. "He was a rare old ranter was this un-reverend Dupee."

Yet another hymn, and finally at 12.30 Bendigo himself spoke. Though now old, he was erect, slender and clean-limbed, with "considerable hardness about his wrinkled face, and his eye was bright and clear as an eagle's". He had a broken finger from his prize-fighter days, when he and the Dupee brothers had been friends. The Reverend introduced him, explaining that after trying for 30 years he had at last persuaded 'Bendy' to preach, though he could not read, "but read his title clear to mansions in the sky". Then he

launched him into the pulpit with a hefty pat on the back.

By contrast Bendigo spoke briefly and fast, but having lost his teeth, not very audibly. Born one of triplets in Nottingham in 1811, known as Shadrach, Meshach and Abednego, in a family of 21 children, he had his first important fight at 25, won contests, had been in prison, and was apparently a reformed drinker, whose friends said on his conversion, "If God can save Bendy, He can save me!" Rambling but sincere, "he sat down long before we expected or wished", and the smooth Dupee filled in with what they had been unable to hear. Bendigo would preach at three services the next week, and take his first Communion, having refused till now as a Teetotaller – so would be given unfermented juice.

Bendigo also preached at the Royal Agricultural Hall in January 1875, when there was concern over the arrival of caravans from all over the country for a large gipsies' fair. "Some Evangelist well known among the lower classes", suggested *The Times*, might do good by a special service. So Bendigo was summoned to speak in one of the smaller halls along with Ned Wright, a converted thief, with Ned's daughter playing a harmonium for the hymns. The sight of so many "respectable persons" attending at first deterred the showmen, but by degrees they ventured in to the number of over 100, in their "rough and peculiar dress, their weather-beaten faces, and their whips and sticks" come to hear these converted bravos, Bendigo the prize-fighter and Wright the thief.

The Rev. Maurice seems much to have enjoyed the experience and the reformed fighter, reflecting that here is a conversion that seems to have worked in getting a man a better life. "A single fact like that … was worth a hundred theories."

THE MISSIONERS

In this grand Victorian period of proselytisation Christian missions overseas among the 'heathen' were matched by home missions to the unrepentant or unconverted. During the great religious expansion they were not mere struggling efforts run by single churches, but campaigns by famous evangelists wishing to address the world, and indeed they seemed to have the genius to do so.

The noted preacher Charles Haddon Spurgeon, born and educated in East Anglia, came to London in 1854. His sermons at Exeter Hall in the Strand proved so powerful that the building, large though it was, could not contain the crowds who flocked to hear him. From 1861 until his death in 1892, Spurgeon was established at the new Metropolitan Tabernacle at Elephant and Castle, which could and did hold up to 6,000.

Spurgeon, though a convinced Calvinist, in time disagreed with changes in biblical criticism, and was to leave the Baptist Union (1887). Yet the Rev. Maurice Davies, who had already heard him at a Tabernacle missionary meeting, felt he aimed at 'Ranters', the Primitive Methodists, though in his view they represented more truly "the original genius of Wesleyan Methodism" better than did later secessionist sects.

Spurgeon preached in Islington in December 1877 during the newly rebuilt Union Chapel's inaugural fortnight. The packed congregation of 3,365 included the Prime Minister, William Ewart Gladstone. Yet Spurgeon was used to more than twice as many. He was an imposing presence, with a fine voice and massive build, and left a more lasting impression than that earlier fiery preacher Edward Irving, whose congregations had become disillusioned by his mystical approach. For one thing, Spurgeon's sermons were said to be rich in humour.

A few weeks later he preached again at Union Chapel, when the Willis organ was inaugurated, but this time the great preacher caused a disagreeable sensation. Following a hymn and organ performance he tactlessly denounced the "sinful waste" of spending money on "worthless noiseboxes" which "drowned the only sound of praise God cared to hear, the human voice", and even went on to declare that he would like to see every organ in England blown up. He was actually roundly hissed.

The gaffe was especially unfortunate in view of the Rev. Henry Allon's 30 years of building up the chapel's early dismal musical performances to their now famously high standard.

89. Charles Haddon Spurgeon.

Spurgeon was very human, and could shock on more than one account. He was once criticised for harmlessly admitting that after a service he liked to smoke a cigar "to the glory of God". [22]

In 1875 Spurgeon had preached at the Royal Agricultural Hall. In the same year, another huge religious turn-out at the 'Aggie' was to hear the famous American evangelists Dwight Moody and his hymn-writer Ira Sankey, who took the Hall for ten weeks. Their meetings held twice a day attracted (it was said) up to 15,000 at a time, and many could not get in. Moody preached, and Sankey's popular hymns from his *Sacred Songs and Solos* were a great hit. [23]

Moody, born on a farm in Massachusetts, was a Unitarian who converted to 'Fundamental Evangelicalism', and from selling shoes in Chicago turned to full-time missioning, worked for the YMCA, met Sankey, and together they made two long evangelising tours in Europe, of which this was the first. They had the support of businessmen, who believed that Moody's eloquence would encourage working men and the poor to live sober, pious and industrious lives.

Dr Thomas Dale, one of many clergy who

hastened to hear Moody, noted that his address, "simple, direct, kindly and hopeful", seemed at first to contain "nothing remarkable. Yet it *told*." A day or two later he actually confessed to Moody that "the work was most plainly of God, for I could see no real relation between him and what he had done". Moody, with a hearty laugh said "he would be sorry to see it otherwise". And throughout the year Dale received about 200 converts at his church taking Communion, of whom about 75 per cent, he reckoned, did not fall away.[24]

The indefatigable Rev. Maurice naturally attended an Agricultural Hall meeting, which appears to have been one of several preparatory services before the missioners opened at Exeter Hall. "Every inch of that vast building was filled", totalling perhaps 15,000 of "all sections of the population of London". To get in at all people turned up early, and during an hour's wait before the service "an excellent choir" sang some of Sankey's best-known hymns, including "Tell me the old, old story". In certain parts their "pianissimo rendering" could be heard throughout the hall. When Moody appeared on the dot of 6.30 the building was completely filled. Moody opened abruptly (Davies recalls) "in a decidedly provincial accent" announcing the doxology "Praise God, from whom all blessings flow". He added, "All sing!" – to which they responded heartily. After a short prayer Moody announced Psalm 100 ("Make a joyful noise unto the Lord, all ye lands"), again adding, "Let all the people sing". "It was a fine sight to see that vast assemblage rise, and a treat to hear their powerful unison."

Another prayer, in silence, followed then Moody made "a special supplication for London", the great city which he prayed God to bless. Sankey then for the first time sang solo, in his rich voice, "Jesus of Nazareth passeth by". This led "an excitable gentleman" rather embarrassingly to propose a chorus, which Moody diplomatically evaded.

After a special setting of "Rock of Ages" came the climax: Moody's address. It was rather unconventional. For example, God spoke to Moses, who was "not the sort of person we should have selected to save three millions of people". Moses asked who he must

say sent him, and God "drew him a blank cheque, and told him to fill it in with the name of Jah [Veh] whenever necessary." There were enough people in that hall (he said) to save London, for which he asked the aid of its ministers – and of London parents.

This "impressive and captivating address" ended with a touching analogy. A poor Liverpool mother had told him of her missing son, "a fine lad of 17", thought to be in London. "Perhaps the lad is before me now. If so, let me tell him his mother loves him still, and so too, like that poor mother, God loves us all." On this symbolic appeal for unity he broke off "as if inspired", calling for Sankey's hymn "Hold the Fort". Dr Henry Allon of Union Chapel pronounced the final benediction.

Davies was greatly impressed. The address had been eloquent but avoided sensation, and with Moody's "quaint touches of humour that provoked a smile", it went straight to the heart.

There followed a month of daily meetings and addresses, and Davies was eager to see if Moody's fervent appeal would prove "ephemeral, as its detractors had predicted", whether North London would profit by it, and how it would go down in the West End. But Moody was so elated that he was unwilling to throw away their success at the Aggie for the sake of, perhaps, a mere 3,000 at the Opera House. Lord Shaftesbury pointed out the potential influence of "one of the upper 10,000", but despite skilful argument Moody insisted on continuing at the Aggie. "His heart was with his Islington Gentiles … I never in all my life saw a man so thoroughly impenetrable to all suggestions as this American Evangelist."

At last Moody's view was accepted, and he continued in Islington while another preacher held evening meetings elsewhere.[25]

The Aggie was not Islington's only venue for evangelising. At Baker's Auction Rooms in Upper Street, opposite Cross Street, in the 1860s the Gospel of the Grace of God was preached on Sunday evenings at 6.30. All seats free, and (as an enticement) no collections taken. Here, for example, in 1860 Mr C Stanley, author of *Railway Tracts* and other pamphlets, preached on an August Friday, and at least one Bishop – of Mauritius – was among those who attended.

Much later, in 1902 the Central London Wesleyan Mission, which needed a London theatre for a gospel campaign, chose to hire the Islington Empire. "In Finsbury alone there must be at least 85,000 persons out of its population of 101,463 who never cross the threshold of a church, or chapel or mission hall." Their effort was a success: 2,500 people turned up at monster Sunday evening services – timed at 8.15 to avoid a possible clash with church services. The theatre was so crammed that hundreds were turned away. Sixty stewards ushered in the crowds, who were given hymn sheets urging "any who desire to lead a new life" to call at the Wesleyan Chapel in St John's Square, while a band played bright music before the mission address, "full of gospel fire".[26]

Much of the information in the first Section is based on Philip Temple's *Islington Chapels*.

1   In 1981, when Union Chapel's congregation had become infinitestimal, a proposal was made to demolish and rebuild as a pastiche of the small original chapel. After strong opposition, notably from the Victorian Society, it was reprieved, restored and under the Rev. Janet Wootton, who served until 2003, has been a famous and florishing institution.

2   *The Builder*, 27 October 1855, p. 516.

3   J Ewing Ritchie, *The Religious Life of London*, London, 1870, pp. 153ff.

4   This Section is based on John S Ellis' useful survey of Methodism in and near Islington, in the *Archway Central Hall Newsletter*, 1977–9.

5   Temple, *Islington Chapels*, pp. 72–3; and information from Derek Seeley of MOLAS.

6   The chapel finally closed in 1929 when the congregation moved to Drayton Park Chapel. The building was demolished in 1932.

7   When the Liverpool Road church closed a new Islington Central Hall was planned, successor in style to the traditional chapel. The first minister, the Rev. Donald Soper, who with his wife moved to Kelross Road, launched his mass-

8   media mission, with broadcasting and, eventually, television.
From 1935 until 1955 it was a Welsh Presbyterian Chapel. The building was then converted into a men's hostel for the Society of St Vincent de Paul.

9   In 1937 it was renamed along with the street as Carnegie Street United Methodist Church, and joined with the Wesleyans and Primitive Methodists, earliest United Methodists Church in London, but destroyed in 1941 by a land mine.

10   The chapel was restored in 1953, and at its centenary in 1970 was claimed to be the oldest building in the district bar the Prison and the Caledonian clock tower.

11   Providence Chapel at Islington Green was then bought by the British Legion, was subsequently in industrial use, including a dress factory, and since the 1990s has been used as offices.

12   Temple, *Islington Chapels*, passim.

13   Ritchie, *The Religious Life of London*, pp. 61ff.

14   *The Tablet*, 18 May 1850; W Ward, *Life and Times of Cardinal Newman*, London, 1913, Vol. II, p. 157.

15   *The Tablet*, 17 January 1852.

16   Temple, *Islington Chapels*, pp. 72–3; and information from Derek Seeley of MOLAS.

17   Alex Bottman, *London Catholic Churches*, London, 1926, pp. 214, 216.

18   Vanderkiste, *Six Years' Mission*, pp. 79ff.

19   *Jewish Chronicle*, 5 August 1955; Charles Booth, *Poverty*, Vol. III, Chapter IV.

20   Information from the Jewish Genealogical Society of Great Britain, VCH, p. 117.

21   Material in the following Sections is based on Ewing Ritchie, *Religious Life of London*, and the Rev. Maurice Davies, *Unorthodox London*, London, 1876.

22   *DNB*, Spurgeon.

23   James A Connell, *The Royal Agricultural Hall*, Islington Public Libraries, 1973.

24   Quoted by E G Rupp in *The Listener*, 17 March 1955.

25   Davies, *Unorthodox London*, pp. 267, 272ff.

26   Posters, Islington Local History Library collection; Rev. John E Wakerley, *A Record of Progress in Central London, 1899–1900*, p.p., London, 1900.

CHAPTER 28

A Still Greater Revolution in Transport

THE RAILWAYS ARRIVE

Until the 19th century was more than half over, in spite of the wheeled traffic clogging the streets of London, most Londoners still travelled on foot. In the second half of the century transport underwent greater change, on four fronts. Omnibus services were expanded and modernised, railways became widespread, there was more new transport – underground railway – and from 1870 tramways introduced a real workmen's service.

The railways themselves, though the cause of great change, did not at first particularly impinge on Islington. Indeed in the first 30 years of steam serving the capital, many Londoners had still never travelled on a train, and with some ¾-million people daily entering the city, street congestion remained a heavy problem.

London's earliest railway, the London and Greenwich line, opened its first section from Deptford to Bermondsey in 1836. By 1837 the London & Birmingham Railway, whose line reached Birmingham in 1838, had opened Euston station. Railways to London from north and west had to terminate north of the New Road and the great ducal estates, hence the siting of Euston and later, King's Cross, St Pancras and Marylebone. Other companies soon lined up in the railway boom, with a hiccup after 1846, with the largest expansion in the 1860s.

Islington, on the fringe of these developments, so far only benefited (or otherwise) in 1850 with the Bow section of the North London Railway (*see below*), and in 1851-2 with the building of King's Cross station to Lewis

Cubitt's design. This relatively modest terminus of the Great Northern line was adorned only by a simple Italian-style clock turret. Within the station the train sheds were covered by a glazed vault, inspired by that great contemporary experiment, the Crystal Palace.

The railways eventually transformed life in Islington as they did elsewhere. It is hard to imagine their extraordinary effect, not only on the countryside, plunging straight ahead unlike the wandering roads, via bridges and viaducts – but on London itself. Not only did they reduce travelling time by avoiding the encumbered streets, but they had an overpowering visual effect. Some towered above congested highways, cutting through in places where buildings in their path had been destroyed, adding unprecedented features to the view. The railway bridge across the Holloway Road was soon as significant an Islington feature as was the Highgate Archway at the north of the parish, or the Regent's Canal cutting through the south.

In Simon Jenkins's view railways proved the worst blow London had suffered since the great Fire of 1666, swallowing labour, capital and materials, despoiling a huge acreage of land, and altering the way of life of thousands. But for people in Islington as in other suburbs, they made it possible for the first time to live far from their work. In the country, in fact. New suburbs, quickly built along railway routes, attracted new inhabitants, so that during the second half of the century inner London's population for the first time actually began to fall.[1]

A central railway terminus for London, such

90. Highbury Station on the North London Line in 1873. It was destroyed in the 2nd World War.

as other cities were to build, was rejected because of the pattern of land ownership, and the decision to bar railways from central London was later a cause of major reorganisation – namely, development of an underground railway when it became imperative to link the main terminals of the different lines.

Compared with, say, London south of the Thames, Islington's participation in the railway revolution was modest. Indeed only two lines crossed the parish, and King's Cross, the nearest major terminal, was just beyond its boundaries. One of the many individual ventures characterising the railway age was the East & West India Docks and Birmingham Junction Railway, begun in 1846 to connect the London & Birmingham Railway with the London Docks. The section from Highbury to Hackney and Bow opened in 1850, shortly followed by connection westward to Camden Town, where it joined the L & B Railway. As yet the only intermediate station was at Kingsland Road, but the eastward section proved instantly popular and was heavily used. In June 1852 another station opened at

Caledonian Road to serve the suburb of Barnsbury. Its trains had no third-class carriages until 1875 and, during its first years, much of the line still ran through open country.[2]

Islington's other line was the Great Northern Railway, for whose King's Cross terminus the old Smallpox Hospital was demolished in 1851. The line ran alongside the parish's western extremity through tunnels, one named Copenhagen after the popular hillside resort through which it cut. Its first local station, Hornsey, was in a country lane – even by 1859 Holloway, only two miles from King's Cross, still had rural features. In 1867 a new branch linked Finsbury Park with Highgate and Edgware. In 1877 a second and in 1886 a third Copenhagen Tunnel were constructed, separating goods from passenger traffic and the up-line from the down. In 1892 a further Maiden Lane tunnel, and new King's Cross platforms, improved facilities. In time Islington boasted seven stations. On the Docks line, which in 1853 became the North London Line, were Highbury & Islington (1849, rebuilt 1873); Caledonian Road & Barnsbury (1852);

91. Canonbury Station in 1905.

Newington & Ball's Pond (1858, replaced in 1870 by Canonbury) and Upper Holloway on the Kentish Town/Barking line. Seven Sisters Road (1861–2) on the Great Northern Line had its name changed to Finsbury Park in 1869, while Drayton Park (1870–72) was on the Great Northern and City Lines. Both of these last were en route from Canonbury to Finsbury Park. Finally came Mildmay Park in 1880.

HOLLOWAY STATION

On the Great Northern Railway, development at Holloway Station, Lewis Cubitt's last commission before retiring may serve as an example of many great changes.

For several years from August 1852 passengers who alighted at Holloway's ticket platform, a narrow and rather dangerous spot, had to climb over two lines to reach a stair to the Holloway Road. A proper down-platform with a waiting-shed was not made until 1860, and a direct stair to the platform only in 1864. Although in regular use from the summer of 1856, the station had to be several times modified, by extra tracks to gain a down main-line, an

up-line, a loop for cattle, goods and coal between Seven Sisters and Copenhagen tunnel mouth, and coal-train facilities. The Seven Sisters signal box, south of Seven Sisters Road bridge on the up (east) side, could now operate night and day.

RAILWAY LANDS

Railway companies tended to buy up large tracts of land for sidings and goods yards, much of it not remaining in gainful use today, so that in many places the line has been bordered by blighted areas, especially around King's Cross, along the already despoiled quarter of Belle Isle, and in much of the land towards Finsbury Park. In the 1860s North London's suburbs, growing with the increased traffic facilities, had a two-way effect: new lines were made to serve new areas, and new areas required new lines. One such was the Edgware, Highgate and London Line, joining the Great Northern near Seven Sisters Road in June 1862. The GNR then requiring $4\frac{1}{2}$ acres more land at Seven Sisters, characteristically regarded it a sound investment to buy seven, and later used part as sidings.[3]

Land was even taken to run a special service for funeral trains. In 1861 when the Great Northern Cemetery Company built a cemetery for north London at East Barnet, an arrangement was made to carry both coffins and mourners by rail. As the GNR had refused to allow such trains to start from King's Cross (1858), a terminus was made alongside the line at Belle Isle, with a covered station and a mortuary in a chapel-like building at York Way. In 1861 a twice-weekly funeral train service was launched, but fares were too high to attract customers, and an attempted charge of £1 for the coffin had to be halved. The service was still not a success. Belle Isle station and buildings fell out of use by the spring of 1865, and the agreement came to an end. The station finally closed when land was needed for a duplicate tunnel (1875). Part of the building survived until the 1950s, when its original purpose had been forgotten and it was replaced by a concrete plant.

RAILWAYS BENEATH THE STREETS

Charles Pearson, the City Solicitor, was the main proponent of an underground railway in London to relieve congestion and to connect the termini of main line railways. This far-seeing proposal for the first underground railway in the world was implemented in 1860 when construction began of what was grandly called 'the Subterranean Railway', between Paddington and Farringdon, via King's Cross. Using the cut-and-cover method, shoring up the sides of the tunnel by brick piers, it followed the line of the New Road, whose name had in 1857 been 'rationalised' as the Marylebone, Euston and Pentonville Roads. The route was chosen partly to avoid affecting property, but the excavations caused massive disturbance to street traffic. The line also had to push a way through gas mains and sewers, and in 1862 a turn southwards encountered a major disaster. This was at the point where the line touched on Clerkenwell, behind the Middlesex Sessions House. During the excavations a temporary bridge was built from here to Farringdon Road (then named Victoria Street) across the submerged Fleet River.

On 15 June 1862, a Sunday evening a few days after heavy rain and thunderstorms, people noticed a 'sinking' on the west side of the adjoining street. It was followed by a sudden rush of sewer water into nearby cellars, breaking through the arch over the Fleet. So this 'Black River of North London' became unexpectedly visible again in all its repulsiveness. For the next three days and nights contractors and officers of the Metropolitan Board of Works struggled to contain the flood, damming the retaining walls to make a barrier; but by Wednesday the roadway was still sinking. About 4 pm. came the worst catastrophe, the ground shook like an earthquake, and workmen fled with shouts of alarm as the heavy scaffolding was flung into the air, crashing to the ground among screams of horrified spectators.

As they watched, the huge new 50–60-foot brick piers were seen to be shifting at the base, and at the foot of the excavation the gravel path moved in a mass, slowly and inexorably giving way to "a dark foetid liquid [which] covered all, and rolled its way towards the mouth of the tunnel, tearing down ... all obstructions, and snapping like straws the strongest piles of massive timber". This revolting flood was the contents of the Fleet and an old burial ground.

The narrator of this, Edward Wood (who was later to complete William Pinks's *History of Clerkenwell*), was standing at the tunnel mouth with the manager and engineers who had been striving to prevent exactly this disaster. All they could do now was frantically dig a channel for the flood to sweep down to the Thames, along the ancient Fleet drain.

The catastrophe had been precipitated by the heavy storms which brought water flooding in huge quantities from Highgate, Hampstead and Kentish Town to concentrate in the Fleet River. At the lower end of Saffron Hill the torrent overflowed into the street, carrying away the temporary bridge and undermining the new foundations. However wide the excavation had been made, it could not have contained such an inundation. [4]

Neither the railway company nor the contractors would admit responsibility for the disaster, and long afterwards legal claims dragged on and on.

In spite of this serious setback the old sewer was rebuilt, the new foundations repaired, and in October the underground railway line was completed, though its opening was delayed by the legal dissension until January 1863 – just two-and-a-half years after work began.

The next stretch of line, to Moorgate, opened in December 1865 without further mishap, and for ten years this remained the terminus of the fragmentary underground railway, the initial section of the Inner Circle Line.

TRAMWAYS

Transport in the metropolis was affordable only to the better-off, until yet another revolution. This was the tram, whose early history had been far from smooth. The brainchild of an American appropriately named George Francis Train, horse-trams were first tried in New York as a street railway, where they proved better than horse buses, the rails giving a smoother ride over the uneven streets. In 1852 trams were introduced in Paris; and after trying them in Liverpool, Train attempted unsuccessfully to set them up in London. In 1860 Joseph Curtis, an engineer, applied to demonstrate a 'tram-bus' on no less a route than Islington's Liverpool Road – but there seems no evidence that this was actually done. His rival George Train meanwhile obtained leave from Hackney Vestry to lay lines in Southgate Road and Shoreditch.

Train also attempted a line from Bayswater to Marble Arch (1861), but in spite of publicity and a champagne launch, bus and cab drivers and carriage-folk alike condemned it as a threat to their vehicles, and the lines were taken up again. After this blunder Train returned to the USA: he should have chosen a less fashionable area where a tram service would have proved a boon. Like Islington.

Although trams were advertised as 'the people's carriage', opposition still prevented their acceptance. In 1865 a Locomotives Act prohibited mechanically propelled vehicles in towns from moving at more than two miles an hour. But in the same year abolition of the long-endured burden of road tolls proved a step towards eventual success.

Not until 1870 was the horse-drawn tram established as public transport, by the London Tramways Act under which three pioneer companies were formed. Yet the Act permitted local authorities (that is, the Vestries) to veto tramways, so the all-powerful City, on grounds of amenity loss and traffic obstruction, prevented the new North Metropolitan Company from laying a line in the City. There was also strong resistance to introducing trams in areas like Knightsbridge and Oxford Street, and they were never admitted to fashionable central London.

Elsewhere, however, lines were forging ahead. In 1871 the London Street Tramways Company laid its first line between Hampstead Road and Kentish Town Midland Railway Station. The next year a line from King's Cross to Kentish Town was laid, and in 1878 another along the Caledonian Road to Holloway. By degrees North London became well served by the new working-man's transport. It was quick, and at a penny a journey, cheap. Tracks were laid round Finsbury Park by the North Metropolitan Company, which later, in 1891, took over rival lines including from Finsbury Park. Tracks were also laid from Moorgate to Holloway via the Angel and Liverpool Road, and along Upper Street to Highbury Station. All through the seventies the service spread.

The journalist George Sala recalls chairing a rowdy public meeting some time in 1882 at "a certain town hall" – possibly Holborn – on "the extension of tramways westward from the new Clerkenwell Road to Theobalds Road … There was a strong anti-tramway party at the back of the hall, who persistently yelled 'Free Streets!' and 'It's a put-up job!'" Led by a burly brewer's drayman, they eventually tried to storm the platform and "smash the chairman" ("the willin in the vite veskit"), while a little old lady in a red shawl, shaking her fist at him, yelled that she was going to lam him as "one of them Jesuits".

Sala approved of having lines along Clerkenwell Road, "that prodigious thoroughfare from west to east, which has been opened up by the Metropolitan Board of Works … there can be no doubt that in these far outlying, densely populated and incessantly busy districts tramways are a distinct boon and blessing".[5]

92. *A horse tram on the Holloway Road, c.1905, with the Marlborough Theatre to the right.*

Each route was distinguished by a different colour, and by the lights on the trams. A newcomer to London had quickly to learn the colours of both omnibuses and trams: Pett Ridge recalled that the Favorite omnibus from Abney Park was green. He had found the early Underground an endurance test, with its "dense, smoke-laden atmosphere", making it impossible to read and difficult to breathe; whereas the new horse-drawn vehicles provided "much of the gaiety of the London streets".[6]

The North Metropolitan Company early extended its service from Highbury station through Canonbury, across Essex Road, and along New North Road to join the Green Lanes/Moorgate route. Most was single-line, with fixed passing places. In 1879 the idea of express trams from Finsbury Park to the City with fares at a penny more was proposed. It was tried with small one-horse cars, no outsides, which could overtake ordinary cars on the passing-loops. But either it did not work, or proved too expensive and was soon withdrawn in favour of the normal 'Brown' two-horse trams, while the 'Yellows' ran via Upper Street.

Another failed attempt was the Liverpool Road branch – a street of unsuccessful experiments, it seems – with an Archway-Moorgate service diverging from the Holloway Road along Liverpool Road to rejoin the Yellow route at Islington High Street. "Probably the least revenue-providing thoroughfare of any length in London through which trams operated", comments Geoffrey Wilson,[7] and it was given up when the LCC took over running the tram service (1913), and Islington's other horse-trams were electrified. Perhaps this story of failures along Liverpool Road is the reason there is no bus service down it today.

The Caledonian Road too came in for a tryout, with the compressed-air tram in 1888, invented by a Frenchman called Makarski and run by the London Steam Company, who put five 38-seat cars on a nearly-two-mile route from King's Cross to near the Nag's Head on the Holloway Road. The steam apparatus below the floor made the tram larger and higher than usual, and it had difficulties at starting, especially on slopes. At the south end was a steep bridge over the Regent's Canal with a rise of 1-in-27, and a quarter-of-a-mile farther on was another rise near Pentonville Gaol.

Here a boy waiting with a cock-horse hooked a horse on to the vehicle on the near side without its stopping, and, jumping on to the driver's platform, unhooked the horse at the top end and rode back down the slope ready for the next car.

In 1896 the North-Met Company also ran special market services for the porters, with half-hourly early cars starting at 3 am. from Highgate, Finsbury Park at 3.15, then joining the Nag's Head-Aldersgate route with a quarter-hourly service.[8]

A famously unsuccessful experiment was the Highgate Hill Cable Tramway, introduced in 1884 on the steep 1-in-11 gradient. It was the first in Europe, though a similar system still flourishes in San Francisco. Ordinary four-wheel trams were used, fitted with a special brake, but there was danger of failure by the cable, the pulley and even the power. Besides, while it was tempting to pay 2d to ascend the steep hill by cable car, few people wanted to pay to come down. So the service did not prosper. After a serious accident in 1894 the line was closed, and disagreements between the three boroughs through which it ran, Islington, St Pancras and Hornsey, prevented its reopening.

The Act of 1870 empowered local authorities to purchase private tramways after 21 years, but this inhibited capital expenditure meanwhile. From 1891 therefore, the new London County Council began serving compulsory purchase notices on the London Street Tramways Company, and prudently acquired complete control. Soon all lines north of the Thames were leased to the North-Met. The Light Railways Act of 1896 further increased tramway building by empowering acquisition of land and reducing restrictions. 'Light Railways' was so ambiguous a term that authorisation for trams could be slipped in under its cover.

The horse-tram age was at its peak by about 1900, when London's 6½ million inhabitants travelled with either North-Met, covering over 51 miles, or London Tramways (24° miles). North-Met had 673 cars and 7,167 horses, and London Tramways 399 cars and 3,835 horses, harnessed in pairs. Each tram required a fleet of eight to 11 horses, valued between £20 and £30.

Electrification was now the power of the future, first demonstrated on trams in Germany in the 1880s. In 1890 the world's first electric railway opened in London between the Bank and Stockwell – and by the end of the century extended to the Angel. The overhead trolley by which they operated, though cheap and reliable, was unpopular enough to keep electric trams out of the smarter suburbs – though as much of an eyesore in workaday Clerkenwell.

But at the end of the century the Royal Agricultural Hall was holding exhibitions by the Tramway and Railway world, and while the horse-tram continued until 1915, and the new motor-bus was already in its infancy, in Edwardian days the electric tram was triumphant as the 'chariot of the people'. [9]

Information on the railways can be found especially in Butcher & Robbins, *History of London Transport*; H G Lewis, *The Railway Mania and its Aftermath, 1845–52*; Sekon, *Locomotion in Victorian London*; and Shepherd, *London 1808–70*, London, 1968.

1   Max Schlesinger, *Sauntering in and About London*, London, 1853, pp. 169–71; Simon Jenkins, *Landlords to London*, London, 1975.

2   Sekon, *Locomotion in Victorian London*, pp. 152f.

3   Pinks, *Clerkenwell*, pp. 361–2.

4   John Wrottesley, *The Great Northern Railway*, London, Batsford, 1979, pp. 81ff, 113ff.

5   George Sala, *Living London*, London, 1883, p. 514. For the history of trams, Charles Klapper, *The Golden Age of Tramways*, London, 1961.

6   W Pett Ridge, *A Story Teller: 40 Years in London*, [?1920] pp. 194, 168.

7   Geoffrey Wilson, *London United Tramways*, London, 1971

8   *Ibid.*

9   Klapper, *Tramways.*

CHAPTER 29

A Mid-century Crisis

SOME STATISTICS

Islington's population had continued rising to a staggering degree, in each of two decades by about two-thirds: between 1841 and 1851 from 55,690 to 95,329 and between 1851 and 1861 to 155,341 and still increasing. By then, having outstripped Finsbury (129,073) and the City (111,784), it was seen as England's most populous parish – yet it was then on the brink of an exodus to distant areas. In 1851 England's towns for the first time exceeded the countryside in population, and swelled still more in the 1860s with the immigration of some 600,000 Irish (though many of these went to Cheshire and Lancashire as much as to London). From the 1880s the arrival began of persecuted Jews from eastern Europe such as Poland and Russia. London's multi-ethnic character was now established.

When such records were first kept in the 1840s, London had 330,000 immigrants, making 17% of the total population, in the Fifties 286,000 and the Sixties 331,000, each 12% of the total. The breakdown for the 1840s was 8,000 Scots, 46,000 Irish and 26,000 'foreign'. By 1841 the Irish represented 3% (82,291) of the total, by 1851, 4.6% (109,000). The largest such increase was in the 1850s, nearly 600,000, mainly young people between 15 and 24, servants and labourers from Ireland, Scotland and the provinces, arriving by the spreading railway network. In 1861 London had more than a quarter-million house servants, often immigrants, and five-sixths of them women.

To accommodate this increase in Islington, in the 20 years from 1831 to 1851 the number of houses doubled from 6,830 to 13,500, and by 1861 soared again to 20,700. By the 1880s and later, 75% of occupants were locally born, of the second or third generation.[1]

We must imagine then a bewildered population having to adjust to the quite sudden transformation of their semi-rural township, still among green fields and farmland with cattle and sheep in the 1840s, into a rapidly spreading suburb.

MID-CENTURY CRISIS

By the 1850s, when not only London's public health but its effect on daily life had reached a crisis, there were at last some practical attempts to deal with it. After the capital had endured the nation-wide cholera outbreak in 1831, it took another to stir the authorities into action. The crisis in the 1850s had an overall effect on local government, on water supply, sanitation, and on housing the poor. The health problem also affected the death rate and the incidence of epidemic (zymotic, as it was then called) and endemic disease.

Even with the parallel of London's post-World War II development, it is hard to imagine what living in such a suburb as Islington could be like in the 1850s. With London expanding in all directions, despoiled fields vanishing under the dreaded 'bricks and mortar', terraces of the most depressing kind lowered on every horizon. As the ever-increasing population were all new to one another, small wonder if London became renowned for anonymity. How could one keep up acquaintance with even a fraction of hundreds of new neighbours?

Late in 1858 an *Islington Directory* (published in 1859), based on personal enquiry and house-to-house visits, was reviewed in the Christmas issue of the newish *Islington Gazette*. It expressed both approval for production of such a guide, and well-founded amazement that, of 16,000 names recorded, no less than 11,000 had changed their address within the past four years.

Despite the vast increase, though, Islington proper still had a population density of only 30 to the acre: Clerkenwell's figure was 170, St Luke's, 245, and in East London it reached 290. In Clerkenwell in 1861 the population was 65,681, which included 1,195 female servants together with upper servants such as house-keepers and cooks at 400. These outstripped individual craftsmen numbers: watch and clock makers 877, goldsmiths and jewellers 725, and printers 720. Only 38 were classed as 'gentlemen' (plus five 'annuitants').

In the crowded and wretched conditions the deficiencies of public health became a serious issue. The City of London's first positive move was to appoint a Medical Officer of Health, Dr John Simon, who put in hard-hitting reports and proposals. For example, noxious businesses were forbidden in the City in 1851, and under the Metropolitan Burials Act of 1852 new burial grounds were authorised outside London boundaries, though the evils of the existing grounds lingered for years. Lord Ashley, at a public meeting in February 1850, blamed as chief objectors to improvement the "owners of small tenements, men who pushed themselves to the front of Boards of Guardians and parish Vestries, and were clamorous about the rating of their property".

An attempt to purify the water supply was made by the Metropolis Water Act in 1852, by which the water companies which drew from the Thames were forbidden to take it below Teddington Lock. All water was to be filtered, and reservoirs within a certain distance of St Paul's were to be covered. This included the reservoir in the centre of Claremont Square, which was now to be drained and piped. But a time-limit of five years was allowed for carrying out these improvements.

Ideas and proposals were not enough to prevent a third cholera outbreak in 1853-4, which did lead to urgent action. The cause was now seen as 'filth', worse in south London than the north, being on lower land and with a poorer water supply. The Southwark and Vauxhall water companies had ignored the law about Teddington Lock. Lack of supervision, non-execution of Acts, Government indifference and the limited powers of the Board of Health together had produced chaos.

Dealing With the Sewers

Meanwhile a series of Commissions considered how to deal with the problems, especially the sewerage system. In 1855 the Metropolitan Board of Works (MBW) was created, and Vestry rule was transformed by London's first attempt at proper self-government. The metropolis was divided into 39 districts, one each for the City and larger parishes (which included Islington), and the 45 smaller parishes were amalgamated into districts. Their representative vestry or district board was to be elected by ratepayers, to manage drainage, paving, lighting etc, each vestry electing a representative to the Metropolitan Board of 45 members, which would control main sewers, new streets and metropolitan improvements, and direct the vestries by bye-laws.

But it was not until Joseph Bazalgette was appointed as Chief Engineer to the MBW that significant improvement was made. And not before time. In Clerkenwell, "numberless houses do not drain into the sewers", 7,000 houses were declared unfit for habitation and in many thousands of houses families had to sleep, live, cook – and die – in a single room. Nearly half of deaths were of infants, as indeed was the case in Islington.

The Bazalgette scheme used *intercepting sewers*. The principle was that three main sewers ran from west to east receiving, or intercepting, the contents of lesser sewers which would no longer drain into the Thames, and carry waste well east of the metropolis for treatment in outfalls. One of these, the Low Level area, ran mainly along the north bank of the Thames; the other two through parts of Islington. The Northern High Level Area, suburban but still with a rapidly increasing population, was defined by the Hackney Brook, which continued to be of vital importance as it diverted all sewage and flood waters from 14 square miles of the upper districts, away from the lower districts and the Thames, and prevented flood danger. This would dispense with the polluted, over-charged Fleet River, now a sewer which was largely uncovered and in parts had fallen in. The route, in detail, started from a Hampstead junction to take the line of the Fleet, crossed Highgate Road, intercepting a second branch of the Fleet, crossed below fields to Tufnell Park Road, widening at various points, down the Holloway Road to Tollington Road. Here it reached 10ft 6in diameter. Thence it passed under the Great Northern Railway and New River Cut. It replaced the open Hackney Brook sewer, falling to Stoke Newington High Street at Abney Park Cemetery; now 11ft 6in wide, it continued thence eastwards to the River Lea.

The Middle Level sewer started from Ealing and took in south Islington. From Oxford Circus along Oxford Street it passed below the maze which later became Clerkenwell Road (Liquorpond Street, St John's Square and Wilderness Row) thence by Old Street to Shoreditch and Bethnal Green, then under the Regent's Canal and East India Dock Railway, crossing the River Lea at Old Ford and ending at Barking Creek.[2]

This revolution in disposing of waste and flood water was the first major reform in London's mediaeval method of drainage.

The intercepting sewer system was heavily criticised. For example, the short-lived journal the *Clerkenwell Times* compared 'The Main Drainage' to highway robbery. "A rogueish, if not a mad scheme, by which every cup of dirty water, and the contents of every slop-pail are to pass off instantaneously from every part of the metropolis, no cesspools being allowed." It derided the changes of destination for the sewage, first near Woolwich, then Erith, Gravesend, even "the German Ocean, full 40 miles from London". The advantages of a distant outfall escaped the writer's comprehension. Further, the scheme meddled with the freedom of the individual, and the editor proclaimed that it would not only "most assuredly fail in its execution", but would prove one of the greatest swindles of the age.[3]

However, significant changes and improvements now on the way affected the whole government of London.

93. Islington Vestry Hall c.1858, designed by H.E. Cooper. On the corner of Upper Street and Florence Street, it later became Islington's first town hall.

A MEDICAL OFFICER

With Vestry government now substantially reformed, progress and public health reports began to receive serious attention. Annual reports were now published by Medical Officers of Health. In Islington he was Dr Edward Ballard, a former lecturer in medicine at St George's Hospital, living at 42, Myddelton Square. The Reports' statistics included numbers of births and deaths, calculation of the present population, comparisons with national annual mortality rates, and an analysis of population by age.

The first Islington report in 1856 showed that of the 1851 population total (95,329, since then calculated as already risen to about 135,000), children under five numbered 12,190, and people between 15 and 25, and 25 and 35 respectively numbered 19,103 and 17,732. In fact, a predominantly young population, and births were almost double the number of deaths. There were barely 3,000 residents over 65.

The main purpose of the reports was to publish progress in sanitary improvements, with inspection of houses, the numbers of new and improved drains, removal of cesspools, conversion of open privies into piped lavatories or at least provision of a water supply, and even supply of dustbins. A large number of cesspools were abolished in 1857 (1,104), a noticeable fall in later reports suggesting that the task was mainly achieved.

The reports make interesting reading, but by the law that if one can count achievement it does not amount to much, they illustrate the problem's magnitude as much as its improvement. They did demonstrate that a turning-point, at least in local government, sewerage and public health, had been reached. Slaughter-houses and cow-houses were among local inspections. The former now had to be licensed, and the 100 in Islington actually required little improvement. Cow-houses totalled 54, containing 924 cows, mostly with fewer than 50 each; though the largest had 293 cattle, presumably Laycock's, though not identified. These were reported as providing too little space per cow and usually with poor ventilation. Some were filthy, or badly paved and drained. The method of removal of dung was considered inefficient, cattle food was usually deteriorating from the poor drainage, and so forth. Many cows brought in from the country succumbed to disease within a couple of months, and the report noted that in general cow-keeping was conducted "so negligently as, directly or indirectly, to create nuisances and to endanger health".

As for public health in 1856, tuberculosis cases in Islington were higher than the London average. Much the worst area was Thornhill ward, with more than 22 per cent. This was in west Barnsbury, where there were a number of ill-built, cramped hillside streets of small houses (mostly swept away in the 1930s), while Barnsbury itself had the best record at only 13.05 per cent. Similarly Thornhill had a bad record for under-5 deaths, and Canonbury, with Upper Holloway and St Mary's districts, had the lowest numbers. The pattern was repeated with epidemic diseases.

Dr Ballard fulminated against the prevailing poverty, apathy, ignorance and neglect. In 1857 house inspections showed that by an order from the magistrates in the east district 94 houses had been ventilated by a window or at least an air-brick, a bald statistic revealing a sad state of affairs. Some landlords were fined for overcrowding. If the Act were strictly applied, however, Dr Ballard reported, scarcely a single tenement inspected would satisfy regulations. He compared the situation in Pentonville prison, where each cell was allowed 800 cubic feet of air, renewable in at most 20 minutes, to these small tenements which had as little as 135 to 220 cubic feet, not renewed. Filthy clothes, excretions, breath, between them contributed to their unimprovable state.

Ballard admitted that the well constructed lodging houses for the labouring classes, beginning to be built, were a step forward, but pointed out their great drawback, that they did nothing for the poorest who needed them most.

Streets suffering 'zymotic mortality' were not only found in Thornhill ward, Stroud Vale and lanes now long demolished, but in such streets as Offord Road and Bingfield Street, all mostly built only a few years earlier. Surprising cases were revealed in Barnsbury: Brooksby and Cloudesley Streets and part of Copenhagen Street. In St Mary's area even Gibson and Milner Squares, Halton Place and Cross Street, had black spots, also a number in Canonbury, and especially in St Peter's ward.

Later years brought slow improvement. The 1859 report, published shortly before the census, showed a fairly good death rate in view of the continuing population rise, but increased by an oppressively hot summer. Scarlet fever had been a danger, and from 1860 smallpox, starting in Upper Holloway (1858) began to spread, because many people were either not vaccinated or given an inadequate dose. Numbers were too high: the worst were 10 cases in Caledonia Street and eight in nearby Netherland Place. In Sidney Grove, St Peter's, where in 1859 a "frightful" scarlet fever epidemic raged, there were nine, in Elder Walk eight. Elsewhere deaths rarely exceeded one in each outbreak.

In 1861 high infant mortality appeared in newly-built areas, like Shepherdess Walk off the City Road, and Mildmay, where (Ballard reported) most new houses had "back street parlours in the basement", and what should have been front kitchens were used as sitting rooms where children spent their time – damp, poorly ventilated and smelling of the drains.

Dr Ballard deplored the long working hours, especially in shops, Sunday work, and the lack of healthy recreational outlets. He particularly regretted the lack of progress on "providing such an invaluable health-resort for our population as the Finsbury Park promised to become". The Park was finally opened in 1869. (*See Chapter 32*)

In 1862 several districts showed a lower death rate, such as in Theberton Street, White Conduit, Highbury Hill and Vale, and Kingsland; whereas Belle Isle, Barnsbury, Battle Bridge and other places had an increase – probably caused by the further population rise, now estimated as 164,986. Belle Isle, in fact, by 1863 had a 31 per thousand death rate of its population, almost doubled from the previous year, and was now worse than Ball's Pond (30.9), while the notorious so-called 'Irish Courts' off the Angel had rocketed to a record 42 per 1,000, and were typical in providing every condition making for disease. (They were demolished only in the 1870s). In a flagrant piece of racism typical of his time, Ballard observed that, being Irish, they were "dirty in their habits, that personal and domestic proprieties have no place in their system of life, and that social irregularities of all kinds abound", presumably implying sexual immorality, incest or child abuse. Yet even among themselves, Ballard noted, there were degrees of depravity. Smith's Buildings inhabitants were superior to those in Rose and Crown Court, who in turn were "not nearly so filthy" as those in Waters Court – and even here there had been great improvements in the past quarter-century.

In the Clerkenwell area in the late 1860s the missioner James Greenwood describes more than 2,000 rooms inspected, almost all "filthy or overcrowded or imperfectly drained, or badly ventilated, or out of repair". In 1,989 inhabited rooms, 1,576 families were living, sometimes with four or five children. Many were crammed with more than one family who had to sleep promiscuously, men, women, children alike, whether sick, dying or even dead, in the same filthy rag or straw bed. Greenwood mentions a few areas where "48 men, 73 women, and 59 children are living in 34 rooms", quoting one room as housing a man, four women and two children, another with 2 men, 3 women and 5 children. He also describes in unpleasant detail the quality of the fetid air, "the product of putrefaction, and of the various foetid and stagnant exhalations that pollute".[4]

Among the poorest, baby farming was not unusual. An inquest on a starving infant in St Luke's in the 1860s revealed that the minder had left the child cold and untended while she was drunk, and that the young mother, a paper-bag maker, never earned more than 6s 3d a week, of which she paid out 4s 6d for care of the baby.[5] More sinister, in 1872 a person in Islington advertised supposed nourishment for an unwanted baby "for ever, and no questions asked, for a 5£ note".[6]

1   Census Reports figures; Cherry & Pevsner, *London 4: North*, p. 649; Shepherd, *London 1808–1870*, pp. 22–3, 84, etc.; and e.g. Rev. Richard Lovett, *London Pictures*, Religious Tract Society, 1890.

2   *Annual Reports of the Sanitary Condition of the Parish of Islington*, (from 1856), (published from 1867); Stephen Halliday, *The Great Stink of London: Sir Joseph Bazalgette and the Cleansing of the Victorian Capital*, Sutton Publishing, 1999, pp. 48ff.

3   *Clerkenwell Times*, 20 December 1855.

4   *Islington Medical Officer of Health Reports*, 1856ff.

5   James Greenwood, *The Seven Curses of London*, London, 1867, pp. 20ff, 34.

6   Advertisement in *The Draper*, 10 May 1872.

CHAPTER 30

Villas for the Middle Class

In 1849 a writer in *The Builder* noted how railways were affecting the now inner suburbs, and quoted as an example a family removing from the Cloudesley Square area to distant Sydenham, and from Myddelton Square to Penge, identified (being as yet little known) as "on the Croydon line".

In 1863 Islington was reckoned to have 20,878 occupied houses, 888 uninhabited and 501 still building, with the eastern half of the parish more built-up than the west. From the 1860s to the end of the century Islington

building spread to the parish limits, and by the time it became a borough in 1899 it was completely built up. Highbury, Finsbury Park, Tollington and Crouch End, Tufnell Park and the Archway area were now thoroughly part of London. Tufnell Park, covering one of the largest areas, was also the most spacious with larger gardens, and its houses displayed interestingly varied detail. Indeed the northern parts of Islington were characterised by variations of style, from bay-windowed row to semi-detached, from gabled villa to high terraces,

94. Middle-class villas in Barnsbury: Belitha Villas c.1905.

with raised basements and front doors reached by flights of steps, to name but a few. Endless strings of undifferentiated low-rise rows, hardly distinguishing street from street, formed parts of Holloway and Finsbury Park.

The development was not generally pleasing. A *Building News* correspondent in 1858 complains how gardens, for example in Highbury, were "desecrated to semi-public use": urban street patterns of terraced rows were inappropriate in the more distant places, where each ought to have its own garden.

As for the style of new housing, the same paper in 1873 attacked Islington, along with Bayswater, Brixton and so on for "lamentable want of taste ... the trumpery allotments which have been dealt out to builders, and

the closely-packed streets and terraces which have arisen". Instead of semi-detached, or well-proportioned villas, between which one could glimpse the country and fresh air, "we have barbarously-stuccoed streets and terraces, of most contemptible architecture, stereotyped *ad infinitum*". Because too few "semi-detached country-looking villas" could be found within easy reach of town, people had to move farther out to the then country, where new suburbs could grow *looking* like suburbs.[1]

Tufnell Park is an interesting example of development of part of an old manorial estate. In the 19th century it was in the hands of the Tufnell family, who in 1822 applied for the necessary Act to reduce copyholds and grant building leases on the demesne. The estate

95. St George's Church in Tufnell Park Road. Its circular interior was used as a theatre-in-the-round in the later 20th century.

Surveyor John Shaw, who died in 1870, designed the earliest houses. His successor was George Truefitt, who had designed many of the villas from the early 1850s, such as 2–11 Grove Place in 1852, and 1–11 Tufnell Park Villas (now part of Tufnell Park Road). By 1870 more had been built by the same architect, along with the Byzantine-style St George's Church.[2] Truefitt himself lived in one of the houses in St George's Grove, and later at 'Fernbank', Carleton Road. Carleton and Anson were Tufnell family names used as street names.

In the mid-17th century the Mildmay family had acquired some 44 acres at the eastern tip of Islington parish extending nearly to Ball's Pond Road. The group of streets with their name was developed in the 1850s: Mildmay Park, 1853–4, Mildmay Street, 1854, and the later Mildmay Road, 1861–2 and Mildmay Grove, 1875–6 (at first known as South and North Grove), with the local church, St Jude's, by A D Gough in 1855.

In 1874 the *Building News* described how the 'Northern Heights', London's north suburbs of Highgate, Upper Holloway and Highbury, attracted people by their "bracing atmosphere, elevated position, fine views, and open situation". As the decades passed, even these one-time outliers lost the fine views, just as had Barnsbury and Pentonville several decades earlier.

Much later came Whitehall Park, built near the Archway in 1891 on the site of an 1860s house of that name in Hornsey Lane, overlooking the whole of London, with new streets built over the estate grounds. Its individual style and decorative ironwork were many years later to qualify it and surrounding streets to be designated a Conservation Area (1973), then unusual for houses of such date and style.

The growth of 'country-looking villas' in spacious gardens in outer suburbs brought into fashion the Queen Anne style, which had spread from London's western suburbs. The *Building News* in 1877, while criticising the pretension, admitted that they had now sprung up "by the hundred ... at Finsbury Park, Holloway, Dalston, Chalk Farm, Hampstead, Kilburn", not to mention south of the Thames.[3]

Yet there were also as many mean rows in Islington as in Battersea, cramming too many in to the acre, with "backyards or so-called gardens". Such trash spread to more distant places where under-paid clerks and over-worked shop assistants had to travel too far by the early morning and late evening trains, only to endure the same living conditions that they could have had in Islington.

Allowing for changes of detail and size, both of which became heavier and larger, the spread of building in and after the 1820s had resulted in an inner and central London of boringly uniform streets, terraces and squares, summed up as "two windows and a door, a door and two windows". Comfort and luxury were internal. With the exception of its historic churches and particular landmarks, observes Charles Pascoe, writing in 1903, "London displayed, till within the last few years, little architectural elegance".[4]

Even middle-class houses were stuffy and ill-ventilated, especially the bedrooms, small and low; gas-light was not yet very common and there were mostly no bathrooms. Grossmith's Mr Pooter in Upper Holloway, with a geyser-fed bathroom, was well housed. Nor was plumbing all that efficient, or well aired.

As new suburbs drew the rich outwards, the earlier terraces, as well as the shoddy developments by some local builders, had been overrun by the poor. London's northern outer suburbs of 1851, Islington, Holloway and Hackney, later housed poorer families in streets vacated by the better-off. The new outer suburbs, at first thinly built-on, were now themselves a grid of streets – like Tufnell Park, Tollington and Hornsey.

1   G R Emerson, *How the Great City Grew*, London, 1862; Donald J Olsen, *The Growth of Victorian London*, London, Batsford, 1976; *The Builder*, 1849, p. 459; *Building News*, 1858, p. 606; 1863, p. 175; 1873, p. 193.

2   Converted into St George's Elizabethan Theatre in 1970, since closed, and in 2004 under negotiation for restitution as a church.

3   *Building News*, 1874, p. 425; 1877, p. 531.

4   Charles Eyre Pascoe, *London of Today*, London, 1903 p. 48.

CHAPTER 31

Housing the Working Class

Treatment of working-class housing in the 19th century was often not very enlightened. Early attempts at improvement foundered through seeing only half the problem. It was one thing to offer respectable, hard-working artisans places in a model lodging-house, quite another to help the teeming under-employed and their families. Neither sweeping away (a favourite term) the squalid courts and alleys round the Angel and Clerkenwell, nor driving new highways – Clerkenwell Road and later, Rosebery Avenue – through old slums, could solve the problem unless new accommodation was available for the dis-placed.

By mid-century improved housing for the poor had been built in many parts of London, like Farringdon Road, Bloomsbury and espe-cially in the slummy parts of the West End such as Seven Dials and Shaftesbury Avenue. A writer in 1903 looked back with incredulity on the barbarous conditions commonplace many years earlier: a man sharing his room with a donkey and ducks, or up to 60 people whose sole water supply was an uncovered water butt, its contents like green slime.

The Artisans' and Labourers' Act of 1868, known as the Torrens Act after William Tor-rens, MP for Finsbury from 1865 to 1885, aimed to make owners maintain their houses in good condition, but made no allowance for either compensation or demolition, and it was little used. Next came the Artizans' and Labourers' Dwellings Improvement Act (the Cross Act) of 1875, which while requiring compulsory purchase, demolition and re-building of houses deemed beyond repair, by contrast offered such generous compensation that parish authorities were reluctant to in-voke it. An amendment fixing compensation at market value, minus the cost of removing the cause of nuisance, still left both Acts under-used.

MODEL DWELLINGS

Philanthropists, meanwhile, were hard at work, notably Octavia Hill, who devoted her life to improving tenants' own attitudes and conditions. For example, her rehabilitation campaign influenced the Northampton estate managers to stop using middle-men, instead employing lady visitors as rent collectors, who also kept an eye on the properties, with beneficial effect.[1] Mrs Hill encouraged thrift among tenants, regular payment of rents, and Evangelical instruction by her missionary-minded ladies. She was good at this, her imi-tators less so.

Housing societies and model dwellings companies did provide better quality hous-ing. But they imposed strict rules, insisting on employers' references, regular jobs (and no 'offensive' homework), no dogs, no gas-light after 11 pm., and so forth. Their army-discipline approach, and the barrack-like building blocks, drew criticism not only from inmates but from the do-gooders themselves, who asked why housing need look so grim.

One leading provider of model housing was George Peabody, born in Massachusetts in 1795 but living since Queen Victoria's acces-sion in London. A merchant and banker, from the 1860s he devoted much of his fortune to building for the poor. Starting with the modest idea of providing drinking fountains, or opening Ragged Schools, he was persuaded by Lord Shaftesbury to undertake model housing. Peabody Buildings were by current standards more airy and less unpleasant-looking than others.

Spitalfields in 1864 was the first of 47 estates eventually built by Peabody in London, and Islington was an early beneficiary. The Greenman Street estate off Essex Road was built in 1866 on the site of the historic Ward's Place, an area then deteriorated into hovels for "the worst characters in London". Four five-floor blocks were built at a cost of £3,600, containing 155 tenements for 650 people, its rooms measuring 9 by 12 feet. For the Dibdin Street buildings nearby, several small streets including Anglers' Gardens were flattened. Later came the estates in Clerkenwell, Farringdon Road (1882), and Dufferin and Whitecross Streets built at much the same time.

Ewing Ritchie in 1880, while deploring London's mean streets and dismal conditions especially round Drury Lane, was impressed by the range of Peabody Buildings, which by then housed nearly 10,000. He reckoned that the Artizans' and Labourers' Dwellings Act had at least released land on to the market, which Peabody for one was buying up. Similarly the Metropolitan Board of Works was removing 16 blocks for new buildings in Pear Tree Court, Clerkenwell, Whitecross Street, Essex Road and elsewhere. This would release 41 acres, enough to house a few thousand more. The Improved Industrial Dwellings Company's properties included a block near the Great Northern Railway goods station, and two near the City Road.[2]

The Metropolitan Association for Improving the Dwellings of the Industrious Classes – a title which defines the limitation on those it was aimed at – followed their early Pancras Road tenement of 1847 with others in

96. *The Peabody blocks in Greenman Street, off Essex Road in 1866.*

97. Corporation Buildings in Farringdon Road, built by the Corporation of London in 1866.

Spitalfields, and in 1874 with Farringdon Buildings in Farringdon Road, five blocks of "novel design" for 260 families. This was high-density building on a site of less than an acre, its tower blocks at right-angles to the road, only 20 feet apart. The flats of two and three rooms were self-contained, provided with sculleries and lavatories. These idealistic projects, regarded as conforming to best practice at the time, employed no leading architects: the Association engaged designers through competitions which were poorly organised and regulated, hence not popular.

Also in 1874, the Improved Industrial Dwellings Company ran a competition for buildings in Goswell Street, on an important site acquired from the Marquess of Northampton. Strict conditions were advertised, again for self-contained flats with separate entrances, ground-floor shops, external staircases to the upper floors, and a flat roof accessible to all. The winner was Henry Macaulay of Kingston, the runner-up Banister Fletcher. Macaulay proposed installing small rear balconies to overcome the problem of the limited site, and of rooms opening off each other (including the lavatories), but this proved more expensive and the company abandoned the idea, reverting to their traditional style.

All these experiments were on small, narrow sites. The same company, for example, bought up a single row of derelict cottages and replaced them with a high over-large block. Only the Peabody Trust built on a more generous scale, which later became the norm. Their blocks might face the street on one side and a court on the other, better than the stinking yards they replaced – but they were still generally admitted to look dauntingly grim.

The Cross Act of 1875, which enabled the Metropolitan Board of Works to lay out the land acquired with only as much accommodation as had been demolished, led to a housing stalemate: the Board was bound to make a loss, and could not pass on the cost to ratepayers.

Not until the passing of the Artisans' Dwellings Act in 1882 was the task of housing eased by reducing the obligations by half – but at the same time it halved the chance to rehouse the displaced. That chance was at last increased in 1890 by the Housing of the Working Classes Act, which for the first time took a comprehensive look at the problem, actually empowering local authorities to provide new housing, while updating the method of action on unfit dwellings. Beaconsfield Buildings, next to York Way, of 1878–9, by the Victoria Dwellings Association to Charles Barry the Younger's design, was considered a fine example of its kind: indeed, such a model that it was not only named after the then Prime Minister Benjamin Disraeli, Lord Beaconsfield, but the foundation stone was laid before a distinguished gathering by the Home Secretary, Assheton Cross. An MOH report in 1906 quoted 379 dwellings, which were provided with 191 WCs off the landings. Eventually there were 15 blocks, providing 430 flats.[3]

The Beaconsfield site, however, was in a declining area, close to the polluted Belle Isle and its notorious factories, and suffered from bad drainage. Further, the early standard was unfortunately not maintained. One inhabitant who lived there for 15 years from 1892 recalled it as 'Bug Island', and that its dust chutes harboured dozens of rats. "One filthy toilet for the use of six families" – too far to trail down at night, so that instead tenants made use of "stinking buckets".

This was to become one of the notorious 'Buildings' which survived far too long into the 20th century, in later decades well below acceptable living standards and, known as 'the Crumbles', a public disgrace. In the 1960s ownership passed to property companies, and in 1966 the Greater London Council took over and began rehousing, yet some families remained as late as 1969. After seven years of campaigning the buildings were finally demolished only in 1971.[4]

Other artisan housing surviving until after the 2nd World War included Popham Cottages, Queens Cottages and Quinns Buildings, off Essex Road, opened with great acclaim in the 1870s and 1880s. The last of the group was demolished by 1971, thanks to tenants' association pressure.

Among important housing blocks which survived longer were Liverpool Buildings in Liverpool Road, opened in 1883, four sets of model dwellings at the corner of Highbury Station Road (but demolished in the 1990s). Much later came the five blocks of Samuel Lewis Buildings, by the Samuel Lewis Trust, between 1910 and 1914, ending at the corner of Laycock Street. Thornhill Houses, at the junction of Thornhill Road and Barnsbury Park, were built in 1902 by the East End Dwellings Company.

ENTER THE LCC

In 1884 a Royal Commission on Housing headed by Sir Charles Dilke investigated the whole spectrum of public health, housing and its legislation and finances, and in 1885 agreed on the need for financial assistance. It had now begun to be accepted that housing was a matter not for the mission-minded but for society generally. The Local Government Act of 1888, which abolished the Metropolitan Board of Works and established the London County Council, paved the way for the new Housing Act in 1890, a wholesale repeal of early legislation and codifying practice.

The 1890 Act simplified improvement, because it was contemporary with the start of local government reformation. Following establishment of the LCC came the creation in 1899 of 28 boroughs in place of the 43 old vestries. The parish of Islington became a borough, Clerkenwell now came under Finsbury, and the two new boroughs continued in their separate ways until 1965.[5]

The new authorities, with the consolidated

Acts in 1890 and decades of earlier experimental help, were enabled to produce municipal housing. In 1894 power was extended to acquiring land outside local boundaries and moving residents wholesale to new estates.

The new LCC was intent on slum clearance, and rather than attempt to upgrade existing housing, much of which was not just beyond reclamation but should never have been built at all, there was large-scale demolition, and the face of London began a radical change.[6]

One of the LCC's early major achievements, in 1899, resulted in the creation of Kingsway and Aldwych. To rehouse those evicted, land was acquired in Clerkenwell and Portpool Road off Gray's Inn Road to build the Bourne estate. But this housing, though much more attractive was still insufficient, and although rehousing was now seen as essential, it was not seen as necessarily in the same area. Here the new trams, now under LCC authority, came into their own, and the creation of more distant housing estates in new outlying suburbs became linked with the provision of new tram routes.

In the last quarter of the 19th century London underwent a transformation, with its new railway terminals, hotels and restaurants of a kind never before known, besides galleries, museums and public libraries, not to mention new schools – and improved housing as well. By the turn of the 20th century the general picture seemed increasingly rosy.

CHARLES BOOTH'S SURVEY

An important contribution to public awareness of the state of housing and poverty was made in the 1890s by the field research of a group of investigators under Charles Booth, a ship-owner much concerned with social questions. Booth's invaluable volumes of *Life and Labour of the People of London*, grading areas by colour codes into good, medium and downright bad, investigated, for example, poverty and the state of religion. His findings proved enlightening. They included the information that in Finsbury, 20 tenants were housed by the breweries, 3,500 by philanthropic societies, 2,000 by a trading company, and only 896 were living in privately owned blocks, of varying quality.

Tenements or flatted buildings in which the societies had invested had by the 1890s become the norm, especially in the then new suburbs. Booth noted that in eleven central London districts in 1888-9, out of 418 blocks providing 31,116 dwellings, Finsbury had the highest number with 79 blocks (7,141 dwellings). Next came Hackney, with 67 (4,190), while the City was lowest with only 8 (420). In three years from 1889 Finsbury added 8 blocks (520 dwellings), Hackney 6 (223), and even Tower Hamlets now had 15. London's inner ring had had a general increase, and new blocks included two in Hackney by the Guinness Trustees and "Mr Hartnell's" two in the recently built Rosebery Avenue.[7]

Booth's findings showed that most of London's best blocks were by the philanthropic societies and other non-profit-making organisations, providing the most space, light, comfort and good sanitation. This largely derived from the influence of the Peabody Trust, the Metropolitan Association, and the Improved Industrial Dwellings Company.

Booth praised the recent improved appearance of model dwellings compared with the earlier when a "plain exterior" was thought enough. For example, while earlier Peabody Buildings had sacrificed stair light to maximise light in the rooms, now stairs were given windows; cupboards, wallpaper and similar minor features were essentials, and all now had fireplaces. They were also spared basement bathrooms, to which heated water had had to be lugged down from the flats. Not surpisingly, tenants had preferred to go out to the public wash-houses.

An LCC analysis of the MBW improvements before 1891 (hence not including Rosebery Avenue) showed that in Peartree Court, Clerkenwell in 1877–8, while 410 people had been displaced, 612 were rehoused, and in Whitecross Street the figures were 3,687 and 3,740. In High Street Islington (the Angel area), 515 were displaced but 800 rehoused, and in Essex Road 1,796 and 3,866. Thus in the late 19th century there was a considerable net housing gain compared with the wholesale eviction of earlier years, which by forcing the poor to cram into already overcrowded alternatives had actually aggravated the problem.[8]

But there was a long way to go. Booth

pointed out how bad building, for example in the Hornsey area, naturally hastened decline, while clearance in Somers Town for railway building had "sent a whole colony of very rough people to the badly built streets near Junction Road". Even the more soundly built Tufnell Park of the 1860s, which had originally attracted better-off people, would probably go down in quality if more streets like Corinne and Hugo Roads, built in 1879 and 1887, were run up. On the other hand the saving of Highbury Fields by handing it over to the MBW as permanent open space, helped maintain standards and halt that area's possible deterioration.

By 1890 when Islington was regarded as having probably the largest population of any parish in Britain, Booth listed its worst areas which marred the general picture of "comfortable circumstances and occasional affluence": south-east of Essex Road, between Packington and Rotherfield Streets were the large blocks built on the site of Anglers' Gardens and possibly re-inhabited by the same families. On former glebe land on the same side of the street, adjoining the former turnpike, were Dorset Street and Orchard Street (later named Dove Road after the building firm), and Wakeham Street. Both sites were, in Booth's rating, 'light blue', that is of 'moderate poverty'. Another light blue area was between Caledonian Road, nearly opposite Thornhill Square, and the western parish boundary alongside the railway.

The other chief blue areas were first, west of the Holloway Road, St Matthias west of Caledonian Road and St Barnabas adjoining the south end of Caledonian Market, and St James's Holloway, centred on George's Road. East of Holloway Road were the notorious Queensland Road district, and a couple of areas of north Holloway, Hampden Road area (subsequently entirely demolished), and a street east of Cornwallis Road, where the then Workhouse was sited. And there was the infamous Campbell Road, running down to Seven Sisters Road. The last two have long been demolished. All these, with other pockets in Pentonville, created a piebald appearance on Booth's map.

In 1890 the *Building News* complained that speculative building had downgraded "once delightful" suburbs, "retreats" for City men, spoiling parts of Hampstead, Highgate, Hornsey and Finsbury, as well as areas south of the Thames. Such new areas were overcrowded by 50–60 houses to the acre, lowering the status of earlier high-quality streets. Yet a few years later the same journal noted that suburbs maintained their character and individuality, naming among these Islington along with St John's Wood and Chelsea. "There are over a score of High Streets in our evergrowing London still retaining their identity", in spite of rapacious landlords and speculative developers flattening out their differences.[9]

Information in this chapter is based on George Godwin, *Another Blow for Life*, London, 1864, and *London Shadows*, London, 1854; Andrew Mearns, *The Bitter Cry of Outcast London*, (reprint), Leicester UP, 1970; *Notes on the Housing Question in Finsbury*, Newman & Thomas (Finsbury MOH Report, 1901); Rev, Thomas Beames, *The Rookeries of London*, 1850 and revised edn, 1852. See also "Dwellings for the Poor", *The Builder*, 25 February 1871.

1   Simon Jenkins, *Landlords to London*, 1974; Octavia Hill, 'Cottage Property in London', in *Fortnightly Review*, November 1866 (published in *Homes of the London Poor*, London, 1875.

2   J W Ritchie, *Days and Nights in London*, London, 1880, Chapter 5.

3   *ILN*, 31 May 1879.

4   *Islington Gazette,* 3 November 1964, etc. Bingfield Park and the Disney-like 'Crumbles Castle', an imaginative childern's play centre, occupy the site.

5   G E Sims, *How the Poor Live*, London, 1889.

6   E M Dence, 'The London County Council and Housing', in *Housing Happenings*, No. 4, 1929. St Pancras House Improvement Society Ltd., Christmas no., 1929, pp. 17ff.

7   Charles Booth, *Life and Labour*, Vol. III, *Poverty*, Pt. I, Chapter 1. See also Cosh, *Squares of Islington*, I, on Rosebery Square.

8   *London Statistics*, I, LCC, 1891.

9   *Building News*, 1890, p. 611; 1893, p. 732.

CHAPTER 32

More Entertainment

REVIVAL AT THE WELLS

Though pleasure-gardens became extinct from the mid-19th century, the music hall emerged as popular entertainment, and there was a revival in the fortunes of Sadler's Wells. The theatre had sunk as low as it could get. Even the road to it from Clerkenwell offered an orgy of shooting galleries, roulette tables, showmen of monstrosities, their patrons thieves and prostitutes, enough to scare off the few cultivated visitors. In the theatre itself (recalled a writer in 1875) audiences were "of the lowest possible class". The *Daily News* in 1856 remembered that it had been "a sink of abomination, its plays a travesty, riots among its degraded audience a commonplace." Indeed, what happened on stage was of little importance, as it was inaudible through the hoots, yells and ribald exchanges of the audience, who stamped, threw missiles and clamoured for comic songs. Dickens describes the depravity in *Household Words*, every performance "resounding with foul language, oaths, catcalls, shrieks, yells, blasphemy, obscenity – a truly diabolical clamour", and interrupted by frequent fights.

Such was Sadler's Wells when in 1844 a remarkable actor took over in partnership with a woman, Mrs Warner. He was Samuel Phelps, one of Macready's company (who had managed first Covent Garden and then Drury Lane), determined to take on the uncouth patrons of the Wells. Forty years old, well built and powerful, probably no-one less tough could have taken up the challenge to "educate his audience" by bringing them Shakespeare. The intrepidity with which

98. Samuel Phelps.

Phelps opened seemed over-rash, when the usual mob appeared and accompanied the show with all the customary interruptions, plus "apples, oranges, nuts, biscuits, ginger-beer, porter, and pipes", while at the doors fish was as usual being fried alongside oyster-stalls.

The partners started by ordering off the motley showmen, a foolhardy gesture, for on

271

opening with *Macbeth*, the dispossessed and friends turned up intent on smashing the place. "They little knew the man they had to deal with", writes a journalist years later. "At the end of the first act the new lessee, then a stalwart and powerful man in the prime of life, appeared in the gallery, in costume, and at once seized the ringleader . . . and literally lifted him out of the gallery. This boldness caused an instant revulsion in the actor's favour. 'Three Cheers for Phelps' – and peace reigned."

By degrees Phelps was able, with police help, to remove the fish-friers and oyster-sellers, despite their frenzied claims to be authorised by the New River Company. He also got rid of the beer-seller inside, as well as the screaming infants in arms, after women smuggled them in under their shawls. He even invoked an old Act forbidding bad language in public, in a handbill distributed with the tickets – and would stop the play to get an offender removed. Before long he could get through even a five-act play to an attentive audience.

In his first season Phelps produced five Shakespeare plays on 106 nights, besides Beaumont and Fletcher, Sheridan and others, and in following seasons introduced new plays, mostly Shakespeare, all well produced and staged with care to detail, including striking scenery.

The best boxes were three shillings, the gallery at 6d now "orderly as a lecture room", and respectable families filled the pit at a shilling. It seemed a miracle, as the audience responded not only in the theatre but in studying the plays at home.[1] It was indeed a minor revolution in the cause of 'culture'.

Over the next 18 years, from 1844 to 1862, devotees in Clerkenwell and Islington turned up faithfully at Sadler's Wells, where Phelps produced thirty Shakespeare plays to regular audiences.

In 1853 the author and journalist Harrison Ainsworth, vividly recalling dismal days of "harrowing melodrama" and "screeching farces" in a dirty, uncomfortable theatre, had evidently not fully appreciated the change when, "greatly daring", he decided on a visit. Descending from the Favorite omnibus near the entrance, to his amazement he found "a dense crowd that besieged pit and gallery door", the galleryites admittedly grubby and

noisy as ever, but the pit-ites almost wholly of the superior ranks of clerks, "got up considerably for the occasion, with gold chains and rings" – badge of the 'gent', he suggests, rather than the 'gentleman'. Doors once open, the crowd pours in among a torrent of oaths and bad language, but a tip to the doorkeeper secures Ainsworth a front seat, able to appreciate the "very decent" orchestra. He finds himself quite impressed by Phelps as Othello and a good supporting cast (except for their regularly calling Phelps "Otheller"): "no unnecessary sawing of the air or insane gesticulation, no tearing of a passion to rags". He is entertained by audience comments ("What a villain that *Iarger* is!") and their tears at Desdemona's fate, but notes that for Londoners they are uniquely quiet and respectful, none of the loud talking and laughter that then characterised the boxes of more fashionable theatres. They did, however, accompany the deepening plot with copious devouring of oranges and occasional swigs from bottles.[2]

Altogether, Phelps's transformation of the formerly deteriorating theatre was enough to create a new audience of devotees.

Phelps also produced concerts, with reputable singers and performers, though one may wonder exactly what was the "inimitable entertainment" provided by the (English) Ethiopian Serenaders, or what was played by the sextet of a cornet-à-pisons, pianoforte, concertina, Gothic harp, violin and flute (1847). For this, private boxes were sold at a guinea and guinea-and-a-half, and even the gallery was upped to a shilling. Phelps even opened the theatre in 1854 for a Temperance meeting by Total Abstainers, apparently attended by thousands.

Sadler's Wells was one of many London theatres refurbished in the '40s and '50s, though except in the boxes seating remained as backless benches. In 1856 there was a move to rebuild, especially as north London's huge population increase had little theatre provision, as great a lack to many people as was the shortage of churches to the Rev. Daniel Wilson. The proposal was to raise £10,000 in £10 shares in order to create a theatre seating 3,000 with adequate space and proper refreshment rooms. This, however, seems not to have been achieved.

The days of fame and fortune sadly came to an end with Phelps's retirement in 1862, and successive managers were a poor substitute. Among other productions there was a return to farces and melodramas, as a Christmas advertisement of 1869 shows, for a local pantomime called *Ye Faire Maide of Merry Islington, or Hoarlequin* (sic) *the Cruel Prior of Canonbury, and the Chivalrous Knights of St John*, written by Mr F. G. Cheatham with "brilliant" scenery by Mr Gowrie.[3]

By the mid-1870s the Wells had become dark and dismantled, thick with cobwebs and dust, still displaying tattered old playbills. Yet despite stained walls and broken windows the building was still sound. There were proposals for its conversion into baths and washhouses, as part of the current cleanliness campaign, and an unexpired lease was advertised at an estimated rental value of £1,000. Another plan was for a skating rink and Winter Garden, then for boxing, and Sunday religious lectures. In 1877 Professor Pepper, a popular science lecturer of the 'Royal Poly', demonstrated fireproof scenery, which at least ought to have been popular in view of theatres' vulnerability to fires. One of his suggestions was for fitting Lawes & McLennan's patent theatre fire-extinguisher, which involved installing perforated pipes across the ceiling to act as a sprinkler once the mains water was turned on.[4]

Desperate attempts were made for legitimate stage revival. In 1878-9 the theatre was again refurbished under the management of Mrs Bateman. The interior was enlarged to hold 2,500 by the architect C J Phipps, designer of 22 other theatres, and the renovation was a real modernisation, thought so handsome as to make the place hardly recognisable. A new saloon above the vestibule looked out over the New River reservoir, the exterior was lit by globe electric lights, and the theatre was now accessible not only by omnibuses but by trams and by King's Cross and Farringdon Stations on the Inner Circle underground, both within walking distance.

The theatre was reopened on 9 October 1879 with a revival of *Rob Roy*, first acted long ago in Edinburgh in 1819, and still very successful though dated in style. It was an impressive production with a cascade of New River water in the glen scene, and generated hopes for the future. Hedging its bets, the theatre also opened on Sundays for religious services. . The outlook did seem promising. In 1881 Sadler's Wells and the Court (at Sloane Square) were praised as the only suburban theatres that "publicly aspire to positions in the first rank", outstripping merely local theatres at Hoxton, Shoreditch and so on.

But the progress slowed to a limp. "A singularly unlucky theatre", pronounced G A Sala in 1882, in spite of attempts by talented actresses to produce favourites like *East Lynne*. The aquatic idea was tried again, using the under-stage tank to represent Henley Regatta (1886). All these gallant efforts failed, and the theatre closed again. It was sold as a venue for touring companies, staging melodramas, pantomimes and variety. *Maria Marten* and *The Man in the Iron Mask* enlivened it in 1890. But with a *fin-de-siècle* renaissance of suburban theatres the Wells now had local rivals, the Grand near the Angel taking the lead. The Wells was refused a variety licence though, in 1893 an enterprising character named George Belmont squeezed in variety under cover of orthodox drama, keeping things going fairly successfully for several more years.

Among Belmont's more spectacular achievements, at the end of 1896, was to introduce the new 'moving pictures', made by the pioneer R W Paul, which had been shown that February at the Finsbury Technical College as the 'Theatrograph'. This was a motley collection of shots, anything from the Tsar at Versailles to laughing children at tea-time. For an audience today probably the most interesting item would be the view of traffic on Blackfriars Bridge, or Sunday morning in Whitechapel. Belmont next staged a number of so-called dramas and more frequently, variety artists, films made by 'the British Biograph' and the 'Historiograph', and plays such as *The Great Detective*, based on Sherlock Holmes. Smoking, though allowed by other theatres, was forbidden, a matter of great complaint. Yet although he claimed to have made it pay, Belmont closed the theatre in May 1902 in order to get away from London to the Continent – and never returned.[5]

THE EAGLE

The Eagle continued not exactly a theatre, not exactly a music hall, more a bit of both. It inspired the song *Pop goes the Weasel*, the tailor's iron supposedly 'popped' at the pawnbroker's at the end of a week of over-spending – very likely on evenings at the Eagle. Long before that, among its playbills one in 1855 advertised "Aerial Trapeze at an Elevation of 70 feet from the Earth, to conclude with the Terrific Ascent of Mlle Josephine Elsler on the Cercle Tension [tightrope], 400 feet long and 60 feet high".

In 1851 Ben Oliver (1805-72), known as Ben Conquest, took over the Eagle and its Grecian Theatre, and by the ambitious scale of his entertainment transformed it into one of the most popular Cockney haunts. The theatre presented ballet, melodrama and pantomime. The famous Cockney song *Villikins and his Dinah* was first sung in 1853 either here or at Highbury Barn. Dancing was a popular feature, supposedly more respectable than at many contemporary pleasure spots, such as Vauxhall in its later decadent years.

One of the music hall celebrities who made her debut at the Eagle was Marie Lloyd, who at the age of fifteen (1885) appeared there under her real name of Matilda Wood. She actually worked in the Eagle's kitchen, but making a stage appearance she so impressed one of the audience that he took her along to the Rosemary Branch to repeat her appearance. She soon established fame under the name of Marie Lloyd, and one of her favourites was *A Bit of a Ruin Cromwell knocked about a bit*.

In 1876 the Eagle was rebuilt for the last time, and though by then surrounded by houses, it retained its pleasure garden. But it was becoming more disreputable, and in 1884 General Booth's Salvation Army bought out Conquest and used the place for mass meetings and for moral purposes such as the musical performances of their uniformed young lady choirs, accompanied by accordions and cymbals. Their interest waned on learning that as the Eagle had a current licence they had to continue to sell alcohol.

In 1898 the Bishopsgate Charity asked the Charity Commissioners to draw up a scheme for building leases on the Eagle site, taking in adjoining property in Shepherdess Walk and Nile Street, with a view to an extensive rebuild. In 1901 the Eagle was demolished, and soon afterwards the present pub, still of that name, was built almost on the site.[6]

HIGHBURY BARN

Highbury Barn was another resort at first criticised for 'Cockneydom' and lack of 'refinement' – as well as later for the rowdiness for which it was eventually closed. In the early 19th century, equipped with the younger Willoughby's Great Room fitted up in the barn itself for a regular Assembly, and for club dinner parties, the Barn twice changed hands. By 1835 it was owned by John Hinton, formerly of the Eyre Arms in St John's Wood, and later by his son Archibald, who between them renewed the resort's then flagging popularity. One of the most celebrated Society gatherings was the 3,000 who sat down at the Licensed Victuallers' dinner in 1841.

But the vogue for these was passing, and as fashion changed, Archibald Hinton introduced musical entertainments, starting at Whitsun 1854 with the band of the Grenadier Guards, but the magistrates refused a licence, claiming it as illegal.

To safeguard the money he had sunk into the Barn, Hinton formed 'the Highbury Club', using as precedent the extremely up-market Almack's,[7] which although not licensed was available to the bluest-blooded aristocrats as ticket holders for an association which ran their dances. The Barn's clientele, far from aristocrats, were "generations of cockneys" who when not dining were drinking stout and smoking: indeed it was "extensively patronized by shopmen and milliners".

In spite of complaints of disorderliness from three clergymen, Hinton obtained his licence. A couple of years later he secured a dancing licence, and in the summer of 1858 opened a grand dancing platform known as the Leviathan, complete with orchestra, covering 4,000 feet, mostly in the open air. It was brightly lit by gas, and attracted huge evening crowds. More gas-lamps were held by female statues lining an avenue, and outside the Barn in the five-acre garden was a lawn with the usual adjoining booths or alcoves.

Hinton gave up in 1860, and in 1861 Edward

99. Highbury Barn in the 1820s.

Giovanelli took over and launched the final, most grandiose stage of the Barn's existence. He built a large hall for balls and suppers, made further changes in the gardens, and engaged singers and the famous gymnast Leotard, later the tightrope walker Blondin, and even the Siamese Twins. In 1865 he too opened a theatre, named the Alexandra after the young Princess of Wales. Not that the entertainments were what the Royal Family would have approved.

The journalist Ewing Ritchie visited here in 1860. Entry, charged at 6d, was through "a dark passage, admirably adapted for a garrotte walk". He was astonished by the appearance of the Master of Ceremonies, a "distinguished swell. His attitude is faultless. His raven hair is parted in the middle; his dark eye is turned in a languishing manner upward to the orchestra."Between dances the MC patrolled the room, but "in an abstracted and poetic manner", as a man with the soul of a Beau Brummell or a Nash.

Ritchie was impressed by the "noble room", none finer in London. Views of "oriental scenery" adorned the walls, and at one end was a gallery, at the other a platform with tables and chairs. The orchestra was seated above the bar. It was less crowded than he had expected, quieter than West End haunts, and the couples were younger – often almost juvenile, the youths proud to be dancing with "young ladies of uncertain occupations", and daringly smoking cigars with their brandy-and-water.

The biggest crowds were on summer Sundays, "on the lawn before the Barn, or in the bowers and alcoves by its side". Over the years the clientele seemed to have changed. "Where are the Finsbury radicals – all beery and Chartist ... the demagogues who duped them ...?" Speech-making had given way to dancing, a hopeful sign of the times, thought Ritchie: it meant less drinking. Before his account went to press, however, ownership of the Barn had changed, and it had already been "gorgeously transformed". Why go to Paris when London could boast such a bower of flowers?

The Barn now became second only to Cremorne in Chelsea, its magnificent ballroom unsurpassed. The modest-sized grounds were well landscaped, with a "crystal platform" for outdoor dancers.

Many were the descriptions by contemporary visitors. Ewing Ritchie, whose account in *The Night Side of London* described the Barn at the end of Hinton's regime and noted the "gorgeous" changes made under Giovanelli in 1861, had spurned it as not very "refined" and its clientele as shopmen and milliners. W S Hayward's *London by Night* of about 1870 is an ill-written fiction about the unsavoury career of a "fallen woman". He describes visiting the Barn with a friend and picking up (apparently innocently) a young seamstress who of course earned very little, and "augmented her income at the expense of her chastity". Reflecting sadly that until women could be offered well-paid employment there would be numerous such girls "compelled to traffic in their honour", he at least admits to the splendour of Giovanelli's dancing room, "second only to Cremorne . . . really a magnificent erection, unsurpassed in the metropolis". The grounds he thought "tastefully laid out", with the advantage of the elegant open-air dancing platform. Indeed, under Giovanelli the Barn had "assumed a high rank among places of its description".

Besides dancing and drinking, Giovanelli offered spectacular stage shows, extravagantly advertised in the playbills: W R Osman's "Grand Gorgeous, Historical, Bustling Burlesque", *The Seven Champions of Christendom*, boasted "pictorial Picturesque Scenery", "Melodious Melodies", "Mechanical Manoeuvres", "Curious Costly Costumes", and gas lighting by a "Metro-o-politan Gastronomer". Characters were described in similarly facetious terms, with the extras "Good, Bad, and Indifferent, Ancient Bricks, Britons, and Fashionable Foreigners". From St George, champion of England, Patrick and Andrew for Ireland and Scotland, Wales, France, Spain and Italy, they ranged to an Ogre, the tyrannical Ptolemy, king of Egypt, his daughter Una (who of course ends by marrying St George), and over-the-top characters from Morocco, Jerusalem and goodness knows where, not to mention a dragon and "Miscellaneous Mummies, Monsters, Dummies, and Domestics".

Nothing, in fact, was left out.

The Barn's darker side was disapprovingly observed in about 1860 by the missionary James Hillocks, contrasting Islington's importance for "Church orthodoxy" with its "bad meeting places". He witnessed "scenes of a most disgusting kind, wicked and abominable", even in and around Upper Street and Highbury Place, from late evening into the small hours, disturbing respectable inhabitants from their sleep. The area was filled with "young sprigs, now called 'mashers', and old rakes, called 'gentlemen', with a large proportion of the rougher element, thieves and cads, and aimless wretches". Drunk men were seen reeling about or prone on the ground, and young women discreetly referred to as "on the road to ruin".

All this unseemliness he put down to the effect of the Barn, which he took care to report to a higher authority. Graphically if over-elaborately, he describes an ageing female pimp, in fine silks and with a fashionable bonnet adorned with a spotless white feather, introducing a young, gaily dressed woman to a rich man, "an overgrown disgrace to his class", his sights limited to the brothel. The girl has just parted from another escort, "a self-conceited fop" jauntily crowned by a white hat, smoking a "superior cigar" and flourishing a cane in his gold-ringed hand. Nearby are two young midshipmen, "flushed" with both drink and cash.

Such scenes are repeated in an atmosphere "vile as well as gay, corruptive, seductive, ruinous". Parties converge on the Barn as "a place of assignation", crowding into the bar where the conversation is "rude, if not lewd", in which the women take equal part.

On the dancing platform the behaviour of a whirling group of riotous young people towards the end of each dance becomes "more and more repugnant". The missionary notes how even some of the bystanders seem shocked. Through the increasingly drunken "brilliant promenade" with its glaring lights Hillocks passes into the dusky "bowers" – merely sheds. Diplomatically silent about what he sees going on, he emerges to find a great change. The "painted beauties" have mostly left, only the old and ugly remain. He stays till morning, "but the scenes were such that I dare not particularise. Strong drink, licentious ways, and vicious habits . . . debased humanity in its worst aspect of unbridled riot."[8]

From 1870, renewal of the Barn's dancing licence was opposed by the locals, and despite a change of management it was closed in October 1871 and went to ruin.

Ten years after the Barn's disgrace and closure, its site was built over and today is marked by a later pub of the same name. Highbury Barn's disappearance from the social scene may be said to mark the final eclipse of the Vauxhall style of entertainment.

STREET ENTERTAINMENT, PENNY GAFFS . . . AND LECTURES

In mid-century the poor who could afford neither plays, panoramas nor halls were amused by street theatre, acrobats, barrel organs and the like. Among free street shows were Punch and Judy, a caravan-load of travelling tumblers and tightrope walkers, dancing children, or perhaps just a boy playing an organ with a monkey. There were hurdy-gurdy players, bagpipers, freaks like albinos – or a peep through a telescope. Even the old mediaeval displays still survived, such as the May-time Jack-in-the-Green, and in November the stuffed figure of Guy Fawkes was hauled around.[9]

Charles Manby Smith in 1852 listed the various street organs, from the grand affair drawn by horse and cart, to the French hand-organist, monkey organist (Swiss or Tyrolean), Irish hand-barrow, and Swiss hurdy-gurdy. He described in detail the 'piano grinders', seen in the morning trooping forth from the "filthy purlieus of Leather Lane", each with his instrument awkwardly strapped to his back, and leaning on the staff on which he then balanced the instrument while playing. This curious contraption, played mechanically, was "a miniature cabinet-piano, without the keys or finger-board". Each player had his own beat, from the toughest with the best instrument, hired for perhaps a shilling, down to the 10-year-old urchin with a "shattered rickety machine" hired at 2d or 3d which he could scarcely drag along. No matter how humble, each had to collect a minimum sum, or he could not go home and expect a supper.

Indoors, the poor could get into the theatres for the "after-piece", when the main play had ended and the more sophisticated audience had left.

And they had the penny gaff. Gaffs were poky establishments without a licence to perform plays, but were not prevented from miming the action in crude, sensational form, all for a penny – at least never more than 3d. They were mostly patronised by children. In the 1860s there were said to be at least 20 within a 5-mile radius of St Paul's, including one in Whitecross Street.

Dramas were sensational, like *Spring-Heeled Jack, The Black Knight of the Road*, both highwaymen, or *Boy Detectives*. Neighbouring newspaper shops sold illustrated 'penny numbers' idealising the highwayman and the thief, and guying the Runners or police.

James Greenwood in 1869 described visiting a gaff near Shoreditch. One entered through a kind of dark large kitchen at the end of a passage, thence up steep stairs to the 'theatre', which had a boarded-up window, a feeble gas jet and no seating or indeed any furniture at all. Within ten minutes of the doors opening the room was full of a youthful audience (mostly boys), screaming and swearing boisterously while emitting clouds of foul pipe smoke, and eagerly applauding, say, Starlight Sal dancing a Highland fling in silk tights and Hessians.

In the 1840s squalid cellars and gas-lit basement kitchens had been popular resorts, with names like the Hole in the Wall, Ben's or Tom's,

the dirtier the better. They were sometimes patronised by young University bloods outdoing each other in consumption of bottles. By the early '70s some of the seamiest haunts had lost popularity, largely superseded, according to Blanchard Jerrold in 1872, by the now popular music halls and refreshment bars with gilding and mirror-glass, which Jerrold thought was a welcome sign of decreased drunkenness. "Let us hope that vice loses half its evil by losing all its grossness." As one proprietor told him, "Twenty years ago they were all drunk before it was dark", while now young men might rather sing, recite, join boating clubs, play cricket, all of which will "surely reduce intemperance and brutal manners among the working class". Just as the spread of knowledge had turned the more educated away from "cock-fighting, the prize-ring, and drinking-bouts".

If this picture was too optimistically rosy, certainly some of the grosser elements of entertainment were losing their savour.

Sundays were a great target. In 1880 Ritchie was reporting on 'improving' Sunday evenings, such as talks by the atheist Bradlaugh, an able lecturer who could fill the barn-like Hall of Science in Old Street with a talk "which would shock many good people if they were to hear him". (Was atheism preferable to drunkenness? contemporaries might have wondered.) Yet Mrs Annie Besant could outdo Bradlaugh, turning Bible and Christian teaching inside out with ridicule. For as little as 3d (top price a shilling) one could endure a long Sunday night lecture, not even lightened by music, which could outstrip what the clergy offered in their churches even with free tea.

A pub near King's Cross advertised "Sunday evening readings for the public", three hours of Shakespeare, Dickens, Thackeray and so on. Ritchie, strenuously seeking the place among the competing gin-palaces, found an upper room into which were filtering some 70 costers, greengrocers, young boys and their girls, to seat themselves at the cheap tables and forms. The reader himself was still downstairs drinking until half-past eight. Eventually he turned up, and launched into his act from a small carpeted platform. "A more fifth-rate, broken-down ranting old hack", says the disgusted Ritchie, "I think I never heard." Dull in the comedy, comic in the pathetic – "nothing better than an excuse for getting boys and girls to sit smoking and drinking."[10]

GIN PALACES AND DEBATING PUBS

Gin palaces had started in the 1830s, their large ground-floor bars a magnificent contrast to the drab lives and grim home conditions of the poor. At the grander end of the scale, from about 1840 the first-class taverns added large, secluded bar parlours at the back, and in the 1880s new or rebuilt pubs offered a choice of several small bars. Flamboyant exteriors began to appear, the better to draw custom, with bastard borrowings from colourful architectural styles.

Such grandiose, luxurious-seeming haunts, dispersed along main roads and brightening the dreary surroundings, attracted the working man as he made his way home. Temperance reformers, struggling to counteract the evils of alcohol, were here confronted by a powerful opponent.

Mark Girouard has suggested[11] a political connection: between 1886 and 1892 under the Conservatives, drinking increased, under the Liberal Government it fell until 1895, only to soar again with the Conservative triumph. Pubs were built on loan capital, but some failed during the Boer War at the end of the century, as innkeepers unable to pay the interest sold at a loss, and many were ruined. Later came a vogue for a respectable family atmosphere, attracting men's wives who could order non-alcoholic drinks – a change favoured by the church – in the new fake-Tudor, Arts and Crafts public houses.

Some pubs maintained standards by becoming intellectual or at least political. The Belvidere at the top of Pentonville Hill was among pubs offering weekly discussion, patronised by (says Ewing Ritchie in 1861) "briefless barristers, braggart third- and fourth-rate literary men, aspiring clerks", admitted free so long as they were prepared to drink all evening. "The speaking is a secondary consideration. The first thing you are required to do is drink."

The discussions, topical or political, lasted from 9 until midnight. After opening by the chairman, a pre-arranged speaker would start the subject, while a watchful waiter hovered throughout to ensure that glasses were constantly refilled. The debates were deadly serious, noted Ritchie. The highlight was some old stager with an inflated view of his own eloquence – apparently shared by the company – as tempers and voices rose. In the disagreeably confined area, the journalist found himself "suffocated by tobacco-smoke, and very unpleasantly affected by the beer and gin-and-water". Worse, he noted a young clerk, not long married, who drank and spent so freely at such a pub that he stole his employer's cash to cover his debts – and ended in Newgate. [12]

THE ROYAL AGRICULTURAL HALL

Islington's unique contribution to Exhibition as entertainment, not as huge as the Great Exhibition of 1851 but in its way as celebrated, was the Royal Agricultural Hall, which from 1862 until the beginning of the Second World War drew huge crowds to a remarkable variety of shows.

The origin of the Hall was serious enough, as a venue for livestock and agricultural implements for the Smithfield Club, formed in 1798 by a group of nobility and gentry. This first showed in Smithfield, then the Barbican, and from 1839 in Baker Street in the basement of Mme Tussaud's waxwork display. The annual shows, patronised by royalty, outgrew their premises and in 1861 three acres of the cattle lairs between Liverpool Road and Upper Street were acquired for a prestigious building designed in cast iron and glass by Frederick Peck of Maidstone. When its foundation stone was laid by Lord Berners on 16 November 1861 the huge structure was already in progress, and when completed it was 384 feet long by 217 feet wide, with a vast arched roof span of 130 feet, and surrounded by a 36-foot-wide gallery supported by cast iron columns. Constructed of a thousand tons of iron, it was lit by 4,000 gas jets, supplemented by seven large chandeliers. The main high-arched entrance in Liverpool Road was flanked by two tall narrow domed towers. Until the 1970s there was a lesser entrance in Upper Street, and over the years smaller halls were tacked on.

100. *The entrance to the Royal Agricultural Hall in Liverpool Road, during its construction in 1861.*

101. *The Smithfield Cattle Show at the Agricultural Hall in December 1862.*

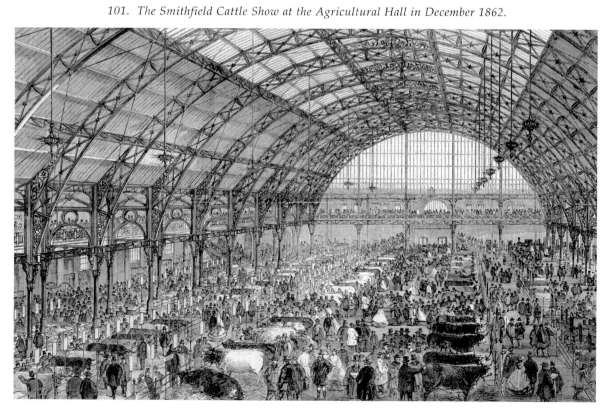

Although intended for agricultural shows, the Hall was rapidly in demand for displays of almost unlimited variety, starting with music recitals and circuses, along with the horse, mule and donkey shows. In 1864 it was the venue for the North-London Working Classes Industrial Exhibition, at Christmas 1863 a mammoth circus (attended by the artist Walter Sickert and his wife Therese Lessore), and in 1866 Lord George Sanger's Circus. From 1865 the Hall was styled 'Royal'. That year the Prince of Wales (the later King Edward VII) opened an International Industrial Exhibition of the worthy if unglamorous work of boys at Reformatory Schools: sack-makers, boot-makers, knitters, ironers, even shoe-blacks. Another display with a moral purpose was the Reform League demonstration in 1866 by members of the working class. The next year a missionary conference was held at which Thomas Barnardo, then a missionary student, was asked to speak in place of a member who was unable to appear. At the end a young servant-girl was so moved that she gave him her savings of 27 farthings for "the heathen at home" which she had intended for foreign missions – Barnardo's first receipt of a public gift. There was also a special service held by the Vicar of Islington, the Rev. Daniel Wilson, for the drovers and shepherds who came to London with their cattle (1868).

The most glamorous event ever was surely the Grand Ball for the Belgian Volunteer regiments, during their visit to England, on 18 July 1867. For this the columns and galleries were painted white and gold, a canopied throne was erected at one end of the hall, and a huge chandelier was hung from the roof. At the other end fountains fed a 'crystal basin' lit by coloured lights. The galleries were divided into suites, while the whole hall was richly furnished and draped. Queen Victoria and members of the Royal Family attended and there were nearly 5,000 guests, half of them from Belgium, who danced until seven next morning to the band of the Grenadier Guards.

The Sixties were also, sadly, a decade of unfortunate accidents. At the time of the circus in 1863 the arm of a new keeper was seized by a tiger as he was pushing straw into the cage, and only after savage blows from the attendants could be freed, but his hand had to be amputated. In 1866 a large crocodile escaped from a water-tank, fortunately after hours, and lashed about until overpowered and lugged back struggling to the tank. A few months later during a pageant at Sanger's Circus a groom stumbled in the procession and was crushed to death by an enormous five-ton triumphal 'car'.

The 1870s saw new departures: a Spanish bull-fight, whose promoters were taken to court for cruel treatment of the animals; the Mohawk Minstrels, and the famous walking races. The much advertised Mohawks, disguised as blacks with burnt cork and garish costumes, appeared from 1876 in the several halls of the 'Aggie', as it was soon affectionately called.

Walking races, started in 1877, were a speciality introduced from America, when the handsome Edward Payson-Weston and Daniel O'Leary, a naturalised American born in Cork, each bet £500, and O'Leary walked 500 miles in 135 hours. Next year 23 men took part in a six-day race, five of whom had to drop out, while the winner, Will Corkey, was so far ahead that he had time to take an hour off and change his clothes. It was a fairly cruel sport, eagerly watched by enormous crowds. At much the same time there were bicycle races on the ludicrous penny-farthing, one of which made a record of 1,172 miles in six days (1879).

On the serious side, another Working Men's International Exhibition was opened by the Prince of Wales in 1870, visited by the Queen and two of the Princesses. This ran for three months. 1875 saw the moral crusade of the American revivalist missionaries Moody and Sankey, whose rousing *Sacred Songs* were popular with the huge congregations. *(See Chapter 27)*

In the Eighties a revival was staged of the ancient Bartholomew Fair, a mediaeval junketing on the site of Smithfield Market which took place annually until suppressed in 1855 for disorderliness – like most such popular survivals. Launched in 1883 by H & T Read and F Bailey, under the title 'World's Fair', along with the sideshows of a country fair, it included Bostock and Wombwell's famous menagerie, and Captain Dudley Vane, the celebrated American lion-tamer with his "highly trained groups of savage animals".

Police were brought in to patrol the building, to reassure "the most fastidious parent" of the entertainment's moral standard.

In spite of precautions, a quite unexpected misfortune happened. A visitor about to try his luck at a shooting saloon, having placed the gun under his arm turned round to speak to the girl attendant, and unfortunately caught the trigger on his coat, shooting the girl in the neck. The police hastened to arrest him, but it was shown to be accidental. Only a few months later, there was another accidental shooting at the same or another shooting gallery.

Frederick Willis, recalling a youthful visit, carried away a distinctly jaundiced impression. Paying 6d to get in, he found what seemed to be Bartholomew Fair "in its most degenerate days". "The din was indescribable, and the heat and fumes from a mighty roundabout, various steam-driven mechanical devices, and hundreds of not over-clean bodies all confined in a rather small hall ... All around were fat ladies, living skeletons, fasting men, dwarfs, giants, 'Lady' wrestlers, dog-faced men ... and a mermaid" – a "mi-ra-cu-lous dis-cover-ree ... from the Persian gulf". Barkers and musical background accompanied every show, all playing different tunes, while the roundabout blared out *March of the Gladiators* and the *Washington Post*. In the centre of it all was the circus ring. Willis is lured into a Fat Lady's booth for 3d, advertised by a huge pair of drawers labelled "These are TOO SMALL For Her Now", and indeed she is seen wearing a scanty shift and hung with "pantomime jewellery". As for the mermaid, disappointingly the fish-tail was obscured by a "ballet dress of seaweed". He is depressed by the sad-looking dwarf, "a poor little deformed woman", pathetically ugly but riotously dressed; dodges the lady wrestlers and the Fasting Man in a glass cage, said to have lived on soda-water for 45 days; and limits his sight of the circus to studying the "veteran clowns in their dirty motley, smoking clay pipes", and the tawdry, tired fortune-tellers.

The World's Fair with its menagerie, circus, fairground roundabouts and shows continued, with modifications, until the 1930s, but in a number of ways was evidently running out of steam.[13]

Another great feature at the Aggie was the Military Tournament from 1880, which included sword contests, tent-pegging, riding displays by the Household Cavalry, and staged battles illustrating what was enthusiastically acclaimed as "the supremely stirring nature of actual warfare". The Royal Navy, not to be outdone, followed up with its own event in a Royal Naval and Military exhibition, and a Naval and Submarine Exhibition (1882), and the Royal Horse Artillery performed a Musical Drive, towing the cannon in close formation.

During the Crimean War the Paris Hippodrome had always ended its programme with a military sketch on the siege of Silistria, ending with the entry of the British army (represented by about 20 players) with detachments of "veritable Lif Gars" and "veritable Iglanders" under command of "le Prince Albert". The Military Tournament at the Aggie was an obvious adaptation of this show.[14]

Crufts, who from 1891 annually held their dog show here, had been preceded by others in the Sixties, when the constant barking had infuriated Barford Street residents, who tried to form an Association for the Suppression of Dog Show Nuisance, but were told that there was no law to prevent it. Other shows included *Arcadia*, "A Veritable Fairyland" in 1887, which featured a vast waterfall pouring 120,000 gallons per hour in an illuminated cascade 45 feet wide, and the tightrope celebrity Jean Blondin, who having crossed Niagara Falls on a tightrope in 1894, at the age of 70, thought nothing of putting on a show at the Agricultural Hall.[15]

These regular spectaculars continued annually until the 2nd World War, when the Hall was commandeered by the Post Office, and after some years of neglect and indeed threats of demolition, was at last restored to public use by Sam Morris in 1986 as the Business Design Centre.

THE DEMISE OF OPEN SPACE
Since Islington had ceased to be a centre of rural delights, visited for its pure water, pure milk, gardens and accompanying pleasures, and become another London suburb, the loss of its open spaces was an ever worsening dis-

advantage. To this day, despite increases to parks, it remains London's borough with the least public space of whatever kind.

Speculative builders were developing areas with thought only for profit, squeezing as many houses as possible on to their land, and soon churchyards and the private squares remained the only green spaces – and trees were ruthlessly felled for building, while greenery in the squares was still immature. *The Islington Athenaeum*, a paper which ran for just eight issues in the early 1850s, devoted much of its space to the subject. Such fields as remained were likely to display builder's boards advertising a "desirable spot of ground" to be let on building leases. Spa Fields, Moorgate, Finsbury Fields, Canonbury Fields, all had gone. Bagnigge Wells and White Conduit Gardens had vanished leaving not a blade of grass. "Everywhere we saw the work of destruction going on, or preparations for its commencement," and unless ground were secured for recreation, they warned, soon it would be impossible to find any.[16]

The warning was not new, yet it was 1837 before the *Penny Magazine* pointed out that all London's parks were on its west side. On the east action was taken in 1847 to form the fine Victoria Park, but North London had not taken up the idea. "All the fields to the north of Islington, about Canonbury and Highbury, are rapidly being absorbed in the brick and mortar system of the town – even now there are hardly any other fields than brick fields." Where would it end, when even Hampstead was in danger?

FINSBURY PARK

Although in 1837 the Commons passed a resolution that on enclosing waste land part must be kept for town recreation, this seemed to be ignored in Islington. The possibility of state grants remained. From 1844 Mr John Lloyd, of Islington, campaigned for 'a park for Finsbury', suggesting to the Commissioners of Woods and Forests an ideal site – even though far from Finsbury – of 800 acres between Highbury and Stoke Newington: 150 feet above sea level, surrounded by good roads, watered by the New River, and needing only a paling to enclose it. He suggested

boundaries of Seven Sisters Road on the north, Lordship Road and Green Lanes on the east, the Docks and Junction Railway on the south, and Highbury on the west. For eight years he argued this laudable opportunity to deaf ears.

At the beginning of 1850 he submitted his plan to Prince Albert. Committee meetings were held, Lord Robert Grosvenor chaired a meeting of 3,000 at Sadler's Wells resulting in a memorial to the Home Secretary and the Chief Commissioner of Woods and Forests, presented by a large deputation of 'influential noblemen' and gentlemen. All seemed well until alarming news came that the ground landlord, Mr Henry Rydon, was about to lay a sewer in order to build. Lord John Russell's Government was prepared to move quickly and sanction a park of 470 acres – but the Government fell. This set a pattern for a series of disasters, until the opening bang ended with a whimper. In 1852 John Lloyd presented the scheme again, to the next Government, and the *London Gazette* announced in November that a park, this time of only 165 acres, was to be formed. Again the Ministry fell.

The next Government received more deputations, more meetings were held, but still no conclusion came. The matter was now urgent, building was beginning to encroach, and as ground value in the area rose, so did the cost.

Details of the unfolding of the story become too depressing to describe. Despite Lloyd's promotion of 'Royal Albert Park' and its glories, including financial (it could become self-supporting), perimeters enhanced by handsome villas, a "splendid drive", picturesque bridges over the New River, temples, pagodas, not to mention the River's reservoirs used for ornamental effect, action still lagged while Henry Rydon was forging ahead. Already by late 1852 he had obtained total ownership of the land. His Highbury New Park, a wealthy suburb laid out and built in the next few years, spelt the end of Royal Albert Park.[17]

The Islington Athenaeum bowed out, declaiming in its penultimate number (16 July 1853) its warning that "the Borough of Finsbury will never have a park, and its inhabitants will for ever have to regret their indifference and supineness".

In the end it proved not quite as bad as that. Meanwhile others had stressed its impor-

102. Token open space for Islington. Highbury Fields – here shown at the Highbury Corner end – with the Boer War memorial and Highbury Place to the right, were acquired for the public in 1885.

tance. *Household Words* in 1850 had argued, "A park for Finsbury is too urgent a demand for a dense population to allow of much time being wasted in knocking at the door of the Treasury. The public must bestir *themselves* in the scheme, and it will soon be accomplished."[18] Similarly the *Lady's Newspaper* in 1850 pointed out how Islington was the only part of London unsupplied with the vital amenity of a public park. They must unite against the builders.

It took time. Six years later, the first issue of the *Islington Gazette* harped on the same theme, looking back nostalgically on the old Shepherd and Shepherdess, Copenhagen Fields and the rest: but now they had a reformed Vestry, and the subject arose again.

The new Metropolitan Board of Works having considered parks among its first priorities, in 1857 secured the passing of the Finsbury Park Act. They were authorised to acquire 250 acres, reserving 20 for building – but the grant was refused, and again the

scheme was put back for years. Eventually land still remaining undespoiled was secured on the old Brownswood estate, part of Hornsey Wood House grounds in a manor originally belonging to a prebend of St Paul's, a hillside park of the Bishops of London. Hornsey Wood Tavern was still a pleasure resort formerly among a few large oaks (a wood long popular for duels), which a later owner had felled, at the same time rebuilding the house and making a lake to rival the New River. Now 115 acres of the land were bought, and in the fashion of the time, everything on it was at once demolished. The site, sloping down on all sides, was bounded by Seven Sisters Road and Green Lanes, a cutting of the Great Northern Railway (with a convenient station adjoining), and the New River at the foot of the slope.

Despite gloomy forecasts of failure by the newspapers the new park, opened on 7 August 1869 by Sir John Thwaites, Chairman of the Board, provided many amenities, cricket, lawn tennis, football, gymnasia, boating and a bandstand, with a flower-house for indoor display. The land was subsequently vested in the London County Council.

And the name 'Finsbury Park', three miles north of that borough and now in Haringey, was retained from some twenty years earlier to signify its purpose, a park for inhabitants of Finsbury.

So far as Islington was concerned, the new park was just outside its limits, as was the smaller, but more attractive Clissold Park.

HIGHBURY FIELDS

A much smaller area farther south was still available, adjoining Highbury Place, where John Dawes had stipulated a century earlier that there should be no building opposite his fine terrace. But only at the end of 1885 were 25½ acres – a paltry figure compared with the grand expanse visualised long ago – acquired from Dawes's descendants by the MBW for £60,000, half being paid by Islington Vestry. Their Chairman of Parks and Open Spaces Committee, John Bradfield, opened Highbury Fields on 24 December. In 1891 a further 2¼ acres were added for £7,500, of which the new LCC and the Vestry paid £3,000 each, the rest being raised by private subscription.[19]

These 27¾ acres, the "whimper" which followed the Royal Albert Park bang, though deservedly popular, have remained Islington's largest open space. Later in the century small acquisitions were made such as the strip of garden opposite Sadler's Wells when Rosebery Avenue was built, Thornhill Gardens opposite Malvern Terrace, and the opening of the gardens of the squares. But further, larger additions since the Second World War still leave Islington under-provided, and the use of City Road Basin for the Islington Boat Club has added, as it were, a valuable dimension to leisure facilities.

For Sadler's Wells in this period see Arundell, *Sadler's Wells*, pp. 133ff, and Sadler's Wells cuttings collection in the Finsbury Library local history section.

1   *Household Words*, Vol. IV, 4 October 1851, pp 25-7.

2   Harrison Ainsworth, *Ainsworth Magazine*, Vol. 24, July–October 1853, pp. 444-6.

3   *The Draper*, 24 December 1896.

4   *The Graphic*, 27 January 1877.

5   Arundell, *Sadler's Wells*, pp. 173ff, 179-80.

6   J F Murray, *World of London*, Vol. II, pp. 77ff; Ritchie, *Night Side of London*, pp. 249f; Seaman, *Victorian London; The Builder*, 21 May 1898, p. 48.

7   Almack's was by then Willis's Rooms.

8   Ritchie, *Night Side of London*, pp. 249f; James Hillocks, *Hard Battle for Life and Usefulness*, London, 1894, pp. 149ff. *London by Night*, [by W S Hayward, *c.* 1870], an ill-written fictitious account of a "fallen woman" describes a typical evening 'pick-up' by young men at the Barn.

9   Thomas Miller, *Picturesque Sketches of London, Past and Present*, London, 1852, Chapter 18.

10   Charles Manby Smith, *The Little World of London*, London, 1857, p. 2; Greenwood, *Seven Curses*, pp. 68, 73; Gustav Doré & Blanchard Jerrold, *London*, 1872; Ritchie, *Days and Nights in London*, 1880, pp. 105f.

11   Mark Girouard, *The Victorian Pub*.

12   Ritchie, *Night Side*, p. 121.

13   Frederick Willis, *A Book of London Yesterdays*, London, 1960 (reprint, p. 198).

14   Arthur W Beckett, *London at the End of the 19th Century*, London, 1900, p. 130.

15   A full account is in Connell, *The Royal Agricultural Hall*.

16   *Islington Athenaeum*, No. 2, 11 June 1853; Lt. Col. J J Sexby, *The Municipal Parks, Gardens and Open Spaces of London*, London, 1905, pp. 309ff.

17   Tanis Hinchcliffe, 'Highbury New Park' in *The London Journal*, Vol. 7, No. 1, Summer 1981.

18   *Household Words*, Vol. I, 3 August 1850.

19   Sexby, *Municipal Parks*, pp. 436ff; *Islington Gazette*, 28 December 1885.

CHAPTER 33

Collins' Music Hall

In the late 19th century the great places for Islington's entertainment were undoubtedly its theatres and music halls. The 'halls', of popular origin, had extended their appeal to the upper classes – though never wholly respectable, nor would genteel ladies be seen there – and later, flashy theatres opened and flourished.

In the 1850s the halls had even rivalled the old theatres, as a combination of glee clubs meeting in taverns, singing-booths such as at Bartholomew Fair, supper rooms providing musical entertainment and taverns with a music licence and saloons like the Eagle or Grecian, catering for the well-to-do worker. An Act of 1843 allowed licences for either plays in 'saloon theatres', without serving drink, or for drink with no entertainment. The latter proving more acceptable to the pub-owner, taverns became home of the future music hall. Pianos would be brought in and sing-songs led by a chairman, later the landlord himself. The chief difference from theatres was their usually free entrance: The profits came from the food and drink. Though many small halls never sought a licence, by 1902 there were 419 licensed houses, and even town halls, schools and public baths might obtain a licence for music and dancing, or theatrical shows.

Stages were built to dubious standards, and theatre fires were a common hazard. In 1878 an Act empowered the Metropolitan Board of Works to make stricter regulations, and insistence on an iron safety curtain drove some halls out of business. The long drinkers' tables were abandoned in favour of stalls at the back

and sides, and eventually the bar was moved outside the auditorium.

Lively working-class themes were the halls' speciality. Their name derived from the pioneer venture, the Canterbury Hall in Upper Marsh, Lambeth, opened in 1852, followed by others adapted from saloons and public houses. One of the most famous was established at Islington Green, the site today of Waterstone's bookshop.

This was the creation of Sam Vagg, an Irish Cockney chimney-sweep who started as a singer in the early music hall boom of the mid-40s, at Sarah Lane's, the Britannia Theatre in Hoxton. This led to his getting a turn elsewhere and becoming successful; he gave up being a sweep and set up his own pub – a plain brick hall with the bar in its foyer, the Lansdowne Arms.

Vagg now retitled himself Collins, dressed in green corduroys, and sang Irish ballads to his customers. Although Sam and his hall became famous, he was active here only three years, during part of which it was closed through a licence dispute, He then enlarged and reopened the place, but died in 1865 aged only 39.

Established singers, and others who made their name in the business, appeared here. Marie Lloyd, who was born in Hoxton and had started at the Eagle (see Chapter 32), was famous for many songs, among them *My Old Man said Follow the Van*, *Oh Mr Porter,* and *A Little of What you Fancy does you Good.* Blond and pretty, with heart-shaped face and blue eyes, she was noted less for a good voice than for her air of helpless innocence combined with

103. Collins' Music Hall c.1908

shortly swallowed up by St Pancras Station. The son of professionals, he excelled in both dance and song, notably in skilful caricature. Leno was famed for peopling the stage with imaginary characters, whom thanks to his skill the audience believed they really saw, while in his *Tour of the Tower of London* his incessant references to the refreshment room would build up such a huge thirst that afterwards everyone rushed to the bar. He could make the most ordinary things extraordinary, not least his ill-fitting shirts, collars and trousers. Dan was another who died in his prime, still not 45.

'Champagne Charlie', or George Leybourn (who also died prematurely, supposedly of exhaustion, in 1884 at the age of 42), lived at 131 Englefield Road. Then there were Albert Chevalier, of *Knocked 'Em in the Old Kent Road* fame, who died at Woodberry Down in Stoke Newington and was buried at Abney Park cemetery in the same grave as his daughter Florrie, also a music-hall artiste; Lottie Collins, famed for *Ta-ra-ra-Boom de-ay*', who lived variously in Tufnell Park Road, Camden Road and at 20 Marquess Road. Florence Desmond, born above her father's bootshop in Westbourne Road, lived in Islington until 1927; Eugene d'Albert lived in Furlong Road; Harry Bedford lived in Halton Road, and G H Chirgwin, 'the White-Eyed Kaffir', in the late '80s lived at 141 Seven Sisters Road. Finally Belle Elmore, victim of her husband, the murderer Henry Crippen, living in Hilldrop Crescent, also sang at Collins'. Other famous artistes appearing there were Lily Langtry, Sir Harry Lauder and Vesta Tilley, and in 1915 Gracie Fields. Marie Lloyd, then living at 24 Dalmeny Avenue, and the young Charlie Chaplin (in 1912) were among the last to hold audiences there in the old way with their strong personality.

The usual arrangement was that the chairman, who engaged artistes and managed the show, sat at his own table where the favoured might join him (and might buy his drinks). Entrance was 2d and 4d, ale a penny a glass; brandy and a cigar cost less than two shillings.

Collins' widow Anna, remarried to Henry Watts, ran the place until her death in 1881, when the hall was still known as the Lansdowne. It was renamed after Collins that

her saucy declaiming of distinctly suggestive songs and *double entendres*. Taken to the Lord Chamberlain's office for one song entitled *She sits among the cabbages and peas*, she got away with it by proposing to exchange 'peas' for 'leeks', which the League of Decency solemnly agreed. Sung at Collins' in this 'respectable' version, it brought the house down.

Marie's personal life was less fortunate, with three unhappy marriages and a daughter whose attempt to follow her career did not succeed. When she died, after collapsing on stage at Edmonton Empire in 1922, it was said that all London went into mourning, ten thousand watching her funeral procession leaving her house at Golder's Green, while in Islington the barrow boys, donning black bands, went off to join the procession, which stretched for a mile.[1]

Among favourite hall performers who lived locally were Dan Leno, one of the great comedians, born in 1860 at 4 Eve Court which was

year by the new owner Herbert Spoke, and Collins' it remained until its demise after a fire in 1958.

A simple brick hall in its early years, with a balcony, and the pub as foyer, from 1897 Collins' was lavishly rebuilt in the old tradition, in Louis XIV style in old gold, blue and terracotta, with blue draperies and old-gold plush tip-up seats, and the stage was nearly doubled in size. There were elaborate gas brackets, ornate mirrors in the bar, and new dressing-rooms under the stage. Bones were found here, evidence that the area had formerly been a burial ground for the Gaskin Street chapel. (*See Chapter 27*) Indeed the theatre was reputedly haunted, with mysterious raps, and supposedly an old Irishman in traditional dress – Sam Vagg no doubt – (in buckskins, gaiters, brogues, shillelagh), seen by Marie Lloyd. In its rebuilt form the hall held 1,800 people.[2]

Late in the century new legislation ruled that food and drink be served in different rooms – a curb which Collins' and the Metropolitan got round by a screen between bar and entertainment hall. And because of the serious fire hazard, there had to be a safety curtain. It bore the legend: "For thine own Especial safety. What! has this thing appeared again to-night? – Hamlet". During an evening there might be twenty turns, lasting three to three-and-a-half hours, the artistes rushing from hall to hall in specially laid-on cabs (or in the case of Marie Lloyd, her own carriage), perhaps four or five times each evening. Twice-nightly shows, which came in only at the end of the century, limited this practice, but they also limited earnings, as managers wanted to keep their artists for both shows, but did not pay them double.

Collins' had its varied moments. In autumn 1899 a programme starting with a selection from Offenbach's *La Belle Hélène* was merely an opener to 22 other items, almost entirely comedians: "Eccentric", "Burlesque", "a vocalist", performers on the "horizontal bar", a display by two "speciality artistes" of the Lupino family, and ending with "Edison's Life-size Pictures".

Early in the 20th century Collins', like some other halls, imported films as sideshows, in booths where for a few pence one could turn the film with a handle, and later there was a projector and screen. In 1904 bioscopes were included as a ten-minute show, and for some years from 1908 the theatre was known as the 'Islington Hippodrome'. But in many places the arrival of films was the kiss of death. Collins' later years were chequered, a melodrama repertory, between the wars a variety house, until its final demise and the selling off of its historic fittings. [3]

Ritchie describes visiting a hall in a supposedly respectable area, not far from Clerkenwell's former Hicks' Hall – perhaps Deacon's, or perhaps even Collins', as he passes the thousands "pushing into the Agricultural Hall, to see the dreary spectacle of an inane walking match". One gets the impression that Ritchie did not care for fun.

Paying his shilling at the Hall – best seats, of course, for so respectable a visitor – he found the house partly divided by a kind of pews, each with a small drink table in the middle. It was already crowded, mostly with young men, many of them soldiers, usually escorting "better-class" maid-servants. The common practice, he noted, seemed to be that the girls were willing to pay, in exchange for having the escort.[4]

The Nineties were the Golden Age of both theatre and Music Hall, when London had thirty West End theatres and as many Halls. Although Music Hall lingered until the mid-20th century it was very much a thing of the past, having given way in turn to films, radio and finally television.

1   Pascoe, *London, 1860–1900*; Seaman, *Victorian London*. There is a wealth of accounts of Collins' Music Hall in periodicals, e.g. *Everybody's*, 4 December 1948; *Standard*, 24 December 1897; *The Listener*, 10 October 1957. See also the Islington Guide, 1962, p. 31; and *Theatre Museum Cards*, HMSO, No. 1, 'Music Halls', by Hazel Holt (1976) and No. 38, 'Marie Lloyd' by R B Marriott (1978).

2   H G Hibbert, *Fifty Years of a Londoner's Life*, London, 1916.

3   Diana Howard, *London Theatres and Music Halls 1850–1950*, Library Association, 1970, No. 168.

4   Ritchie, *Days and Nights in London*, p. 68.

CHAPTER 34

The New Prisons

MIDDLESEX HOUSE OF CORRECTION

When transportation of criminals to America ended with the War of Independence in 1776, prisoners had to be 'temporarily' confined in dismasted old ships, the 'hulks' beached along the Thames. In fact these continued until 1858. New prisons were necessary, and it was the time of the philanthropist and prison reformer John Howard, campaigning for improved conditions, but they were long in coming.

Howard favoured building a new 'House of Correction' for Middlesex on a site uphill from Clerkenwell, with a good water supply, good access for provisions and, he mistakenly thought, a healthy situation. The site chosen adjoined Cold Bath Fields (in the present Rosebery Avenue near Mount Pleasant Post Office). Though the original design was by the architect Charles Middleton the actual building, with some revisions, was by the speculative builder Jacob Leroux, the initiator of Canonbury Square and Somers Town. The prison opened in 1794, with some scandal over inflated costs, and indeed some 40 years later during the cholera outbreak it was found that parts had been so shoddily built that the fabric harboured disease.

Prisoners were transferred here from Clerkenwell New Prison, which thus became redundant and was demolished in 1804. At first Cold Bath Fields had 232 cells, but it was several times enlarged over the years, for example in 1832 by a women's ward for 300, in 1840 by a vagrants' ward for 120.

It proved neither a desirable nor a healthy situation. On one side was the insalubrious Fleet River, on the other some famous rubbish tips, and with swampy intervening land, its nickname Mount Pleasant was yet not wholly ironic, for in the mid-18th century there had been a failed attempt to grow grapes on the slopes, and Vineyard Walk was the name of a local lane.

John Howard's benevolent intentions of 'correction' combining regulated labour, religious instruction and solitary confinement, aimed at reform as well as punishment, but this quickly foundered as no attempt seems to have been made to introduce any such system. It was revealed after a few years that "men, women and boys were indiscriminately herded together ... without employment or wholesome control", while "smoking, gaming, singing and ... brutalising conversation" were rife,[1] and the tyrannical Governor, Thomas Aris, walked around with a knotted rope inflicting blows at will. One unlucky prisoner described bare, unfurnished cells, with windows containing only iron grates, exposing the cells to the weather. (Windows were not glazed until 1837.) William Pitt himself, who visited in 1799, found neither fire nor candles, outdoor exercise for only one hour a day, and apparently solitary confinement.

The poets Coleridge and Southey composed a famous satirical poem, *The Devil's Walk*, describing how the Devil on a visit admired the prison:

> And he was well pleased, for it gave him a hint
> For improving his prisons in hell.

Riots by indignant crowds outside the prison in August 1800 were matched by riots inside, only ended by the appearance of a

104. Cold Bath Fields Prison, by Thomas H. Shepherd.

company of Clerkenwell Volunteers. A Government Commission of Inquiry followed, resulting in Aris's dismissal, and the worst abuses were righted.

Governor Townsend, a former Bow Street Runner, was in charge when in 1813 the journalist and essayist Leigh Hunt and his brother were imprisoned for two years for Hunt's libel on the Prince Regent in his magazine *The Examiner*. But conditions for him were exceptionally lenient, for he was allowed visits from his family, and could continue editing his journal, not to mention being able to walk in the Governor's garden. Then in 1820 the Cato Street conspirators were briefly imprisoned here before transfer to the Tower.

The dreary aspect of the prison seemed to affect the whole neighbourhood. Grubby houses were downgraded to cheap lodging-houses, and nearby were brass-founders in Dorrington Street and saw-mills in Phoenix Place. North of the prison were yards for building contractors' materials, and waste land where local boys played as best they could.[2] The prison itself covered nine acres, but its interior was completely hidden by its high brick perimeter wall. On the entrance front half an acre of rough grass behind a railing separated the street from the gate, which was surrounded by a black-lettered inscription announcing the place's identity.

The gates and their surrounding arch sported a pair of huge model fetters. On either side a *cheval de frise* surmounted the adjoining walls, and notice-boards displayed various prohibitions. To the right of the gateway the rear of the Governor's house formed part of the exterior wall, its lower windows barred, its upper shuttered. Only a couple of hundred yards from Sadler's Wells and the same from the Angel, this cheering view marked the approach to Islington from the west for nearly a century.

In 1830 there was a further upheaval over opposition to the Stamp Act, and as many who demonstrated against it were imprisoned here an attempt to free them was feared. With additional arms summoned from the Tower, and by fortifying the house of the Governor Col. George Laval Chesterton, the prison was so well prepared that the expected attack was abandoned.

Peel's Prison Act of 1823 was a step towards prison reform, promoting the idea of prison labour. The treadmill, first used at Brixton Prison in 1817, was introduced at Cold Bath Fields for those condemned to hard labour. At first the object of work was less to aid productivity than to keep prisoners occupied for their own good – and occupied they were. Ten hours a day were allotted to this exercise, with a draconian target of 12,000 "feet of ascent" daily. The system was to keep a row of men constantly tramping, and as one stood down another took his place until his own stint was up. Not surprisingly this proved to have such serious physical effects that eventually the stint was reduced to the considerably milder 1,200 per day, and the six treadmills were reduced to one, under cover, which took 160 men at a time.

The Governor meanwhile had early set about reforming abuses, not least by dismissing the corrupt turnkeys who were notoriously not only tyrranical but open to bribery. Less laudably, in 1834 he introduced the 'silent system', at a time when there were 914 prisoners, who were overnight forbidden further communication of any kind, by speech or sign.

By the 1860s there had been many changes and additions. The main felons' prison was quadrangular with wings, the vagrants in radial wings. There were also two chapels. Below the Governor the staff of 120 comprised two chaplains, a surgeon, 35 warders including a chief, 78 sub-warders, four clerks, and an engineer, storekeeper, miller, baker and schoolmaster. The treadwheel now at least performed useful work, as part of a mill grinding up to 30 hundredweight of flour a day, enough to supply three prisons. The Annual Report of 1861 pointed out how this switch had had a beneficial effect, the men responding to the knowledge that their daily grind was of some use. It was considered that even though it had the silent system, this productivity had resulted in fewer floggings than in other prisons.

Concerted labour also produced oakum-picking, mat and shoe making, tailoring, carpentry, bricklaying and painting, most of it directed towards prison maintenance, for all of which the men received small wages. As for their carefully regulated diet, it varied according to the length of time served. Everybody received a pint of cocoa and $6\frac{2}{3}$ ounces of bread daily for breakfast and the same amount of bread at dinner and supper. Those serving more than two months had meat four times a week and soup three times, those between 14 days and two months had meat and soup only twice weekly. The long-term prisoners had a pint of gruel at supper, the rest only $\frac{1}{2}$-pint, indeed those serving only a fortnight lived chiefly on gruel, with a pint each daily for breakfast and dinner, and half a pint at supper.

Only 36 prisoners were registered in the prison at its opening, and 1,702 in 1862, the numbers rising steadily almost annually. Most were classed as 'felons' and nearly two thirds as many for 'misdemeanours'. They cost the state £21 19s 4d per head per year. There was of course the perennial problem of overcrowding, up to 800 more prisoners than there were cells, with men assigned to large dormitories where they either swung a hammock or almost literally paved the floor with beds.

There were two religious services on Sundays in each of the two chapels, and on Christmas Day and Good Friday, with monthly Holy Communion. The chaplains daily visited the infirmary, the schools and prisoners undergoing punishment, and kept in touch with the families of juveniles. Selected books were supplied, Catholic and Protestant Dissenters were allowed to see their own clergy, and the prison was now pronounced healthy, well drained and in good repair. Yet it was also known by yet another name – 'the bastille' – which became 'the Steel'.[3]

In 1873 there were 1,875 prisoners and only 1,626 cells, which caused a complaint from the Prisons Inspector, and a further wing was recommended. In 1877 the treadwheel, mill and bakery were destroyed in a fire, and in the same year the Home Secretary and the Prison Commissioners visited, as did William Gladstone the following year. The prison was taken into the Prison Commissioners' orbit, but only a few years later, in 1884, it was abolished by Act of Parliament, and in 1889 it was demolished. Soon after, Mount Pleasant Post Office was built on its site.

OUT-OF-TOWN PRISONS

By a curious series of developments first Clerkenwell, then Islington, became the homes of most of London's prisons. At first it was not so strange. The usual London method for dealing with the obnoxious was to banish it to the capital's outskirts. Clerkenwell, where the custom started in the 17th century, was first given the New Bridewell, then the New Prison, the two long existing side by side but with different functions. The Bridewell was a so-called 'House of Correction', the New Prison a 'House of Detention' for criminals awaiting trial, or charged with lesser offences.

The out-of-town precedent, as we have seen, was followed when the new Middlesex House of Correction was built in 1794 in Cold Bath Fields, and in 1818 the New Prison, greatly enlarged, was mostly rebuilt on a larger site on demolition of the older Bridewell. Finally in this area, the *new* New Prison was itself demolished and rebuilt, in 1845–6 as a House of Detention for men and women. Underground tunnels connected it with the Sessions House.

Here in 1867 took place the 'Fenian Outrage', a misconceived attempt to blow up the outer wall in order to rescue the Fenians imprisoned there. The authorities had been alerted and all the explosion achieved was to kill six local inhabitants and injure 120 others. The instigator, Michael Barrett, was hanged in 1868 – the last in England to die by public execution. The prison was closed in 1886.

Clerkenwell's association with prisons ended in 1889 with the demolition first of Cold Bath Fields, and then of the House of Detention which was replaced by Hugh Myddelton School.

Clerkenwell's connection with the law, too, ceased after the First World War. The Middlesex Sessions House on Clerkenwell Green had been substantially enlarged in 1860 by the architect Frederick Pownall, but with the creation in 1888 under the Local Government Act of the County of London (comprising parts of Middlesex, Surrey and Kent), Middlesex Sessions were merged with those of Surrey. The County's Guildhall in Westminster became the headquarters of Middlesex Justices and County Council, and while joint sessions were still held at Clerkenwell, this caused problems and it was decided to relinquish the building. Its remaining courts were to be removed to a new building (1913) in Newington Causeway, but the First World War delayed this until January 1921, when the new County of London Sessions opened there and the Clerkenwell building was sold. Since 1978 it has been the London Masonic Centre.[4]

PENTONVILLE PRISON

Islington took over Clerkenwell's connection with prisons. First came Pentonville Prison, a 'Model Prison', built in the classical style. Its foundation stone was laid in 1840 by the Marquess of Normanby, watched by MPs and philanthropists concerned with the need for improvement.

Some dozen years later Holloway Gaol was opened in 1852, disguised this time as Warwick Castle – in order not to offend the view of the Marquess of Northampton, who could see it from Canonbury. Starting as a mixed prison, it was only later limited to women.

There were differences between the two new gaols. Pentonville, whose architect was Sir Joshua Jebb, Surveyor-General of Prisons, was designed on the radial lines later generally adopted, modelled on a penitentiary in Philadelphia The object was to avoid 'contamination' between prisoners, in a layout which prevented contact, for the purposes of solitary confinement and the 'silent system'. Even exercise was segregated, when prisoners wore masks so that they could not glimpse each other's faces, and in chapel were confined in separate boxes unable to see anyone but the preacher and a warder or two.

Their ingenuity, however, provided means of communication, at least in chapel. "Half a dozen different ways of coughing expressed as many different things, shuffling the feet and cracking the finger joints had their special signification, and sniffing and sneezing their respective meanings."[5]

It was intentionally a grim life. In 1853 the

105. The Gatehouse of Pentonville Prison, Caledonian Road, 1840s.

editor of the *Islington Athenaeum*, while aesthetically overwhelmed by Pentonville's stately appearance, "a magnificent, costly and extensive pile … a massive gateway of great architectural beauty" – magnificence probably lost on its inmates – pointed out that the £20,000 needed annually for maintenance would have been better spent on founding or enlarging schools. He contrasted it, for example, with the humble appearance of the nearby Caledonian Asylum for Scottish orphans. "The schools", declared the writer hopefully, "would eventually do away with the necessity of prisons of such dimensions." [6] A hospital block was built in the 1870s, the first purpose-

built prison hospital in the country. (It was replaced only in 2002.)

In the 1860s solitary confinement was seen as salutary, though even then it was recognised that if carried too far it could lead to madness. Yet the remedy was not seen in nutrition for the mind as well as body.

At this time a prisoner cost about £59 a year, Spartan though his life was. Pentonville had two principal warders and 13 discipline warders, besides 15 trade instructors. After rising at 5.45 in the morning and breakfasting on ¾-pint of cocoa and 10 ounces of bread, the prisoner spent 12 hours in hard work, lengthened by the brief meal-times, and went

106. The newly-erected Holloway Prison. It was built for the City of London and was therefore known at the time as New City Prison.

to bed at 8.45 pm. Meals were rigorously measured. Meat, served once a day, was ¾-pound "weighed when cooked, without bone", with a pound of potatoes, preceded by half a pint of soup, with bread. The soup's vegetable content was also strictly measured. Supper was just a pint of gruel with another five ounces of bread. If on punishment diet, the wretched man received only a pound of bread and three pints of water a day.

On the separate system, the day's work was done in the prisoner's cell, each furnished only with a hammock, a stool and table, and a covered stone privy. There were 560 cells, three storeys of rows in each radius, the upper two opening on to galleries.

The rule on Silence was carried to such extremes that even plumbing was constructed to prevent the pipes being used for communication, and the very work was silent – tailoring, or making brushes, rugs and mats. On the other hand the diet was thought liberal, and there was what was considered a good library, with books and periodicals for such spare time – mostly on Sundays – as there was.[7]

HOLLOWAY PRISON

Life in Holloway might seem a mite jollier, though again, the prisoners probably thought little of its architecture: "a feudal castle apparently, just what you might expect to see on the Rhine, but certainly not . . . in the immediate proximity of the Cattle Market". The style may have pacified not just the Marquess but the owners of the neighbourhood's "genteel villas and desirable residences". So wrote Ewing Ritchie in 1870.

Holloway, said to have cost only £100,000 to build, whereas Pentonville, including its fittings, was reckoned at £200,000, was on a 10-acre site bought by the Corporation of London and originally intended for a cemetery in the 1832 cholera epidemic. The prison was designed in 1852 as a House of Correction for the City of London. The architect, James Bunning, again adopted Pentonville's radial system, with four wings, and here too prisoners were kept separate, exercising in the yards in single file at least three yards apart, hands behind their backs and gazing straight ahead. The inspectors in 1857 praised it as a successful method.

Ewing Ritchie paints a fairly rosy picture of the relatively comfortable life offered to prisoners from impoverished homes, "with its cleanliness and fresh air, wholesome food, educational advantages, and considerate attendance ... in spite of its drawbacks of the treadmill". Might this temptingly good treatment for the wrongdoer, he wondered, become an incentive to dishonesty? [8]

At the start Holloway held 436 prisoners. Among famous inmates were Oscar Wilde, awaiting trial in the 1890s, where he was visited by Lord Alfred Douglas; and not long afterwards Dr Jameson, leader of the abortive Jameson Raid on Johannesburg.

In 1878 the Government took over the prison from the City, which retained the now very valuable surrounding land. Not until 1903 did Holloway become a women's prison, and in the decade following 1905 many suffragettes were held there.

Until 1972 Holloway's architecture lent a distinction, however sinister, to the uninspiring surroundings, but the handsome Gothic entrance was then, during a general rebuilding designed by Robert Matthew Johnson-Marshall & Partners, demolished to some local disappointment.

Two decorative griffins from the old building (the device harking back to the time when it was a City of London prison) were incorporated in the new buildings, as well as the glass foundation stone on which is inscribed "May God preserve the City of London and make this place a terror to evil doers".

1 George Laval Chesterton, *Revelations of Prison Life,* London, 1856, pp. 16, 17; Henry Mayhew & John Binney, *The Criminal Prisons of London and Scenes of Prison Life,* New York, 1968 (1st edn 1862), pp. 277ff.

2 Henry Mayhew, *The Great World of London,* (1856).

3 Among many accounts of Coldbath Fields Prison are Southey's *Letters from England* [Espriella], pp. 280-1; Flora Tristan's *London Journal,* pp. 115ff.; Ewing Ritchie, *Days and Nights in London,* Chapter 13; Greenwood, *Low Life Deeps,* pp. 139f.

4 *The History of the Crown Court at the Inner London Sessions House,* Middlesex Guildhall, 2002; *The History of the Crown Court at the Inner London Sessions House,* Middlesex Guildhall, 2003.

5 Henry Vizetelly, *Glances Back Through 70 Years,* London, 1893, Vol. I, p. 405; Mayhew & Binney, *Criminal Prisons,* pp. 112ff.

6 *Islington Athenaeum,* 16 July 1853, editorial.

7 Thomas Coull, *History of Islington.* London, 1864; James Greenwood, *The Wilds of London,* London, 1884, pp. 41ff.

8 *VCH,* p. 33; Ritchie, *The Religious Life of London,* London, 1870, pp. 93ff.

CHAPTER 35

The New Markets

THE CALEDONIAN CATTLE MARKET

In 1852 the City Corporation acquired the historic pleasure-ground Copenhagen House and 75 acres, for £460,000, in order to establish an out-of-town cattle market to replace Smithfield. The land was carefully divided, reserving part for roads, the new market covering 30 acres, seven of which were kept for abattoirs, five for cattle and three for sheep lairs. Only 15 acres were to be used for the market space proper.

This new site was no ordinary field, but one that had figured in recent history. In Copenhagen Fields political gatherings had been held on this side of the parish, notably the Trades Union meeting in 1834. More recently in 1851 the Hungarian patriot Louis Kossuth, in exile in London since the failure of the 1848 revolutions, had addressed a large crowd here. On a happier note, the fields were used for games of cricket, which continued adjoining Maiden Lane even after the land was bought for the market.

A cattle owner who no longer had the heart to send animals to Smithfield, who visited the new site in 1852, had imagined "a nice place . . . with acres of open space", no houses, and decent accommodation and water supply for the beasts. He pronounced himself very disappointed. "Whichever way I looked, there was nothing but houses. On the Islington side they are as densely packed as in Cow Cross, Smithfield. Then towards the Regent's Park there are thousands of handsome villas, and all the vacant ground seemed to be let on building leases." He was not mollified by the sight of a walking race in progress alongside Copenhagen House, with supporters "swarming the grounds" – though he admitted the ale was good. At the present rate of building, he calculated, the new market would have to petition for another move after as little as two years, and in spite of the adjacent railway it would be just as difficult to move the cattle, while as large an area of housing would be "poisoned with stench and disgusted with bad language, as there is round Smithfield."[1]

But the move went ahead. It was probably more controversial than the campaign a century and a half later to move the Arsenal Football Ground, with fears of traffic problems and the effect on the environment. A writer in the *Illustrated London News* (28 August 1852) bewailed the prospect of covering "the beautiful fields" with buildings which "will soon cover one of the most delightful spots near London". It was a sign of the times: despoliation was happening all over the place.

On 26 November 1853 a deputation from Islington waited on the Lord Mayor on the effect of market days on the Sabbath. It consisted of vicars, curates and other incumbents, churchwardens, deacons and elders of the now numerous churches in Islington, including Union Chapel, Baptist, Wesleyan and Presbyterian. For years (they claimed) they had endured the herds passing through the parish on Sundays on their way to Smithfield, and because of the Monday market they regretted that drovers, butchers, salesmen, publicans and other tradesmen were prevented from attending church. Once Islington became the centre for the new market the situation would deteriorate further into "a monstrous evil ...

fraught with injury to the best interests of the community". Years earlier, Sabbath violation had been the concern of a Select Committee of the House of Commons, which debated moving the cattle market day to Tuesday, and since then a rising population had aggravated the problem. The Rev. Daniel Wilson followed the deputation by a Memorial, and at the Lord Mayor's suggestion a petition signed by 16,000 was presented in a large bound volume to the Court of Common Council (April 1854), with a supporting letter from the Bishop of London. And as late as January 1855 *The Builder* was considering the effect of thousands of visitors converging on the new site by its only two access roads, Maiden Lane (York Way) and the Caledonian Road, and was discussing means of diverting the extra traffic by alternative approaches and opening other roads.

The new Caledonian Market, for cattle, sheep and horses, opened on 13 June 1855, claimed as the largest in the world. It could take 3,000 cattle, 10,000 sheep, and had lairs for 1,600 bullocks and 36,000 sheep, brought from all over the country and from abroad now mainly by the nearby railway, which lessened the need for droving, or from local lairs. Market days were fixed as Monday for cattle, Thursday also for sheep and pigs, Friday for horses, mules and donkeys, and milch cows.

The opening was presided over by Prince Albert, with a ceremonial luncheon. The layout and buildings, by the City Architect, J B Bunning[2] were much praised. A large marquee, for 1,700 people, whose elaborate decorations included medallions used at the Guildhall for the visit of the Emperor Napoleon III, was erected. It showed appropriate designs such as ploughs, scythes and sickles, and the armorial bearings of the chief grazing counties and the countries from which Free Trade now allowed importation of meat. Flags were hung in the interior, bands played and more than a thousand sat down at long tables to "a substantial and elegant repast" supplied by Mr Staples of the Albion in Thornhill Road.

Forty-seven carriages deposited members of the Common Council, and the Lord Mayor and Corporation arrived at 1 pm. to receive the Prince and his suite at the main entrance to the market. Proceeding on an inspection they were greeted with cheers from the "well-dressed" spectators; then to the pavilion, where the chair of state recently used at the Guildhall was installed. Here the Prince stood amid a semi-circle of functionaries while the Recorder read an address on the City's satisfaction at providing this much-needed amenity (which they had resisted for so many years), "in deference to the suggestions of the national Legislature", with other pious assertions. In reply the Prince, referring to the difficulties attending such a major removal, affirmed that opposition would soon cease and farmers would soon appreciate this benefit conferred by the Corporation. "Beautifully delivered", his speech was greeted by cheers. The guest list was distinguished: Earl Spencer, Lords Breadalbane, Stanley of Alderley, Salisbury and Berners, Ministers including from the USA, MPs and visiting mayors. The Prince drew a laugh by admitting that he would be delighted to be invited to "the inauguration of similar undertakings".

There was now no turning back. "Fields no longer, except brick-fields", this recently rural area had grown "a plentiful crop of streets".

The market's 15 acres were paved, 3 million blue Staffordshire bricks were used in the building, more than 13,000 feet of railings were supplied to pen the beasts, 35,000 sheep could be herded in 1,800 pens, and proper sewers and two spacious slaughter-houses were provided. The railway companies promised special stations and facilities for cattle to arrive on Saturdays and rest over until market day. Indeed the railways had so facilitated transport that what used to take five or six weeks, from North Scotland to London, was now reduced to two days.

A certain number of acres were allotted to the animals, with iron-pillared sheds and drinking troughs, while the drovers and graziers were provided with taverns. Before long these were supplemented by four solidly-built hotels, one at each corner. In the central block, the Polygon or Bank Buildings, were six banks, three railway offices, a telegraph office and offices for the Clerk of the Market and the architect. The spacious site contrasted with Smithfield's pens crammed to the point of cruelty; cast iron, the favourite material of the

107. Flea market day at the Caledonian Cattle Market in Market Road.

day, imparted lightness and grace, and the tall central tower was "a graceful novelty in commercial architecture". All in all, it was found hygienic and provided all the convenience Smithfield had lacked.[3]

There were of course teething troubles: driving cattle through the streets did not cease overnight – but now they were different streets, leading from south London and West India Docks, and though twice as far as before, over more convenient roads. Nor was there to start with any means of watering the sheep, which were brought in once a week. But in general the vote was for success. In its first three hours of business the new market handled the sale of 7,000 beasts and 26,000 sheep, a higher number than Smithfield had been able to deal with.

Bunning's central clocktower, faced with Portland stone and crowned with an open arcaded bell-stage, with a balustrade and a pyramidal roof, dominated the site and soon became a local landmark. The bell in the tower tolled the times of market opening and closing, and the clock, a precursor of Big Ben, by the same maker, was claimed as the largest of its kind in London. It presided over a geometrically planned enclosure, pens and sheds laid out at right angles. The extensive cast-iron railings, adorned with cattle heads, were designed by J Bell.

To many Londoners the area was a revelation. Ewing Ritchie, visiting in 1859 when the market was still a fairly new experience, noted that it was sited past "the model gaol, and lying in that *terra incognita* stretching away to Camden Town and the steep of Highgate Hill, where juvenile Cockneys some 20 years ago played, and called the waste Copenhagen fields". He remarks on the City's obstinacy over removing the nuisance of Smithfield, and its regular policy of first denying the nuisance's existence and then "yielding to public indignation".

Summer was the busiest season, and hours were strictly limited to 2 am-2 pm. Unlike

Smithfield the market was an enclosed space, guarded by gates and police, and its four large pubs were now built, with names unfamiliar to fashionable areas, Butcher's Arms, White Horse, Lamb, Red Lion, while the men, who came for business on Mondays and Thursdays, were "of a class not visible elsewhere in London. Farmers, graziers, jockeys, jobbers, pig-drivers, salesmen, drovers", and they were there from the earliest hour.

The animals were shut up from Saturday midnight for 24 hours, released on Sunday night, to a scene of confusion and noise, "the lowing of oxen, the tremulous cries of the sheep, the barking of dogs, the rattling of sticks on the bodies and heads of the animals, the rough and ragged appearance of the men, the shouts of the drovers, and the flashing about of torches … a wild and terrific combination". Yet while the animals had no idea where they were going, the dogs did, and knew each animal too. By daylight the melée was over, and when the buyers arrived all was amazingly orderly and even clean, "a strong contrast to Smithfield".

The bewildered animals had been assembled from Northamptonshire, Leicestershire, Scotland, Ireland – even from Holstein or Spain (these last being "rather like buffalo, cream-coloured with long horns"), for the foreign trade was much increased.[4]

By 1857 tens of thousands of animals, mostly from Holland and Denmark, were being imported and sent straight to London by train: a change expected to bring the farmers' ruin, but in fact proving among the most profitable lines. London was now consuming annually meat from more than a quarter of a million bullocks and nearly a million and a half sheep, not to mention other meat. Only the large dealers came to the Cally, others went to the 'dead meat market', then in Newgate but soon to move to the Smithfield site. On Fridays was the horse and donkey market, much used by costers.

In 1875 the drovers too gained from the new site when a large hostel was opened, known as Drovers' Hall, between the two large hotels in North Road. The architects were Lander and Bedells[5], and the building in "ornamental pressed bricks" had a pilastered arcade, and ornamental tiles made by the Architectural Pottery Company. On its two floors were 15 three-room suites, committee rooms and a reading and club room, with a dais for lectures and "other means of improving this class of our fellow-creatures, who need it not a little", condescendingly observed the *Illustrated London News*.[6]

Changes did not stop there. Within a quarter-century the market had spawned "a poor man's market" of a new kind, operating from sunrise to sunset and selling "anything saleable, either alive or dead". Once the horse-copers and costers had established themselves, other dealers began to turn up, to profit from the crowds attracted by the new market. They paid only a 6d fee, so it became a good outlet for otherwise unsaleable stock.

On one side a "sort of 10th-rate Tattersalls" grew up, dealing in wild, unbroken shaggy horses brought over from Scandinavia and Russia – roughly ill-treated, sometimes just for fun. Donkeys were also sold off when no longer needed after the season. Beyond was a knock-down market for anything in the horsy line, whether for stables or smithies, spurs, bits, carriage lamps, currycombs and a great deal of broken-down junk, but also decent sets of harness, saddles, reins and so on. Then there were areas dealing in turn with industrial equipment for carpenters, smiths, shoemakers, house-painters, bookbinders, anything ranging from organ pipes and piano keys to parts of telescopes, door furniture and musical instruments. Blending with this came furniture and kitchen goods, adjoining clothes stalls set up in the calves' pens. In another corner animals other than horses were sold, pigs (now cheap, because farm labourers had supposedly given up pork in favour of beef and mutton), poultry, and cage-birds – canaries from Germany, and parrots. Near these were costers' carts and barrows; elsewhere other carriages, vans, old cabs. There were even stalls selling patent medicines.

Refreshments were also available: fried fish with a hunk of bread, eels stewed in their own jelly à la Bismarck – all for a penny, though sausages and bread were charged three-half-pence. Not to mention whelks, cockles and mussels, trotters, oysters, hot potatoes or ham sandwiches, and to drink, lemonade and ginger-beer. Or one could visit the pubs.[7]

This was in the Seventies. By the 1890s the cattle market was established in its final form as a 'People's Fair'. The cattle market was held on Tuesday and Friday, the latter an especially busy day, with not only horses and carts but the Pedlars' Market held in the Hide Market and on the 'stones' round the pens – often known as Rag Fair. Other days were given over to pigs and poultry, and hay and straw. By the end of the century 'antiques' became all the rage, sometimes providing amazing bargains for under-valued pieces.

So the Cally became a famous part of London Life, traditionally known as offering for sale anything from a pin to an elephant: furniture and clothes, food and flowers, books and tools, a centre for huge crowds, who came as much for the fun as for the bargains. This part of London folklore flourished until ended by the Second World War in 1939.

THE STREET MARKETS[8]

Islington's surviving street markets of to-day, Chapel Market and Exmouth Market, were surprisingly among its latecomers, most of the rest being frowned on by the vestries and eased out by degrees. A survey of London street markets in 1893 showed that Islington's

chief numbered five, and Clerkenwell's (which included Chapel Street) four, with two in the St Luke's area, of which Whitecross Street with 117 stalls was largest of all. Some were declining, and because they were considered to encroach on the streets and impede traffic, in most cases vestries were anxious to see them off. While Farringdon Road was noted as being "long established", on the whole they were of mid-19th-century origin.

In Islington only Essex Road was of much consequence, with 109 stalls, though Caledonian Road had once boasted 74; otherwise there were a mere eight in Seven Sisters Road, five in the Holloway Road and two in Copenhagen Street. Clerkenwell's Chapel Street market was larger than any of these with 131 stalls; Farringdon Road had 66, Exmouth Street 61 and Goswell Road 20, Cowcross Street three. This does not include single costers, of whom there were 95 in Essex Road, 65 in the Cally, and 102 in Chapel Street.

The wares were mostly fruit and vegetables, some flowers, and a few other foods such as fish, meat and groceries, rivalled by confectionery. But there were also many "non-perishables": earthenware, hardware, drapery and even furniture, and a few sold second-hand clothes, games and other sundries. For certain

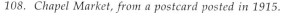

108. Chapel Market, from a postcard posted in 1915.

goods the leading markets were Chapel Street and Whitecross Street for drapery (30 and 17), and Farringdon Road for books and music.

In Islington the earliest market was evidently the Essex Road stalls, dating from the 1830s. They extended northwards from Colebrooke Row and unlike most street markets had a good residential area on one side, with medium-class shops adjoining, though on the other were densely populated working-class streets which provided the chief customers.

Being on a main road then carrying trams, the market was regarded as a public nuisance, preventing carriages and carts from pulling up outside the shops – yet its value was not only to the poor. Local shopkeepers, 14 of whom actually owned stalls, welcomed the market as a means of keeping out costers, and for the profit it brought to the area. Indeed at that time the market was greatly increasing, and like most others was especially busy on Saturday nights. Of its 70 food stalls, 45 were greengrocery and seven flowers or fruit, the remainder chiefly meat and fish; there were also seven furniture stalls, six earthenware, five for rugs and carpets, and miscellaneous sales included drapery, ironmongery and old iron – a typical range of goods.

The next oldest market was in the Caledonian Road, established about 1840 but by the Nineties decreasing. It ran on both sides of the street from what is now Keystone Crescent for about 70 yards, and on the west side much farther, from the canal bridge as far as Copenhagen Street and at intervals farther still. This too was a thickly populated main road served by trams, with good medium-class shops and streets of artisans' and railway workers' houses.

In contrast to Essex Road, despite its length and a potential of over 70 stalls, it then had a daily maximum of only 20 stalls, some of which belonged to shopmen, and apart from greengrocery and fish its range of products was not particularly profitable. With wide pavements the market proved no great inconvenience for traffic except on the busy Saturdays and from the usual stacked boxes and baskets on the pavements. Yet its use for the poorer classes was accepted and (having a vested interest themselves) shopkeepers were

sorry for it to go.

Earlier markets in nearby Copenhagen Street and the Holloway Road near the station had by that time dwindled, and similarly Seven Sisters Road now had only a few flower barrows at street corners in season on Saturdays.

Chapel Street, to-day regarded as 'Islington' though strictly in the old Clerkenwell parish, was by contrast a former residential street, where Charles Lamb and later the Storer brothers had lived, and the market's rise from the 1860s was resented by inhabitants. A glance at the buildings above the barrows and shops lining it today reveals that the street had originally been private houses (and even had rear gardens). In 1868 a local doctor complained to the Vestry that a butcher had set up a stall outside his house, which suggests that others had already infiltrated the street. Complaint was to no avail. In 1879 the market was officially recognised (though the street was not renamed Chapel Market until 1936).

From about 1880 the houses became flats let to artisans and the street from Liverpool Road to Penton Street was entirely lined with stalls, leaving no possibility of further expansion. Here the customers were not merely local but also came from areas like Holloway and Highbury, or anywhere offering a penny tram-ride, especially on Saturdays. For the public it was a popular centre, known as the "most crowded market in north central London", though the Vestry wished it could be limited to perishables and second-hand clothes, and. wanted to insist on licences and seek discretionary powers, such as giving preference to local dealers.

Chapel Street stalls were fairly evenly divided between food and non-food – 63 and 68, and of the former, 29 were owned by shopkeepers. Most of the rest were drapery, old clothes, furniture, earthenware, as sold in most markets, and its trade was (said the report) of "rather a better class" than most. But spreading along both sides of the street and even parts of the pavement the market caused a complete stoppage to traffic, especially on Saturdays. Nowadays no-one would attempt to use it as a traffic thoroughfare, except on Mondays.

Exmouth Street market was even later in origin, officially denominated a market after the completion of Rosebery Avenue in 1892, which cut across the southern end of what had like Chapel Street originally been a well-to-do middle class street (again renamed 'Market' only later, in 1939). Shops were later established on both sides, serving a highly populated and respectable working-class district, with side-streets mostly let as tenements for artisans. Again it was almost impassable on Saturdays, but less of a hindrance to traffic, which had mostly been diverted to the new Rosebery Avenue. It then had a total of 61 stalls, 41 of them food stalls, again more for greengrocery than for meat and fish. Nearly half of the other 20 stalls sold drapery, the rest china, ironmongery and so on. Here only seven were owned by shops.

In all these cases the number of stalls reckoned did not include the costers.

Farringdon Road was rather different. Running north from Charterhouse Street to Farringdon Station and thence as far as Clerkenwell Road, it was in an area predominantly warehouses and offices, while on the east side ran the boundary wall of the underground railway. The street had been created only in 1855–6 and named Victoria Street, a meld of old Coppice Row, Ray Street and Oldham Place, and renamed Farringdon Road in 1883. In 1869 James Dabbs set up his first bookstall at the northern end, then adding more, and until the 1990s a row of bookstalls survived, run by the late George Jeffrey.

Increasing as a market in about 1890, it then remained mostly non-food stalls, 33 of books and prints, 12 others, and 21 food stalls of which only 14 sold fruit or flowers. There were also many sellers from trays. All these were costers, there were no shops. The Holborn Board of Works tried to evict the costers in 1892, and were greeted with strong opposition.

In the late 1880s the bookstalls were cleared away, but soon trickled back again, many closing up before evening. The busy market did not interfere with wheeled traffic, but the pavements were thronged with crowds who streamed from their workplaces in the middle of the day.

Nearby, Cowcross Street boasted just three fruit stalls, and along the east side of the City Road, another less densely populated area of 'respectable' artisans, there was a market at Shepherdess Walk, by the '90s much decreasing, mostly vegetables and causing no obstruction. In fact shopkeepers regretted the decline and would have liked to attract more trade.

Much the largest market, outnumbering Chapel Street in size, was Whitecross Street, though by the 1890s considered much reduced from its earlier extent. In a district of shops, warehouses and a few factories, it filled both sides and overran slightly to the side streets, again thickly populated by occupants of model dwellings, old tenements and lodging houses. Here were 130 food stalls, as usual mostly vegetables and meat, only 14 each of fruit and flowers. Of 67 others, a quarter sold drapery and the rest were equally divided between china and glass, old clothes, leather and footwear, and iron goods; a number were unclassified.

Again the market's wide coverage meant interruption to traffic, though business was seasonal and supposedly decreasing. But by about 9 o'clock on a Saturday evening road and footpath were alike densely crowded – so that it might be said to exist solely for the market, with no heed paid to the passage of walkers. As in Chapel Street, customers came from up to a mile away, a boon to local shops. Here too the Vestry were keen to limit trade to perishables, and confine traders to local licence-holders.

Much of the hostility to street trading was aimed at the costers, who were unpopular with the authorities and the police, and always being moved on. By the 1890s London was said to have about 30,000. In September 1892 the costers staged a large open-air meeting in Hyde Park, with a procession, and banners demonstrating against Holborn's proposal to evict them from Farringdon Road. A deputation waited on the Holborn Board of Works, but failed to persuade them. The official argument was, as usual, hindrance to traffic.

The market that had recently replaced the old Fleet Market had, the argument ran, been a failure thanks to costers' competition. In the costers' view this was irrelevant, and they presented a petition signed by 20,000 of the public. Most had been established from the mid-80s, and their leader, named Roberts, had been there 20 years. Roberts offered concessions, limiting hours, size and sites. The Board of Works issued a number of summonses, the costers formed a defence committee and appealed for funds to form their own union, at a meeting at the Patriotic Club on Clerkenwell Green.

At a Court hearing at Clerkenwell Sessions, they claimed their rights under the Street Traffic Act of 1867, arguing that their site against a blank wall was no obstruction. They also claimed immunity from interference save from the police – not from the Board or the Commissioners of Sewers; besides, strictly they were within City, not Holborn limits. And Farringdon as a turnpike road did not come under the Metropolitan Local Management Act Section 147. They had done their homework.[9]

In fact when in 1860 the Meat, Poultry and Provision Market was established by the Act authorising part of old Smithfield market to be used for the dead meat trade, and part of the site was outside the City, it was declared for the purposes of the Act to *be* part of the City, in the Ward of Farringdon Without.

Farringdon Market was declared inconvenient and cramped, and closed in 1892, and the Fruit, Vegetable and Flower Section of the Metropolitan Markets was established north of Charterhouse Street. Under the 1867 Act, further, no market for cattle or horses was to be set up within seven miles from St Paul's.[10]

A COSTER'S LIFE

Costers sold practically anything: eels, whelks, pigs' trotters, from clothes and cutlery to birds and matches. Yet by the mid-19th century it was they who sold one in three of the capital's cabbages, half its apples and pears and much of the cheap fish, which included herring and oysters as well as winkles. They were a supportive fraternity, always under pressure, usually earning barely enough to keep going or pay the hire for their donkey or barrow. Wet Saturdays were the worst threat – a failure of their best chance to pay off debts. The saddest sight (claims one writer) was a poor coster obliged to give up, now trying to sell his sole assets, barrow and pony, on a succession of wet Saturdays on the 'stones' at the Cally. Many had to hire the barrow, and the largest of the 'barrow markets' was in Lloyd's Row in Clerkenwell, the little street that had grown up on part of the site of Islington Spa.

Many costers were descended from coster families. Others might be trades-people down on their luck and some were even out-of-work actors, or struck-off solicitors. The life was both hard and precarious: few hours' sleep, early departure to fetch the barrow (in Clerkenwell sometimes the donkey had to share the family home), collecting the load of wares to stock the barrow, standing often in the rain all day, then to return home soaked and find some way of drying off his clothes. Several hundredweight of vegetables or fruit sometimes had to be hand-pushed the whole way.

They took their fun where they could get it, a wedding procession for the more successful, a joint outing if the weather were good, and the solidarity by which fellows helped out the more down-and-out.

"Buffeted from pillar to post – men who help their fellows as no other class does", they struggle "for sixteen hours out of the 24 [and] live literally from hand to mouth. Perpetually at war with the local authorities, who are determined to clear them notwithstanding that they are indispensable to the poor."[11]

Widespread but extremely under-privileged was the livelihood of the coster and his barrow. He might, in fact, be more likely to own his donkey than his barrow, and either was expensive. One of them in 1881 described the bond between man and beast, how he would always

> "make sure he gets his grub regular ... I look after him, too, as I would a brother." At the Caledonian market the donkey cost £5, yet ten years earlier cost only half that amount. "Everything's gone up" – the perennial cry. "Nothing with legs" now costs less than £2, "and nothing good under a fiver". One reason was the competition, as the number of costermongers had risen so high. Carts were relatively cheaper, up to £5 second-hand, "and the harness, wot's been used, from five shillings to a sovereign".[12]

At the end of the same decade George Sims went to observe conditions round St Luke's, "almost exclusively inhabited" by costers. It was an eye-opener. He went early, before they had taken out their loads, and saw "the rooms and yards piled up with rotting vegetable refuse", and the "fetid" single room where couples lived with their family, stacked overnight with the unsold food. By morning "the green-stuff was decidedly faded and languid. It was piled on the barrow, and then soused with dirty water, and so wheeled away to be cried up and down the streets of London. No wonder diseases are spread."

Costers had no choice: They were limited to places like waste sites where condemned houses had been demolished, parking their barrows overnight, taking home a wheel to prevent their being stolen. As such areas were limited, up went the prices. For example at Green Arbour Court, one man was paying eight shillings a week for "one miserable room", and locally "the very vilest accommodation" was let at a similarly exorbitant figure. Even slum rents were from half-a-crown upwards, and five shillings was considered dear.[13]

STREET DEALERS

Finally there was the outdoor trade of street-dealers to be seen in most of the main streets, and Charles Manby Smith, writing in 1857, paints a vivid picture of the "commercial Bedouins" of the City Road between Finsbury Square and the Angel, whose infinite variety may serve for the rest.

First he sees a fiddler who is also playing a set of bells with his feet – a one-man band. Next, near the wooden Highlander such as adorned the front of many a tobacco-shop, a loud-voiced knick-knack seller holds a tray of home-made gadgets ranging from candle-end savers to mousetraps. Another is selling 'secret remedies' for removing grease, mending china and sharpening blades, and beside him is 'Fowler Jack', a bird-seller. Next comes 'Penny Peter', named for the penny wares with which his hand-cart is stocked; toys, ninepins, boxes, pens, paper and ink, cups and mugs. He has returned from a day selling to servants and children at Somers Town and Pentonville, and is now in wait for the home-bound crowd from the City. Beside him is a

couple of children, a ten-year-old girl quite skilfully playing popular tunes on a violin while her little brother holds the collecting-box (they are said to be orphans supporting three younger siblings).

Next, stealing a march on the penny cart, is an inverted umbrella spread with paper pictures for a farthing – portraits and topographical or other wonders from "some old Cyclopaedia". Next, Sam Scollop with his bench of oysters, sold all the year round and popular with "street-porters, coal heavers, hod-men, costers, sweeps, scavengers". Then a barrow of pineapples, cut into penny portions, and coconuts cheaper still.

A ballad-seller, a broadsheet vendor ("Last Shocking Murder!"), a crippled sailor with a sailing-ship model, a legless miner with his "terrible picture of the explosion" which mutilated him, a blind man who can "read you a chapter with his finger", and a poor woman cutting pieces of wood into fire-screens. Even the side-street taverns are haunted by conjurors and jugglers . . . and all are trying for a penny or less from the workman walking home (no transport for him, of course). A far cry from the City Road of today.[14]

1   *Household Words*, V, 1852; *Bell's Weekly Messenger*.

2   Sir Walter Besant, *London in the Nineteenth Century*, London, 1909, p. 139.

3   *Leisure Hour*, 1856.

4   Ritchie, *Here and There in London*, London, 1859, pp. 210ff.

5   Of John Street, Bedford Row.

6   *ILN*, 31 May 1875.

7   *Leisure Hour*, 1879.

8   Much of this section is based on *London Markets*, Special Report of the Public Control Committee relative to Existing Markets and Market Rights . . . , LCC Public Central Dept., London, 1893.

9   *Pall Mall Gazette*, 17-29 September 1892.

10   Besant, *London in the Nineteenth Century*, pp. 116, 117.

11   C Duncan Lucas, "Coster-Land in London", in *Living London*, ed. G R Sims, London, 1902, Vol. II, p. 79.

12   John Thomson & Adolf Smith, *Street Incidents*, London, 1881, p. 57.

13   G R Sims, *How the Poor Live*, London, 1889, pp. 75-6.

14   Charles Manby Smith, *The Little World of London*, London, 1857, p. 384.

CHAPTER 36

Poor People's Jobs

NOXIOUS TRADES

The following account of local industries is admittedly of some of the seamier jobs of the day. Despite complaints of their anti-social nature, the nuisance industries at Belle Isle continued and increased. They were centred round York Way between the railway bridge, Vale Royal, Almina Road (no longer existing) and Brandon Road. A glance at the *Post Office Directory* of 1860 shows, apart from the occasional chandler's shop, beer seller or pub, almost continuous workshops and yards: horse slaughterer, toothbrush maker, tallow melters, varnish makers, japan makers, a manure works, soap makers, lucifer match makers, printer's ink makers . . . there was even still a cow keeper. Alongside the railway on the west side of the road (in St Pancras parish) there was also a cattle station, and several potato salesmen supplying the potato market on the railway.

The ironically titled Pleasant Grove also contained a row of cottages, homes for some of the luckless workers, and Brandon Road, hemmed in by factories, had cottages on both sides and was crammed with the barrows of the many costers who lived there.

Charles Dickens, in chapter 4 of *Our Mutual Friend* (1865), describes this area between Battle Bridge and Holloway where Mr Wilfer lived, as "a tract of suburban Sahara, where tiles and bricks were burned, bones were boiled, carpets were beat, rubbish was shot, dogs were fought, and dust was heaped by contactors ... the light of kiln-fires made lurid smears on the fog.".

In 1874 the journalist James Greenwood paid a grisly visit to this hellhole, on a summer's day that had a temperature of 80 degrees in the shade. Following his nose he was led to Belle Isle by its stink, where "you will be sensible of leaving civilisation behind you". In one cul-de-sac, opposite some cottages, a pair of gates led to a red-brick building labelled 'Cemetery Entrance'. Here were kept the bodies destined for out-of-London burial, awaiting loading on the special train. *(See Chapter 28)* In front of the building, visible beyond iron gates red with rust, was a pathetic attempt at a kitchen garden, a "ghastly failure": "barren, sickly, yellow-cabbage stalks" strangled by rank weeds. Some dozen "shoeless, almost breechless young Belle-Islanders were swarming over the wall ... pitching old tin pots and other gutter refuse upon a sort of high-up window ledge".

This was merely an outpost. Belle-Isle proper was reached, handkerchief to nose, through an archway, heralded by the large horse-slaughtering yard of "the late celebrated Mr John Atcheler". Here every week hundreds of lame, diseased or worn-out horses were killed, their carcases "daily boiled in the immense coppers and carried away every evening by a legion of industrious barrow men". Alongside the yard with its nauseating smell was a public house frequented by the pole-axe men and knife-wielders who, anchoring the corpse with a hook, removed the emaciated flesh from the bones. Bloodstained as they were in hands and face, these "terrible looking fellows" lined up at the bar "merry as sandboys", while at the gateway the "savage young Belle-Islanders" prodded with pointed sticks at the miserable horses, all skin and bone, as they stumbled in.

Even the smell here was nothing compared with Pleasant Grove, some 50 yards farther on, a repository of every imaginable unsavoury trade: bone boilers, fat melters, chemical works, firework makers, lucifer factories, and dust-yards staffed by scores of women and girls, knee-high in the refuse they were employed to sift. The long row of cottages in the middle, often housing more than one family, was overrun by small children playing among the garbage. A group of older children watched "a giant, stripped to his waist", as he smashed with a sledge-hammer the skeletons of the horses dragged from the "stripping department", while other boys were playing a form of cricket between the dust-heaps, a pile of old hats and broken crockery for wickets, an old bed leg for a bat, and "for ball *the head of a kitten*". It sounds like an embodiment of the horror comics rampant in the 1950s. This gang, playing in the scorching sun, were factory-lads in their dinner-break, their clothes stained all kinds of unnatural colours from their work.

Beyond was Brandon Road, housing several hundreds in the cottages lining both sides, "hemmed in . . . by stench-factories. The odour makes the nostrils tingle" – the eyes water, even the tongue tastes acid. Yet here these scores of families live, eat and sleep, in cold winters and airless summers. That many were costers was demonstrated by the rows of barrows and carts, from which every night unsold goods were lugged into the hovels, bruised fruit and rotting vegetables stored, on the same floors where they slept on straw-filled sacks, and next day made up into "pies and puddings by the thrifty poor", while split herrings were to be seen by the hundred hung up to "cure".

This repulsive account was written not for prurience but to goad the authorities to intervene and to shame the middle-classes into action. Greenwood doubted whether factory inspectors or school board visitors ever set foot here, particularly when the stunted, half-starving children, many of them under nine years old, ragged and filthy came trooping out of the match factories and other works where they were employed, among infected materials which undermined their health.

Other dangerous local employments for boys elsewhere were in sawmills with circular saws, or lemonade bottling factories, such as Webb's behind Islington Green, where they might be injured by bursting bottles: masks protected the face, but not the hands. Industrial accidents were common enough.

Maiden Lane (York Way) generally was described in 1853 as "the El Dorado of hungry donkeys, numberless small patches of unenclosed grass, half lumbered with bricks and building materials" – potential building sites. Among the rubbish and broken bricks browsed the donkeys whose owners could not keep them indoors. They were also fed on sackfuls of the rank grass and vegetation growing alongside open drains and culverts, by Bob, a man with eight children whose wife kept "a small ginger-bread and apple stall" in front of the grimy cottages. Curiously enough Bob, son of a railway navvy, prospered in this job, could dress better, painted and whitewashed his father's cottage, kept two donkeys in "a neat tarred shed". He was to be seen "in a field not far from the Seven Sisters Road" with his young brother, gathering herbage while the donkeys were tethered to a hurdle in a nearby lane.[1]

Another tough job, winter this time, which Greenwood encountered in 1881 was that of the ice-gatherers along the still country roads leading to Highgate or Hampstead, where already long before 7 o'clock workers swathed in ragged comforters hastened in carts and barrows, to garner the harvest of last night's frost with drags, hooks and poles. Some carts were drawn by gaunt-ribbed horses and ponies, many were dragged by hand. The poorest had only a hooked pole and a pickaxe. The poleman and his mates would wade in, break up the ice into manageable pieces and, themselves frozen and draped with icicles up to their knees, drag the ice to their carts. The faster the better, for the carter must be early at the icewell to avoid having to queue for an hour or so before unloading. They were paid 4d a load.

This particular ice-well or 'shade', one of few in London, was in the Caledonian Road near the cattle market. Greenwood described it as "a brick-built, windowless, 'round house', with some sort of machinery that looks like a gigantic mouse-trap surmounting its roof", and "a terrible pit, 72 feet in depth ... and 42 in circumference". He visited it at night, among the "flickering lamps to light the men at the various 'shoots' while the levellers with shovels flattened out the spikes of broken ice in freezing temperature, always in danger of slipping, "pounding and shovelling while all the time load after load went shooting down, crashing and clattering, and making the glassy splinters fly about their purple ears". He was relieved to hear one of them actually whistle a lively tune, and even see another wipe perspiration from his face as he took a hearty swig of beer.

This ice-well, when packed to the ceiling, held 3,000 tons, totalling 7,000 loads of all sizes. Including the cost of the barrow-loads and charges for the pair-horses, 3,000 tons of rough ice were reckoned to cost £700, "carted and delivered". On the receiving end, merchant, fishmonger or confectioner paid two shillings per hundredweight (£2 a ton), so the 3,000 tons brought in £6,400, a gross profit of £5,300. The ice was packed so closely that wastage was small, though by degrees it became compacted, and on removal had to be hacked with axes. It created its own refrigeration and needed no further cold air supply.

The season began in May, and by July the ice-well was emptied, but such was the demand in London that much of the supply came from Norway. The ice-king was Carlo Gatti, owner of the Islington well,[2] who started as a pastry-cook in Hungerford Market off the Strand. By 1856 he was styling himself confectioner, and shortly became a limited company with branches at Holborn Hill and Whitechapel High Street, and in 1860 was established at New Wharf Road. Gatti, a successful business man, by 1881 owned besides Hungerford Hall – "grandest café in the kingdom" – billiard saloons, music halls in Villiers Street and Westminster Bridge Road, and in Battersea and Finsbury Parks. From 1894 the firm was Gatti & Stevenson Ltd, ice merchants at New Wharf Road, and from 1900 was United Carlo Gatti, Stevenson & Slaters Ltd.

Another equally disagreeable industrial job, which again brought great profit to the proprietor, was that of scavenger in the dust-yards. London's rubbish had long been stacked on its outskirts in increasing heaps, a famous one being at Mount Pleasant on the edge of Clerkenwell, much of whose impacted dust, by then fit for making bricks, had been dug out and shipped to Moscow for rebuilding after its burning in 1812 during Napoleon's invasion. And if not this, then one near at hand was described by Dickens as the livelihood of Mr Venus in *Our Mutual Friend* (1864–5). The yard described by Greenwood in 1867 was in Dodd's, off the New North Road, adjoining the Regent's Canal, measuring some 160 by 70 yards, lined on one side by the dust-carts and on the other by "great mounds of ordinary dustbin muck". Plunged into these, 30 or 40 women and girls, aged anything between 16 and 60 were wielding huge sieves with which to catch the contents of the 'feeders' shovels. While the older women were dressed randomly, in all but rags, the girls sported even fashionable bonnets and carefully oiled and tended hair-styles. Most of them wore mittens, and all wore lace-up boots like carmen, and voluminous sackcloth aprons. Here they worked from before most people got up until darkness fell, hours between which they scarcely tasted food. At about noon one of them would brew tea in an old kettle, and this sustained them with just a slice of bread and perhaps a herring. Yet all looked healthy, cheerful, rosy and fat. Medical evidence purported to show this as among the healthiest occupations, despite London's dire experiences of cholera and bad sanitation. It seemed to have something to do with working in the open air.

Mr Dodd's system was to contract with firms for his dustmen, euphemistically termed Collectors and paid 10 shillings a week and perks, to bring in a fixed number of loads a day. The sifters who sorted 'hard core' from 'fine core' sat with several baskets at hand, and as they worked quickly through the unsavoury contents of each new heap, the items would be unerringly thrown over one or other shoulder or tucked under an arm. In this way they salvaged "rags, and bread, and bones, and bits of metal, and cabbage-stumps, and offal, and bits of iron, and old tin pots, and old boots and shoes, and paper, and wood, likewise broken glass". What was left was merely "breeze and ashes". All the woman could keep for herself was bits of wood. The breeze, ashes and manure, and the hard-core, "broken crockery, oyster shells, broken bottles &c., went for foundation of new roads. The rest sorted by the women, went to the foreman." A large brick building alongside the canal, with a tall chimney, was a warehouse where the rags were sorted, washed and dried.

Immediately inside the door a vast gulf was almost entirely filled with thousands of old boots and shoes, from dainty satin dancing-slippers to scruffy Wellingtons and brick-makers' clodhoppers burnt by lime, all mildewed, rat-eaten, cobbled with string. These, according to the foreman, were mysteriously destined for the Jews. Then there was about a ton of paper of all kinds, fairly clean, sold at half-a-crown a hundredweight. A vast basket of what looked like muddy wood or broken brick proved to be bread, "pig-wittles".

Finally, Greenwood was shown the iron doorway opening into the furnace, a huge dark chamber, its floor a gridiron of bars, making him think nervously of the Spanish Inquisition. His guide relentlessly pushed him on, amid the smell of burning to find a lot of crates and baskets. Here they disposed of the quantities which even Mr Scorch could find no use for, "worn-out oil-cloth, old bonnet-boxes, cocoa-nut matting". Above their heads through a large hole with a sliding iron door, the rubbish was shot to fall on the grating and be consumed by the roaring fire constantly burning beneath.

As a slight relief there was the wash-house, in which rags were cleansed at least to some extent in two huge vats, each holding several gallons of water, which were connected by a spout to a pump. The rags trundled into the first vat, with much stirring and pumping, were gradually converted from "inky blackness to relative cleanliness", then taken out and wrung, before finishing in a drying-room with a tiled fireproof floor. Larger rags were hung on wire lines, smaller spread on a mesh screen, and dried off by large braziers. In this steamy, oppressive atmosphere James Greenwood was happy to bring his visit to an end.[3]

STREET WORK

While many of the unattractive employments were of a stationary nature, others had to be

carried on in the street: hawkers and porters, match sellers, knife-grinders, shoe-blacks, street entertainers, bill-stickers and drink-sellers, milkmen selling direct from the can. The most disagreeable were connected with street and household cleansing, the rubbish collectors, crossing-sweepers, chimney-sweeps, rat-catchers, cesspool cleaners and 'nightmen' or dung-collectors. Many of these men had nowhere to live but slept on the street, for even a doss-house cost twopence or threepence a night. Nor did the poor often enter shops, but bought their necessities from street sellers.

A large proportion of the poor and the street-workers were children. For example sweeps still employed climbing boys long after they were officially forbidden in 1840, and in spite of the findings of a Select Committee in 1862, boy chimney-sweeps were to be found well into the 1870s.

In the last quarter of the century the street armies expanded after a slump in farming. Getting the vote in 1884 was too late to save the farm labourers and just as they had a century earlier they drifted from the land to the towns. In 1886 nine per cent of the population was reckoned to be unemployed.

THE BOOT BLACKS

One outdoor employment seen to be well-run, even beneficial, was the boy boot-blacks. The idea came to a well-to-do philanthropist in 1851, John McGregor, soon known as 'Rob Roy', who seeing a chance to find jobs for boys with the forthcoming Great Exhibition, trained a couple of them in shoe-cleaning, and sent them off into the streets. They were a great success, in spite of at first being pelted with flour by street boys envious of their smart red uniforms.

McGregor and his supporters increased their range, investing ten shillings per boy in uniform and equipment, and his 'City Reds' were soon followed by West End Greens, Marylebone Whites and Islington Browns. Rob Roy used to go out with them in turn, have his boots cleaned and seize the opportunity to urge passers-by to do the same. At the end of the day the boys' takings were divided: a third they kept for themselves, a third was

109. A cheerful representative of the Shoe-Black Brigade.

pudding, at the Refuge in Church Street (now Gaskin Street). Other boys were housed in Clerkenwell.

The philanthropy continued. For example, in 1882 40 of the Islington brigade had their annual outing in September to Southend, starting from Fenchurch Street at 8 in the morning and with a wagonette drive through the town, which attracted much attention – especially as some boys showed "more or less skill in equestrianism".[4]

This venture was a success on the whole, and having started in 1851 with 36 boys, in 1876 when the idea had spread throughout London, there were 385. The boys' own weekly earnings averaged between 12 and 15 shillings; although there was some friction between 'regulars' and 'independents' – that is, non-members of the official brigade. By the 1880s girls were being increasingly employed in factories – because they were cheaper. Boys' wages rose, girls' didn't. [5]

banked for them, and a third the society took for expenses, for the boys were also given lodgings under the society's care.

The Islington and North London Shoe-Black Brigade and Refuge held their fifth annual meeting in June 1863 at the Myddelton Hall in Almeida Street, with the Earl of Harrowby in the chair, and several local clergymen, including the Vicar of St Mary's, the Rev. Daniel Wilson, and the Rev. Henry Allon of Union Chapel in attendance, along with two MPs and the Prebendary of St Paul's. In the preceding year 33 of the boys, dressed in new uniforms, had been taken as a treat to the International Exhibition, and at Christmas were given a dinner of roast beef and plum

1   James Greenwood, *In Strange Company*, London, 1874; Charles Manby Smith, *Curiosities of London Life*, London, 1853, p. 141.

2   James Greenwood, *Low Life Deeps*, London, 1881, pp. 152ff. The ice was brought by canal to Gatti's premises at Battlebridge Basin, now part of Islington Canal Museum in New Wharf Road, where the ice wells can still be seen.

3   James Greenwood, *Unsentimental Journeys*, London, 1867, pp. 64–71.

4   *Holloway Press*, 9 September 1882.

5   See e.g., John Thomson & Adolf Smith, *Street Incidents*, London, 1881, p. 98; *The Ragged School Shoe-Black Society*, An Account of its Origins, Opinions and present condition (pamphlet), Shoe-Black Society, July 1854; *The Times*, 16 March 1959; *Islington Gazette*, 5 May 1959.

CHAPTER 37

Education for All

BOARD SCHOOLS

After Disraeli's parliamentary Reform Act of 1867 enfranchised most male town householders and urban workers, and almost doubled the electorate to nearly two million, the new voters helped to eject the Conservative Disraeli and re-elect Gladstone and the Liberals. In 1870 William Forster, Quaker and Vice President of the Council under this reforming Government, presented an Education Bill which for the first time offered state-funded education to all children.

This at last faced up to the thorny problem of religion in schools, steering a middle way between the Scylla of subsidising the church-supported societies, thus offending Dissenters, and the Charybdis of withdrawing that support in favour of wholly secular, Government-aided schools, offending the established Church. The bitterly argued debate ended in compromise, allowing existing schools to continue until Government-subsidised schools were built (from 1871), administered by locally elected school boards, at which religious teaching was excluded.

Well under half of children were reckoned to be attending private schools, and in London 80,000 at no school at all, and less than half of existing schools were deemed efficient. For London about a quarter of a million school places were needed, especially in areas like Finsbury, Tower Hamlets, Southwark and Marylebone.

School Boards were set up in 11 areas (Finsbury had six members, Hackney four), and the Metropolitan Board of Works was empowered to make building loans. Results

110. Caledonian Road Board School.

were fairly swift: in 1871, as a first instalment, London had 20 new schools already open. From 1873 80 schools were built, and many voluntary schools transferred to the Board until it controlled 540. By 1876 education was compulsory, though until 1892 when it also became free, only the poorest children were exempt from paying a small fee. In 1918, the school-leaving age was raised to 14.

Board Schools, named from the new Board of Education created in 1899, had wider resources than the former voluntary schools. As denominational teaching was excluded, clerics were debarred from teaching in them, and the lay teachers might interpret religion in their own way. Many Anglican clergy were indignant at the exclusion: for example the Rev. George Allen, vicar of St Thomas's Church in Hemingford Road, whose own schools had opened in 1867 a few years after the church itself. Allen believed fervently in the value of church schools for every parish, with a strong religious basis including Sunday teaching. He detested the Board School system and strongly protested against pupils leaving to join the new schools, similarly urging teachers not to join them either.[1]

School Boards were abolished in 1902 by a new Conservative Education Act under Arthur Balfour. Education Committees in the 40 new local Councils now controlled the state-aided schools, funded from the rates, and secondary schools opened where none existed, establishing an educational system which theoretically allowed every child a virtually free education even to University entrance level. Among the chief objectors now, as in 1870, were Non-conformists, some of whom were ready to go to prison rather than pay the required rates.

At primary level the new schools were less promoted, thanks to a persistent attitude that over-educating working-class children would cause discontent at their opportunities in life. But the secondary schools had greater scope, and their school-leavers were seen to benefit from new job opportunities, in government and local government clerical jobs, and expanding into banking, insurance and commerce.[2]

By 1890 Charles Booth reckoned in his Poverty Survey that London now had no less than 388 Board Schools, attended by 441,609 children, a quarter of whom, 110,054, were classed as very poor, including criminal. Only 6,075 were reckoned to be "upper working class", that is, children chiefly of small shopkeepers, minor clerks, foremen etc. Nearly 200,000 still attended Church of England and other voluntary schools, including 32,000 of them at Catholic schools.

Nearly 10 per cent of board school children were found to be underfed (in a period of unusual distress), though curiously enough it was in Finsbury, Hackney and Southwark that the better-fed were to be found, as well as the highest proportion who paid a fee. Surprising, as Booth notes that the lowest grade of pupils, including the 21,000 at 'Special Difficulty' schools, lived usually on the outskirts of crowded, insanitary areas. But once away from the narrow, filthy streets, in school the children were "orderly", and many at Missions, who were habitually barefoot, were given free boots, even clothes, and free food.[3]

The new Board Schools abandoned the old all-purpose halls, in which the entire school was kept under a master's eye, and instead were built on a classroom system. Between 1871 and 1884 E R Robson, architect to the Board, J J Stevenson and others, built 289 London schools for more than 300,0000 children, in the fashionable Queen Anne style, bringing some distinction to the capital's more unprivileged districts. Eagle Court School, off St John's Lane, was the prototype of London Board Schools, segregating girls and boys. Cost per pupil was said to be £10, an extravagance for which the architects were criticised. But by the 1890s the buildings' high quality was seen to be in glaring contrast to the drab old charity and National schools: tall, spacious and in the humble low-rise surroundings, distinctive.

After the 1902 Act, under the local councils new architectural styles were introduced: first Edwardian Baroque, as in the new Town Halls, and later, Neo-Georgian, often with a preference for single-storey.

TEETHING PROBLEMS[4]

The 1870 Act was not a magic wand that suddenly and miraculously provided universal education, and opening a Board School did not immediately mop up all the local children still needing education. Although most of the new schools could accommodate up to or even more than a thousand – say 300 each of boys and girls, and over 300 infants – after a couple of years the authorities were congratulating themselves if a school was even half full. On the other hand, after a few years some had to expand. Truancy was a problem, and the varying state of children's welfare showed a need for more than just education. A look at some of the new Islington schools shows how un-expected problems lasted for a number of years.

First, a success. Bowling Green Lane School in Clerkenwell, opened in 1875, was among the most distinguished of the new establishments. It was soon so overflowing that the future of the adjoining House of Correction site, closed in 1886, was easily solved: the School Board bought up the whole 2½ acres and buildings for £20,634, and on the site created a new large school with centres for cookery and laundry, and departments for teaching the blind, deaf and mentally retarded. The school moved there in 1886, though the buildings were not completed until 1893 when Bowling Green Lane pupils transferred to it. (In 1899 junior boys moved back to the Bowling Green Lane site to become Hugh Myddelton Junior School.) Thus rebuilt, restyled and re-named Hugh Myddelton School, the institution was considered so advanced that its official opening in 1893 was performed by the Prince of Wales (later King Edward VII) and his brother the Duke of York. Accommodating 600 each of boys and girls and 800 infants, it also ran continuation evening classes. An early truancy problem, because of the poverty of the area – and anyway boys tended to leave at the age of 13 – was met by offering free breakfasts and dinners for more than 300 of the most deprived children.

Hugh Myddelton was soon a show school, drawing visitors from different parts of the world, such as in 1902 His Imperial Highness Prince Chen of China, and in 1904 Paris Municipal Council representatives, all eager to profit from its example. After several years of improvements and reorganisations, in 1934 it was recognised as a 'demonstration school' (yet until shortly before the 2nd World War it had no electricity).[5]

Thornhill Road School, which opened in 1881 with 1,200 places, in 1895 had to enlarge. At the opening of its new premises that July General Francis Moberley, Vice-Chairman of the Board, remarked on generally irregular school attendance in the Finsbury Division – 79 per cent, just under the London average of 80.5 per cent – and how Thornhill being nearly full had done well, able to claim that with its higher standards it had drawn children from non-Board schools.

But not all early Board schools were of the same standard, some needing improvement within a few years. When reorganised, Thornhill had halls on three storeys, making for healthier conditions, and introduced 'innovations' such as cookery classes for girls, and manual training for boys. Girls were also taught drawing, General Moberley rather naively observing that "in some of the Board schools the girls had taken to it very kindly".[6] A much later school, Ambler Road off Blackstock Road, opening in 1888, was at first only half filled, despite being equipped with five classrooms in each of its three departments, an art room for 50 pupils, and up-to-date lighting and heating.

There had been tension with neighbouring Hornsey, an area which (said the Hon. Lyulph Stanley at the opening) "has not been greatly inclined to provide for their own children". This part of Islington's fringe was also rather cut off, by the railway and by Seven Sisters Road. Blackstock Road (opening in 1888) and Gillespie Park (1878) could not accommodate all the local children. From 1894 the School Board put pressure on the Education Department, which in turn pressed Hornsey to build this new school at Ambler Road. Delayed by site difficulties, it cost rather more than average, but had more accommodation. This was actually the Board's 430th London school, the total of children in education now being 514,000. Yet (said the Hon. Mr Stanley) even with this number they were not quite there, and with one more school, this part of London might claim its educational facilities were complete.

At Gifford Street School off Caledonian Road, which opened in 1877, Harry Gardner in 1915 [7] recorded how at his appointment there as Second Master in 1883 his chief impression was how shabby the children were, "badly clothed and many of them evidently insufficiently fed". So the managers started a 'Penny Dinners' service in a nearby hall. (This would be the Gifford Hall Mission.) Gardner, acting as observer, took daily case notes, whose publication attracted notice and led to many donations. The Congregational Union in Farringdon Road acted as almoners, providing many of the children with boots and clothes.

In 1886 Gardner was awarded a £40 prize, offered by Sir Francis Peek, for an essay on Penny Dinners. In this he urged establishment of "scientific polytechnics" to rectify Britain's lagging behind Germany in science and industry, and of 'Trade Evening Schools' to continue boys' education and prevent their drifting into dead-end jobs. Bound copies of his essay were presented to Members of both Houses of Parliament, *The Times* praised his work, and Mr Mundella of the Education Office came to see him. Early in 1887 Gardner became Headmaster of the Hornsey Road Ragged School, a small backwater off the Holloway Road, less abjectly poor but with "a great deal more vice", and most of the children were inbred.

On the suggestion of Mr Z Merton, who was keen to promote Trade Schools, Gardner found premises in nearby George's Road, a cul-de-sac and a rookery of poverty-stricken courts. It was an abandoned public house which had never secured a licence because there were too many already, and was on a short lease at £40 a year. They fitted it up, chiefly for carpentry, with an upstairs book-bindery, and in the cellars a plumber's shop, employing as caretakers an Irish carpenter and his wife. Boys of 13 and over, taken on for two-hour evening classes at 3d a week, did especially well in carpentry. The secretary, G Q Roberts, an Oxford graduate and writer for *The Hospital*, later became Secretary to the London Hospital, then to St Thomas's Hospital.

However, while the school attracted boys of rather 'better class' the more deprived tended to ignore it. Furthermore, they were not making much impression in George's Road. One of Charles Dickens's daughters, who visited, recommended abolishing the weekly charge. The road was dangerous in winter and they found better though dearer accommodation at a former bookbinder's in Hornsey Road, a "respectable neighbourhood" and a more promising site. A rear extension on the former garden was turned into a carpenter's shop, and the basement, after an unsuccessful trial at bookbinding was given over to carpentry, with three teachers.

The place now again became a success, and boys of 'better' background profited from the training, though the school still never attracted the 'lower', more deprived boys.

The philanthropic Mr Merton spent some £11,000 to equip the new institute, on overheads, wages, repairs, tools and materials, including replacing gas by electricity, with electric lathes instead of foot-operated in the turning-shop. On Wednesday and Saturday evenings there was a gymnastic class and the reading room was kept open, for which Merton supplied bound volumes of the best magazines. Many of the boys took the opportunity to go into the building or carpentry trade, and a few were aided to emigrate to New Zealand.

In 28 years from 1887 the Institute, as it was called, admitted at least 5,000 boys, and though not all stayed long enough to benefit it became a pioneer venture in handicraft training.

Meanwhile at the Forster School in Hornsey Road conditions remained unimproved. Formerly a Ragged School, it came under the School Board in 1871 with little allowance made for the effect of the children's ill-fed state on their learning power, nor had they decent clothes or shoes. In vain teachers pointed out to Board inspectors that this affected their work, only to be told that the Board was "not a charitable institution". During Gardner's years this improved, again thanks to Mr Merton, who ordered a large gas cooking-stove to be installed in the cellar, supplied basins, plates and cutlery, and during winter provided 50 of the poorest boys from each department with "a nourishing dinner" four times a week, soup on two days, pudding one day, substantial sandwiches on the fourth. Merton also provided for the children who even in winter turned up in broken-down boots, or none at all, and suffered all day with sodden feet. Thanks to a clothing fund, they now had new boots, worn till they too fell to pieces, then applied for more.

When the LCC was set up, the Council realising that hundreds of children in poor districts were suffering from malnutrition, finally took over school dinners.

From 1888 Merton even took care to provide some fun, organising a day trip to the country, at first in vans to parks in north Middlesex or Hertfordshire; then in 1892 a trip to Southend by train proved such a success that until the First World War it became an annual event.

These struggles of one school and the early circumstances of its pupils, exemplify Islington's teething troubles in universal elementary education.

Revealingly enough, the saints' names usually given to the National Schools run by the church were eschewed by the School Boards, which resolutely entitled their new schools with utilitarian names, mostly of their streets: Shepperton Road (1879), Hungerford (1894–5). By degrees Ragged Schools, superseded by the new institutions, faded away, and the church schools similarly gave way to the Board schools – for example St Peter's National School in Devonia Road, opened in 1840 alongside the then new church, closed about 1878, its buildings later used by the German church. St Silas in Penton Street, a National School since about 1862 (when it functioned in Half Moon Crescent), was transferred to a Board school.

CHANGE AT OWEN'S
The 1870 Education Act caused some opposition until grammar schools were reorganised. The spread of elementary education put many private schools out of business, and in 1889 and 1890 71 such schools closed, though 38 others opened.

In the 1890s Booth singled out Owen's School for special mention. A visit there in 1865 by the Schools Inquiry Commission had reported 120 boys aged between 10 and 14, chiefly sons of local tradesmen. Tuition was free; but improvement in standards was highly recommended.

Booth quoted Owen's as a good example of the haphazard growth of endowed schools, increasingly out of touch, until in the 1850s and 1860s the Charity Commissioners, under Charitable Trusts Acts, revised many schools' educational endowments. These proving inadequate, in 1869 the Endowed Schools Commission was appointed with greater powers, to divert endowments back to education.[8] General reorganisation followed including of schools in Hackney and Hoxton, and schools such as Haberdashers' Aske's. In 1874 the Commission was disbanded to make way for a special department in the Charity Commission.

Owen's, still endowed through Hermitage Fields and its 41-acre Essex farm, provided "grammar, fair writing, ciphering, and casting of accounts". Thanks to this, Islington and Clerkenwell between them could boast "one of the most efficient secondary schools in London", and (Booth declared), Islington was fortunate that, had Alice Wilkes's famous mishap occurred elsewhere, it might now have been as ill-provided for schools as was the rest of London.

About two-fifths of the farm income was used for the school, and rent from the Fields for the ten widows in the almshouses, but with the rise in London's land values too much went to the almshouses, too little to the school.

Under the Endowed Schools Act, the Brewers' Company was expected to produce plans for improvement, which they achieved in 1873. These included abolition of the old almshouses in favour of pensions for Clerkenwell and Islington widows, their site to be used for enlarging the school and providing a playground. Three hundred or more boys could thus be accommodated, paying fees of about £3 a year. An equally revolutionary change was to be the inclusion of a girls' school to open in Rawstorne Street, for similar numbers and of the same standard. An adjoining site was to be acquired to accommodate more boys.

Through these changes the school status would be raised to official secondary school rank, and it would cease to be a 'free' school.

The last proposal was fulfilled when in 1877 the Owen's Foundation assisted the North London Collegiate and Camden School for Girls to finance new buildings, on the understanding that some free places would be available for their girls.

This was agreed in 1878, and the Headmaster's salary was revised up to £100, with a £1 per scholar capitation fee. Entrance was to be by examination instead of 'election', annual examinations and reports were introduced, and the leaving age was fixed at 15, with 'Alice Owen Exhibitions' to aid scholars to continue to adult colleges. Finally, a revised syllabus included mathematics, English grammar and literature, two languages, history, geography, science, drawing and singing.

The school's scope was so widened that it graduated to secondary grammar school standard. After agreement with the Governors, in 1879 the almswomen moved out – not without deep regret – and their houses were demolished. Early that year Mr John Hoare resigned as Head, and the Second Master, Thomas Hawkins Way, served as temporary head until 1881. Way, an able man and no mere stand-in, prepared the school for its future expansion, and in 1880 first entered pupils for the Cambridge Local Examination, the boys thenceforward proving increasingly successful. From 1881 when James Easterbrook took over as Head the number of boys by degrees increased to 300. For this the school was divided into Upper and Lower, with Thomas Way in charge of the latter until his retirement in 1906, a worthy second to Easterbrook, who himself was Head until 1909.

The buildings, now greatly enlarged (and still incomplete) involved demolition of the old Headmaster's rooms at the front in favour of new classrooms on two floors, and for the first time the Head was obliged to live outside the school, arriving daily in a hansom. The almshouses site was eventually asphalted, allowing space for a gymnasium. The old almshouse gateway became the playground gate. All games were played here until in 1890–91 ground off Priory Road in Hornsey was rented from the New River Company.

With school numbers now rising to nearly 400, Easterbrook took over a St John Street house opposite the Crown and Woolpack and later three shops in Goswell Road (1894 and 1895), converted for chemistry classes and an art school with language classrooms above, and improvised entrance from the main school. In 1896 some of the Company's capital was employed to replace these converted buildings by a new East Wing, much of it designed by the Headmaster himself, plain but admirably functional and including electric light and hot-water radiators. When this was opened in 1897 Dame Alice's statue was installed in the entrance hall. Still the school expanded, by 1903 numbering 450, and though Easterbrook did not achieve his wish for a proper Assembly Hall and a swimming bath, with acquisition of more St John Street houses in 1904 it reached its final size.

Yet probably the most revolutionary change was building the girls' school in 1886, spurred by the example of the North London Collegiate School of 1850. Girls' schools had

been proposed under the Endowed Schools Act (1869–74), and Owen's 1878 inclusion of girls had indeed been Dame Alice's intention two and a half centuries earlier. Houses in Owen's Row were now acquired, on whose site the architect E H Martineau designed a large red-brick school of three storeys and basement, including classrooms for art and music, and with a playground behind.

The pioneer headmistress was Miss Emily Armstrong, with a St Andrews degree, who had taught at Dr Williams's School, Dolgelly, from which she brought her Second Mistress and some of her pupils. She gradually built up the new school to 300 girls, with a syllabus at grammar school level, notably introducing her own interests of botany and biology. Pupils entered for the various current certificates, including the new London Matriculation, and university entrance.

Furthermore, what was then the innovatory Swedish gymnastics were introduced, and among games, cricket as well as tennis and netball, at a rented sports ground at the Spaniards in Hampstead.

Miss Armstrong's Christian principles and strong personality made a great mark on the school, and when she invited her friend, the philosopher Herbert Spencer, to suggest a school motto, he supplied: "Instead of being made – make yourself" – very characteristic of the times. Miss Armstrong was Headmistress until 1914, and died in 1930.

Meanwhile under Mr Easterbrook, Owen's boys were continually successful in Cambridge Local Examination and also entered for London Matriculation, the London Chamber of Commerce and other exams, and excelled in Honours, Firsts and prizes. Sports were also developed at outside football and cricket grounds, and the modern school trappings of library, debating society, Old Boys' Club – and a school cap – all became part of Owen's.

In 1906 Easterbrook achieved the great honour of election to the Headmasters' Conference, raising Owen's to public school status, and in 1908, in his fifties, he married – one year before his retirement, when he was appointed a School Governor. He died in 1923.

With this headship, lasting 28 years, Owen's had been transformed into a school of the modern age.[9]

THE PUBLIC LIBRARY BATTLE

Since libraries are an integral part of a rounded education, even the provision of universal education would be incomplete without them. They had long been available to the middle and upper classes, as private possessions or by admission to a professional or national collection. The British Museum Library was exclusive to scholars, others belonged to institutions, for scientists, physicians, zoologists and so forth, maintained by subscription. A working man could not use a library unless he belonged to a Mechanics' Institute. This situation took a very long time to change.

Islington's early history of public libraries was a sorry one, rather a non-history though probably hardly worse than in many other parts of London. Between them politicians and ratepayers strongly resisted their establishment, and finally it was rich industrialists who got them established at all.

The first of several Public Libraries Acts was in 1850, so timid that it was largely ignored, the second in 1855 evoking such a stormy reaction, at least in Islington, that it was rejected. The crux of the Act was its putting the onus of decision on the ratepayers, in towns and municipalities of more than 8,000 population. The very maximum imposed on the rates would be ld in the pound, equivalent in a year (argued supporters to no effect) to the cost of a pot of ale, to which a library offered a worthy alternative.

Unfortunately the country was then in the midst of the Crimean War, a sufficient excuse to reject the whole idea. Professionals and middle classes were not eager to pay for the educational uplift of the working classes who would be the chief beneficiaries, and the necessary two-thirds vote was far from achieved.

In 1870 Benjamin Lucraft and supporters attempted to introduce public libraries to Islington by petitioning the Vestry, arguing that they would raise the standards of the working class, whose improvement in education and hence capabilities was essential if British manufactures were to compete with the fast progressing Continent. Public libraries and museums, which were included in the Act, would "lead many to a higher pitch of morality and industry having within their reach a more wholesome and pure source of recreation." They lost.

Lucraft tried again in 1874, supported by Dr Leoni Levi, a Jewish statistician born in Italy. After being greeted with bureaucratic vagueness by the Vestry, they called a meeting at the Agricultural Hall, for which they had some 500 ratepayer supporters; but of the 2,000 who attended most were antagonistic, and rowdy heckling prevented several of the speakers from being heard at all. In the face of the anti lobby the *Islington Gazette* published an impassioned column (24 November) on the need to lessen popular ignorance, crime and pauperism. The unruly meeting also spawned an indignant correspondence, mostly anonymous, one deploring the "howling roughs", taxing the Vestry with corruption and insisting that "there never was so strong an argument in favour of public libraries" as the ratepayers' behaviour at the meeting. Another writer from Gibson Square said that the very disorderliness of the "pipe-smoking clique" shouting down all supporters had convinced him of the rightness of the cause. While the parish was able to lay out money on the new Workhouse, it was unwilling to raise a halfpenny on the rates "to find a working man the materials for reading". That halfpenny could have raised nearly £2,000, less than they paid for Workhouse officials.

By 1887, when Islington's population at 283,000 had nearly doubled over the past quarter-century, and no less than four Public Library Acts had been passed, only four London parishes had adopted it: Westminster (St Mary & St John, 1856), Wandsworth (1883), Fulham and Lambeth in 1886. Again Dr Levi, this time supported by a Highbury tea-merchant, Robert Major Holborn – offered both money and books to the cause which again had no success. Instead Robert Holborn made his donation of £600 to Clerkenwell, which was willing to adopt the Acts.

The adoption in Clerkenwell was to some extent due to H W Fincham, the historian-Librarian of the Order of St John at St John's Gate, who persuaded Holborn to transfer his offer from Islington to Clerkenwell, and who served on the new Library Committee from its inception. Clerkenwell thus got well ahead of Islington, for the Skinners' Company leased them the site for the library on part of their

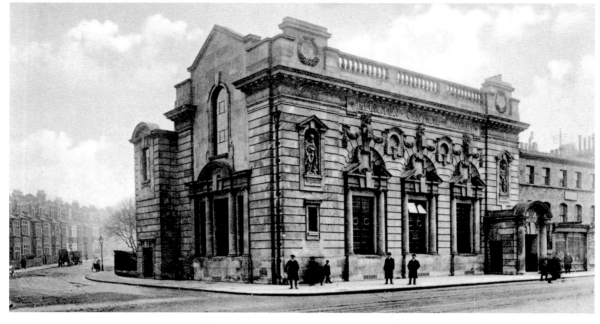

111. Islington's Central Library in Holloway Road.

land appropriately named after them, and the Finsbury Public Library was opened in 1890 by the Lord Mayor of London, Sir Henry Isaacs, remaining in Skinner Street until 1967 when it was moved to a new building in St John Street.

Levi died in 1886 and Holborn, still writing in aid of the cause, in 1892. In other parts of London by 1900 no less than 30 local authorities had freed themselves from the 'penny rate' limitation and adopted the Act, aided by the philanthropists Passmore Edwards and the Scots-born Andrew Carnegie, who had made a fortune in America and used much of it to endow public libraries both there and in Britain.

In 1897 the matter was again revived in Islington; this time the campaign was led by the Irish Thomas Lough, MP for West Islington, himself lacking in education but devoted to working-class causes. At his instance Passmore Edwards put up £5,000 capital for a Central Library and £2,500 each for two branches. Yet again the poll was defeated, by an 'Islington Public Libraries Rejection Committee' and a volley of hostile pamphlets and letters, one of which insisted that the initial capital would soon be outweighed by the cost

of annual maintenance, and sneered that they would only be subsidising "Mary Jane with novels".

At last in 1899 the reformation of local government, which had created 28 Metropolitan Boroughs in place of the old vestries, came to the rescue, authorising the new Councils, not the ratepayers, to resolve on adoption. The change still took time, for once again the old argument was made that public libraries would serve only as a source of popular novels and a meeting-place for dating couples – a cynical attitude to improving the lot of the working man which died hard.

Not until 1904 did a deputation, this time from 'Islington Libraries *Promotion* Committee' led by Thomas Lough, present a petition signed by 796 ratepayers. Chief among the opposition was Alderman George Samuel Elliot, long an opponent, who claimed that it was not in the election manifesto and was therefore unconstitutional; but the Mayor, Andrew Torrance, who was a friend of Carnegie, moved adoption of the latest Acts of 1892 and 1893, proposing to limit the rate charge to a mere 2d, and the vote was carried 36 to 19 – after a struggle of half a century.

The Central Library, to a design of Henry T Hare, was built in Holloway Road, rather grandiosely adorned with statues of Spenser and Bacon, and opened in October 1907. By a stroke of irony the lavish ceremony, accompanied by the band of the Coldstream Guards, was presided over by Alderman Elliot – who incidentally was to become Major of Islington 13 times and died in 1925. As Mayor in 1915 he was to lay the foundation stone of the Essex Road or South Islington Library; the architect was Mervyn Macartney.

Two branch libraries were begun at the same time. These were the North Branch in Manor Gardens, again designed by Henry T Hare and partly financed by Andrew Carnegie, and the remarkably original West Library in Thornhill Square, by Beresford Pite, with its sculptured letters in panels above the windows, and a cupola above. This too was opened by Alderman Elliot, in 1907. So this deplorable history ended at last in triumph.[10]

In 1872 the former Welsh Charity School on Clerkenwell Green, which for more than a century had been put to various uses, became a meeting-place for the radical London Patriotic Society, and for 20 years from 1892 was used by the Socialist 20th Century Press. Here in 1902–3 the exiled Lenin had an office while he was publishing the revolutionary periodical, *Iskra*, and was living in Holford Square. Since 1933 the building has been the Marx Memorial Library, its exterior restored in 1969 to its 18th-century appearance.

Provision for local museums, also rightly regarded as promoting popular education and culture, had also been included in the Public Library Acts, but for this Islington had to wait until the late 20th century for even a modest establishment to be achieved, through the efforts of an enthusiastic band of volunteers.

HIGHER EDUCATION

In the 1890s first Clerkenwell, then Islington, embarked on higher education. First came the Northampton Institute, on 1½ acres of land presented by the Marquess of Northampton, and appropriately on the approximate site of the one-time Northampton Manor House – which had from the late 17th century become by turns a private lunatic asylum, a girls' school and finally in the 1860s the Manor House School for boys.

In 1893 the design was put up for competition, and was won by E W Mountford, who had also built the Battersea Polytechnic. It was a difficult site, triangular and partly right-angled, and at first only the north west corner was available. Here Mountford placed a great hall, swimming bath and gymnasium, and a grand principal entrance under a central tower, with a frieze of symbolic figures. In a grand, if unavoidably asymmetrical style combining French Baroque and Queen Anne, it opened in 1898 at a cost of £80,000.

Fees to students were fixed, in the phrase of a contemporary, "within the reach of every respectable working man and woman". Indeed, as part of the new thinking, women were admitted, and the syllabus was designed to attract workmen of several trades, especially artisans and apprentices, for them to learn processes, aimed at serving as "a complete polytechnic" – as it was renamed in 1907 on the dissolution of its parent institute the City Polytechnic.

Mainly technological and trade in scope, by the mid-20th century it specialised in engineering, mathematics, applied physics, chemistry, and optics and horology (the National College of Horology opening here in 1947), and was again renamed, as a College of Advanced Technology. From 1966, when it had further expanded, it finally became the City University, rebuilding extensively in Northampton Square, much of which was unfortunately demolished for the rather unexciting new buildings.

The Northern Polytechnic in Holloway Road was also begun in 1896, with funds made available by the Clothworkers' Company and by public subscription, and its Great Hall (later its theatre) was opened the following year. This too was centred on science and engineering, and also included building. Like the Northampton it gave evening classes for working men, but of its 2,600 students 500 attended by day. By 1905–9 there were nine departments, of several sciences and kinds of engineering, architecture and the building trades, and also including English, foreign languages and literature.

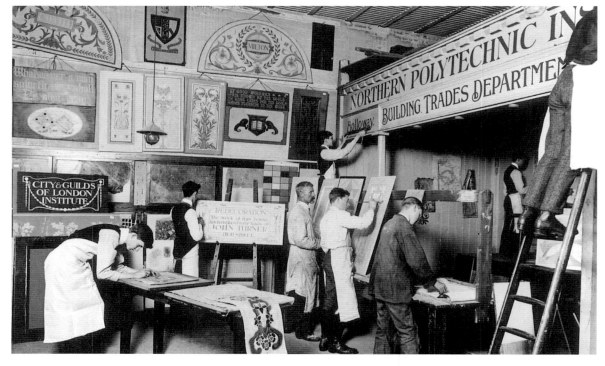

112. At work in the sign-writing department at the Northern Polytechnic.

A description in 1894 defined the college's object as "to promote the industrial skill, general knowledge, health and well being of young men and women belonging to the poorer classes of Islington".[11] This was expanded when in 1971 it was designated a Polytechnic, amalgamating with the Northern and North Western Polytechnics, and it became the University of North London, with expansion and rebuilding. Finally, in August 2002, by a merger with the London Guildhall University, it was renamed London Metropolitan University.

A highly original building designed by Daniel Libeskind, was opened here in 2004.

1   *St Thomas' Parish Magazine*, Jubilee edn, 12 July 1910; *VCH*, pp. 120–122.

2   Alastair Service, *London, 1900*.

3   Booth, *Poverty*, 1890, pp. 196ff.

4   Accounts of Board Schools in this Section are based on press cuttings in the Is;ington Local History Library.

5   During the Second World War Hugh Myddelton School was evacuated and with the subsequently much reduced local population was closed, becoming instead the Kingsway College.

6   *Islington Gazette*, July 1895.

7   From 1968 the Catholic St William of York School, but sadly demolished in 2001.

8   Booth, *Poverty*, 1889, Vol. III, pp. 252–3.

9   Dare, *Owen's School*, pp. 62, 64ff. In 1976 Owen's School removed to Potter's Bar.

10   R H Hidson, *The Birth of a Library Service: Islington 1855–1904*, Islington Local History Education Trust (1990); Potter Collection III, British Library.

11   Hugh B Philpot, 'Institute London', in Sims, *Living London*, 1889, Vol. II, pp. 192–3.

CHAPTER 38

The Suburban Theatre

In 1850 London had only 18 theatres of all kinds – the two old-established 'Patents' Drury Lane and Covent Garden, and Haymarket in the summer, originally with exclusive right to legitimate drama; seven others in central London and the rest farther afield, ranging to Astley's Amphitheatre in Lambeth, the Victoria (later the Old Vic) in Waterloo Road, and Sadler's Wells. These alone staged 'legitimate' plays. The rest mostly ran to opera, operetta and melodrama, and usually at a loss.

From the 1840s and '50s William Macready and Edmund Kean began to make theatre 're-spectable', and Society then made it fashion-able, dressing up for the stalls, and so on. The reign of Samuel Phelps brought Sadler's Wells early fame for almost two decades before that theatre again took a down-turn after his re-tirement in 1862. At a lower level the Eagle's Grecian Theatre, and others in Hoxton and Whitechapel always catered for the superior working-class.

Theatre building began to spread after Squire Bancroft's company took over an old theatre off Tottenham Court Road, rebuilt it as the Prince of Wales Theatre in 1865 and until 1880 successfully produced the comedies of T W Robertson. After this, until the end of the century, theatres were built and rebuilt all over London to the number of 112, most of them opening in the 1880s, while the actors who played in them were accepted in society and leading players were even knighted. Lesser actors might earn only a guinea a week, but leading actors £50, and the most out-standing up to £100.

Perhaps for this reason ticket prices rose to ten shillings and half a guinea at West End theatres, putting them beyond the reach of many families, and from 1890 the suburbs began to compete by opening their own thea-tres. So that by the late 1890s London's sub-urbs, within the circumference of Camberwell on the south and Holloway on the north, had as many as 23 theatres.

Despite the fact that licences (except for the two 'Patent' theatres and the Haymarket) were for music and dancing, with speech prohibited unless with music, this was inter-preted very broadly to include ballet, panto-mime and equestrian shows (such as at Astley's). "It being considered hard that the inhabitants of St George's Fields, Lambeth, Islington, Marylebone, etc., should be com-pelled to make a positive journey in order to enjoy the rational amusement of the theatre", proprietors in those places regularly broke the law, and usually got away with it.[1]

One of Islington's earliest theatres, and with the most chequered history, was the building variously known as the Philharmonic Hall, the Empire and the Grand Theatre, which stood in Islington High Street (east side), near the Angel junction. With its recurring fires, it was a veritable Phoenix. It opened as the Philharmonic in 1860, designed by Finch, Hill and Paraire and intended for "first-class concerts". In spite of this ambitious objective, it started with shows by Sam Collins, 'the Great Vance' and other popular entertainers, though during the 1860s it did stage works by Bellini and others with the English Opera Company. A leading soprano

113. *The Islington Empire, so named from 1911, on the east side of Islington High Street. It was the fourth theatre on the site, and was formerly known as the Grand.*

was Emily Soldene, a lawyer's daughter living in Duncan Terrace, especially successful in Balfe's *Bohemian Girl* and Offenbach's *Geneviève de Brabant*. The Hall had a bad patch when it was known unaffectionately as 'the Spittoon' and 'the Dustbin', but in 1871 Charles Morton, 'father of the music hall', secured a licence to run it as a theatre. In 1873-4 he succeeded with French light operas by the popular composer Charles Lecocq.

The original building was burnt down in 1882, but rebuilt the next year with a temple-front design by the noted theatre architect Frank Matcham; it was appropriately re-named the Grand Theatre. Here among others Harry Hemsley, years later to be the ventriloquist child impersonator, appeared in 1885 at the age of eight, and in 1887 Seymour Hicks, aged 16, first appeared in a drama, *In the Ranks*. Also, in 1886 it was here that Shelley's *The Cenci* was first produced by the Shelley Society, in which Philip Ben Greet played the Papal Legate.

At the end of the following year the theatre

was again burnt down, by a fire which started in the scenery – indeed in less than 10 years no less than eight London theatres and music halls had been destroyed by fire. The famous Captain Shaw of the Fire Brigade, called after midnight to the Grand's blaze, noted in his official report how it also destroyed 20 dwellings of the adjoining Myddelton Buildings of the Industrial Dwellings Company, and about 15 in their Torrens Buildings behind, off the City Road. In each case, he noted bleakly, "insurance unknown".[2]

There was another sad effect, as the theatre's rear wall fell on the stables behind used by the London General Omnibus Company, killing several horses and seriously injuring an employee – besides putting more than 200 people out of a job.

Once again Frank Matcham rebuilt the theatre, this time incorporating fireproof features; learning from the disaster how the iron and concrete proscenium had withstood the fire, he coated the pillars with concrete. The new theatre, in Louis XV style, was upholstered in the crimson velvet now fashionable for theatres, and the drop-curtain was painted with a scene of Actaeon and Diana. The Crush Room was in 'Singalese style', whatever that was.

A dozen years of success followed, notably with Henry Irving in *The Bells*, and performances by the companies of Lewis Waller and George Alexander, the Carl Rosa Company, as well as popular pantomimes. Other famous performances included Dorothea Baird as Trilby, Martin Harvey in *The Only Way* (based on *A Tale of Two Cities*), and the musical *The Belle of New York*. Here too was said to be Lottie Collin's premiere of *Ta-ra-ra-boom-de-ay* (1891).

But after a successful decade the Grand was burnt down a third time in 1900 – and rebuilt in 1901.

Like Sadler's Wells, the Grand was sought after by worthy institutions to spread moral uplift. In 1902 the Central London Wesleyan Mission, which had been trying to lease a theatre for their gospel services, eventually succeeded in securing the Grand for monster evening services, holding 2,500 – which was indeed a success. "In Finsbury alone", they had warned, "there must be at least 85,000 persons out of its population of 101,463 who never cross the threshold of a church, or chapel or Mission-hall".

Activities would start with a parade by a fine brass band through the streets, which soon gathered a crowd. At 8 o'clock the doors would open (the hour carefully chosen not to clash with church services), and the band led singing from the stage. There were 60 stewards to usher in the crowd and dole out hymn sheets urging the readers who "desired to lead a new life" to call on the Rev. John Wakerley at the Wesleyan chapel then in St John's Square. Wakerley was a highly successful missionary, and his red-hot gospel addresses drew packed houses at the Grand, with hundreds proverbially turned away.

In 1903 the theatre was hired for a working-class rally, and in 1904 a meeting for the unemployed, at which Keir Hardie and Ramsay Macdonald spoke.

Becoming a variety theatre in 1907 it was renamed the Empire in 1908, and more meticulously in 1911 "the New Islington Empire (late the Grand)". Its last true variety show was presented in 1932, and from then on it played as cinema and variety combined.[3]

HOLLOWAY THEATRES

Under its several identities the Empire/Grand long preceded the theatres which made *fin-de-siècle* Islington such a popular entertainment venue. These successors had varying origins, and mostly came to an ignominious end, usually some half-century later. First of these was the Parkhurst Theatre of 1890 – quite a long way out of town in the Holloway Road, opposite the Nag's Head. It was in fact intended as a public hall, of which there was a serious shortage, but application for a licence was turned down by the new London County Council, then in its green days and overcautious about public entertainment. The owner, J R Perfect, decided to make it a theatre and after hasty alterations to the interior, secured a Lord Chamberlain's licence. It opened to the scepticism of those who doubted the success of a suburban theatre.

The 'pretty Parkhurst', as it was soon affectionately known, was launched with a play called *Nixie*, under the actor-manager Lewis Waller, and at once proved a great success. Public taste soon converted to the idea of a suburban venue, and it did so well that in 1898 it had to be enlarged; but in Edwardian days its prosperity ended with the competition of the new Marlborough Theatre. And, from now on, there was also competition from cinemas, and the Parkhurst bowed to fashion and converted to a cinema in 1909.[4]

The Parkhurst reigned supreme as a Holloway theatre for nearly a decade before the Holloway Empire opened in December 1899, designed by W G R Sprague, a regular theatre architect. At no. 564, even farther up the Holloway Road, this was more strictly a music hall, at first named the Empire Theatre of Varieties, and the earliest to be built as a regular twice-nightly house. Owned by the London District Empire Palaces, its manager was Oswald Stoll. The favourites Lily Langtry, Vesta Tilley, and the young George Formby all played here, besides Harry Tate and Marie Lloyd. Home from 1903 of famous and future performers, this too became a cinema in 1924. By 1953 it seemed likely to become a blouse factory, but in 1956 it was derelict.

Islington's other theatres were Edwardian: the Marlborough, at 383 Holloway Road, was another Matcham building, which opened

114. *The Holloway Empire at 564 Holloway Road. It opened in December 1899, but by 1924 was being used as a cinema.*

115. *The Coronet Cinema in Essex Road.*

322

116. The Carlton Cinema in Essex Road, now a bingo hall.

with the Carl Rosa company in October 1903 (during which Eugene Goossens conducted Act II of *Faust*). Before long it had shown a splendid series of productions: *East Lynne*, the *Adventures of Brigadier Gerard*, based on Conan Doyle's stories, Frank Benson and his Company, Julia Neilson and Fred Terry in *The Scarlet Pimpernel*. Matheson Lang appeared as Mr Wu, and the Courtneidge family and Gilbert and Sullivan were other favourites. In 1908 came *The Merry Widow*, in 1912 Martin Harvey in *The Only Way*.

The Marlborough had been built on a field, and up to the time of the First World War was flanked by solid Victorian houses. During the war, however, the theatre became a variety house, and in 1919 was one of the earliest to be converted to a cinema. It closed in 1962.

Finally, the Finsbury Park Empire on the corner of St Thomas's Road was opened only in 1910, owned by Moss Empires, yet again a Frank Matcham design. It was really a music hall, featuring Nellie Wallace, Florence Desmond, Gertie Gitana, Kate Carney, George Robey and other famous names. One favourite performer was the escapologist Harry Houdini. In its early days came the Scottish comedian Sandy McNab, who had had the grisly idea of buying Harvey Crippen's house at 39 Hilldrop Crescent (off Camden Road) and opening it as a museum of Crippen relics.[5] Neighbours complained of the tasteless enterprise, and he instead turned it into a boarding-house, much frequented by artistes performing at the Finsbury Park Empire.

117. *The Electric Cinema facing Islington Green. The building survives and is now a restaurant.*

118. *Sandy McNab outside Crippen's house, 39 Hilldrop Crescent. He christened the building McNab House and decorated it with thistles.*

Chronological histories of Islington's theatres are given in Diana Howard, *London Theatres and Music Halls 1850–1950*, Library Association, 1970, *ad loc.* Posters, cuttings and other information are in the Ellis Ashton Collection, British Library, and Islington Local History Library Collection.

1   Pascoe, *London 1850–1900*, p. 126; and see, e.g. J Robinson Planché, *Recollections and Reflections*, London, 1872, Vol. II, p. 73.

2   H G Hibbert, *Fifty Years of a Londoner's Life*, London, 1916, pp. 73–4; Howard, *London Theatres*, p. 122; *Daily Telegraph*, 30 December 1887.

3   *Islington Guide*, 1962.

4   The Parkhurst was demolished in 1930, and rebuilt as a department of the then Northern Polytechnic.

5   The Empire closed in 1960 and was used for storage, and demolished in January 1965. A 9-storey block of Council flats later covered the site. The Hilldrop Crescent house was pulled down in 1954 and replaced by flats.

CHAPTER 39

Elections, World Wars & 'The Game'

POLITICS AND ELECTIONS

Politically, neither Islington nor Finsbury were of any account, even as rotten or pocket boroughs, until the 1832 Parliamentary Reform Act, when Finsbury was allotted two Members of Parliament. Its electoral area included not only Clerkenwell and Islington parishes, but also St Luke's, Stoke Newington, St Giles in the Fields, St George's Bloomsbury and smaller areas, and institutions as, for example, Lincoln's and Gray's Inns and the Charterhouse. Of the constituency's then population of 224,839, only 10,309 were eligible to vote, and in that first post-Reform election only 7,344 did so. Indeed the composition of the first post-Reform MPs was still fairly aristocratic, Finsbury's numbering 18 knights or baronets, four who became peers and one the son of a peer.

Until the 1880s Finsbury was mainly Liberal, then for the next 20 years largely Conservative. Not until the London Government Act of 1885 did Islington qualify for its own MPs, when it was allotted four, Finsbury continuing with two.

When Finsbury's first MP, Sir Robert Grant, became Governor of Bombay in 1834, his successor was Thomas Slingsby Duncombe, Old Harrovian and dandy, but a Liberal of Radical tinge, known as 'Honest Tim'. He was popular for campaigning for the Chartists, whose monster petition of 1842 he presented to Parliament – it was so large that even to get the roll into the House it had to be split into sections. Duncombe was regularly re-elected until his death in 1861.

His fellow-member from 1835 was Thomas Wakley (after whom a local street was named), son of a Devon squire, who had run away to sea, then became a surgeon, was Middlesex Coroner, and had already twice stood unsuccessfully for Parliament. He petitioned for the return from transportation of the Tolpuddle Martyrs, attacked the unpopular Workhouse system, and helped raise the standard of medical aid for the poor. Bad health, and the pressure of his combined Coroner's profession and, Parliamentary work, made him give up his seat in 1852, but he continued as Coroner, and as editor of *The Lancet*, until not long before his death in 1862.

Wakley's successor, Thomas Challis, an Alderman and Mayoral candidate, also found politics too demanding and stood down in 1857, and was followed by an Islington Vestryman, William Cox, who served twice.

The Finsbury hustings, held at Clerkenwell Green, saw some rowdy scenes. 'Hustings' were tent-like pavilions erected for the occasion, as a stage from which candidates and canvassers harangued the public, and until 1872 there was no secret ballot. Polling closed at 4 pm. as the voters, privileged men, were unlikely to have to keep working hours. In 1857, when Cox was elected, some 10,000 people gathered in the hope of hearing fiery speeches. They were so annoyed by hearing only a mere 'independent' voter from a window in the Crown Inn where Cox's committee had assembled, that fighting broke out and had to be quelled by the police.

Among early unsuccessful candidates were Henry Hobhouse, brother of Lord Byron's friend Sir John Cam Hobhouse, and Dudley

Perceval, son of the assassinated Prime Minister, Spencer Perceval. But far more interesting was the pioneer of calculating machines, or early forms of computer, Charles Babbage (1792–1871). As Professor of Mathematics at Cambridge he contested the first two Finsbury elections, being ignominiously defeated in the second (1834) with only 379 votes.[1]

One Finsbury MP was Joseph Chamberlain's brother Richard. Also important was William McCurragh Torrens (Member 1865–85), an active Radical and former member of the Irish Bar who originated the 1868 Artisans' Dwellings Improvement Act. And a noted Member was Britain's first Indian MP, Dadabhai Naoroji, a Liberal, a Parsee professor who had been three times President of the Indian National Congress. After several unsuccessful attempts he scraped in by only five votes in 1892 and sat for three years, facetiously known by fellow-MPs who insisted they could not pronounce his name as "Mr Narrow Majority". He was an active Home Ruler, and in his own country was the first Indian professor, founded two newspapers, and was a leader in Indian literary and scientific societies. He is commemorated today in the name of a short street off Margery Street.

Islington started in 1885 with four MPs (and Finsbury was until 1918 increased to three), divided over the points of the compass, North, South, East and West. A first Islington Member in 1885 was the Liberal Henry Ince, who sat for only a year; the Conservative Sir George Bartley served until 1906. Until 1931 Islington was divided between Conservative and Liberal; the first Labour Member, Robert Young, sat from 1929–31 for North Islington.

Political development over a century is of some interest. In the early days, with a more limited electorate, the candidates whether successful or otherwise were members of the gentry, often with minor titles, and voting was fairly even between Liberal and Conservative. After 1885, with Islington separately represented, voting was almost wholly Conservative until 1900, and from 1906 became Liberal until the end of the First World War. A social analysis of the electorate in 1910 is revealing. The social tone declined as one moved south: Islington North included Upper

Holloway, "comparatively salubrious", and until 1910 regarded by the *Daily Telegraph* as mainly "upper middle class", which may surprise some people to-day.

East, which included Highbury, had "aristocratic aspirations", especially Highbury New Park and its adjoining streets, enough to outweigh the bordering Hackney influence: yet there was a strong base of "Liberal Nonconformity" until at least 1910.

West and South were both mainly working-class, the former thanks to railway employees, though with many middle-class, and South covered the old village area, Barnsbury, and the poverty-stricken Pentonville, though of higher "quality" farther north. West was Liberal, South divided between the two parties.[2]

Throughout the 20th century only three women sat for Islington, Dr Ethel Bentham in 1929 for North, and in 1931 briefly Mrs E L Manning (East), both Labour, followed by Thelma Cazalet-Kerr, Islington East's last Conservative Member, from 1931-45. At the end of the Second World War she was succeeded by Sir (later Lord) Eric Fletcher.

Since then Islington has been predominantly Labour, except when George Cunningham and colleagues moved to the SDP in the 1980s while still in office. In the 1960s the Fascist-leaning Union Movement made an attempt, when Sir Oswald Mosley contested Shoreditch and Finsbury, and his colleague Dan Hermiston was spectacularly unsuccessful in South West Islington. In 1950 the first Communist stood, followed in the 1960s by the stalwart Marie Betteridge, a grand campaigner though never elected.

In 1918 Finsbury, with a falling population was reduced to one member, and in 1950 was incorporated into South West Islington. Islington's members were reduced to three and then with redrawing of boundaries in 1983, to two, since when the Labour Jeremy Corbyn and Chris Smith have represented North and South Islington between them.[3]

Among leading politicians associated with Islington was Joseph Chamberlain, one-time Colonial Secretary – and by his two marriages father of two other distinguished politicians Sir Austen and Neville Chamberlain. He lived at 25 Highbury Place, where John Wesley used to visit a century earlier. Chamberlain, who lived there from 1845 to 1854, liked the house so much that on moving he carried the name 'Highbury' with him for his house in Birmingham.

Much later Fenner Brockway (1888-1988), prolific political activist and writer, and in 1954 a founder of the CND, moved in 1908 to 60 Myddelton Square, which became the base for the Independent Labour Party. Brockway was several times Secretary of the ILP and from 1931-33 its Chairman. A conscientious objector, he was imprisoned at Pentonville in 1916 and 1917. In 1964 he was created the first Labour life peer and in 1975 unveiled a plaque at his former home. He was also present at the unveiling of his statue in Red Lion Square in 1984.

Barbara Castle (created a life peer in 1990), when Secretary of State for Transport under Harold Wilson (1965–8), moved with her husband Ted Castle to John Spencer Square.

Prime minister Tony Blair was living at 1 Richmond Crescent at the time of his move to Downing Street in 1997.

ISLINGTON IN THE FIRST WORLD WAR [4]
With the outbreak of the first World War in 1914, young men eagerly flocked to join the army or navy, even several hundred from the notorious Campbell Road or 'Campbell Bunk' off Seven Sisters Road, regarded as a hotbed of crime. Anti-German feeling was so high that shops kept by Germans were attacked, and at Smithfield some butchers were nearly drowned in the horse-troughs by porters. Not only did people anglicise German-sounding surnames, but even street-names were changed – for example, Bismarck Road in Highgate became Waterlow Road.

The Workhouse, then in Cornwallis Road, was turned into an internment camp, where by 1917 3,000 Germans had been either confined, or deported. Feeling was so high that in 1917 the place was stormed for four nights in succession, and had to be defended by Special Constabulary based at Upper Holloway Police Station.

On today's 61 Farringdon Road a plaque records that 'These premises were totally destroyed by a Zeppelin raid during the world War on September 8th, 1915. Rebuilt 1917.' A

year later came the famous Zeppelin flight over north London – it was struck down and met its end at Cuffley in Hertfordshire. And at Passing Alley of bowdlerised name, off St John's Lane, a plaque records its damage by a German bomb in December 1917.

A famous wartime prisoner held at Pentonville Gaol was the Irish patriot Roger Casement, where the politician Fenner Brockway got a glimpse of him from a cell window.

The first bomb from an aeroplane raid on London was supposedly on Highbury Fields in 1917, where an anti-aircraft gun and searchlights were set up, and a shelter was made at Holloway Road Underground station. Houses in Alwyne Road were damaged, and one of the worst raids seriously damaged the Easter pub in Eden Grove, off Seven Sisters Road, with a number of casualties. Civilian casualties were taken to the Royal Northern Hospital in Holloway Road.

At the end of the war in November 1918, Islington had an RAF exhibition of captured German aircraft. There were the usual celebratory street parties with flags and banners, and hostilities were barely over before memorials were being planned – at the Royal Northern Hospital in practical form by building a casualty department, and a Nurses' Home, financed by donations and Islington's War Memorial Fund. Other places adopted more traditional memorials, such as a window and roll of honour at St Mary Magdalene church, and the somewhat nondescript monument on Islington Green, unveiled even just before the war ended.

THE SECOND WORLD WAR [5]
The Second World War was a very different experience, with its prolonged and direct effect on civilians and their homes. First there was the famous evacuation of children to the countryside and the provinces, heralded by broadcast instructions in the last days before war was declared, giving just one day's notice. Children arrived at school next morning with their kitbags (no suitcases allowed), had them labelled, and were off to the nearest station. Many came back – about 35 per cent – and their schools reopened, when the expected air raids did not happen and the 'phony war' set

in, until the fall of France in summer 1940. Then fresh evacuations were hurriedly made as the Battle of Britain raged.

Like many parts of inner London, Islington suffered badly from the bombings of 1940 and 1941, and again during the V1 and V2 attacks from the late summer of 1944.

Raids started over London Docks on 1 August 1940, then over the City. Blanket incendiaries caused huge fires. The first bomb on Islington fell on 24 August on the corner of Canonbury Park North and South, behind Willowbridge Road, at 11.15 pm. During 27 days in September there were 15 raids, in October 18 over 28 days, then diminishing until the next summer. Damage was widespread. St Mary's parish church was effectually destroyed (22 September, apart from its tower and spire). In one of the worst raids, on 15 October, a parachute mine made a direct hit on Dame Alice Owen's School, killing more than 100 people trapped there. In 1941 many houses in Mildmay Grove were destroyed and others damaged by blast (rebuilt in 1959 as Queen Mary's Court flats); Mildmay Street, Park and Avenue were also hit, and the local library and station damaged. The last severe Battle of Britain raid was on 19 May 1941, when in Rosebery Avenue a serious fire in the building adjoining Clerkenwell Fire Station severed the links with other fire stations and damaged water mains; Pentonville Prison was hit and Holford Square, one-time home of Lenin, was also partly destroyed (and later regrettably entirely obliterated and rebuilt). In 1942 the Russian Ambassador presented the borough with a bust of Lenin.

Other 1941 casualties were the Northampton Institute (now City University), killing whole families, totalling about 400 people, who were sheltering in the basements. Such disasters were dealt with by the heavy-duty Rescue Squad, partly served by specially released prisoners. The Charterhouse too was badly damaged, and the Church of the Holy Redeemer hit by incendiaries. Meanwhile the 17th-century Oak Room at New River Head was removed to safety 'for the duration', a phrase then in frequent use. Sadler's Wells, like many other theatres, closed and the cast went on tour – yet Gainsborough Film Studios, on the borders of Hackney and Islington, kept on producing, mostly films with a topical flavour like *We Dive at Dawn*. Caledonian Market too closed, for the last time on that site as it turned out, and the area was used to store munitions.

Though Islington lacked parks, it had squares whose gardens were dug up for air-raid shelters, while their fine railings were ripped up, supposedly to use for building planes and tanks – pointlessly as it proved. A Mayor's Spitfire Fund was launched to which everyone contributed, including more than 200 people 'sightseeing' a garden where a land mine had fallen, paying 1d each towards the fund.

There were barrage balloons – one over Arlington Square – and a large naval gun installed in the railway tunnel passing through Mildmay Grove, to be brought out during raids, while Lewis guns were driven around on lorries. Back gardens were dug for Anderson shelters, the empty schools were converted into fire stations, taxis commandeered for use by the armed services. Water tanks were set up in many streets for an instant supply against incendiaries and the multi-bomb, 'Molotov breadbaskets'. Shrapnel littered the streets in the mornings, while unexploded bombs, phosphorus and parachute mines were taken off to Hackney Marsh for detonation.

Black-out enforcement was strict, air-raid wardens patrolling the streets with an eye for chinks in blinds and curtains, so that in run-down Islington many an old-fashioned window shutter proved a godsend. Many such houses were still for many years to come lit by gas, had no bathrooms, and were in multi-occupation.

The face of London changed for good. In 1940, in Islington alone, 17,993 houses were damaged or destroyed, in 1941 19,303 – though many were repaired at the time, some more than once. Houses damaged included 3,097 'seriously', 1,253 'extensively', and of people killed and injured 958 casualties were fatal, 2,090 serious, 3,000 slight.

While the home front now had a lull from raids and immediate danger, shelters were still in use, and privation, limitation of social life, shortages, rationing and reduced travel enforced changes. In 1944 the pace hotted up again with Hitler's 'secret weapon', the V1s and V2s, 5,000 V1s coming over in little more than a month, and later, V2s landed at up to ten a day until March 1945. The Home Front suffered continually, the people wearied and services were dislocated. Civilian staff was short, social centres like day nurseries were damaged, and air raid deaths were higher than in 1941. And as anyone who could leave London did so, Islington's population fell – from 272,300 in 1939 to as low as 183,470 in 1941. During the succeeding lull it rose as people returned, but even in 1945 remained less than 200,000 – with fewer houses still undamaged for them to live in.

Islington's first V1 fell at Highbury Corner at 12.44 midday on 27 June 1944, killing 26 people, injuring more than 150, destroying Highbury Station and the Cock Tavern, the end of Upper Street, the end of Compton Terrace, and houses in St Paul's Road. (This historic cross-roads on the Great North Road was eventually reorganised as a roundabout, until in 2004 a re-creation of the cross-roads was proposed.) This was not the worst raid – a bomb in December hit the Prince of Wales pub in Mackenzie Road, killing 69 and injuring more than 250, 114 of them hospital cases. Another serious raid was on 5 November, a Sunday afternoon in Boothby Road, damaging two neighbouring north Islington roads, killing 33, seriously injuring 85 people and slightly injuring 134.

Damage to a public building which led to lasting change was by a bomb which hit Mount Pleasant postal sorting office, to replace which the Agricultural Hall was commandeered (1943). It continued as a sorting office until 1971, then lay empty and deteriorating while its fate was debated, from demolition to rebuilding.

The total number of bombs recorded in Islington was 559, with 76 unexploded, 15 parachute mines, 16 flying bombs and two rockets. Streets and institutions damaged or destroyed included Dame Alice Owen's and Starcross Schools, Finsbury Park Station, King's Cross Depot and the London Fever Hospital, some hit twice, even three times. Recovery after the war was painfully slow, as it was elsewhere in London. Only in the late 1950s, with the re-discovery by the professional classes of Islington's run-down but still attractive post-Regency houses did prosperity – in places only – begin to return.

'THE GAME'[6]

For more than 90 years the Arsenal Football Club has been synonymous with Highbury, and for many Islington inhabitants has played an important part in their leisure time. Founded in 1886 at the Royal Arsenal, Woolwich, whose name they adopted, they moved in 1913 to Highbury to the more spacious grounds of St John's College of Divinity. Dropping the name 'Woolwich' was first of many significant innovations – and as 'Arsenal' they were now at the top of the alphabet, and remain the only senior English team without a place-name in its title.

Arsenal were promoted to the Football League Division One in 1904, but were relegated in 1913, the year they moved to Highbury. They were promoted again in 1919, and have remained in the top division – it is now called the Premiership – ever since.

The club has had two golden eras, the first under the management of Herbert Chapman (1925–34) when they won the League three times, and since 1996 under Arsene Wenger they have won the Premiership three times and the FA Cup twice. In the season 2003–4, they won the Premiership without losing a game. In all, they have been League or Premiership champions 12 times and cup winners 9 times.

It was the enterprising Herbert Chapman who got the name of the local Underground station, Gillespie Road, changed to 'Arsenal'.

Beset by the financial need to increase its seating capacity, and unable to extend because of houses around, Arsenal took the decision to remove its stadium to the south where a hinterland of yards, waste facilities and old railway lands provided the space they needed. After protracted negotiations and enquiries the new stadium is now being built. It remains to be seen if Holloway Road station, which will be the nearest, will be renamed!

1   Pinks, *Clerkenwell*, London, pp. 141–2; *DNB*, Babbage; Islington Local History Library collection.

2   Henry Pelling, *The Social Geography of British Elections, 1885–1910*, London, 1967, pp. 32–49.

3   *VCH*, p. 82; Islington Local History Library collection.

4   Jerry White, *The Worst Street in London: Campbell Bunk, Islington, between the wars*; Routledge, 1986; Ken Weller, *"Don't be a Soldier!" The Radical Anti-War Movement in North London 1914–1918*, London, Journeyman Press, 1985; Islington Libraries Local History collection. (YA 130, YA 795).

5   For the 2nd World War, personal references in Islington Local History Library, e.g. Beth Voden, *One Over the Baker's Dozen*, Centerprise; Florence & Charles Nelson, *Bugs in the Bed*; Alan Ricketts, *A Child of the Twenties*; Harry Walters, *The Street*, Centerprise Publishing Project, Hackney, 1975; Alderman (later Mayor) D McArthur Jackson, JP, Scrapbook 1939–40. See also Michael E Reading, "Remembering Islington under Attack", The V Weapon Campaign, 1944–5 (pamphlet), March 2004.

6   I am indebted to Jim Lagden and John Richardson for invaluable information on the history and fortunes of the Arsenal Football Club.

CHAPTER 40

Envoi

A Social Change

The state of Islington in the years before the First World War can be seen as a microcosm of the Edwardian Age. Then England appeared at the peak of its power and influence, with the upper classes entrenched in ever grander country houses and estates, and the aspiring servant-employing upper middle class probably richer and more influential than ever before. Yet it was carrying the seeds of its own decay, even before an epoch ended and a generation was destroyed by the monumental crash of the War.

Islington had its colleges, its new LCC Board Schools, and it had its modern shops, some of them rivalling popular and fashionable central London shopping venues. It had its own popular theatres and music halls, in the tra-

119. Run-down Islington. The junction of Islington Green and Essex Road c.1910.

331

120. Grimy, soot-covered Islington. This is Gibson Square in 1938.

dition of Merrie Islington of centuries earlier. And though its century-old terraces and squares were now dated in style, it had more modern developments of spacious rows and villas with gardens: the Victorian parts of Canonbury – quintessential leafy suburb – Highbury, Tufnell Park and new streets in the north of the borough. And to complete the parallel, it had its shaming contrasts in the life and housing of the poor.

As opposed to Percy Fitzgerald's exuberant view of Islington's originality and lively social life, in 1903 Walter Besant was gloomily writing, "As regards simple absence of joy, Hoxton, Haggerston, Pentonville, Clerkenwell, or Kentish Town, might contend . . . with any portion whatever of the East End proper."[1]

He indeed put his finger on the extremes of prosperity, comfortable inner suburb and slummy small streets and tenements. That has now been repeated at the turn of the succeeding century, trendy Islington famous for fashionably revamped terraces, squares and villas, and problem estates – estates intended to solve the housing difficulties of the poor – a distinction similar to Mrs Gaskell's in *North and South*. The wheel has, as it were, come full circle.

In the early 20th century decline set in. The spread of the Underground Railway to villages on the fringe of fresh countryside which themselves rapidly became suburbs, lured those who could afford it from the dirt and smoke of what was becoming inner and central London, to more tempting surroundings. Yet many old-established families remained, witnessing change and deterioration in their neighbourhood, while struggling or unorthodox writers like Evelyn Waugh and later, just after the Second World War, George Orwell, found it an acceptable place to settle: it might be thought quaint but it was down-at-heel.

The evacuation and destruction of the Second World War seemed to put paid to all prosperity and pleasant living. The once agreeable terraces were shabby, multi-occupied, one or more tenant to each room. Other houses decayed or were demolished without a pang, while successive Councils rebuilt without compunction, with no attempt to marry new building in style or scale.

In place of more than 3,000 houses destroyed, by 1958 Islington Council and the LCC respectively had built 1,622 and 1,051 new dwellings. Yet by 1967 there were still 59 per cent of inhabitants in multi-occupation, and 7 per cent lacking basic amenities, the highest in London. In 1951 Islington was recorded as the most densely populated borough in the capital, and with the least open spaces. It still has.[2]

Then in the late 1950s, first Canonbury, then Barnsbury, Highbury and the canal area, were rediscovered, restored, reoccupied, houses changing hands at knock-down prices while existing tenants were bought out or sometimes simply evicted. In some areas Rachmanism was rife. By degrees south Islington became not a slummy, decayed area with a few reclaimed and newly-painted houses, but a smart suburb with a few sore thumbs sticking out here and there, tempting such income-groups as it had never had in its early developing years . . . and then no sore thumbs at all.

This didn't happen at quite the speed that journalists, who were among the incomers, liked to pretend, Fleet Street (as it then was) being conveniently near for young newspapermen's families to move to the pretty houses and restore them. Early incomers were positive, environmentally minded, eager to renew the borough's lost pride and beauty. Over the following decades it became another popular suburb, at house-prices its 1960s' pioneers could never have afforded. As years passed reclamation spread to the more Victorian areas farther north. It still attracts many active, responsible professionals, and has tempted actors, radio and TV personalities, writers, artists, a number of whom have indeed made notable contributions to the area. But many newcomers have been happier to benefit from what the pioneers achieved for them than to try putting anything back into it.

Modern Islington has long been a very cosmopolitan society, its population including in turn, immigrants from Ireland, the Caribbean, then Cyprus, both Greek and Turkish, then refugees from oppressed countries in Africa and East Asia. Today 27 per cent of its population is from ethnic minorities, whose arrival has been reflected not only in lively contributions to schools and work-places but in shops – especially food-shops – and in proliferating ethnic restaurants.

A TRANSFORMED UPPER STREET

Meanwhile along Upper Street, ousting the run-down traditional shops there appeared, first antique shops, then estate agents and lawyers, and finally a plethora of restaurants. But instead of luring quality shopping the borough acquired supermarkets. A few good butchers and grocers survived and flourish here and there; a few famous street markets also struggle on, notably Chapel Market which always feels under threat though deservedly popular. Opposite, Chapman Taylor's N1 Shopping Centre of 2002 has added the sort of dress-shops and stores that had already begun to appear in Upper Street. There are also several commercial art galleries, and modern sculpture is represented in Wolfgang and Heron's conceptual wings at the N1 Centre.

The most aggressively original new building must be the addition to London Metropolitan University in Holloway Road. Designed by Daniel Libeskind, opinions on it range from squashed shoebox to most inspiring/imaginative/fun.

Camden Passage was transformed in the 1960s from a collection of junk-shops to a successful antiques market, and became a leading contributor to recovering prosperity for Islington, though in 2005 there are hints of possible decline in its trade. In 1999 on the same site a Sunday farmers' market was established.

In 1970 Dan Crawford introduced London's original pub theatre at the King's Head in Upper Street, setting a fashion for others and launching many young actors and plays to West End success. An enterprise which left a positive mark on the lives of many young people in Islington was the youth theatre formed by Anna Scher in 1968, and established in Barnsbury Road. This creative venture, pioneered by its charismatic and imaginative founder, inspired many schoolchildren over some thirty years, launching a number into dramatic careers. But after Anna suffered a breakdown in 2001, in a dispute which, whatever the rights of the case, was not sensitively handled, she was not reinstated by the charity, and in 2004 she was suspended despite strong local protest. Further, Council funding was then substantially cut. Anna, undaunted, continued classes at the Blessed Sacrament

121. Camden Passage in the 1950s.

Starting with permission for two local schools to make a temporary garden, it has blossomed in all senses. Locally run and appropriately named after the 17th-century herbalist, Nicholas Culpeper, it is like a miniature paradise, with shrubs, walks, flowerbeds, ponds and a wildlife area full of hidden delights.

From being served chiefly by buses, the area profited in the 'Sixties from the new Victoria Line – not without a vigorous local campaign to prevent a soulless vent-shaft wrecking Gibson Square, and receiving instead an elegant Roman temple designed by Quinlan Terry. Though London Transport missed a trick through bypassing the Angel between King's Cross and Highbury Corner. And like every other part of London Islington, from a relatively car-free area has become traffic-loaded, with the usual parking problems, new culs-de-sac and one-way streets.

The Angel itself narrowly escaped a massive roundabout with underpass and flyover in the 1970s, fortunately abandoned as a result of campaigning led by the Islington Society.

Islington is one of the London areas that has suffered least from the surfeit of tower-block housing in the 1960s and 1970s, thanks to the policy of Alf Head, who became Borough Architect in 1964. He prevented further demolitions and saw the importance of what remained. Today Islington has the highest number of listed houses in London.

Unemployment, which rocketed in the '70s and '80s, has fallen to less than 8,000. In 2003 the population, slightly up from the 2001 Census figure, stood at 176,103, little over a third of the figure in 1901 (436,701). But the area is still divided between haves and have-nots, the latter more in the north, on the borough's fringes and in the large Council estates in the south. The merger with Finsbury Borough in 1965 caused much local resentment, although Clerkenwell/Finsbury retains its individual character. Since before the turn of the 21st century Clerkenwell too has been pressed into social rehabilitation, with blocks of offices updated and revamped or turned into well-equipped flats, increasing its living-in population for the first time in decades, and again new restaurants open in all directions. Here the Museum of the Order of St John at St John's Gate has extended and enriched its display.

Church in Copenhagen Street.

Another youth venture, which has strongly affected Islington children, has been the Little Angel Puppet Theatre, founded by John Wright in Dagmar Passage behind St Mary's parish church, which has become world-famous among children and adults alike.

Later the Almeida at the one-time Literary and Scientific Institution re-established Islington's suburban theatre tradition of a century earlier. This has, in the last year or so, been completely refurbished. In the '90s the magnificently rebuilt Sadler's Wells theatre (architects RHWL and Nicholas Hare) has added distinction to Rosebery Avenue. The seedy cinemas of the fifties, when not converted to Bingo halls, have been upgraded or added to by smart newcomers, some, like Screen on the Green, of cult-movie style. Compensating for the shortage of public open space, a notable amenity for young people has been the Islington Boat Club, started in 1970 by Crystal Hale and moving to its present City Road Basin site in Graham Street in 1985. An admirable addition to the small number of parks is the Culpeper Community Garden off Tolpuddle Street, begun in 1982 on the site of demolished houses, hence at 'basement level'.

122. Dereliction in Canonbury Square in the 1950s.

123. A house in Barnsbury Road in 1954, before 'gentrification' began.

Further, with the demise of Fleet Street, the only national newspapers not to move to Canary Wharf moved into Finsbury/Clerkenwell, the *Guardian* to Farringdon Road, the *Independent* (though briefly) to City Road. A new local paper, the *Highbury and Islington Express*, was launched in 1996, though like the 150-year-old *Islington Gazette* it subsequently moved office out of the borough. In November 2003 the free newspaper *Islington Tribune*, based in Camden Road, joined the now vigorous local press. All maintain a lively readers' correspondence.

Environmental societies now flourish in different parts of the borough, starting with the Islington Society in 1960, and in 1987 a local museum was launched and survives, if rather creakily.

While in the 1950s and '60s fine if run-down property changed hands at what by any standards were ridiculously low prices, today Islington is among London's top ten 'least accessible' housing areas. Only one-third of the housing stock is owner-occupied and a fifth is privately rented. Approximately half is estimated as 'social renting' from the Council or housing associations. At 36 per cent Council-rented, Islington is the third highest in the country, and for owner-occupation the fourth lowest.[3] On the housing market, a modest late Victorian or Edwardian terrace house in the north of the borough may change hands in the region of £½ million; a similar-sized house in fashionable pre-Victorian south Islington may be offered from £700,000 upwards, and larger houses in the grander streets have well passed the million mark. In 2003 the earnings gap was estimated at 83.6 per cent, leaving young would-be buyers unable to afford the most modest of houses.

In the 1960s Islington became gay, in the contemporary sense of the word, when it proved an agreeable refuge for the then still persecuted homosexuals. By the 1990s it was also again gay in the 'merry' sense, with its sprinkling of all kinds of small theatres, the rebuilt Sadler's Wells and the flood of restaurants along Upper Street and neighbouring areas.

In the new century redevelopment of the King's Cross area for extension of the Channel Tunnel Rail Link began to affect the surroundings, especially the Caledonian Road, where industries had declined, drug dealing and prostitution had become a problem, and there were derelict buildings. But by 2004 new developments, notably by P & O, were in progress, and round what was beginning to be named the Regent's Quarter shops, commercial offices and housing were part of the plan. Meanwhile artists, tempted by local low rents, were also beginning to move in.

Yet, nasty shocks abound. In 2003 gun crime was reported as 15 per cent, while Holloway Gaol was reckoned as Britain's worst prison. In spring 2004 seven Islington wards were rated by the North Central London's Strategic Health Authority as among Britain's 20 most unhealthy areas, with 150 deaths per 100,000 from coronary heart disease. The worst wards ranged from Holloway and Tollington to Bunhill and Clerkenwell. Poor diet and insufficient exercise were quoted as the chief causes (while central Islington, ironically, was bulging with gourmet restaurants). TB cases were also shown to have risen by a disturbing amount and road deaths were quoted as sixth highest in London in the six years to 2002. This was followed in 2003 by a proliferation of 'traffic calming' road humps.

Islington was also claimed to have one of the highest pollution rates in London, itself among the worst in major European cities. This was the place where in the 18th century people flocked from London for the sake of their health.

In Spring 2004, despite its popular reputation for glamour and affluence, Islington's 'pockets of poverty' condemned it as England's eighth most deprived area – among London boroughs only Tower Hamlets and Hackney ranking worse. Islington was granted £18 million of neighbourhood renewal fund money, whose allocation at the local end aroused some controversy.[4] Not long afterwards local inhabitants entered with a verve in a contest to name the borough's worst streets. In the standard of healthy criticism Islington certainly stands high.

A survey in the autumn of 2004 revealed that more than a third of Islington residents were smoking addicts, and it was one of only nine English boroughs with more than 40 per cent smoking-related deaths. More than half were overweight, two-thirds took too little exer-

cise and some 30 per cent tended to drink more than the recommended limit. It also had London's second-lowest birth rate. In fact, if these dismal statistics can be believed, many Islington inhabitants appeared to be well under par for fitness.

In December 2004, however, there appeared to be hopeful signs. Whereas in 2002 Islington local authority had been adjudged by the Corporate Performance Assessment as "poor", it now appeared as Britain's fastest-improving authority, moving up three places to "good". This included, for example, schools, care services and the environment; in spite of, for example, such controversial changes as the closing of Angel primary school for rebuilding as flats, the intended sale of Finsbury Town Hall, and the unpopular closing of Arthur Simpson Library in favour of a new library elsewhere.

At much the same time a borough project was launched for improving the 'A1 corridor' – namely the Great North Road from the Angel via the Holloway Road to the unlovely Archway area. It included the effect of a rebuilt Arsenal stadium, a waste recycling centre, and improvements to Highbury Corner.

All this contrasts sharply with the popular press images of Islington since the 1990s and their *on-dits* of trendy Islington dinner-parties. Again a centre of gaiety and active social life as it was up to a century ago, Islington is seen by some, unaware of its contrasts, as a famously fun place, while in some areas women say they are afraid to go out at night. The rich are richer, the poor poorer. Whether the 20–21st century version is as vibrant as the old, is for the current generation of inhabitants to determine.

Statistics and reports of surveys are based on reports in the local press, *Islington Gazette, Highbury and Islington Express,* and *Islington Tribune* (launched November 2003

1   Percy Fitzgerald, *London City Suburbs as they are To-day*, London, 1903, pp. 28-9; Walter Besant, *As we are and as we may be*, London, 1903, p. 288.
2   National Statistics Office; *VCH* 11.
3   Islington Council Census Department.
4   *Islington Gazette*, 6 May 2004.

Glossary

Beadle: A parish officer empowered to punish minor offenders.

Bellman: An official who rings a bell, especially in the streets, before the making of public announcements; a town crier.

Carucate: As much land as a team of oxen can plough in a season.

Copyhold: In English law, the right of holding land by copy of the roll originally made by the Lord of the Manor's court steward.

Cottar: Peasant occupying a cot or cottage for which he must give labour.

Cow-lair or layer: An enclosure where cattle could be housed on the way to or from market.

Curtilage: Court attached to a dwelling.

Demesne: Lands adjacent to a manor-house not let out to tenants; the grounds personally used by the Lord of the Manor.

Headborough: A petty constable; head of a tithing.

Hide: Enough land for a household (variable in law).

Liberty: Area adjoining the City within which certain privileges were allowed.

Sexton: Parish officer attending the clergyman, who rings the church bell, digs grave-pits etc.

Socage: Tenure of lands by service fixed and determinate in quality (soc = inquiry, jurisdiction).

Steer: Young ox, especially castrated, between 2 and 4 years old.

Stot: Young ox or steer.

Toft: Homestead, hillock.

Villein: Free villager. In the 13th century, a serf, free of all except his lord, 'not absolutely a slave'. Later becomes a copyholder.

Virgate: (= rod-like). Land measure, usually 30 acres.

Abbreviations

DNB: *Dictionary of National Biography*

IG: *Islington Gazette*

ILN: *Illustrated London News*

LAMAS: London and Middlesex Archaeological Society

LMA: London Metropolitan Archives

MCR: *Middlesex County Records*, Old Series, Middlesex County Records Society, 1888

MOLAS: Museum of London Archaeology Service

VCH: *Victoria County History*

VM: Vestry Minutes, Islington Local History Library.

Sources and Bibliography

Main primary sources:
Colvin, Howard, *A Biographical Dictionary of British Architects 1600–1800*, 3rd edn, John Murray, 1995.
Cromwell, Thomas, & Storer, J & H S, *Walks Through Islington*, London, 1835.
Dictionary of National Biography.
Lewis, Samuel, Jr, *History of the Parish of St Mary, Islington*, London, 1842.
Nelson, John, *The History of Islington*, London, 1811.
Pevsner, Nikolaus, *The Buildings of England, London, except the Cities of London and Westminster*, Penguin Books, 1951.
Pevsner, Nikolaus, & Cherry, Bridget, *The Buildings of England, London 4: North*, Penguin Books, 1998.
Pinks, William J, *The History of Clerkenwell*, with additions by Edward J. Wood, London, 1865.
Victoria County History of the County of Middlesex, Vol. VIII, *Islington and Stoke Newington Parishes*, OUP for Institute of Historical Research, 1985.
Willats, Eric A, *Streets with a Story*, The Book of Islington, Islington Local History Trust, 1988.

Other primary sources:
Annual Reports of the Sanitary Condition of the Parish of Islington, London, 1856 ff.
Borough of Islington Guide, 1962.
Islington Vestry Minutes, 1665 ff. [MSS]
London Statistics, LCC, 1891 ff.
The Ragged School Shoe-Black Society, An Account of its Origins, Opinions. Shoe-Black Society, 1854.
Tibberton Square 1839–1979, Islington Council, 1979.

Periodicals:
Archway Central Hall Newsletter, 1977–9
Ainsworth's Magazine
Bell's Weekly Messenger
Builder, The
Building News
Clerkenwell Times
Daily Post
Daily Telegraph
Draper, The
Everybody's
Fortnightly Review
Gentleman's Magazine, The
Graphic, The
Hewitt's Journal
Holloway Press
Hornsey Historical Society Bulletin
Household Words
Illustrated London News
Islington Athenaeum
Islington Gazette
Islington, Hornsey, Highgate and Kentish Town Family Newspaper
Jewish Chronicle
Lady's Newspaper, The
Leisure Hour
Listener, The
London Chronicle, The
London Journal, The
London Magazine, The

Mirror, The
Northampton Herald
Pall Mall Gazette
Penny Magazine
St Thomas's Parish Magazine [Hemingford Road, Islington]
Tablet, The
Times, The
Traveller, The
Warehouse & Drapers' Trade Journal
Weekly Dispatch

BIBLIOGRAPHY
Adbergham, Alison, *Shopping in Style*, London, Thames & Hudson, 1979.
Adbergham, Alison, *Shops and Shopping*, London, 1964, revised 1981 (George Allen & Unwin).
Arundell, Dennis, *The Story of Sadler's Wells 1683–1977*, David & Charles, 1978.
Baker, Frank, *John Wesley and the Church of England*, London, Epworth Press, 1970.
Bateman, Rev Josiah, *The Life of the Rt Rev. Daniel Wilson, DD*, London, 1860.
Beames, The Rev Thomas, *The Rookeries of London*, 2nd edn, London, 1852.
Beckett, Arthur W, *London at the End of the 19th Century*, London, 1900.
Bennett, A M, *London and Londoners in the 1850s and 1860s*, London, 1924.
Berry, Fred, *Housing: The Great British Failure*, London, 1974
Berry, C G, *London's Water Supply 1903–1953*, Metropolitan Water Board, 1953.
Besant, Walter, *London in the 19th Century*, London, 1909
Boarding School and London Masters Directory, London, 1828.
Booth, Charles, *Life and Labour of the People in London*, Second Ser., *Industry*, 1909; Vol. III, *Poverty*, 1902; 3rd Ser., *Religious Influences: London North of the Thames*, 1902.
Boswell, James, *The Life of Samuel Johnson*, Folio Society, 1968.
Bottman, Alex, *London Catholic Churches*, London, 1926.
Brayley, Edward Wedlake, *History and Descriptive Accounts of the Theatres of London*, London, 1826.
Butcher, T C, & Robbins, Michael, *A History of London Transport*, London, 1963.
Carlyle, Thomas, *Two Notebooks of Thomas Carlyle*, ed. Charles Eliot Norton, New York, Grolier Club, 1898.
Carlyle, Thomas & Jane, *The Collected Letters of Thomas and Jane Welsh Carlyle*, N. Carolina, 1970 ff.
Cave, Lyndon F, *The Smaller English House*, Robert Hale, 1981.
Chantreau, Pierre, *Voyage dans les trois Royaumes d'Angleterrre, d'Ecosse et d'Irlande*, Paris, 1792.
Chesterton, George Laval, *Revelations of Prison Life*, London, 1856.
Colman, Rev Henry, *European Life and Manners*, Boston & London, 1849.
Cornwall, Barry, *see* Procter, Bryan Waller.
Cosh, Mary, *A History of St Stephen's Church*, Canonbury, p.p. St Stephen's Church, 1989.
Cosh, Mary, *The Squares of Islington*, Parts I & II, Isling-

ton Archaeology & History Society, 1990 & 1993.

Coull, Thomas, *History of Islington*, London, 1864.

Creevey, Thomas, *Creevey*, ed. John Gore, London, 1948.

Cymmrodorion, Transactions of the Honourable Society of, for 1956 (published 1957).

Daniel, George, *Democritus in London*, London, 1852.

Daniel, George, *Love's Labour's Not Lost*, London, 1863.

Darby, H C & Campbell, E M J, *The Domesday Geography of S E England*, OUP, 1962.

Dare, Reginald A, *A History of Owen's School*, Wallington, 1963.

Davies, Rev. Maurice, *Unorthodox London*, London, 1876.

Day, John R, *The Story of the London Bus*, London Transport, 1973.

Defoe, Daniel, *A Journal of the Plague Year*, Folio Society, 1960.

Dibdin, Thomas, *The Reminiscences of Thomas Dibdin*, New York, 1970.

Dickens, Charles ('Boz'), *Memoirs of Joseph Grimaldi*, ed. by Boz, London, 1838.

Dickens, Charles, *American Notes*, London, 1842.

Dickens, Charles, *Our Mutual Friend*, London, 1864-5

Doré, Gustav, & Jerrold, Blanchard, *London*, London, 1872.

Emerson, G E, *How the Great City Grew*, London, 1862.

Emerson, Ralph Waldo, *The Letters of Ralph Waldo Emerson*, ed. Ralph L. Rusk, New York, 1939.

Espriella, Manuel Alvarez, *see* Southey, Robert.

Essex-Lopresti, Michael, *Exploring the New River*, 3rd edn, London, 1997.

Evelyn, John, *The Diary of John Evelyn*, ed. E S de Beer, OUP, 1959.

[Feltham, J] *The Picture of London*, London, 1802.

Fincham, H W, *The Order of the Hospitallers of St John of Jerusalem*, London, 1924.

Fitzgerald, Percy, *London City Suburbs as they are Today*, London, 1900.

Forshaw, Alec, *Smithfield*, London, Heinemann, 1980.

Fox, Henry Edward, *The Journal of Henry Edward Fox, 1818-1830*, ed. Lord Ilchester, London, 1923.

Foxe, John, *Actes and Monuments*, London, 1563.

Franklin, Benjamin, *The Papers of Benjamin Franklin*, ed. Leonard W. Labaree, Yale UP, 1965, 1966, 1973.

Gillies, Robert Pierse, *Memoirs of a Literary Veteran*, London, 1851

Girouard, Mark, *The Victorian Pub*, 1975.

Godwin. George, *Another Blow for Life*, London, 1864.

Godwin. George, *London Shadows*, London, 1854.

Grant, James, *Lights and Shadows of London Life*, London, 1842.

Greenwood, James, *Dining with Duke Humphrey*, London, [1884].

Greenwood, James, *In Strange Company*, London, 1874.

Greenwood, James, *The Seven Curses of London*, London, 1869.

Greenwood, James, *Unsentimental Journeys*, London, 1867.

Halliday, Stephen, *The Great Stink of London: Sir Joseph Bazalgette and the Cleansing of the Victorian Capital*, Sutton Publishing, 1999.

Harrison, M, *London Growing*, London, 1865.

[Hayward, W S] *London by Night*, [c.1870] (fiction).

Hazlitt, William Carew, *The Hazlitts*, London, 1912.

Hibbert, H G, *Fifty Years of a Londoner's Life*, London, 1916.

Hidson, R H, *The Birth of a Library Service: Islington 1855-1904*, Islington Local History Education Trust, [1990].

Hill, Christopher, *The World Turned Upside Down*, London, 1972.

Hill, Octavia, *Homes of the London Poor*, London, 1875.

Hillocks, J J, *Hard Battle for Life and Usefulness*, London, 1894.

Hinde, Thomas, ed, *The Domesday Book*, Guild Publishing London, for English Tourist Board, 1985.

Hollingshead, John, *My Lifetime*, London, 1895.

Hone, William, *The Every-Day Book and Table Book*, London, 1826.

Howard, Diana, *London Theatres and Music Halls 1850–1950*, Library Association, 1970.

Inwood, Stephen, *A History of London*, Macmillan, 1998

Irving, Washington, *Journals of Washington Irving (1823-1824)*, ed. Stanley T. Williams, Cambridge, Harvard UP, 1931.

Jenkins, Simon, *Landlords to London*, Constable, 1975.

Jephson, Henry, *The Sanitary Evolution of London*, London, 1907.

Jerrold, Douglas, *Mrs Caudle's Curtain Lectures*, London, 1846 (reprinted 1902).

Klapper, Charles, *The Golden Age of Tramways*, London, 196

LAMAS Transactions, Vol.39, 1988.

Lamb, Charles, *Last Essays of Elia*, London, 1833.

Lamb, Charles, *The Letters of Charles Lamb*, ed. E V Lucas, London, 1935.

Lennox, Lord William Pitt, *Fifty Years of Biographical Reminiscences*, London, 1863.

Lennox, Lord William Pitt, *My Recollections from 1806 to 1873*, London, 1874.

Lewin, H G, *The Railway Mania and its Aftermath 1845-52*, London, 1968.

Lewis, Samuel, jr, *A History of the Parish of St Mary's, Islington*, London, 1842

London Markets, Special Report of the Public Control Committee, LCC, London, 1893.

Survey of London, King's Cross Neighbourhood, Vol. XXIV, LCC, 1952.

Lovett, Rev. Richard, *London Pictures*, Religious Tract Society, 1890.

Marks, Stephen Powys, *The Map of Mid Sixteenth Century London*, London Topographical Society, 1964.

Marple, Maurice, *Wicked Uncles in Love*, London, 1972.

Mayer, Joseph, *Memoirs of Thomas Dodd*.

Mayhew, Henry, *The Great World of London*, London 1956.

Mayhew, Henry, & Binney, John, *The Criminal Prisons of London and Scenes of Prison Life*, New York, 1968.

Mearns, Andrew, *The Bitter Cry of Outcast London*, (reprint), Leicester UP, 1970, Reprinted GLC 1972.

Middlesex County Records, Vols. I, III, Middlesex County Records Society, [c.1880s].

Miller, Genevieve, *Adoption of Inoculation for Smallpox in England and France*, Philadelphia.

Miller, Thomas, *Picturesque Sketches of London, Past and Present*, London, 1852.

Mitton, G.E., *Clerkenwell and St Luke's*, London, 1906.

Moritz, Carl Philip, *Journeys of a German in England in 1782*, London, 1924.

Morris, Simon, & Mason, Towyn, *Gateway to the City*, Hornsey Historical Society, 2000.

Montagu, Lady Mary Wortley, *The Complete Letters of Lady Mary Wortley Montagu*, ed. Robert Halsband, Oxford, 1965.

Murray, John Fisher, *The World of London*, London, 1845.

Musson, David, *Memories of London in the Forties*, Edinburgh & London, 1908.

Museum of London Archaeology Service (MOLAS),

Archaeological Evaluation Reports, March 2000.

Northumberland, Duchess of, *The Diaries of a Duchess*, ed. James Greig, London, 1926.

Oliphant, Mrs Margaret, *The Life of Edward Irving*, London, 1862.

Ollard, Canon Sidney, *Short History of the Oxford Movement*, London, [1915].

Olsen, Donald J, *The Growth of Victorian London*, London, 1971.

Olsen, Donald J, *Town Planning in London*, London, 1964

Palmerston, Henry Temple, 3rd Viscount, *The Letters of Viscount Palmerston to Laurence and Elizabeth Sulivan, 1804-63*, Camden 4th Series, Vol. 23, Royal Historical Society, 1979.

Pascoe, Charles Eyre, *London of Today*, London, 1903.

Pelling, Henry, *The Social Geography of British Elections, 1885–1910*, London, 1967.

Pepys, Samuel, *The Diary of Samuel Pepys*, ed. Henry B. Wheatley, London, 1904.

Pigot & Co, *London and Provincial Directory*, 1828–9.

Planché, J Robinson, *Recollections and Reflections*, London, 1872.

Place, Francis, *The Autobiography of Francis Place*, ed. Mary Thale, Cambridge UP, 1972.

Procter, Bryan Waller ['Barry Cornwall'], *Literary Recollections*, London, 1936.

Pugh, Edward [= David Hughson], *Walks Through London*, 1817.

Ridge, William Pett, *A Story Teller: 40 Years in London*, [?1920].

Ritchie, J Ewing, *Days and Nights in London*, London, 1880.

Ritchie, J Ewing, *Here and There in London*, London, 1859.

Ritchie, J Ewing, *The London Pulpit*, London, 1854.

Ritchie, J Ewing, *The Religious Life of London*, London, 1870 .

Ritchie, J Ewing, *The Night Side of London*, London, 1861.

Robinson, Henry Crabb, *The Correspondence of Henry Crabb Robinson with the Wordsworth Circle (1810-1866)*, ed. Edith J Morley, Oxford, 1927.

Rogers, Samuel, *Reminiscences and Table Talk of Samuel Rogers*, ed. G H Powell, London, 1903.

Rogers, Samuel, *Recollections of Samuel Rogers*, London, 1859.

Rudden, B, *The New River, A Legal History*, Oxford, 1985.

Sala, George, *Living London*, London, 1883.

Sala, George, *Gaslight and Daylight*, London, 1859.

Schlesinger, Max, *Sauntering in and about London*, London, 1853.

Seaman, L C B, *Life in Victorian London*, London, 1973.

Sekon, G A, *Locomotion in Victorian London*, London, 1938.

Service, Alastair, *London, 1900*, London, 1979.

Sexby, Lt. Col. J J, *The Municipal Parks, Gardens and Open Spaces of London*, London, 1905.

Seymour, Robert, *Humorous Sketches*, London, 1838.

Shepherd, Francis, *London 1808-1870, The Infernal Wen*, London, 1971.

Shirren, A J, *Samuel Rogers: the Poet from Newington Green*, Stoke Newington Public Libraries, 1963.

Silliman, Benjamin, *A Journal of Travels in England, Holland and Scotland. . . in the Years 1805 and 1806*, 3rd edn (enlarged), New Haven, 1820.

Sims, G R (ed), *Living London*, London, 1902.

Sims, G, *Ballads and Poems*, London, 1883.

Sims, G, *How the Poor Live*, London, 1889.

Sisley, R, *The London Water Supply*, 1899.

Smith, Albert, *The Adventures of Mr Ledbury, and his Friend Jack Johnson*, London, 1886.

Smith, Charles Manby, *Curiosities of London Life*, London, 1853.

Smith, Charles Manby, *The Little World of London*, London, 1857.

Southey, Robert, *The Life and Correspondence of the late Robert Southey*, ed. by his son the Rev. Charles Cuthbert Southey, London, 1849-50.

[Southey, Robert], Alvarez Espriella, *Letters from England*, ed. Jack Simmons, London, 1951.

Stanton, F M, *Norman London, with a Translation of William FitzStephen's Description*, London, Historical Association, 1934.

Stow, John, *The Annales of England (1585-7)*.

Stow, John, *Survey of London, brought to the present by John Strype*, 1720 (1893 edn).

Stow, John, *Survey of London (1592 & 1603)*, Sutton Publishing edn, 1994.

Strype, John, *Annals of the Reformation*, London, 1824.

Sunderland, Septimus, *Old London's Spas, Baths and Wells*, London, 1915.

Temple, Philip, *Islington Chapels*, RCHME, 1992.

Thomson, John & Smith, Adolf, *Street Incidents*, London, 1881.

Thornbury, Walter, *Old and New London*, London, 1883.

Tomalin, Claire, *Life and Death of Mary Wollstonecraft*, Penguin Books, 1992.

Tristan, Flora, *Flora Tristan's London Journal, 1840*, London, 1980.

Unwin, George, *Gilds and Companies of London*, London, 1908.

Vanderkiste, R W, *Six Years' Mission. . .Among the Dens of London*, London, 1854.

Vizetelly, Henry, *Glances Back through 70 Years*, London, 1893.

Wakerley, Rev John E, *A Record of Progress in Central London, 1899-1900*, London, 1900.

Ward, Robert, *London's New River*, London, Historical Publications, 2003.

Ward, W, *Life and Times of Cardinal Newman*, London, 1913.

Wardroper, John, *The World of William Hone*, London, Shelfmark Books, 1997

Weale, J, *The Pictorial History of London*, London, 1854.

Weller, Ken, *"Don't Be a Soldier!" the Radical Anti-War Movement in North London 1914-1918*, London, Journeyman Press, 1985.

Wesley, John, *The Journal of the Rev. John Wesley, A.M.*, ed. Nehemiah Curnock, London, 1909.

White, Jerry, *The Worst Street in London: Campbell Bunk, Islington, between the Wars*, London, Routledge, 1986.

Whitefield, George, *Journal of a Voyage from London to Savannah*, London, 1737.

Wight, John, *Sunday in London*, London, 1833.

Willis, Frederick, *A Book of London Yesterdays*, London, 1960.

Willis, Nathaniel, *Pencillings by the Way*, London, 1835.

Wilson, Geoffrey, *London United Tramways*, London, 1971

Wroth, Warwick, *The London Pleasure Gardens of the Eighteenth Century*, London, 1896.

Wrottesley, John, *The Great Northern Railway*, London, Batsford, 1979

Yates, Edward, *His Recollections and Experiences*, London, 1884.

Ziegler, Philip, *The Black Death*, Folio Society, 1997